ALSO BY THOMAS SCHATZ:

HOLLYWOOD GENRES

OLD HOLLYWOOD –
NEW HOLLYWOOD

ABOUT THE AUTHOR

Thomas Schatz is professor of Radio-TV-Film at the University of Texas in Austin. He is the author of *Hollywood Genres*, the definitive text on Hollywood's most popular story forms, and his writing has appeared in *Wide Angle, Cineaste,* and *Premiere*. A regular lecturer for the American Film Institute, Schatz also writes and consults for various PBS programs on American film and television. He lives in Austin with his wife and three children.

THE
GENIUS
OF THE
SYSTEM

HOLLYWOOD FILMMAKING IN THE STUDIO ERA

Thomas Schatz

A METRO PAPERBACK

HENRY HOLT AND COMPANY

Metropolitan Books
Henry Holt and Company, Inc.
Publishers since 1866
115 West 18th Street
New York, New York 10011

Metro Paperbacks® is an imprint
of Henry Holt and Company, Inc.

Library of Congress Cataloging-in-Publication Data
Schatz, Thomas.
The genius of the system: Hollywood filmmaking in the studio era
/ Thomas Schatz.—1st Metro pbk. ed.
p.   cm.
"A Metro paperback."
Originally published: 1st ed. New York: Pantheon Books,
1989. With new pref.
1. Motion pictures—California—Los Angeles—History.   2. Motion
picture industry—California—Los Angeles—History.   3. Motion
picture studios—California—Los Angeles—History.   I. Title.
PN1993.5.U65S3   1996   96-1707
384′.8′0979494—dc20   CIP

ISBN 13: 978-805-04666-3
ISBN 10: 0-805-04666-6

Henry Holt books are available for special promotions
and premiums. For details contact: Director, Special Markets.

First published in hardcover in 1989 by
Pantheon Books, a division of Random House, Inc.

First Metro Paperback Edition—1996

Designed by Beth Tondreau Design

Printed in the United States of America
All first editions are printed on acid-free paper. ∞

P1

for my father

CONTENTS

ACKNOWLEDGMENTS

The research for *The Genius of the System* took me to various archives, libraries, and depositories around the country, all of which are listed in the bibliographical section at the end of this book. I would like to acknowledge those institutions here at the outset, and to thank various individuals for the generous and able assistance I received on this project.

I am deeply indebted to Leith Adams and to Ned Comstock of the Department of Special Collections, University of Southern California —Leith for his help with the Warners materials and Ned for his help with the MGM and Universal files. They also provided valuable ideas and advice as this project took shape. At the Academy of Motion Picture Arts and Science's Margaret Herrick Library, my research was arranged and assisted by Sam Gill. Anne Schlosser helped me access and sort through the George B. Seitz Collection in the American Film Institute's Louis B. Mayer Library. At the Wisconsin Center for Film and Theatre Research, I was assisted by Harry Miller and Maxine Fleckner.

The support I received from the University of Texas and its Humanities Research Center while researching and writing (and rewriting) this book was enormous. I am especially grateful to W. H. (Deacon) Crane, Ray Daum, Paul Bailey, and Prentiss Moore for their assistance in the Hoblitzelle Theatre Arts Library at the Humanities Research Center, and also to Thomas Staley, Director of the HRC. Permission to quote from materials in the Selznick Collection at the HRC was granted by Selznick Properties, Limited. Jeffrey L. Selznick and David Thomson were gracious enough to review this manuscript and offer constructive suggestions for revisions. My thanks also go out to Dean Robert Livingston of the University Research Institute for financial support during the early stages of my research, and to Dean Robert Jeffrey of the College of Communication for similar assistance. I am most indebted, finally, to Bob Davis and Horace Newcomb, who as my friends and colleagues, and as successive chairs of the Radio-TV-Film Department, were upbeat and supportive throughout the five-year life span of this project. I would also like to thank my graduate students at the university for their support, encouragement, and patience, with special thanks to Chris Anderson for his research and editorial assistance.

Many other individuals helped in many different ways, and I am particularly grateful to Edwin Sharpe, Kathryn Burger, Greg Beal, Joann Lammers, Don Hartack, and Hilary Radner. I'd also like to acknowledge Dudley Andrew and Bruce Gronbeck of the University of Iowa for providing me a place to hole up while I began work on the manuscript.

M Y deepest gratitude goes to Sara Bershtel, my editor. This book would not have been taken on without her encouragement, and it would not be even half what it is now without her counsel and tireless assistance. Sara commented throughout this project on the similarities between book publishing and moviemaking, and indeed she played the role of "creative producer" from its inception to the final cut. Thanks also to Peter Biskind, a leading film writer and editor in his own right, who first suggested that I take on this subject and who monitored it from a distance.

Preface:
The Center
of Gravity

When *The Genius of the System:
Hollywood Filmmaking in the Studio Era* was first published I wrote that
I thought it "a necessary book." I did and I do. Its reappearance now will
enable it to join that slender selection of film books essential to scholars
and a lasting delight to fans. The current edition is justified by many
distinctions, as you will see, including a timeliness no one could have
foreseen when it was originally published.

I should confess my subjective credentials and bias right away. My first
job in the movie business was in the studio system that is the main subject
of this book. It was at MGM as the sixties turned into the seventies. Leo
the Lion was wheezing his last *Ars Gratia Artis* gasp, but remnants of the
studio's structure and one-time glory lingered, if only in reproach. The
first picture I ever worked on was photographed by William Daniels, who
had been Garbo's great cinematographer and was still under studio contract in 1969; editing was overseen by the legendary and formidable
Margaret Booth, who had worked for Irving Thalberg and edited pictures like *Camille* and the original *Mutiny on the Bounty*. Within
months, MGM's props, sets, costumes, and much of the magic they represented (including Dorothy's ruby slippers from *The Wizard of Oz*) were
on the auction block, placed there by a newly installed chief executive
from television known as "the smiling cobra." Later, as the seventies
became the eighties, I was myself production head of a major company,
United Artists. By then a torpor seemed to paralyze much of the

industry, and uncertainty and fickle audience taste were, like death and taxes, the only certainties.

As one of those involved with the legendary disaster *Heaven's Gate,* I played my role in that uncertainty-verging-on-panic. I have done my mea culpas elsewhere, but as I've shed considerable blood of my own in the corridors of power (and powerlessness) which are the concerns of the book in your hands, I claim a certain bruised authority in regarding it as "necessary."

It is so, I think, because Thomas Schatz provides the most insightful and well-researched examination of the studio system at its height that we have. He leads the reader with compelling narrative skill through Hollywood's Golden Age: how it grew, how it achieved what he calls that "delicate equilibrium" and "marvelous symmetry" that had so much to do with why the silver screen turned momentarily golden.

The Genius of the System is far more ambitious than a mere history of the studio era. With a scholar's detachment, a critic's sensitivity, and the tenacious shrewdness of a detective, Mr. Schatz sweeps away the confusion, hearsay, and misinformation film history is plagued with. He expertly reveals what I think of as the center of creative gravity at the heart of the studio system and of this century's art form. I envy the first-time reader of these pages the experience of discovering that center with him. Mr. Schatz makes getting there as fascinating as it must have been to be there at the time, in a manner wholly persuasive and inordinately entertaining.

That should be enough to make any book "necessary," but there is more. In the time that has passed since *The Genius of the System* first appeared, the studio system has undergone yet another series of developments — even convulsions — that make the issues and content of this book more contemporary and pertinent than ever.

Studios that seemed hidebound or moribund a decade ago (think of Disney) are immensely powerful and promise to be more so before you turn the page. Warner Bros., for years the most successful of the major companies, has itself undergone a bust-and-boom cycle over the last decade and is today a wholly different entity from what it was when this book was written. Columbia, Universal, MGM, Paramount, 20th Century-Fox, and United Artists are all resurgent and, for all intents and purposes, different companies run by different people for different audiences.

The movie business has always been unstable — or, to put it another way, dynamic. Public taste and the mysteries of the creative process evolve with the societies they mirror and sway. Their ability to do so, as Mr. Schatz demonstrates, is part of "the genius of the system." As the New Hollywood searches to establish its own "equilibrium," its own "symmetry," we may be on the verge of — of all things — another Golden Age. The elements in today's crucible are remarkably like those Mr. Schatz discusses: talent; technological change; and — last but never least — money.

First, talented people make the movies. Crass, greedy, power-mad as they are (and some of them are), they will endlessly search for their own profane forms of the Holy Grail. Without some kind of crusading tenacity and aspiration they wouldn't last a minute in what they reverently call "The Business," and there wouldn't be any movies without them. Fortunately, they are not in short supply. There are probably more creative people per square inch in Hollywood than anyplace on earth, and most of them, I suspect, would much prefer doing better work than they're doing.

Secondly, the technological changes of recent years and those yet to come are as volatile and full of promise as any we have ever known. Cable, satellite systems, and the ubiquitous VCR have brought tens of millions of viewers back to the movies. They may not be Billy Wilder's "wonderful people out there in the dark," communally sharing an experience from the seats of the grand movie palaces of old, but those were mostly just real estate, anyway. The point is that the theatrical film still drives the market, whether from a satellite twenty thousand miles in the sky or down at the corner video rack. More importantly, the theatrical film still drives the imaginations of the talent — filmmakers and executives.

Which brings us to money. It's always All About Money, which is ignoble and all that, but movies simply can't be made without it. Ask any filmmaker. It is an art that is also an industry, and, as Mr. Schatz demonstrates in these pages again and again, the relationship between money and creativity need not be malign. The two can and often do interact in what is fashionably called "synergy," one enhancing or enabling the other. *Schindler's List* was made by Steven Spielberg, but it was made by "Indiana Jones," too, just as David O. Selznick's *Gone With the Wind* depended less on Margaret Mitchell than on Selznick's track record with (among other things) *King Kong.*

Schindler's List was also leveraged by Spielberg's blockbuster *Jurassic Park* and "green-lighted" by Universal-MCA — which is to say, by Lew Wasserman and Sid Scheinberg, then the powers directing the Universal empire. MCA itself has changed hands since then, of course, with control of the company going to Edgar Bronfman, Jr., of Seagram's.

These are scarcely the studio power brokers of old, of course. In fact the power of today's conglomerated moguls dwarfs that of their Golden Age predecessors. Today's moguls — Rupert Murdoch, say, of 20th Century-Fox, or Michael Eisner of Disney, or Gerald Levin of Time

Warner — are heads not of studios but of global multimedia empires. Mr. Murdoch owns not only his studio, but far-flung newspapers and a television network and a book publishing company. Mr. Eisner recently acquired ABC (and Michael Ovitz) to add to his several movie companies and theme parks. Mr. Levin heads not just Warners, but what used to be Time-Life, as well as HBO.

These are men, or corporate entities, wielding power so immense that we are right to be concerned about their influence and attentive to their vision. They may well bring "genius" to it; their possibilities to do so are awesome and the alternative is awful to contemplate. No "smiling cobra" ever wielded such power or had such potential to cover himself — and us — with glory. One can only hope that the unworthy will flash for a moment and fade away, and that the good yet to come — about which some next-century historian may write his or her own *Genius of the System* — will remain, maybe even endure. It's happened before; just read these pages. The idiosyncratic- or autocratic-seeming decisions of the Mayers, Zanucks, Thalbergs, and Selznicks did not prevent the first Golden Age, after all; they helped create it.

As for the future of the movies . . . the audience is there; the money is there; the talent is there. You and I are part of all that — our standards, our expectations, our demands. We are part of "the system," as Mr. Schatz knows. I invite you to contemplate that as you discover the riches that follow for yourself.

STEVEN BACH

THE
GENIUS
OF THE
SYSTEM

The American cinema is a classical art,
but why not then admire in it what is most admirable,
i.e., not only the talent of this or that filmmaker,
but the genius of the system.

— ANDRÉ BAZIN, 1957

Introduction:
"The Whole Equation
of Pictures"

Walking at dawn in the deserted Hollywood streets in 1951 with David
[Selznick], I listened to my favorite movie boss topple the town he had
helped to build. The movies, said David, were over and done with.
Hollywood was already a ghost town making foolish efforts to seem
alive. . . .
But now that the tumult was gone, what had Hollywood been?
—Ben Hecht, 1954

David Selznick had a flair for the
dramatic, and no one knew that better than Ben Hecht. The two collaborated on some of Hollywood's biggest hits—movies like *Gone With
the Wind* and *Notorious* and *Duel in the Sun*—and often enough the
making of those films was as rife with conflict as the films themselves,
thanks to Selznick's ego and his unconventional working methods. In
fact, Selznick, a "major independent" producer in the age of the big
studios, saw his entire career in epic-dramatic terms: David amid a
slew of Goliaths. But in the early 1950s that scenario was changing
rapidly. In 1953 Selznick wrote Louis B. Mayer, MGM's recently deposed studio boss, that all of Hollywood's "old companies" were still
geared to a "business that no longer exists." Selznick felt that everything from the production studios in Los Angeles to the worldwide
marketing and distribution networks were predicated on a notion of
moviemaking—and of movies themselves—for which there was "no
longer a market."

This was scarcely a cause for celebration, since Selznick was learning how little real independence he had from the entrenched movie
companies and their way of doing business. He was barely fifty years
old and his earlier blockbusters were virtual prototypes for the independent productions that now ruled the marketplace, and yet he felt
himself going under with the old studios. By the decade's end he was
ready to write his own as well as Hollywood's epitaph. Selznick told

one of his former partners in 1958 that their "old stomping ground" had become "very mixed up and unhappy." He went on to eulogize the pioneers and moguls, a vanishing breed now that the industry was a half-century old, and he closed with the observation that Hollywood's "big companies" were staying alive only through the momentum and the motion pictures created in earlier years.

The big companies like MGM and Paramount and Warner Bros. continued to survive, of course—indeed they flourished in the age of television and the New Hollywood. But things had changed since that halcyon era when Selznick and Hecht and Mayer were making movies. Gone was the cartel of movie factories that turned out a feature every week for a hundred million moviegoers. Gone were the studio bosses who answered to the New York office and oversaw hundreds, even thousands, of contract personnel working on the lot. Gone was the industrial infrastructure, the "integrated" system whose major studio powers not only produced and distributed movies, but also ran their own theater chains. Something was "over and done with" in the early 1950s, all right, but it wasn't the movies. It was the studio system of moviemaking and the near-absolute power that the studio wielded over the American movie industry. The Hollywood studio system emerged during the teens and took its distinctive shape in the 1920s. It reached maturity during the 1930s, peaked in the war years, but then went into a steady decline after the war, done in by various factors, from government antitrust suits and federal tax laws to new entertainment forms and massive changes in American life-styles. As the public shifted its viewing habits during the 1950s from "going to the movies" to "watching TV," the studios siphoned off their theater holdings, fired their contract talent, and began leasing their facilities to independent filmmakers and TV production companies. By the 1960s MGM and Warners and the others were no longer studios, really. They were primarily financing and distribution companies for pictures that were "packaged" by agents or independent producers—or worse yet, by the stars and directors who once had been at the studios' beck and call.

T H E collapse of the studio system was bound to provoke questions like Ben Hecht's—"What had Hollywood been?"—and the answers have been plentiful but less than adequate. Hecht himself answered as so many of his industry colleagues did, with an anecdotal, self-serving memoir laced with venom for the "system" and for the "Philistines" who controlled it—and who paid Hecht up to $5,000 a week for his services as a screenwriter. Hecht was an essential part of that system, of course, though he hardly saw things that way, and his reminiscence was less revealing of Hollywood filmmaking than of the attitudes of eastern-bred writers toward the priorities and the power structure in the movie industry. Hecht's answer did provide yet another piece of evidence to be factored in, along with countless other interviews and autobiographies, critical studies, and economic analyses. But the accumulated evidence scarcely adds up, and our sense of what Hollywood had been remained a vague impression, fragmented and contradictory, more mythology than history.

Promising to change all that, a cadre of critics and historians in the 1960s and 1970s cultivated a "theory of film history" based on the notion of directorial authorship. As the New Hollywood emerged from the ashes of the studio era, proponents of the "auteur theory" proclaimed that what the Old Hollywood had been was a director's cinema. They proclaimed, too, that the only film directors worthy of canonization as author-artists were those whose personal style emerged from a certain antagonism toward the studio system at large —the dehumanizing, formulaic, profit-hungry machinery of Hollywood's studio-factories. The auteurist's chief proponent was Andrew Sarris, who in his landmark study, *The American Cinema: Directors and Directions, 1929–1968*, cast the studio boss as the heavy in Hollywood's epic struggle and reduced American film history to the careers of a few dozen heroic directors. Keying on an observation by director George Stevens that as the industry took shape, "the filmmaker became the employee, and the man who had time to attend to the business details became the head of the studio," Sarris developed a simplistic theory of his own, celebrating the director as the sole purveyor of Film Art in an industry overrun with hacks and profitmongers. The closing words of his introduction said it all: "He [the director] would not be worth bothering with if he were not capable now and then of a sublimity of expression almost miraculously extracted from his money-oriented environment."

Auteurism itself would not be worth bothering with if it hadn't been so influential, effectively stalling film history and criticism in a prolonged stage of adolescent romanticism. But the closer we look at Hollywood's relations of power and hierarchy of authority during the studio era, at its division of labor and assembly-line production process, the less sense it makes to assess filmmaking or film style in terms of the individual director—or *any* individual, for that matter. The key issues here are style and authority—creative expression and creative control—and there were indeed a number of Hollywood directors who had an unusual degree of authority and a certain style. John Ford, Howard Hawks, Frank Capra, and Alfred Hitchcock are good examples, but it's worth noting that their privileged status—particularly their control over script development, casting, and editing—was more a function of their role as producers than as directors. Such authority came only with commercial success and was won by filmmakers who proved not just that they had talent but that they could work profitably within the system. These filmmakers were often "difficult" for a studio to handle, perhaps, but no more so than its top stars or writers. And ultimately they got along, doing what Ford called "a job of work" and moving on to the next project. In fact, they did their best and most consistent work on calculated star vehicles for one particular studio, invariably in symbiosis with an authoritative studio boss.

Consider Ford's work with Darryl Zanuck at 20th Century-Fox on a succession of Henry Fonda pictures: *Young Mr. Lincoln, Drums Along the Mohawk,* and *The Grapes of Wrath.* Or Alfred Hitchcock doing *Spellbound* and *Notorious,* two psychological dramas scripted by Ben Hecht and prepared by David Selznick for his European discovery, Ingrid Bergman. Or Howard Hawks working for Jack Warner on *To Have and Have Not* and *The Big Sleep,* two hard-boiled thrillers with Bogart and Bacall that were steeped in the Warners style. These were first-rate Hollywood films, but they were no more distinctive than other star-genre formulations turned out by routine contract directors: Universal's horror films with Boris Karloff directed by James Whale, for instance, or the Paul Muni biopics directed by William Dieterle for Warners. Whale and Dieterle are rarely singled out for their style or artistry, and each would have been lost without the studio's resources and regimented production process. But that doesn't diminish the integrity of films like *Frankenstein, The Old Dark House,* and *The Bride of Frankenstein,* or *The Story of Louis Pasteur* and *The Life of Emile Zola.*

The quality and artistry of all these films were the product not simply of individual human expression, but of a melding of institutional forces. In each case the "style" of a writer, director, star—or even a cinematographer, art director, or costume designer—fused with the studio's production operations and management structure, its resources and talent pool, its narrative traditions and market strategy. And ultimately any individual's style was no more than an inflection on an established studio style. Think of Jimmy Cagney in *Public Enemy,* staggering down that dark, rain-drenched street after a climactic shoot-out with rival gangsters, gazing just past the camera and muttering "I ain't so tough," then falling face-down into the gutter. That was a signature Warner Bros. moment, a narrative-cinematic epiphany when star and genre and technique coalesced into an ideal expression of studio style, vintage 1931. Other studios had equally distinctive styles and signature moments, involving different stars and story types and a different "way of seeing" in both a technical and an ideological sense. On a darkened, rain-drenched street at MGM, for instance, we might expect to find a glossy, upbeat celebration of life and love—Mickey Rooney in another Andy Hardy installment, struggling to get the top up on his old jalopy while his date gets soaked, or Gene Kelly dancing through puddles and singin' in the rain. Over at Universal a late-night storm was likely to signal something more macabre: Count Dracula on the prowl, perhaps, or Dr. Frankenstein harnessing a bolt of lightning for some horrific experiment.

These are isolated glimpses of a larger design, both on screen and off. Each top studio developed a repertoire of contract stars and story formulas that were refined and continually recirculated through the marketplace. Warners in the 1930s, for example, cranked out urban crime films with Cagney and Edward G. Robinson, crusading biopics with Paul Muni, backstage musicals with Dick Powell and Ruby Keeler, epic swashbucklers with Errol Flynn and Olivia de Havilland, and in a curious counter to the studio's male ethos, a succession of "women's pictures" starring Bette Davis. These stars and genres were the key markers in Warners' Depression-era style, the organizing principles for its entire operation from the New York office to the studio-factory across the continent. They were a means of stabilizing marketing and sales, of bringing efficiency and economy into the production of some fifty feature films per year, and of distinguishing Warners' collective output from that of its competitors.

The chief architects of a studio's style were its executives, which any number of Hollywood chroniclers observed at the time. Among the more astute chroniclers was Leo Rosten, who put it this way in *Hollywood: The Movie Colony,* an in-depth study published in 1940:

> Each studio has a personality; each studio's product shows special emphases and values. And, in the final analysis, the sum total of a studio's personality, the aggregate pattern of its choices and its tastes, may be traced to its producers. For it is the producers who establish the preferences, the prejudices, and the predispositions of the organization and, therefore, of the movies which it turns out.

Rosten was not referring to the "supervisors" and "associate producers" who monitored individual productions, nor to the pioneering "movie moguls" who controlled economic policy from New York. He was referring to studio production executives like Louis B. Mayer and Irving Thalberg at MGM, Jack Warner and Hal Wallis at Warner Bros., Darryl Zanuck at 20th Century-Fox, Harry Cohn at Columbia, and major independent producers like David Selznick and Sam Goldwyn. These men—and they were always men—translated an annual budget handed down by the New York office into a program of specific pictures. They coordinated the operations of the entire plant, conducted contract negotiations, developed stories and scripts, screened "dailies" as pictures were being shot, and supervised editing until a picture was ready for shipment to New York for release. These were the men Frank Capra railed against in an open letter to *The New York Times* in April 1939, complaining that "about six producers today pass on about 90 percent of the scripts and edit 90 percent of the pictures." And these were the men that F. Scott Fitzgerald described on the opening page of *The Last Tycoon,* the Hollywood novel he was writing at the time of his death, in 1940. "You can take Hollywood for granted like I did," wrote Fitzgerald, "or you can dimiss it with the contempt we reserve for what we don't understand. It can be understood too, but only dimly and in flashes. Not a half dozen men have been able to keep the whole equation of pictures in their heads."

F I T Z G E R A L D was thinking of Irving Thalberg when he wrote that passage, and it would be difficult to find a more apt description of Thalberg's role at MGM. Nor could we find a clearer and more concise statement of our objective here: to calculate the whole equation of pictures, to get down on paper what Thalberg and Zanuck and Selznick and a very few others carried in their heads. After digging through several tons of archival materials from various studios and production companies, I have developed a strong conviction that these producers and studio executives have been the most misunderstood and undervalued figures in American film history. So in a sense this is an effort to reconsider their contributions to Hollywood filmmaking; but I don't want to overstate their case or misstate my own. Hollywood's division of labor extended well into the executive and management ranks, and isolating the producer or anyone else as artist or visionary gets us nowhere. We would do well, in fact, to recall French film critic André Bazin's admonition to the early auteurists, who were transforming film history into a cult of personality. "The American cinema is a classical art," wrote Bazin in 1957, "so why not then admire in it what is most admirable—i.e., not only the talent of this or that filmmaker, but the genius of the system."

It's taken us a quarter-century to appreciate that insight, to consider the "classical Hollywood" as precisely that: a period when various social, industrial, technological, economic, and aesthetic forces struck a delicate balance. That balance was conflicted and ever shifting but stable enough through four decades to provide a consistent system of production and consumption, a set of formalized creative practices and constraints, and thus a body of work with a uniform style—a standard way of telling stories, from camera work and cutting to plot structure and thematics. It was the studio system at large that held those various forces in equilibrium; indeed, the "studio era" and the classical Hollywood describe the same industrial and historical phenomenon. The sites of convergence for those forces were the studios themselves, each one a distinct variation on Hollywood's classical style.

This book explores the classical Hollywood by interweaving the histories of four representative companies from the rise of the studio era in the 1920s until its decline in the 1950s. Three of the companies were actual studios—Warner Bros., Metro-Goldwyn-Mayer, and Universal—and the fourth was a major independent producer, David Selznick, who climbed the executive ranks at MGM, Paramount, and RKO before creating Selznick International Pictures in 1935 and becoming a virtual studio unto himself. We will examine how these companies "worked" in both a literal and a figurative sense, tracing not only their production operations but also their marketing and sales strategies, their corporate structures and management systems. Our ultimate objective is the filmmaking process itself, which will be pursued primarily through dozens of case studies of the making of individual movies. These case studies as well as our view of the larger industrial context will be based on actual industry documents—interoffice memos, corporate correspondence, and other general records, along with the budgets, schedules, story conference notes, daily production reports, censorship files, and other materials generated for each production. Because of the complexity, cost, and fragmentation of studio filmmaking, Hollywood left its legacy not only on celluloid but also on paper, and that documentation provides a comprehensive and reliable account of the studio system at work.

Limiting this book to four representative companies was no arbitrary decision. The Hollywood studio system was, as economists and the federal courts well understood, a "mature-oligopoly"—a group of companies cooperating to control a certain market. So a close look at any one company necessarily takes them all in, and indeed all of Hollywood's important production outfits figure into this book. But looking at one studio cannot convey the richness and diversity of Hollywood filmmaking, while looking closely at them all in a single volume would be impossible due to the mass of information involved, and also the difficulty of integrating so many corporate histories into a unified narrative. The inevitable result would be a series of disjointed, cursory sketches of a dozen or so companies with only a vague sense of the overall picture.

Interweaving the stories of Warners, MGM, Universal, and Selznick will enable us to look closely at individual companies and still keep an

THE HUB OF FILM PRODUCTION

STUDIO	ACRES	EMPLOYES	EXECU-TIVES	BUILD-INGS	STAGES
1 FIRST NATIONAL	76	1500	30	56	13
2 UNIVERSAL	365	2000	20	63	16
3 FOX (MOVIETONE)	108	2500	19	34	9
4 HAL ROACH	10	166	8	12	3
5 PATHE	69	350	12	35	4
6 ASSOCIATED	5½		2	7	4
7 SENNETT	22	300	4	8	3
8 M G M	53	1500	8	15	15
9 WARNER BROTHERS					
10 FOX (HOLLYWOOD)	13½	2500	19	22	6
11 PARAMOUNT	26	1500	27	11	14
12 UNITED ARTISTS	26	390	10	21	7
13 R K O	15	1500	10	16	7
14 CHRISTIE	4	(inactive)		9	4
15 EDUCATIONAL	3	75	10	8	4
16 TEC ART	2	80	10	14	4
17 METROPOLITAN		500	11	22	9
18 CHAPLIN	5	100	6	9	2
19 TIFFANY	10	75	11	12	7
20 DAVIS	2	30	2	3	2
21 COLUMBIA	10	250	3	10	6

22 HERALD-WORLD WEST COAST OFFICE
23 DARMOUR

STUDIOS RENTING SPACE

DARMOUR — Bob Curwood Productions—Trem Carr Productions.
EDUCATIONAL — Jack White Comedies—James Cruze, In.
METROPOLITAN — Caddo Productions—Harold Lloyd—Christie—Halperin Brothers—Lloyd Hamilton—Robert L. Bruce—Benwatte Productions—Sono Art Productions—Broughton-Reed Productions—Halstone Productions—Gilham & Reed Productions—Fine Arts—Stanish Latin American Film Bureau.
PATHE — Gloria Swanson Productions.
TEC ART — In-peration—Walt Disney—Chesterfield Productions—Brazilian southern Cross Productions—Carewe—William Miller Productions—Burr-Hines Enterprises—Pickwick Pictures—Conrart Synchrotone—Masout Productions—Technicolor—Gotham Productions—Cineton Company—Superior Dramet Company—Al Nathan—Burton King—Rearrus—Leo Young—Mayfair Productions—Jesse Weil Productions.
UNIVERSAL — Ken Maynard Productions—Charles J. Rogers—Hoot Gibson Productions.
UNITED ARTISTS — Picture Productions—Pickford Productions—Fairbanks Productions—Joseph M. Schenck—Arthur Hammerstein.

Map of Los Angeles published in the 1930 Motion Picture Almanac, *giving the location and vital statistics of Hollywood's two dozen studios at the dawn of the classical era.*

eye on the development of the industry at large. As will become obvious in the following chapters, a studio's style and production operations were closely related to its market skew, and these four companies were representative of the dominant marketing strategies during the studio era. MGM and Warners were "integrated majors," along with 20th Century-Fox, Paramount, and RKO. These five studios developed their own theater chains, and they dominated the first-run movie market—the palaces and deluxe downtown theaters in major urban centers, where most of the box-office revenues were generated. The five major studios were the supreme powers in the industry, and each developed a distinctive production and market strategy relative to the number, size, and location of its theaters. Universal's marketing and production operations were considerably different since it had no theater chain and was thus a "minor" studio—though Universal was considered a "major minor" along with Columbia because its production output and distribution network were on a par with those of the majors. But Universal had nowhere near the capital or the resources of the majors, so it developed a more regulated, factory-oriented operation. The result was low-grade product and second-class status for Universal, although after the war the company would find itself ideally suited to network TV, with its brutal economies and demands for quickly produced, formula-bound product.

Selznick was another story altogether. While the big studios emphasized efficiency and productivity, Selznick and other major independents like Sam Goldwyn and Walt Disney produced only a few high-cost, high-yield pictures annually. These filmmakers were in a class by themselves, turning out prestige pictures that often tested the economic constraints and the creative limits of the system, or challenged its usual division of labor and hierarchy of authority. But the so-called independents were closely tied to the studio system, and especially to the integrated majors. They borrowed the majors' personnel, leased their production facilities, and relied heavily on their first-run theaters. The independents needed the system for its resources and its theaters, while the system needed them to cultivate the "high end" of the market and to keep the first-run theaters stocked with quality product—an obvious benefit to the majors since they took a sizable exhibitor's fee on these releases.

The market strategies developed by Warners, MGM, Universal, and Selznick influenced but in no way determined production operations and house style. The movies were a "vertical" industry in that the ultimate authority belonged to the owners and top corporate officers in New York. But the New York office couldn't make movies, nor could it dictate audience interest and public taste. And whatever the efforts to regulate production and marketing, moviemaking remained a competitive and creative enterprise. In the overall scheme of things, the West Coast management team was the key to studio operations, integrating the company's economic and creative resources, translating fiscal policy into filmmaking practice. This demanded close contact with New York and a feel for the company's market skew, but also an acute awareness of the studio's resources and heavy interaction with the top filmmakers on the lot, particularly the directors, writers, and stars.

Because of the different stakes involved for each of these key players, studio filmmaking was less a process of collaboration than of negotiation and struggle—occasionally approaching armed conflict. But somehow it worked, and it worked well. What's most remarkable about the classical Hollywood, finally, is that such varied and contradictory forces were held in equilibrium for so long. The New Hollywood and commercial television indicate all too clearly what happens when that balance is lost, reminding us what a productive, efficient, and creative system was lost back in the 1950s. There was a special genius to the studio system, and perhaps when we understand that we will learn, at long last, what Hollywood had been.

I

THE 1920s: BEGINNINGS

I

Universal: The System Takes Shape

The train ride West was aboard the Twentieth Century Limited. The year was 1920 and Carl Laemmle was en route from New York to Los Angeles in yet another effort to bring Universal's far-flung operations into a closer accord. Like most movie companies, Universal had its "home office" on one coast and its "factory" on the other, and as the stakes in the movie business steadily went up, there seemed to be more than just a continent separating the two. What Laemmle desperately needed was someone who understood the business interests of the New York office and could oversee operations at Universal City, his company's massive production facility outside Los Angeles.

Though Laemmle was president and founder of Universal Pictures, he wasn't the man for the job. He was a businessman and a showman, but he knew precious little about the actual making of films. In that sense Laemmle was a prototype of the American movie mogul, that rare breed of first- and second-generation immigrants, most of them Jews from Eastern Europe, who pioneered the film industry. Like William Fox and Adolph Zukor, Marcus Loew and the Warners, Laemmle got his start just after the turn of the century in the nickelodeon business in a major industrial city. And like the other moguls—the ones who survived, anyway—he eventually expanded into production, but his heart and his savvy were always at the "audience end" of the movie business, in marketing and sales.

Laemmle started in Chicago in 1905, building up a string of store-front theaters. Within two years he had his own distribution "exchange," the Laemmle Film Service. Both ventures were doing well until his supply of product was threatened in 1909 by the Motion Picture Patents Company—the so-called Trust controlled by Thomas Edison that demanded license fees on production and projection equipment. Laemmle defied the Trust by creating the Independent Motion Picture Company to produce his own pictures, and in 1912 he merged IMP with several other renegade outfits to form the Universal Film Manufacturing Company. By the early teens the Trust's power was waning and Laemmle had won sole control of Universal, and had sold off his theaters to concentrate on production and distribution. He consolidated production operations on a 230-acre ranch just north of Hollywood, California, where independents were colonizing to evade the Trust and to exploit the climate and real estate values, both of which were ideal for filmmaking. In March 1915 construction was completed on Universal City, a massive studio capable of turning out some 250 serials, shorts, newsreels, and low-cost feature films per year. The factory operation enhanced efficiency and productivity, but Laemmle was unable to find a satisfactory management setup. By 1920 over a dozen top executives had come and gone, and the three-man team now running Universal City were faring no better than their predecessors.

Thus Laemmle's trip West for an on-site evaluation and quite possibly another management change involving his traveling companions, Nat Ross and Irving Thalberg. Ross was a writer-director from Universal's modest New York studio whom Laemmle wanted to consult as he looked over the West Coast plant. Ross struck Laemmle as having executive potential, but if things didn't work out in the studio's front office he could always go back to directing. Irving Thalberg was quite another story. He clearly was executive material, and there was no telling how far he might go in the movie industry. Thalberg had joined Universal in 1918, barely out of high school, working as a $25-per-week secretary in the New York office. He was a quick study with remarkable instincts for the business, and soon he was working almost exclusively for Laemmle. Among Thalberg's duties was taking dictation as Laemmle screened and evaluated Universal's upcoming releases in his private projection room high atop the Mecca Building at 1600 Broadway. Before long Thalberg was not merely transcribing but was editing Laemmle's comments and providing commentary of his own.

It was during those screening sessions that Thalberg began to reckon the complex equation of filmmaking, with its curious melding of art and commerce, craft and technology, story and spectacle. Laemmle

Portrait of "Uncle Carl" Laemmle taken in 1915, the year he consummated his company's move West with the inauguration of the Universal City studio.

came to rely on Thalberg's insight, but he wondered if the youngster's talents were being squandered in New York. In the spring of 1920 Laemmle decided to find out. He planned to go abroad after sorting things out on the West Coast, and he really wouldn't need Thalberg while scouting talent in Europe and surveying Universal's vast foreign distribution network. Laemmle figured that Thalberg's time would be better spent at Universal City, learning production firsthand and perhaps contributing his own ideas. Once they got to California Laemmle looked over the plant, took a series of meetings with studio chief Isadore Bernstein and his two associates, and decided to stay with the present management setup. But he did install Thalberg and Ross in the front office as consultants and executives-in-training, though with no real authority over production operations.

Thalberg was awestruck with Universal City. It was a virtual world unto itself, a self-contained municipality devoted exclusively to making motion pictures. There were restaurants and shops and even a police force, but most impressive were the production facilities. Universal's largest shooting stage was 65 feet by 300 feet—roughly the size of a football field—with another stage at 50 by 200 feet. Both were enclosed and electrically equipped; in fact, a dramatic moment during the studio's dedication in 1915 had been the activation of the electrical system by Thomas Edison, Laemmle's former nemesis, who supervised the wiring of the plant. Besides the enclosed and open-air stages, the street sets and "back lot" for location work, there were extensive auxiliary facilities, from film processing labs and cutting rooms to prop

and costume shops, construction yards, and even a zoo to supply supporting players for some of Universal's more exotic productions.

Thalberg took to his new assignment, but as he immersed himself in
the everyday production activities he steadily alienated the studio's
management troika. Bernstein was particularly intolerant of this office
boy who until a few weeks ago was living with his mother and had
never been west of Jersey, let alone on a Hollywood movie lot. When
Laemmle returned from Europe, Bernstein went back East to vent his
spleen. Laemmle heard him out, consulted with various executives on
both coasts, and made a series of key decisions. Nat Ross, who showed
little promise in the front office, was put under contract as a staff director. Bernstein and his two associates were put in charge of the physical
operations of the plant. And Irving Thalberg was given sole command
of production at Universal City, answerable only to Carl Laemmle
himself. Thalberg's weekly salary was boosted from $60 to $90, and
Laemmle assured him that if things went well both his pay and his
status would improve considerably.

At the outset Thalberg was little more than a studio-based functionary of Laemmle and the New York office. Laemmle spent a good deal
of time at Universal City breaking in his new production chief, and the
two were widely regarded as Hollywood's unlikeliest power brokers.
Even studio personnel were amused when the aging mogul and the
boyish executive prowled the lot. Thalberg was frail and delicate because of a sickly childhood and a chronic heart condition, but at five
feet six he towered over "Uncle Carl," as the diminutive mogul was
known to his employees. Laemmle's unabashed nepotism was legend
—humorist Ogden Nash once quipped, "Uncle Carl Laemmle has a
very large faemmle." Everyone at the company, including Thalberg
himself, suspected that he was being groomed for membership in the
Laemmle clan, since besides playing surrogate son at the studio he also
was courting Carl's daughter, Rosabelle.

Thalberg's match with Rosabelle didn't take, and his rapport with
Laemmle proved short-lived as well. Much has been made over the
years of the clashes between Thalberg and Erich von Stroheim, Universal's headstrong director. But equally important were Thalberg's
ongoing and steadily escalating battles with Carl Laemmle. Though
Laemmle was the most affable and compassionate of movie czars, he
was fiercely independent and self-assured. He went into production in
defiance of the Trust, and in carving out his company's destiny he
developed strong convictions about what it took to satisfy audiences
and turn a profit. As Thalberg got a feel for production, he realized how
much Universal City's operations and the company's general market
strategy were shaped by those convictions.

Irving Thalberg (upper right) shortly after his arrival at Universal City, with the studio's management team. At lower left is Isadore Bernstein, whom Thalberg eventually replaced as production chief.

Laemmle's strongest convictions—and his major differences with Thalberg—involved stars and "feature-length" films. (A feature in those early silent years was any movie with a running time of more than three reels, or about thirty minutes—a total that steadily expanded to eighty or ninety minutes by 1920.) Laemmle actually had promoted stars and features in his earlier days with IMP to distinguish his products from those of Edison, Biograph, and the other Trust-based companies. Those outfits had resisted features and big-name stars, reasoning that they were not cost-efficient from a production standpoint, they were too risky from a sales standpoint, and they compromised the producer's control. Laemmle may have shared those sentiments, but he was willing to subdue them while battling the Trust. He even helped advance the star system back in 1910 by recruiting the "Biograph Girl," Florence Lawrence, and aggressively publicizing her films. But once federal antitrust action and competition from independents eroded the Trust's power, Laemmle reverted to his earlier biases. "There is room at Universal," Laemmle asserted in a 1913 trade paper ad, "for every Showman who has got his bellyful of features, feature stars, and their attending evils." He softened a bit on features as they became more prevalent in the mid-teens, but not in his attitudes toward stars. In a 1915 advertisement, Laemmle extolled Universal as "the first producer to buck the star system—the ruinous practice that has been responsible for high-priced but low-grade features."

From his earliest years in production and distribution, Laemmle had been committed to what he termed a "scientifically balanced program" of shorts, newsreels, serials, and modest features. The Universal City plant was designed and equipped to roll out these program jobs like so many Model-T's off the assembly line. Unlike automobiles, though, motion pictures were expected to be different from one another. Laemmle was convinced that such distinctions could be minimized through a policy of "regulated difference," so long as certain production values were maintained. Once the production process and story formula were established for, say, Universal's five-reel westerns with Harry Carey, a competent filmmaker like Jack (later John) Ford could crank them out, often using the same footage for action scenes, with only routine adjustments in story and character. That strategy held through the war years, but by the late teens the marketplace was chang-

Entrance to a motion picture "palace," circa 1920.

ing. Feature-length narrative films became the industry staple, and the most successful features were calculated star vehicles. This was underscored in 1919 when three of the biggest stars in Hollywood's silent era—Charles Chaplin, Mary Pickford, and Douglas Fairbanks—joined forces with producer-director D. W. Griffith to create United Artists. UA's sole function was to distribute its founders' high-class (and high-priced) features, enabling them to operate without the constraints of the emergent studio system. UA's stars produced their own pictures, which were targeted for the "first-run" market, where attendance and thus profit potential were greatest.

Universal had all but written off the first-run market by 1920. The downtown deluxe theaters that had been cropping up in big cities since the mid-teens seated thousands of moviegoers, and they developed exhibition practices that were altogether different from those of the "subsequent-run" houses. To exploit the vast numbers and the varied life-styles and work habits of their market, the big-city movie palaces ran A-class features at inflated prices virtually around the clock, except in peak business hours—primarily evenings and weekends—when they offered "presentations" that included not only a feature film but a stage act and full orchestral performances as well. What's more, a first-run theater might run a hit feature for weeks or even months at a time, as long as public interest held. Once the picture exhausted its first-run market, it worked its way through the subsequent-run circuits, playing to the same audiences that Laemmle went after in the first place. There Universal offered "program" fare ideal for an evening of family viewing: a three-hour package of shorts, newsreels, and low-grade features that changed weekly. Laemmle's decision to skew Universal's pictures away from the first-run market and toward independently owned neighborhood, small-town, and rural theaters had made sense in the past. It regulated both output and income, since there was less competition and a steady audience in these outlying theaters. But Thalberg doubted that such a strategy would hold up much longer. The nation was in the midst of an urban-industrial boom, and as the population shifted to big cities Universal was appealing to an ever-shrinking market while its competitors were adjusting to the changing marketplace. Studios like Fox and Metro were upgrading feature production and they also had begun to build, buy, or otherwise gain control of their own theater chains, concentrating on the first-run market. Likewise, major exhibition outfits like First National and Loew's Incorporated were expanding into feature production. Thalberg figured that Universal's only recourse was to get back into the theater business, which Laemmle had abandoned years earlier, and to accelerate feature production.

Laemmle appreciated Thalberg's concerns, but he advised his studio chief to concentrate on the supply side and let the New York office worry about marketing and sales. Thalberg's point, however, was that production and marketing were no longer distinct, that any notion of the "studio system" now reached far beyond the studio itself. He was concerned that as Universal's competitors merged their production, distribution, and exhibition operations into vertically integrated combines, they would consign nonintegrated companies to second-class status. Then even with Universal's solid production and distribution operations, Laemmle's resistance to A-class star vehicles and to theater acquisition would relegate Universal to an inferior—and eminently less profitable—position in the industry.

Universal didn't disdain features altogether, of course, but the majority of its features were "programmers," inexpensive five-reelers designed to top off an evening's viewing. These low-grade westerns, melodramas, and action pictures were dubbed Red Feather releases and underwent a disciplined production and marketing process. Universal's A-class Jewel releases, conversely, were longer-running star vehicles, often shot on location with period sets and costumes. They comprised no more than a half-dozen of the literally hundreds of films that the studio cranked out each year. Executives on both coasts tended to perceive the Jewels as being "outside the system," unfettered by the production and distribution policies governing Universal's lesser films. In fact, the Jewels were the most undisciplined and inefficient projects on the lot—or rather *off* the lot, which was where prestige filmmakers like Erich von Stroheim and Rupert Julian liked to work.

Thalberg was determined to change all that. Universal depended on a steady flow of product, and Thalberg felt that both the flow and the quality of all its products had to be controlled if Universal was to compete with the other industry powers. Universal City was often derided as Hollywood's consummate movie factory, and Thalberg was quite comfortable with the analogy. Like other modern industries that relied on mass production and mass merchandising, the cinema developed its own version of the assembly-line system with an appropriate division and subdivision of labor. The director was crucial to that process, and Thalberg saw no reason to limit the director's freedom and creative control over actual shooting, so long as he recognized the nature and limits of that authority. This wouldn't come easily for filmmakers like Stroheim and Julian, who considered themselves not just directors but also writers, editors, and producers. And in Stroheim's case, the problem was further complicated by his privileged relationship with Carl Laemmle, who was much impressed by Stroheim's continental airs and German accent, by his expert performance as the

Lobby card for Blind Husbands, *which indicates the prestige status of both film and filmmaker.*

strutting, white-gloved autocrat, and by the glint of class and prestige that Stroheim brought to an otherwise déclassé factory.

Stroheim had been ensconced as Universal's resident artiste since his 1918 debut, *Blind Husbands*, a lavish sex farce that he not only wrote and directed but starred in as well. *Blind Husbands* was a huge success, generating a succession of upper-crust comedies set in exotic locales, with an emphasis on spectacle and extravagance and a remarkable attention to detail. In 1919 he made *The Devil's Pass Key*, and when Thalberg arrived in 1920 Stroheim was preparing his third feature, *Foolish Wives*. Again Laemmle was indulging his star director. The sets, for instance, included a life-size replica of a street in Monte Carlo that was constructed on the back lot, even though most of the shooting was to be done on location on the Monterey peninsula in northern California.

Thalberg did not question Stroheim's skill as a director, writer, or actor—although by 1920 his performance both on and off the screen as the stiff-necked Prussian was wearing a bit thin. But Thalberg was determined to rein in Stroheim's talent and increase the profit margin on his pictures, thus demonstrating that the pursuit of excellence was not a license for waste. And if one thing characterized Stroheim's film-making, it was waste; he squandered time, film stock, resources, and money. Before Stroheim took *Foolish Wives* on location, Thalberg called a series of meetings to go over the schedule and budget. When Stroheim refused to attend, Thalberg suspended the project. Laemmle backed his new production chief, and so Stroheim acquiesced—at least until he had his picture off the lot. Stroheim gambled that once the project was approved and under way, he would regain the upper hand. His instincts were right. Laemmle valued Stroheim too highly to let Thalberg's discipline amount to anything more than a slap on the wrist. Once the company reached Monterey, discipline gave way to inspiration, and both budget and schedule were forgotten.

While Stroheim devoted most of 1921 to *Foolish Wives,* Thalberg attended to studio operations, instilling the same discipline and efficiency in feature production that already typified the making of serials and shorts. Directors like Jack Conway, Tod Browning, and John Ford relished Thalberg's commitment to feature production and adapted readily enough to his methods, wherein shooting scripts, production schedules, and detailed budgets were seen as requisites rather than impediments to productivity and quality control. Some, like Ford, had directed shorts and two-reelers and had no desire to control script development or editing. Like any capable director, Ford expected complete authority when he was shooting, and he got it so long as budgets and schedules were respected. Others, like Tod Browning, were talented writers, and Thalberg encouraged them to work on their own scenarios. But whatever the director's creative impulses, the films themselves were deliberate star-genre formulations only a notch or two above Universal's programmers. Among the more successful features produced under Thalberg, for instance, were the Priscilla Dean melodramas written and directed by Tod Browning and John Ford's westerns starring Harry Carey.

Thalberg rarely intervened during actual shooting. No intervention was necessary considering his editorial role during script development and preproduction planning, and then later during the cutting. Thalberg was a strong proponent of the "continuity script," a carefully prepared scenario that broke a picture down shot by shot and served as a virtual blueprint for production. He also sharpened his sense of story, even taking story credit (as "I. R. Irving") on a modest 1921 programmer, *Dangerous Little Demon.* That was the only time in his entire career that Thalberg had a screen credit, a measure not only of his modesty and confidence ("credit you give yourself," he often said, "is not worth having"), but also of his authority at the studio. Thalberg's power was only incidentally a matter of individual pictures. The "product" of his efforts, so far as Thalberg was concerned, was Universal's steady output and its efficient production operation.

L A T E in 1921 Stroheim returned to Universal City to complete *Foolish Wives*, and he found the stakes had changed in his absence. Thalberg was much impressed with the footage shot in Monterey, but he made it clear that the remaining scenes would be shot with the benefit of budget and schedule. Still *Foolish Wives* cost over $1 million, fully five times the cost of all five of Ford's 1921 westerns put together, with Stroheim generating a staggering 320 reels of film—over fifty hours of footage. He cut the picture down to just over twenty reels, insisting that the three-and-a-half-hour sex farce play exclusive engagements at special admission prices as a two-part feature. Thalberg doubted that would please either audiences or exhibitors, and he instructed Stroheim to recut the picture. When the filmmaker refused, Thalberg locked him out of his editing rooms and supervised recutting himself.

Foolish Wives was released as a Super-Jewel early in 1922 at standard feature length and did well at the box office, although critical reaction was split. Stroheim's technique was uniformly praised, but his overt misogyny was beginning to alienate critics, who were tiring of his portrayals of women as silly, sex-starved strumpets. The reaction at Universal was split as well. Stroheim complained that his picture had been mutilated, while Thalberg lamented the waste of time, money, and resources. By now Laemmle's sympathies were with his young studio chief, and when Stroheim initiated his next project, *The Merry-Go-Round,* certain conditions were carefully spelled out. The picture would be shot on the Universal lot and supervised personally by Thalberg; Stroheim would direct but not act in the picture, thus minimizing any problems should he walk off the picture; and even though the conception was Stroheim's, the script was to be done by staff writer Harvey Gates. The handwriting was on the wall, and just after *The Merry-Go-Round* started shooting Stroheim walked off the picture—and off the lot. He signed with Goldwyn Pictures to do an adaptation of a grim, naturalist novel, *McTeague*, which he planned to shoot on location in San Francisco and in Death Valley.

Stroheim was not sorely missed at Universal, though his departure evinced a disturbing trend. A number of promising directors bolted for other studios where the opportunities—and the salaries—were better and the conditions less constraining. Thalberg had imposed those constraints to improve Universal's operations and its output, but without a genuine commitment to the first-run market, he was beginning to wonder whether the effort was wasted. As other companies continued to expand and vertically integrate, Thalberg doubted Universal could keep pace with Fox and Paramount and First National, whatever its commitment to feature production.

But Thalberg forged ahead despite his misgivings, putting together an adaptation of *The Hunchback of Notre Dame* in late 1922 to assert both his own and Universal's potential for quality filmmaking. The picture was a display of disciplined extravagance featuring a back-lot reproduction of the Notre Dame cathedral and a breakthrough performance by Lon Chaney, whose portrayal of the grotesque title character was as spectacular as the lavish sets. As Thalberg supervised editing, however, he felt that the picture lacked the scope he was after, especially in the crowd scenes outside the cathedral. Without seeking Laemmle's approval, he sent the project back before the cameras to restage the crowd scenes. The retakes went well, and Thalberg was confident that the added expense would be offset by increased revenues when the picture was released. But Laemmle had a less upbeat appraisal of the situation. Not only had Thalberg poured additional money and resources into the picture without New York's OK, but he had pushed it into the realm of the prestige epic. Now only a road-show release in select first-run theaters throughout the country, with reserved seating and a hefty promotional budget, could adequately

Universal City in 1923, the year Thalberg left the studio. In the upper right is the Monte Carlo set for Foolish Wives.

A closer view of the Monte Carlo set.

exploit the picture. That would mean competing head-on with other road-show releases like De Mille's *The Ten Commandments* and Fairbanks's *Robin Hood.*

That was exactly what Thalberg wanted, of course, and Laemmle's reaction only proved how little Thalberg could hope to change Universal's direction. Relations between the two executives already were strained, since Laemmle had failed to come through with the long-term contract and stock option deal Thalberg requested. Thalberg's salary was now $400 a week, and Laemmle was willing to raise it by another $50. But Thalberg wanted a piece of the company or possibly even a partnership. Laemmle obviously was no more inclined to make that kind of commitment than he was to pursue first-run theaters or to commit to A-class feature production, so Thalberg began looking elsewhere for work. Within a few weeks he met with Louis B. Mayer, a crude but enthusiastic producer in his late thirties who ran a small studio on Mission Road outside Los Angeles. Mayer's company concentrated on first-run features for release through Metro and First National, and though Mayer knew the business end he needed someone to oversee production. Thalberg liked the setup, so in mid-February 1923 he left Universal and signed with Louis B. Mayer Productions as vice president and production assistant at a salary of $600 per week.

The Hunchback of Notre Dame was released a few months later to widespread popular and critical acclaim. It was Universal's biggest hit of 1923 and it vaulted Lon Chaney to stardom, but its success had no real impact on the company's production and release policies. There would be others after Thalberg who also tried to push Laemmle into theater acquisition and first-run feature production, but Laemmle was never convinced to abandon the conservative program strategy devised decades earlier. It's been said that Laemmle was unique among the film industry pioneers in that he lacked the qualities most often associated with the movie mogul: the ruthless, competitive drive, the open greed, the instinct for the jugular. Laemmle was fiercely independent and competitive early on while battling the Trust, but once Universal City was built he became increasingly complacent and set in his ways. Before the age of vertical integration, Universal dominated the motion picture business through sheer size and output; no other company was as productive or as prominent during the teens. But Universal slowly, inevitably declined during the 1920s. The studio had its niche, to be sure, and produced a few important, successful features along with the steady flow of shorts and programmers. But with the emergent studio era, Laemmle's steadfast program strategy and his aversion to theater acquisition destined Universal to minor status in a major-league game.

2

MGM: Dawn of the Thalberg Era

Another movie mogul with serious misgivings about vertical integration in 1923 was Marcus Loew. Like Carl Laemmle, Loew got his start in the theater business back in 1905, although not with nickelodeons. Loew took a somewhat higher road, building up a circuit of first-class vaudeville houses and music halls in the Northeast. The growing popularity of moving pictures drew him into film exhibition, and by the late teens Loew's Incorporated was the dominant theater chain in New York City, the world's busiest motion picture market. By then Loew was committed to the picture business, and he was determined to keep pace with the rapid expansion of movie industry giants like Paramount and First National. In early 1920 he bought Metro Pictures, whose nationwide distribution setup and modest studio in Los Angeles made Loew's, Inc., a fully integrated company overnight. The following year, construction was completed on Loew's new corporate headquarters, a sixteen-story office building at Broadway and Forty-fifth, atop the palatial 3,200-seat Loew's State Theater.

By 1921 Marcus Loew's son Arthur had parlayed Metro's network of film exchanges into a unified international power, but Loew's production problems persisted. Metro simply could not deliver the quantity or the quality of product needed for Loew's distribution and exhibition setup. And when a slump hit the industry in 1923, Loew was sorely tempted to unload the Metro studio and concentrate on what he knew best, the marketing and sales end of the business. But Loew's outlook changed in January 1924 when Joe Godsol offered to sell him Goldwyn Pictures. Like Loew's-Metro, Goldwyn was an integrated company with uneven strengths. It was weakest in distribution and exhibition, although its holdings did include the 4,500-seat Capitol Theater on Times Square, the world's largest movie palace—and a most attractive selling point for a theater man like Marcus Loew. The strength of Goldwyn Pictures was its massive production facility in Culver City, just west of Los Angeles. Thus a merger would result in a perfect fit: Loew's theater chain, Metro's distribution network, and the Goldwyn studio.

Loew relayed Godsol's proposal to his first lieutenant, Nick Schenck, who had been with him since 1906 and ran the motion picture operation. Schenck was definitely interested. He booked the New York theaters and, like Marcus Loew, he was fed up with second-rate movie product. So Schenck pursued the Goldwyn deal while Robert Rubin, a top Loew's executive who had come over in the Metro merger, began scouting for management executives to run the Culver City studio. What Loew's needed, Schenck told Rubin, was someone who could manage the Goldwyn plant efficiently and still turn out the quality features that Loew's first-run theaters required. Rubin courted a number of filmmakers and top movie executives, including Sam Goldwyn, the feisty, talented producer who had left his own company during a power struggle in 1922. Goldwyn wasn't interested in running the merged studio, nor were the other top prospects, and as the field narrowed Rubin began leaning toward Louis B. Mayer.

The thirty-eight-year-old Mayer was coarse and outspoken, which Rubin attributed to his background as a Russian-born street kid who had been a junk dealer before getting into the nickelodeon business back in 1907. But Mayer knew the movie business, having run theaters and worked distribution—including a stint at Metro, where he had first caught Rubin's eye. Mayer's drive and chutzpah as a successful independent producer further convinced Rubin that he was the kind of man Loew's needed for its newly merged studio. Another key factor was Irving Thalberg, who oversaw production operations for Louis B. Mayer Productions. Rubin was impressed with the discipline and efficiency of Thalberg's operation, which turned out A-class product from Mayer's meager facility on Mission Road outside Los Angeles. Equally important, especially for Rubin and Schenck, was the youngster's feel for commercial story properties and his sense of what passed for taste and quality among feature film audiences.

During the spring of 1924, Schenck had hammered out the details of the merger, which was essentially a "paper deal." The only cash transaction involved the purchase of Sam Goldwyn's remaining stock. Loew's Incorporated bought Goldwyn Pictures for $5 million and Louis B. Mayer Production for $75,000, indicating the difference in market value between the two companies. Both purchases included contract talent, from directors and stars to technicians, craftsmen, and laborers, but the principal cost item was the Culver City plant. Built in the mid-teens by studio pioneer Thomas Ince as the home of Triangle Pictures, the forty-acre expanse featured glass-enclosed stages (designed to use available sunlight for shooting), a three-story office building, and an array of shops, labs, dressing rooms, storage facilities, and bungalows for its staff.

Mayer's chief asset, conversely, was the intangible resource of a studio management team—something Loew would pay a great deal more than $5 million for over the coming years. The so-called "Mayer group" was composed of Louis Mayer, Robert Rubin, and twenty-four-year-old Irving Thalberg. Mayer was named Vice President and General Manager of Metro-Goldwyn at a salary of $1,500 per week; Thalberg was Second Vice President and "Supervisor of Production" at $650 a week; Rubin was Secretary, based in New York, at $600 a week. Besides their salaries, Schenck offered the trio an unprecedented bonus incentive. They would divide 20 percent of all MGM's profits among themselves, with Mayer getting 53 percent of that cut, Rubin getting 27 percent, and Thalberg 20 percent. In order to qualify for their profit share, the Mayer group had to deliver a minimum of fifteen pictures per year—a good indication of Loew's hunger for product. The contracts also stipulated that Mayer's name be "prominently displayed" in all film prints and advertising, although the company was officially called Metro-Goldwyn. Within a year "Mayer" was incorporated into the title, and the new company adopted the name Metro-Goldwyn-Mayer.

Another important but rather curious component of the merger was Cosmopolitan Pictures, a company created by newspaper czar William Randolph Hearst to promote its sole resource, actress Marion Davies. Hearst "discovered" Davies in 1918 when she was a Ziegfeld chorine, and he created Cosmopolitan Pictures, which released through Goldwyn, to make Davies a star. The Hearst-Davies partnership extended into their personal and domestic lives as well, and although Hearst had not divorced his previous wife his rapport with Davies was widely known. Davies was more than a kept woman or a manufactured star, though; she had genuine talent as a light comedienne. But her value to the new company was nothing compared to Hearst's. His vast chain of newspapers and magazines could provide steady, favorable treatment for MGM's pictures and its stars, and they also were an excellent source of story material. Shortly after the merger, Mayer affirmed the couple's value by building an elaborate fourteen-room "bungalow" for Davies at Culver City and announcing that Hearst would supervise all her pictures under the Cosmopolitan banner.

Schenck closed the deal on April 10, 1924, with the merger set to take effect in late May. News of the deal was leaked a week later—by Hearst's papers, aptly enough—and Mayer planned a gala inauguration for Saturday, April 26. Mayer played the role of the studio patriarch to the hilt at the ceremony, basking in the attendant adulation that included a congratulatory telegram from Secretary of Commerce Herbert Hoover. There was much speechifying, and among the recipients of Mayer's praise were "seventeen of the great directors in the industry calling this great institution their home." During that speech one of the seventeen, director Marshall (Mickey) Neilan, got up and left, followed by his wife and star, Blanche Sweet, and the cast and crew of *Tess of the D'Urbervilles*. The headstrong Neilan later explained that he already had sacrificed a half-day's shooting for the event and that Mayer's display was "taking too goddamn long."

T H E unceremonious departure of Mickey Neilan and company was something of a portent. He had clashed before with Mayer on various independent productions in the late teens, but that was before centralized studio production really began to take hold. Neilan was none too pleased about the emerging "studio system," nor were other prominent Metro and Goldwyn directors like Rex Ingram, Maurice Tourneur, and Erich von Stroheim, all of whom suspected that the MGM motto, "Ars Gratia Artis," had little currency where their own artistry was concerned. (Actually, the art-for-art's-sake slogan was conceived by publicity wizard and occasional lyricist Howard Dietz when he worked for Goldwyn; it was retained by the new company along with another Dietz conception, Leo the trademark lion.) Neilan's concerns about the new regime were borne out soon enough. He finished shooting *Tess* without interference, but his "director's cut" and the picture's release version turned out very differently—and the difference indicated the changing values and power structure in the industry. At a preview screening Louis Mayer was put off by the film's closing, in which the heroine is hanged for murdering a man who sexually assaulted her. He told Neilan to replace the finale with a "happy ending" wherein Tess is miraculously spared by a last-minute reprieve. Neilan protested loudly, even taking his case to Thomas Hardy, who had written the novel, but to no avail. MGM owned the rights to the story and could

Nicholas Schenck, standing behind a portrait of Marcus Loew, addresses the crowd at the April 1924 inauguration of MGM's Culver City studio.

Harry Rapf, Louis B. Mayer, and Irving Thalberg at the April 1924 inauguration.

adapt it as it pleased, stated Mayer, who was convinced that he understood the sentiments and tastes of movie audiences better than either Neilan or Hardy.

Rex Ingram learned of the merger while in North Africa, where he was directing Alice Terry and Ramon Novarro in *The Arab*, a costume epic based on his own script. Not until Ingram returned to Culver City to cut *The Arab* did he realize that Thalberg's "supervisory" system threatened his control over pre- and postproduction and perhaps even his shooting. After completing *The Arab*, Ingram informed Loew and Schenck that he refused to submit to anyone's authority. The Loew's executives weighed Ingram's ultimatum, influenced no doubt by his wife Alice Terry's market value, and also by the success of *The Arab* and of a reissue of their 1921 hit, *The Four Horsemen of the Apocalypse*. Loew's capitulated, setting up a production unit for Ingram in the south of France—on the Riviera, yet—where he could write, direct, and produce Terry's films. Ingram's preferential treatment was as much a function of his wife's star status and the instability of the new studio setup as it was an acknowledgment of his filmmaking talent. Mayer realized that, but still he let Schenck know he was unhappy with the decision. As Mayer and Thalberg settled in and their authority was challenged by other directors, though, they gradually were supported by the New York office. In the months following the Ingram episode, Mickey Neilan and Maurice Tourneur each gave a similar ultimatum, and each wound up leaving MGM.

The heaviest conflicts over the director's authority and creative control, as fate would have it, involved Erich von Stroheim. The Thalberg-Stroheim battles resumed with *Greed*, Stroheim's overlong, hyperrealistic adaptation of Frank Norris's *McTeague*, done for Goldwyn before the merger. Joe Godsol had nixed Stroheim's downbeat seven-hour adaptation, and even after Stroheim cut the picture to four hours in late 1923, Godsol still deemed it unreleasable and shelved it. The Mayer group was aware of the problems with *Greed*, and as a condition of the merger they refused to take any responsibilty for its completion. But the $470,000 debit weighed on MGM's books and on Thalberg's mind, so he decided to recut the picture. He saw little commercial viability for the grim tale of lust and avarice, whatever its length, but he hoped it might recoup some of its production costs and enhance MGM's prestige. Though Stroheim was still under contract, he refused to "butcher" his masterpiece any further. When Rex Ingram finished *The Arab*, Thalberg asked him to work on *Greed*, and Ingram cut another hour from the film before leaving for France—a suitable distance, he felt, from a studio whose directors were asked to cut one another's work. Thalberg had no such qualms, of course, and he was not about to release the dour saga as a three-hour road show. Working with various staff writers and cutters, he pared the picture down to a standard feature length. MGM released the film in December 1924 to little fanfare and even less audience interest.

Despite the problems with *Greed*, Thalberg still believed he could control Stroheim's tempestuous but undeniable talent. Early in 1925 he agreed to let Stroheim do an adaptation of *The Merry Widow*, a popular operetta whose style, spectacle, and romance appealed to both men. Stroheim was assigned to write and direct, but only on the condition that he include certain popular scenes from the original and that he not act in the picture, again just in case he bolted or had to be removed from the picture. Script development went well, but once the picture went into preproduction friction began to develop over casting, budgets, and costume design. The problems escalated during shooting, and though Stroheim finished the picture, he and Thalberg knew long before it was over that it would be Stroheim's last for MGM.

I N G R A M , Neilan, Tourneur, and Stroheim were all products of the early silent film era, when the director ruled not only the set but the entire production process. All four were writers as well as directors

King Vidor (behind the camera in jacket and spectacles) lining up a shot in The Big Parade.

and considered editing an essential aspect of the director's role. Each also considered himself his own producer. But with centralized production and the division of labor under the emerging studio system, they found themselves at odds with the very industry they had helped create. None could adjust to the steady fragmentation and the increasing constraints of studio filmmaking, and by the time sound hit in the late 1920s, solidifying the studio-based production process, each of their careers was effectively finished.

There were other directors, like Clarence Brown and King Vidor, who learned their craft during the teens and distinguished themselves as silent filmmakers, but then adjusted to—and in many ways helped to shape—MGM's increasingly complex production system. Under that system it was no longer the director's responsibility to orchestrate the entire filmmaking process from conception and story development through editing to release. That responsibility steadily shifted to the producer. But some directors, like King Vidor, parlayed their efficiency and commercial success into a relatively higher degree of authority within the system. Whereas Clarence Brown was the consummate company man who rarely questioned Thalberg's authority, Vidor had a career marked by continual negotiation and compromise. He yielded to the system's demands on most projects in exchange for an occasional innovative or offbeat project—*La Bohème* in 1926, for instance, with Lillian Gish starving to death in a Parisian garret, or *The Crowd* in 1928, a somber parable about an anonymous Everyman lost among the urban-industrial masses.

Vidor's privileged status came after *The Big Parade*, a 1925 hit that established John Gilbert as MGM's first homegrown star and Vidor as its top director in the late silent era. And equally important, that breakthrough hit validated Thalberg's production system and his own savvy as an executive. Scheduled as a modest "Gilbert Special," *The Big Parade* scarcely began as a prestige project. Vidor had directed two routine star vehicles with Gilbert in 1924, and while mulling over Gilbert's next picture, Thalberg and Vidor decided on a war story. Thalberg tried to get the screen rights to *What Price Glory?*, the hit play by Maxwell Anderson and Laurence Stallings. Failing that, and after a futile search through the story department files, Thalberg hired Stallings himself to collaborate with Vidor and scenarist Harry Behn on an original war story. They came up with a tale centering on a singularly unheroic but sensitive doughboy whose combat experiences during the Great War are softened by a fleeting affair with a French farm girl. Gilbert was cast as the soldier and Renee Adoree as his "love interest," and the picture was budgeted at $205,000.

Most of *The Big Parade* was shot at the studio during the summer of

1925; Thalberg also dispatched a second unit to Fort Sam Houston near San Antonio to pick up shots of troop movements and such—hence the film's title. While screening Vidor's rough cut and witnessing the picture's impact on preview audiences, Thalberg sensed that MGM had a hit and he immediately went to Louis Mayer. Employing much the same strategy he had with Universal's *The Hunchback of Notre Dame* two years earlier, Thalberg argued that the picture would be vastly improved—and it profit potential enhanced—by building up the crowd scenes and expanding its overall scope and spectacle. Mayer agreed, and he ran interference with Schenck while Thalberg sent the picture back into production. After reshooting many of the battle sequences, Vidor took his production unit back to Texas to restage the now-legendary sequence depicting an army column of some 3,000 men, 200 trucks, and 100 planes overhead, stretching endlessly toward the horizon. While Vidor was away, Thalberg had staff director (and former cinematographer) George Hill shoot additional night battles, which also were added to the release version.

In all, the retakes on *The Big Parade* pushed its costs to $245,000, the going rate for an A-class feature in those years and well worth the additional investment so far as Thalberg was concerned. The postproduction work also confirmed what was emerging as one of Thalberg's basic tenets of studio filmmaking—namely, that the first cut of any picture was no more than the raw material of the finished product. Studio screenings and sneak previews would determine when a picture needed more work, and Thalberg would decide just how much—but not without input from Mayer, of course, and not without considering the scheduling and requirements of other projects. This preview-retake process was indeed extravagant, and no other studio adhered to it as a matter of policy. Culver City, in fact, was known as "retake valley" because of Thalberg's postproduction strategy. But Thalberg figured that the public was the ultimate arbiter of a movie's quality, that only an audience could decide if a picture really worked. If postproduction was handled as efficiently as preparation and principal photography, then the extravagance of rewrites, retakes, and fine-tuning would prove profitable in the long run.

That strategy paid off after the November 1925 release of *The Big Parade,* which opened simultaneously at the Capitol and the Astor in New York to overwhelming public and critical acclaim. Financial records from the period are scarce, but reliable sources indicate that it grossed in the neighborhood of $5 million. Only one other picture from Hollywood's silent era enjoyed that kind of box-office success, and that was *Ben-Hur,* another Loew's/MGM release that opened in December 1925, just weeks after *The Big Parade. Ben-Hur* was equally important

The huge success of The Big Parade, *released in late 1925, brought credibility to the newly merged MGM and to Irving Thalberg's production system.*

to MGM's growing reputation, but it was hardly an MGM picture in the same sense; nor was it as profitable as *The Big Parade.* The Mayer group had inherited the biblical epic from Metro Pictures, which by 1924 had already invested considerable time and money in its production. The project was so shaky that Mayer refused, as he had with *Greed,* to include *Ben-Hur* in the initial production quota. It was on location in Italy at the time of the merger and foundered there for another year before Thalberg brought it back to Culver City and personally supervised its completion—at roughly ten times the cost of *The Big Parade.*

The concurrent release of *Ben-Hur* and *The Big Parade* in late 1925 marked a watershed for Loew's/MGM and the Culver City operation. *Ben-Hur* was the last of the premerger projects, many of which required a crisis-management approach to get them finished and into release, while *The Big Parade* signaled a more stable, cost-efficient, and productive process. That process had stabilized by late 1925, which was affirmed in October when Schenck agreed to renegotiate the Mayer group's contracts. For their part, the Mayer group promised to deliver at least forty-four pictures per annum to Loew's. In return, they were guaranteed a minimum annual bonus of $500,000 and a new salary scale. Thalberg's weekly income took the biggest leap, going from $650 to $2,000. Mayer's climbed from $1,500 to $2,500 per week, and Rubin's from $600 to $1,000. Loew's also put up a half-million dollars to expand both the studio facilities and the production staff.

The success of *The Big Parade* and other MGM pictures indicated how well not just the studio but also Loew's market strategy was working. Loew's/MGM was a vertically integrated outfit, but it owned or controlled far fewer theaters than did Paramount, Fox, or First National —nowhere near a sufficient number to guarantee a profit for any given MGM release. And even though other major studios were acquiring new houses in the mid-1920s, pushing their theater holdings to five hundred and more, Loew and Schenck were content with some one hundred theaters. Their reasoning was simple enough. Since anywhere from 50 percent to 75 percent of their revenues came from the first-run theaters, due to the huge seating capacities and steady flow of customers, they decided to concentrate on that end of the market. Expansion-oriented companies like Warners, Paramount, and Fox had a different outlook. Large theater chains meant extensive real estate holdings, which increased the company's assets and also its financial leverage. Moreover, some outfits, like Warners and Paramount, relied heavily on block booking and blind bidding, whereby independent ("unaffiliated") theater owners were forced to take large numbers of the studio's pictures sight unseen. Those studios could then parcel out second-rate product along with A-class features and star vehicles, which made both production and distribution operations more economical.

Loew's/MGM disdained that strategy—or at least modified it by skewing its production operations toward a steady output of first-class product for first-run theaters. MGM did produce low-cost comedies and formula westerns, of course, but its proportion of A-class features was well above any other studio's. The integrated companies did not block-book in one another's chains and competed openly in the first-run markets, where pictures generally played as long as they continued to draw audiences. So with its emphasis on the first-run markets, Loew's/MGM was the most genuinely competitive company in the business. There was considerable risk but also a greater profit potential in that approach, which clearly was paying off. In 1926, its second full year in existence, Loew's/MGM was the most profitable company in the industry, clearing $6.4 million.

Coordinating studio operations at Culver City with the sales and marketing strategies back East was essential to that success. The "star vehicle" was the primary coordinating principle for executives on both coasts, who steadily came to see the studio system and the star system as inextricably linked. But it's worth noting that star vehicles were perceived differently by those executives, depending on their particular vantage point within the system. When Schenck and his cohorts in New York translated one season's box-office receipts into the next season's budget, they conceived it in terms of "star units"—so many Lon Chaneys or Norma Shearers or Lillian Gishes, depending on their reading of public demand. Mayer's task, in turn, was to translate the assigned budget into that season's production program. What for Schenck were vaguely defined commodities became specific genres for Mayer, Thalberg, and their staff.

While New York saw a "Lon Chaney" as a marketable commodity to be moved through the distribution-exhibition process, Mayer and Thalberg saw it as a certain type of story that demanded a certain mobilization of MGM's resources. More specifically, a Lon Chaney was likely to be an offbeat character study—often of a disfigured or mentally unbalanced criminal—a tradition most notably established at Universal by *The Hunchback of Notre Dame* and *The Phantom of the Opera*. Frequently, Lon Chaneys were written and directed by Tod Browning. They were nominally supervised by Thalberg but required little of his input, given Browning and Chaney's excellent track record at MGM. A Chaney cost anywhere from $200,000 to $250,000, just below the studio's average cost for A-class features. The relatively low cost was due primarily to two factors: Chaney's films rarely required a major studio player to costar—indeed Chaney occasionally played more than one role himself—and Browning generally contributed the story and scenario as well as the direction. Since half the cost on MGM's top features usually went for star, director, and story/continuity alone, doing without a high-priced costar and doubling up Chaney's and Browning's responsibilities meant substantial savings for the studio.

A "Norma Shearer" was likely to be a romantic melodrama, often an intrigue of bourgeois marriage and adultery and thus a costarring vehicle, perhaps featuring two other players if the ever-popular romantic triangle was employed in the story. Standard features costing about a quarter-million dollars, Shearer's vehicles were supervised by one of Thalberg's associates and scripted by a middling scenarist like Hugh Herbert and directed by a capable but undistinguished employee, say Robert Z. Leonard or Jack Conway. A "Lillian Gish'" was quite another matter. As a long-standing star and serious actress who was given story approval when she was signed personally by Nick Schenck, Gish was likely to appear only in prestige productions closely supervised by Thalberg himself and directed by one of MGM's top directors, probably Victor Seastrom or King Vidor. The script was apt to be an adaptation of some presold story property from Broadway or nineteenth-century literature, written by a top scenarist like Frances Marion. The total cost of a Lillian Gish vehicle in 1926–27 would be in the $400,000 to $500,000 range, and, as the executives on both coasts soon learned, it could not be expected to return much profit.

As with any other star vehicle, the costs for director/stars/story on a Gish picture represented roughly one-half the total production costs, even though its budget might be twice that of a standard feature. Consider, for example, the relative costs for a standard Chaney vehicle, *The Road to Mandalay*, and Gish's *The Scarlet Letter*, two early 1926 releases:

	MANDALAY	SCARLET LETTER
Director/stars/story	$ 90,776	$214,450
Continuity	1,189	20,846
Remaining cast	7,042	26,988
Production manager	812	2,175
Cameramen	3,250	8,244
Lighting	2,810	5,401
Editors	1,839	2,400
Sets	9,705	32,642
Props	5,547	7,533
Wardrobe	2,000	19,517
Location expenses	1,211	275
Film and labs	12,072	20,938
Titling	1,500	3,000
Publicity	1,750	5,015
Misc.	12,225	27,266
Studio overhead	21,000	33,600
TOTAL	$174,728	$430,290

The Road to Mandalay was shot in five weeks (thirty days), by director Tod Browning, who coauthored the story and script with Herman J. Mankiewicz. *The Scarlet Letter* was adapted from Hawthorne's novel by Frances Marion, directed by Victor Seastrom, costarred Lars Hanson and Karl Dane, and was allotted forty-eight days for production.

MGM produced an occasional nonstar feature, although these were rare and usually had some obvious hook to draw audiences. A good example of this type of feature was *The Fire Brigade*, a 1926 project scheduled for a twenty-eight-day shoot and budgeted at $249,556. The picture starred May McAvoy, a "featured player" at MGM, and was directed by William Nigh. The second-class status of the project was obvious from the budget, with only $60,000 going for director, cast, story, and continuity. But the attractions in *The Fire Brigade* were spectacle, special effects, and fiery destruction rather than star and director. The budget allowed $25,000 for photographic effects and another $66,000 for sets, a relatively high figure since many of the sets for the picture had to be not only built and "dressed" but destroyed as well.

S T A R S were the prize commodity at Loew's/MGM, although directors and writers were highly valued as well. These were employees whose talents could not be easily defined and cultivated, who could not be trained and regulated like other craftsmen and technicians. But as important as they were to feature filmmaking, they had precious little control over their individual careers or their pictures. At MGM, it was Louis Mayer who controlled their careers, at least where contracts and principal casting were concerned. There were rare occasions when Schenck or Loew cut a deal, but for the most part Mayer negotiated with and signed the studio's star performers, directors, and writers, thus supplying the key resources for Thalberg's production operations. Mayer was a consummate tactician and psychologist, well known for his ability to cultivate and control MGM's top talent, especially its stars. He was aware that he could not shape an actor's personality or foist just any player on the audience. "The public makes the stars," Mayer was fond of saying—and this attitude was a complement to Thalberg's reliance on public previews to test-market MGM's pictures. But while Mayer and Thalberg relied on audience feedback to confirm their judgments, both were adamant about the judgments being their own. Success necessarily bred confidence, and with MGM's prosperity their dual control over the production process steadily tightened.

That control was challenged, or course, since stars tended to have powerful egos and were well aware of their box-office clout. Mayer in fact had rather significant battles in 1927–28 with two top stars, Greta Garbo and Lillian Gish, and each of those skirmishes was revealing of the star's authority at MGM and of the complex interplay of star persona and studio style. A few weeks after MGM secured Gilbert's stardom in *The Big Parade*, the studio released *The Torrent*, a routine melodrama featuring one Greta Gustafsson, whom Mayer had discovered a year earlier while scouting talent in Germany. She changed her name to Garbo, and in *The Torrent* she displayed that rare combination of beauty, personality, and dramatic ability that was the essence of stardom. Garbo's breakthrough came in late 1926 when she was teamed with Gilbert for *Flesh and the Devil*, and when that picture hit she demanded that her $600-per-week salary be adjusted to reflect her market value. Mayer refused and Garbo bolted—all the way to her

Waiting at the station: (left to right) studio boss Louis B. Mayer, supervisors Harry Rapf and Hunt Stromberg, production chief Irving Thalberg, along with MGM's top silent-era star, John Gilbert.

native Sweden, in fact, where she remained for seven months until Mayer and company came around to her demand of $5,000 a week. Mayer caved in not only because of Garbo's market value and star appeal, but also because her screen persona was so well suited to MGM's prestige strategy and emerging high-gloss style which favored romantic melodrama and light comedy set in a contemporary milieu populated by glamorous, sophisticated characters.

Lillian Gish provided an interesting counterpoint to Garbo. She came to the studio an established star, but one whose personality was distinctly at odds with MGM's style and whose degree of control over the production process—by way of script approval, granted by Schenck when he signed her—put her at odds with Mayer and Thalberg's system. Gish delivered strong performances in *The Scarlet Letter* (1926) and *The Wind* (1928), two brooding dramas directed by Victor Seastrom which Thalberg appreciated for their critical prestige, but which Mayer found utterly distasteful. Mayer was so displeased with the downbeat finale of *The Wind*, in which Gish descends into madness and awaits certain death after killing a man who had molested her, that he demanded a more favorable outcome for the virtuous heroine. As he had with *Tess*, Mayer sent the picture back into production for a revised ending. Gish protested bitterly, as did Seastrom, but Mayer stood firm—and without protest from Thalberg, who had personally supervised the production. *The Wind* was the last picture Gish or Seastrom did for MGM, and their departure was as inevitable as Mayer's buckling under to Garbo's salary demand. Gish's penchant for grim realism and "serious" drama had no place at MGM, where quality and style were a function of polish, poise, and glamour—qualities personified by Garbo, who would never work for any other studio but MGM.

Louis Mayer kept the stars in line and under contract, and Irving Thalberg kept them busy. They relied on a number of key executives for assistance, none of whom had any real visibility outside the studio. Mayer's right-hand man where the plant itself was concerned was E. J. "Eddie" Mannix. Ironically enough, Mannix first came to Culver City as a confederate of Nick Schenck, who sent him out West in late 1925 to keep an eye on Mayer and Thalberg after their new contracts guaranteed them a bigger portion of Loew's/MGM profits. There may have been an intimidation factor involved, since Mannix gave the impression of being something of a thug. Decades earlier, when Nick Schenck and his brother Joe were still in the amusement park business, Eddie Mannix had been a bouncer at one of their parks. The Schencks soon learned that Mannix had a mind for business and a knack for diplomacy in labor-management relations, so he wound up in the front office. Once he got used to California, Mannix found he liked Hollywood and that he had much in common with Louis Mayer. Before long he was a fast friend of the MGM boss, and under Mayer's guidance he learned the movie business and sharpened his management skills. Within a year of his arrival Mannix was managing the studio at executive rank and even supervising an occasional feature.

So Mayer managed the human resources and Mannix the facilities, and both worked closely with Thalberg to plan the overall production program. This required meticulous scheduling and script development, close collaboration with the various department heads to ensure efficiency and to maintain production values, and careful supervision of each picture. Thalberg relied on a coterie of close associates to facilitate actual production. There were five key "Thalberg men": Harry Rapf, Bernie Hyman, Hunt Stromberg, Al Lewin, and Paul Bern. Others came and went, of course, but these men worked closest—and longest—with Thalberg once his system stabilized. Generally referred to as supervisors, the five were forerunners of the Hollywood line producer. They worked closely with Thalberg to prepare projects for production, and then they monitored shooting, keeping an eye on budget and schedule as well as the day-to-day activities on the set. Each of them was handpicked by Thalberg, and each was fairly unique in terms of training and talent. Bernie Hyman was similar to Thalberg in personality and upbringing—a New York street kid with a public school education who was introverted and somewhat cerebral, but with a sense of humor and a quick wit. At MGM, Hyman tended to supervise the middle- and low-budget pictures. He shared those duties with Harry Rapf, who came to movies via vaudeville and carnival shows. His tastes were cruder and his judgment more pragmatic than those of his colleagues, but Rapf was a highly efficient and capable supervisor. The other three Thalberg men came up through the writers' ranks. Hunt Stromberg started as a reporter in the Midwest, came to the Coast to work as a publicist, and then became an independent producer before joining MGM in 1925. Both Paul Bern and Al Lewin had solid academic credentials, Bern from the American Academy of Dramatic Arts and Lewin from New York University and Harvard. Both started at MGM as screenwriters and became head of the scenario department before graduating to supervisor status.

These five associates were closely involved in the preparation and execution of individual productions, but the production operation at large was Thalberg's. His supervisors may have anticipated the producers of later years, but to see them in the 1920s as anything but functionaries in a centralized producer system is to underestimate the nature and degree of Thalberg's authority. Although he refused to take screen credit on any MGM film and was unknown to the general public, everyone in the studio—and indeed in the industry—was aware of Thalberg's role at MGM and his contribution to its success. The Loew's officers were acutely aware, as well, which Schenck reaffirmed in October 1926 when he cut Thalberg yet another new contract. Just one year after Loew's had raised Thalberg's weekly salary from $650 to $2,000, Schenck doubled it to $4,000 and set Thalberg's minimum annual compensation, including his bonus, at $400,000.

T H E best evidence of Thalberg's value was MGM's output and Loew's box-office revenues, both of which were produced by the system he put together and maintained at Culver City. To appreciate that system in its early years—and particularly before the coming of sound —we might take a freeze-frame of studio operations in mid-1927, assembled from the memos, reports, and "recapitulations" that were circulating at the time. A July 1927 roster of MGM's principal contract personnel listed nine executives, forty-five actors, forty-one writers, and twenty-five directors. The executives were Mayer, Thalberg, Mannix, and six supervisors. Among the forty-five actors under contract

were eight "Stars" and thirty-seven "Featured Players." The reigning
stars were Lon Chaney, Jackie Coogan, Marion Davies, John Gilbert,
Lillian Gish, William Haines, Ramon Novarro, and Norma Shearer.
The featured players included two costarring comedy teams and also
such near-stars as Joan Crawford, Lionel Barrymore, and Greta Garbo.
(By September 1927 Garbo would be in the star category and Gish
would be gone altogether.) During that month, MGM had seventy-
seven projects in some stage of development, from preliminary story
outline to final lab work. As of July 25, ten pictures were in production,
seven were completed and "in the can," two were "reissues" of earlier
hits, and the remaining fifty-eight were in some stage of preproduction. The dominant organizing principle of MGM's production operations clearly was the star. Other than a few "dog stories" and all-
star "Super Specials," the seventy-seven projects were grouped according to the leading "personality" in each picture.

Thalberg personally supervised roughly one-third of the productions,
with his supervisors sharing responsibility for the others, and their
duties also were keyed to Metro's star roster. While Thalberg took on
an array of top-star vehicles, each of his supervisors tended to work
regularly with only one or two stars. The supervisors generally were
assigned their projects when the annual budget and schedule were
being worked out, long before writers, directors, or the other cast and
crew were assigned. Thus the supervisors played a key role in story
and script development, and also in overall production design—all of
which generally was done prior to the director's coming aboard. A
"Weekly Directors Report" that July indicated that twenty-three of
MGM's twenty-five contract directors were working on an assignment.
The directors generally came on a picture just before shooting, though
they did participate in final script preparation and then, after shooting,
in the preparation of the first cut of the picture.

So even with the increased specialization and division of labor that
were so essential to studio filmmaking, Thalberg's system was no
assembly-line operation. There was a good deal of interaction and collaboration among the principal creative personnel, all of which was
orchestrated by Thalberg and one or more of his associates. This necessarily minimized the director's sense of ownership of or authority
over any given project. Sam Marx, who was head of MGM's scenario
department after Thalberg's system was firmly in place, noted that
"team spirit was implicit in the studio's directing staff." This was evident in the collaboration during preproduction, and also in Thalberg's
preview-retake policy. Directors "often embellished the work of their
fellow directors," recalled Marx. "Thalberg would want retakes, and
rather than recall the original director [from a subsequent assignment],

he asked another to do the added scenes. It happened all the time." Marx admitted that "the system had its shortcomings; it wasn't one that appealed to directors accustomed to a less regimented way of making movies."

C L E A R L Y "regimentation" was the operative term here, but it was hardly discipline for its own sake. In the late 1930s when the Hollywood studio era was at its zenith, F. Scott Fitzgerald noted that "people in the East pretend to be interested in how pictures are made," but their real fascination was with "the pretensions, the extravagances, and vulgarities" of Hollywood. "Tell them pictures have a private grammar like politics or automobile production," he said, "and watch the blank look come into their faces." That observation is from *The Last Tycoon*, Fitzgerald's fictionalized homage to Thalberg, and the metaphor seems appropriate. Thalberg was one Easterner who not only learned the grammar of pictures, but also found out how it could be rearticulated systematically and on a massive scale. Thalberg was not the most powerful man at Loew's/MGM, nor was he the most artistic individual at the studio. But he occupied a critical position in the system—poised, in effect, between New York and L.A., between capitalization and production, between conception and execution. He developed a system that kept those forces in equilibrium, and he carved out his own role as studio production chief in the process. It was a role that Thalberg virtually created and defined, and by the late 1920s, it was the single most important role in the Hollywood studio system.

3

Selznick at MGM: Climbing the Executive Ranks

By 1927 Irving Thalberg's central-producer system was being heralded as a model of filmmaking efficiency, productivity, and quality control. Other studios developed similar management setups in the late 1920s, most notably Paramount under B. P. "Ben" Schulberg and the fast-rising Warner Bros. under Darryl Zanuck. Among Hollywood's growing roster of production chiefs, Thalberg was perhaps the most heavily involved in the day-to-day filmmaking process, shuttling endlessly from one script conference or editing session to another. But there was only so much that even Thalberg could do, and he relied heavily on his executive staff and his corps of supervisors to keep Metro's production system running smoothly.

The most promising member of Thalberg's executive staff in mid-1927 was David Selznick, a twenty-five-year-old dervish who, since joining MGM in late 1926, had climbed from script reader to head of the scenario department and then was promoted to supervisor status. Selznick's meteoric rise at MGM was remarkable considering that he'd been in Hollywood barely a year, and considering, too, the animosity between Louis Mayer and Selznick's father, Lewis J. Selznick. Indeed, when Harry Rapf suggested that Mayer take on Selznick as a production assistant, Mayer flatly refused. That reaction was directed not at David Selznick but at his father, who had been a top distributor of independent pictures in the teens and thus was one of Mayer's chief competitors. Mayer and Lewis Selznick were bitter rivals, and Rapf

*Studio portrait of David O. Selznick
shortly after he joined MGM.*

watched them feud firsthand as a Selznick employee. He also watched young David learn the business, starting as a story analyst in his mid-teens and running the publicity department and publishing a weekly newsletter, *The Brain Exchange,* for Selznick Pictures by age eighteen. Since then David had had some success producing newsreels in New York, so Rapf figured the youngster might fit in as either a story analyst or a production assistant. But Rapf also figured to keep his job with Metro, so when Mayer flared at the very name of Selznick, Rapf simply let the matter drop. But not David Selznick. While surveying the Hollywood landscape after his recent arrival, he made up his mind that MGM was ideal for someone with his skills and ambition. Supremely confident, Selznick felt he was overqualified for anything Harry Rapf could hire him to do. But he had to start somewhere in Hollywood, and he was determined that it be MGM. So after Mayer turned him down, Selznick simply went over Mayer's head to Nick Schenck.

Schenck happened to be in Los Angeles in October 1926, and he also happened to owe David Selznick a favor. Several years earlier when Schenck was engineering the Metro-Goldwyn merger, problems arose over the screen rights to *Ben-Hur.* One of the partners in the company that owned the rights to the Lew Wallace novel was thinking of selling his share to Lewis Selznick, who in 1923 was looking for a way back into the movie business. Schenck met with Selznick, imploring him not to complicate the delicate merger negotiations. Young David had come along to the meeting, and in a typically impetuous gesture his father turned to him for counsel. David had been advising his father for years on adaptations and "literary" acquisitions, and he suggested that his father stay out of the deal—advice that cost Lewis a fortune but paid off for David some three years later. In that October 1926 meeting, David explained to Schenck that he only wanted a chance to prove himself. The Loew's executive felt he deserved a shot and overruled Mayer, instructing him to give Selznick a two-week trial. And so the youngster was put on the payroll at $75 per week as a reader in the story department.

S T A R T I N G anywhere but at the top was out of character for a Selznick, but David figured he wouldn't be there long. He was right; a few years later he joined the echelon of "boy wonders" in the movie industry who were overseeing production at a major studio while still in their twenties. Like Thalberg and Zanuck and Hal Wallis, Selznick was among Hollywood's second generation of moguls, who still felt the pioneer's lust for power and wealth but were entering an industry whose foundation was already set. The first generation of moviemakers had begun with virtually nothing, while Selznick and Thalberg and the rest came into filmmaking with a feel for the business and with a certain cinematic literacy—an idea of how the production system might be run and of what it could accomplish. But Selznick was also different from the other Hollywood wunderkinder in his fierce independence and his fascination with actual production. More in the mold of a Sam Goldwyn than a Thalberg or a Zanuck, Selznick was drawn to the minute details of moviemaking, including shooting, rather than concentrating on pre- and postproduction and the running of a vast production company.

Although Selznick's governing ambition was to produce his own movies on his own terms, he had no trouble redirecting his talents and energies to accommodate the MGM machine. He certainly had the right tools: he was bright and aggressive, with remarkable organizational skills and an obsessive drive to succeed. Within days of his arrival, he began firing off memos to Rapf, Thalberg, and even Mayer, suggesting story ideas, titles, script revisions, and ways of enhancing the efficiency of various production departments. One of the more interesting memos written during his two-week trial period urged Rapf to secure a print of *The Battleship Potemkin*, a recent film by Soviet filmmaker Sergei Eisenstein. "It possesses a technique relatively new to the screen," wrote Selznick, "and I therefore suggest that it might be advantageous to have the organization view it in the same way that a group of artists might view and study a Rubens or a Raphael."

Mayer and Thalberg were impressed with Selznick's management skills, and after the trial period they put him on contract at $150 per week to oversee the writers' department. Selznick described his new role in a November memo to Rapf. "So long as the firm has 40 or 50 writers, generally responsible to 5 executives and directly chargeable to none," wrote Selznick, "there can be no effective supervision." He felt that "under the present supervisory system it is futile [for a supervisor] to keep in touch with the work of 50 writers." Thus his new assignment, which was "to weed out those writers whose work is ineffectual for the purposes of the firm; to direct the efforts of those who show me more ability into channels consistent with the company's policies—policies which necessarily can be known only to the executives, and consequently only to the writers under a policy of supervision." But Selznick realized that his quest to economize must not detract from the department's basic function. "Cutting down the payroll is an important consideration," he noted, "but I realize that even more important is the obtaining of story material."

Selznick upgraded both the productivity and the efficiency of the department as he climbed to assistant and then to associate story editor early in 1927. His first task as associate editor was to pare down to thirty the number of writers on at least six-month contracts, virtually all of whom were on salaries considerably higher than his own. A handful were earning four figures per week. At $3,000 weekly Frances Marion was the studio's highest-paid staff writer; a few others were down around $1,250, and the majority in the MGM writing stable earned about $500 per week. A dozen or so scenarists were on a per-picture basis. Playwright Marc Connelly, for instance, was doing an original screenplay for $10,000 in early 1927, and June Mathis was adapting Channing Pollock's *The Enemy* as a Lillian Gish vehicle for a flat fee of $20,000. Those writers were a rather exclusive group, taking a project through story and script development without heavy input from Selznick or enforced collaboration with any of MGM's staff writers. They did meet regularly with Thalberg for story and script conferences, though, and there was no assurance that their work wouldn't be rewritten after they were off the payroll. MGM's staff writers enjoyed few of the same privileges. Even a top staffer like Frances Marion expected her scenarios to be reworked, polished, or otherwise revised by other writers while she was still on the project.

Selznick arrived at MGM just before talkies hit, when silent filmmaking was at its height and the division of labor among scenario writers was fairly acute, which made virtually every writer a specialist and collaboration inevitable. Writing for silent pictures was an art all its own, and each of Metro's staff writers was a specialist who had mastered some aspect of that art. Some developed stories at the early "treatment" stage, when the scenario was no more than a one- or two-page outline. Others were considered "script doctors," who came in for the last-minute rewrites or even a total overhaul before a completed scenario went into production. Still others were "comedy constructors," doing everything from isolated gags to entire story lines. Another group were "title writers," specializing in dialogue or bits of story information that appeared on title cards during the picture. By the mid-1920s most filmmakers—producers and directors as well as writers—tried to minimize the use of title cards and to deliver narrative information visually. But the cards were necessary, and clever intertitle writing was a highly valued skill.

One of the few Hollywood-bred writers who could do it all was Anita Loos. She began writing scenarios in the teens, before the system took

Anita Loos, shown here with her husband and sometime collaborator, director John Emerson, was a top scenario writer from Hollywood's earliest years. In 1926, the year Selznick arrived at MGM, Loos left Hollywood to write fiction and stage plays.

hold and when motion picture writing meant coming up with a story premise for directors who generally shot "off the cuff." As the studio system took hold, her own narrative and technical skills developed, and she even wrote a few how-to manuals on the intricacies of scenario writing. By 1926 she was MGM's top writer and one of the few who could take an idea through to a final shooting script. But the tremendous success of her 1925 satire, *Gentlemen Prefer Blondes*, which was serialized in *Harper's Bazaar*, encouraged Loos to head East and adapt her best-selling novel for the stage. A rare case, Loos reversed the usual journey from East to West Coast, but she left behind a distinctive style of comedy writing. Its chief practitioner at MGM was Robert Hopkins, who became a fixture as an intertitle and dialogue writer of the "Anita Loos School"—that is, he had a penchant for hyperbole, wisecracks, and double entendre. Though weak on plot construction, Hopkins could spew venomous one-liners and the kind of zingers that directors and other writers knew could put over a scene. Such a talent was much in demand at the studio, even before sound came in, and Hopkins would literally prowl the lot and supply bits of dialogue as needed. Some writers and producers even penciled "Hopkins line here" into screenplay drafts, counting on MGM's resident wit for an appropriate ad-lib. Hopkins rarely received screen credit for his work, and a talent so esoteric scarcely fit into Selznick's sense of a disciplined staff operation. But still his unique ability was recognized and cultivated for nearly two decades at the studio.

Another staff writer with a rather unconventional but valued talent was Kate Corbaley. At $150 per week, Corbaley was one of the few staffers whose salary was in the same range as Selznick's, and her option was coming up when Selznick took charge of the writers' ranks. Corbaley had been working with Hunt Stromberg, and Selznick suggested that if Stromberg no longer needed her, "we could use her to splendid advantage as an editorial supervisor." Her option was picked up, though her specialty at MGM was not in editorial but rather as Louis Mayer's preferred "storyteller." Mayer was not a learned or highly literate man, and he rarely read story properties, scripts, or even synopses. He preferred to have someone simply tell him the story and he found Mrs. Corbaley's narrational skills suited him. She never received a writing credit on an MGM picture, but many in the company considered her crucial to Mayer's interest in stories being considered for purchase or production at any given time.

With little impact on the actual substance of stories or scripts during his tenure in the scenario department, Selznick concentrated instead on streamlining the writing process and charted the development of the myriad projects in the works. He redesigned MGM's daily and semiweekly recapitulation forms to include more detailed information on the status of projects in preparation and production, and he reviewed daily the progress of every staff writer. Even after he moved up in the story department and became a supervisor, he continued to file daily reports on all writers and on all active studio projects. Charting the progress of writers and projects became somewhat easier with the introduction in late May of the "Dead Line Date," conceived by Selznick and ratified by studio manager Eddie Mannix. A May 1927 memo from Mannix to all story department personnel announced the new policy: "Commencing today, we are introducing a 'time limit' check on writers, to be known as the 'DEAD LINE DATE.' Hereafter writers shall be allowed: For First Drafts of Original Stories—two weeks; For Treatments—two weeks; For First Drafts of Continuity—three weeks." This further regimented the screenwriting process, which many writers resented. But Selznick was lucky enough to avoid their wrath, since another member of the editorial staff was given the task of "tabulating and enforcing" the deadlines.

Selznick's first assignment as a full-fledged supervisor was to oversee several low-budget westerns starring Tim McCoy. A year earlier, Mayer and Schenck had decided to compete with the sagebrush serials and program westerns being trotted out by almost every other studio. Mayer signed "Colonel" Tim McCoy to a one-picture deal in May 1926 at $250 per week. The picture went well, and by 1927 McCoy was set for six pictures and listed among the studio's stars—though his weekly salary of $300 was only a fraction of Garbo's or Gilbert's. McCoy's films generally were shot in two weeks for about $75,000, roughly one-third the cost of an average MGM feature. The director assigned to the Selznick-supervised McCoy pictures was W. S. "Woody" Van Dyke, who started in the business as an actor and assistant to D. W. Griffith, then began directing in the later teens. Van Dyke signed a one-year deal with MGM in 1927 at $600 per week, and among his first assignments were the McCoy westerns.

Van Dyke and Selznick were eager to impress the studio brass and move on to more ambitious projects, and in preparing McCoy's next two pictures they devised a plan to showcase their skills. On July 15 Selznick reported to Rapf that "W. S. Van Dyke has been preparing the next two McCoys—TIN SOLDIERS and BALAKLAVA—simultaneously, as we expect to shoot much of these two pictures together." By mid-August the two westerns, whose titles were changed to *Wyoming* and *Spoilers of the West*, were set to start. Van Dyke took them into production in late August on a nine-day schedule, and he managed somehow to bring the two pictures in on time. What's more, the simultaneous shooting schedule kept costs at a minimum:

	WYOMING	SPOILERS
Director	$ 7,021	$ —
Production manager and asst.	887	137
Cameramen	1,491	499
Editors	494	224
Cast: stock company	7,291	2,500
Cast: picture talent	4,345	500
Extra talent	7,614	783
Story and continuity	554	1,081
Sets	7,222	1,043
Props	3,171	751
Wardrobe (women's)	595	464
Wardrobe (men's)	1,364	274
Lighting	191	667
Location expenses	7,800	540
Film and lab	3,647	3,082
Titles	88	103
Publicity	110	—
Misc.	2,572	1,538
Studio overhead	5,000	5,000
TOTAL	$61,457	$19,186

Turning out two features for $80,000 in less than two weeks had the desired effect: Selznick and Van Dyke scored a more important assignment. Selznick was given two more McCoy westerns, but these were done strictly by the book with second-rank directors while he and Van Dyke turned their attention elsewhere—to the "high end" of MGM's production spectrum, in fact, and a project so distinctive in terms of both subject matter and technique that no one quite knew what to do with it. The project, *White Shadows in the South Seas*, had been languishing on the production schedule for months while director Robert Flaherty prepared the film in his own inimitable fashion. He had won international acclaim five years earlier with a documentary feature, *Nanook of the North*, which was years in the making due to Flaherty's complete autonomy as a filmmaker and his practice of living among his subjects to understand their way of life before trying to capture them on film.

That made sense for an independent documentary filmmaker and ethnographer, perhaps, but not for a director on MGM's payroll. By fall 1927, Flaherty had been in the South Seas for some six months, and

Publicity photo of cowboy star Tim McCoy appearing in Wyoming, *Selznick's first supervisory assignment at MGM.*

Hunt Stromberg, the film's nominal supervisor, was doing very little to move the project along. Sensing Thalberg's impatience, Selznick suggested that Thalberg put him and Van Dyke on the picture. He also lobbied for a stronger action-adventure plot and only a semidocumentary production approach. Thalberg agreed, convinced that the project needed a fresh approach and that Selznick and Van Dyke could provide it. Hunt Stromberg was all for strengthening the dramatic elements in *White Shadows,* and he immediately set a staff writer to work on a revised treatment. Flaherty's documentary soon became the story of a down-and-out American whose latent idealism is brought out by the love of an unspoiled native girl. Both his love and his idealism are tested when a pearl bed is discovered, and the hero must deal with his own incipient greed and the hordes of whites who come to plunder the Edenic island.

But Selznick was moving a bit too quickly for his own good—at least so far as Stromberg was concerned. Stromberg was amenable to a story overhaul, but he wasn't about to let Selznick usurp his authority.

Stromberg went to Thalberg, telling him that he still wanted to supervise the picture and that Flaherty was still his director of preference. Thalberg acquiesced, bowing to Stromberg's seniority and his promise as a prestige-level producer. Selznick was informed that he was to assist Stromberg and that Van Dyke would codirect only certain portions of the picture.

Selznick was outraged, not only because his ambitions were thwarted but because he was convinced that his approach to *White Shadows* was both commercially and logistically superior to Stromberg and Flaherty's. (And indeed it proved to be; Thalberg eventually yanked Flaherty and replaced him with Van Dyke, who shot the picture as he and Selznick conceived it, using Flaherty's footage to provide a sense of atmosphere for the film.) Flashing the cocky self-confidence that would carry him to the top of the industry in the next decade, Selznick barged in on Thalberg and his associates during their daily luncheon ritual in MGM's executive bungalow. As the other supervisors watched in disbelief, Selznick questioned their mentor's judgment and challenged his authority. Again Thalberg backed Stromberg, but Selznick persisted. "I told Thalberg in the rather strong language of youth that he didn't know what he was talking about," Selznick later recalled, "and I was fired."

Thalberg cooled down by the next morning and reconsidered the dismissal. He did not want to lose Selznick, who had worked wonders with MGM's story and editorial departments and kept tight control over its writers. And considering the sensational impact of Warners' newly released talkie, *The Jazz Singer,* those departments were likely to need even more attention in the near future. So Thalberg sought out Selznick and calmly told him that he would be reinstated after an apology. But none was forthcoming. Perhaps Selznick felt more chagrined and angry about the previous day's confrontation than Thalberg realized, or perhaps he already knew that Paramount was in the market for a top production executive. Or maybe Selznick simply felt he had gotten what he wanted out of his tenure at MGM and it was time to move on. Whatever his reasoning, David Selznick left MGM in November 1927 and began negotiating with Ben Schulberg for a position at Paramount.

4

Warner Bros.: Talking Their Way to the Top

Sidling from MGM over to Paramount in 1927 made perfect sense for someone with big plans as a producer and a studio executive like David Selznick. He wanted to go with the biggest and the best, and at the time Metro and Paramount were the unquestioned powers in the American movie industry. But as Selznick began his courtship with Paramount in November, a single movie was sweeping the nation which threatened to shake up the Hollywood power structure. And by the time he signed in December, *The Jazz Singer* was a bona fide sensation, certain to transform not just Warners' fortunes but the industry at large, particularly since MGM and Paramount had adopted a wait-and-see attitude toward sound pictures. *The Jazz Singer* snapped them out of their complacency, although for the time being the major powers would have to play catch-up with the upstart Warners.

A governing irony in Warners' rise and the "talkie revolution" generally was that Warner Bros. developed sound not to differentiate its products or to revolutionize filmmaking, but to bring itself in line with the other majors. Warners' theater circuit included only a few first-run houses, and sound would enable the company to offer the kind of stage acts and musical shows that moviegoers had been getting in the downtown palaces from Loew's and Fox and Paramount. Darryl Zanuck, then the studio's most prolific screenwriter, later recalled that Harry Warner "didn't give a damn what the characters were saying on the screen, and I have to say that I didn't bother about it much either. We all thought Harry had a point when he said, 'Do you realize what this means? From now on we can give every small town in America, and every movie house, its own 110-piece orchestra.' " This same view was expressed in the nationwide press release announcing Warners' foray into sound, issued in April 1925 through publicity chief Hal Wallis. "Warners will enter a policy of talking pictures," Wallis announced. "Our researchers show that this is practical and will bring to audiences in every corner of the world the music of the greatest symphony orchestras and the voices of the most popular stars of the operatic, vaudeville, and theatrical fields."

The fraternal Warners—Harry, Albert (Abe), Sam, and Jack—were well aware of the risk involved in their decision to pursue sound films. But the decision scarcely represented a desperate attempt to stave off bankruptcy, as some have argued, nor was it an isolated, go-for-broke effort. It was, rather, one facet of a calculated strategy to lift Warner Bros. into the ranks of the integrated majors. The chief architects of Warners' expansionist efforts were company president (and elder sibling) Harry Warner and financial guru Waddill Catchings, from the Wall Street firm of Goldman Sachs, retained by Harry in 1925. Bringing in Catchings was a key decision in Warners' development, in many

Production supervisor Harry Rapf, at far left, with the four Warner brothers —Sam, Abe, Jack, and Harry—in the company's early years.

ways as important as the commitment to sound production. The Warners had been trying for years to upgrade their operations, but their efforts had been tentative and haphazard at best. In Waddill Catchings they had a strategist with the business savvy and the financial leverage, via Goldman Sachs, to direct their climb to the top. And Catchings saw in Warner Bros.—and in the movie business generally—the same kind of growth potential that he had already exploited in the retail chain-store business working with companies like Woolworth's and Sears Roebuck.

Like virtually all their fellow pioneers, the Warners started out in the nickelodeon business and were forced by the Trust to shift into distribution. When they finally came West in the late teens, Warners was still primarily a distribution outfit, though it had had some success in 1918 with its first feature, *My Four Years in Germany,* a biopic about America's German ambassador that was produced back East. After the move to Hollyood Jack Warner, the youngest and most flamboyant of the siblings, rented a production facility and set to work. He produced a fifteen-part serial for release in 1920, then a half-dozen features over the next two years. In 1922 the company moved out of its rental digs and into Warner Brothers West Coast Studio, built on a ten-acre site at Sunset and Bronson. Although it was dwarfed by other movie factories, the Sunset studio signaled Warners' serious commitment to movie production. In 1923 the company became fully incorporated—as "Warner Bros."—and the studio was upgraded with half of a $500,000 financial package put together by Los Angeles banker Motley Flint. The other half went into the screen rights to three David Belasco hit plays (including *The Gold Diggers,* which would figure heavily in the studio's Depression-era fortunes), and also into the production of a "dog picture," *Where the North Begins.* The latter marked the debut of Rin Tin Tin, Warner's first real star and thus its first bankable commodity, whose box office held up through nineteen pictures over the next seven years.

With the refurbished studio, the prestige of the Belasco deal, and the success of Rin Tin Tin, Warner Bros. started looking like a competitive company. Its products were pitched and its image polished by Hal B. Wallis, who started in theater management and in 1922, at age twenty-three, took over Warners' publicity department. Over the next few years Wallis had ample opportunity to develop his marketing skills. Warners produced thirteen features in 1923 and seventeen in 1924, and signed heavyweights John Barrymore and Ernst Lubitsch to multipicture contracts. Barrymore, already a stage and film star and just off his huge Broadway success in *Hamlet,* made his Warners debut in

Beau Brummel in 1924. When the picture hit, Harry Warner loosened his notoriously tight purse strings and signed "the great profile" to a long-term contract at $12,750 per week. Lubitsch, a top filmmaker from Germany's Ufa studio, made his Warners debut in 1924 with *The Marriage Circle*, the first of five pictures he did for the studio.

It was in 1925 that Harry Warner decided to go all out, allowing Jack a budget for thirty features and bringing in Waddill Catchings to expand their distribution-exhibition operation. Catchings arranged the purchase of the Vitagraph studio in Brooklyn along with its thirty-four distribution exchanges, giving Warners a national distribution operation. He also arranged financing for Warners to expand its first-run theater holdings. By late 1926 the company added ten first-run houses to its chain, including the massive Warner Theater in New York, and had leased another six, including the palatial Orpheum Theatre in Chicago. Brother Sam Warner, meanwhile, initiated the company's pioneering sound effects. In April of 1926 Warner Bros. formed a partnership with Western Electric to create the Vitaphone Corporation. Under the aegis of that partnership, Sam Warner produced hundreds of one- and two-reel shorts—mainly vaudeville skits done with synchronous sound tracks—at the Vitagraph facility in New York.

A S Warners entered its hell-bent expansionist phase in the mid-1920s, its corporate personality began to take shape. Warner Bros. was unique to begin with, since it was Hollywood's only family-owned-and-operated outfit, run by brothers from an immigrant clan of Eastern European Jews. The company's internal power structure reflected a rather complex set of sibling relationships, particularly between Harry (born in Poland in 1879), who took his role as generational patriarch quite seriously, and Jack (born in Canada in 1892), who was equally sensitive about his status as baby of the family. The division of executive labor was complicated enough in any movie company, and in Warners' case it was fueled by a sibling rivalry between Harry and Jack that persisted throughout their—and the company's—life span, with the familial pecking order reinforcing the usual tension between the New York office and the studio.

Jack's status and authority within both the family and the company grew steadily as production operations expanded and output increased during the 1920s. But as the stakes went up at the studio, Jack was required to play a more administrative role and to move ever further from the actual filmmaking process. Jack was scarcely a creative type to begin with, though, and as Warners' schedule grew to thirty then forty pictures per annum during its expansion, both Harry and Jack

realized the value of having someone like Irving Thalberg on the lot.
They found their production chief in 1924, but they scarcely realized
it when they signed a twenty-two-year-old writer named Darryl Zanuck to a $250-per-week contract. The Warners hired Zanuck after hear-
ing the brash, diminutive, hyperkinetic youngster pitch story ideas for
their Rin Tin Tin series. Zanuck wrote the only Rin Tin Tin picture of
1924, *Find Your Man,* and he also scripted the first and most successful
of the canine's four 1925 features, *The Lighthouse by the Sea.* By then
it was obvious that Zanuck, after little success as a fiction and magazine
writer, had a knack for turning out silent movie scenarios. He worked
quickly and understood the basics of dramatic construction, and could
come up with dozens of variations on any given theme. Perhaps most
important, Zanuck had a gift for turning out what he termed "hokum"
—sentimental, melodramatic, and utterly predictable stories, long on
action and plot but short on thematics or character development. Eventually Zanuck's writing skills, along with his organizational savvy and
his feel for popular tastes, encouraged Jack Warner to upgrade his role
in the overall production setup. Scripting the Rin Tin Tin adventures
had become second nature, so Zanuck supervised other contract writers on those projects while he developed a whole range of stories and
scripts.

Harry and Jack Warner had come to learn the importance of story
and scenario development, and the value of the final shooting script in
the studio production process. Thus someone like Zanuck was price-
less. As Jack Warner later recalled, Zanuck "could write ten times
faster than any ordinary man. He worked Saturdays, Sundays, and
nights in those days. He was a very professional writer. He could leave
on Friday and come back Monday with a script." Zanuck was so prolific, in fact, that he wrote under four different names—Melville Cross-
man, Mark Canfield, and Gregory Rogers, as well as his own—to
downplay the studio's dependence on his writing talents. His ability
to dash off stories also brought him into the annual budget-setting and
scheduling process. Before Jack Warner went East for the annual sales
convention where he laid out the program for the upcoming season,
Zanuck would crank out story synopses not only for properties and
scenarios already acquired and in preparation, but also for stories made
up on the spot, many of which would find their way into production
during the coming year.

B Y 1927, Jack Warner and Darryl Zanuck were playing roles at Warners Bros. similar to those Mayer and Thalberg played at MGM. Jack
ran interference with the New York office, managed the studio at large,
handled contract negotiation, and made important cast and crew as-

signments. Zanuck supervised scenario development and much of the everyday production activities; his weekly salary increased tenfold along with his creative and executive responsibilities. But whatever the similarities to MGM, Warners' Sunset studio was no Culver City, and Zanuck was no Thalberg. Warner Bros. had nowhere the working capital or the resources of Loew's/MGM, and Zanuck's authority was not commensurate with that of Thalberg, who oversaw all production, received a cut of the studio profits, and had executive officer status. Nor was there a middle-management system at Warners, a corps of production supervisors answerable to Zanuck. Instead, Zanuck handled the standard action pictures and melodramas, which constituted most of Warners' output, while either Jack Warner or a producer-director like Ernst Lubitsch oversaw the more prestigious projects. Thus Warner developed something of a split personality by 1927, with its production efforts divided between Zanuck's routine features and the occasional prestige projects.

This split widened with Warners' move into sound, since aside from shorts, the new technology was reserved for important productions. Warners' first sound feature was *Don Juan,* a costume romance starring John Barrymore which was given a full-blown prestige release in the fall of 1926, opening as a road show in select houses with reserve seating and at inflated prices. This was not a talkie per se—there was no spoken dialogue, only a musical score and a sound-effects track. Despite a massive promotional campaign, public response to *Don Juan* was disappointing. In fact the film was much less successful than the previous Barrymore vehicle, *The Sea Beast,* a lavish adaptation of *Moby Dick* released as a silent in 1926. The lukewarm response to *Don Juan* gave the Warners pause, coming in the midst of a conversion involving not only its theaters but the Sunset studio in Hollywood, where four new sound stages were under construction. After several profitable years Warners showed sizable losses in 1926, which temporarily stalled both theater acquisition and the conversion of its own houses. The losses were not unexpected, given the cost of sound conversion, and they did not diminish the company's commitment to sound—or Sam's commitment anyway, and Sam was persuasive enough to keep Harry and Abe from bailing out.

There were no plans to cut production, although the commitment to prestige pictures was scaled back. Harry and Jack decided not to renew the contracts of John Barrymore, Ernst Lubitsch, and several other top artists in 1927, focusing Warners' high-stakes production efforts on *The Jazz Singer,* which, at a cost of $500,000, was their most expensive picture yet. A program of forty releases was planned for the coming season, most of them standard features supervised by Zanuck. He wrote either story or script for thirteen of them (under all four names), including two of the four Rin Tin Tin pictures, which by then were virtual insurance policies against box-office failure.

That insurance was hardly necessary after the October release of *The Jazz Singer*, which took the public by storm and took the Warners somewhat by surprise, after *Don Juan*'s weak reception. *The Jazz Singer* was Hollywood's first effort to incorporate song lyrics and even some spoken dialogue into a feature film, and the effort was primitive indeed. The plot was pure melodrama, the acting laden with panto-mime and excessive gesture, and virtually all of the dialogue was pre-sented through intertitles. But 1927 audiences were captivated by the film, particularly when vaudeville star Al Jolson spouted his trademark ad-libs to the orchestra, the other players, and even the audience. "C'mon, Ma—listen to this!" gushed the dynamic Jolson before break-ing into "Blue Skies," and those snatches of dialogue had as much impact on audiences as the song that followed.

Released a full year after *Don Juan*, *The Jazz Singer* finally affirmed Warners' commitment to sound production. The picture grossed $3 million and sent Harry Warner headlong into further expansion and theater conversion—though without the assistance of his brother Sam, who died of a cerebral hemorrhage on October 5, the day before *The Jazz Singer* premiered. Only weeks after *The Jazz Singer*'s release, construction was completed on the last of the four sound stages at the Sunset studio, and plans were finalized for complete conversion to sound within another year. The new stages were 90 feet by 150 feet and specially soundproofed, with mobile booths for the cameras and separate glass-enclosed booths for sound recording. Work began im-mediately on a slate of "part-talkies," with the efforts on both coasts—at Vitagraph as well as at Sunset—to produce an "all-talking" feature. In December 1927, Vitaphone released an all-talking two-reeler, *Solo-mon's Children*, and in July 1928 Warner Bros. released *The Lights of New York*, a Vitaphone two-reeler that was expanded by director Bryan Foy to a modest feature length (fifty-seven minutes). That pushed its production costs from $21,000 to $75,000, but the eventual box-office take on *The Lights of New York*, Hollywood's first all-talking feature, was over $1 million.

T H E timing of Warners' sound conversion could not have been better —at least for Warner Bros. Back in February 1927, Paramount, MGM, and United Artists had decided to wait at least one year before com-mitting to sound. By the time they began conversion, Warners had completed its sound stages and had its theater conversion well under way, and it also got the jump in developing related technologies to

Theater magnate Sid Grauman and Jack Warner pose with the sound equipment for Grauman's Egyptian Theatre, which was delivered and installed under armed guard to prevent sabotage by Warners' competitors.

Al Jolson in a musical number from The Jazz Singer, *which heralded the arrival of "talkies" although it contained very little spoken dialogue.*

facilitate sound production. By the fall of 1928, Warner Bros. was fully converted and thus far ahead of any other studio in satisfying the public's appetite for talkies. Warners flooded the market with sound films, and Harry Warner made the most of the company's temporary advantage. Working once again with Waddill Catchings of Goldman Sachs, he completed his company's decade-long expansion strategy in three bold strokes. In September 1928 Warners purchased the Stanley Corporation of America, with its 250 theaters in 75 cities and 7 states—including the Strand on Broadway, one of the nation's premier movie palaces. In October, Warners bought 42,000 shares (out of a total of 75,000) in First National, a fully integrated company with an extensive distribution system and a massive studio facility in Burbank, just north of Los Angeles. Warners closed out the year by absorbing the Skouras Brothers Theaters in St. Louis, solidifying Warners' chain in the Midwest. Box-office revenues in 1928 were such that Harry paid all of Warners' outstanding debts and the company still netted over $2 million.

Warners spent most of the following year consolidating its newly acquired power. The company had yet to establish a house style, since its growth had been too quick and uneven to stabilize either its market strategy or its pool of resources, but perhaps that would change with Zanuck's promotion to full-blown production chief in 1929. There was little to distinguish Warners' early talkies other than their sound tracks, but still the money poured in. Warners was on a roll, and not even the October 1929 stock market collapse slowed its momentum. In fact the crash actually improved Warners' position in the industry, since it forced William Fox to liquidate his holdings in First National in order to raise cash for his own overextended company. On November 4, 1929, exactly one week after Black Tuesday, Harry Warner bought the remaining stock in First National, completing his company's remarkable decade-long climb.

II

1928-1932:
THE POWERS
THAT BE

5

Selznick at Paramount: From Boom to Bust

The 1920s were years of tremendous growth and prosperity for the movie industry, with the coming of sound providing a final surge in Hollywood's fortunes at decade's end. The talkie boom was so strong, in fact, that Hollywood was all but oblivious to Wall Street's momentous crash in late 1929. And as the stock market's collapse sent shock waves across the nation in 1930, moguls and studio heads were touting the movies as a "Depression-proof" industry. Indeed, 1930 was Hollywood's biggest year ever, as theater admissions, gross revenues, and profits reached record levels. Economic reality quickly caught up with the movie industry, though, and the studios paid dearly for their blissful ignorance. Falling attendance, depleted reserves, and tight fiscal policies staggered the studios by 1931–32, especially those that had expanded most aggressively in the 1920s.

Hollywood weathered the storm, of course, but not without massive adjustments to its way of making movies and doing business. The late 1920s and early 1930s brought a realignment and consolidation of corporate power, a widespread effort to economize production, and a more efficient utilization and exploitation of corporate resources. The general results were twofold. First, the survivors emerged as Hollywood's dominant powers, the so-called Big Eight: the five integrated majors (Paramount, MGM, Fox, Warners, and RKO), the two dominant nonintegrated minors (Universal and Columbia), and United Artists, which wasn't a studio but a releasing company for major independents. Second, because the studios were forced to streamline operations and rely on their own resources, their individual house styles and corporate personalities came into much sharper focus. Thus the watershed period from the coming of sound into the early Depression saw the studio system finally coalesce, with the individual studios coming to terms with their own identities and their respective positions within the industry.

DAVID SELZNICK spent those watershed years at Paramount Pictures, a longtime Hollywood power that took sound conversion in stride but then fell heavily when the Depression finally hit Hollywood. Selznick's tenure with the company, in fact, was bracketed by these two industry upheavals: the coming of sound and the coming of the Depression.

Selznick's clash with Thalberg and his abrupt departure from MGM in November 1927 came at an opportune time. Experienced production executives were in demand throughout the 1920s as the studio system took hold, but in late 1927 with *The Jazz Singer* sweeping the nation and Warners' competitors gearing up for talkie production, Selznick was an especially hot commodity. Besides his stint as a Thalberg supervisor, he had been head of MGM's scenario department and writing staff. Warners already was proving that the coming of sound may have been a technological revolution, but it hardly revolutionized the studio production process. If anything, the costs and logistical complexity of sound increased the need for a closely supervised, assembly-line system. The key to that system was the shooting script, which mapped out all aspects of production—from camera work and dialogue to the shot-by-shot construction of the picture—before the actual filmmaking machinery was set into motion.

Paramount was taking an aggressive approach to sound conversion, with plans to be fully converted by the late 1920s and to release a full program of talkies for the 1929–30 season. Ben Schulberg, the Managing Director of Production in Hollywood, saw Selznick as someone who could facilitate the transition to sound and streamline the whole process of scenario development. So in December 1927 Schulberg hired Selznick as his executive assistant to oversee Paramount's story department and writing staff, and to recruit new writers who were adept with spoken dialogue. Eager to cast his lot with MGM's rival and still convinced that the surest way to the top at any studio was via the scenario development, Selznick welcomed the opportunity. He spent most of 1928 getting Paramount's story department and writing staff into shape, following much the same course he had at MGM a year earlier. He also did some important recruiting for the studio, taking on a job that had been initiated by a most unlikely talent scout, Herman Mankiewicz.

Mankiewicz had come West a few years earlier as a screenwriter, having struggled as a journalist and playwright in New York. After a stint at MGM he segued over to Paramount, where Ben Schulberg offered him $400 per week plus a guarantee that the studio would buy up to four original stories per year at $5,000 apiece. With the threat of talkies, Schulberg asked Mankiewicz to start courting dialogue writers from among his newspaper and theater cronies in New York. Thus was created the "Herman J. Mankiewicz Fresh Air Fund," which brought Ben Hecht, Charles MacArthur, Laurence Stallings, Gene Fowler, Nunnally Johnson, and a number of other eastern writers to Paramount. Mankiewicz was typically cavalier and cynical about the venture, as he displayed in a now-legendary telegram to Ben Hecht: WILL YOU ACCEPT 300 PER WEEK TO WORK FOR PARAMOUNT PICTURES? ALL EXPENSES PAID. THE 300 IS PEANUTS. MILLIONS ARE TO BE GRABBED OUT HERE AND YOUR ONLY COMPETITION IS IDIOTS. DON'T LET THIS GET AROUND.

Selznick sustained Mankiewicz's recruiting efforts, bringing out a number of prominent eastern writers, as well as Herman's brother, Joe Mankiewicz, and also a few stage directors like George Cukor and John Cromwell. But Selznick's most important contributions were in the scenario and writing departments, and as he brought them up to speed, his own status at the studio steadily rose. In working with Schulberg at Paramount, though, Selznick soon learned that Paramount's power structure and chain of command were altogether different from those at MGM, and that the difference had considerable impact on the way Paramount made movies.

The chief differences between Paramount and MGM had to do with market strategy and the relationship between the studio and the New York office. Like MGM, Paramount had merged its way to integrated status in the late teens and the 1920s. Company president Adolph Zukor had started in the theater business; he'd even been partners with Marcus Loew for a time just after the turn of the century. Zukor went into production in 1912 to compete with the Trust, and then in 1916 he merged his production company, Famous Players, with a national distribution company, Paramount Pictures. Zukor soon won control of the merged company, bringing in independent producer Jesse Lasky as his second-in-command. By the late teens "Famous-Players Lasky" began developing a national theater chain and thus pioneered vertical integration on a nationwide scale. Zukor expanded production and exhibition throughout the 1920s, making a key move at mid-decade in a merger with the Chicago-based theater outfit Balaban and Katz. By then Loew's and Fox had tied up New York, the nation's top movie market, but the Balaban and Katz deal gave Zukor control of Chicago, the nation's second biggest market.

The merger also brought in the peculiar genius of Sam Katz, who already had transformed exhibition practices in the Midwest. Katz moved his staff to New York after the merger and revamped Zukor's operation. He handled booking and advertising out of the New York office, and he also helped monitor and regulate the company's cash flow. He remodeled the company's exhibition arm along the lines of the retail chain stores that were sweeping the nation during the 1920s —not unlike what Waddill Catchings was then doing at Warner Bros. It was largely at Katz's behest that many of the company's theaters took the name Paramount, and the title Paramount-Famous-Lasky was even abbreviated to Paramount to accommodate Katz's sales and marketing campaign. The expansion of Paramount's theater operation continued during the early sound era, with Katz converting the theaters to sound while Zukor closed out the decade with a massive theater-buying binge. In 1928–29 Zukor added five hundred houses to the Paramount chain, pushing the total beyond twelve hundred—nearly ten times the size of the Loew's/MGM chain.

Selznick was awed by Paramount's sheer size, but he came to resent its impact on studio operations. Simply stated, Paramount was a much more market-driven company than MGM. It operated through a classic "top-down" model, with Zukor and Lasky, the President and the Vice President in Charge of Production, respectively, dictating the company's sales and production strategies from the New York office. If they consulted anyone on an important marketing decision it was not studio chief Ben Schulberg in Hollywood but rather two other corporate officers in New York: exhibition chief Sam Katz and his counterpart in distribution, Sidney Kent. Zukor and his chief officers—Lasky, Katz, and Kent—read the market, evaluated Paramount's resources and the currency of its stars and genres, and set the annual budget and program accordingly. Only then were the studio executives brought in to assist Lasky with the scheduling and the important cast and crew assignments.

The key figure in this power structure was Jesse Lasky. He was the linchpin, the executive with filmmaking savvy who knew the company's resources and finances, its market skew and production capabilities, and who could factor them into a profitable program of pictures. Unlike the vice presidents in charge of production at other companies, Lasky operated out of New York, splitting his time between the company's Manhattan headquarters and its modest East Coast studio on Long Island, which turned out occasional prestige pictures and low-

Paramount's headquarters in New York's Times Square, seen here in 1927, the year Selznick joined the company.

The ground floors of the Paramount Building housed the Paramount Theater, one of New York's foremost motion picture palaces.

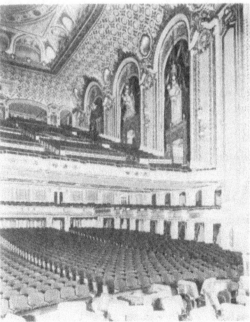

budget programmers. With Lasky's physical and philosophical proximity to the New York office, Paramount lacked the kind of interpersonal dynamic between the vice president and the production chief at other studios—between Mayer and Thalberg at MGM, for instance, or between Jack Warner and Darryl Zanuck at Warners. It also lacked the bicoastal antagonism between production and sales that typified those other companies, and that helped foster whatever climate for innovation and creativity there was at the studio.

For the 1929–30 program, Zukor and his colleagues in New York handed down a budget of $20 million, which Lasky then translated into a production schedule with assistance from Schulberg and Selznick, and from Walter Wanger, who managed the East Coast studio. In the span of some two weeks, Lasky and the others put together a slate of seventy pictures at an estimated total cost of $19,765,000. The pictures were in four categories—New Showworld Specials, Leader Specials, Commander Specials, and Personalities—grouped according to budget, star, and release strategy, with the clearest distinction setting off the eleven Showworld Specials from the other fifty-nine projects on the schedule. The Showworld Specials were Paramount's prestige offerings for the season, designed to carry two or more stars and usually based on some presold commodity like a hit play or best-selling novel. The Showworld Specials alone took up $6 million of the $20 million budget, each costing an average of just over a half-million dollars. Thus they represented only about one-eighth of Paramount's total output but nearly one-third of its budget. Unlike MGM with its emphasis on the first-run market, Paramount was a volume outfit that relied heavily on subsequent-run theaters. That meant block booking and blind bidding with Paramount's ten or so top features, all sure box-office winners, selling the entire program to exhibitors outside the Paramount chain. Among the more notable Showworld Specials on the 1929–30 docket were *The Cocoanuts,* a Marx Brothers comedy budgeted at $500,000; *The Love Parade,* a Lubitsch-directed musical starring Maurice Chevalier and Jeanette MacDonald with an estimated cost of $650,000; and *The Virginian,* a western starring Gary Cooper and Walter Huston that was budgeted at $425,000.

The other fifty-nine projects were straight star vehicles and formula pictures in the $175,000 to $325,000 range, averaging $243,000 per picture. Most carried one star along with a featured player or two, and none were based on presold story properties—in fact most were not even titled as yet. These were generally identified by the personalities involved, with their budgets indicating the status of the star or the near-star involved. A Maurice Chevalier was pegged at $325,000 and a Clara

Bow at $300,000, for instance, while a William Powell and a Gary Cooper were each set at $225,000.

PARAMOUNT'S two-tiered market strategy, with its occasional prestige productions and glut of standard features, corresponded to the studio operations and management structure of its West Coast plant. Schulberg and Selznick supervised the standard features but simply monitored the high-class projects, intervening only when production problems warranted it. These projects were produced, for the most part, by Paramount's star directors—notably Ernst Lubitsch, Josef von Sternberg, and Rouben Mamoulian. That's not to say that these filmmakers operated outside the company's purview, particularly Jesse Lasky's. Because of the cost and potential market value of Paramount's prestige pictures, and also because they tended to be adapted from stories that had succeeded in some other medium, Lasky usually had a pretty clear conception of the end product even when the annual budgets and programs were set. But in almost direct opposition to MGM or Warners, where the higher the stakes the more likely the studio boss and production chief were to be involved, at Paramount the high-cost, high-risk pictures involved the least amount of executive control or front-office interference. Thus Paramount was something of a "director's studio" where its prestige productions were concerned, and there was much less continuity in terms of style or market appeal between its top features and its routine releases.

Significantly, Lubitsch, Sternberg, and Mamoulian all spent some of their early years in Europe, where producer-director status was commonplace. Each managed to win producer-director status at Paramount even after sound came in. Sternberg was Paramount's most successful and powerful house director in the late 1920s, moving freely between Hollywood and Ufa—a Berlin-based studio partly owned by Paramount. Sternberg brought to his American pictures a certain Germanic style and a number of German performers as well. And interestingly enough, he used his success not as leverage for individual authority and autonomy (à la Stroheim), but rather to assure that he could work regularly with select Paramount personnel.

Selznick was well aware of Sternberg's privileged status. In June 1929 Schulberg set out on an extended tour of Europe and left Selznick in charge of the studio. Before departing Schulberg circulated a memo endorsing Sternberg's desire to work regularly with Jules Furthman. The idea, as Schulberg put it, was that "if an efficient writer and an efficient director work together constantly they are bound to do better work." Selznick later recalled that while running the studio, "I varied the extent of my controls," and that in Sternberg's case, "I abided by Schulberg's instructions that I was to let him do as he pleased." Sternberg himself was away during much of Schulberg's absence, working on *The Blue Angel*, a Paramount-Ufa coproduction starring Emil Jannings and newcomer Marlene Dietrich. Both Sternberg and Schulberg were much impressed with Dietrich, so much so that Schulberg signed her to a Paramount contract and she returned to the States with Sternberg.

An English-language version of *The Blue Angel* was a moderate hit, and in early 1930 Furthman began writing *Morocco* as a follow-up for Dietrich and Sternberg. In July Paramount's story editor, Edward J. Montagne, sent Furthman's script to Selznick and Schulberg. With it he sent a lengthy critique that provides a clear indication of Sternberg's status and authority at the studio, and of Paramount's regard for its new star. "Here is a carefully tailored garment," wrote Montagne, "selected and measured with Marlene Dietrich in mind." He considered it ideal as "a vehicle which will permit Miss Dietrich to exhibit her personality and versatility to the American public." Montagne allowed that "from the standpoint of story, *Morocco* is just average," but he felt that Sternberg could "get much more out of the scenes . . . than appears on paper." Montagne's closing comment was the most telling of all: "In brief, it is a case of looking to Dietrich and von Sternberg to lift this story far above its normal story strength, which would be severely questioned if a less able director and a less colorful star were going to tackle the job."

The star-director-writer combination clicked on *Morocco,* laying the foundation for a distinctive production unit at Paramount composed of Dietrich, Sternberg, Furthman, and cinematographer Lee Garmes. Indeed, Selznick's fascination with a "unit-producer" system first took hold as he watched this team turn out a succession of exotic romantic melodramas—*Morocco, Dishonored, Blonde Venus,* and *Shanghai Express*—all of them huge hits.

Had *Morocco* been prepared for a "less able director"—or a less conventional or less commercially successful one—the studio would have done more than simply question the project. This was demonstrated clearly enough in another prestige project, *An American Tragedy,* which was then in preproduction. Zukor had purchased the screen rights to Theodore Dreiser's controversial novel late in 1927 for $90,000, a considerable sum even for a presold commodity. The property lay dormant until 1930, when Lasky assigned it to another of Schulberg's European discoveries, Soviet filmmaker Sergei Eisenstein. While Sternberg and Furthman were preparing *Morocco,* Eisenstein was adapting the Dreiser novel, which he also was to direct.

Josef von Sternberg (in safari garb) with rising Paramount star Gary Cooper, on the set of Morocco.

Like Schulberg, Selznick was impressed with Eisenstein; indeed he had sung the Russian's praises to his MGM superiors some three years earlier after seeing *The Battleship Potemkin.* But the Dreiser script led Selznick to an altogether different—and more pragmatic—assessment of Eisenstein's talent. In an October 1930 memo to Schulberg, Selznick stated that Eisenstein's draft was "the most moving script I have ever read . . . positively torturing. When I finished it, I was so depressed that I wanted to reach for the bourbon bottle." But Selznick didn't leave it at that. "As entertainment," he went on, "I don't think it has one chance in a hundred." He saw Eisenstein's project as "a glorious experiment," with its heavy use of "interior monologue" (voice-over narration of the characters' thoughts) and of montage; he also conceded that it was dramatically in line with Dreiser's novel. But he doubted that Paramount could risk so radical an interpretation in so important a project. Selznick mused that "the advancement of the art" of cinema was "not the business of this organization," nor was the offering of "a most miserable two hours to millions of happy-minded young Americans."

Selznick's reference to the upbeat attitude of young moviegoers indicated naiveté or outright ignorance of the Depression's impact, but Schulberg concurred with his evaluation of the script. After consulting with Lasky he pulled Eisenstein off the project. That cost the company over $30,000 in compensation to Eisenstein, but that was a modest sum in the scheme of things. Paramount already had invested three times that amount in securing the property, and the company also had grown accustomed in recent years to writing off "abandoned" or "worthless" scripts. (Before 1928, the studio wrote off less than $50,000 per year; that figure escalated to just over $150,000 in 1929. In 1930 the total reached $390,000, including the Eisenstein project. Clearly, the influx of new writers and the changing demands of project development after sound came in were taking their toll.) Schulberg had the script rewritten and, after *Morocco* was completed, he put Sternberg and photographer Lee Garmes on *An American Tragedy*. Sternberg's penchant for lush, dense visuals and baroque stylization, along with his rather cynical regard for romantic love, gave the Dreiser adaptation a distinctive edge but without too extreme or "depressing" an interpretation.

INTERVENING in a project like *An American Tragedy* was outside Schulberg and Selznick's usual realm of authority. The two managed all feature production below the prestige level, playing a variation of the studio boss/production chief tandem at outfits like Metro and Warners. But the Paramount executives lacked the authority or the creative control enjoyed by Mayer and Thalberg or by Jack Warner and Darryl Zanuck. Selznick described Schulberg as a "mill foreman," and he saw himself as a creative producer whose talents were squandered at a factory like Paramount. Occasionally he got the chance to test his skills, as when a disastrous preview of *The Four Feathers* in 1929 required an eleventh-hour overhaul. Selznick conducted a massive salvage job on the adventure drama, reconstructing the story and setting up a program of retakes, and then he personally supervised the reediting. The picture was a mild success, and it put codirectors Merian Cooper and Ernest Schoedsack on the industry map; it also fueled Selznick's desire to get out from behind a desk and onto the lot, making movies rather than administrative decisions.

For the time being, though, Selznick mainly confined himself to producing memoranda—a skill that was already becoming legend in

Hollywood. Most of his Paramount memos went to Ben Schulberg and story editor E. J. Montagne, and most of them involved scenario development for the standard features. It was here that Selznick and his fellow executives, caught up in an endless discourse on stars, story formulas, and production costs, were most "creative." This interplay of budget, star, and genre was crucial to studio filmmaking—the three were, in effect, the holy trinity of the studio system and an obsession for executives like Selznick, Schulberg, and Montagne. Consider an exchange in August 1929 about Richard Arlen, who had vaulted to stardom in *Wings* a few years earlier but whose stock was declining. After brainstorming with Montagne, Selznick passed along this advice to screenwriter Bartlett Cormack. "The Arlen budget is very limited," said Selznick of its $175,000 cost estimate, "so while Dick falls most naturally into the soldier-of-fortune and the man-who-came-back formulas, we cannot go in for big production values." He also discouraged Cormack from "anything that would take a great deal of shooting time, such as an abundance of exteriors." Their best option, as Selznick saw it, was to try Arlen in "the George M. Cohan type of romantic melodrama."

Another Paramount player whose market value was fluctuating in 1929–30 was Jack Oakie—although his stock was on the rise—and again the budget-star-genre factors had to be recalculated. New York wanted to upgrade Oakie from feature player to star and refashion his comic persona along the lines of Harold Lloyd. A project was initiated in 1930, tentatively titled "On the Spot," which Montagne commented on when he sent a draft of the script to Schulberg and Selznick. Montagne felt that they had "a very amusing comedy, following the Harold Lloyd formula, well constructed, which should prove a good vehicle for Oakie." But Montagne was concerned that it didn't follow the formula closely enough. He went on to suggest that "if we are going after this formula, we might as well follow the policy of one who had it down to a science," and he provided a detailed analysis of the story's failure to accommodate the Lloyd formula.

Selznick and his colleagues were experts in typecasting, though occasionally they couldn't get the star and story type to jibe. Early in 1930, novelist and sometime screenwriter Dashiell Hammett joined Paramount's writing staff at $400 per week, with another $5,000 promised for each original story. One of the first stories he sold the studio was *The Maltese Falcon,* based on his novel. Selznick liked the story and was convinced it would make an ideal vehicle for George Bancroft, a burly masculine type who had first hit playing a gangster heavy in the silent epic *Underworld.* Bancroft had a narrowly defined screen persona and severe limitations as an actor, but Selznick saw the role of

Sam Spade as a chance to broaden his range. He had Hammett start the adaptation and got Schulberg to agree with the casting idea. But when Montagne read Hammett's novel, he urged the executives to reconsider. "I cannot see Bancroft in it at all," said Montagne, arguing that "the method of recital" made the novel work and that the story's "easy, casual, whimsical" style was embodied in the hero. "This man works mentally, not physically as a Bancroft would," wrote Montagne. "The only man we have who could put Sam [Spade] on the screen is Freddie March." At the time Fredric March was considered a light comedy type, and there was little inclination for off-casting at Paramount. So Montagne's inspired casting idea was dropped and Hammett's story was sold to Warner Bros., where it was done a few months later as a low-budget thriller.

S E L Z N I C K spent 1930 immersed in his administrative duties at the studio, and he developed a grudging admiration for the Paramount machine. Zukor and Lasky's market-driven strategy and formulaic products were paying off, with profits in 1930 of $25 million—over ten million ahead of Paramount's nearest rival, MGM. It was a good year for Hollywood in general, with profits at an all-time high and theater admissions pushing a hundred million per week, fully twice what they had been only five years before. A few of the more cost-conscious outfits like Warners and Universal were economizing, but for the most part it was as if the October 1929 stock market collapse had never happened—or if it had, as if the Depression had only increased the public's appetite for the movies.

By early 1931 Selznick was earning $1,500 per week, and his contract was due for renewal at the same salary level. But his duties and responsibilities were increasing steadily and he felt that a raise was in order. The proposed 1931–32 program indicated Selznick's value to the studio, which he pointed out in a memo to Schulberg. Of the sixty-five productions on the schedule, Selznick figured that "there are about forty pictures on which I must act virtually as supervisor." He considered the situation "impossible," noting that "at our outstanding contemporary, Metro-Goldwyn-Mayer, the equivalent of my work is handled by no less than six high-salaried executives." Selznick reminded Schulberg that he had "personally supervised, during the past three years, more pictures than any other three executives combined," and that he had "originated several times more story ideas that saw production than any other single individual in the studio."

Schulberg and the New York powers were persuaded. Selznick's option was picked up at $2,000 weekly, and his supervisory assignments were adjusted, along with the overall management setup. A revised 1931–32 program was issued in April, listing seventy productions on an estimated budget of $24 million. Most of those were standard features. Selznick was assigned to only five, and the rest were spread among eight associate producers, most of whom were culled from the writers' ranks and all of whom fell under Selznick's purview. Again there was a clear distinction between the standard features and the prestige productions. Schulberg was the nominal supervisor on the sixteen prestige projects, termed Rialto-Rivoli pictures after the company's first-run palaces and budgeted at an average of $506,000. But most of those were directors' pictures, for Sternberg, Lubitsch, Mamoulian, and would require Schulberg's involvement only if problems came up. The estimated costs for the fifty-three remaining "Paramount Specials" and "Star Units" averaged $286,000.

But the Depression finally caught up with Paramount, and the envisioned 1931 program never left the drawing board. Zukor and Katz had been pretty cavalier—if not downright reckless—in disregarding the worsening economic conditions. As attendance fell and money grew tighter in the spring of 1931, it was clear that Hollywood was in for a serious siege in the coming months. In late May Paramount's board of directors faced up to the deteriorating market conditions, bringing in John Hertz, a partner in the Wall Street firm of Lehman Brothers, to chair their finance committee and to exact whatever measures were necessary to keep the company operating. Hertz recommended that the production budget be cut by one-third, that all company personnel take heavy salary cuts, and that distribution operations be scaled back.

Selznick would have none of it. He felt he deserved his recent salary increase, and he was not about to stay on for a lower salary while his executive duties and authority had been increased. In a letter to Schulberg on June 15 he refused the pay cut, but the company stood firm. On July 15 Selznick formally resigned in a letter to Jesse Lasky, citing "differences of opinion which it was increasingly apparent would be impossible to reconcile." By then Selznick had already made plans for his own independent production company, and he was confident that despite the economic climate he could make a go of it.

6

Universal: Renaissance and Retrenchment

Any reversal of fortunes is bound to be fraught with irony, and the fate of Universal Pictures in the early 1930s was ironic indeed, since the Depression hit just as Junior Laemmle's campaign to upgrade production was taking off. Carl Laemmle, Jr., son of the company's founder and eager candidate for Hollywood's echelon of boy wonders, had taken over production in April 1928, when Carl Sr. gave him Universal City for his twenty-first birthday. Many dismissed this consummate act of nepotism out of hand, assuming that Carl Laemmle would continue to dictate policy from New York. But Junior had big plans for Universal, and the aging mogul had every intention of indulging his son.

Junior's plans were much the same as those proposed by Thalberg in the early 1920s and later by Al Lichtman, Universal's savvy young business manager. Both had wanted to upgrade feature production and compete in the first-run market, and Uncle Carl had indulged them both up to a point. He even initiated a theater-buying campaign in the mid-1920s, at Lichtman's encouragement. By the time Junior took over, Universal Theaters Inc. had grown to just over three hundred houses. Most of those were subsequent-run theaters in less desirable markets, though, geared more to Universal's long-standing "program" strategy than to first-run releases. Junior figured the theaters were out of line with his upscale production plans and that converting them to sound would only drain the company's resources, so they were sold to finance

Carl Laemmle, Sr., with Junior Laemmle in 1929, one year into Junior's tenure as studio chief at Universal City.

his run at the prestige market. At the studio, Junior cut back shorts and programmers by some 40 percent, channeling his resources into top-grade feature production. He began going after presold properties and big-name stars, directors, and writers.

Junior personally supervised two of the most ambitious projects on Universal's 1929 schedule: *Broadway,* an all-talking, all-singing version of a 1927 stage hit, and *All Quiet on the Western Front,* an adaptation of Erich Maria Remarque's best-selling war saga. Both were to be big pictures that Laemmle felt would reorient Universal's style and corporate image. They would have scope via heavily populated, well-choreographed production scenes—whether musical numbers or battles—and solid production values throughout. Laemmle assigned Hungarian-born staffer Paul Fejos to direct *Broadway,* and he brought in cinematographer Hal Mohr, who had shot *The Jazz Singer* for Warners. Fejos and Mohr were encouraged to develop dynamic, imaginative musical numbers, and they responded by devising a crane that mobilized the camera and brought a fluidity to the dance sequences that was unprecedented in Hollywood sound pictures.

Broadway was a success, but then so were musicals from every studio in the early sound era. A more distinctive effort in Junior's campaign was the production of *All Quiet on the Western Front*. He commissioned playwright Maxwell Anderson, who had written *What Price Glory?*, to adapt Remarque's bleak tale about the horrors of trench warfare. He also looked outside Universal for a director, signing free-lancer Lewis Milestone through agent Myron Selznick, David's older brother, for $3,500 per week. Because of Milestone's limited experience with sound, Laemmle signed another of Myron Selznick's clients, former stage director George Cukor, then at Paramount, as "dialogue director" for $750 per week. Milestone was an experienced and versatile talent, and as soon as he arrived at Universal City he began testing Laemmle's authority. Laemmle responded well, proving to have the creative knack and the management skills to handle both a prestige picture and a headstrong director.

Milestone's main concerns involved the Anderson screenplay, which, he pointed out to Laemmle, captured the grimness but not the subtle optimism of Remarque's novel. The original story followed a group of idealistic German schoolboys who in 1914 are inspired by their schoolmaster to enlist, and then one by one are killed or maimed at the front. The last to die is Paul, the story's central character. Milestone felt that the thrill and spectacle of the battle scenes would counter the downbeat aspects of the story, but he also believed that the boys' compassion and humanity should emerge as the strongest statement against the futility and horror of war. Anderson's *What Price Glory?* had used a love story to interject a similar theme, but in this case Milestone wanted it to emerge from Paul's own character as he comes to appreciate the value and beauty of life, even amid the carnage of trench warfare. After considerable negotiation, Laemmle agreed to bring in another writer, Del Andrews, to help Milestone overhaul the script. Anderson then returned for another rewrite, and later while Milestone prepared to shoot, playwright George Abbott did a dialogue polish. Laemmle monitored but didn't interfere with this convoluted writing process, and the result—for which all four writers received screen credit—was a strong, sensitive screenplay.

Milestone handled principal casting, though with considerable input from both Laemmle and Cukor. In fact, it was Cukor who suggested Lew Ayres for the lead. A promising feature player earning only $200 per week, Ayres displayed just the combination of naive idealism and world-weariness that Milestone wanted in Paul. For the supporting roles they cast more familiar—and thus more expensive—actors, notably Louis Wolheim (at $3,500 per week) as Sergeant Katczinsky, the hardened veteran who whips the boys into shape, and John Wray ($1,000 per week) as Himmelstoss, the mild-mannered postman who is transformed by warfare into a sadistic brute. Zasu Pitts was set to play

Paul's mother, and in an inspired bit of off-casting, dapper silent co-median Raymond Griffith was cast in a key bit part as the French soldier discovered in a bomb crater by Paul, who then impulsively stabs him and waits in anguish as he slowly dies.

All Quiet went into production in November 1929 with a sixty-three-day shooting schedule and an estimated budget of $891,000. Most of the picture was shot in the controlled environment of the studio, en-abling Milestone and cameraman Arthur Edeson to execute elaborate crane and tracking shots, and also to create a growing sense of darkness and despair. As the story moves from Paul's hometown to the barracks, and then to the trenches and the charred, surreal expanse of no-man's-land, the film traces a harrowing descent—not only into the maelstrom of carnage and death, but into the depths of Paul's own psyche. The battle scenes are all furious action and confusion, challenging many assumptions about the immobility of the camera in early sound films (as had the dynamic musical numbers in *Broadway*), and they came as almost welcome distractions from Paul's growing sense of futility and malaise. "We live in the trenches and we fight," Paul explains at one point. "We try not to be killed. That's all." His disillusion deepens until the film's final moment, when Paul reaches out to touch a butterfly and is killed by a sniper's bullet—a scene that Milestone and Edeson improvised on the set, using the director's own hand for the closeup.

By the time Milestone closed production in February 1930, Laemmle was convinced Universal had not only a big but a truly im-portant picture. Preview audiences had no trouble with the potentially depressing subject, and they seemed genuinely taken with Lew Ayres's performance. Using comic actor Ray Griffith also paid off: his slow death in the bomb crater where he and Ayres are pinned down by gunfire was the film's most haunting scene. One element of the picture that preview audiences didn't buy, though, was Zasu Pitts's performance. Pitts had done many dramatic roles but recently was scoring as a comedienne, and her portrayal of Paul's mother drew a mixture of laughter and confusion from viewers. So Laemmle sent the picture back into production, with Beryl Mercer filling in for Pitts. The retakes were completed in early April, pushing *All Quiet* even further over budget—to $1.45 million, nearly twice the estimated cost. The cost overruns concerned Laemmle, of course, but his concerns van-ished with the picture's New York premiere on April 30, 1930—exactly one year after he took over the studio. The picture was an immediate hit, both commercially and critically, and later that year the newly created Motion Picture Academy, in its third annual award ceremony, voted *All Quiet on the Western Front* the best picture and Lewis Mile-stone the best director of 1929–30.

Coming in the wake of *Broadway* and another hit musical, *Show Boat*, *All Quiet* was a clear affirmation of Universal's new market strategy, and of its new studio chief as well. Junior Laemmle, at age twenty-two, was bringing new stature and credibility to Universal and proving how quickly things could turn around in the movie business. But despite the A-class hits and new market profile in 1929–30, Laemmle had some expensive flops, too, and not even the hits had done as well as they could have, since Universal's sales and distribution setup was not geared to exploit first-run releases. So with Junior's upgraded production strategy depleting Universal's cash reserves, the company needed to borrow. But money was getting tight in 1930 and Universal lacked the real estate holdings to leverage any sizable loans, particularly after selling off its theater holdings. The only answer was to cut back production, to revert to the closely regulated, high-efficiency system that Carl Sr. had relied on for decades.

Junior Laemmle's foray into prestige production had been a remarkable feat, but even more remarkable was the way he scaled back production and economized operations as the Depression hit. In the eighteen months from August 1930 to February 1932, Laemmle stopped supervising individual pictures altogether, concentrating instead on the entire feature schedule. During that period, Universal produced thirty-four features, less than half its output in the preceding eighteen months. And the era of million-dollar budgets was over. The thirty-four pictures were budgeted at $7,581,000, and their final cost was $8,060,000—an average of $237,000 per picture, only 6 percent over budget. The average shooting schedule was twenty-six days. The following figures indicate the budgetary range of the thirty-four releases, including both estimated and final costs:

BUDGET RANGE	NO. OF PICS (BUDGET EST.)	NO. OF PICS (FINAL COST)
over $500,000	0	0
400,000–500,000	2	5
300,000–400,000	3	2
200,000–300,000	16	14
100,000–200,000	11	9
50,000–100,000	2	4
below 50,000	0	0

Equally stringent economies were applied to Universal's subfeature operations—its five-reel programmers and its one- and two-reel shorts. Programmers were shot in two to three weeks for less than $75,000, while shorts and serials were cranked out in two to three shooting days per reel and at a per-reel cost of $8,000 to $10,000. For a time, Universal's low-budget units also shot separate foreign-language versions of selected features. These were generally done with a different cast and crew than the original, but with the same sets, costumes, and scripts (in translation). The savings were substantial—entire features could be done for $40,000 to $70,000 in two to four weeks—although within a few years new sound-dubbing facilities would provide Universal an even more economical means of producing foreign-language versions of its pictures.

As expected, 1930 was a rough year for Universal: losses totaled $2.2 million, while the other studios continued to flourish. But a year later the situation was reversed. As the Depression sent a shudder through the entire industry in 1931, the Big Eight's combined profits fell from over $50 million in 1930 to $6.5 million. Universal was the only Big Eight company that improved its economic position over 1930, turning a profit of $400,000 in 1931. Though Universal had reverted to its program strategy, the general quality of its features was up and its less distinguished six- and seven-reelers proved to be ideal "second features" as double billing became standard practice outside the first-run market. And in general, Universal's balanced offering of features, five-reelers, shorts, serials, and newsreels delivered more for the moviegoer's money in outlying urban areas and in the small-town and rural markets where sagging attendance meant keener competition. Its programs also provided more frequent interruptions, enabling exhibitors to try everything from bingo games to dishware giveaways between pictures. This turned an evening at the movies into a four-hour marathon at many theaters and proved to be a marketing bonanza and a revenue boost to theater owners.

T O cut costs and enhance marketability in 1930 and 1931, Laemmle concentrated on formula pictures even at the feature level. The shift to low-cost genre production forced Universal to operate within its means and exploit its own resources, and only then did its house style and market strategy really coalesce. Pictures like *Broadway* and *All Quiet* had brought unprecedented credibility and prestige, but for Universal they were acts of cinematic and institutional bad faith, hardly the basis for a consistent studio operation or a reliable market strategy. Under Laemmle's new program, Universal cultivated a few standard movie formulas like women's pictures and gangster sagas, but its signature genre in the early 1930s was the horror film. Universal's wholesale commitment to horror pictures came with the success of *Dracula*, a late-1931 release, which the studio followed up with a succession of horror classics in 1932, including *Frankenstein*, *The Mummy*, and *The*

Old Dark House. The horror picture scarcely emerged full-blown from the Universal machinery, however. In fact, the studio had been cultivating the genre for years, precisely because it played to Universal's strengths and maximized its resources.

The most important of those resources were a function of Universal's sales and marketing setup. Over the years Carl Laemmle built a strong international distribution system, particularly in Europe. To ensure the viability of Universal's pictures on the Continent, Laemmle signed scores of European filmmakers during his annual trips abroad. Many of those recruits were German—as was Laemmle—and were schooled not only in the European tradition of gothic horror, but also in the German Expressionist cinema of the late teens and the 1920s. They brought a fascination for the cinema's distinctly unrealistic qualities, its capacity to depict a surreal landscape of darkness, nightmare logic, and death. This style sold well in Europe, and it also distinguished Universal's products in the U.S. market. And equally important, it was a relatively inexpensive look to reproduce on the screen. The dark, foreboding atmosphere of Universal's horror pictures cut the costs and complexity of lighting and set design—indeed, it became standard practice to construct only the portion of a set that would be visible through the shadows or fog.

This rather odd form of narrative economy was vitally important to a studio with limited financial resources and no top stars to carry its pictures. And in casting, too, the studio turned a limitation into an asset, since the horror film did not require romantic leads or name stars. What was needed was an offbeat character actor, and in fact Universal's one big star during the 1920s, Lon Chaney, was essentially a featured player known not for his own personality or physical star qualities, but for the horrific parts he played, most notably in *The Hunchback of Notre Dame* in 1924 and *The Phantom of the Opera* in 1926. Chaney had since bolted for MGM, but there were a number of dynamic character actors at Universal—contract players like Conrad Veidt, Boris Karloff, and Claude Rains—who later climbed to stardom via the horror film.

In the late 1920s, the filmmaker at Universal most adept at mustering its resources for horror production was Paul Leni. Another German expatriate recruited by Laemmle, Leni was an expert at translating Expressionist style into the language of Hollywood. His training as a painter led to early film work in set design and art direction, and he eventually became a director at Ufa before coming to Universal. His debut picture in America was *The Cat and the Canary*, a 1927 silent that set the pattern for Universal's "old dark house" formula. The picture, which depicted a brood of greedy relatives converging on a remote mansion for the reading of a will, worked well despite its second-rate cast. But the star of the picture clearly was Leni. His integration of lighting, set, and costume design created a sense of atmosphere that proved both unsettling and captivating to American audiences. He scored again in 1928 with *The Man Who Laughs*, starring Conrad Veidt as a man whose face was distorted at birth into a permanent hideous grin. Veidt's performance recalled Chaney's role in *The Phantom of the Opera*, a picture that was invoked again in 1929 when Leni used the same opera sets for *The Last Warning*, a gothic murder mystery. Leni had another hit, but his promise as a master of the macabre was cut short that same year by a case of blood poisoning, which killed him at age forty-four.

Despite Leni's death, the horror film was becoming a staple on both sides of the Atlantic for Universal by 1930. No other company was so fascinated with the horrific, not even Paramount with its strong European connections. In fact, early in 1930 Paramount studio boss Ben Schulberg toyed with the idea of doing *Dracula*, but his studio colleagues would have none of it. "At your request, some months ago, I felt out all our supervisors on *Dracula*," reported Paramount story editor E. J. Montagne in an April 1930 memo to Schulberg. "We did not receive one favorable reaction." Sharing their sentiments, Montagne suggested that despite the interesting subject, he felt it was "the type of story which would be more palatable for Europe than the U.S." due to the "strictly morbid type of theme." Montagne was also concerned about Hollywood's newly devised Production Code, created specifically to uphold the moral standards of movies. He realized that the stage version of *Dracula* had been successful on Broadway, but he was concerned that "the very things which made people gasp and talk about it, such as the blood-sucking scenes, would be prohibited by the code and also by censors because of the effect of these scenes on children."

Junior Laemmle shared some of those concerns, but the success of *Dracula* on stage and Universal's own success with "morbid" subjects convinced him to take it on. He decided to adapt the 1927 stage version of *Dracula* by Hamilton Deane and John Balderston, not only because it had proven itself with American audiences but also because of the copyright problems in Germany over *Nosferatu* in 1921. The producers of that German Expressionist classic insisted that it was based on a popular legend and not on Bram Stoker's novel, but the courts decided otherwise. So Laemmle opted for the stage version, and in fact he planned *Dracula* during Universal's first-run phase and envisioned it as a prestige production. Like *All Quiet on the Western Front*, which was being shot at the time, *Dracula* was based on a presold property and involved outside talent—in this case Tod Browning and Lon Chaney. Laemmle borrowed the director-star duo from MGM, but Browning and Chaney were no strangers to Universal City; in fact, both had started doing features at Universal under Thalberg. Nor were they unfamiliar with the horror tradition: they did a series of bizarre projects for Metro, including *London After Midnight*, a 1927 vampire picture. But both Browning and Chaney were uneasy with MGM's steady shift to more glamorous stars and a high-gloss style, and felt that Universal was more amenable to their interests, what with its influx of European talent and burgeoning horror tradition.

Laemmle bought the rights to the play and put Tod Browning to work on the adaptation while Lon Chaney finished his first talkie at MGM. But the project hit an unexpected and most unfortunate snag later in 1930 when Chaney learned he had throat cancer. Within only a few months he was dead, at age forty-seven and after some 150 films. Browning was devastated by Chaney's death, and he never really recovered his professional footing after that—a curious comment on the director-star symbiosis. But Browning did press on with *Dracula* after Laemmle signed Bela Lugosi, who starred in the stage version and had worked once with Browning at MGM. One can only speculate what Lon Chaney would have done in the role, though by now anyone but Lugosi as Dracula seems inconceivable. This is a good indication, more than half a century after the filmic fact, of the powerful association between star and character, star and genre. From the black-caped Lugosi's first utterance in a Universal film, "I am Dracula," the screen persona was forever fixed. With his pinched features and thick accent, and his hair slicked into a tight skullcap, Lugosi's Count Dracula was evil incarnate, a creature from the dark side who transfixed viewers because he dared to exist at all, to give substance to the unspeakable.

Dracula was shot in the fall of 1930 and was the most ambitious production under the new streamlined operation. It was a dark and highly stylized film whose technique owed as much to Karl Freund's lighting and camera work and to Lugosi's performance, so excessive and yet so restrained, as it did to Browning's direction. The shoot was scheduled for seven weeks, and though it ran eight days over and required another two days of retakes, Laemmle and Browning kept the production within its $355,000 budget. There was little postproduction done on the film, since Universal had yet to develop "postdubbing" facilities (for rerecording blown lines or poor readings) and since no score was recorded for the picture. Laemmle and Browning had decided to keep music to a minimum, using only an occasional strain from Tchaikovsky's *Swan Lake*. Laemmle previewed *Dracula* in November—within days, ironically enough, of the Academy Awards cer-

Bela Lugosi, Hollywood's vampire prototype, became a subgenre unto himself with the success of Dracula.

emony that brought Universal its first best-picture Oscar for *All Quiet on the Western Front.* But by then the war epic, like the world war itself, was ancient history as far as Laemmle and company were concerned. Universal had produced *Dracula* in one-half the time and at one-fourth the cost of *All Quiet,* and now all that remained was to see whether it played as well in general release as in preview.

Laemmle was sure it would—so sure, in fact, that he closed the *Frankenstein* deal several weeks before *Dracula's* February 1931 release. The Lugosi picture promptly took off at the box office, and Laemmle was more convinced than ever that the horror film was an ideal formula for Universal, given its resources and the prevailing market conditions. He was convinced, too, that he had made the right decision with *Frankenstein,* which had little presold appeal but now had the success of *Dracula* to generate audience anticipation. Mary Shelley's original novel did have some currency as a literary cult classic, of course, and since its publication in 1818 there had been countless stage versions, including a recent adaptation for the London stage by Peggy Webling. Laemmle decided to use Webling's stage version of *Frankenstein*, bringing in playwright John Balderston, who had co-authored the stage version of *Dracula*, to work with staff writer-director Robert Florey on the adaptation. Florey was also penciled in to direct, and at that point he was the governing creative force behind *Frankenstein*. Born in Paris and trained as a filmmaker in Europe, Florey envisioned an even more distinctly Expressionistic style for *Frankenstein* than Browning went after in *Dracula*, turning for inspiration to such German masterworks as *The Golem* and *Metropolis*—both of which were shot by Karl Freund, whom Florey hoped to use on *Frankenstein*. Florey also wanted Lugosi for the role of Dr. Frankenstein, although the new Universal star was unwilling to commit to the project.

At that point a curious turn of studio politics came into play, which had a major impact not only on *Frankenstein* but on Universal's horror tradition in general. Although Florey had been making films for ten years, he had limited feature experience and had done only one talkie. And since he was relatively new to Universal, he had little leverage or credibility at the studio. James Whale, meanwhile, was an established British stage director who was successfully making the transition to movies. He had recently directed an adaptation of the stage hit *Journey's End*, a British war picture starring Colin Clive that was shot in Hollywood to utilize its advanced sound facilities. Whale then directed the dialogue scenes in Howard Hughes's aviation epic, *Hell's Angels*, before signing with Universal in early 1931. Laemmle wanted Whale for an adaptation of Robert E. Sherwood's play *Waterloo Bridge*, a watered-down version of *Camille* designed for Mae Clarke, best known at the time for taking a grapefruit in the face from Jimmy Cagney in *Public Enemy*. Whale was only lukewarm on that project, and in order to secure him on a long-term basis, Laemmle had to give him the pick of Universal's upcoming projects to do after *Waterloo Bridge*. Whale decided on *Frankenstein*, assuring Laemmle that he could overcome the casting problems by getting Colin Clive to play Dr. Frankenstein and Lugosi to play the monster. Laemmle agreed and assigned Florey to start work instead on an adaptation of Poe's "Murders in the Rue Morgue."

Though he had no real knowledge of German Expressionism and little enough experience in the cinema, Whale threw himself into *Frankenstein* once he completed *Waterloo Bridge*. By early summer, Colin Clive was set to play the doctor, but Lugosi flatly refused to play Frankenstein's monster. So Whale searched the studio for someone who was right for the part. He came up with Boris Karloff, a British actor with stage experience and considerable breeding who was mired in second-rate gangster roles. Whale sensed something in Karloff's menacing but oddly sensitive countenance, and he convinced Laemmle to let makeup artist Jack Pierce go to work on him. In turn Whale yielded to Laemmle's insistence that he take Mae Clarke in a supporting role as Dr. Frankenstein's fiancée.

While Pierce worked on Karloff, Whale concentrated on the picture's visual design with cinematographer Arthur Edeson, who shot *Waterloo Bridge* and shared Whale's excitement about doing a horror film. *Frankenstein* was to be made under carefully controlled conditions, using

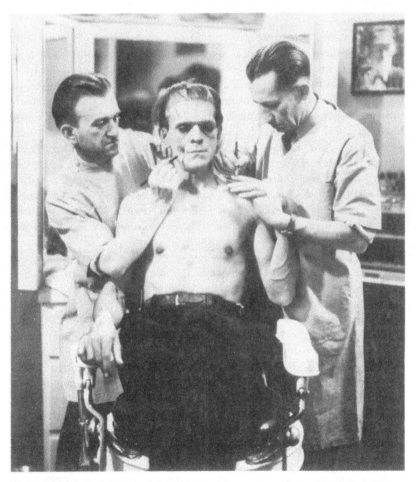

Makeup artist Jack Pierce (left) and an assistant transfigure Boris Karloff into Frankenstein's monster.

many of the same sets Milestone and Edeson had used for *All Quiet on the Western Front*. Whale and Edeson studied Florey's script and production design and screened a number of German Expressionist films. The film's initial spectacle, borrowed from similar scenes in *Metropolis* and *The Golem*, would depict Frankenstein in his laboratory, bringing his monster to life during a fierce electrical storm. The climax would come in a spectacular fire, set by the superstitious and thoroughly terrified townspeople, which destroys Frankenstein and his creation. By late July the production design was completed and so was Pierce's design of the monster, which increased Karloff's size by a foot and a half, his weight by sixty pounds, and his menace factor by an incalculable degree.

Frankenstein went into production in late August 1931, scheduled for a thirty-day shoot. Whale planned to shoot "in continuity"—that is, in the same chronology as the story—because of his own stage background rather than because of any specific demands of the project. As soon as he shot the "birth" of the monster, it was obvious he had made the right decision in casting Karloff. Many experienced actors could have handled the hulking mannerisms and frightening capacity for destruction, but Karloff captured the creature's vulnerability and brought a touch of humanity and pathos to the role. The creature's fear of fire, his submission to his creator, his confused fascination with a little girl before he inadvertently kills her—these qualities and others created sympathy for what was in essence an agent of mindless destruction. Whale made sure that these flashes of humanity remained just that: momentary flashes in an otherwise dark and terrifying story. Lighting and production design were essential here, creating a sense of evil that by film's end, as the townspeople track down the monster, pervades the entire landscape.

Production closed in early October, five days over schedule and well over the $262,000 budget, though Whale did keep the final cost under $300,000. He supervised editing and within two weeks had what he felt was a solid release version of the picture. Junior Laemmle was equally pleased with Whale's work, but after seeing the rough cut he was certain that the end of the picture needed to be changed. His concerns were twofold. The finale, in which both Frankenstein and his monster are killed, seemed vaguely dissatisfying; Laemmle suspected that audiences might want a glimmer of hope or redemption. He also had a more pragmatic concern about killing off the characters—and thus any possibility of sequels. Like *Dracula*, this story was based on a unique and provocative premise. Laemmle now regretted letting Professor Van Helsing drive that stake through Count Dracula's heart, since it consigned the original character to the grave (though not the premise, which Laemmle regenerated a few years later). Laemmle was not about to make the same mistake by letting that angry mob do away with the mad doctor and his monster.

Whale was adamant about keeping the picture intact, so Laemmle agreed to preview Whale's version and gauge the audience reaction. The previews confirmed Laemmle's suspicions and he ordered the ending revised, but Whale came up with a solution that did only minimal damage to his apocalyptic finale. The actual demise of Clive and Karloff was simply cut, leaving their fate in doubt. Then in a brief epilogue—which Whale shot in a single day—the young doctor is seen convalescing from his injuries and reunited with his loved ones, as his father toasts the Frankenstein family.

Laemmle felt much the same way; he too wanted *Frankenstein* to succeed and to propagate. Universal had created a monster, long may it run amok—and indeed it would, becoming one of the most frequently retold tales in movie history. Equally important in the short term was *Frankenstein*'s commercial success, confirming the popularity of the horror film and Universal as its prime purveyor. By November Robert Florey had closed *Murders in the Rue Morgue*, which he shot in only twenty-three days for less than $200,000, and in January 1932 Laemmle sent two more horror films into preproduction: *The Mummy* and *The Old Dark House*. Karl Freund, who shot *Dracula* and *Rue Morgue*, graduated to director for *The Mummy*, a project scripted by John Balderston and designed in much the same vein as *Dracula* and *Frankenstein*. It was yet another tale of the "undead" with strong sexual and religious undercurrents. Karloff portrayed the title character, a mummified Egyptian ruler whose grave is disturbed by British archaeologists and who thus wreaks all sorts of havoc. Freund attended more to visual style and atmosphere than to narrative logic, but the result was another solid hit for Universal, securing Freund's place in the directors' ranks and Karloff's as the studio's top star.

Karloff expanded his range in *The Old Dark House*, stealing the show from an all-star cast that included Charles Laughton, Melvyn Douglas, and Raymond Massey. The picture was a pronounced departure from the other horror films of 1931–32, not only because there was no monstrous Other as protagonist, but also because of its offbeat comic tone. Directed by James Whale, melding the haunted-house formula and the comedy of manners à la Ernst Lubitsch, *The Old Dark House* followed a group of well-heeled travelers taking refuge from a storm in a household of murderous eccentrics, with Karloff's butler the most eccentric of them all. Audiences were pleased with the results, which indicated the range of Whale's and Karloff's talent and the flexibility of the horror genre—how easily the surreal logic and visual stylization of the form

This European village set at Universal City was used for a wide range of pictures, including All Quiet on the Western Front, Frankenstein, *and* The Bride of Frankenstein.

could be pushed into parody and self-conscious humor. Whale's deft manipulation of the genre became a trademark of his best work—and Universal's best horror films of the mid-1930s—culminating in *The Bride of Frankenstein.*

Frankenstein, Rue Morgue, The Mummy, and *The Old Dark House* all scored well for Universal in 1932, with *Frankenstein* by far its biggest hit—just as *Dracula* had been the year before. Another hit for Universal that year was *Back Street,* a John Stahl melodrama based on a best-seller by Fannie Hurst and starring Irene Dunne, on loan from RKO. It was a slick, well-produced weepie, which Stahl pushed into the prestige realm, but it did well at the box office and Junior Laemmle felt it offered exhibitors and audiences an alternative to Universal's run of horror features. But still Universal's lifeblood was the horror film. The cycle just kept turning, and by now other studios were getting into the act—MGM with *The Mask of Fu Manchu* and Tod Browning's *Freaks,* Paramount with *Dr. Jekyll and Mr. Hyde,* Warners with *Dr. X.*

Even the "poverty row" outfits that produced only low-budget pro-grammers had tapped into the genre, a sure sign of its currency. None of this worried the Laemmles, though. It only reinforced the horror film's commodity value in the movie marketplace, and Universal was by far the best equipped to turn it out.

The overall market for pictures was down, though, and even with the success of its horror films, Universal lost $1.7 million in 1932. That hit the Laemmles hard, but it was nowhere near what the majors were losing—all but MGM, anyway, which continued to turn a steady profit. The other integrated studios were losing big, siphoning off income and even assets to cover production costs and make the mortgage payments on their theaters. Universal was still smarting from Junior's fling with prestige production, but the decision to sell off its theater holdings had been fortuitous indeed. Carl Sr. was particularly happy about the move. He always preferred the role of a major minor—a company with a solid production and distribution setup but without the burden of a theater chain. Now as the Depression deepened that strategy made more sense than ever.

7

MGM and Thalberg: Alone at the Top

Of all the Hollywood studios, MGM was least affected by the stock market crash and ensuing Depression. The general economic climate and declining theater attendance cut into revenues, of course; no company could escape that. But while the other studios struggled, Metro flourished, taking in profits year after year and actually increasing its corporate assets. The consistent quality and appeal of its movies was an obvious key to Metro's success, but equally important was the market skew of Loew's, Inc. In the early 1920s Marcus Loew and Nick Schenck had decided against wholesale theater expansion, concentrating instead on the first-run theater market and on Loew's vast distribution network. When Schenck took over after Loew's death in 1927 he sustained that policy, holding the number of houses at about 150 while Warner and Fox pushed their theater total over 500, and Zukor took Paramount-Publix to over 1,000. Due to its relatively small chain, Loew's was not hit so heavily by costs for sound conversion, and once the Depression cut into attendance and revenues, Loew's was not faced with the kind of mortgage payments that drove its competitors to the brink.

Loew's stability throughout the late 1920s and early 1930s enabled MGM to operate pretty much as usual. Talkies were a disruption, but the studio handled sound conversion smoothly enough. By mid-1928 musical scores and sound effects were added to its films (along with three roars from Leo before the opening credits); MGM released part-talkies in late 1928 and its first all-talking pictures early in 1929. Then in February Metro released *Broadway Melody*, Hollywood's first "All Talking! All Singing! All Dancing!" production. It was a huge hit, winning the best-picture Oscar for 1928–29 and proving that MGM had entered the sound era without missing a beat—or a stock dividend. Wall Street's collapse later that year had virtually no effect on MGM, and Loew's first-run strategy meant that even as the Depression hit, the studio could still concentrate on A-class releases while the other majors downgraded feature operations and cut production costs.

The crash itself marked an upbeat moment at MGM, oddly enough, since it thwarted William Fox's attempted takeover of Loew's, Inc. Fox was perhaps the most aggressive of the Hollywood moguls, and during the 1920s he had not only expanded theater holdings but also developed his own sound system, Fox Movietone, to compete with Warners' Vitaphone system. Flush from the talkie boom, he moved on Loew's/MGM in an effort to reduce Hollywood to the "Big Two"—Paramount and Fox. Acquiring the Loew's chain gave Fox over one thousand theaters in the United States and another four thousand overseas, putting him head-to-head with Paramount-Publix and giving him almost complete control of New York City, the world's premier motion picture market. Equally attractive to Fox was the MGM operation, with its fifteen stages and fifteen hundred employees, by now considered the most capable corps of filmmakers in the business. MGM also boasted "all the stars in the heavens," and they were complemented by Hollywood's top writing staff and, of course, a top management team in Mayer and Thalberg.

Because the Mayer group owned no stock in Loew's, they were not privy to the takeover deal—not even Robert Rubin in New York knew of it until Schenck and Fox held a press conference to announce the deal in March 1929. Schenck engineered the buyout, acting on behalf of the Loew family, which wanted out of the entertainment business after Marcus's death. Schenck's own future with Fox was uncertain, though he took some eight to ten million dollars—accounts vary—as "commission" on the sale of the Loew's family stock to Fox. Mayer and Thalberg were vital to the package, but neither wanted anything to do with William Fox. Mayer used his influence with Hearst and others, including President Herbert Hoover, to undercut the deal, and he applauded when the Justice Department initiated an antitrust case against Fox in late 1929. But Fox was undone even before a ruling was handed down. En route to meet Nick Schenck for a summer golf game, he was in an auto accident that killed his chauffeur and left him near death. He was still recovering in October when the stock market collapsed, which left Fox's overextended paper empire—composed mostly of stocks and bonds—in shreds. By early 1930 the merger was off, Fox's creditors took control of his company, and the wily mogul was out of the movie business.

T H E Fox fiasco put another wedge between Schenck and the Mayer group, and from all appearances it brought Mayer and Thalberg into a closer accord. They bought pieces of property and built beautiful new homes on the same stretch of beach, not far from Hearst and Davies, and in early 1930 Mayer gave Thalberg a bigger cut of the Mayer group's annual 20 percent profit-sharing bonus. While Rubin's cut remained at its original 27 percent, Mayer cut his own share to 43 percent and increased Thalberg's to 30 percent—roughly a quarter-million-dollar pay hike, considering MGM's 1929 profits of $12 million.

Appearances and bonus cuts aside, though, the rapport between Mayer and Thalberg was cooling. There were various reasons, both personal and professional, for the growing estrangement. Thalberg was now thirty years old and happily wed to Norma Shearer, who had their first child in 1930. Both of Mayer's daughters were married that same year, giving him two other surrogate sons to deal with, both of whom were movie executives. Edith wed William Goetz, a supervisor at Fox, and Irene married David Selznick, who by then was second-in-command at Paramount. Meanwhile Thalberg was becoming more obsessive about his work at the studio, and Mayer more actively sought the limelight.

Mayer had reached elder-statesman status in the industry, particularly after his campaign in 1927 to create the Academy of Motion Picture Arts and Sciences. Despite its promotional function and its avowed objective to "improve the artistic quality of the film medium," the Academy also served to keep film artists in line. In 1926, the studios created the Central Casting Corporation to improve working conditions and signed a Basic Agreement with actors to keep a lid on outright unionization. But when Actors Equity threatened to organize the performer ranks, Louis Mayer convened Hollywood's power brokers and suggested that they create their own "union." The result was the Academy, technically an offshoot of the Motion Picture Producers and Distributors Association of America (MPPDA), which served as arbitrator in any disputes between the studios and Academy members, who were separated into five groups: producers, directors, writers, actors, and technicians. That effectively stalled the organization of "above-the-line" labor, a considerable coup for Mayer and for the studios in general. The success of the academy solidified Mayer's own power and prestige, encouraging him to look beyond the movie colony for action. His archconservative views of business and politics were reinforced by

By the early 1930s, Irving Thalberg's marriage to Norma Shearer was consuming an increasing amount of his time and energy.

Louis B. Mayer, meanwhile, was rubbing elbows with the power elite of the Free World. Here, Mayer (right) and William Randolph Hearst flank Winston Churchill.

William Randolph Hearst, who introduced Mayer to the privileged realm of the nation's power elite.

Mayer was away from Culver City for weeks and even months on end in the early 1930s, but that had little effect on studio operations. Thalberg and Eddie Mannix, Mayer's chief lieutenant, kept the film-making machinery running smoothly. Working out of neighboring offices on the second floor of MGM's executive building, Mannix managed the plant while Thalberg oversaw production, and with the growing complexity of talkies both were spending more time in their offices and less time prowling the studio lot than they had in the silent era. Thalberg's days were a succession of script conferences and editing sessions, always in concert with one of his supervisors and one or more writers, directors, or film cutters. As always, they concentrated on producing well-crafted star vehicles, a doubly challenging goal after sound came in due to the demands of talkies. In fact, a curious phenomenon at the time was how differently Metro's male and female players fared during the early sound era.

Norma Shearer and Joan Crawford climbed quickly to top stardom in the late 1920s. Marion Davies, already a leading lady thanks to Hearst's support, proved in her early talkies that she had real star quality as a light comedienne. Garbo was silent until late 1929 in *Anna Christie;* the ads proclaimed "Garbo Talks!" and the public took immediately to her husky voice and Swedish accent. *Anna Christie* was also a breakthrough for Marie Dressler, perhaps the most unlikely star in MGM's history. A massive, homely sixty-year-old, Dressler was a sensation playing a hard-drinking waterfront floozy who is befriended by Garbo. After decades of stage and screen work, Dressler was an overnight star, and her popularity grew through another half-dozen 1930 releases, peaking a year later in another boozy waterfront fable, *Min and Bill.* This time Wallace Beery played the comic drunk while Dressler had a Mother Courage role for which she won both an Oscar and the number-one spot on the coveted exhibitors' poll, an annual ranking of the ten biggest box-office stars. Dressler held that top spot for three straight years, defying the governing wisdom that equated female stardom with glamour and adding a new dimension to MGM's house style.

While Metro's female stars were on the rise, its male stars had little success making the transition to sound. Tim McCoy did four silent westerns in 1928–29 but never even attempted a talkie. Lon Chaney died in 1930 after only one sound film. William Haines, always good for half a dozen light comedy hits per annum, faded quickly once sound came in. Latin lover Ramon Novarro declined as well, lingering into the 1930s as a second-billed costar in costume romances. The most dramatic fall was that of John Gilbert, who in 1928 was signed by Nick Schenck to a new five-year, multimillion-dollar contract. That ill-advised vote of confidence destined Gilbert to an extended and very visible decline, due less to his high-pitched nasal voice than to his inability to adjust an exaggerated pantomime style to the subtler technique of talking pictures. Gilbert claimed loudly—in a full-page ad in *Variety*, in fact—that he was done in by Mayer and Thalberg, but there was little to support that claim. After leaving MGM in 1933 Gilbert did a low-grade feature—his last—for Columbia; by 1936 he was dead, a victim of alcohol, a weak heart, and his own hubris.

Buster Keaton could have made a stronger case for victimization by MGM, but the comic genius was characteristically tight-lipped about his fall from grace. Back in the teens and early twenties, Keaton had worked with his own unit and at his own pace, relying on spontaneity, off-the-cuff shooting, and ad-libs. Thalberg indulged this approach during MGM's early years, as did United Artists when Keaton went there in the mid-1920s. Keaton did some of his best work for UA, and his popularity was peaking when he returned to MGM in 1928. The move proved disastrous. The constraints of sound production and of Thalberg's system were simply too much for Keaton, abetted as they were by alcoholism and a failing marriage. He hung on into the early 1930s, but by then his career was effectively over.

But Metro developed a new crop of male stars, including romantic types like Clark Gable and Robert Montgomery, to play opposite its glamour queens in light comedies and romantic dramas, which were still the staples of MGM's output. The other emergent male stars— child actor Jackie Cooper and two middle-aged character actors, Lionel Barrymore and Wallace Beery—were less suited to MGM's polished, high-class fare, but Thalberg found the right vehicles for them, as well. There was also the usual crop of near-stars among MGM's feature players, including Myrna Loy, Maureen O'Sullivan, Franchot Tone, and Robert Young.

METRO'S stars and feature players were its most visible resource, but equally important was the writers' stable, which in the early 1930s added many celebrated playwrights, novelists, and journalists. After the coming of sound, MGM signed such noted eastern writers as Maxwell Anderson, Michael Arlen, Robert Benchley, Stephen Vincent Benet, F. Scott Fitzgerald, Moss Hart, Ben Hecht, Sidney Howard, Samuel Hoffenstein, George S. Kaufman, Charles MacArthur, Elliott Nugent, Dorothy Parker, and S. J. Perelman—along with dozens of others. It's worth noting, though, how few eastern writers made it as screenwriters. The most successful transition was made by journalists

The new crop of male stars developed at Metro in the early 1930s included Clark Gable, shown here with his frequent costar, Joan Crawford.

like Ben Hecht and Robert Benchley, who were accustomed to deadlines and copy editors and writing for an anonymous public that liked its information meted out in economical and dramatic doses. Journalists often had a better ear for dialogue than playwrights or novelists, whose language usually sounded anything but natural when spoken on-screen. Perhaps most important, journalists shared with veteran screenwriters a tendency to think of their work more as a craft than as an art. They rarely considered what they wrote their own, and put little stock in creative control and individual autonomy. Like any other writers, journalists bitched about having their copy mutilated and having to write down to the masses, but they understood the movie business —and that it was a business.

For those writers used to working at their own pace and with more authority, movie writing was dehumanizing, artistically stifling, and a trifle bizarre, particularly at MGM due to Thalberg's approach to story and script development. Thalberg thought nothing of putting half a dozen of his best writers on a project at different times—or even at the same time working separately—to keep the approach fresh and to vary the interpretations of the material. A more frugal studio like Universal or Warners used as few writers as possible on any project, and a few privileged writers actually worked alone from treatment through to shooting final. Writers at MGM occasionally received solo writing credits, but that rarely meant they worked alone on the script. Charles MacArthur received solo credit in 1932 for *The European*, for example, but six other writers contributed to the project. Equally rare were projects where a single writer stayed aboard from start to finish, working continually as other writers came and went. When it did occur it was usually with top staff writers like Frances Marion and Anita Loos, who specialized in story and character development but also wrote creditable dialogue. Still, their work invariably was polished by dialogue specialists whose contributions may or may not have been credited.

All this was business as usual for Marion and Loos, who honed their skills in the silent era, when writing simply meant talking through a story idea with a director. Their skills developed along with the studio system, as story ideas gave way to scenarios and then to shooting scripts and dialogue continuities. Talkies demanded an even more regimented system of preparation and production, and Loos and Marion grew accustomed to the writer's functional and subservient status within the filmmaking process. Loos left Hollywood in the late 1920s, long enough to write a best-selling novel and hit play, and during that sabbatical she developed a better understanding of eastern writers. But still she had no illusions about her craft or her creative control when she returned to Hollywood during the talkie boom.

The controlling force, of course, was Irving Thalberg. He decided what properties were worthy of development, when a story was ready to be scripted, and when a script was suitable for production. Thalberg preferred presold properties that had proven themselves in the marketplace as fiction, drama, or even as news feature. But the majority of Metro's scripts were based on more routine fare, and for these Thalberg relied on his story department, which culled the more promising stories from thousands of prospects it examined annually. In any given year during the early 1930s, MGM's readers filed reports on over 1,000 novels and original scripts, over 500 short stories, and on 1,500 plays and 1,300 works in foreign languages. To facilitate story selection, Thalberg came up with "The Ten Commandments for Studio Readers." These commandments were:

1. Your most important duty is to find great ideas. You'll find them buried under tons of mediocre suggestions.
2. Read at least two newspapers daily. Photoplays sell best which are based on timely topics. . . .
3. Analyze all material on the basis of the players who are working for us. . . .
4. Remember you are dealing with a pictorial medium. . . .
5. Make a close notation of all books you see the public reading.
6. See at least two full-length motion pictures each week, one from this company, one by a competitor. . . .
7. Everything else is secondary in your work to the finding of a strong dramatic situation . . . an interesting clash between the principal characters. . . .
8. Prove your ability to recognize creative material by writing and submitting to us stories of your own.
9. Be proficient in one language besides your own. The competition for good stories is so keen that the supply written in English was long ago insufficient.
10. Above all, train yourself to recognize sincerity in a story. Talking pictures, particularly, have made the public very sensitive to false notes in plots.

Stories that met these criteria were passed to story editor Sam Marx and eventually to Thalberg, who was considered the best judge of a commercial property in the business, with a knack for seeing just how a story might be reworked to suit both the public's taste and the studio's resources. Once Thalberg decided on a property, he generally hammered out a story outline with one of his supervisors and a "story constructionist." Full story and script development, with the usual procession of writers, took six months to a year—though sometimes it reached truly outrageous proportions. On an adaptation of Arthur Schnitzler's novella *Daybreak*, for example, story and script development lasted from October 1927 until March 1931 and involved over a dozen different writers and teams, including a draft by Schnitzler himself in September 1930. Credit for adaptation and continuity went to two of the very first writers on the project; dialogue credit went to someone who worked on the script three years later. Additional dialogue was supplied during shooting, and supervisor Bernie Hyman scripted twenty-eight pages of retakes, all uncredited.

The case of *China Seas,* initiated in late 1930 but not released until 1935, was even more extreme. In December 1930 Thalberg received a five-page reader's report on the Crosbie Garston novel about an English merchant captain who saves his ship from typhoons and pirates, and later gives up his boyhood sweetheart for a mysterious and seductive Chinese heiress. The report opened and closed with the same exclamation: "YOU MUST READ THIS BOOK!" Thalberg read the book, liked it, and assigned three different writers—including Garston —to work up separate treatments. All three were submitted in August 1931. Garston's was a ten-page "suggestion for a treatment." Richard Sharpe's was a straightforward prose rendition that, he explained in a memo, reworked the story along the lines of Maugham's *East of Suez,* with additional inspiration from two Garbo films, *Flesh and the Devil* and *The Temptress.* The most intriguing treatment was John W. McDermott's sixty-six-page tone poem, which opened with these lines:

> The harbor at Hongkong—
> The Kin Lung is pulling out.
> 'Red' Gaskell, the skipper
> Is on the Bridge—
> Shouting orders—wisecracking to—
> 'Ribbing' Ralston, the second mate,
> Cursing, laughing, bullying—
> Snarling, gnarling, joking—
> A hell of a fellow—
> He'd kill his grandmother
> For a laugh!
> That's what they said about him.
> Up and down the China coast—
> Each trip he vowed
> Would be his last!
> The East!
> God! How he hated it!
> Vile—peccant—foul—
> Rotten—stinken—Chinks! . . .

Thalberg and supervisor Harry Rapf worked over the treatments with various staff writers, and by fall they settled on a story line. That initiated a four-year process that involved over two dozen writers, half a dozen directors, and three supervisors. Al Lewin finally took *China Seas* into production early in 1935; it was one of the biggest box-office hits of the year.

To those unfamiliar with studio filmmaking, this seemed like madness; perhaps so, but there was method in it. Thalberg hit his stride in the early 1930s, and his studio machine turned out a steady supply of quality hits. It was a disciplined operation that Thalberg ran, but as the process of story and script development indicated, it was not all that economical. From the high-gloss look and all-star casts of its pictures to the army of well-paid writers and dependence on presold properties, there was a logic of excess, a calculated extravagance at Metro. In fact, by the early 1930s, Thalberg's system was in many ways less efficient and less systematic than any other studio's. But Thalberg was convinced his strategy would pay off in the long run—quite literally, in terms of long-running releases—so long as he controlled the entire process. Thus the importance of the Thalberg conference. In an endless succession of meetings, Thalberg worked with his supervisors and writers, directors, and department heads, editors and composers, shaping each Metro picture. He shepherded each story property as it went through script development and into final preparation before shooting, then monitored production itself through written reports and the screening of dailies, then oversaw the postproduction process of editing, previews, retakes, and reediting until the picture was ready to be scored and sent to New York. Thus, without ever stepping onto the set, Thalberg was intimately involved in every MGM production.

The development of *Grand Hotel,* perhaps the consummate expression of the MGM style during Thalberg's regime, provides an ideal glimpse of this process, of the steady transformation of another "property" into a distinctive MGM product. Serious script development on *Grand Hotel* began late in 1931, but Metro's involvement had begun well over a year earlier. The original novel by Vicki Baum was published in Germany in 1929, and by 1930 it had been translated into English and had become a huge international best-seller. The Mayer group's New York–based partner, Robert Rubin, who kept an eye on the stage and fiction markets back East, cut a deal for MGM to help finance a Broadway version of *Grand Hotel* in exchange for the movie rights to the play. Rubin's modest investment—reportedly only $15,000—paid off; *Grand Hotel* was a solid stage hit. The deal stipulated that the MGM version be delayed until at least fifteen months after the play's November 1930 opening, so by the time Thalberg started moving on it in the fall of 1931, *Grand Hotel* was the most promising project on MGM's docket.

There were other promising projects, of course, pictures like *Arsène Lupin,* which set Lionel and John Barrymore at odds as a detective and a jewel thief, and *Beast of the City,* which exploited Jean Harlow's recent success as a hard-bitten siren in male action films. Both Harlow and John Barrymore were newcomers to Metro who figured in Mayer and Thalberg's future plans—though not in crime films. Barrymore was ideal for the studio's sophisticated comedies and light romances, though he still hadn't agreed to anything beyond a one-picture deal. Harlow, whose long-term contract had just been purchased from independent producer Howard Hughes, struck Thalberg as having potential as an offbeat, sexy comedienne. In fact, he had already convinced Mayer to give her the lead in *Redheaded Woman*, a best-selling sex farce still in script development about an amoral hustler who beds her way to wealth and happiness.

There were also two Garbo vehicles then in the works, *As You Desire Me*, and *Mata Hari*. They were more typical MGM projects but still reflected Thalberg's efforts to vary the casting of his stars to keep their work and their screen images relatively fresh. *As You Desire Me* was an adaptation of Pirandello's melodrama about a woman who, while having an affair with a novelist, suffers amnesia and rediscovers her love for her husband. *Mata Hari* was a less ambitious project, a spy thriller-cum-romance that both Thalberg and Garbo considered a light diversion. Thalberg worked with different supervisors and writing teams on the two Garbo projects to vary her characterization, but he

MGM's massive Culver City facility in 1932.

ensured consistent production values by putting director George Fitz-maurice and William Daniels, Garbo's personal cameraman, on both pictures.

Garbo also figured in the *Grand Hotel* conferences, which began in earnest in late 1931 after writer-director Edmund Goulding completed a rough draft of William Drake's stage play. But *Grand Hotel* was by no means simply a Garbo vehicle. It was essentially an ensemble piece that Mayer and Thalberg agreed should be an all-star picture. By November 1931 several of the key parts, including Garbo's, were already set. She would play Grusinskaya ("Grus"), the dancer whose fame and youth have begun to fade. Joan Crawford was to play Flaemmchen, the gritty stenographer who takes more than dictation from the business-men who employ her. For the role of Preysing, the obnoxious industri-alist who secures Flaemmchen's services while at the Grand Hotel to execute a business deal, Thalberg wanted Wallace Beery. But Beery resisted; he was feeling fatigued after doing *The Champ* for MGM, and he also felt somewhat intimidated by the demands of the Preysing role. However, Thalberg wanted Beery, particularly once *The Champ* took off at the box office. Not only would *Grand Hotel* secure his stardom, but the Preysing role was a nice counter to Beery's comic-pathetic title character in *The Champ*, a broken-down fighter whose love for his son motivates a suicidal return to the ring. So Thalberg pressured his emerging star. Knowing Beery's penchant for scenery chewing, Thal-berg assured him that his would be the only principal character to speak with a German accent, and also that Goulding was eager to ex-ploit his primitive nature.

Beery finally agreed, which left two other key roles to fill: the fatal-istic Baron and the fatally ill Kringelein. The part of the Baron would probably go to the fast-rising Clark Gable, who was still wet behind those oversize ears but seemed ideal for the charming but penniless aristocrat who steals the dancer's pearls but falls in love with her in the process. The Kringelein role was more complex and tougher to cast. A naive, sweet-tempered bookkeeper from one of Preysing's factories who is dying of an incurable disease, Kringelein squanders his savings on the Grand Hotel's everyday luxuries, determined to enjoy his last weeks of life. Goulding wanted Buster Keaton for the role, and Thal-berg agreed it was inspired casting. But Mayer balked because of Kea-ton's drinking and his undisciplined behavior on the set, so for the time being no one was set to play Kringelein.

Goulding completed his screenplay draft in early November 1931, and at that point he, Thalberg, and Bern started a series of script con-ferences. As usual, the sessions themselves were transcribed by a stu-dio secretary for later use in rewriting. The transcriptions were invaluable, since at some point in virtually every conference Thalberg would launch into detailed analysis, often running on for minutes at a time, laying out the entire story line or untangling some particular script problem. Paul Bern rarely spoke during the sessions, and when he did it generally was to affirm one of Thalberg's ideas. Thus the *Grand Hotel* conferences were an extended dialogue and process of negotiation between Goulding and Thalberg. The two relied heavily on the stage version by William Drake, who by contractual agreement was to get writer's credit. But the play was stage-bound and much too long, and the principal roles and plot lines had to be adjusted to suit MGM's players.

The dynamics of the Thalberg-Goulding interplay demonstrated Thalberg's talent and confidence but also his knack for diplomacy—he knew when to stroke Goulding and when to bear down. During an early session, for example, they disagreed over the revision of a scene. "Have you got the play here?" Thalberg asked Goulding. "To me the play was so far better, Eddie. In my humble opinion." Such diplomacy vanished when Goulding pushed too hard, as he did while defending a certain cut later in that same conference. "Over my dead body you'll cut that scene," Thalberg asserted. "Nothing in the world would make me do that—unless I saw it on the screen and was convinced."

Interestingly enough, Goulding was consistently more mechanical and practical in deciding how and what to cut. Thalberg's concerns centered on story structure and the "emotion" of the piece, scarcely what one might expect of a studio executive. A typical exchange occurred during an early script conference. Goulding reminded Thalberg that "footage is our great problem," to which Thalberg responded, "First we get our story and then cut it down."

Thalberg found the mechanics of the various subplots to be fairly obvious and banal; his real fascination was with the overall pattern created when the stories were interwoven. "This is a lousy play that succeeded only because it was lousy," he stated at one point. "It's full of life—a painted carpet upon which the figures walk. Audiences love those damn things, if they are done properly." Thalberg's governing analogy was not to weaving or painting, though, but to music. "To me the whole thing is a beautiful symphony," he said at one point, and he often referred to the subplots as "leitmotifs."

Thalberg felt that in the film version of *Grand Hotel*, two of the subplots should dominate: the love story involving Grus and the Baron, and the fate of the industrialist Preysing. In the opening moments of the story, a lonely and distraught Grus returns from a performance and is on the verge of suicide in her dark hotel room. But she has unknowingly interrupted the Baron, who is there to steal a valuable string of pearls. He watches her from the darkness, intervenes during her suicide attempt to avow her beauty, and within moments the two fall deeply in love. The next morning the Baron promises to leave Berlin with her but only if he can raise sufficient cash, for he refuses to accept her offer of money. Meanwhile, Preysing, sacrificing his honor and integrity to save his own company, desperately maneuvers a Berlin company into a merger under false pretenses.

Thalberg felt that these two expository scenes should be directly interwoven. "We have the ability to be able to cut, which they can't do on the stage," he said to Goulding. "I mean cut from scene to scene." Thalberg laid out the pattern for interweaving the two scenes, then summarized for Goulding: "We've had two terrific scenes intercut. One: Preysing and his problem. The other: Grusinskaya and her problem. There is the backbone of the story."

These two plots converge late in the film, when Preysing finds the Baron stealing his pocketbook from his hotel suite; in a rage of anger and guilt he kills the Baron. Thalberg believed Preysing should commit the murder with a revolver, to underscore the detached and arbitrary nature of the act. But Goulding wanted a more impulsive and brutal killing, with Preysing striking the Baron with a telephone. "I don't feel that the use of the telephone for the murder is nearly as effective as shooting," argued Thalberg. "I'll tell you why, Eddie. Because the thing you got in the play was that he didn't have to kill him —it was cruel on his part to kill him." Thalberg picked up a copy of the play and read the scene aloud, then looked up at Goulding. "I tell you, there's a scene," he said, and began looking for the same scene in the novel. Then, as so often happened during these conferences, Thalberg was called away from his office.

The discussion continued in Thalberg's absence, and when he returned Goulding told him, "I sold Paul the scene in the script of the murder." Thalberg turned to his supervisor for confirmation. "I was completely wrong in that respect," Bern admitted. "I'm sold on Eddie's scene. After all, shooting with a revolver, anyone can do." Bern's conviction clearly enhanced Goulding's case, since Bern rarely disagreed with Thalberg. Thalberg did eventually come round to their viewpoint—and with good reason. Not only did Goulding's version of the killing suit Preysing's brutal character, but it tied in with an important thread running through the story. Goulding and Thalberg had decided to open the picture with a montage of telephone calls to establish the various subplots and also the hotel's general din of activity. Phones were to be used throughout, not only to deliver information but to interweave plot lines and to provide transitions. This approach culminates in a poignant scene late in the film when Grus, after returning to the hotel from her last performance and unaware of the Baron's death, phones his room. Elated over her successful closing and her newfound love, she insists that the operator let the phone ring to awaken the Baron. As the dead man's phone rings on, she speaks as if he were listening, promising love and future happiness.

Another story problem that was hashed out in conference—and another demonstration of Goulding's savvy and Thalberg's flexibility—involved Kringelein's discovery of the Baron's need of cash (to leave with Grus), yet without letting it compromise their growing friendship. Thalberg complained that in Goulding's script, the Baron "is definitely asking Kringelein for money," thus diminishing audience sympathy. Thalberg wanted to bring the scene back in line with the stage version, even if it meant additional footage. Goulding felt that the situation could be set up more dramatically and economically. The two traded ideas and then Goulding hit on a solution.

"Then, Irving, will you do this?" asked Goulding, proposing that they add a single line to the scene as he'd rewritten it. The kindhearted Kringelein would simply ask the Baron, in his timid, deferential manner, "Was the Baron joking when he said he was in need of money?" Thalberg mused for a moment and again he yielded to Goulding's judgment. "That's good," said Thalberg. "It's all right. Now the rest is all right, isn't it?"

I N late November 1931, Thalberg set Goulding to work on another rewrite while he attended to various other projects at hand. He monitored the rough cut of *Beast of the City* with supervisor Hunt Stromberg and, anxious to establish Harlow as a Metro player and to move her into *Redheaded Woman,* scheduled previews for mid-December. The *Redheaded Woman* script hadn't come together to his satisfaction, though, so he decided to try F. Scott Fitzgerald on the project. Fitzgerald was back in Hollywood for the first time since 1927, when his success as a novelist was at its height. But his fiction writing had not been going well of late, nor had his personal life, and Fitzgerald looked to Hollywood for a bit of diversion and ready cash. Thalberg was willing to risk a four-week assignment on *Redheaded Woman,* hoping Fitzgerald's experience as Jazz Age bard might give the story and dialogue a bit of flavor. Always one to hedge his bets, however, Thalberg kept Anita Loos apprised of the project in case Fitzgerald didn't produce.

Arsène Lupin finished shooting that same month, and the success of the Barrymore brothers as costars started Mayer and Thalberg rethinking their casting for *Grand Hotel.* Jack Barrymore was perfect as a suave jewel thief in *Arsène Lupin*—an ideal warm-up for the role of the Baron, and Jack made it clear that he was interested in *Grand Hotel*

The all-star ensemble featured in Grand Hotel: *(from left) Lewis Stone, Lionel Barrymore, Wallace Beery, Joan Crawford, Greta Garbo, John Barrymore, and Jean Hersholt.*

only if his brother Lionel played Kringelein. The idea was intriguing for both its marketing and its dramatic possibilities. Lionel Barrymore was essentially a character actor, though he had attained full-fledged star status at MGM. He could certainly handle the Kringelein role, and he, too, wanted to work with his brother in *Grand Hotel*. But what secured the roles for both Barrymores was Jack's agreement to sign a long-term studio pact. So in December 1931, only weeks before production opened, the principal roles in *Grand Hotel* finally were set.

Goulding completed his rewrite that same month, sending *Grand Hotel* back into conferences. Actual production was now only weeks away, and these were preproduction sessions with a very different tenor than the earlier story conferences. The discussions became more direct and practical, the negotiations less congenial, and the general atmosphere more intense. As Goulding and Bern awaited Thalberg's arrival for their initial preproduction conference on December 9, Goulding pulled out his revised script draft. "I want Irving's feelings on this, page by page," he said to Bern. "Three meetings would take us through the script."

This time around the focus was on setting and technique, and on the mechanics and execution of the project. Thalberg was especially concerned with pacing and atmosphere. "I miss the increasing tempo in these damn scenes," Thalberg complained about Goulding's rewrite. "I'm a great believer in curtains. Work it up to a point—bang—look—fade out before an audience is up to you—while they are still wondering, 'What did he mean?' Fade out." Thalberg had several ideas for enhancing the tempo. One was the use of overlapping dialogue, initiated during the opening telephone montage, accompanied by dissolves and transitional montages. He wanted to generate "a slight confusion . . . there is a feeling of new people piling in. I see the people coming in from all directions." Thalberg also wanted to come out of the opening montage with a scene that established the size and extravagance of the hotel. He suggested that Goulding follow a bowl of soup, ordered from room service, in its journey from kitchen to hotel suite. This might even be done in a single take, which would offset the opening montage. "The novel thing is to go from a dining room through a noisy kitchen, from a woman who screams because [hot] soup is spilled over her to a man who says, 'It's cold!'"

Goulding, interestingly enough, resisted the idea as being too costly —something that scarcely seemed to faze Thalberg. "No we won't cut that," said Thalberg of the soup scene. "When I'm spending $500,000 in round figures and I see an opportunity to do something that's a little bit extraordinary—it's being in the picture will depend on how well you do it." The scene eventually was dropped, but as always, Thalberg was pretty cavalier about budgets and production costs. So far as MGM's money was concerned, he told Goulding, "It's just as important to see that it's spent as to see that it isn't." And he felt pretty much the same way about footage: "I would rather take the picture out [for preview] two thousand feet over length and cut it down afterwards." Goulding found this attitude maddening, but Thalberg considered it utterly practical considering the vagaries of the marketplace and of public taste.

The key dramatic concern during the December conferences was the Baron-Grus relationship. Goulding's rewrite had the two exchanging vows of love that first night, after the Baron prevents her suicide and they are instinctively drawn to one another. Thalberg felt the avowals should come the next morning, after the two spend the night together in her suite. "This is sex," he said to Goulding; "you don't want tenderness until morning." Goulding's rewrite also withheld from the audience the fact that the Baron was in Grus's room to steal her pearls, saving that revelation until the next morning. That eliminated several expository scenes, where the Baron's relationship with a ring of thieves and his plans for stealing the pearls are established. This would save precious footage, and Goulding also felt it would bring more emotion to the love scene. But Thalberg vetoed the idea, reasoning that the audience's knowledge was essential and that the emotion would be there regardless, particularly with Garbo and Barrymore playing the scene. Goulding persisted: "If you know the Baron is a thief—" he began, and Thalberg finished the sentence for him: "You have motive in every line." Goulding conceded the point. "I'm overruled," he said.

Perhaps the most portentous exchange during the preproduction meetings involved Kringelein's drunken, life-affirming speech, made at the close of an all-night, high-stakes card game in which he wipes out his well-heeled and more experienced opponents—including the Baron, whom he had staked to the game. Lionel Barrymore, by the way, was developing a reputation for his climactic tirades. The most recent was in *A Free Soul,* in which he played a lawyer who delivers an impassioned plea to a jury and promptly drops dead. The performance won Barrymore an Oscar, but Thalberg wasn't after anything quite so melodramatic this time out. Still, he was worried that Goulding cut too much of the speech from the play. Barrymore needed more time to build the emotion before he collapsed, done in by the alcohol and his illness as well as the rush of excitement. The timing was also important. The speech had to begin with all the card players in the room and end with them gone, giving the Baron an opportunity, after Kringelein's collapse, to steal his cash—a temptation that he resists. Thalberg also wanted Barrymore to steadily shift the speech from the players to the movie audience as the emotion built and the players filed out.

Thalberg insisted that another line or two be added, but he and Goulding had trouble agreeing on exactly what was needed. "You select your line," said Goulding, growing a bit testy. "It's silly for you to say, 'I believe in this but I won't insist.' " Thalberg backed off somewhat, but he did make one request. "I would like that one more line," he told Goulding. " 'It doesn't matter that life be long, but that one feel it entirely—drain it to the last.' Then collapse." Thalberg waited for the effect to sink in. "That scene alone can make a picture," he said.

Goulding took *Grand Hotel* into production in January 1932, and shooting continued without a hitch until late February. As expected, the Barrymore brothers dominated, although Garbo, Beery, and Joan Crawford also turned in solid performances. The production was not exceptionally ambitious by studio standards; it was scheduled for only six weeks, and budgeted at just over $700,000, with star salaries and sets the heftiest line items. Thalberg could see from the dailies that Goulding had the shoot well in hand, so he tended to other projects. Preview response back in December to both *Beast of the City* and

Director Edmund Goulding working with John Barrymore and Joan Crawford in a scene from Grand Hotel.

Arsène Lupin demanded rewrites and retakes, and both pictures were released in January to favorable response—nothing spectacular, but enough to generate some enthusiasm for the upcoming Harlow and Barrymore vehicles. Scott Fitzgerald's rewrite of *Redheaded Woman* had not panned out, so Thalberg decided to take him off the project and bring in Anita Loos. Loos was a great admirer of Fitzgerald's and felt bad about Thalberg's decision, even though she felt he was right. Looking back on that incident, Loos wrote that "there was a knack to dramatic writing which some very legitimate talents can't master," and that Fitzgerald's scripts "just wouldn't play." She knew Thalberg wanted the kind of sexual banter and playful eroticism that had become her trademark, and she delivered just that for the Harlow vehicle. The Loos rewrite of *Redheaded Woman* ensured its popular success, but embarrassed and enraged Fitzgerald, as did her solo screenplay credit.

E D I T O R Blanche Sewell prepared a rough cut while *Grand Hotel* was still in production, which she and Goulding reworked when he finished shooting. The project then moved back into Thalberg's baili-wick. In late February he began a series of cutting conferences with Goulding, Bern, Sewell, and William Daniels, preparing for the usual run of previews and reedits, and, undoubtedly, rewrites and retakes as well. That was a ritual that all of Thalberg's associates knew well enough—it was, as MGM story editor Sam Marx called it, "the equiv-alent of Broadway's 'taking a show to New Haven.' " Years earlier, Thalberg had the Pacific Electric System cut a spur right onto the MGM lot where a chartered car could pick up a coterie of studio exec-utives and ten-or-so cans of rough-cut footage and deliver them to a theater in some outlying suburb of Los Angeles. If the reaction was favorable and the picture felt right to the studio brass, there would be a friendly bridge game and perhaps even a few drinks on the ride back to Culver City. But if the picture didn't click and Thalberg rode home in silence, lost in thought and staring at the passing landscape, the others knew the picture was going back into production.

The ride back from the first preview of *Grand Hotel* was a quiet one. For the next few weeks Goulding, Thalberg, Sewell, and Bern took a series of all-day meetings, convening in the morning in Thalberg's office to hash out rewrites. After lunch they met in Thalberg's private projection room, replete with desks, pianos, and velvet armchairs, to decide how the envisioned retakes would work with the existing foot-age. Thalberg felt that the only real problem portions in *Grand Hotel* were the love scenes between the Baron and Grus. Their initial scene, when the Baron prevents Grus's suicide and then stays and makes love to her, would be completely rewritten and reshot. Only a portion of the love scene that takes place the next morning—when the Baron tells Grus that he is actually a thief and she assures him that it doesn't matter —needed to be redone. These were the only substantive changes in the picture, and Thalberg demonstrated his confidence in Bern and Goulding by letting them handle most of the retakes themselves once they had agreed on the changes.

Further previews in late March assured Thalberg that *Grand Hotel* was ready for release; it opened in April and was an immediate hit. In fact, *Grand Hotel* proved to be the biggest hit in one of MGM's biggest years ever. While the rest of the Big Eight were mired in red ink in 1932, MGM turned a profit of $8 million. The studio had five of the top fifteen box-office hits that year, and one-third of the major Oscar nominations. *Grand Hotel* had but a single nomination—for best picture, which it won. That seems appropriate, actually, since its individual elements, all fairly routine by Metro's standards, combine to create a whole that both exceeds and eminently justifies its parts. *Grand Hotel* was the archetypal MGM picture during Thalberg's regime. It emphasized glamour, grace, and beauty both in its polished setting and in its civilized characters. But as with so many Metro pictures, its surface gloss and seemingly escapist fare belied deeper concerns. All its characters are doomed or desperate individuals, yet each suffers life's misfortunes with style; each manifests grace under pressure. That façade is shattered when Preysing, after compromising his company and his marriage, loses control and kills the Baron. For that moment we ponder our primal, brutal, and uncivilized instincts. But balance is soon restored and the surviving principals leave the Grand Hotel—Preysing under arrest, Grus alone but stoic, Kringelein and Flaemmchen bound together for France and another fling before his life slips away. All have glanced into the abyss and been severely shaken, and all have recovered their poise. That recovery, evident in the final moments of so many MGM films, is both heroic and vaguely cynical. What *Grand Hotel* is about, finally, is the triumph of style.

Metro's style was embodied by its stars and given substance in light and shadow by its top artists and craftsmen—by Edmund Goulding and Blanche Sewell, along with cinematographer William Daniels, recording engineer Douglas Shearer, art director Cedric Gibbons, and costume designer Adrian. Significantly, these six were credited on individual cards in the opening titles of *Grand Hotel*, along with the stars and playwright William Drake. Equally significant was the absence of a producer's credit on the picture. There was no indication of how those various individual efforts were melded into a coherent, seamless whole. Even with the studio relying so heavily on his judgment, Thalberg still disdained producer credit or any other fanfare—a distinct oddity in 1930s Hollywood, a world so utterly dependent on displays of ego and so obsessed with appearances.

Thalberg's contract ran out in April 1932, just as *Grand Hotel* went into release. There were offers from other studios and from independent producers, but Thalberg was not about to give up what he had built at MGM. Still he was dissatisfied with his present pact. His salary of $6,000 was certainly adequate, particularly now that salaries everywhere else were being cut. But Loew's/MGM was going strong despite the Depression, and Thalberg understood his value to both companies. Schenck and Mayer agreed, and their solution was to hold the salary but increase yet again Thalberg's cut of the Mayer group's 20 percent profit share. Thalberg's cut was boosted to 36½ percent, and again the increase came from Mayer's cut. Now he and Thalberg had equal cuts, while Rubin kept the same 27 percent cut he was allowed in the 1924 agreement. The deal placated Thalberg, although it further fueled Mayer's resentment of MGM's boy wonder, putting him in an odd kinship with Nick Schenck. Both Mayer and Schenck appreciated Thalberg's accomplishments, but they were beginning to wonder how much they would have to give up in the coming years to keep their young studio chief happy.

Thalberg took little notice. MGM was on a roll and his consuming passion was to maintain that momentum. He still tried an offbeat project now and then; some of them hit, as did *Tarzan the Ape Man,* and some, like Tod Browning's bizarre circus story, *Freaks,* did not. For the most part, though, Thalberg continued to turn out high-grade vehicles for Metro's expanding roster of stars. The success of *Grand Hotel* encouraged Mayer to go after yet another Barrymore—sister Ethel, who had sworn off movie acting in the late teens. During the early summer of 1932 Thalberg put together *Rasputin and the Empress,* a lavish costume biography designed for Lionel and Ethel Barrymore in the title roles, with Jack playing the Prince who eventually kills Rasputin. The success of *Redheaded Woman* after its June release kept Harlow on a path to top stardom, and Thalberg decided to team her with the fast-rising Clark Gable. Gable gave Metro something it sorely needed, a rugged leading man who appealed to women without alienating male viewers, while Harlow's earthy, frank sex appeal was altogether unique among MGM's refined and distant leading ladies. Together, thought Thalberg, they might bring another dimension to Metro's tradition of high-gloss romances—maybe they'd heat things up a bit, as Garbo and Gilbert had in the late silent era.

Gable and Harlow were teamed in *Red Dust,* a steamy saga of adultery and redemption set in the jungles of Indochina, and *China Seas,* the pirate adventure that had been stalled in script development for well over a year. Thalberg figured the Gable-Harlow angle might give *China Seas* new life, and he also hoped that putting Paul Bern on it might soothe his deepening depression. By the time Harlow's MGM career ignited, Paul Bern had taken the actress under his protective wing—something he had done with a number of troubled or insecure starlets over the years. Harlow welcomed a man who appreciated her intelligence and personality, someone who, as she confided to director Jack Conway, "doesn't talk fuck, fuck, fuck all the time." She and Bern were wed that summer, but the marriage proved shaky and ill-advised from the start. For years now Bern had been the subject of Hollywood gossip. There were rumors that he was impotent and something of a palace eunuch for the likes of Harlow, that he was into kinky sex, that he was homosexual. Thalberg and the other supervisors, always a close-knit group, tried to deflect or simply ignore such talk, and Thalberg did his best to keep Bern distracted with the *China Seas* project.

Bern spent much of August 1932 revising and amalgamating recent story treatments. On September 3 he submitted his own nine-page version of the story, essentially a melding of earlier treatments but with one notable alteration: a finale depicting the hero's death in an act of ritual suicide. Bern's climax has the hero rescuing his virginal American fiancée, Joan, from Chinese villains, after which he "destroys the illusions" of his innocent love by telling her about his acts of piracy and philandering. Joan "shrinks from him in horror and disgust," and he returns to his Chinese lover, Yu Lan, and to the mysterious clan he has become involved with. Bern closed his treatment with this final scene:

> Within the house, a different judgment is waiting for him. He has violated the Code—he has betrayed the secret of the Band. Stoically he goes back to the inner chamber where the others are gathered. He bares his arm, and in the presence of Yu Lan submits to the torture— finally dying in Yu Lan's arms.

Two days later it became evident that Paul Bern had been narrating more than just a Gable-Harlow fantasy. On Labor Day, September 5, 1932, Bern himself was dead—also in a ritual suicide with bizarre sexual overtones. Fortunately for the studio, the houseboy who discovered Bern's body and the cryptic note he left for Harlow contacted Louis Mayer instead of the police or the newspapers. (The note read, "Dearest dear: Unfortunately this is the only way to make good the frightful wrong I have done you and to wipe out my abject humiliation. You understand that last night was only a comedy. Paul.") Mayer managed to contain the story and avoid a scandal thanks largely to Hearst, whose papers subdued their usual hunger for sensationalism and actually watered down the story for public consumption.

Thalberg was devastated by Bern's suicide. An oft-repeated anecdote around MGM at the time involved Thalberg and the funeral of silent-film star Mabel Normand in 1930. On the day of the funeral, Thalberg and several writers were caught up in a particularly intense script session. They were making headway, so Thalberg kept the session going not only in a limo en route to the funeral but inside the church during the actual service. Bern's death hit Thalberg closer to home, though, and the funeral did more than interrupt a sacrosanct Thalberg conference. He wept openly during the service and didn't come into the studio for several weeks. He also began worrying about his own compulsive nature and his obsessive commitment to his work. Thalberg's health had been improving somewhat in recent years, especially since he and Shearer started taking summer pilgrimages to Europe "for the waters." But he was by no means a healthy or robust man, and clearly the physical and emotional strains were getting to him. Thalberg told Mayer he wanted to scale back his commitment to the studio. He was thinking seriously about taking a year off, or perhaps even leaving MGM.

Mayer immediately sent for Robert Rubin and Nick Schenck, and there ensued a series of emotional confrontations in Schenck's hotel room. The Loew's president reminded Thalberg that his contract, renewed only months before, guaranteed his services for five years. Thalberg waved off his contractual obligations and openly defied Schenck. Their exchanges grew so heated that Rubin eventually brought in Nick's brother Joe Schenck, then chief executive of UA, to act as mediator. It was eventually decided that Thalberg would stay on at MGM only if he were made a partner in Loew's itself. Nick Schenck begrudgingly granted Thalberg the option to buy up to 100,000 shares of Loew's private issues at a fraction of their market value. Mayer and Rubin were offered similar options but for fewer issues—Mayer for 80,000 and Rubin for 50,000.

M A Y E R and Schenck had decidedly mixed feelings about Thalberg's flare-up and the settlement. The entire studio revolved around him, which was proving to be both a blessing and a curse. Mayer, fearing for MGM's prestige market and seeing a way to offset Thalberg's increasing authority, suggested that they bring in other producers to lighten Thalberg's load. Schenck supported the plan and Thalberg showed no resistance, so Mayer began courting Walter Wanger, David Selznick, and a few other top-flight filmmakers. Walter Wanger was then a vice president at Columbia Pictures, and he jumped at the chance to produce films on his own, using MGM's resources. Selznick also liked the idea of returning to active production, but he had reservations about joining Metro as an in-law to Mayer and a competitor to Thalberg, whom he described as "the greatest producer the industry has yet developed."

Selznick was hardly alone in that estimation of Thalberg. By 1932 the Thalberg legend was spreading beyond the movie colony, and it accelerated with the December issue of *Fortune* magazine. The business journal ran an in-depth piece on Metro-Goldwyn-Mayer, surveying the studio's assets, production operations, and top personnel. *Fortune* described Metro's total domination of the industry, praising Nick Schenck and Louis B. Mayer for their business acumen. Mayer was described as MGM's only vestige of "the old regime of fun peddlers, secondhand jewelers, and nickelodeon proprietors" who pioneered the motion picture industry. He was now acknowledged as "probably the most dignified personage in Hollywood." The real focus of the piece, though, was Irving Thalberg. "For the past five years, M-G-M had made the best and most successful motion pictures in the United States," *Fortune* asserted, and "everyone in Hollywood" thought Thalberg was responsible: "He is what Hollywood means by M-G-M." After describing MGM's supervisory system, retake policy, and endless conferences, *Fortune* reinforced the mystique of Irving Thalberg. "Tutored by a sharper master than adversity—success—he is now called a genius more often than anyone else in Hollywood."

The piece closed with a summation of MGM's three corporate strengths. First was the studio's "corporate smoothness, that amity among executives"—a comment indicating how well the recent conflicts had been kept quiet. "Second, there is Mr. Thalberg's heavy but sagacious spending. . . . M-G-M would seem to have shown conclusively that although vast expenditure is no guarantee of good results, economy is decidedly not the secret of profitable movie production." As its third strength, *Fortune* cited "the kind of picture M-G-M makes with its money," describing the studio's style not in terms of quality writing or direction but rather its stars and production values: "The glamour of M-G-M personalities is part of a general finish and glossiness which characterize M-G-M pictures and in which they excel."

Thalberg was genuinely unimpressed by such accolades, while they only refueled Mayer and Schenck's resentment. Schenck in particular was adamant about realigning the power structure at MGM, but Mayer insisted they wait until after he had traveled abroad for the Christmas holidays. Thalberg and Mannix kept things moving back on the West Coast, welcoming the new year with MGM's annual party. Operations were suspended for a rare evening of festivity, and this year even

Thalberg joined in. But that night Thalberg's overworked heart and chronically weak constitution simply gave out, and he collapsed. His condition was not life-threatening, but still it shook the studio to its very foundation. Mayer received word and immediately returned to Los Angeles. En route he tried to imagine MGM without Thalberg, but the image simply didn't compute. Across the continent, Nick Schenck conjured up the same image as he boarded a west-bound Twentieth Century Limited. He liked what he saw.

8

Selznick at RKO:
At the Helm of a
Foundering Studio

Whenen Louis Mayer came courting
in 1932, he offered David Selznick lavish budgets and creative control
as an MGM producer, with his pick of the studio's stars, story properties, and top personnel. Selznick, shocked by the offer, finally realized
how serious the power struggle at Culver City really was. If Mayer's
offer was on the level, it meant a realignment not just of Thalberg's
status and his supervisory system, but of MGM's entire production
operation. Selznick hesitated, however; the outcome of the power
struggle was still in doubt, and he knew all too well how Louis Mayer
really felt about giving his producers that kind of authority and creative
control.

Selznick found that out back in 1931 when he left Paramount to
create an independent company composed of several separate filmmaking teams that together would produce a dozen or so first-rate features
per year. Each unit would be headed by an established filmmaker.
Lewis Milestone and William Wellman had already expressed interest,
and Selznick hoped to bring in one or two others after he had worked
out financing and distribution. Selznick had pushed the same idea at
Paramount when he advised Ben Schulberg in 1931 that "the best way
out of the pit of bad and costly pictures in which we are now sunk is
through breaking up production, in whole or in part, into smaller
units." Paramount had let Sternberg and other top directors create
informal units, but the company wasn't about to formalize the process

A resolute David Selznick with his bride, Irene Mayer Selznick, during their 1931 travels in search of backing for Selznick's independent production venture.

or practice it on a widespread scale. So Selznick was not surprised when Schulberg dismissed the idea—it was what he expected of the studio's "mill foreman." But Paramount vice president Jesse Lasky was receptive to it, seeing an opportunity to cut Paramount's risk by relying on Selznick's new company as a source of first-run pictures.

Selznick went East in the late summer to raise money for his independent venture, and he polished his sales pitch, coincidentally enough, on Ben Schulberg's son Budd, whom Selznick saw fairly often during his stay in New York. Young Schulberg was in prep school at the time and he revered David Selznick as a surrogate older brother and as Hollywood's crown prince. Schulberg later broke into screenwriting as an employee of Selznick's, and he looked back to the fall of 1931 as the period when their friendship matured and when he first came to understand Selznick's zeal for independent filmmaking and unit production. Whenever he could get away, Schulberg commuted to New York City to do the Manhattan speakeasy circuit with David and his bride, Irene Mayer Selznick.

"Still in his late twenties," recalled Schulberg, "David had a fleshy, sensuous face, an exuberant intelligence, and a feisty independence."

What struck Schulberg most were the "pouring words from a bottomless well, good words, great words, needless words all gushing forth together, flooding one's mind." At the time Selznick's main topic was the Hollywood factory system. "Instead of the system Paramount and the others employed," said Schulberg, "with supervisors standing in for the studio chief but never completely responsible for the finished product, David advocated a more personal approach, with supervisors becoming full-fledged producers heading their own independent units —a system of creative decontrol."

But these were ideas whose time had not yet come, not if Louis Mayer and the other studio heads had their way. When it became evident that Selznick's plans might succeed, Mayer called a meeting of Hollywood's power brokers to head off the threat of unit production. Mayer said he could live with a supervisory system, where productions were monitored by middle-management types—whether they were called supervisors, associate producers, "Thalberg men," or whatever. But giving producers creative and administrative authority over their own units threatened the industry's traditional power structure. Creative and administrative control, so far as Mayer was concerned, should remain in the hands of the owners and top executives. Mayer's colleagues concurred, and Selznick's independent venture was finished. Within weeks Jesse Lasky withdrew his support, and Lewis Milestone signed an exclusive deal with United Artists' Joe Schenck. Selznick saw the handwriting on the wall. He knew that even if he raised the capital, without studio support he would never get adequate distribution and exhibition, nor could he borrow the necessary talent to produce top-flight features.

So Selznick set aside his plans and scheduled a meeting with David Sarnoff. A boy wonder in his own right, Sarnoff was the president of RCA and chairman of the board of RKO-Radio, an RCA subsidiary. Encouraged by the booming picture business and the potential for talking pictures, Sarnoff and Boston financier Joseph Kennedy created RKO back in 1928. They merged several film companies into a fully integrated major, RKO-Radio Pictures, with RCA providing the sound, and the new studio immediately took off. In 1930, its second full year of operation, RKO pulled in profits of nearly $3.5 million. But business had been so good during the talkie boom that it was impossible for a major studio *not* to make money. Only when the Depression hit in 1931 did Sarnoff realize how inefficiently the studio was being run. He was impressed when Selznick looked him up in New York to pitch his unit-production scheme, and he suggested instead that Selznick take over his two West Coast facilities, RKO-Radio and RKO-Pathe. Selznick declined the offer, but after running into Louis Mayer's roadblock, he reconsidered. Selznick and Sarnoff met again in October 1931 in New York and quickly worked out the details. David Selznick, at age twenty-nine, became RKO's "vice president in charge of production" at a salary of $2,500 per week.

Selznick knew when he came aboard that RKO was in deep financial trouble—expected losses for 1931 were in excess of $5 million. His task, essentially, was to reverse the downward trend by cutting costs and upgrading the market value of RKO's releases. Sarnoff assured Selznick that although RCA was beginning to feel the economic squeeze, the parent company would supplement RKO's expenses if the average picture costs could be kept down around $250,000. That meant Selznick would have to rely on the studio's internal resources, which would be tough. Creating RKO as an integrated major had required massive capitalization, and the Depression hit just as the company was getting on its feet. So the studio lacked not only sound management but also resources; it didn't come close to having the artists, technicians, story properties, or production facilities that the competing majors had. That had not really been a problem in the past, since RKO's theater holdings, especially its first-run houses, had scored hefty profits and offset its weak production arm. But an RKO chain of 161 theaters no longer meant automatic revenues—just the opposite, in fact—and thus Sarnoff's effort to stabilize and upgrade production operations.

Selznick immediately merged the two West Coast studios and went to a supervisory system, though he hoped to use a few of RKO's top filmmakers as unit producers within another year or so. He established the RKO-Radio facility as the base of filmmaking operations, with Pathe serving as a rental facility when it wasn't required by RKO. He assembled a staff of seven associate producers, two of whom, Pandro Berman and Merian Cooper, also served as his executive assistants. "Pan" Berman had been around since the studio's creation and had kin at both RCA and RKO. But nepotism aside, Selznick was impressed with the twenty-six-year-old Berman and was glad to have him as an assistant. Cooper was another story—a flying ace in the world war and then an adventurer, documentary filmmaker, and, briefly, employee of Paramount Pictures. Cooper left the movie business to help get TWA off the ground, but he longed to come back. He had his doubts about RKO, but Selznick promised to let him develop his own projects, including a "gorilla picture" that no other studio would touch.

With the help of Berman and Cooper, Selznick evaluated all RKO personnel. Many studio employees were fired or laid off, and those who weren't had sixty days to prove their value to the company. The only bona fide star at RKO was Irene Dunne, but there were a few second-rank stars like Richard Dix and Dolores Del Rio and some promis-

The front office at RKO in 1931, the year David Selznick took over the studio.

ing newcomers like Joel McCrea. Selznick hired a few free-lance stars for one- and two-picture deals, notably Constance Bennett and John Barrymore, each of whom came in for $125,000 per film. Selznick also cultivated new talent; among the future stars whose screen tests he arranged were Katharine Hepburn, Lucille Ball, and Fred Astaire. RKO's directorial staff was nearly as weak as its star stable. Selznick sacked most of the directors when he came aboard, and by June 1932 only three were on contract for a full year: Wesley Ruggles at $2,250 per week, Gregory La Cava at $2,000, and George Cukor at $1,500. There were a few others on six-month deals, but most of the remaining directors—from heavyweights like William Wellman to relative unknowns earning $500 per week—were signed on a per-picture basis.

Despite the meager resources, Selznick soon had RKO running smoothly and efficiently. He gave himself the title of Executive Producer—in fact, Selznick claimed he coined the term—but supervised only the most important features, concentrating instead on studio administration. His associates oversaw the routine productions, with Cooper taking most of the load; he supervised seven of RKO's thirty projects during the first six months of 1932. By mid-year, though, most of Cooper's energies went into his "gorilla picture." *King Kong* was easily the most ambitious RKO project initiated during Selznick's regime, and it was virtually the only prestige picture that Selznick left alone once it was approved and under way. Cooper later commented that Selznick "never interfered, never tried to tell me what to do." The studio boss simply ran interference on the project, securing New York's approval of its $500,000 budget and then getting additional financing as the costs escalated to nearly $675,000.

Selznick's own creative efforts were devoted mainly to the productions of Cukor and La Cava, who between them did eight pictures in 1932, with Selznick involved either as executive producer or supervisor. If any style emerged during Selznick's tenure at RKO, it was in these pictures, particularly those directed by Cukor. A relative newcomer to Hollywood and close friend of Selznick's, Cukor shared with Selznick a predilection for sentimental dramas with forceful heroines, relatively heavy themes, and lavish production values—qualities the two would cultivate, whether together or apart, for years to come. The most distinctive Selznick-Cukor films at RKO were *A Bill of Divorcement*, *What Price Hollywood?*, and *Little Women*. All three were resisted by the New York office as commercially suspect, but all three were pushed through by Selznick and were sizable hits. And all three had distinctive Selznick qualities. *A Bill of Divorcement* was a melodrama of ill-fated love—both familial and romantic—privileging the heroine's viewpoint and her obsession with a mysterious father figure. It centered on the problems of a headstrong young woman, played by Katharine Hepburn, when her father (John Barrymore) returns unexpectedly after years in a mental institution. The picture hit, affirming Selznick's confidence in Cukor and in the viability of adult dramas. Equally important was the overnight success of Katharine Hepburn, the first of many Selznick discoveries.

The fast-rising female star also turned up in *What Price Hollywood?*, but this time as a fictional character. The film was based on Selznick's own story idea about a star-crossed romance between a young ingenue and a talented but self-destructive filmmaker who eventually commits suicide to avoid impeding the girl's rise to stardom. Again there was an intense relationship between an older man and younger woman, with the woman as central character, and again there was a sentimental treatment of rather heavy themes. *Little Women*, though a lighter project, was another sentimental woman's picture, this time with Katharine Hepburn and Joan Bennett. Prepared by Selznick late in his tenure at RKO, it revealed his emerging interests in costume dramas, period romances, and literary adaptation.

Outside these few prestige hits, Selznick's accomplishments at RKO were administrative—cutting expenses and maximizing the studio's limited resources. His strategy was to turn out a feature every week and to keep picture costs in the $200,000 to $375,000 range, with an

John Barrymore and an early Selznick "discovery," Katharine Hepburn, in a publicity still for A Bill of Divorcement.

occasional half-million-dollar picture offset every five or six weeks by a low-budget western costing about $35,000. The strategy was remarkably successful. In a single year he reduced overall expenses at RKO's West Coast facility by roughly one-third without sacrificing output or quality. In 1931, the year before his arrival, RKO-Radio and Pathe had put out forty-two features on a budget of $16 million; Selznick produced forty-one in 1932 for $10.2 million. He also reduced the operating costs at the studio from $21.7 million to $19.3 million. But Selznick could do nothing about the general industry slide—the declining attendance and massive theater shutdowns. Nor could he help RCA, which was beginning to feel the effects of the Depression in 1932. He kept production costs right at the $250,000 average, as per Sarnoff's initial instructions. And though Sarnoff held to his earlier promise to supplement RKO's production costs, the $175,000 that RCA was putting into each picture was proving to be a severe drain on its financial resources.

A shake-up in RKO's executive echelons also affected Selznick's fortunes in 1932. At mid-year an executive purge elevated B. B. Kahane to president of RKO-Radio Pictures, while former NBC president Mer-

lin ("Deac") Aylesworth became president of RKO-Radio, the integrated parent company of the various RKO subsidiaries. Selznick got
along well with Kahane, but he found Deac Aylesworth meddlesome,
power-hungry, and altogether ignorant of the movie business. Their
rapport was strained but tolerable until late in the year, when Selznick's contract was up for renewal. During the negotiations, Aylesworth made it clear he planned to restrict Selznick's casting and script
approval, and that he intended to control the purchase of all presold
story properties from New York. Selznick had no intention of running
the studio unless he had complete authority in these areas, and the
contract discussions quickly deteriorated. Interestingly enough, Selznick wanted authority in these areas but not control—that he planned
to give to his unit producers. He had told Kahane back in June 1932
that "a production schedule of forty or more features is too much for
one man to supervise," and that he wanted the producer to "assume
complete charge of stories and talent." So while Selznick was again
pushing his unit-producer idea, Aylesworth was threatening to reduce
him to a mere plant manager.

It was at this point that Louis Mayer came calling with the MGM
offer, which was doubly ironic given the impasse with Aylesworth as
well as Mayer's earlier efforts to short-circuit Selznick's unit-production plans. Selznick had turned Mayer down, citing the appearance of
nepotism, his unwillingness to compete with Thalberg, and his allegiance to RKO as his reasons for staying. But Selznick's good faith was
not returned in kind by RKO, and by mid-December negotiations had
stalled. When Henry Luce of *Time* magazine got wind of the story and
asked for a statement, Selznick's reply indicated that unit production
was still an issue. Selznick wired that he was leaving RKO due to its
"inability to agree on production policies particularly with respect to
putting into effect 'unit system' theory of production of which I am the
father." Selznick also told Luce that he wanted to reduce RKO's feature
production to about two dozen, with that output being "supplemented
by four units, each to make one to four pictures [per year], headed
respectively by King Vidor, Lewis Milestone, Walter Wanger, and Merian C. Cooper."

David Sarnoff was not about to let Selznick get away, however. He
dispatched Kahane to Los Angeles on December 19 and wired Selznick
that same day with hopes that he and Kahane would come to a "mu-
tually satisfactory understanding." Sarnoff also confided that RCA had
"major financial problems," and they all would survive only through
"teamwork and faith in each other." Within a week, Selznick and Kahane agreed to a new fourteen-month contract; Selznick's weekly salary remained at $2,500, but he would get an additional 20 percent of

the net profits on all RKO productions. Features were to be budgeted at no less than $200,000 and were to be billed on screen and in all advertising as "A David O. Selznick Production." Aylesworth was satisfied with the figures, but he still refused to give Selznick final authority over budget, casting, and script. Again Selznick broke off negotiations, declaring himself "a free agent," and again Sarnoff intervened, this time taking over the negotiations personally. Selznick repeated his demand for "the final word in story purchase and assignment, as well as in all other production matters." He granted Kahane authority "in matters of finance and policy," but argued that no one should wield "veto power" over his production decisions. And in a particularly telling aside to Kahane, Selznick wrote: "Certainly Irving Thalberg has never been subject to the word or approval of Nicholas Schenck; on the other hand, Ben Schulberg was responsible to New York executives and you have seen the result."

The Schenck-Thalberg rapport was also strained at the time, and Selznick knew it—but that only underscored his point. The key issue for Selznick or Thalberg or any other studio executive was authority over production operations. It was obvious that as the Depression hit, the corporate powers in New York were increasingly unwilling to grant that authority, but Selznick could not see himself working without it. The lack of it soured him on RKO, and the promise of it, even as a unit producer, drew him to MGM. Selznick was also drawn to MGM for economic reasons—it was not just Mayer's offer of $4,000 a week and his promise of budgets in the $500,000 to $1,000,000 range, but also the general economic health of Loew's/MGM. Selznick had relished the challenge of piloting RKO through the Depression's stormy seas, but only if he was navigating and giving the orders. The RKO and RCA executives in New York insisted on charting the studio's course, however, so Selznick felt he had no choice but to leave.

Among Selznick's last decisions at RKO was to approve a screen test for one Fred Astaire, a dancer and stage star from Broadway who was having trouble in Hollywood: there were concerns that he was skinny and balding and too old for the movies at age thirty-three. Selznick's decision paved the way for RKO's famed Astaire-Rogers musicals, which were produced by Pan Berman and were the studio's only solid star-genre formulation during the 1930s. But the New York office eventually let Astaire get away, and it squandered Berman's talents just as it had Selznick's and Merian Cooper's and those of various other top production executives. In fact, RKO had the most uneven and disjointed studio operation in Hollywood during the classical era, and never really did develop a consistent house style.

MGM was a different story, of course, and whatever reservations

Selznick had about Mayer's offer were all but forgotten when Thalberg fell ill in January 1933. It was obvious that Thalberg's convalescence would be lengthy, and Selznick now realized that if and when Thalberg returned, the power structure at Metro would never be the same. On February 2, he wrote a formal letter of resignation to B. B. Kahane, and later that week Louis B. Mayer announced to the press that David Selznick was joining Metro-Goldwyn-Mayer as a unit producer.

9

Warner Bros.:
The Zanuck Era

The power struggle between Schenck and Thalberg at MGM had a curious parallel over at Warners, where company president Harry Warner and production chief Darryl Zanuck were locked in a furious battle for control of not only production operations but the hearts and minds of Warners' employees. Like Thalberg, Zanuck played an ambivalent role at the studio, poised as he was between the owners and the salaried employees, balancing the studio's economic and creative interests. That ambivalence was even heavier for Zanuck because he'd worked his way up through the studio ranks as a writer, and it was intensifying in early 1933 as Roosevelt's economic recovery plans mandated wage cuts throughout the film industry. Thalberg's recent collapse put him on the sidelines as things heated up, but Zanuck was in the thick of the fray, openly defying Harry Warner's announced salary cuts. And at both studios, the company president faced the same question: whether the vice president in charge of production who effectively shaped and maintained the house style was indispensable.

At the time, Warners without Zanuck was as inconceivable as MGM without Thalberg—perhaps more so, since Zanuck was a centralized producer without the benefit of "Zanuck men" or the overall support system of MGM. Back in 1930, when Zanuck took charge, Warner Bros. was a company with considerable power and resources but no real personality. Up until then Harry Warner had been the key force at

Warner Bros., the brains and guts behind the company's tremendous growth from a second-class outfit to a major studio. But the Depression, coming after Harry Warner's heavy spending for sound conversion, theater acquisition, and studio expansion, forced Warners to adopt a more conservative, cost-efficient strategy. Low-budget production was stepped up and budgets for A-class features were reduced. Harry declared a moratorium on musicals, which not only were costly but had glutted the market in the early talkie era. Costume pictures and period pieces were all but eliminated as well, with the exception of George Arliss's occasional biopics, which were the closest Warners came to prestige production. Harry Warner saw himself in the early 1930s as the Henry Ford of the movie industry, and the studio as a factory that produced consistent, reasonably priced products for a homogeneous mass of consumers. There was no room in such a system for exceptions or excess. "Anyone who got over $2,000 a week he hated instantly even if he never met him," Zanuck once said of the tight-fisted, conservative Warner. "In Harry's mind, everybody was a thief, including Jack for condoning extravagances."

Though Zanuck was earning $5,000 a week by then, he avoided Harry Warner's shit list because of his obvious value to the company— which by now was considerably greater than Jack's. Of course, Jack Warner, who assumed much the same role as Louis Mayer at MGM, was vital to studio operations. He was the most visible of the Warners and handled contract negotiations and scheduling as well as plant operations. But whatever Jack's importance to the studio, Darryl Zanuck was the institutional catalyst. Zanuck assumed command of all production in November 1930, when operations were consolidated at First National in Burbank. He soon whipped the studio into shape and in the process he fashioned the most distinctive house style in Hollywood. That style—a model of narrative and technical economy—was ideally suited to Harry's fiscal policies. Warners shunned the high-gloss, well-lit world of MGM and Paramount, opting instead for a bleaker, darker world view. Warners' Depression-era pictures were fast-paced, fast-talking, socially sensitive (if not downright exploitive) treatments of contemporary stiffs and lowlifes, of society's losers and victims rather than heroic or well-heeled types. And perhaps most distinctive in Warners pictures were the lack of naive optimism and a disdain for romantic love as either a motivating plot device or a means to a narrative resolution.

As with any studio, the house style at Warners was keyed to its star-genre formulations, and here, too, economy was the key. There were a few established high-priced stars like William Powell and Joe E. Brown on the roster—holdovers from the late-twenties talkie boom.

Darryl F. Zanuck, the production chief and moving force at Warner Bros. in the early 1930s.

But a new crop of stars was developed in the early 1930s along with a more cost-effective, genre-based production strategy. Emerging stars like Jimmy Cagney and Edward G. Robinson were willing—at least in the early stage of their careers—to work more often and for lower salaries, and they had little leverage over their pictures or their roles. They were ruthlessly typecast, usually in films that required only a single star. Economy, too, reinforced Warners' aversion to romantic stories, which were invariably costarring vehicles, more expensive to produce than action pictures with individual male stars, and more disruptive of the studio's production schedule.

There were glimpses of Warners' Depression-era style back in the 1920s, particularly in the screenwriting "hokum" Zanuck dashed off under any one of his four pen names. Once Zanuck became production chief in 1930, his taste permeated Warners' entire program. He emphasized male action films and promoted a stark vision and hard-bitten dramatic style at every opportunity—in script conferences, preproduction meetings, editing sessions, and even while prowling the sets.

Milton Sperling, then a young Warners employee (later a producer), recalled Zanuck pacing the set of *Public Enemy;* he was dressed as usual in riding breeches and boots, pounding his sawed-off polo mallet into his fist for emphasis, and "repeating to [director] Willie Wellman and his crew that they mustn't let a drop of sentimentality seep into the action."

As Warners' new stars and genres caught on with the public, there were inevitable struggles with its contract players, many of whom displayed the same combative demeanor in contract negotiations with Jack Warner that they displayed on-screen. The earliest battles, aptly enough, were with Warners' resident tough guys, Edward G. Robinson and James Cagney. The two vaulted to stardom in a pair of pictures that established the gangster film as Warners' foundation genre in the Depression era. Robinson's breakthrough came with *Little Caesar,* released in January 1931, and Cagney's came three months later with the release of *Public Enemy.* Because Robinson had done *Little Caesar* without signing a long-term deal, its runaway hit status gave him the leverage to go after a lucrative long-term contract. In February 1931 he signed a two-year, six-picture deal at $40,000 per picture, although the studio balked at giving him any control of story, script, or casting.

Cagney was already on long-term contract at $400 per week when he did *Public Enemy,* and he spent much of 1931 and 1932 lobbying for a new pact. Jack Warner refused to renegotiate and eventually Cagney refused to perform, so Warner put him on indefinite suspension. Intervention by the Motion Picture Academy resolved the dispute, and Cagney's weekly salary was raised in late 1932 to $3,000 per week. But both Robinson and Cagney soon realized that with their salaries and commodity value increasing, the studio was bound to grow more obstinate in refusing their demands for different roles or for even minimal input into decisions having to do with story selection and script development. Zanuck indicated the studio's regard for such requests in late 1932 in his response to Robinson's bid for input during script development. "We will accept anybody's ideas or suggestions," reasoned Zanuck, "but the treatment of the subject in script form should be left largely to the judgment and intelligence of our 'system.' "

Warners' female players had an even tougher time dealing with the "judgment and intelligence" of Warners' system, due to the male skew of its principal stars and genres, as well as its aversion to costarring vehicles. An ill-advised talent raid on Paramount early in 1931, just before the gangster sagas hit, brought Kay Francis and Ruth Chatterton to Warners. Both were established stars who commanded huge salaries but scarcely fit Warners' changing style and market strategy. Francis earned $3,000 per week in 1931–32, and Chatterton a staggering $8,000 per week while doing only three pictures a year. More promising were the ingenues that Warners signed in the early 1930s, including Bette Davis, Ruby Keeler, and Joan Blondell. Davis dominated this group in terms of salary and status, but she lagged far behind her male colleagues in the star categories. After signing in 1931 for $400 per week, she did nine pictures over the next thirteen months, none of any real note. Her option was renewed in December 1932 for $550 weekly, but still no one at the studio seemed to know quite what to do with her. Warners' commitment to women's pictures was marginal, and Kay Francis won most of those roles. Davis was relegated to costar status in male-oriented crime films or to an occasional lead in an urban melodrama, often as a distaff version of Warners' male stars—perceived, as one sales executive put it, as "a female Jimmy Cagney."

Like Robinson and Cagney, Davis was ruthlessly typecast; this ensured her market value but steadily restricted her screen persona. Not only did Warners resist "off-casting" its emerging stars, but Jack Warner also resisted loaning them out, since work for other companies upset Warners' schedule and threatened to dilute or offset the screen personality being refined at Warners. The stars resented this policy, and several of them, particularly Davis and Cagney, not only battled Jack Warner but took frequent suspensions rather than submit to studio authority. But in the long run there was little any star could do, since in those years the standard industry practice was to tack on the suspended time to the end of a player's contract, thus making it impossible to "sit out" and become a free agent.

W H I L E Warners' system proved inflexible for its stars, production efficiency demanded that directors, writers, and other top personnel be fairly versatile. Production at Warners was even more centralized than at MGM, since there were no "Zanuck men," no counterparts to Thalberg's team of supervisors. Nor were as many writers involved in rewrites until screenplays satisfied someone with Thalberg's refined tastes. Warners' staff writers preferred Zanuck's approach, since it improved the chances of their work—and their names—making it to the screen. Zanuck also avoided the kinds of specialized units that often developed around a specific star-genre combination. The closest Warners came to such a unit was for George Arliss's biopics—*Disraeli* (1929), *Alexander Hamilton* (1931), and *Voltaire* (1933)—with director Alfred Green and writer Maude T. Howell. For the most part, writers and directors were expected to work effectively with various genres and studio players.

Warners directors, in particular, were attuned to a factory-based assembly-line production system. Even top staffers like Roy Del Ruth,

Al Green, Michael Curtiz, Archie Mayo, and William Dieterle could expect to work on four or five films per year with little involvement in pre- and postproduction. They were relatively well paid, with salaries ranging from $1,000 per week for Dieterle to $2,700 per week for Del Ruth, but their duties did not include story or script development, or the supervision of a "director's cut." Rarely did they have time even to consult on a rough assembly edit while a picture was being shot. Their time was devoted to an intensive shooting session on each project, and as soon as principal photography on one picture was finished they were assigned to another. Generally only free-lance directors could expect to exercise much influence over pre- and postproduction. Howard Hawks, for example, directed two pictures for Warners in 1932, *The Crowd Roars* and *Tiger Shark*. He earned $50,000 per picture, and his contracts gave him authority over both scripting and editing, although the shooting script and the final cut on each picture was subject to Jack Warner's approval.

Only one contract director, Mervyn LeRoy, had that kind of authority at Warners in the early thirties. LeRoy was without question Warners' most important house director; from 1930 to 1933 he did twenty-three films for the studio, including *Numbered Men, Little Caesar, Five Star Final, I Am a Fugitive from a Chain Gang,* and *Gold Diggers of 1933.* These and other LeRoy projects were commercial and critical hits, and they contributed heavily to the burgeoning Warners style. LeRoy's success was rewarded with a steady increase in authority and in salary, which climbed from $600 per week in 1929 to $2,750 per week in 1933. His ascent as a filmmaker was yet another indication of the rampant nepotism in the industry: he got his start at Paramount in the wardrobe department because he was Jesse Lasky's cousin, and his opportunities at Warners owed something to his relationship with Harry Warner's daughter, Doris, whom he wed in 1934. But the key to LeRoy's status and power at Warners was not merely a matter of kinship. The key, rather, was his feel for the contemporary idiom and milieu—a sense of realism that he shared with Zanuck—along with his remarkable efficiency as a movie director.

Quite simply the most productive director of A-class features on the lot, LeRoy was quite capable of cranking out six to eight pictures per year, on schedule and under budget. In the Hollywood production system of the 1930s, a director of top features was expected on any given shooting day to generate roughly two and one-half minutes of finished film—that is, printed takes that were ready to be edited into the rough cut of the picture. When a director failed to maintain this pace, the consequences for the studio were costly, since added production days meant increased expense, along with scheduling and logistical problems. There were no "slow" directors at Warner Bros. Michael Curtiz, the only other staff director with anywhere near LeRoy's track record and status, consistently supplied 2'30" per shooting day. But Curtiz's speed was nothing compared to that of LeRoy, who tore through shooting scripts at a pace of five to six minutes per day. What may have been lost in terms of technical or dramatic nuance was compensated for, especially in the minds of studio executives, by pure economy. This in turn gave LeRoy more freedom and authority than were allowed to his studio colleagues—although he had precious little time to exercise them, considering his frantic pace.

LeRoy's productivity and speed were especially important to the studio in the early 1930s as Warners developed its penchant for topical issues and current events. More than any other studio, Warners concentrated on immediate social and economic conditions in Depression-era America for its subject matter. Zanuck valued those filmmakers—writers and technicians as well as directors—who could take a news headline or magazine piece, a recent novel or Broadway hit, and transpose it to the screen quickly enough to exploit its social currency. Consider Warners' production of *Five Star Final*, which LeRoy directed in 1931. Louis Weitzenkorn's topical hit play, which was then touring the country, traced the sins, guilt, and redemption of a newspaper editor when his "yellow journalist" tactics destroy an innocent girl and her family. Zanuck convinced the Warners to shell out $50,000 for the property, which he saw not only as a hot property but as a vehicle for Edward G. Robinson—a chance to satisfy the star's demand for different screen roles, but without really altering his persona as the street-wise crime boss.

Two staff writers completed an adaptation within a few weeks of the purchase, following Zanuck's instructions to modify the role of the newspaper editor for the gritty, energetic Robinson. Production was budgeted at $290,000 and scheduled by early April. LeRoy spent one day rehearsing and began shooting on April 14. The picture was shot in continuity, with LeRoy staying precisely on its four-week schedule (twenty-four shooting days, including Saturdays). The project went into postproduction in May and was in the can by June, and Warners actually had to hold up release for two months since a condition of the play's purchase was that the film not be released before September 31, and not within thirty days of its stage run in any major U.S. city. *Five Star Final* opened on September 10, 1931, at the Winter Garden, a 1,700-seat theater on Broadway. It was Warners' longest-running release of the year, outdrawing the studio's more costly and more ambitious releases, even its annual Arliss biopic, *Alexander Hamilton*. *Five Star Final* was a solid critical success as well, ranking seventh in the prestigious *Film Daily* annual critics' poll and scoring an Oscar nomination for best picture.

A S Zanuck, LeRoy, and other filmmakers at the plant pushed beyond the norms of entertainment and realism, Harry Warner found himself having to placate his colleagues in the New York office. He subdued brother Abe's chronic concerns about market conditions, and he deflected complaints from sales executives about the brutality and violence of so many Warners pictures. Harry was willing to let Zanuck and Jack tackle sensational subjects, as long as they kept costs down and audience interest up. Technically, most Warners pictures were on a par with those from Universal or even from a B-grade outfit like Monogram, and had nowhere near the polish of a standard feature from a competing major. That was a function of cost, of course—in 1932, Selznick convinced struggling RKO to commit to *minimum* budgets of $200,000, while Warners rarely spent that much on its standard features. But Warners' topical stories were produced quickly and inexpensively, and the distinctive subject matter compensated for their meager production values. They had little critical or prestige value, though. *Five Star Final* had been a step in the right direction, and by 1932 Harry Warner was looking for a major hit not only to solidify public acceptance of Warners' style but to establish its credibility with critics and especially with first-run distributors.

The studio came through with *I Am a Fugitive from a Chain Gang*, a picture that marked a high point in Zanuck's regime and the coming of age of Warners' Depression-era style. It didn't come easily. Zanuck and the Warners faced resistance to the project on both coasts, but they pulled together and quite literally muscled the film through the institutional machinery. Thus its production provides a good idea of executive authority and interaction at Warners in the early 1930s, and the complex decision-making process involved when one of the studio's more controversial productions was in the works. That process involved not only Zanuck and the Warners but also Hal B. Wallis, who took producer credit on the picture. After working his way up through theater management and advertising, Wallis had become a top executive at Warners; in fact it was Wallis who ran the First National plant while it was being converted to sound in 1929–30. He was now Zanuck's executive assistant and the closest thing to a supervisor on the lot, although his limited authority was evident enough in his $900-per-week salary—not even one-fifth of Zanuck's, and less than that of many top writers. Though only two weeks of his salary were charged to the picture, Wallis did assist with the day-to-day details during production.

Still, it was Zanuck who orchestrated *I Am a Fugitive from a Chain Gang.*

Both Jack Warner and Darryl Zanuck had been interested in Robert Burns's autobiographical exposé, *I Am a Fugitive from a Georgia Chain Gang,* when it was serialized in *True Detective Mysteries* from January through June 1931. The story involved a man who is unjustly accused of a crime, convicted by an incompetent judge, and sentenced to serve time on a chain gang; there he suffers unspeakable brutality and hardship before escaping to live on the run. In early 1932 Warner and Zanuck decided to go after the project, and in February Warner went to New York to secure the screen rights and the star for the picture. On February 27 Warner paid Burns $12,500 for his story, which by then had been published as a novel by Vanguard; then Warner immediately entered serious negotiations with Paul Muni to play the title role. Muni was a Broadway star just breaking into film, and judging from his recent performance in *Scarface,* the Howard Hughes–Howard Hawks film, Muni was an ideal Warners type—surly, iconoclastic, capable of sudden bursts of violence. Warner signed Muni in mid-March at $3,000 per week to star in Burns's exposé, scheduled to start shooting later that summer.

Predictably, there were problems with both the legal and sales departments when they learned of the project. Jack subdued the studio lawyers, while Harry soothed the boys in New York. Zanuck, meanwhile, dealt with unexpected opposition at the studio. On February 19, a few days before Jack purchased the rights, Warners' story department filed a report on Burns's novel "at Mr. Zanuck's request." It included a thirteen-page synopsis, a two-page summary, and a one-page commentary. The report closed with this: "Comment: this book might make a picture if we had no censorship, but all the strong and vivid points in the story are certain to be eliminated by the present censorship board. My reasons for not recommending the book for a picture are as follows." The story editor then listed seven specific reasons, most of them having to do with the violence of the story and the hostility the film was bound to generate in the Deep South. The editor was right on the latter score, as was the legal department: the state of Georgia tried to ban the film and sued Warners to prevent its release.

Remarkably enough, even heavier misgivings were voiced in the directors' ranks. On Zanuck's instructions Wallis assigned the picture to Roy Del Ruth, who was then Warners' highest paid director. In a lengthy memo to Wallis, Del Ruth declined the assignment—an action permissible only for a top director, and not without a good explanation. And Del Ruth felt he had one. "This subject is terribly heavy and

morbid," he explained; "there is not one moment of relief anywhere."
Del Ruth went on to argue that the story "lacks box-office appeal," and
that it seemed especially ill-advised now, "when the whole public is
depressed to the extent that many of them are leaping out of windows."
He noted that the ending of the story, with the hero still on the run,
was "unusual" but that it was "not one that the mob [that is, the public]·
will like." Toward the end of his rambling memo Del Ruth stated that
"the above views are merely my impressions of the story—it will probably make a good picture for Muni, and he will probably be great in it,
but I doubt it will ever meet such a hearty approval from an audience."
In closing, Del Ruth again declined the assignment: "I personally do
not care for a story of this kind," he wrote, "and would not like to make
it."

Zanuck pressed on, assigning the treatment to staff writer Brown
Holmes, who was assisted by a most unlikely collaborator—the fugitive himself. In early April Zanuck received a wire from the New York
office informing him that the "author of *I Am a Fugitive from a Georgia
Chain Gang* is coming out" to assist with the screenplay. Robert Burns
was "under cover and traveling under a phony name . . . because the
state of Georgia is after him for having escaped." The wire closed with
an amusing understatement: "You may find Burns a little erratic, but
you are used to all kinds of people so I am sure you will handle him
and get the best out of him." Burns arrived in early April—he was
known around the studio as "Mr. Crane"—and a few days later Wallis
sent a memo to "Crane-Holmes," informing his writing team: "I am
anxious to have a treatment in Mr. Zanuck's hands no later than April
25th. . . . We will get together tomorrow for a preliminary discussion
and I would like to go into treatment immediately as I want to get an
okayed treatment before Zanuck leaves, so that the continuity can be
done in his absence."

The treatment was completed by April 25, and a more experienced
studio writer, Sheridan Gibney, worked with Holmes on the continuity
script, which was completed in five weeks. After a solo rewrite by
Gibney, Zanuck assigned the project to yet another writer, Howard J.
Green, demanding a rewrite by June. (Green, at $600 per week, was
only a notch above Gibney's $500-per-week status.) In a deposition for
the Georgia lawsuit a few years later, Green recalled the circumstances
of that rewrite. The script, said Green, "was unsatisfactory to Mr. Zanuck in many respects. He had a series of conferences with me about it,
after which I wrote a revised screenplay which changed the original
story considerably." Green described his work as "a job of dramatic
construction, editing, tightening." Zanuck instructed him not to name
Georgia or any other state in his script, and Zanuck also insisted that

Green minimize the polemics against chain gangs. "If I had had my way," admitted Green, "I am afraid that the script would have been a blasting tirade against the entire system. Mr. Zanuck sensed this and upbraided me for it. He wanted both sides of the case presented and insisted that I incorporate into my script sincere arguments in favor of chain-gang systems."

The arguments for a chain-gang system in the shooting script were scarcely persuasive, but they were enough to intensify the dramatic conflicts and to avoid any serious legal problems—even with Georgia, as it turned out. (Warners won the suit.) By July Zanuck felt that Green's script was on the right track, and on the twenty-first all department heads were notified that the picture would start one week later. Not until then did Zanuck decide on a director, tapping Mervyn LeRoy for the assignment. LeRoy was then preparing a picture entitled *42nd Street* for shooting in September, but he agreed to abandon that project temporarily and direct *I Am a Fugitive*. LeRoy, Wallis, and various department heads came up with a budget of $195,845—less than for a second-rate feature at MGM or any other major. Of that total, the above-the-line costs were barely $50,000; story and continuity costs were $18,882; Wallis earned $1,800 for two weeks' work as supervisor; LeRoy earned $13,200 for eight weeks at $1,650; and Muni earned $16,750 for five and a half weeks' work.

LeRoy shot *I Am a Fugitive from a Chain Gang* on five sound stages at the Warners' studio, using the back lot for occasional exterior work. The picture was finished exactly on schedule in thirty-four days, with LeRoy cranking out footage at his usual pace. He averaged 5'30" of finished film per day through most of the shoot, even though Muni, who was in almost every scene, required a good deal of attention because of his limited experience as a film actor. Muni turned in a strong if somewhat theatrical performance—his gestures are a bit exaggerated, his speech too carefully projected. But Muni's acting was compatible with LeRoy's typically unobtrusive style of directing. LeRoy's position as storyteller in *I Am a Fugitive* is removed from the action, rarely directing the viewer's attention or commenting on the action via close-ups and cutting. Most scenes are shot as tableaux, with an almost documentary detachment. LeRoy does make an occasional effort to get inside Muni's character, as in the sequence after Muni's escape when he looks longingly at a prostitute. For that scene, LeRoy set up a series of glance-object cuts: tight shots of Muni staring at the woman, intercut with close-ups of her body. The intensity of that moment is rare in the film—and in Warners sagas generally—and its rarity tells us something about the usual interplay of technique, thematics, and production design in Warners pictures. It also says something about the interplay of

Star Paul Muni and director Mervyn LeRoy (both seated) take a break from the breakneck shooting pace on I Am a Fugitive from a Chain Gang.

narrative economy and cost-efficiency. LeRoy's detached style required fewer camera setups, since he seldom broke down the dramatic space for close-ups, shot/reverse shots, and glance-object cutting.

Ultimately, our perspective is akin to that of somebody watching a rat in a maze—the hero is victimized by social conditions and by circumstances beyond his control. But there is precious little time for us to contemplate the social implications or to demand a closer rapport with the hero, since all of our energies and his are consumed by his inexorable flight. As in so many of Warners' male-oriented sagas, the subtleties of character development and narrative complexity—and ultimately of visual technique—give way to a curious momentum, with the hero's obsessive, hell-bent quest moving the picture along at a frantic pace. This offsets LeRoy's essentially static camera in individual scenes, giving the impression of a rather dynamic visual style. This dynamic quality is reinforced by the frequent use of montages as transitional devices, another trademark Warners device. *I Am a Fugitive* and countless other early-1930s Warners pictures, particularly the crime sagas, were laden with these high-speed, quick-cut passages, these flashes of narrative condensation. Significantly, the footage for these transitions was shot silent by a second unit, and thus montages were a cost-cutting device as well as a means of narrative continuity. All in all, the visual and narrative technique in *I Am a Fugitive* indicated how Warners' top directors turned the constraints of tight budgets and schedules to their advantage, translating Harry Warner's demand for cost-efficiency into an economical narrative style, one that was ideally suited to the stories they told.

Zanuck was directly involved in shaping that style, not only through script development and production design, but also in his involvement on the set. Unlike Thalberg, who fashioned MGM's style from his office and cutting rooms, Zanuck was on the set constantly, often providing counsel regarding a camera angle or a story problem. Legends abound concerning Zanuck's brainstorms on the set or in the editing room, and one of the more telling incidents occurred with *I Am a Fugitive*. Jack Warner decided to preview the film in October once it was edited—an extravagant move for the company, again underscoring the importance of the picture. Audience reaction to the preview assured Zanuck that Warners had a hit, but also that the film needed a stronger closing, so he rewrote the film's tag scene, which in the preview version simply depicted Muni on the lam. The new epilogue had Muni's fugitive meeting his former girlfriend in the dead of night. She is horrified by his condition, living like a hunted animal, and asks how he survives. Backing into the shadows, Muni mutters, "I steal," and then disappears into the night. The scene is perfect—one of those moments when story, performance, and technique perfectly coalesce. That one moment also undercuts the heroic posturing and pro-social values of more conventional films, even other Warners crime films, celebrating individual initiative and freedom but recognizing the inhumanity and injustice in Depression America.

I Am a Fugitive from a Chain Gang opened in November 1932 at the Strand on Broadway, Warners' largest first-run theater (2,758 seating capacity). Initial reports from the sales force indicated both uncertainty about the picture and excitement about its reception. On November 11, the day of the New York premiere, Zanuck received a wire from Dan Michalove reporting that the first day's gross receipts were $5,100, the Strand's biggest take since the opening of *Little Caesar*. He went on: NEWSPAPERS UNANIMOUS MOST TOUCHING BRILLIANT MOST TERRIFYING DRAMA EVER OFFERED TALKY AUDIENCE AND MOST IMPRESSIVE REALISM YET TO COME TO SCREEN. He concluded with the hopeful suggestion that THIS IS PICTURE THEATERS OF AMERICA HAVE BEEN WAITING FOR. Charles Einfeld, Warners' director of publicity and advertising, sent Zanuck a similar salvo that same day: FUGITIVE BIGGEST BROADWAY SENSATION IN LAST THREE YEARS, enthused Einfeld. CANT REFRAIN FROM WIRING YOU TONIGHT AS WARNER PROSPERITY TURNS THE CORNER IN 209 OTHER CITIES WHERE FUGITIVE OPENED . . .

The following day Michalove reported receipts of $7,950, adding that on its second day *I Am a Fugitive* PLAYED TO MORE ACTUAL ADMISSIONS THAN ANY PRODUCTION IN HISTORY OF STRAND THEATRE FOR ONE DAY. Realizing that Warners had a blockbuster on its hands, Michalove had only praise for Zanuck and the studio. He closed the wire with this rather remarkable statement: ENTIRE SALES DEPARTMENT JOINS ME IN SENDING CONGRATULATIONS TO YOU AND ENTIRE STUDIO PRODUCTION FORCE WHO MADE THIS TREMENDOUS EPIC AND MUST ADMIT YOU PEOPLE WERE RIGHT WHEN WE ASKED YOU TO CUT DOWN ON BLOOD AND BRUTAL SEQUENCES AND YOU REFUSED. AUDIENCES THROUGHOUT AMERICA HAVE VINDICATED YOUR DECISION.

Besides grudging admiration and even humility, that comment expressed the complexities involved in the making of a single Warners picture, in the refining of its house style, and in the relations of power between the home office and the studio. Harry Warner's fiscal policies shaped but scarcely dictated production policy, and the balance of Warners' economic and creative forces was continually renegotiated by Zanuck and company on one coast and the marketing and sales executives on the other. That balance shifted with *I Am a Fugitive,* which was acclaimed by critics as well as audiences. It was heralded as a Depression-era masterpiece, with the National Board of Review calling it "not only the best feature film of the year, but one of the best films ever made in this country."

T H E success of *I Am a Fugitive* affirmed the burgeoning Warners style, although Zanuck himself hardly needed affirmation. He was so confident in the studio's direction, in fact, that even before *I Am a Fugitive*'s release he went ahead with a Warners-style musical, despite Harry Warner's edict against the genre. Zanuck was aware of both the expense and the declining popularity of musicals, but he was convinced, along with Mervyn LeRoy, that the "backstage musical" could be revitalized with an infusion of Warners' Depression-era ambience. On August 15, 1932, Warners closed a deal with novelist Bradford Ropes, paying $6,000 for the movie rights to his as-yet-unpublished novel, *42nd Street,* the story of an obsessive stage director who mounts a Depression-era musical despite heavy odds and his own declining health. By then Zanuck had already started two staff writers on an adaptation, and he and LeRoy had been preparing the production. The film was scheduled to start shooting in mid-September, with LeRoy directing the dramatic sequences and a newcomer named Busby Berkeley handling the musical numbers.

The decision to bring in Berkeley was as significant as the decision to try a Warners-style musical in the first place. Berkeley was a stylist in his own right, with a distinctive approach to musical production that became as important a defining characteristic of Warners' backstage musicals as the established house style. Berkeley came to Hollywood

Choreographer and musical director Busby Berkeley, Warners' most distinctive stylist, in an aptly framed publicity photo taken in 1933.

in 1930 to choreograph Sam Goldwyn's *Whoopee,* and he stayed on largely at LeRoy's encouragement and despite the musical's declining market. LeRoy saw that Berkeley was developing something more dynamic than the stage-bound treatment of most movie musicals, and as LeRoy's own stock went up he was determined to work with Berkeley, whatever the disparity between their styles of filmmaking. Berkeley's early training had been as a choreographer of military parades and marches, which helps explain his fascination with elaborate stage routines and overhead shots of chorines in kaleidoscopic displays. But an equally important Berkeley technique was the use of a single, highly mobile camera for dance numbers. He insisted that it was "the camera that must dance," a notion that energized his choreography and drew audiences into the performers' space onstage—and that put him distinctly at odds with LeRoy and his fellow Warners directors.

LeRoy did not direct *42nd Street,* even though he had prepared the picture. *I Am a Fugitive* left him out of commission due to exhaustion from overwork, and Zanuck was unwilling to wait for his recuperation to start the musical. Ropes's novel was published in mid-September, and Zanuck wanted to capitalize on its success. He also had struck a deal for Warner Baxter, a loan-out from Fox for $5,000 per week, to play the manic, harassed director. In mid-September fifty-seven "chorines" were signed at $66 per week, and Ginger Rogers was signed a few days later for four weeks at $500 per week. By then the picture was ready to go, and Zanuck figured several of his house directors could handle the dramatic scenes. He assigned staff director Lloyd Bacon, and on September 28, 1932, production opened on *42nd Street.*

The way Zanuck and LeRoy planned the picture—whether consciously or otherwise—reinforced the dissonance between its dramatic and musical sequences. The picture was done by Bacon and Berkeley working with two separate units in two different studios. The Bacon unit shot on six sound stages at the First National studio from September 28 to October 29, with retakes done on November 2 and 3, and completed the nonmusical portion of the film in thirty days of shooting. The Berkeley unit shot at Warners' Sunset studio from October 19 to November 16, although it was actually in production for only eighteen days, including five days for rehearsals of the "42nd Street Finale," shot from November 12 to 15. Actual shooting went smoothly for both units, with Zanuck monitoring production and Sol Polito handling the cinematography for both Bacon and Berkeley. But even with Polito lighting and shooting for both directors, there was little consistency or continuity between the dramatic and musical portions of *42nd Street.* The entire film builds toward the climactic premiere of the show-within-the-show, and those "finished" numbers were staged by Berkeley. The earlier rehearsals had been presented as just that—as rough, unpolished performances—and were shot by Bacon's unit. Those rehearsals, like the dramatic sequences throughout, have the look and feel of Warners' Depression-era dramas, while Berkeley's musical numbers are marked by an exuberant excess, a technical polish, and a visual dynamism that was unprecedented in Warners' pictures.

By the time *42nd Street* was in postproduction, LeRoy was back on the lot, working with Zanuck and Berkeley on a follow-up, *Gold Diggers of 1933*. It would be Warners' third adaptation of Avery Hopwood's play *The Gold Diggers*, which was done twice as a silent back in the 1920s. In mid-November Zanuck started his writing staff on the adaptation. "I want to retain as much of the old picture as possible, especially the great comedy sequences," wrote Zanuck to his story editor, adding that the writers should "smarten up the situations." Zanuck also wanted "to keep this quiet and not let anyone know what we are working on." He planned to announce the remake of *The Gold Diggers* after the release of *42nd Street*, so that it could come "like a big news break." And it wasn't just the public and the industry that Zanuck planned to surprise with the news. Apparently, Harry Warner was unaware of the remake and still had no idea that *42nd Street* had been done as a musical.

By December the writing team of James Seymour and David Boehm was on the project, and they had regular conferences with Zanuck and LeRoy through that month and into January 1933. Also attending was Robert Lord, another top Warners writer who contributed story ideas and acted as informal supervisor on the project. This klatch of Warners' writers gave the backstage story the same Warners ambience as *42nd Street*. But despite its basis in the grim realities of the Depression, *Gold Diggers of 1933* also relied on the conventions of romantic comedy. The original play, an exercise in wish fulfillment, traced the efforts of two sisters to break into the big time. Now the story focused on three hustling showgirls (Ruby Keeler, Joan Blondell, and Ginger Rogers) who pursue not only dancing careers but also three wealthy men (Warren William, Dick Powell, and Guy Kibbee). The plot is a hodgepodge of mistaken identity and screwball romance, with all three of the love stories resolved magically to make way for Berkeley's final tour de force, "My Forgotten Man."

In *Gold Diggers*, unlike *42nd Street*, Berkeley's work would figure into more than just the finale. Zanuck wanted the upscale production numbers interspersed throughout, and not only onstage but in quasi-dramatic scenes as well—as when Dick Powell croons to his showgirl neighbors through their adjoining apartment windows. In fact, Zanuck and LeRoy decided to overhaul the opening of the picture to establish the Berkeley style from the outset. The initial treatment and the conference notes called for a semidocumentary montage opening, with "various shots of closed theaters, empty ticket agencies, deserted office buildings." But this was replaced after a series of meetings with Zanuck in early January with the following:

> Picture opens on the stage of a theater. A performance is in progress. The camera pulls back to reveal that the theater is empty and we realize that it is only a dress rehearsal. The idea of the number is that there is no depression—"happy-happy-throw your money away!" the chorus is yelling, flinging handfuls of gold coins into the air. A gang of sheriffs walks in and starts dismantling the set—stripping the girls, etc.

This would become the now legendary "We're in the Money" number, which Ginger Rogers and other chorines perform wearing oversize coins. A bizarre celebration of capitalism, commercial entertainment, and the commodification of female sexuality, it also was an ideal counter to "My Forgotten Man," Berkeley's closing lament for the anonymous victims of World War I and the Depression

As with *42nd Street*, *Gold Diggers* was shot with two separate units, and again there was a strong disparity in terms of technique and narrative style between the musical and dramatic sequences. LeRoy's unit shot on a thirty-day schedule from February 16 through March 23, and Berkeley's from March 6 to April 13. Again Polito was the cinematographer for both units, with Sid Hickox filling in if schedules conflicted. And again the musical numbers were more polished and dynamic than the dramatic sequences, due largely to the different resources and working methods of the two directors. Their work on *Gold Diggers* did indicate, though, that the backstage musical could be refined into a coherent narrative form and thus might be as important a breakthrough for Warners as *I Am a Fugitive* had been a few months earlier.

Berkeley started shooting the musical numbers for *Gold Diggers* on March 6, 1933, four days before *42nd Street* was due for release. But Zanuck and nearly everyone else in Hollywood had something very different on their minds that day. On Monday, March 6, the newly elected Franklin D. Roosevelt declared a nationwide bank holiday to inaugurate his National Recovery Administration. That week the Hollywood studios, by agreement with the Motion Picture Academy, and in support of Roosevelt and the NRA, initiated an eight-week pay cut of 50 percent for all salaried employees earning over $25 per week. Harry Warner was a vocal supporter of the strategy, and in fact he instigated pay cuts at the studio without consulting or even informing

This elaborate set for Berkeley's "Shadow Waltz" number in Gold Diggers of
1933 *was far from typical at Warners, known at the time for its realism and
economical production methods.*

Zanuck. In an overt test of his own authority, Zanuck informed the
Warners that the cuts were unnecessary and he reinstated previous pay
levels. This was certainly a bold assertion, considering Warners' losses
of just over $14 million in 1932. But Zanuck genuinely believed that
Warners had licked the Depression. Still, Harry Warner reinstated the
cuts, and he even threatened to extend them beyond the period initially imposed.

Zanuck was furious and shaken, but in the coming weeks his mood
shifted from rage to stone-cold resolve. He conducted studio business
with an air of detachment and was all but oblivious to the tremendous
impact of *42nd Street* after its March 10 release. Zanuck realized now
that a partnership at Warners was impossible; siding with the workers
in the salary flap only confirmed his status with the company. "Harry
held the purse strings," quipped Hal Wallis about the feud, "and Darryl made a mistake in crossing him." Studio insider Milton Sperling,
who was wed to one of Harry's daughters and understood the Warner
clan all too well, thought Zanuck "had been conned into believing that
he was the crown prince, whereas, though head of production, he was
just like the rest of the studio employees."

The struggle between Zanuck and Harry steadily intensified, coming to a head in early April, when Warner told Zanuck he would not be reinstating full salaries on the date prescribed in the Academy agreement. Zanuck demanded that the agreement be honored, but still Warner refused. By now dissension was spreading throughout the Warners plant, and Jack asked MPPDA President Will Hays to help resolve the dispute—something Louis Mayer had tried a few months before when Thalberg and Nick Schenck were locked in a similar combat at MGM. But there was no chance of resolving this dispute and keeping the executive ranks intact. On April 14, Zanuck met Wallis at the Brown Derby in Hollywood to discuss his plans. Their meal was interrupted by Harry Warner, who asked to speak privately with Zanuck. After a heated exchange, Zanuck returned and spoke in confidence to Wallis. According to Wallis, Zanuck told him, "I'm leaving Warners and I'm not coming back. Joe Schenck offered me a job and I'm going to take it." Later, when Warners threatened Schenck with a lawsuit for raiding his executive staff, both Schenck and Zanuck denied that they'd discussed a possible partnership before Zanuck resigned on the morning of April 15, 1933. Yet on April 21, Warners' former production chief and the United Artists executive pooled their resources and filmmaking

Darryl Zanuck (left) and Joe Schenck (center) shortly after creating Twentieth Century Pictures. On the right is biopic star George Arliss, who left Warners to sign with Twentieth.

talents to create Twentieth Century Pictures, an independent company that would release through UA.

N O T even Darryl Zanuck's overactive imagination could have conjured up what lay ahead: Twentieth would become a major independent and within another two years would take over the bankrupt Fox Film Corporation, and 20th Century-Fox would stand as a major industry power under Zanuck for another twenty years. Zanuck's success after leaving Warners reaffirmed his creative and administrative talents, and it reaffirmed, too, the viability of a central-producer system, which Zanuck sustained at Fox long after Warners and other companies had gone to a unit-production system. Zanuck's abrupt departure from Warner Bros. shook the company to its very foundation, but he did not prove to be indispensable—no more than Irving Thalberg over at MGM. Both Zanuck and Thalberg had built successful production operations and distinctive studio styles, but by 1933 those very accomplishments rendered them expendable. The machinery they designed was geared to run—with or without them.

III

THE 1930s: GOLDEN AGE

10

MGM in the Mid-Thirties: Charmed Interval

After touting itself as Depression-proof in 1930, Hollywood took quite a fall when the Depression finally struck. At the height of the talkie boom in 1930, the Big Eight's combined profits had been over $55 million. In 1931 they were down to $6.5 million, and in 1932 the Big Eight showed net losses totaling $26 million. The industry hit bottom in early 1933, with the five integrated majors—Paramount, MGM, Warners, Fox, and RKO—hitting the hardest. Three of the five—Paramount, Fox, and RKO—went into bankruptcy or receivership in early 1933, and in all, the stock value of the five majors fell from nearly a billion dollars in 1930 to under $200 million in 1933. Paramount's fall was the most dramatic. In 1930 its profits were $25 million and its assets just over $300 million; by late 1932 the company was bankrupt. Like the other studios that went under, Paramount continued to operate but with tremendous losses. After fiscal reorganization, its assets were down to $117 million. Warners displayed the grim determination of a survivor, but it, too, was on the brink of collapse; between 1930 and 1933, $60 million in assets—fully one-quarter of its corporate worth—were siphoned off to cover its losses and debts. MGM was the only major studio that held its market value and continued to turn a profit in the early 1930s. Net revenues did fall steadily, from a peak of $14.6 million in 1930 to a low point of $4.3 million in 1933, but just staying in the black during that period was an accomplishment. And while the market value of the other majors plunged, Metro's assets held steady at $130 million.

Clearly the movie industry needed help in early 1933, and thus the inauguration of Franklin Delano Roosevelt could not have been more timely. When he was sworn in in February, Roosevelt declared a week-long bank moratorium for early March to assess the economic damage, and then kicked his National Recovery Administration into gear. There were none of Herbert Hoover's promises that prosperity was just around the corner, but indeed it was for the movie industry. Hollywood was a Depression-era success story, and it owed its resurgence largely to Roosevelt's economic recovery measures. FDR's plans centered on the National Industrial Recovery Act (NIRA), which went into effect in June 1933. The NIRA strategy, basically, was to promote recovery by sanctioning certain monopoly practices among major U.S. industries. There was potential for worker exploitation and abuse in such a plan, so the NIRA also authorized labor organizing and collective bargaining.

The NIRA's impact on Hollywood was twofold. First, the long-standing but informal collusion among the Big Eight to control the marketplace now had government sanction, and the Hollywood powers made the most of it. In fact, Hollywood's own trade association, the Motion Picture Producers and Distributors Association (MPPDA) wrote the Code of Fair Competition required by the NIRA, committing to paper such unwritten laws as blind bidding and block booking, whereby the nonaffiliated theaters were forced to take the studios' output, sight unseen. Equally important were "zoning" and "clearance" policies, which specified where a picture would play and for how long, thus minimizing a studio risk and ensuring favorable treatment of its affiliated theaters. The second significant result of the NIRA was that Hollywood became more union-oriented, with the division and specialization of filmmaking labor now mandated by the government. Thus the NIRA provided federal approval and support of the studio system both as a widespread strategy for market control and, within the studio-factories themselves, as a specific mode of production. What had been a loose affiliation of movie companies and a vaguely defined production process now became a codified, regulated totality. Significantly, the NIRA would be declared unconstitutional by the Supreme Court in 1935, but the ruling had little immediate effect on the movie industry. By then Hollywood was on the rebound and power had been consolidated so effectively by the studios that it would take the Justice Department and the courts until the late 1940s to wrest it away.

As the studio system solidified during the mid-1930s, production management changed substantially. In the early studio years, the system was keyed to the central producer—to top production executives like Thalberg, Zanuck, and Lasky. The central producer worked with the studio boss to cultivate the company's resources and personally supervised all production, shaping the studio's policies, procedures, and ultimately its house style. But by the early 1930s each studio's production and market strategies were pretty well set; Hollywood's central producers had done their jobs well and thus were no longer as crucial to the system. What's more, certain production chiefs like Thalberg and Zanuck had simply become too powerful, threatening the corporate control by studio owners and top executive officers. So the studios steadily phased out or downgraded the central producer's role, and developed management systems with a clearer hierarchy of authority and a greater dispersion of creative control.

With the central producer's role either phased out or downgraded in the 1930s, there were fewer "creative executives" at the management level. Thus the long-standing split between conception and execution, and between capitalization and production became more acute. Studio bosses like Louis Mayer and Jack Warner regained power—but they were administrators, not filmmakers. And even with the regulation of the system and consolidation of studio power, the cinema was still a competitive business demanding quality, innovation, and differentiation of product. In fact, as the industry pulled out of the Depression in 1935–36, first-run and prestige productions were more profitable than ever. Consequently, studio executives were compelled to give more authority and creative freedom to select personnel, particularly above-the-line artists on first-run features.

Taken together, the impact of the NIRA and the internal shifts in management brought the studio system into clearer definition and gave it greater balance as well. Federal regulations helped to consolidate power, standardize production practices, and create a more genuinely integrated system; but at the same time they allowed filmmaking artists, technicians, and laborers more power—both individually and collectively—within the system. The result was a greater balance of power and of the industry's various economic, institutional, and aesthetic imperatives than ever before. That balance did not come overnight, and each studio had its own skew, depending on its resources, market fix, corporate structure, and key personnel. But once that balance was reached, it signaled Hollywood's coming of age—indeed, the coming of its golden age. By the late 1930s the Hollywood studio system reached full equilibrium, generating a remarkable run of pictures that were equally successful as commercial commodities, as popular entertainment, and as cinematic art.

M G M had created a prototype for the dominant management system in the 1920s, and it did the same in the 1930s. Metro's shift from a central-producer to a unit-production system was pronounced, since it involved not only Thalberg's ouster but also the arrival of David Selznick and Walter Wanger, who left their respective jobs as central producer at RKO and Columbia. The management shake-up at Metro was motivated largely by Nick Schenck and Louis Mayer's desire to reassert control over studio operations, but Thalberg's ill health played a key role in their efforts. Schenck had always fretted about Thalberg's delicate condition, but he felt a perverse sense of relief when he learned of Thalberg's illness in January 1933. The occasion brought Schenck to the West Coast for the second time in recent months to handle a Thalberg-related crisis; but he had a different mind-set this time out. The way Thalberg had been appeased with a stock option deal after Paul Bern's suicide still rankled Schenck—no employee deserved a piece of the parent company, not even Thalberg. Schenck felt it was time to rein in the young production chief, and when Thalberg fell ill he saw an ideal opportunity. His plan was to keep MGM's supervisory system intact, but without a centralized producer. Surely the coterie of Thalberg men, after years of schooling in Thalberg's office and screening room, could sustain the system on their own. Mayer would hire a few other top producers to handle Metro's more ambitious projects, and if Thalberg returned to the studio, he, too, could concentrate on prestige pictures.

Mayer scarcely needed persuading. He enjoyed MGM's success, but resented the steady loss of authority over recent years to Thalberg. After meeting with Schenck, Mayer immediately moved on the Wanger and Selznick deals. Wanger was eager to leave his post at Columbia as vice president and production chief under Harry Cohn, and on January 10, 1933, he signed with MGM to work "in the capacity of an executive and producer of motion pictures" for $2,000 per week. On that same date, Wanger's signing was reported in *Variety*, along with two other pieces that signaled the shake-up at MGM. One story reported that Mayer "took charge of active production at Metro due to the illness of Irving Thalberg last week," and that he delivered a cost-cutting lecture to Metro's "associate producers, supervisors, and executives." The other dealt with Thalberg's "breakdown," which was described, interestingly enough, as "a flu relapse rather than any nervous disorder." There was no mention of a coronary or even of Thalberg's heart condition; clearly Schenck and Mayer wanted to signal the transition without sounding an alarm, and without implying that MGM's boy wonder would be out of commission for an extended period.

Thalberg's tenure as central producer was over, though, and that fact hit home when Mayer finally signed David Selznick in early February. Thalberg had known of the Wanger deal and was perfectly comfortable with the idea of bringing in a top supervisor with the stature of, say, a Hunt Stromberg. But he was not apprised of the Selznick courtship, nor of the contractual terms—and when Selznick signed, it was obvious why Thalberg had been kept in the dark. Selznick's contract gave him a weekly salary of $4,000 for two years, plus first option on the studio's stories, stars, and key production personnel, and promises of prestige-level budgets and marketing efforts. After Mayer had signed his son-in-law, he went to Thalberg's home to explain the deal, and the MGM partners broke into a bitter quarrel. The exchange was so heated that afterward Mayer, in a rare gesture, wrote Thalberg a letter of apology and explanation. "Certainly we [Mayer and Schenck] could not permit the company to go out of existence just because the active head of production was taken ill and likely to be away from business for a considerable length of time," wrote Mayer. "I consider it my duty and legal obligation under our contract to take up the burden anew where you left off." Thalberg responded with a perfunctory apology of his own, but he saw the handwriting on the wall. And rather than sit by while Mayer and Schenck realigned the studio power structure, he left with wife Norma Shearer and a few friends for an extended sojourn in Europe.

S E L Z N I C K hit the ground running at MGM, and his initial race was against the specter of Irving Thalberg. His debut project was *Dinner at Eight*, an adaptation of the George S. Kaufman–Edna Ferber play that Selznick saw as an all-star vehicle in the tradition of *Grand Hotel*—and as an ideal opportunity to prove he could compete on Thalberg's turf and on Thalberg's terms. This, too, would be a stylish ensemble piece, a comedy-drama featuring an array of high-society types whose fates intertwine. Mayer had promised Selznick free rein and open access to Metro's resources, and Selznick got both on *Dinner at Eight*. After signing, he started top writer Frances Marion on the script and made arrangements for George Cukor to come over from RKO as soon as he had finished *Little Women*. Selznick instructed the casting office to "make arrangements for Wallace Beery, Jean Harlow, Clark Gable, Marie Dressler, Lionel Barrymore, Lee Tracy, Louise Closser Hale. We will discuss, upon completion of the script, whether or not to have Joan Crawford play the girl." On February 22 Selznick sent a memo to story editor Sam Marx indicating when Marion would complete the continuity and requesting "a dialogue writer for only a week's work"—preferably Anita Loos or some other "dialogist" of the "modern school." Marion finished on March 6, but Loos was unavailable so Selznick used Herman Mankiewicz for a dialogue polish.

Cukor was tied up until April, so Selznick started preproduction without him. He worked with Adrian on the costumes, with Cedric Gibbons on the sets, and with cinematographer William Daniels on the overall design of the picture. These were the principal craftsmen on *Grand Hotel*, and together they again created a sophisticated, high-sheen milieu for *Dinner at Eight*. Selznick planned a thirty-day shoot starting in late April on a $500,000 budget, most of which went to the script ($123,000, including screen rights), the cast ($85,000), and the sets ($150,000). The cast varied from Selznick's original request, but still it included Metro's ranking stars: Marie Dressler, Wallace Beery, the Barrymore brothers, and Jean Harlow. Production closed on time and at a final cost of $515,000—some $200,000 less than *Grand Hotel* —indicating that Selznick could work efficiently even with Metro's top talent. *Dinner at Eight* also proved he could deliver MGM's distinctive blend of glamour and wit, light comedy and world-weary cynicism. The picture was due for release in late summer, and after several successful previews Selznick was confident it would sell. But he also hoped it would appease the industry critics who had derided his arrival at MGM as a flagrant example of industry nepotism. (One particularly venomous trade paper headline had read, "The Son-in-Law Also Rises.")

Selznick was also eager to prove himself to Thalberg, who announced in early summer that he would be returning in July. Selznick grew more anxious as the summer wore on, and he actually asked on several occasions to be released from his MGM contract. Mayer routinely refused those requests, but he, too, was anxious about Thalberg's return, fearing that there would be fireworks. Signs of the changing power structure were everywhere—especially the opulent side-by-side "bungalows" (outfitted by Cedric Gibbons) that Mayer built for Thalberg and Selznick as their respective unit headquarters. Selznick and Mayer were both pleasantly surprised when Thalberg returned in July 1933 and seemed to accept the changes at the studio. He was gracious and upbeat toward Selznick, and genuinely excited when *Dinner at Eight* emerged in August as a solid critical and commercial hit. Thalberg also seemed open to his new role as unit producer; he realized there was no going back to the old regime—not that he wanted to. The demands of the central-producer system had become too heavy, and Thalberg welcomed the chance to scale back and devote himself to a few high-quality pictures per year.

Several of Thalberg's former associates were less amenable to the change, however, and asked permission to resume working with Thalberg during pre- and postproduction. Mayer and Schenck nixed the request, allowing only "informal" input from Thalberg on anyone else's pictures. Mayer was especially adamant about regaining control over Metro's production operation, even though his creative input was essentially nil. His creative limitations potentially gave Metro's producers more autonomy over their own productions, which Thalberg, Selznick, Wanger, and Hunt Stromberg relished. But second-string producers like Bernie Hyman, Laurence Weingarten, Harry Rapf, John Considine, and Monta Bell continued to rely on Thalberg—and with tacit studio approval. So by late 1933 MGM was developing a modified central-producer/unit-producer system, with four top producers operating independently while one of them, Thalberg, maintained a degree of influence over MGM's more routine productions.

The only glitch in this setup involved Walter Wanger, who was on the outs with Mayer after his very first MGM production, *Gabriel Over the White House.* That left-wing political fable struck Mayer as an affront to all right-thinking Americans, especially his old friend Herbert Hoover. But an even greater affront was Wanger's box-office performance. Only one of his first five MGM productions turned a profit, and that was *Queen Christina*, Garbo's first appearance on-screen in nearly a year. Success with that venture was virtually automatic, but Garbo was so dissatisfied with Wanger that she refused to work with anyone but Thalberg or Selznick thereafter. Wanger's stock was falling,

David O. Selznick in his "bungalow" office at MGM, just after becoming a unit producer in 1933.

and it hit bottom when he became enmeshed in a triangulated romance between his close friend, agent Charles Feldman, an actress named Jean Howard, and Louis Mayer. The Metro boss was in his late forties and had been married to the same woman for some thirty years. But like many of his colleagues, he occasionally took more than just a professional interest in an aspiring starlet. His ardor was pretty serious in Jean Howard's case, and when she threw him over to wed Feldman, he blasted all involved with one of his "You'll never work again in this town" harangues. One of the targets was Wanger, who had helped facilitate the Feldman-Howard courtship. Wanger left MGM in the spring of 1934 and he created Walter Wanger Productions in September, only a few weeks after Feldman and Howard's wedding, in which he served as best man.

Wanger was hardly missed at MGM. By then Thalberg, Selznick, and Stromberg had hit their stride, and their unit productions dominated the studio's output. These three produced fourteen pictures in 1934—one-third of MGM's releases and virtually all of its big hits. While Wanger had never quite fit in, Selznick's credibility grew with each subsequent success. He followed *Dinner at Eight* in late 1933 with *Night Flight,* an aviation vehicle for Gable, and then *Dancing Lady,* a quasi-musical with Gable and Joan Crawford. These films proved he could adjust to Metro's style and market skew, but in 1934 he began to display his own cinematic interests and his range and savvy as a filmmaker. The first of his three 1934 productions was *Viva Villa!,* a biopic of the famed Mexican bandit starring Wallace Beery as Pancho Villa. There were problems throughout the production, notably with the location shoot in Mexico, with director Howard Hawks's refusal to follow orders, and with Ben Hecht's potentially libelous screenplay. Selznick handled the problems, eventually bringing the production back to the studio, revamping the story, and replacing Hawks with staffer Jack Conway. The budget swelled to just over $1 million, but the picture grossed $1.7 million on release.

Selznick's other two 1934 projects, *Manhattan Melodrama* and *David Copperfield,* were considerably more important to both MGM's and Selznick's own development. While both enabled Selznick to broaden his range as a producer, the former established a new costarring team—William Powell and Myrna Loy—at Metro, and the latter changed the studio's attitude toward literary adaptations. *Manhattan Melodrama* was a gangster saga starring Clark Gable, William Powell, and Myrna Loy, with Gable and Powell as adopted brothers who fall for the same woman (Loy) but wind up on opposite sides of the law. At film's end Powell's D.A. sends Gable's wisecracking, self-sacrificing hood strutting to the electric chair. *Manhattan Melodrama* was, rather atypically for MGM, an exercise in low-budget filmmaking that Selznick and director Woody Van Dyke (who had worked together on low-budget Tim McCoy westerns back in 1927) knocked out in just three weeks for only $300,000. In terms of production values, story, and technique, it was a Warners-style gangster epic—in fact, Powell came over on loan from Jack Warner. But there were some significant departures from the Warners model, particularly in terms of casting and characterization. *Manhattan Melodrama* was essentially a romantic melodrama, a love story as well as a saga of a ruthlessly self-serving hood. Thus the trio of stars, and the upbeat finale in which Gable's death clears the way for Powell and Loy's happiness.

That finale was pure MGM, and it also was the kind of adjustment to the gangster genre that Joseph Breen of the "Hays office" was looking for. The so-called Hays office was an agency of the MPPDA and was named for its first president, Will Hays. Its function was to monitor movie content and uphold the Production Code, a doctrine of ethics that Hays commissioned a Jesuit priest and a Catholic publisher to write in 1930. Code enforcement had been fairly lax until 1933, when widespread criticism of excessive sex and violence in movies led the MPPDA's board of directors, at Hays's behest, to sign a "Reaffirmation of Objectives" of the Production Code. This they did on March 5, 1933 —the same date, significantly enough, that FDR's bank holiday went into effect. Just as the bank holiday heralded heavy federal regulation via the NIRA, the Reaffirmation was the first step toward widespread industry self-censorship via the Production Code Administration—the PCA or "Breen office," named for Hays's successor, Joseph Breen. Of particular interest to Breen in regard to gangster films was the Code's insistence that "the sympathy of the audience should never be thrown to the side of crime, wrongdoing, evil, or sin." Pictures like *Manhattan Melodrama* played it both ways, of course, splitting our sympathies between Gable's gangster and Powell's civic leader. But the finale tipped the balance toward righteousness, satisfying Breen's demand for "moral retribution" and "compensating moral values."

Manhattan Melodrama satisfied not only the Breen office but the public as well, grossing well over $1 million and revitalizing the career of William Powell, who had been faltering at Warners. Selznick was pleased with its success, but by the time it was released he was immersed in his next project, *David Copperfield*. This was MGM's last release of the year and perhaps its best, and it was an even clearer example of Selznick's growing confidence as a Metro producer. Though his contract gave him control over story selection, Dickens's classic was not on MGM's agenda and the New York office was adamant in its opposition to literary adaptations, particularly highbrow period pieces and costume dramas that were not only costly but were deemed a bit much for the average viewer. Selznick took on the East Coast philistines, and the terms of their debate were indicated by a memo that Selznick sent in February 1934 to Loew's sales and distribution executives. "There is no question in my mind," stated Selznick, "that the public has finally decided to accept the classics as motion picture fare." He noted that these stories had withstood the test of time and that they were a welcome change from "the outmoded [movie] formulas that the public knows even better than the producers." According to Selznick, there were "millions of fans" who knew movies better than the average producer, and thus were "even more familiar with the hackneyed situations than the makers of the films who have been grinding them out with machinelike efficiency and standardization." Selznick acknowledged that there were "very few producers with sufficient understanding" of the classics and "very few directors with sufficient taste and talent to transcribe them with an accuracy of spirit and mood."

Selznick finally convinced the powers at Loew's/MGM that he had the understanding and George Cukor had the taste and talent to handle *David Copperfield*. The picture was more an ensemble piece than a star vehicle, with Selznick's most recent discovery, Freddie Bartholomew, playing young David. Still it cost over a million dollars, due largely to its sixty-nine-day production schedule—a far cry from Van Dyke's pace on *Manhattan Melodrama*. Actually, there were vast differences between the two products, as is obvious from this comparison of various line items on their respective budgets:

	MANHATTAN MELODRAMA	COPPERFIELD
Story/cont.	$ 45,720	$ 69,457
Direction	13,146	113,585
Cast	76,427	46,769
Extras	32,051	20,213
Cameramen	6,140	33,608
Lighting	5,896	19,062
Sets	32,969	104,038
Props	9,897	42,019
Wardrobe	6,288	33,544
Location	99	4,348
Film/lab	11,044	46,818
Sound	7,811	31,864
Cutting	2,350	9,566
Music	2,475	45,914
General overhead	59,227	171,726
TOTAL	$304,292	$1,069,254

Copperfield was a huge hit, grossing nearly $3 million in its eighty-six-week run and doing exceptional business abroad. A few weeks before its release, Selznick had informed the sales office in New York that the picture "will roll up an enormous gross in the British Empire, which will more than justify its production cost." He was right. Of *Copperfield*'s $2.8 million gross 25 percent came from Commonwealth countries, versus 54 percent in the United States and Canada and 21 percent from "other foreign." This trend continued for Selznick's pictures, peaking a year later with *A Tale of Two Cities,* another Dickens story that scored 31 percent of its $2.4 million gross in the Commonwealth.

Selznick's efforts in 1934 to refine Metro's style and expand its repertoire of story types were complemented by Thalberg's productions, particularly his remake of *The Merry Widow* and his highbrow biopic, *The Barretts of Wimpole Street,* starring Norma Shearer as poetess Elizabeth Barrett Browning. Hunt Stromberg, meanwhile, solidified his status as a top producer—as a bona fide unit producer, in fact—via an altogether more conservative route. Stromberg's two key projects in 1934 were *The Thin Man,* a classy detective comedy starring William Powell and Myrna Loy, and *Naughty Marietta,* a light operetta featuring Jeanette MacDonald and Nelson Eddy. Both Strombergs were directed by Van Dyke and written by Frances Goodrich and Albert Hackett, and both pictures hit. These hits were reformulated in 1935 by the same filmmaking team and with the same sets of costars; *After the Thin Man* and *Rose Marie* also hit, and Stromberg's status at Metro was secured. So were the two formulas with their respective above-the-line collaborators.

It's worth noting that the two Stromberg unit formulas were reworkings of successful Selznick and Thalberg productions—the *Thin Man* series from the Powell-Loy pairing in *Manhattan Melodrama,* and the MacDonald-Eddy operettas from *The Merry Widow,* which Ernst Lubitsch directed for Thalberg. But while Selznick and Thalberg produced the prototypes, they left to Stromberg the task of "grinding them out with machinelike efficiency and standardization." Both Selznick and Thalberg jealously guarded their autonomy and regarded each production as a distinct venture, differentiated not only from their competitors' high-class products but from other MGM productions as well. They avoided rehashing their successes and rarely used the same above-the-line personnel from one project to the next. Thus neither really developed a production unit as such at MGM. That was particularly ironic in Selznick's case; he had been a proponent for years—since his stints at Paramount and RKO—of just the kind of unit production that Stromberg was doing.

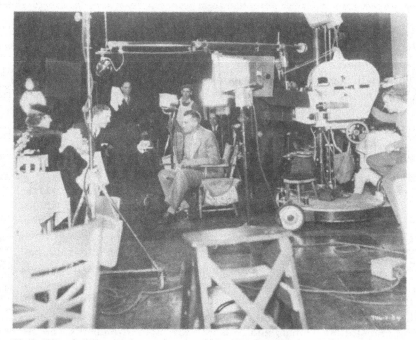

W. S. "Woody" Van Dyke on the set of The Thin Man, *a breakthrough film for him and also for stars William Powell and Myrna Loy.*

Thalberg, on the other hand, had avoided even the appearance of second-rate production tactics or formulaic filmmaking when he was running MGM, but clearly that was changing. Any other studio would have churned out Tarzan movies like so many sausages after *Tarzan the Ape Man* hit in 1932—which indeed was Mayer's inclination. But Thalberg convinced him to limit production to one Tarzan movie every two years, hoping to keep the premise fresh and to maximize profits. Mayer stayed with that strategy for the Tarzan pictures after he took full charge of the studio, but he displayed no such restraint when it came to reformulating other successful releases or to regulating the production process. His reasoning was clear enough. With costs steadily mounting and audiences growing more accustomed to B pictures and programmers during the Depression, he was looking for ways to economize. In fact, Mayer put together a production unit under Lucien Hubbard whose output looked suspiciously subpar by MGM standards —although the term *B movie* was strictly taboo at Metro. So by 1935 Metro was developing a three-tiered production system, with Thalberg, Selznick, and Stromberg handling the prestige output, the second-string producers supervising more routine fare, and Hubbard cranking out relatively inexpensive products.

That balance of feature offerings was ideal, given current market conditions, but it proved to be short-lived. The first sign of its undoing came early in 1935 when Selznick announced that he was leaving MGM to start an independent company that would produce a few prestige pictures per annum for release through United Artists. There were several reasons for Selznick's decision. He was apprehensive about Mayer's growing conservatism and concern for cost-efficiency, which were at odds with Selznick's filmmaking interests. They were at odds, too, with the improving economic climate, which, as Selznick saw it, demanded an increase in top-grade pictures. And more than anything else, Selznick wanted to make movies on his own lot and on his own terms, without studio bosses or New York executives calling the shots. He relished the talent and resources available at MGM, but there were obvious limits to his authority and control. That would all change with the creation of Selznick International Pictures.

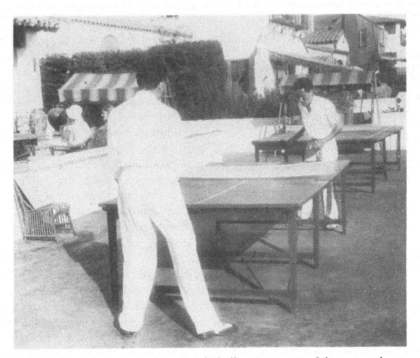

By 1935 Selznick (back to camera) and Thalberg were two of the top producers in Hollywood and friendly competitors both on and off the MGM lot.

Selznick officially resigned in late June 1935, but he stayed on through December to complete his last two MGM productions, *Anna Karenina* and *A Tale of Two Cities*. Both were sizable hits, grossing over $2 million apiece, and were further evidence of Selznick's confidence and his sensibilities as a prestige-level producer. They also solidified MGM's commitment to lavish adaptations of literary classics. Thalberg later claimed that it was the success of *Copperfield* that encouraged him to do *Mutiny on the Bounty*, a project that Mayer had nixed when Walter Wanger asked to produce it in 1933. Thalberg's adaptation of the Nordhoff and Hall epic, released in 1935, grossed well over $4 million—MGM's biggest hit since *Ben-Hur* a decade earlier.

W I T H Selznick leaving to start his own company and the market for top-grade independent productions heating up, Thalberg, too, began thinking about an operation of his own. Early in 1936 he went to Nick Schenck to propose a company that would be separate from MGM but with access to its facilities and personnel, and would release through Loew's. Schenck was intrigued—he was always in the market for first-run product—but Mayer was opposed to the idea. Thalberg's pictures were essential to MGM's overall program, and there were still several MGM producers who still counted on Thalberg's supervision. The development of *San Francisco* in early 1936 was a case in point. *San Francisco* was a historical romance starring Gable, Spencer Tracy, and Jeanette MacDonald, and because its producer was Bernie Hyman, Thalberg's input was considerable. Thalberg sat in on the conferences and suggested that Anita Loos, who was doing the screenplay, use the Gable-Laughton relationship in *Mutiny on the Bounty* as a model for the rapport between the Gable character, a smooth self-centered saloon owner, and Tracy, his lifelong friend who has become a priest. Gable's pursuit of MacDonald's virginal singer provides the more obvious and conventional romance, but the Gable-Tracy courtship is at the heart of the story. Loos later commented that "to Irving Thalberg every film had to be a love story," adding that "it wasn't at all necessary for the affair to concern people of the opposite sex."

Mayer relied heavily on Thalberg's films and on the kind of counsel he gave Bernie Hyman and Anita Loos on *San Francisco,* but he grew increasingly meddlesome and contrary when Thalberg wanted to try a bit of off-casting or an unconventional story, particularly once Selznick was off the lot. Schenck overruled Mayer and gave Thalberg the go-ahead on two projects early in 1936: *The Good Earth,* from a Pearl S. Buck saga about Chinese peasant farmers, and *Romeo and Juliet,* with

Shearer (at age thirty-six) playing Shakespeare's adolescent heroine. Thalberg resented Mayer's interference, and he disliked having to ask Schenck for anything. He knew many of his projects were risky, but the risks nearly always paid off for the studio. Most recently, for example, he had brought over the Marx Brothers from Paramount, where they had been fading badly. *A Night at the Opera* reversed their decline in rather a spectacular fashion in 1935, and Thalberg was developing a surefire follow-up, *A Day at the Races*, for the 1936 program. He had another low-risk, high-yield project in the works with *Camille*, a classic women's picture costarring Garbo and a promising young male lead, Robert Taylor. Thalberg felt these more than offset the risks he was taking with *The Good Earth* and *Romeo and Juliet*, and the hassles with Mayer only reinforced his desire to set up an independent production outfit.

Thalberg's schedule in the summer of 1936 forced him to set aside those plans, though, at least for the time being. *Romeo and Juliet* proved particularly troublesome, requiring extensive retakes when previews went badly. Despite Thalberg and George Cukor's efforts, the picture never quite came together and did only mediocre business when it was released in late August—although a Shakespeare adaptation was always good for Metro's prestige. Thalberg was disappointed, since he had so few opportunities to work with his wife these days. Shearer was doing only one picture per year now that there were two children at home to care for, and at age thirty-six, she was talking about retiring from the screen. Thalberg dismissed such talk—he'd always been able to come up with the right parts for Shearer, and he would again. To subdue his disappointment over *Romeo and Juliet* he redoubled his efforts on *Camille* and *A Day at the Races*, which were still in production. Before they finished shooting, however, he decided to get away for a few days. Over the Labor Day weekend, he and Norma and several other couples and industry friends holed up at the Del Monte Club on the Monterey peninsula. Most of the time was spent playing bridge, Thalberg's abiding passion outside the movie business. They played into the wee hours throughout their stay, and the long evenings in the cool California air left Thalberg with a head cold, which grew worse when he returned to Los Angeles. By the following weekend he was bedridden, and within another few days he had contracted pneumonia. For almost anyone else this would simply have been a difficult illness, but for a thirty-seven-year-old filmmaker with a bad heart and chronically weak constitution, it proved fatal. Early Monday morning, September 14, 1936, Irving Thalberg died at home in his sleep.

T H E entire industry was shaken by Thalberg's death, which, in the deepest sense, was the end of an era. Hollywood lost more than its resident genius; it lost the man who first learned to calculate the whole equation of pictures, who understood the delicate balance of art and commerce in moviemaking. Thalberg developed a management style that was efficient without being inflexible, disciplined without being inhumane, extravagant without being wasteful. Appropriate gestures marked Thalberg's passing: all of Hollywood shut down for five minutes as his funeral began, and MGM suspended operations for that entire day. It was decided that *The Good Earth*, his last project, would carry the dedication "To the memory of Irving Grant Thalberg." And so for the first time since MGM's founding, Thalberg's name appeared on one of its pictures. There were countless epitaphs and pronouncements after his death, but perhaps none was more appropriate than the line Thalberg had insisted on for Kringelein in *Grand Hotel*: "It doesn't matter that life be long, but that one feel it entirely—drain it to the last."

Irving Thalberg's death came at a time when MGM's total dominance of the movie industry was seemingly unassailable. Metro's profits in 1935 had been $7.5 million, more than the rest of the Big Eight movie companies combined. Metro's take surpassed $10 million in 1936, when it dominated the critics' polls and Academy Award ceremonies as well. Of the ten Oscar nominees for best picture in 1936, five were MGM productions: *San Francisco, Romeo and Juliet, A Tale of Two Cities, Libeled Lady*, and the eventual winner, *The Great Ziegfeld*. Four of the top ten box-office stars were from MGM, and in an era when a two-million-dollar gross was considered exceptional, MGM's pictures often reached that total. Consider these figures on eight of Metro's top 1936 releases:

	DOMESTIC RELEASE DATE	DOMESTIC RENTALS	FOREIGN RENTALS	TOTAL GROSS RECEIPTS
Mutiny on the Bounty	11-8-35	$2,256,187	$2,071,392	$4,327,579
A Tale of Two Cities	12-27-35	1,106,696	1,057,059	2,163,755
Rose Marie	1-31-36	1,676,291	1,448,845	3,125,136
Wife Versus Secretary	2-28-36	1,346,089	669,499	2,015,588
San Francisco	6-26-36	2,861,160	2,049,401	4,910,561
The Gorgeous Hussy	8-28-36	1,451,901	473,266	1,925,167
The Great Ziegfeld	9-4-36	3,069,785	1,416,204	4,485,989
Libeled Lady	10-9-36	1,593,189	883,942	2,477,131

Metro's lead held throughout the 1930s, but it steadily diminished. The other studios were pulling out of the Depression, and Metro was hardly the same without Thalberg. MGM's success before 1933 was due largely to Thalberg's accomplishments as central producer; its success from 1933 to 1936 was a tribute both to the system Thalberg had already established and to Thalberg's own work as a prestige producer. In fact, that three-year period was a charmed interval for MGM, a short-lived golden age when the studio reached a balance of power and of commercial, popular, and critical performance that was still a few years away for its competitors. Metro could not maintain that equilibrium without Thalberg's and Selznick's productions, and without the informal supervision that Thalberg provided Metro's second line of producers. And besides the lack of Thalberg's counsel and his pictures, there was a perceptible change at the studio that virtually everyone who worked there during the Thalberg era has noted. The force of his personality and his will had shaped MGM, and though the studio would go on without him, it would never be quite the same.

11

Selznick
International Pictures:
Going Independent

Going independent in mid-1930s Hollywood, at least for anyone intent on producing top features, meant going with United Artists. And that in turn meant an ambivalent rapport with the studio system, and especially with the integrated majors. UA was founded in 1919 by three of Hollywood's biggest stars—Mary Pickford, Douglas Fairbanks, and Charlie Chaplin—along with star director D. W. Griffith. From the outset, UA was a distribution company designed to release its founders' high-class productions. But it was by no means a studio. In fact, it was created as a veritable declaration of independence from the emerging studio system, which its founders saw as a threat to their power and autonomy. UA gradually changed as the founders' careers tapered off and the studio system took hold, and by the 1930s it was a different operation altogether. Though UA was still a distribution company, now it was dominated by independent producers. Whatever their claims to independent status, these producers relied heavily on the major studios in three crucial areas. Although a few of them had their own modest production facilities, they generally had to lease studio space from one of the majors for their more ambitious productions. They also borrowed top personnel from the majors, particularly stars, directors, writers, composers, and cameramen. And perhaps most important, they relied on the majors' first-run theaters when they released their pictures. The major studios, in turn, relied on UA for all the same reasons—that is, as a way of keeping their facilities and personnel busy between studio projects, and as a source of product for their bigger, more profitable theaters. A successful UA release brought revenues to the majors, since they held on to roughly one-third of the gross revenues (as a distribution fee) on any release screened in their theaters. With weekly movie attendance back up to eighty million per week in 1935 and the economy showing signs of life, first-run production was heating up and so was the demand for UA product.

There was some concern, however, about UA's capacity to deliver in 1935. While UA's founders had not produced a single picture in the previous year, two of them—Chaplin and Pickford, the only ones still active in the company—did manage to alienate UA's chief suppliers. In an ill-advised power play, Chaplin and Pickford blocked a merger effort by Joe Schenck and Darryl Zanuck, whose Twentieth Century Pictures delivered nine of UA's twenty releases in 1934. Schenck and Zanuck were sufficiently outraged that they bolted UA in early 1935, and Schenck began working on a merger between Twentieth and the Fox Film Corporation. David Selznick was waiting in the wings, however, and promised to deliver at least ten pictures per annum to UA. He also would replace Schenck as the chief executive of the company, coordinating the production efforts and schedules of the various UA producers. Those were heavy responsibilities, but Selznick seemed up to the task. His years at MGM, Paramount, and RKO schooled him well in production management, and his recent stint as a unit producer at MGM proved he could turn out profitable first-run product.

Since Selznick was by now a known commodity as a Hollywood prestige producer, he had no trouble financing Selznick International Pictures (SIP). He raised the initial seed money of $400,000 in Los Angeles, with half coming from his brother, agent Myron Selznick. That investment was motivated less by fraternal piety than by Myron's utter pragmatism; he knew the investment would be returned many times over when his free-lance clients paid him 10 percent of their SIP salaries. In New York, Selznick scored another $300,000 from "small" investors and then went after the big money, persuading John Hay "Jock" Whitney and his family to invest $2.4 million. That put Selznick over $3 million, the sum he needed to capitalize SIP. Thus in the summer of 1935 Selznick became president, chief executive officer, and sole producer of a company committed to prestige production—all this at age thirty-three and without investing a dollar of his own.

The new company did have a board of directors, which was chaired by Jock Whitney and composed mainly of New York bankers and financiers. The board granted Selznick virtually absolute authority, so there was no New York office dictating budgets, schedules, and market strategy. Whitney appointed two studio executives who represented the board's interests—Henry Ginsberg as vice president and general manager, and John Wharton as treasurer—but neither exercised any real authority over SIP operations. Control was in Selznick's hands, and he aptly indicated both his authority and his overall strategy for SIP with a December 1935 pronouncement to the board. "There are only two kinds of merchandise that can be made profitably in this business," said Selznick, "either the very cheap pictures or the very expensive pictures." So far as Selznick was concerned, "there. is no alternative open to us but to attempt to compete with the very best."

That meant fewer pictures at higher costs, with Selznick himself preparing, supervising, and fine-tuning every SIP product, devoting more time and attention to each picture than he ever could have as a studio executive. "In the making of good pictures," said Selznick after the birth of SIP, it was "so essential for a producer to collaborate on every inch of script, to be available for every conference, and to go over all details of production that it is physically impossible for him to

David Selznick, Jock Whitney, UA executive Lloyd Wright, and Kay Brown announce the creation of Selznick International Pictures.

give his best efforts to more than a limited number of pictures." Like all "creative" producers, Selznick considered himself an excellent judge of talent and commercial story properties, a capable writer and film editor, and a demanding production executive. To fully exploit those talents, he planned to assemble an administrative and technical staff capable of keeping one picture in front of the cameras, while one other project was being prepared for production and another was being prepared for release. In other words, SIP was to have one picture being scripted, one being shot, and one being edited at all times. Selznick would personally oversee operations, shuttling from script conferences to screenings of dailies, to previews and editing sessions. If he could keep preproduction, shooting, and postproduction on each picture to about six weeks each, then SIP could turn out eight or ten first-rate features per year.

That was the plan, anyway. But it didn't quite jibe with the realities of the marketplace or with Selznick's complex personality and his working methods as an independent. Early on at SIP, Selznick proved to be both showman and sophisticate, crassly commercial and exploitive yet a man of cultured tastes. He was a disorganized, impetuous perfectionist who would plan out a day's shooting and then, in a flash of insight and without notice, discard that plan and improvise another. He was supremely confident and equally insecure; he relished a challenge and took on impossible tasks, yet no script was ever quite ready for production, no picture was ever quite ready for release. In terms of efficiency and productivity, Selznick clearly was lost without the discipline of a full-blown factory grinding away or a New York office controlling finances and demanding a steady output. With fewer constraints on his obsessive rewriting and reshooting, previewing and reediting, it took SIP fully five years to deliver the ten pictures promised to UA for the first year. But while productivity was down, profits were up. As Selznick came to realize, working as an independent in the late 1930s, more money could be made turning out one or two big hits per year than eight or ten competitive A-class features.

SELZNICK proved that fact clearly enough with *Gone With the Wind*, the biggest blockbuster in movie history. In fact, the nature and destiny of SIP—its corporate identity and its very life span—were curiously entwined with that one project, which Selznick initiated in the summer of 1936. At the time SIP was still in its formative stages, since Selznick spent the last six months of 1935 finishing *Anna Karenina* and *A Tale of Two Cities* at MGM, and devoted the first six months of 1936 to *Little Lord Fauntleroy* and *The Garden of Allah*, two lavish costume pictures he had prepared while he was still at Metro. When he left MGM he simply purchased the screen rights to *Fauntleroy* and *Allah* and took the scripts with him. Both projects were virtually ready to start shooting and demanded relatively little attention, allowing Selznick to concentrate on SIP's future direction. That in turn led to the initiation of *Gone With the Wind*, which marked the birth of Selznick International Pictures.

Margaret Mitchell's novel first came to Selznick's attention via Kay Brown, SIP's East Coast story editor. In May 1936, a month before its publication, Brown sent Selznick a copy of Mitchell's manuscript and a fifty-seven-page condensation of the novel. "I am absolutely off my nut about this book," she wrote Selznick. "I beg, urge, coax, and plead with you to read it at once." With *The Garden of Allah* still in production, Selznick had no time to read the novel, so he read the condensed version and passed the manuscript to Val Lewton, his West Coast story editor. Lewton dismissed Mitchell's novel as "ponderous trash," but Selznick was taken with the story. He feared a bidding war, though, knowing that Mitchell's agent already had nixed an offer of $35,000 from Zanuck. Selznick had paid MGM $62,000 for *Allah,* and he was not up for another huge investment, particularly for a novel with no presold value.

Once Jock Whitney had read the novel, he joined Brown in trying to sell Selznick on doing the adaptation. Whitney's motives were more complex than Brown's, though, since he saw *Gone With the Wind* as an ideal project for Pioneer Pictures, another independent company that he was backing—and one that had a six-picture deal with Technicolor. That company had come out with a three-color process in 1932 which was costly but was catching on with viewers; the surge in prestige production meant more and more films were being done in Technicolor. Pioneer was created in 1934 by Merian C. Cooper, who had worked with Selznick at both Paramount and RKO. He, too, was excited at the prospect of doing the Civil War saga as a Technicolor spectacle, and Selznick himself began coming around to the idea when the advance sales of Mitchell's book indicated a possible best-seller. In the summer of 1936, the entire project came together in a series of important deals. In late June, Selznick took charge of Pioneer and, though that company and SIP never formally merged, the six-picture commitment with Technicolor was transferred to Selznick International. Cooper, meanwhile, was made a vice president of SIP at $2,000 per week. Two weeks later, with Mitchell's saga now out and selling in record numbers, Selznick wired Brown: "If you can close *Gone With the Wind* for $50,000, do so." She did, so Selznick began thinking about another production facility. SIP was housed in a rather modest studio built by Thomas Ince back in the teens, and it hardly seemed adequate

This formidable edifice, originally built by Thomas Ince and later acquired by RKO, became the headquarters for Selznick International after Selznick took over the entire RKO-Pathe facility in 1937.

after the Pioneer and *Gone With the Wind* deals. Selznick had been leasing space from RKO on a limited basis, and he decided to take over the entire RKO-Pathe facility, beginning in February 1937 when he planned to start shooting *Gone With the Wind* (or simply *Wind*, as it was known at SIP).

Selznick hoped to produce one or perhaps two other pictures while he was preparing *Wind*, so he signed William Wellman that same summer to a one-year, two-picture deal at $2,750 per week. George Cukor, who had followed Selznick from Paramount to RKO and then to MGM, was signed to direct *Wind*, and he was to devote himself entirely to its preproduction. Meanwhile Wellman, who was a writer as well as a director and had experience in the Warners trenches, would keep the SIP machinery busy with a few A-class, Technicolor star vehicles. In fact, Selznick had already decided on his first picture: a rehash of *What Price Hollywood?*, which he and Cukor had done for RKO in 1932. Again Selznick came up with the story idea, and it typified his cinematic interests and tastes. It was to be a romantic melodrama with comedic overtones, a story of ill-fated love, of fame and fortune won and lost, and of tragic consequence. The story would center on a woman's devotion to a dynamic, self-destructive mentor who wins her love, assists her climb to stardom while his own career fails, and finally kills himself to keep from ruining her career.

Selznick had Fredric March and Janet Gaynor lined up to star—both at flat fees of $125,000 for eight weeks—and his "Hollywood story" was keyed to these two performers. Selznick was neither typecasting nor off-casting, though, but rather letting both March and Gaynor revert to types they played back in the late 1920s. March was now one of Hollywood's top male stars and almost exclusively doing costume roles in historical biopics. He longed to return to light comedy and a modern wardrobe, his specialty at Paramount in the early sound era, and Selznick planned to give him that chance. Gaynor's role marked a return to an even earlier image, when she played a waiflike innocent in such silent Fox hits as *Seventh Heaven* and *Sunrise* in 1927. By the 1930s she was considered to have outgrown that woman-child persona, but Selznick felt she could still handle that type of role.

Selznick fleshed out his story idea with Wellman in July 1936, suggesting "It Happened in Hollywood" for the title. When he was satisfied with the plot structure, he brought in an untried youngster, Robert Carson, on a week-to-week basis at $250 per week to collaborate with Wellman. Within two weeks Wellman and Carson had a detailed treatment, but one that veered away from Selznick's conception. Theirs was a fairly heavy-going saga of the heroine's struggles to the top, closing with an upbeat wedding-cum-redemption finale. Selznick sent Wellman a memo stating that "the story to date is very good" and that Carson "looks promising," but he advised Wellman against "going into continuity" until they made a few adjustments. Selznick wanted "the same comedy spirit" as in the earlier RKO picture, with any grimness reserved for the finale—which *had* to involve the mentor's suicide. Wellman and Carson returned to the Hollywood story while Selznick supervised retakes and assembled a preview version of *Allah*. By late August Wellman and Carson had not only finished the story but a continuity script as well.

Selznick was uneasy about his writers' moving so quickly with the script, but he did want to get the project under way. So he scheduled a meeting at his home in early September and instructed his scenario assistant Bobby Keon to distribute copies of the Wellman-Carson script to various technicians and department heads. That was great news to Wellman, who since completing the script had been directing retakes on *Allah* and sitting in on story conferences for *Tom Sawyer*, which Selznick was considering as a future SIP production. Wellman felt that he was working his way into Selznick's system and winning his employer's respect, and he was eager to start his own picture. But his confidence was shaken during the preproduction meeting, when both he and his script suffered a severe thrashing. Wellman was devastated, though the experience did afford him valuable insight into Selznick's psyche and his working methods. He realized now that Selznick demanded much more input into a script's development than other executive producers, independent or otherwise. He was not content to approve a story outline and then let his writers develop the screenplay on their own. Wellman also realized that his new boss tended to become increasingly anxious—even a bit paranoid—when a project neared the shooting or release stages. Selznick simply could not be satisfied with a shooting script or a final cut, so with both the Hollywood story and *Allah* on the line, he was particularly temperamental.

Wellman said almost nothing during the meeting, but then wrote a lengthy epistle the next day in which he stroked Selznick's ego, haggled over story changes, and generally tried to reassert some control over the project. He noted Selznick's obvious "hostility" at the meeting, which he considered perfectly understandable. He realized now that he had been "too goddamned ambitious" by going ahead with the continuity script instead of staying with the story outline, since it short-circuited Selznick's usual way of "attacking" the story and scenario as they developed. Wellman admitted that there were problems with the story, especially the lack of humor in portraying the self-destructive Norman Maine. But he felt that the heroine's character should not be altered, particularly now that the lead roles had been cast. He was most adamant about the finale he and Carson had written, in which the heroine, Esther Blodgett (whose stage name is Vicki Lester), is convinced by her great-grandmother to stay in Hollywood after Norman's suicide. Wellman felt that with a vulnerable innocent like Janet Gaynor in the lead, this finale would be not only convincing but quite poignant.

In a deft rhetorical maneuver, Wellman acknowledged Selznick's authority over the initial conception of the project but reasserted his own command over its development. This was a story, reasoned Wellman, that after "originating" with Selznick was something that the two of them "wrote together." And considering Selznick's "multiple duties" in the overall SIP operations as well as actual filmmaking, he really hadn't had adequate time to evaluate either the project itself or Wellman's contribution.

Within a few days they had a fix on the story, with Norman's character assuming a more comic tone and Esther's remaining essentially as Wellman and Carson had written her. Once the story and characters were set, Wellman began preparing the shoot while Selznick sought out a continuity and dialogue specialist. Failing to secure Hecht—always his first choice for such a task—Selznick signed Rowland Brown in mid-September at $850 a week. But he was not impressed with Brown, and within a few days he replaced him with Dorothy

Parker and Alan Campbell, who signed on at $1,750 per week for five weeks. They delivered an acceptable continuity script by late October, when production opened as per the Technicolor schedule. But that scarcely signaled their departure or the script's completion. About the only thing that Selznick was fully satisfied with at that point was the title, "A Star Is Born," which was suggested by Jock Whitney. Selznick felt the story line was close but that much of the dialogue needed work, and he still wasn't satisfied with Norman's suicide scene or the epilogue wherein Esther makes her first public appearance after his death.

So writing continued after production opened, and in a rather fragmented and haphazard fashion. Campbell and Parker continued to work on their own, handling the dialogue and bits of action. Carson collaborated with Wellman when he had the chance, and he occasionally worked with Selznick as well. (Though Carson rarely interacted at all with Campbell and Parker, the three shared screenplay credit.) Also contributing to A Star Is Born during production were Budd Schulberg and Ring Lardner, Jr., whom Selznick had hired as "junior writers" at $75 per week to hone their screenwriting skills and serve as troubleshooters on various SIP projects. The pair showed promise and actually had some influence on Star, most notably on a scene that didn't wind up in the picture. That scene had Norman killing two motorists while driving drunk, which Schulberg and Lardner argued—at some length in a carefully prepared report—transformed the story into a "social problem" melodrama. Selznick bought their argument and on November 6, one week into production, he told studio manager Henry Ginsberg to "advise the necessary departments that the automobile accident is out."

O N C E Wellman started shooting in late October, he was unaffected by the flurry of rewrites and the myriad other distractions. Schooled at Warners and Paramount, he worked with speed, confidence, and a healthy sense of detachment. By November 19, the seventeenth day of shooting, Wellman's assistant director reported that 49½ of the shooting script's 108 pages had been finished. Wellman was averaging nearly three pages daily, generating an average of 3'25" of printed footage and roughly fifteen camera setups per day. Selznick rarely visited the set during production, confining his input to memos and wires, which he dictated incessantly to any and all involved. When principal photography began to wind down, he and his chief editor, Hal Kern, began a rough cut of the picture, and at that point, Selznick resumed more direct control of the picture. His concerns were usually with a line or a bit of business he felt didn't play or was difficult to cut together. On December 3, for example, Bobby Keon informed Wellman that Selznick wanted an "entire scene retaken," and closed the memo: "The dialogue for this scene will be supplied Monday." Occasionally, Selznick dictated Wellman's camera work and shot breakdown as he reconstructed a scene at the editing bench. On December 17, for example, he sent Wellman a rewrite of Norman's suicide scene, complete with an elaborate montage of Norman's memories at the moment he goes under water. Selznick suggested that the montage could be shot by Russian montage specialist Slavko Vorkapitch. Accompanying the rewrite was a note from Keon: "Following is the way Mr. Selznick would like to have the sequence shot. If you disagree with him, will you please discuss it?"

Selznick clearly was in his element at this stage of a project's development, wrestling with the various problems that emerged as the picture came together during editing. Besides the suicide scene, the toughest problem in *A Star Is Born* involved the tag scene, when Esther decides to face the public at the premiere of her new picture, a few days after Norman's funeral. In the shooting script, Esther col-

Technicolor camera mounted above the coffee shop set in A Star Is Born, *for a shot of Janet Gaynor and Fredric March during their initial courtship.*

lapses outside Grauman's Chinese Theatre after seeing imprints of her dead husband's hands and feet in the concrete and the message, "Good Luck, Norman Maine." Judging from responses in the studio projection room and at preview screenings, Selznick could see the scene was not working—but he felt it was close. He showed it to John Lee Mahin, an MGM staff writer whose judgment he respected, and together they worked out a solution that Selznick conveyed to Wellman:

> I believe we can retain Gaynor's entire approach up the aisle in front of the Chinese, simply retaking the reaction to the footprints, more or less as is; with her pulling herself together; the announcer asking her if she will say a few words; . . . Gaynor saying she will, advancing with all the pride in the world, throwing her head back, with tears in her eyes, and saying "This is Mrs. Norman Maine speaking."

This poignant but upbeat finale did in fact close the release version of *A Star Is Born*, and it remains one of the more moving moments in any of Selznick's films. It's worth noting, though, that Selznick hedged his bets by having Wellman shoot an alternate take with the line, "This is Vicki Lester speaking." Not until he previewed the "Mrs. Norman Maine" version was he certain that it worked.

The first sneak preview for *Star* was held on Saturday, January 23, at the Fox Pomona Theater in suburban Los Angeles. Although theater manager Bob Cannon assured Selznick that the picture and the audience response were "excellent," the preview cards and Selznick's own judgment told him that a release version was weeks—perhaps months —away. Taking his cue from Thalberg, Selznick regarded the first cut of any picture as simply the raw material, with its eventual reshaping determined largely by the reactions of preview audiences. The tag scene comprised one-half page of the twenty-seven pages of retakes; most of them were scripted by Selznick, and, all told, they accounted for about one-sixth of the finished film. With his usual speed and efficiency, Wellman shot the retakes from late January through February, with the final revisions involving Norman's suicide. Neither the original scene nor the montage version was playing well with preview audiences, so on March 1, 1937, Selznick had Wellman shoot yet another version. The scene was an ingenious display of narrative economy: it opens with a shot of Norman's feet at the water's edge; then his robe falls into the frame and the feet exit into the water. That was all that was used for the suicide scene in the release version.

The retakes on *Star* pushed its closing costs to $1,173,639, with March and Gaynor's salaries accounting for fully one-quarter of that total. Max Steiner composed the score once Selznick settled on a final cut, and the picture was ready for release by early April. The premiere was scheduled for April 20 at Grauman's Chinese, but Selznick couldn't wait to get a public assessment of the finished film. On April 12, he sent a wire to the New York office: "At 10:30 the other night I held a sneak preview all by myself, completely unannounced, for the audience at the last show of the Village Theatre in Westwood. Picture played sensationally."

On its initial release, *A Star Is Born* took in $2.37 million in gross revenues, but returned a net profit to SIP of only $100,000 due to UA's marketing and sales policies, which Selznick found much inferior to MGM's and was determined to correct. Still, Selznick had to be pleased with the visibility the picture gave his new company. It put SIP on the industry map, doing well with the critics and scoring half a dozen Oscar nominations—for best picture, best director, best actor and actress, best original story, and best screenplay. The only winners, ironically, were Wellman and Carson for original story, resulting in Wellman's now-legendary gesture at the Academy banquet when he took his statuette over to Selznick's table and offered it to the producer, saying, "Here, you deserve this—you wrote more of it than I did."

S T A T U S and credibility were vital for an independent producer, and the success of *A Star Is Born* brought both to Selznick. It also proved that he had a first-rate production outfit at SIP. Selznick himself was the only key above-the-line player, and for the time being he was willing to hire stars, directors, and top writers to one- or two-picture deals. He could handle the creative end, with his support staff keeping the wheels turning. His essential technicians were art director Lyle Wheeler, editor Hal Kern, and color cameraman Howard Greene. His chief studio administrators were production manager Ray Klune and assistant director Eric Stacey. Story editors Val Lewton and Kay Brown were also important, with Brown keeping Selznick abreast of the East Coast theater and publishing scenes and Lewton acting as an in-house script consultant and story editor, and handling all communication with the Breen office. Selznick also kept anywhere from six to ten writers on staff, although none of them did the important screenwriting on any SIP project.

With his production staff shaping up, Selznick was determined to keep them busy. He had signed Wellman and March for two pictures, and he planned to use them again in another Technicolor project after *Star* was released. But *Gone With the Wind* was nowhere near ready to start, and Selznick did not want his studio sitting idle between Wellman projects. So even before *Star* was finished Selznick began looking for another project, preferably a relatively low-stakes black-and-white picture. As with his first two SIP productions, he looked to MGM for a property with some presold value that was virtually ready to go. He found one in *The Prisoner of Zenda*, an adventure drama replete with swordplay, palace intrigue, and star-crossed romance. The story, set in the mythical kingdom of Ruritania, follows a British subject on holiday who happens to be a distant, illegitimate relative of a man about to be crowned king of Ruritania. The prospective king is kidnapped before the coronation, but his supporters replace him for the ceremony with the vacationing Brit—who takes his crown and the heart of his queen as well. MGM owned the rights to the story, which was done as a silent in 1913 and 1922. Metro had been developing a sound version, but the project was on hold.

On December 17, 1936, the same day Selznick dreamed up the suicide montage for *A Star Is Born*, he agreed to pay Metro $100,000 for the rights to *The Prisoner of Zenda* and for all related materials in the MGM files. That included a dozen different treatments, drafts, continuities, and other versions of the story. (Selznick was particularly interested in recent drafts by Ben Hecht, Wells Root, and Jules Furthman.) Still it was a hefty price for the property—and indeed there were other reasons for buying *Zenda*. Besides the current trend toward swashbucklers and swordplay sagas, a recent event in England sold Selznick on the project. England's Edward VIII decided to abdicate his throne after falling in love with an American divorcée, whom he intended to marry. Edward's abdication was a story in itself, but it also meant a coronation later in the spring or summer. Selznick saw fabulous worldwide promotional possibilities in such an event, especially in the British Commonwealth countries, where his pictures did very well.

The fact that Selznick signed British romantic star Ronald Colman for the lead and John Cromwell to direct suggested he was more interested in the love story and its pomp and circumstance than the action-adventure angle. Selznick's tastes were growing more precious, sentimental, and melodramatic with each passing year, and Cromwell tended to reinforce those qualities—though rarely to the benefit of the pictures involved. Selznick's was a distinctly feminine sensibility. Just as Cukor was considered a "woman's director," Selznick was proving to be a "woman's producer." And as this tendency became more pronounced, there were certain projects—*Zenda* being one of them—in which Selznick needed to collaborate with directors or writers like Wellman, Woody Van Dyke, or Ben Hecht, who balanced his sentimentality with cynicism, his refinement with something more rugged or offbeat, his melodramatics with a livelier treatment.

A strong director not only checked Selznick's enthusiasms, but curbed his interference as well. This was especially important after

Selznick went independent and his quest for quality and control often lapsed into autocratic perfectionism. The making of *Zenda* was plagued by Selznick's unnecessary interference and his arbitrary firing of key personnel. The screenplay was done by Donald Ogden Stewart, a leading stage and screen writer, but it was overhauled so extensively that Stewart did not even merit screen credit on the release version. Cinematographer Bert Glennon, who won an Oscar two years later for *Stagecoach*, another black-and-white adventure film with its share of intimate scenes, was fired early on when Selznick found his camera work unsatisfactory. And Cromwell's own work in the action scenes and the climactic love scene was deemed inadequate; all of these scenes were redone during postproduction by other directors. *Zenda* also marked a falling out between Selznick and composer Max Steiner, whose association went back to the early sound era at Paramount.

By spring 1937 SIP was falling behind in its commitments to both UA and Technicolor—the latter being a major source of concern, since Technicolor equipment and personnel were limited and scheduled well in advance. Jock Whitney was adamant that Selznick complete *Zenda* and start another Technicolor project by mid-June. Wellman and Fredric March were now ready to go, but Selznick had no script, though he was intrigued with Whitney's suggestion that SIP try a screwball comedy. So he closed a deal with brother Myron for the services of Carole Lombard (at $18,750 a week), a top comedienne he wanted to team with Fredric March. He then wired Ben Hecht in New York, asking him to come up with an idea for an original story. Selznick promised that if he liked Hecht's story, he would hire the writer to script it at $5,000 per week, and pay a $30,000 bonus if he finished the screenplay within a month.

Hecht was an ideal choice for several reasons. He and his partner Charles MacArthur had set off the 1930s cycle of fast-paced, fast-talking, irreverent comedies with *The Front Page* and *Twentieth Century*. Hecht also had a reputation for wielding the fastest typewriter in Hollywood. His speed was due not only to a background in journalism (where deadlines and production schedules were a way of life), but also to an outspoken love-hate relationship with the movie industry. This was a writer who won an Academy Award for his first screenwriting assignment (on *Underworld* for Paramount in 1928), and used the Oscar as a doorstop; who couldn't resist the money or the life-style in Hollywood, but couldn't stand to live there more than a few weeks at a time; and who by the mid-1930s had actively promoted his reputation as the industry's consummate gadfly. Consider the first few stanzas of "Hecht's Prayer to His Bosses," an illustrated poem he sent out as a Christmas card to Hollywood's top executives:

Good gentlemen who overpay
Me fifty times for every fart,
Who hand me statues when I bray
And hail my whinnying as Art—
I pick your pockets every day
But how you bastards break my heart.

Knee deep in butlers, smothered half
In horse-shit splendors, soft and fat
And worshiping the Golden Calf
I mutter through my new plush hat
"Why did you steal my pilgrim's Staff?
Why do you make me write like that?"

Selznick and Hecht went back a long way—in fact, Selznick had signed an agent's agreement with Hecht back in the early 1920s, and actually brought some of Hecht's fiction with him on his first trip West, hoping to sell it as movie material. They had worked together during Selznick's studio years, and since creating SIP he had been trying to find a project for Hecht. When Hecht agreed to his offer, Selznick decided to head back East and get the script moving, even though several important scenes in *Zenda* remained to be shot. He arrived in New York City on May 7, a date that marked the genesis of *Nothing Sacred*, the best of the SIP/UA pictures in the late 1930s—and also the beginning of the most chaotic and embattled four months in SIP annals.

O N Selznick's arrival in New York, Hecht handed him a six-page treatment he had written while Selznick was en route from Hollywood. It was only a sketch—referred to on the cover sheet as "Original Story by Ben Hecht for Lombard-March"—which set up the characters and situation. Hecht's original sketch bears little resemblance to the eventual shooting script, though there are certain screwball comedy motifs common to both: a massive hoax based on mistaken identity, an antagonistic romance between equally irreverent characters from vastly different backgrounds, and the victory of homespun savvy over the avarice of city slickers. While these motifs remained, however, the basic story changed radically once Selznick got involved.

Hecht's "original" should be considered, though, if only to appreciate Selznick's contribution to the eventual screenplay. The story opens in the "entertainment slums of Havana" at the "Trocadero Café." Its hero is "Philip Anstruter—47," once a "great Yale halfback" and now "tall, dark, still powerful looking, a heavy drinker, married to a society girl in New York." Anstruter is traveling with a group of eight bored Americans (his wife is not among them), "who belong to a special class, more than a class—a cult, whose God is a combination of swank, superiority, and emptiness." These are a people "with neither ideas nor ideals," who are "sincerely unimpressed by everything, including themselves."

The night we meet Anstruter and his cohorts in Havana, our hero is smitten by Dolly Dean, a singer in the Trocadero who is, says Hecht, "a cut above the wenches hitherto revealed." The group moves on, but Anstruter stays at the café to pursue Dolly; before leaving, the others remind him that they are to set sail for New York the next morning on a dowager's yacht. Dolly responds to Philip's overtures, and the two embark on an all-night binge of passion and alcohol. By the time their heads clear the next day, Philip's cash is gone and the yacht has sailed. Dolly spends her savings on a seaplane that flies them to the yacht, and Philip convinces her to go with him to New York. At that point we fade out for a three-month hiatus. After the fade-in we find the couple in Dolly's Manhattan apartment, with their resources depleted and Philip scheming to marry Dolly off to some local blueblood. His plan is to "fix her up with a story of family connections, and if it is the last thing he does, he'll put her over."

Thus ends Hecht's "story"—little more than a synopsis of an opening act, and not quite what Selznick had in mind. Selznick was particularly concerned about the unsympathetic central characters and the censorable situation involving the hero's marriage and his adulterous rapport with Dolly. Hecht considered these points, brainstormed with Selznick, and hammered out a new story outline by that evening. This version, entitled "Nothing Sacred," retains the Havana opening, but now the hero is one Thomas Coogan II, a bachelor war hero at odds with his industrialist father, who is fighting for control of a railroad empire. Again the hero passes off the heroine, Margaret, as a high-society type, maneuvering her into an engagement with a Mr. Brown, one of the senior Coogan's business rivals. This story was a thinly veiled rehash of You Can't Take It With You, a recent George Kaufman–Moss Hart stage hit that Robert Riskin and Frank Capra were getting set to adapt for Columbia. As in the Kaufman-Hart play, there was redemption all around: Margaret redeems Tommy, Tommy redeems his father (just before the patriarch's death near the end of the story), and in an upbeat finale, the two lovers set out to redeem New York City, with Margaret chirping, "Come on—we'll go back with him [Tommy's dead father] to the shanty on the railroad tracks, and I'll show you the only way to lick New York, to lick failure—by being like he was."

Selznick couldn't digest this can of low-grade Capracorn, at least not from Ben Hecht. What Selznick wanted was a wisecracking newspaper story with a breakneck pace and genuinely screwball romance, something like *The Front Page* or *It Happened One Night*. But he wasn't discouraged; Hecht's creative juices were flowing, and Selznick was certain that the two of them would come up with something. So while he monitored *Zenda* via cables back and forth to the studio, Selznick holed up with Hecht in the Waldorf Astoria to start rewriting. Within a week the pair had created the story of Hazel Flagg (to be played by Lombard), a small-town girl mistakenly diagnosed by her alcoholic physician as having "radium poisoning." She allows herself to be exploited by reporter and con artist Wally Cook (Fredric March), even after learning of her doctor's mistake, and Wally parlays her malady into a major news event. Before long Hazel is a cause célèbre and the toast of New York, she and Wally have fallen in love, and she has no idea how to tell either Wally or the city of New York that her illness is nonexistent. Unfortunately, Hecht and Selznick had no idea either. Both were pleased with the characters and the basic plot setup, but they could not come up with a satisfactory plot resolution. Conscious of the Technicolor schedule and his contracts with Lombard and March, however, Selznick wired SIP to gear up for production. Meanwhile he and Hecht started working on the continuity script during a three-day train ride back to Los Angeles. Most of the script was completed on that cross-country trek, although the collaborators still hadn't come up with a suitable finale.

Once back in Hollywood, Selznick turned his attention again to *The Prisoner of Zenda*. His production manager had wired him back in mid-May that Cromwell's picture was ready to preview, but when Selznick looked at Hal Kern's rough cut, he reached an altogether different conclusion. The sword-fighting sequences simply didn't work, nor did the climactic love scene between Colman and costar Madeleine Carroll. Reshooting the love scene could wait, but Selznick wanted the numerous action scenes restaged and reshot immediately. He borrowed veteran action director Woody Van Dyke from MGM, teaming him with the equally flexible and fast-working James Wong Howe. During the seven straight days of retakes spanning June 5 to June 11, Van Dyke and Howe averaged twenty camera setups per day. That gave Selznick, working with Hecht on the screenplay and Wellman on final preparation for shooting, a week to get *Nothing Sacred* ready to go. On Saturday, June 12, he sent a wire to Jock Whitney in New York. "*Nothing Sacred* started shooting this morning," he told his board chairman. "You wanted comedy—boy, you're going to get it, and be it on your own head."

As was becoming standard operating procedure at SIP, Selznick started the picture without a completed shooting script. So Wellman

Fredric March, Walter Connolly, and Ben Hecht on the set of Nothing Sacred.

had to shoot in continuity, since the outcome of the story was still in doubt. This suited him just fine, because he could take a more improvisational approach—which many comedy directors preferred. And surprisingly enough, it seemed to suit Selznick as well. On July 2, Selznick dictated a twenty-three-page memo to "Messrs. Hecht and Wellman," detailing his reactions to Hecht's rewrites and Wellman's dailies, and generally blowing off steam over the story and script problems. Selznick felt that Wellman's on-the-set revisions were enhancing the project, but they were creating other problems logistically. For example, Selznick liked the rapport between Lombard's heroine and Dr. Downer (Charles Winninger), the boozy physician who misdiagnoses her condition. "As the picture is developed on the screen," said Selznick, "and largely due to the charming touches Mr. Wellman had added, a relationship of affection between Hazel and Downer comes through and should be planted in the first scene." That meant further rewrites and retakes, and Selznick wanted Wellman to "shoot the whole scene over" rather than do a "patchwork job" by redoing portions of the existing scene.

Selznick was far less complimentary concerning Hecht's work. He was especially concerned about "the picture going completely to pieces on nutty comedy" toward the end, after the hoax is revealed. Instead of staying with the lovers, Hecht focused on Wally's blustering editor, Stone (Walter Connolly), and on the newspaper's role in deceiving all of Gotham with Hazel's supposed poisoning. "It is five o'clock in the morning and I have been dictating continuously for a couple of hours," lamented Selznick as he pondered the troublesome finale. "My mind is in a fog, but this much shines through clearly, to me at least: We need a situation involving Hazel and/or Wally, and not a situation involving the impersonal newspaper and the mostly unimportant Stone." Selznick wanted Hecht to come up with a quick-hitting resolution and tag scene that would expose the hoax and reaffirm the couple's love, and without too much ado. He recalled what Hecht and MacArthur had done in wrapping up *The Front Page:* "When the girl-vs.-journalism [conflict] was solved, there were three or four lines and the play was over," recalled Selznick. He insisted that he was at least as good a collaborator as Hecht's former partner, Charles MacArthur, and that there was no reason why he and Hecht couldn't come up with as effective a finale as the one in that earlier screwball hit.

Hecht replied to Selznick's critique via wire, begging him not to cut or otherwise alter certain scenes, especially one in which Hazel decides to throw herself into the East River rather than expose the hoax, which she knows will compromise Wally and his paper. Selznick considered the scene too heavy-handed for a comedy and wanted it cut, but Hecht urged him to let Wellman shoot it. Hecht was certain that "tampering with that [scene] will dislocate the picture," and he assured Selznick that Wellman could pull it off. Hecht closed the cable with a promise to have the rewrites to Selznick within a few days, pleading with his impetuous employer-collaborator not to do anything drastic in the meantime.

Unfortunately, Hecht's cables were funnier than his script revisions. A few days later Selznick hired George Oppenheimer from MGM at $700 per week to work with Lardner and Schulberg on *Nothing Sacred*'s finale. Oppenheimer was a logical choice, given his recent success on *Libeled Lady,* a comedy with William Powell, Myrna Loy, and Spencer Tracy about an heiress who wins a huge lawsuit against a muckraking tabloid. Selznick charted his progress and the production as well, and worked with Wellman each evening to revise and polish the next day's scenes. This was not an efficient way to operate, and it was especially difficult on Wellman. On July 15, for example, Wellman shot six script scenes, seven added scenes, and four retake scenes, getting 2'23" in seventeen setups. That evening, Selznick sent Ginsberg and the other department heads this memo:

> I have been able to squeeze in some time with Bill Wellman during his dinner tonight, and the packing case scene is now complete in its rewrite. . . . I'd suggest that Freddie Spencer get this at once from Mr. Wellman's penciled notes as rewritten in my office and see to it that the actors get this. . . . I will cover the café scene with Mr. Well-

man tomorrow at lunch and will get with him on script again tomorrow when he finishes work. This means that we will not have to work out time tomorrow, Friday afternoon, for script conferences.

Selznick and Wellman reworked the suicide scene, which was shot two days later on "location" in the Studio Tank—ie., in a large pool on the back lot. Wellman and his production unit were a week behind schedule, but they finally had overtaken the rewrite teams and had run out of pages to shoot. With production costs at nearly $5,000 per day and his two stars taking home over $35,000 per week, Selznick was prepared to close down the shoot. "I am in such a tailspin on *Nothing Sacred*," Selznick wrote Ginsberg, "that I should like to be prepared, if it becomes necessary, to call off production and get the rest of the script so lined up that we can do it quickly when we get started again." He decided to hold out for another week, putting Wellman to work on rear projection and special effects shots while he wrestled with the script. Selznick decided to bring in playwright George Kaufman for a few days of intensive but well-paid work—if he could only find him. Kaufman was en route to a retreat in Vermont, and as Selznick was tracking him down he got word that Oppenheimer and Lardner had licked the script problem. The solution came via a *Cosmopolitan* story, "Letter to the Editor" by James Street, that SIP had purchased in June for $2,500. In the new finale, Stone and various other prominent public figures, all of whom have exploited and benefited from Hazel's martyrdom, decide to sustain the hoax by announcing her death. There follows a tag scene with just the brevity and wit Selznick had wanted. While New York mourns Hazel's death, the lovers are honeymooning aboard an ocean liner, reveling in their newfound anonymity, their future blissfully uncertain.

T H E Oppenheimer-Lardner breakthrough on *Nothing Sacred* came just as retakes on *Zenda* were completed, and by late summer *Nothing Sacred* was ready for preview and *Zenda* ready for release. *Zenda* opened in September 1937 at the Radio City Music Hall, and somehow it held together on-screen, capturing the public's imagination just as Selznick had anticipated. During that same week Selznick previewed *Nothing Sacred* in Los Angeles and again the reaction was favorable, even though the picture was screened in rough cut with stock music and slides for intertitles. The only hitch was the opening scene—a favorite of Hecht's—involving a counterfeit sultan who flimflams Wally and the paper. Selznick wired Hecht that "a hundred preview cards all of which are excellent confirm our impression that this sequence laid a terrific egg and is the only weakness in the picture." Trusting the collective judgment of his audience, Selznick cut the sultan gag, opening instead with a montage of New York City and Hecht's dedication to the "Skyscraper Champion of the World . . . where the Slickers and Know-It-Alls peddle gold bricks to each other . . . and where Truth, crushed to earth, rises again more phony than a glass eye."

That prologue was perfect, setting just the right tone for an affectionate swipe at New York's gullible, sentimental, and sensation-seeking populace. Selznick decided to preview *Nothing Sacred* in New York City to make sure they had not pushed things too far—the New York area, after all, generated about 15 percent of a picture's domestic revenues. Sneaks were held in October in Manhattan and the Bronx, and again the audience reaction was positive. Selznick also got a favorable reading from the state censors. In fact, another reason for previewing *Sacred* in New York City was Selznick's concern over the amount of potentially censorable material in the film, from Hecht's usual off-color wisecracks and double entendres to bits of comic violence and the heavy drinking throughout the story. Like most states, New York had its own censor board which operated independently of the PCA. New York had a notoriously strict board, and Selznick wanted its stamp of approval before going to a final cut. He got it on October 4 and wired SIP editor Hal Kern the next day that the picture "passed New York censors without a cut."

Selznick knew that once he got *Nothing Sacred* past a tough state censor board like New York's, he was bound to win approval from the PCA. After a few hassles with Breen over excessive "drunkenness" and sexual innuendo, the picture was indeed approved on October 21. But although Breen passed the picture, he still voiced severe reservations about it. "As I told you in New York City," he wrote Selznick in his letter of approval, "we are reluctant to approve your picture, *Nothing Sacred*, because of details showing Freddie March kicking Carole Lombard in the posterior. While the shot may not be offensive, per se, it nevertheless is in conflict with our practice. . . . In view, however, of the fact that to delete this shot from the picture will cause you great difficulty, we are reluctantly approving the picture with this shot in it."

Selznick was accustomed to Breen's holier-than-thou attitude. "Joe Breen and his merry men," as Lewton called them, found something morally objectionable in virtually every SIP project. Heavy lobbying had been necessary on *A Star Is Born*, for instance, to convince Breen that the ill-fated hero's alcoholism and philandering were essential to his characterization. *Zenda* caused problems due to an illegitimate birth that occurred several generations before the story takes place—a seemingly innocuous plot point but a necessary one, since it explains the physical similarities between the vacationing Brit and the Ruritanian monarch. Breen was concerned, however, that there was no indication in the story that the long-dead fornicators had suffered "moral retribution" for their sin. In fact, negotiations grew so troublesome, due to Selznick's rewriting during production, that Lewton had to relay all references to lineage over the phone for PCA approval as they were being shot.

Even more obstinate on *Nothing Sacred*, Breen complained for weeks after the film was approved. On December 7, shortly after the film went into general release, he wrote a personal letter to Will Hays, voicing his own distaste for the film and asking Hays, in effect, to overrule the PCA. "Can't you stop the showing of *Nothing Sacred?*" pleaded Breen, who was distressed over the "brutality" of the Lombard-March relationship. (Besides the kick March delivers to Lombard's posterior, the two also exchange socks to the jaw late in the film.) Breen feared that after *Nothing Sacred* "we will have a run of brute pictures, just when we were beginning to enjoy the fine plays which resulted from your cleanup campaign. Don't let them spoil it all." Breen sent a copy of the letter to Selznick, who replied that he hoped "Mr. Hays does not permit himself to get upset by individual letters of this kind." But both Breen and Selznick realized that with Code Certificate No. 3744 already affixed and some 350 prints of the picture in release, there was no chance of Hays rescinding approval.

Whatever his personal misgivings about this or that individual picture, Breen realized that his office demanded a reasoned and flexible professional response. In fact, as an MPPDA official, Breen was obligated to maintain harmonious relations within the industry. This often required more subtle forms of interaction and negotiation—that was demonstrated in the midst of the Breen-Selznick flap over *Nothing Sacred*. On November 30, 1937, Val Lewton sent a memo to Selznick about an off-the-record conversation he had just had with Breen. Lewton, who was sworn to secrecy, informed Selznick that "Mr. Breen told me that we have nothing whatsoever to worry about with Warner Bros.' *Jezebel*." The reference was to a Bette Davis vehicle with obvious similarities to *Gone With the Wind* (it was set in the Old South just before the Civil War). Breen confided to Lewton that he had read the *Jezebel* script the night before and that its story varied substantially from Mitchell's—and thus that Selznick needn't worry about Warners stealing his story or his box office thunder. Breen even provided a brief plot synopsis of *Jezebel* for illustration. Later that day Selznick instructed Lewton to "thank Joe for me" and assure him that the information would be kept confidential.

That exchange spoke volumes, not only about Breen's paradoxical role in the movie industry, but also about the industry itself in the mid-

1930s. The studios were meshing into a vast interlocking system, unified by standardized production and marketing practices, a code of acceptable content, and an increasingly stable system of technical and narrative conventions. These manifested a narrower sense of audience interest and public taste, which in turn limited what passed in Hollywood as a viable story property. The prospect of anything truly innovative or distinctive being produced in Hollywood was becoming more remote by the mid-1930s, even at the prestige level, where competition was fiercest. In fact, *Jezebel* was only one of several instances in the fall of 1937 that had Selznick fretting about his efforts being duplicated by his competitors. In September he had to rush *Zenda* into release ahead of Frank Capra's production *Lost Horizon*, another Ronald Colman fantasy-adventure set in a mythical kingdom. And in November, *Nothing Sacred* came out within days of Paramount's *True Confessions*, another Carole Lombard comedy that turned on a case of mistaken identity and a sensational news story.

The SIP releases held their own at the box office, though, which was doubly gratifying to Selznick. He clearly had a feel for industry trends and audience tastes, and he exploited those trends and tastes more effectively than his competitors. By December 1937 Selznick's competitive savvy was on nationwide display in five features: *Little Lord Fauntleroy* (474 prints in circulation), *The Garden of Allah* (545 prints), *A Star Is Born* (494 prints), *The Prisoner of Zenda* (360 prints), and *Nothing Sacred* (350 prints). That output of five releases in fourteen months marked the most prolific period of Selznick's entire career as a producer—but it was only half what he had promised to deliver United Artists in a single year. Selznick was not all that concerned, however. As his obsessive preoccupation with *Gone With the Wind* grew, so did the conviction that a single blockbuster, if properly exploited and released, could outperform a dozen top features combined at the box office. Selznick planned to test that assumption with *Wind*, but he also planned to hedge his bets by turning out routine A-class pictures. In 1937 he started courting top "producing directors" like Capra and John Ford and Alfred Hitchcock, who could pick up the production slack at SIP while Selznick devoted himself to *Gone With the Wind*.

12

Warner Bros.:
Power Plays
and Prestige

The prospect of *Jezebel* or any other Warners picture worrying an independent prestige-level producer like David O. Selznick would have been unthinkable five years earlier. But *Jezebel* was a far cry from the hell-bent urban crime dramas that Warners cranked out during Darryl Zanuck's regime, and Warners itself was a very different studio. It was Zanuck's departure, in fact, that first signaled a series of changes for the studio in the mid-1930s— changes in production and management operations, in economic conditions and market strategy, and ultimately, in Warners' house style. After the Zanuck era, Warners underwent a decentralization of creative and administrative control, much the same as MGM did in 1933. Schenck and Mayer eliminated the role of central producer altogether at Metro, but the Warners had neither the resources nor the corps of producers to go that route. Instead they initiated a supervisory system under Hal B. Wallis, a longtime Warners employee who had been Zanuck's executive assistant for the past three years.

The first sign of Wallis's upgraded executive status came even before Zanuck left. On March 19, 1933, while Zanuck and Harry Warner were battling over 50 percent pay cuts for all studio employees, Wallis's salary was raised from $900 to $1,100 per week. Then on June 14, 1933, three months to the day after Zanuck's abrupt resignation, Wallis signed a new contract giving him a salary of $1,750 weekly and defining his duties as being "of an executive and/or administrative character in connection with the supervision and general overseeing of production." So Wallis clearly was Warners' new production chief, though at a salary well below the $5,000 per week Zanuck had been earning. And in a business where paychecks were a barometer of power and authority as well as success, the disparity was significant. Wallis would oversee studio operations, but he was by no means a central producer à la Zanuck. In the mold of Paramount "mill foreman" Ben Schulberg, Wallis was a company man whose strengths were administrative, and he relied on his writers and supervisors for creative input. By late 1933 every Warners picture was assigned a supervisor, many of whom were culled from the screenwriting ranks. Some writer-producers like Robert Lord and Robert Presnell had been supervising informally for some time, and these "hyphenates" were the key creative personnel and the highest-paid supervisors on the lot; Lord earned $1,750 and Presnell $1,000 per week in late 1933. The lowest-paid supervisors were straight middle-management types like Henry Blanke at $500 and Lou Edelmen at $300. But whatever their writing skills, Warners supervisors oversaw script development as well as production, and then helped prepare a rough cut before passing the project back to Wallis and Jack Warner.

These changes on the Warners lot were not immediately evident on the screen. In fact, judging from Warners' output in 1933 and 1934, it was almost as if Zanuck had never left. The studio turned out a steady supply of efficient and predictable products—backstage musicals and urban melodramas, action pictures and crime films "torn from the day's headlines" that typified Warners' early-thirties style. But even in a backstage musical like *Dames* or a crime saga like *Bordertown*, we can glimpse changes in the production and management process. Both pictures were under Wallis's administrative control and were supervised by Robert Lord, who was to oversee script development and monitor actual production. There were problems on both pictures, though, reflecting not only the difficulty of shifting to a supervisory system but also the consequences of dispersing authority into the creative ranks.

D A M E S was initiated in August 1933, some six weeks after the release of *Gold Diggers of 1933*, Warners' biggest hit of the year. The Warners wanted a follow-up, so Wallis put Robert Lord to work on a story idea with choreographer and dance director Busby Berkeley, who was suddenly the hottest thing in Hollywood. Lord brainstormed with Berkeley, and the two came up with a story idea and title, which Wallis relayed back to Jack Warner. Wallis told Warner to "register the title *Dames*," and told him that the picture would be "done with a stage background, with Dick Powell in mind as the dance director patterned after Busby Berkeley and Ruby Keeler as one of the girls in the chorus." Wallis put Lord and screenwriter Tom Buckingham on the project, and by early October the two had a script draft and a new title, "Stage Struck"—neither of which Wallis liked. Wallis decided to bring in another writer-producer, James Seymour, who had coscripted *42nd Street* and *Gold Diggers of 1933*. Wallis gave Seymour specific instructions to reprise his earlier hits, and the result was a story about a struggling songwriter who falls for a chorine, which Seymour described to Wallis as derivative of *Gold Diggers* but "much more up to date," with a female lead "tailor-made for Keeler." Wallis was satisfied and sent the project into preproduction, with Seymour supervising and Archie Mayo assigned to direct. Mayo was the first of three directors for *Dames*, and the fact is that any number of Warners directors could have handled the "book" portion of the picture. But only Berkeley could have done the choreography and musical direction.

Busby Berkeley was a rare commodity at Warners, a specialist and true visionary amid a corps of interchangeable directors. He signed a new seven-year contract in February 1934 that identified him as a director, but Berkeley's work was so specialized and distinctive—and commercially successful—that he was given a remarkable degree of authority. He conceived, designed, choreographed, directed, and even edited the musical numbers himself. The elaborate sets and costumes in his musical numbers, the fluid camera work and dramatic angles, the clarity and precision of the images themselves—all were uncommon qualities in Warners' pictures. They were even exceptional in the musicals themselves, setting off the numbers from the rest of the picture, creating a tension between story and music, between reality and artifice. Despite this tension there was a curious integrity and coherence to these Warners musicals, since Berkeley's densely populated numbers and his penchant for reducing human forms to machinelike, syncopated displays complemented the offstage sagas of struggling songwriters and anonymous chorines working together to survive the Depression.

There was a logic of excess to Berkeley's work, which Wallis both appreciated and continually fought to keep in check. Berkeley had his own unit for the musical numbers on *Dames*, as he'd had on *42nd Street* and *Gold Diggers*, and it operated outside of any supervisor's purview. Berkeley had virtually complete creative control, with Wallis repeatedly pulling rank to keep him in line. Wallis overruled Berkeley's casting decisions and insisted that Berkeley never cast without consulting him. He nixed Berkeley's idea for a "pussy song," arguing that "we are accused of obscenity in our pictures enough as it is without reason, and besides there is no use besmirching the name of Berkeley with filth." Wallis's greatest concern, though, was Berkeley's casual disregard for the budget in his production numbers. The "I Only Have Eyes for You" number, for example, was budgeted for thirty-six performers and a set cost of $15,000. But by the time he was ready to start shooting, Berkeley wanted 250 chorines and a $50,000 set. "We have been warned not to have this kind of number in the picture," Wallis informed Berkeley before set construction for the scene began, "and I, personally, will not approve anything of this kind."

There were no such problems with director Ray Enright, a model of Warners efficiency who took over the picture only a week before shooting began. By then Robert Lord was back on *Dames* supervising the Enright unit, with Wallis screening their footage in his home each evening on a projection system installed by the studio. But still Berkeley remained the dominant creative force, cutting and scoring the musical numbers and advising Wallis on the rest of the picture. When Jack Warner screened the film and decided that a certain production number needed to be redone, Berkeley staged, directed, and edited the scene. Although Wallis demanded to see the number rehearsed before it was shot, the number was Berkeley's. So was the picture itself, in large measure, which Wallis acknowledged in a postproduction memo concerning the credits and billing: "The title *Dames* is to be followed by the name of the director and Busby Berkeley in equal-size type." *Dames* was in final cut by mid-July, and it opened on August 16 at New York City's Strand theater.

O N the following day back at Burbank, *Bordertown* went into production. That project was equally illuminating in terms of Warners' changing management and production operations, though for altogether different reasons. The primary reason was Paul Muni, who was without question the most powerful star at Warners in the mid-1930s. Back in June 1933, just after Zanuck's departure, Jack Warner signed Muni to a two-year, eight-picture deal, paying him $50,000 per picture and allowing concessions that were given to no other star on the lot. These included approval of story, role, and script; billing as sole star, both on-screen and in all advertising; loan-outs only on consent, with story and role approval, and at a fifty-fifty split with Warners on any salary overage; and permission for Muni "to render his services as he sees fit upon the legitimate stage" between film projects. The only previous Warners star who had enjoyed that kind of authority was George Arliss, who followed Zanuck to Twentieth that same summer of 1933. The Warners figured they had an even better bet in Paul Muni, who had just hit in *Scarface* and *I Am a Fugitive from a Chain Gang*. They saw

Muni as a hybrid of Cagney and Arliss, part surly tough guy and part cultured stage star.

Muni himself initiated *Bordertown* when he sent Carroll Graham's novel to Wallis in March 1934. The story centered on a Mexican lawyer who, blinded by both the American success ethic and a wanton Anglo seductress, forsakes his own people and degenerates into a murderous criminal. Wallis sent the novel to Jack Warner, who liked its possibilities as a crime saga and approved its purchase for $5,000. Wallis put Edward Chodorov on script development, instructing him to "give the character as much motivation and sympathy for the things he does as possible," to accommodate Muni. Two weeks later Chodorov submitted a treatment that, he told Wallis, provided "complete justification for the initial murders" committed by the hero, although "after this he emerges as a completely cold Little Caesar."

Chodorov's invocation of Edward G. Robinson's legendary gangster-hero might have pleased Wallis and Warner, but it could not have come at a less opportune time. Two weeks later, on April 11, 1934, while Chodorov was working on the screenplay for *Bordertown*, the Catholic Church officially announced the formation of the Legion of Decency. The Legion was created by the nation's bishops expressly to battle "indecent and immoral pictures, and those which glorify crime or criminals." The chief weapon was abstention. A Catholic was expected to pledge not only to avoid "pictures that are dangerous to my moral life," but also "to stay away altogether from places of amusement which show them as a matter of policy." This all went largely unnoticed at Warners—until Cardinal Dougherty of Philadelphia ordered a boycott of all movie theaters. There were boycotts against specific films in other cities like Boston and St. Louis, but only in Philadelphia was there a general boycott against all movies and theaters. There were some 800,000 Catholics in Philadelphia, but well over a million people of all denominations participated in the boycott. In fact, *Newsweek* magazine reported in early July that the movement had spread well beyond the Catholic constituency, and "no less than 65,000,000—half the population of the country—were under official church pressure to boycott indecent and un-Christian films."

The Warners had gotten their start in Pittsburgh with a string of nickelodeons, and by the mid-1930s they controlled the entire state of Pennsylvania. Out of 152 affiliated theaters in the state, 140 were Warners', including almost all the first-run houses in Pittsburgh and Philadelphia. So the boycott got the Warners' attention, and it got the MPPDA's as well. It was during the boycott that the Production Code Administration was created and Joe Breen was installed as president.

The code would be enforced beginning July 15, 1934. No script could go into production without PCA approval; no film could be released without a PCA seal. For the time being the Catholic bishops were appeased—and both the Legion and the PCA were now permanent fixtures of the movie industry. So the heat was off the theaters, but it was on in Hollywood. And for the time being, at least, the studios were more than willing to submit to the PCA. Hollywood could scarcely deal with a widespread theater boycott, and there were also veiled threats of government censorship. If Breen's self-censorship outfit could forestall those external threats and maintain more favorable public relations, the studios would learn to live with it.

As it turned out, *Dames* and *Bordertown* were two of the first Warners pictures to require PCA approval. There were a few minor problems on *Dames*—a reference to bribery and a brief suggestion of nudity in a silhouette shot—but these were cleared up easily enough. On July 19, Jack Warner received a letter from Breen informing him that "the version we saw this morning in your projection room of your production *Dames* is acceptable under the provisions of the Production Code." *Bordertown* was a different story, however. By early July Chodorov had taken it through two script drafts, both of which were savaged by the PCA. "The general background of the story is very low toned," wrote Breen to Warner, "with practically no compensating moral values." Breen was particularly concerned about the "sympathetic" Muni character, who lives "in adultery" with a prostitute and "becomes a murderer, gambler, and crook, always trying to 'go American.' " He also expressed dismay that "the race distinctions between Mexican and American" might offend "our southern neighbors." Breen advised Warner that "it would be difficult, if not impossible, to produce a picture from this script which would meet the requirements of the Production Code."

It was clear that wholesale revisions were in order, so Wallis brought in a new writing team under Robert Lord's supervision. Lord came through, and the massive rewrites not only gutted *Bordertown* but set a pattern for future compromises with the Breen office and marked an overnight transformation of Warners' crime sagas. Muni's character was watered down from a "completely cold Little Caesar" to a well-intentioned but hot-tempered lawyer whose only crime is punching out a rival attorney during a trial. He is disbarred and winds up running a seedy casino across the border—which puts Muni on the margins of society but scarcely in the gangster class. And rather than take up with an Anglo prostitute, in this version Muni spurns the advances of the casino owner's libidinous wife. To remove the obvious impediment, she kills her husband, and this murder leads to a climactic trial and, eventually, to the hero's redemptive return, at the behest of his mother and a neighborhood priest, to his own Hispanic people. Lord had a new script ready in three weeks that Wallis sent to the PCA. After a personal meeting between Wallis and Breen on August 10, Jack Warner was informed that there were "no definite Code violations" in the script, although numerous "details" needed to be "cleared up." That meant Wallis could schedule the shoot, and he sent word to director Archie Mayo that production would start the following week.

It also meant that Jack Warner finally had to decide on a female lead. Muni wanted Carole Lombard, but Warner was leaning toward Bette Davis. The gifted, headstrong Davis was at a turning point in her career in August 1934. After two and a half years at Warners, Davis had done sixteen films and had bitched nonstop about her roles, her work load, and her pay, which by then was $750 per week. Back in February 1934 Warner had decided to placate her—and get her off his case—by loaning her to RKO to play the cockney prostitute in an adaptation of Somerset Maugham's *Of Human Bondage*. It was an inspired bit of casting, and in that RKO picture Davis, at age twenty-six, first displayed the nature and range of her talent. While the RKO picture was in postproduction, she went back to Warners and more second-rate roles. She played a home-wrecking secretary in *Housewife* and then was assigned a supporting role (as secretary Della Street) in a low-budget Perry Mason thriller, *The Case of the Howling Dog*. Davis refused to report, and Jack Warner promptly suspended her. Two weeks later RKO released *Of Human Bondage*, which changed Jack Warner's attitude rather quickly. The response to the picture was such that Davis, as *The Los Angeles Times* put it, was "welcomed back into the fold with embarrassing effusion." Jack Warner's first effusive gesture was to give her the part of the adulterous Marie in *Bordertown*.

Bordertown, scheduled for six weeks and budgeted at $343,000, went into production on August 17. The shoot went well, though there was a mild flap over Davis's performance at one point that indicated the limits of Wallis's authority over—and his understanding of—the filmmaking process. Some three weeks into the shoot, Wallis sent a memo to Archie Mayo after seeing the dailies of a scene that was to appear toward the end of the picture. "I don't like the way you played Bette Davis at all in the scene in the construction set," said Wallis. "It's about time she's starting to crack . . . [yet] she plays it like Alice in Wonderland." Wallis instructed Mayo to retake the scene "and make it in a more emotional-hysterical way." He even specified what camera angle and setups would have to be redone.

Lord sent a return memo that same day. "I emphatically disagree with your criticism," he said. "I think Archie has directed the scene

Lobby card for RKO's Of Human Bondage, *which gave Bette Davis second billing but the first real chance to display her distinctive skills and personality on screen.*

perfectly. At least, he has directed the scene as I, who wrote it, intended it to be directed." Lord reminded Wallis that they were shooting out of continuity and explained how carefully he and Mayo were setting up Davis's "growing insanity." Lord reasoned that "if we start Miss Davis cracking up and screaming too early, we will have absolutely nothing left for her in the later clinching scenes." Wallis let the scene stand, and once the film took shape during postproduction, it was clear that Lord had been right. Several successful previews confirmed that Warners had another hit in the works, one that would require only minimal retakes if they could get past the PCA. Breen himself came to the studio on November 11, 1934, and reported to Jack Warner later that day that the picture merited Code approval.

Bordertown was released in January 1935, the first of many crime pictures by Warners that year—pictures like *G-Men, Special Agent,* and *Dr. Socrates.* These, too, were vintage Warners in terms of technique, budget, and narrative economy, but they also had been sanitized to accommodate the PCA. Clearly, the hard-edged antisocial type popularized by Cagney and Robinson and Muni had quite literally been outlawed by the Breen office, and so had his "low-toned" back-ground and amoral world view.

The type would undoubtedly have faded from Warners' repertoire even without Breen's encouragement, given the improving economic climate at Warners in 1935 and the generally upbeat mood in the in-dustry and nation at large. After losing over $20 million in 1932–33, Warners suffered losses of only $2.5 million in 1934 and Harry Warner fully expected to turn a profit in 1935. This was the year in fact when Warner planned to start competing with MGM, Paramount, and Fox on their own terms. That meant prestige productions, which hadn't been on Warners' agenda since the 1920s, but the studio was now ready to go that route. Not only had Warners adjusted its management and pro-duction operations in 1933 after Zanuck's departure, but it also initi-ated a series of deals that were key to a first-run strategy. The most important of these were the $40,000 purchase of Hervey Allen's best-selling historical romance, *Anthony Adverse,* and a two-year pact with free-lance director and two-time Oscar winner Frank Borzage, calling for six "Frank Borzage Productions" that were to be, in the words of his contract, "of the highest type and character as is practicable, having due regard to the efficient and economic operations of [Warners'] busi-ness." In fall 1934 Warners signed German stage legend Max Rein-hardt "in connection with the directing, staging, creating, and producing of *A Midsummer Night's Dream,*" which he had staged the previous summer at the Hollywood Bowl. Warners was willing to spend a million dollars on a film version and bill it as "A Max Reinhardt Production." Later in 1934, Warners cut what was without question the most important deal in its climb to prestige status, a deal with William Randolph Hearst.

The decade-long partnership between MGM and Cosmopolitan Pic-tures had soured in recent years, as Marion Davies's appeal waned and she kept losing roles to Norma Shearer that Hearst wanted for her. So the newspaper czar and *ersatz* independent producer decided to leave MGM, and he did so with characteristic flair. In November 1934 he cut a twelve-picture deal with Warners; he also cut Davies's elaborate two-story bungalow into three sections and had it moved from Culver City to Burbank. Warner Bros. agreed to finance, produce, and distribute the twelve "Cosmopolitan Productions," four of which would star Da-vies. Warners would retain "full charge of production and the sole and absolute power and control over all matters in connection therewith." After recovering its production and distribution costs, Warners would split all profits evenly with Cosmopolitan. A major benefit of the deal for Warners was access to Hearst's publishing empire as a source of story material and publicity. The contract promised Warners "lists and manuscripts of all stories appearing or about to appear in the Hearst newspapers, *Cosmopolitan* magazine, *Good Housekeeping, Harper's Bazaar,* and other magazines published by William Randolph Hearst." The contract also stated that "Cosmopolitan will cause to be published in newspapers controlled by William Randolph Hearst, without expense to [Warner Bros.], adequate advertisement and publicity in connection with . . . the promotion of Cosmopolitan productions."

The Warners did not expect much from Davies, and indeed her four pictures for them closed out her career. But they expected quite a bit more from Hearst, thanks to his publications and also his leverage with first-run exhibitors, developed over the past decade at MGM. Warners tested those expectations only weeks after the Hearst deal by initiating two ambitious Cosmopolitan projects, *Captain Blood* and *The Story of Louis Pasteur,* two "costume pictures" geared to the same prestige market for which they had produced *Midsummer Night's Dream* and *Anthony Adverse.* Historical epics, swashbucklers, and biopics were undergoing a full-scale revival in the mid-1930s, particularly through the efforts of two Warners alumni, Darryl Zanuck and George Arliss. The two did *Voltaire* just before leaving Warners, and then at Twentieth Century Pictures they scored with two other biopics: *The House of Rothschild* in 1934 and *Cardinal Richelieu* in 1935. Along with these high-minded Arliss vehicles, Twentieth also turned out several epic romances like *The Affairs of Cellini, Clive of India,* and *Les Misérables* —history with a measure of sex, swordplay, and the old Zanuck hokum.

Warners followed the same dual trajectory of history and hokum in 1935 with *The Story of Louis Pasteur* and *Captain Blood. Pasteur* clearly was modeled after the Arliss biopics; it was another solemn celebration of a European Great Man and champion of enlightenment, modern science, and liberal humanism. Muni took readily to the genre. Like Arliss, he had been trained in theater and he never let anyone forget it. Both on and off the screen, he was given to histrionic excess, long-winded tirades, and an inflated sense of his own status as an artist and social crusader. The biopic provided an ideal idiom for those conceits, and Warners was obliged to indulge Muni since he had story and role approval. But Wallis minimized the risk by capping *Pasteur*'s budget at $330,000.

Warners had fewer reservations about its swashbuckler, *Captain Blood,* even without the likes of Muni cast in the lead. Based on a 1922 best-seller by Rafael Sabatini, the story was a heady blend of action, romance, and European politics, and Jack Warner wanted someone in the Douglas Fairbanks style for the surgeon-turned-pirate, Peter Blood. But Warner and Wallis had trouble finding anyone with Fairbanks's rare amalgam of charm, athleticism, and sex appeal. They had considered Fredric March for the title role, but signed him instead to play the more cerebral and subdued Anthony Adverse. Ronald Colman was considered for the part, as was Robert Donat, but Warner eventually decided to look closer to home, and he came up with Errol Flynn. Still in his mid-twenties and with no real acting experience, Flynn had the face, the physique, and the general élan for the role—and for major stardom as well. Flynn won over the Warners brass with his first screen test for *Blood*, and when he tested opposite nineteen-year-old Olivia de Havilland in late March 1935, the costars were set. The Flynn–De Havilland chemistry was unmistakable, though a bit incongruous, with De Havilland's subdued charm and virginal innocence offsetting Flynn's overt sexuality and dashing, reckless personality. At times, due to her maternal aura as well as his endearing childishness, she seemed more like Flynn's mother than his lover.

Captain Blood was in production by late summer, with a budget of $1.2 million and steadily rising expectations on the lot. Writer Casey Robinson stayed on the shoot to adjust the dialogue and accentuate the action for Flynn, and director Michael Curtiz learned to rely less on Flynn's acting skills than on his mere screen presence. Preview audiences were enthusiastic, so Warners rushed *Captain Blood* into a holiday release. It opened in New York at the Strand on Christmas day, ten weeks after *A Midsummer Night's Dream*. Both movies did well commercially and critically to confirm Warners' changing market strategy. Both also received an Oscar nomination for best picture, and *A Midsummer Night's Dream* made the National Board of Review's top ten—a first for Warners since *I Am a Fugitive* back in 1932.

The Reinhardt project was very much an isolated case, giving Warners' credibility a boost but scarcely providing a platform for any future projects. *Captain Blood* was quite another matter. In Errol Flynn Warners seemed to have found a possible successor to Douglas Fairbanks, at a time when no one else in Hollywood seemed able to take up Fairbanks's cutlass. The studio renewed Flynn's option and increased his salary to $750—a paltry figure compared to Muni's or Cagney's salary, but five times what Flynn had been making a year earlier. Wallis and Curtiz initiated another Flynn–De Havilland vehicle, *The Charge of the Light Brigade*, solidifying its commitment to the costarring team and to the costume epic, with its peculiar blend of history and legend, of action and romance. Flynn was at the narrative epicenter of those fantasies, which Jack Warner affirmed with successive pay hikes. Flynn's option was picked up in November 1936, just after the release of *Light Brigade*, giving him $800 weekly. By December the picture was a hit and Warners was preparing its biggest Flynn epic yet, *The Adventures of Robin Hood*. In a grandiose gesture, Jack Warner "tore up" Flynn's contract and signed him to a long-term deal starting in February 1937 at $2,250 per week. Meanwhile De Havilland was learning that Warners was still very much a man's world. She was set to play Maid Marian opposite Flynn's Robin Hood, but her $500-per-week contract of April 1936 remained intact.

I F prestige were defined only in terms of excess and box-office performance, then the Flynn blockbusters certainly qualified. But the term also implied critical acclaim and top Oscars, and that brand of prestige was supplied by the Muni biopics. In 1936 *The Story of Louis Pasteur* ranked higher than any recent Warners release in the polls of both the *Film Daily* and the prestigious National Board of Review. Muni also won an Academy Award for best actor, giving Warners its first major Oscar since 1929–30, when Arliss won for *Disraeli*. In 1937 *The Life of Emile Zola* did even better than *Pasteur*, both critically and commercially, and finally brought Warners a best-picture Oscar, culminating its climb to prestige status. But Warners Bros. was an institutional creature of habit, and once the costume epics and biopics took hold so

Director Michael Curtiz with two of Warners' newest and brightest stars in the mid-thirties, Olivia de Havilland and Errol Flynn, on the set of The Charge of the Light Brigade.

did the studio's reflex to standardize and economize. However risky and innovative *Captain Blood* and *Pasteur* may have been in 1935, within two years both types of movies were hardening into formulas, into standard operating procedures at the studio and standardized products in the marketplace.

That process was facilitated by Warners' supervisory system, which was beginning to look like a unit-production operation in 1937. That was the year, in fact, that Warners' supervisors began getting "associate producer" credit on-screen. Predictably, Warners' units tended to center on the studio's star-genre combinations, invariably involving a top staff director as well as a contract player—as with the Flynn–De Havilland epics directed by Michael Curtiz, the Berkeley musicals with Dick Powell, and the Cagney crime dramas directed by Lloyd Bacon. Warners' most efficient and most accomplished production team was the biopic unit, whose key personnel were Muni, supervisor Henry Blanke, director William Dieterle, and cinematographer Tony Gaudio. There was always a certain tension between innovation and standardization in unit production, which was especially acute with prestige pictures because they were, by definition, the studio's most distinctive and inventive products. It was this factor, more than the play of personalities or the economic stakes involved, that made biopic production at Warners such a complex and embattled process. The making of *Zola*, coming in the wake of *Pasteur*'s success, provides an ideal glimpse of this process at Warners.

The Life of Emile Zola was initiated early in 1936. At the time Muni was on loan to RKO, but Blanke, Dieterle, and Gaudio were actively reformulating *Pasteur*'s success with a Great Woman biopic, *The White Angel,* starring Kay Francis as Florence Nightingale. Meanwhile literary agent Heinz Herald came to Blanke with a story about the French novelist Emile Zola's heroic defense of Alfred Dreyfus, a military officer victimized by the bureaucratic ineptitude and ingrained anti-Semitism of France's judiciary and military systems during the 1890s. Blanke and Muni both liked the idea, so Wallis, the executive producer on the biopics, assigned Herald and another German expatriate, Geza Herczeg, to develop it further. In June Herald and Herczeg submitted an eighteen-page treatment entitled "Emile Zola: The Conscience of Humanity," whose opening two-page precis made it clear that "the Dreyfus affair" was the heart of the story, and that Zola's earlier literary career would be the "backstory." It also was clear that this project was designed along the lines of *Pasteur*. "Pasteur fought bacteria, while Zola opposed lies," wrote Herald and Herczeg in the opening pitch. "Like Pasteur, who had to face obstacles, Zola had to suffer from defamation, prison, flight, and deportation." What's more, Zola "decided quite by himself to be a crusader of truth and be crucified." They closed with Zola's own proclamation that "the Truth is on the march and nothing can stop it," a notion that they felt had "never been more timely than today."

Wallis passed the treatment on to Jack Warner, who then got story approval from Muni; Warner agreed to pay the authors $3,000 for the treatment and another $10,000 for a continuity script. By November, they had completed a two-hundred-page draft, which staff writer Norman Reilly Raine transformed into a "revised temporary" during the following month. Meanwhile Wallis worked with various department heads on scheduling, budgeting, and the initial production design process. Blanke supervised final script preparation, which meant juggling input from the three writers as well as from Wallis, Muni, and Dieterle, each of whom had his own conception of the project. In early February a "script final" was ready, and ten days later Wallis circulated an estimated budget of $699,000—over twice the cost of *Pasteur* but only half what Warners was spending on Flynn's pictures. The above-the-line costs were remarkably low: $37,000 for story and script, $32,000 for Dieterle, $12,000 for Blanke, and a flat fee of $50,000 for Muni. At another major the above-the-line costs on a top star-genre picture comprised one-third to one-half of the budget, but Warners was able to keep that portion of the budget to about one-fifth on *Zola*.

Wallis's role in the process was primarily administrative and Jack Warner's involvement was only marginal—during the initiation and final approval of the picture. As on most Warner productions, Jack Warner handled property acquisition for *Zola* and then saw little of the project until it was ready for preview. But while there was little contact between Warner and Wallis on the picture, there was heavy interaction at the next juncture in the hierarchy of authority. Wallis and Blanke's working relationship was one of continual struggle and negotiation, the two men virtually embodying and acting out the studio's contrary impulses for standardization and innovation. While Wallis was inclined simply to reformulate *Pasteur*, Blanke—more than Dieterle or Muni or anyone else involved—fought for what he considered the integrity of the project. He and Wallis battled over every phase of the production, from casting and costume design to camera work and performances and even the title of the film.

It became obvious early on that Wallis's sense of history extended only as far back as Muni's last picture. Blanke understood the logic of reworking *Pasteur*, but he wanted a more authentic re-creation of the actual Zola-Dreyfus episode. The two first flared over Muni's makeup. *Zola* was Muni's third straight historical drama (including the RKO loan-out) in which he played a bearded Frenchman. In a November

1936 memo to Wallis, Blanke said "our greatest problem on this production" was keeping Muni's appearance "as different from Pasteur as possible." Wallis disagreed, arguing that Muni's box-office clout was not to be compromised for the sake of historical accuracy. This conflict came to a head in February, just before production began, when Blanke had makeup specialist Perc Westmore use "additional flesh compositions" in recreating Zola's facial appearance. After seeing the makeup tests, Wallis feared they would "lose the Muni personality." Countermanding Blanke's instructions, Wallis told Westmore to "make [Muni] up for the character so far as hair and beard is concerned and still retain for the audience the impression that Paul Muni is playing the part." Blanke acquiesced, but soon he and Wallis were haggling over the female lead. Wallis wanted Josephine Hutchinson cast as the woman behind the Great Man. Blanke objected, reminding Wallis that "she played the wife of Pasteur in a picture laid in France in the same period as Zola." Wallis insisted on exploiting Hutchinson's residual box-office appeal, and the two finally compromised; Hutchinson was cast in a minor but important role as Dreyfus's wife.

The most severe preproduction hassle between Wallis and Blanke involved costume design. Wallis assigned Milo Anderson, who had done the costumes for Pasteur with only minimal attention to authenticity and detail. Blanke wanted Zola to display "more of the genuine touch of the period," and Wallis agreed to let Blanke bring in another designer, Ali Hubert. But Wallis then rescinded his approval on the recommendation of studio manager T. C. "Tenny" Wright, who was trying to keep costs down. In a rage, Blanke told Wallis "to talk with Mr. Warner and see that I may be relieved of my duties" if Hubert was taken off the picture. "We [supervisors] get little enough credit for what we are doing," lamented Blanke, "but one likes to have at least the feeling that one is responsible for the quality and good taste of some of the pictures, even if nobody else knows about it." Wallis backed off, and Hubert served as technical adviser and shared costume designer credit with Milo Anderson on Zola.

Shooting began in March, scheduled for forty-two days, with Dieterle and company working as quickly as they had on Pasteur. During the first week Dieterle and Gaudio averaged just under twenty setups per day, generating a remarkable 29'30" of finished footage. They sustained that pace, slowing only for the now-legendary courtroom scene that culminated in Zola's impassioned plea for social justice. Dieterle shot Muni's tour de force in a single six-minute take in which Muni addressed the camera, which was situated in the jury box. Wallis sent congratulations to Dieterle and Muni after he saw the dailies, but he doubted that the scene would work as a single take. Wallis suggested that Dieterle shoot more "coverage" of the crowd and also that he "protect himself with a tight two-shot" of Muni and another character to facilitate editing. But Blanke supervised a rough cut of the scene and he felt that it played perfectly. "I would consider it a waste of money to shoot any more of this," Blanke told Wallis, reasoning that crowd scenes were costly and difficult to shoot. Besides, the shots were unnecessary since "the main characters in the courtroom and their actions are so fascinating that you can hardly cut away from them." And about Muni's speech, Blanke simply stated, "We did not figure on spoiling it by intercutting with anything else."

While Blanke readily played on Wallis's frugality when it served his own purposes, he was severely critical when it compromised the quality of the project. Like most Warners pictures, *Zola* was shot out of sequence. Among the last scenes to be shot were those depicting Zola's early development as a writer and his friendship with painter Paul Cézanne. In a daily exchange of memos in early April, Wallis and Blanke debated the merits of Ben Weldon's performance as Cézanne. Wallis admitted that he cast Weldon "to save money," but still he felt the performance was satisfactory. Blanke insisted that neither the performance nor the cut scenes were working and the picture would open on a decidedly weak note. Wallis finally relented and on April 17, Vladimir Sokoloff was brought in and the Cézanne scenes were reshot in a single week. Those retakes pushed *Zola* ten days over schedule, with the picture closing on May 10. By then Blanke and Wallis had reached another compromise, this one involving the title, and again the key issue was whether to adhere to the norms set by *Pasteur*. Wallis had been holding out for "The Story of Emile Zola," while Blanke lobbied for various alternatives: "The Truth Is on the March," "I Accuse," "Destiny," and others. In late April Wallis and the Warners finally agreed on "The Life of Emile Zola"—a curious decision since little of Zola's life was actually depicted in the film.

During postproduction Wallis's involvement was minimal. He spent two days going over the rough cut, dictating ideas for tightening and polishing scenes, and later he suggested cuts to accommodate Joe Breen and the PCA. (The picture managed to tell the Dreyfus story without the word *Jew* ever being uttered, although Dieterle did highlight the anti-Semitism issue with a bit of telltale camera work, pulling in for a close-up on the word when it appeared on a military document.) By late June *Zola* was close to a final cut and was previewed, without Max Steiner's score, at Warners' theater in Hollywood. The preview went well, and most of July was devoted to scoring. *The Life of Emile Zola* premiered on August 11, 1937, and was an immediate sensation. A week later Harry, Jack, and Abe Warner took full-page ads in various

Los Angeles papers, offering congratulations "to Mr. Muni and his fellow players, to director William Dieterle, to the writers, to the nameless and numberless studio workers and technicians who gave their share in its shaping. They, and they alone, own the glory of having created a masterpiece." Two of the workers who remained nameless— not just here but in the countless rave reviews of *Zola*—were Hal Wallis and Henry Blanke. Their enforced, embattled collaboration was crucial to the picture's creation and its success, but they scarcely expected recognition. Indeed, the critical raves and box-office revenues were reward enough. *Zola* did exceptional business, it was named the year's best picture by the Academy and *Film Daily*, and it placed second in the National Board of Review's annual poll.

W H I L E Warners' star-genre units were solidifying in the mid- to late-1930s, another very different kind of unit production emerged at the studio. The prestige pictures and other A-class features made up only half of Warners' output of sixty pictures per year. To supplement them and to keep the entire Warners system operating at full capacity, the studio relied on the newly organized Foy unit. Bryan "Brynie" Foy

The nucleus of Warners' biopic unit: director William Dieterle, star Paul Muni, executive producer Hal Wallis, and unit producer Henry Blanke.

had started in vaudeville, breaking into movies as producer-director of vaudeville shorts at Warner's Vitagraph studio in New York in the 1920s. Having achieved sudden and unexpected notoriety when he did Warners' first all-talking feature, *The Lights of New York*, in 1927, he was directing low-budget features in Hollywood by the early 1930s, and by 1935 he'd become the studio's B-movie specialist on a salary of $750 per week. In 1936 Warners doubled his salary and put him in charge of all B-movie production, which totaled twenty-nine releases in 1936 and thirty in 1937.

The Foy unit's function, in essence, was to keep Warners' facilities, personnel, and second-rate talent operating at top efficiency while supplying a steady flow of low-cost product. Warners' B pictures gave costars and featured players from the A ranks like Ann Dvorak or Barton MacLane an opportunity to star, and they were directed by the likes of B. Reeves Eason, Nick Grinde, and William McGann, who also did second-unit work on A-class features. Even the scripts for many of Foy's productions were recruited from the A ranks. Two 1932 hits, *Tiger Shark* and *Five Star Final*, for instance, were redone in 1936 as B pictures under the titles *Bengal Tiger* and *The Voice of Life*. Schedules ranged from fifteen to twenty-five days and budgets from $50,000 to $125,000; pre- and postproduction ran three to four weeks. Executive input was minimal. Since few of the pictures were star vehicles or based on presold properties, Jack Warner was rarely involved before the final cut. Wallis monitored each production, but the process was so mechanical that it required little real input. Thus Foy had considerable authority, although it was over a process of assembly-line moviemaking. But Warners had the most productive and efficient B-picture unit among the majors, and Foy was well paid for his success. His weekly paycheck was up to $2,000 by 1938, putting him on a par with those associate producers who supervised only a half-dozen projects per annum.

With the prestige productions settling into a regulated process and Foy's B-picture unit going strong, there was a marked return in 1937 to Warners' tradition of efficient filmmaking. But even as things leveled off, Warners was clearly operating on a higher plane. *The Life of Emile Zola* was the hit of the year, the 1937 profits were nearly $6 million— twice the 1936 take—and *Fortune* magazine closed out the year with a piece on Warners' "ten-year zoom . . . from the rank of outsider to the biggest thing in show business." That "zoom" was attributed to Warners' system, to its executive corps and its production operation rather than to any "producing genius." The company "used to have one of those in Darryl Zanuck," said *Fortune*, but he "has never been officially replaced." Now production operations were "in the hands of a jocose penny watcher, Jack Warner, his methodical assistant, Hal Wallis, and a half-dozen almost anonymous supervisors." Jack was described as the "supreme head of Warner Bros. production," though *Fortune* suggested that he "would not be Harry's brother if he did not look upon the making of movies like any other kind of factory production, requiring discipline and order rather than temperament and talent."

There was a certain truth to that viewpoint, since Warners was a well-regulated studio and a classic top-down operation, with power descending through its executives and into the filmmaking ranks. But Warners was scarcely a smooth-running "factory" whose recent surge was accomplished without its share of "temperament and talent." Those qualities were rarely flashed by its directors, who were indeed a disciplined lot in an era when the producer-director was emerging as an important filmmaking force. Mervyn LeRoy had tried vaulting to that privileged status in 1936–37, when Harry Warner gave him his own independent unit. The result was four overblown failures and LeRoy's abrupt segue to MGM. Once LeRoy left, the only director who worked regularly at Warners in the late 1930s with any real administrative and creative authority was free-lancer Howard Hawks. He invariably signed one- and two-picture deals that paid him well and gave him much greater control than any of Warners' staff directors. For instance on a 1936 project, *Ceiling Zero*, Hawks got $6,000 per week and contractual rights to "collaborate" during both the scripting and the editing of the picture, which was billed as a "Howard Hawks Production."

Ceiling Zero was even more illuminating in terms of its star's authority. In fact, Warners' stars were the most talented and temperamental individuals on the lot throughout the 1930s. *Ceiling Zero* was made to placate James Cagney, who was locked in a bitter dispute with Jack Warner and Hal Wallis over casting and project quality. Cagney wanted more "serious" dramatic projects and an occasional musical, and he was not satisfied with the likes of *Ceiling Zero*—which critic Otis Ferguson called "the best of all airplane pictures" but Cagney dismissed as just another action yarn. Cagney was dead serious, and he was willing to bolt Warners to prove it. In 1936 he successfully sued for release from his $4,500-per-week contract, contending that Warners' vehicles were not commensurate with his standing in the industry. Cagney had the contractual leverage and the box-office clout to defy Warners, and he encouraged other Warners stars to follow suit. Several tried, but without Cagney's success—not that any of them really expected to succeed. Bette Davis, George Brent, Kay Francis, Ann Dvorak, and others fought Warners in the courts during the 1930s, less in hopes of defeating the studio than of gaining some degree of control over their careers.

C A G N E Y ' S battles with Warners were well publicized, but Bette Davis's were equally intense and even more significant, not only in terms of her career but of the studio's house style as well. Cagney's victory over Warners was a hollow one; within two years he was back making the same kind of pictures he had sued the company to avoid. Davis, meanwhile, battled the entrenched Warners system and traditional male ethos, managing somehow to reshape her screen image into a star persona that was as powerful and provocative—and distinctly feminine—as any in the industry. Her struggles with Jack Warner extended throughout her eighteen-year tenure at Warners, from 1931 to 1948. But the most dramatic and important skirmishes were in the mid- to late-1930s, culminating in the production of *Jezebel*.

The release of *Bordertown* in January 1935 bolstered the image that Davis established a few month earlier in *Of Human Bondage*—the image of an intense, ruthless, sexually aggressive woman who relied on her will and wits to get what she wanted. But Warner and Wallis failed to exploit these qualities, casting Davis in a second-rate woman's picture and then two routine crime thrillers after *Bordertown*. Not until late 1935 was she given roles that she could really work with: an alcoholic, self-destructive actress in *Dangerous*, and a naive love-struck waitress in *The Petrified Forest*. *Dangerous* was released in December while Davis was doing *The Petrified Forest*, and though it brought her an Oscar nomination it scarcely improved her stature at the studio. Her next assignment was in *Satan Met a Lady*, a cut-rate version of Dashiell Hammett's *The Maltese Falcon*. Davis found both the part and the picture unacceptable and she refused to report. A suspension changed her mind and she did the picture—her sixth that year and the twenty-third for Warners in four years. Her next assignment was *Golden Arrow*, in a role so weak that Kay Francis had taken a suspension to avoid it, and when production closed in February 1936 Davis resolved not to start another picture without a new contract and the assurance of better roles.

This was not an unreasonable endeavor, considering Warners' move to prestige production and Davis's own market value, which climbed even higher in late February 1936 when she captured the best actress Oscar for *Dangerous*. In early March, two weeks after finishing *Golden Arrow* and only days after the Academy Awards ceremony, Davis was offered the lead in RKO's *Mary, Queen of Scots*. Set to direct was John Ford, who had just won best director and best picture for *The Informer*. Davis desperately wanted the role, but when Jack Warner received a

A key event in Bette Davis's career—and in her ongoing battles with Jack Warner—was her 1935 Academy Award. Davis is pictured here with Victor McLaglen, who won the Oscar for best actor that same year.

memo on RKO's request to borrow Davis, he simply returned it with "Not interested" scrawled across the bottom. That was the last straw; Davis resolved to stay out of pictures altogether until her status at the studio changed. She took a six-week "layoff"—a leave without pay, though not a suspension. She went back East, where she was big news after the recent Oscar, and through the press she lambasted Hollywood's power brokers. "Film Bosses 'Headache' to Bette Davis," blared *The Evening Journal*, wherein she openly castigated Warners and declared she would not return for retakes on *Golden Arrow*. That same date (March 25, 1936) the *World Telegram* ran a banner headline: " 'They'd Make All the Women Wed the Men,' Cries Bette Davis." This time she took on the studio's willing submission to the Breen office.

While Davis was in New York, her agent sent Warners a list of her contract demands. She wanted a new contract on these terms: five years, with salaries escalating from $100,000 to $220,000 per year (she was then earning $64,000 per year); a maximum of four pictures annually; star or costar billing with her name above the title and in type size equal to that of her costar; the services of either Tony Gaudio, Sol

Polito, or Ernie Haller on camera; three months' consecutive vacation each year with the right to do one outside picture. Davis refused to start another picture without the new pact, and she was promptly suspended. That led to weeks and then months of negotiation. By midsummer Davis was offered $2,000 per week and a vague promise of better roles, but still she held out. In mid-August, she sailed to England to work for an independent company, Toeplitz Productions. Warners sued to prevent Davis from signing, and the case was tried in London in October 1936. Warners prevailed, although its British attorney voiced his surprise at the outcome. He agreed that the studio "should have the right to suspend" and also "to discontinue payment of salary." But he suggested that "there should be a limit to the period which the Producer can add on to the existing period of the contract"—that is, the time that can be tacked on to actors' contracts when they refused to perform, thus preventing them from sitting out and becoming "free agents."

Davis accepted the judgment and took a different tack. She went after Warner through his attorneys, who conveyed to Warner that after the trial Davis "was very subdued and in a much more chastened spirit," and that she would return to work without any "modifications" of her existing contract. At the close of this report, though, several "requests, as mere suggestions," were relayed, intended for "the mutual benefit of [Davis] and the Company." The studio's attorneys then began pleading Davis's case, reiterating her earlier demands for Jack's "sympathetic consideration" and even suggesting that the studio cover her court costs. Warner held firm but he got the message; Davis might have lost this skirmish, but the war would go on. And Warner himself, having been without his top actress for nearly a year, was ready to compromise. He already had set several routine Davis projects in motion, beginning with *Marked Woman,* a crime thriller. But he also bought Davis a property that he knew she wanted, one that featured a difficult role he now believed she could pull off. Davis expressed her appreciation to Warner in a handwritten note in January 1937. "I am thrilled to death about *Jezebel,*" she wrote. "I think it can be as great, if not greater, than *Gone with the Wind*—thank you for buying it."

DAVID SELZNICK'S two-year "Search for Scarlett" was just getting under way in early 1937, and Bette Davis was a leading contender for the part. There was no real chance of her playing Scarlett O'Hara, since her improving market value only reinforced Warners' opposition to her doing any outside work. Still Davis coveted the role, and what with her Oscar, the lawsuit, and the best-selling status of Margaret Mitchell's novel, Warner was inclined to give it to her—or to give her a reasonable facsimile in *Jezebel*, a play by Owen Davis that had run on Broadway in 1933–34. The story was set in the Old South and centered on Julie Marston, a spoiled southern belle whose head-strong behavior costs her the love of a young Yankee banker. After he breaks their engagement and leaves New Orleans, Julie realizes her loss and connives to get him back, even after he weds someone else. A yellow fever epidemic gives her her chance: though the two seem destined to a tragic end, it finally unites Julie with her beloved after he contracts the disease.

Actually, Warners had almost bought *Jezebel* for Bette Davis back in 1935. But there were misgivings about the property, which Wallis's assistant Walter MacEwen summarized in a February 1935 memo. No doubt the story "would provide a good role for Bette Davis," said MacEwen, "who could play the spots off the part of a little bitch of an aristocratic southern girl." But he doubted whether "a picture built solely around her in an unsympathetic role would be so well liked." MacEwen suggested "a touch of the good old regeneration through suffering," which would make her character "a wiser and more palat-able person after the final fade-out." Wallis concurred, but a succession of writers and supervisors failed to work out a suitable adaptation, and in March 1935 Wallis decided against buying the property.

The stakes obviously had changed since then, and in January 1937 Warner bought the rights to *Jezebel* for $12,000. The story problems remained, however, though this time around Wallis hoped to resolve them by placing more emphasis on Julie's suffering after her fiancé's departure. Another parade of writers, directors, and supervisors tried and failed to make the story work. Their sentiments were best ex-pressed by Edmund Goulding, a writer-director who came to Warners from MGM and had just directed Davis and Henry Fonda in *That Certain Woman*. In a July 1937 memo to Wallis, Goulding said he found the "background and characters" of the play "intriguing," and he felt that it was "quite possible to put a vivid picture upon the screen." But he was convinced the project was doomed because, with or without the plague and the redemptive finale, "the picture can only tell the story of the triumph of bitchery."

Another six weeks of script revisions only reinforced that estimation, and in late August Warner and Wallis began looking outside the studio for help. They decided on William Wyler, a director under contract to independent producer Sam Goldwyn. Still in his mid-thirties, Wyler had come a long way since his apprentice years directing shorts and five-reel westerns for Universal. He had recently handled such A-class Goldwyn projects as *These Three* and *Dodsworth*. He had two dozen features to his credit over the last decade, and he also had gained a reputation as a capable script doctor. Warner signed him to write and direct for fifteen weeks at $6,250 per week, with instructions that *Jezebel* be ready to shoot by late October. Wyler came aboard on September 6, 1937, and between rewrite sessions with Abem Finkel and Clements Ripley (who eventually received screen credit), he worked on preproduction with associate producer Henry Blanke and various department heads. A "final draft screenplay" was approved on October 13, the same day Jack Warner closed a deal with independent producer Walter Wanger, getting the fast-rising Henry Fonda in a straight swap for Joan Blondell. A start date of October 25 was set, with a seven-week shooting schedule and a preliminary budget of $783,508.

Wyler knew when he started shooting that the script still needed work, but his and Fonda's upcoming commitments and Warner's production schedule demanded that he start production in late October. Wallis kept Finkel and Ripley on the project for rewrites, but Wyler had someone else in mind. John Huston was then a much traveled thirty-year-old writer, actor, painter, and former prizefighter, just off a theater stint in Chicago. He had worked for Universal in the early 1930s, where he met Wyler, and he decided in 1937 to take another shot at movie writing. He reworked his short story, "Three Men and a Girl," as a movie treatment. "I then called Willie Wyler," Huston later recollected, "asked him to put me up for a while, took a plane to California, and sold the treatment to Warner Brothers for $5,000, with a contract . . . to write the screenplay."

Warners signed Huston on September 18, 1937, and while Huston was staying with Wyler the two began talking about *Jezebel*. Wyler was impressed with Huston's ideas and when production opened in late October, he asked Wallis to put Huston on the picture. Three days later Wallis sent a memo to Blanke explaining that Huston was "to sort of represent [Wyler] in collaboration with the writers and yourself." He added that Wyler "knows Huston personally, spends a great deal of time with him, and will see him at night, and he maintains that Huston knows exactly his feeling and thoughts about the script, and his views on the last half of it."

Bette Davis also was getting to know Wyler personally and seeing him at night. The two became lovers soon after Wyler arrived on the lot, and the affair brought an end to Davis's troubled marriage to bandleader Ham Nelson. Wyler and Huston worked evenings throughout the shoot, with heavy input from Davis, rewriting the script, polishing the dialogue, and blocking out each day's camera setups. Thus Davis helped shape the project and John Huston got a crash course in filmmaking and in the politics of sex and power in Hollywood. Warners tolerated the affair and the unconventional writing setup, since neither threatened the project's development—on the contrary, both seemed to enhance it.

Wyler's shooting of *Jezebel* was another matter. From the opening weeks of production, his deliberate and seemingly excessive methods caused concern. "Possibly Wyler likes to see those big numbers on the slate," wrote Wallis to Blanke early in the shoot, "and maybe we could arrange to have them start with number 6 on each take; then it wouldn't take so long to get up to 9 or 10." By late November Wallis had lost his sense of humor, and unit manager Bob Fellows was sounding the alarm almost daily. Appended to Fellows's production report of November 24, for example, were these comments: "To date Wyler has averaged a little better than two [script] pages per day for twenty-five days. . . . I do not believe anyone is aware of just how slow Mr. Wyler is. Company delayed from 9:00 A.M. to 11:30 A.M. changing script and rehearsing new scene with Miss Davis and Mr. Fonda. Picture is nine days behind schedule."

Like any production manager, Fellows was basically an efficiency expert, and he was used to operating with staff directors like Mike Curtiz or William Dieterle, who followed the shooting script, put their actors through their paces, and brought pictures in on time and under budget. Wyler, conversely, freely reworked the script, and often called for one take after another without saying a word to the performers about what he wanted done differently. He also designed intricate camera setups and elaborate movements, often using long takes, reframing, and deep-focus shooting to involve several planes of action in a given shot. This demanded heavy rehearsal and meticulous work by both cast and crew—demands that were altogether new to most Warners personnel.

Soon both Wallis and studio manager Tenny Wright were badgering Blanke about the time and money Wyler was costing the studio. A memo in early January about the previous day's shoot typified Wallis's attitude as the picture fell further behind schedule: "The first [take] was excellent, yet he took it sixteen times. Doesn't this man know that we have close-ups to break up a scene of this kind? . . . What the hell is the matter with him anyhow—is he absolutely daffy?" Wallis's anger was fueled by the fact that he could do little besides fire off memos to Blanke, who as associate producer was to represent the interests of the front office but without alienating the director or disrupting the project. Blanke was equally frustrated. This was no unit production, and an outside director like Wyler was not about to adjust his working methods at the behest of a mere supervisor.

Even with the delays and the escalating costs, Wyler's authority over the shoot was never directly challenged. There was a suggestion in mid-December that William Dieterle be brought in to make sure the scenes with Fonda were completed before December 17, when Wanger needed him back, but Bette Davis refused to work with anyone but Wyler on the production, so the issue was dropped. Wyler did manage to close Fonda by the seventeenth, but by mid-January Wyler was so far behind schedule that John Huston was tapped to direct a scene in which one of Davis's suitors and the younger brother of her former fiancé fight a duel. The sequence was shot "on location" at the Warners ranch and marked Huston's directoral debut some three years before *The Maltese Falcon,* his first credited work as a Warners director.

This was another violation of the studio's standard operating procedure; Huston was, after all, an untried director and fledgling writer who had been under contract for only a few months. But Warner and Wallis permitted such violations since they didn't want to upset their temperamental star or her director, who clearly was getting from Davis the performance of her career. Her Julie Marston struck the perfect balance of bitchery and captivating charm, of euphoria and barely sub-

William Wyler, seated at left, directing Bette Davis in Jezebel.

dued hysteria, evoking both sympathy and grating irritation. It was equally evident as the rough cut came together how important Wyler's skills as a director were to the picture and to Davis's performance. Warner and Wallis were not used to making such distinctions, since their factory-oriented system required that staff directors be more adept as technicians and traffic cops than as narrative artists. But Wyler's direction was bringing Julie Marston to life, shaping the viewer's conception of both character and story. This involved more than simply lighting and shot composition, although Wyler and cinematographer Ernie Haller did capture Davis's physical beauty as no previous Warners filmmakers had. Even more important was Wyler's ability, through camera work and cutting, to situate Julie as the governing sensibility of the story. Through the calculated use of point-of-view shots, reaction shots, glance-object cutting, and shot/reverse-shot exchanges, Wyler orchestrated the viewer's identification with and sympathy for Julie, which were so essential if the story was to "play."

Wyler's artistry cost Warners both time and money; the *Jezebel* budget climbed from $783,000 to $1,073,000 as the project fell some five weeks behind its seven-week schedule, finally closing on January 17. The extent of Wyler's "inefficiency," at least by Warners' standards, was most evident in the daily production reports. Consider these figures from a single week of shooting on both *Zola* and *Jezebel*:

THE LIFE OF EMILE ZOLA (Dieterle, 1937)

3/15/37	4 scenes	16 setups	37 takes	3:00
3/16	10	25	58	5:50
3/17	3	22	44	4:05
3/18	21	23	47	3:45
3/19	3	31	52	6:50

JEZEBEL (Wyler, 1938)

11/1/37	5 scenes	4 setups	25 takes	1:45
11/2	1	8	57	0:20
11/3	2	6	43	1:25
11/4	3	4	36	1:50
11/5	3	14	69	2:05

In the early 1930s, LeRoy set the standard of productivity at Warners, and his working methods had been a key to its house style as well—he was a master at translating on-set efficiency into narrative economy. LeRoy had left, but staff directors like Lloyd Bacon and William Dieterle still cranked out films at nearly the same rate. Note Dieterle's pace on *The Life of Emile Zola,* a period piece featuring Warners' highest-paid star shot in eight weeks on a budget of $699,000. And note too its connections with the traditional Warners style. Its elliptical story developed at a frantic pace, replete with montages and ellipses, yet the overall pacing was countered in individual scenes by the minimal camera work and cutting. Dieterle usually framed the action in medium or medium-long shots, cutting to close-ups, reactions shots, or point-of-view shots only when absolutely necessary—which was not often, given his pacing and Muni's stage-bound performance. Thus *Zola* had much the same feel as Warners' earlier crime sagas, despite obvious social and thematic distinctions.

The same was true of *Marked Woman,* the Davis crime thriller that Lloyd Bacon directed earlier in 1937. The story elicits sympathy for Davis's heroine, an amoral hustler who goes straight when mobsters kill her innocent sister, but neither her performance nor Bacon's direction draw the viewer into the narrative or lift the picture above the ranks of a routine Warners thriller. Its performances, production values, and narrative structure seem altogether primitive compared to those of *Jezebel,* which was paced much more evenly and deliberately —never as frantic and elliptical as *Zola* or *Marked Woman* in its transitions, and never as ponderous in its dramatic sequences. And perhaps most important, to watch *Jezebel* was to be wedded to Julie Marston's consciousness, to adopt her way of seeing and perverse logic in making sense of her world and her plight.

A hit both commercially and critically after its March 1938 release, *Jezebel* brought Davis another Oscar and solidified Warners' commitment to quality women's pictures. Suddenly the "female Jimmy Cagney" rap and the urban crime thrillers were behind her, and Davis starred over the next few years in some of the greatest melodramas in Hollywood's history, including *The Sisters, Dark Victory, The Old Maid, All This and Heaven Too, The Letter, The Great Lie, The Little Foxes,* and *Now Voyager.* Each of those roles was a variation on the contradictory Julie Marston, with Davis cast either as an emasculating shrew or as a charming innocent. Davis had fought for the Marston role, and Warners, to its credit, went with it once *Jezebel* hit. The process of struggle and negotiation was fairly dramatic in Davis's case, since the transformation of her screen persona went against the studio's traditional male ethos—an ethos that dominated not only its screen fare but its executive offices as well. But in fact Warners' other top stars were undergoing much the same process in the late 1930s and with similar results. The Warners were learning that prestige filmmaking meant giving more power to top contract talent and allowing wider variation in the studio's basic star-genre formulas.

The lesson came hard, particularly for Jack, but the results were altogether positive. Davis, Flynn, and Cagney made the exhibitors' 1939 top-ten poll, and in 1939–40 Warners turned out a succession of pictures that displayed a remarkable penchant for variation and reformulation. Flynn scored yet again as the heroic Brit in *The Sea Hawk*, but also as an American westerner in *Dodge City* and *Santa Fe Trail*. Cagney reprised his gangster persona in *The Roaring Twenties* but also hit in a war picture, *The Fighting 69th*, and in a screwball comedy with Bette Davis, *The Bride Came C.O.D.* Robinson parodied his gangster persona in *Brother Orchid,* and, after Paul Muni left the studio, he took over the biopic with *Confessions of a Nazi Spy, Dr. Ehrlich's Magic Bullet,* and *A Dispatch from Reuters.* Marking a high point for Warners at decade's end, these and other hits proved that the studio could turn out first-rate pictures and compete consistently with Metro, Paramount, and Fox. They also marked a period of equilibrium, when the studio struck an ideal balance between efficiency and excess, convention and innovation, administrative constraint and creative freedom. They proved that Warners, after two decades of struggle, had come of age.

13

Universal: Playing Both Ends Against the Middle

Universal survived the Depression's toughest years, 1931–33, by operating within its means and turning out modest genre pictures, programmers, and serials. Junior Laemmle had scaled back feature production and his own aspirations as a prestige-level producer when the Depression hit, and he began doing double duty as studio boss and production chief. He held Universal's losses to $1.7 million in 1932 and $1 million in 1933, during a two-year period that saw Warners lose $20 million and three other majors fall into receivership. The horror film was crucial to Universal's survival, with pictures like *Dracula, Frankenstein, The Mummy, The Old Dark House,* and *The Invisible Man* doing solid business and setting the parameters for the studio's signature genre. The quality and consistency of these films were due largely to the Laemmle-assembled and -supervised production unit, whose key above-the-line personnel were stars Boris Karloff and Bela Lugosi, director James Whale, writer John Balderston, and cameraman-turned-director Karl Freund.

By 1934 it appeared that Laemmle, who turned twenty-seven that year, had the business and leadership skills to chart the studio's resurgence. Universal actually finished 1934 in the black—just barely, showing a profit of $200,000, but enough to start Junior thinking again about the first-run market. That train of thought was hardly surprising, considering the general economic recovery and steadily improving market conditions, and indeed executives at other studios were thinking along the same lines. It was in 1934 that Warners, for instance, began shifting its relatively modest, factory-oriented operation into a higher gear. But Warners was equipped to make that shift because, unlike Universal, it had the facilities, the personnel, the management structure, the financial leverage, and the theater chain that were necessary not only to turn out top features but to regulate the overall process. Universal had excellent production facilities, but it was sorely lacking in every other area. Laemmle believed he had the base on which to build, however, and the way he saw things, Universal could ill afford *not* to compete with the other studio powers for its share of the first-run market.

In 1934–35 Laemmle began building up the musical and the woman's picture, hoping to create the same dependable production units and star-genre formulas that he had with the horror film. At the same time he steadily expanded horror production, even at the low-grade feature level. By the mid-1930s Universal was turning out sixty-minute horror programmers like *The Black Cat, The Raven,* and *The Man Who Reclaimed His Head.* These featured the genre's top stars—Karloff, Lugosi, and now Claude Rains—who often worked together to give the picture a veneer of quality. But the pictures were produced quickly by second-class staffers on budgets of well under $200,000. Laemmle increased A-class horror production as well, and he was able to do so without pushing up production costs, even when top studio talents like Whale and Balderston were involved. *The Bride of Frankenstein,* for instance, went into production in January 1935 with a thirty-six-day shooting schedule and a budget of only $293,750. Above-the-line costs were $65,000, including $15,000 for Whale and $5,900 for Junior Laemmle, who personally supervised the production. The picture went ten days over schedule and closed at $397,000—still a bargain for a top feature, especially one whose box office was virtually assured.

It's also worth noting that *The Bride of Frankenstein* was no routine sequel designed to rehash the original and cash in on its success. That may have been what Laemmle had in mind when he started Balderston working on "The Return of Frankenstein" in early 1934, but when Whale came aboard during script revision, the project took an odd and inspired turn, veering into screwball romance. Whale had walked a fine line between horror and high kitsch a few years earlier in *The Old Dark House,* and he wanted the same effect here. Colin Clive and Boris Karloff, back as the doctor and his creation, both had theater experience and welcomed the chance to broaden their roles. They were upstaged by Elsa Lanchester, though, who played Dr. Frankenstein's distaff creation and also appeared in an introductory prologue as Mary Shelley, the author of the original novel. Lanchester's histrionics in the title role, particularly her singular distaste for her prefabricated

The set for Dr. Frankenstein's laboratory, constructed at Universal City for The Bride of Frankenstein.

mate, gave *The Bride of Frankenstein* a curious edge, pushing the horror genre into the realm of black comedy. The picture was a solid hit, further demonstrating the appeal and flexibility of the genre and thus its importance to Universal. But Whale was growing unhappy: he was frustrated by the fact that after four successful years at Universal he was still turning out horror pictures, while a director like John Stahl was doing prestige jobs with more authority and higher pay. He made it clear that *The Bride of Frankenstein* would be his last horror picture.

Laemmle was sympathetic, but he also was very high on Stahl, who came up through the MGM ranks in the 1920s doing women's pictures and was Universal's top house director in the early 1930s. Stahl did the studio's only prestige pictures—and its biggest hits—in the early 1930s, producing one picture per year that could compete with MGM's routine fare. The first was a 1932 adaptation of Fannie Hurst's best-selling weepie, *Back Street,* starring Irene Dunne, on loan from RKO. Stahl scored again in 1933 with another melodrama, *Only Yesterday,* this one starring newcomer Margaret Sullavan. Encouraged by the improving economy and the horror genre's continued success, Laemmle gave Stahl the go-ahead in early 1934 on a more ambitious melodrama, *Imitation of Life,* based on another Hurst best-seller. The picture was a lavish star vehicle for Claudette Colbert, whom Laemmle borrowed from Paramount for a flat fee of $90,000. The story, which cost Laemmle another $25,000, was vintage Hurst. It concerned a young widow and mother who braves the Depression with admirable grit, builds a fortune, but learns, at last, the transcendent value of mother-love. An early indication that Stahl's adaptation would be an exercise in excess—at least by Universal standards—was the fact that nine different writers worked on the adaptation. Continuity costs reached $21,000 on the picture, and, added to Stahl's $60,000 salary, the above-the-line expenses alone were $196,000—the cost of a routine horror picture.

Laemmle was concerned about Stahl's excess, so he assigned one of his executive assistants, Henry Henigson, to keep an eye on the project when Stahl started shooting in June 1934. Henigson was the closest thing yet to a supervisor or associate producer on a Universal picture, but he really had little authority over the production, which ran twelve weeks and cost $665,000. Stahl supervised the editing, bringing in the final cut at 106 minutes—on par for his films, but a half-hour longer than most Universal features. The increase was significant, because it showed how far afield his melodramas were from Universal's usual releases, even its top horror features. That was the idea, of course, and the risk paid off. *Imitation of Life* was targeted for the first-run market and emerged one of Hollywood's biggest money-makers in 1934–35. It also brought the studio its first Oscar nomination for best picture since *All Quiet on the Western Front* four years before.

The Laemmles' spirits were soaring in early 1935. Universal had a first-run hit, a modicum of credibility, and it was actually turning a profit. *The Bride of Frankenstein* bolstered their confidence even more, and when Whale started lobbying for better assignments, Junior Laemmle was ready to listen. Junior had been stifling his own desire to compete with the majors for years, but now it looked like Universal could resume its stab at the first-run market. Laemmle planned a half-dozen prestige projects for 1935, most of which he would supervise personally, with Stahl and Whale directing the two top pictures. Laemmle gave Stahl the go-ahead on *Magnificent Obsession*, a million-dollar melodrama starring Irene Dunne, while Whale was assigned the most ambitious project of the year—and perhaps the decade—an all-star remake of Universal's musical hit, *Show Boat*.

T H I S step was the biggest mistake of Laemmle's career, although it made perfect sense at the time. The first-run market was booming in 1935, and Laemmle wanted a piece of the action so badly that he refused to recognize how ill-equipped Universal was for such a strategy. Maybe Universal could handle one or two big-budget melodramas per annum, but was it ready for a blockbuster musical? And could Laemmle afford to let James Whale, his top horror director, abandon the house genre? Karl Freund had recently bolted to MGM, which wanted a horror unit of its own, so letting Whale swear off horror production left the genre in the hands of second-rate talent at Universal, just when it was reaching its commercial and creative peak. And Laemmle's own decision to produce *Show Boat* was equally ill advised; the studio simply could not afford to disrupt its management system and lose its studio boss and production chief. Without a supervisory system or a firmer hand on the controls, Universal was headed for trouble.

The clear and present danger was the erosion of efficiency and discipline just when they were needed most. Stahl's production of *Magnificent Obsession*, on which he was to be credited as producer-director, was a perfect example. Laemmle tried to bolster studio control by putting E. M. Asher on as associate producer, but it was obvious even during script development that Asher's authority over the extravagant, self-important Stahl was virtually nil. The picture was based on a 1929 best-seller by Lloyd C. Douglas, a clergyman who turned to fiction writing late in life. *Magnificent Obsession*, his first novel, was about a playboy whose carelessness causes the death of a man and the blindness of his widow. The profligate turns to medicine and metaphysics, eventually restoring the woman's eyesight and winning both her love and a Nobel prize for his efforts. This unlikely yarn was laden with sermons and weighty asides, but somehow Douglas made it all work—which was more than Stahl and his writers could do. Laemmle paid $12,500 for the rights to the novel, then shelled out another $65,000 to a dozen different writers who worked on the adaptation.

While the script went through one rewrite after another, Stahl and Asher handled the casting. The role of the widow went to Irene Dunne, who cost Universal $75,000 for eleven weeks, plus $7,500 for each additional week. For the male lead Stahl wanted Robert Taylor, a twenty-four-year-old contract player at MGM with matinee-idol looks but little experience. Asher balked at using an untried male lead with Dunne, and Laemmle shared his concern—even though the youngster would cost him only $2,400 per week. But Stahl shot a screen test on July 5, only a week before shooting was to begin, which sold Laemmle on Taylor. A few days later, there was a major run-in after Asher informed Stahl that he was removing writers George O'Neil, Sarah Mason, and Victor Heerman when the picture went into production. "If any writers are taken off *Magnificent Obsession* at this time, or during the next two weeks," fumed Stahl in response, "you are doing it at your own risk, and I absolutely forbid it." He had always worked with at least one writer on the set, and he saw no reason to change that practice now. He closed with the assertion: "This is absolutely final."

Stahl got his way and the writers stayed on throughout the shoot, pushing the writers' combined salaries to $49,250. But Stahl's power play and the additional expense had meager results—he never did get a satisfactory script. He shut down production on the scheduled closing date in late September after sixty-seven shooting days, but a rough cut indicated that the picture was far from complete. Stahl spent several days rewriting furiously and preparing retakes, and on October 3 Dunne and Taylor were back on the set. Twenty-five shooting days and $200,000 later, Stahl officially closed *Magnificent Obsession*. By then the script-star-director costs alone reached $272,000 and the total cost of the picture was $947,697. And perhaps most remarkable of all, in ninety-two shooting days Stahl exposed 456,000 feet of film—roughly eighty hours of footage that was edited down to under two hours in the release version.

Stahl was confident the picture would hit, but Laemmle could not afford to wait until its release for an influx of cash. Universal's overall box-office returns were well below expectations, and its cash reserves were depleted due to preproduction costs on *Show Boat* and location problems on an ill-fated biopic, *Sutter's Gold*. Sets and props alone for *Show Boat* cost $86,000, with another $47,000 going for wardrobe.

Whale was set to start shooting in December, at which point salaries for Irene Dunne, Paul Robeson, Helen Morgan, and the other stars would consume enormous amounts of cash—nearly $300,000 by the time the picture was finished, with Whale costing another $90,000. Things were even worse on *Sutter's Gold*, which Laemmle had hoped would carry Edward Arnold to genuine stardom. Arnold, a heavyset character actor who Laemmle felt was Universal's answer to Lionel Barrymore, portrayed pioneer John Sutter in his epic journey from Switzerland to California. Laemmle allowed a liberal location budget and brought in director James Cruze for the shoot, hoping for the same scope and grandeur in *Sutter's Gold* that Cruze had brought to his silent western, *The Covered Wagon*. But as the rushes came back to Universal City, Laemmle grew increasingly discouraged.

The cash shortage was so serious that in December Carl Sr. came West to meet with his son. Junior defended his strategy with much the same rationale that David Selznick was giving his own board of directors at SIP at the time. "There are two kinds of merchandise that can be made profitably in this business," said Selznick; "either the very cheap pictures or the very expensive pictures." For Selznick this was an either/or proposition, and he went with the top features. But Junior Laemmle saw it as a both/and deal for Universal. The difference, of course, was that Selznick's entire production operation was focused on a single kind of product and a single marketing strategy, whereas Junior Laemmle was trying to target Universal products for virtually the entire market range, from subfeatures and programmers to prestige pictures. Junior was convinced that the low-cost product could cover the overhead while the high-cost, high-risk pictures would enable him to compete for a share of the lucrative first-run market. His father agreed, and he secured $750,000 cash from Standard Capital Corporation, a Wall Street firm run by J. Cheever Cowdin that specialized in bailing out financially troubled companies. The conditions were rather stiff. If Laemmle failed to repay within ninety days, Cowdin had an exclusive option to take over Universal via stock purchases of $5.5 million.

In late December things were looking up. *Magnificent Obsession* opened during the holidays, and the rushes from *Show Boat* were excellent. But by February the mood on both coasts had changed once again. *Sutter's Gold* was in postproduction and seemed beyond hope of even modest success. And it was now clear that Whale was out of his element in a big-budget show musical. He was working slowly and his overhead was murderous. The average cost per shooting day on *Show Boat* was $16,350 (versus $8,630 on *Bride of Frankenstein*). Even with Junior personally supervising production and spending virtually every minute on the set, things were not moving quickly enough. Costs on *Show Boat* were well over a million dollars, and the overruns were eating up the revenues on *Magnificent Obsession* as fast as they came in. Closing production by mid-February and rushing the picture into release now seemed out of the question. As the shoot carried into March, the Laemmles could only pray that Cowdin would cut them another deal or simply decide not to exercise his option.

Those prayers were not answered. Capital Standard bought 80 percent of Universal's common stock after the allotted ninety days, thus acquiring control of the company. Cowdin installed a new president, Robert H. Cochrane, whose association with Laemmle went back some thirty years. Carl Laemmle was paid a cash settlement of $1.5 million and "promoted" to chairman of the board. And while the sixty-nine-year-old mogul was kicked upstairs, Junior Laemmle was unceremoniously kicked out and succeeded by former RKO exec Charles R. Rogers. The Laemmles were effectively gone—not only from Universal but from the movie business at large. After trying without success to set Junior up as an independent, Carl Laemmle died in 1939. And though Junior was still in his twenties when he lost Universal, his career was over. He dropped out of sight after his father's death and lived out his years in relative obscurity in Hollywood.

A S I D E from replacing the Laemmles atop the management structure on both coasts, Cowdin's takover had little effect on the personnel at Universal. There were, however, changes in Universal's production and marketing strategies. Junior's costly prestige efforts had forced him to cut overall feature production from thirty-nine releases in 1934–35 to only twenty-seven for the 1935–36 season. That total was back to forty for Cochrane and Rogers' first year, and the two planned fifty for the next. Costs per picture would be reduced to increase output, though not too severely thanks to the hits that Junior left behind. *Show Boat*, released in May 1936 after six months in production and at a final cost of $1,275,000, finished (along with *Magnificent Obsession*) among the industry's top twenty-five box-office performers of the year. Rogers and Cochrane welcomed the revenues, but there would be no new projects on that scale, and those that Junior Laemmle had in the works were cut back considerably. The most notable of these was *My Man Godfrey*, which free-lancer Gregory La Cava was writing, producing, and directing for Universal. La Cava's penchant for improvising on the set and his disregard for budgets and schedules were legend, but Rogers made it clear that the picture's $586,000 bottom line was inviolate. The bulk of the expenditures were for costars William Powell, on loan from MGM at $12,500 weekly, and Carole Lombard, secured through

Myron Selznick for a flat fee of $45,000. With La Cava earning $102,250 and coscenarist Morrie Ryskind staying on throughout the shoot, *My Man Godfrey* had one of the more top-heavy budgets of any picture on the lot. Above-the-line costs were $260,000, nearly half of the total budget.

My Man Godfrey was a classic Depression-era screwball romance, and thus a rarity for Universal. Powell played a Boston blue blood slumming in a hobo camp to see how the other half lives when he's rounded up by Lombard and a group of her socialite friends, on a scavenger hunt for a "forgotten man." Powell and Lombard embark on an embattled courtship, and in a series of comic complications Powell takes a job as butler for Lombard's family, bails her father out of a business crisis, opens a nightclub called The Dump where he puts his down-and-out cronies to work, and winds up in the arms of Lombard at film's end. This fantasy of enlightened capitalism, reconciled class conflict, and romantic love unfolds at such a frantic pace and with such inspired lunacy that there's no time to ponder motivation or narrative logic. Audiences and critics were swept up by the picture, which scored huge profits, rave reviews, and seven Academy nominations. Final costs reached $656,000, but La Cava's production was remarkably economical. He shot *My Man Godfrey* in thirty-five days, only two days over schedule, and required no retakes. He exposed just 110,000 feet of film stock for the picture—less than one-fourth the amount exposed for *Magnificent Obsession.* Clearly La Cava had not done multiple takes of every setup, nor had he shot coverage from a variety of angles, hoping for inspiration during cutting. He knew what he wanted on the set and he got it without wasting time and footage.

My Man Godfrey was a pleasant surprise for the new regime, which welcomed the revenues and accolades it brought Universal. Cochrane and Rogers dismissed the whole thing as a fluke—an unexpected return on Junior's ill-fated investment in prestige production. They had plans of their own for upgrading production at Universal, though not at the feature level. They were convinced that it was in subfeatures—serials, shorts, and programmers—that Universal could best exploit the market. They upgraded serial production when they came in, increasing budgets and moving beyond westerns into sci-fi and jungle sagas. In September 1936 Ford Beebe, the studio's serial maestro, started *Jungle Jim,* a twelve-episode cliff-hanger based on a popular comic strip and calculated to exploit the success of MGM's Tarzan pictures. It was scheduled for twenty-two shooting days on a $120,000 budget. Essential to this and other Universal serials, Beebe served as a virtual unit producer as well as a director in getting a serial under way, then moving on to another. Once Beebe had established the narrative and technical conventions and worked out the logistics on *Jungle Jim*, he did the same on a serial crime thriller, *Radio Patrol*. Then he started *Secret Agent X-9*. All of these serials had twelve to fifteen weekly installments, each of which ran two reels—just under twenty minutes. They were budgeted in the $125,000 range, with schedules of four or five weeks—roughly one reel of finished film per day. Beebe and his colleagues consistently brought them in on time, under budget, and with a minimal expenditure of resources. *Secret Agent X-9*, for example, was a twelve-episode thriller that closed on schedule at twenty-six days and $4,000 under its $133,500 budget. The project was allotted 100,000 feet of exposed footage, and 85,156 feet were printed—that's roughly sixteen hours to be cut down to about four hours of screen time. Compare Beebe to a feature director like Stahl, who exposed over eighty hours of film for *Magnificent Obsession,* which ran less than two hours, or even to La Cava, who exposed over twenty hours for his ninety-minute feature, *My Man Godfrey.*

S T U D I O boss Charles Rogers scarcely expected the same efficiency from his feature directors that he got from Ford Beebe, but he did try to tighten up feature operations in 1936. He installed M. F. (Martin) Murphy as production manager to keep tabs on all feature production, from the moment a project was started until it was finally shipped to New York for release. Rogers also adopted a supervisory system, which was long overdue. In fact, it may have been too late for any consistent supervisory policies in Universal's feature operations, since top directors like Stahl had never learned to deal with—let alone submit to— direct executive supervision. The reason for this, quite obviously, was the peculiar absence of production management personnel at Universal. Serving as studio boss and sole executive producer, Junior Laemmle had supervised production with practically no executive assistance. For all practical purposes, the role of associate producer did not exist at Universal, which, in the 1930s, put the studio in a class by itself in Hollywood. It may have cut down on expenses for executive salaries, but in the long run it cost Universal dearly. Without a supervisory or unit-production system, the kind of star-genre formulations so essential to consistent feature production were virtually out of the question.

Among the first producers developed by Rogers, and certainly the most successful, was Joe Pasternak, who shepherded a string of hit Deanna Durbin musicals through production in the late 1930s. Pasternak's arrival was not a strategic move on Rogers's part, though, but rather it was the result of previous cutbacks overseas. One of Carl Laemmle's last cost-cutting efforts before the takeover was the shutting

Deanna Durbin and Judy Garland were both under contract at MGM in 1936. Garland won the tic-tac-toe game and a long-term Metro contract as well, but it was Durbin who first reached stardom at Universal.

down of Universal's production operation in Germany, and a number of its employees still on contract wound up at Universal City. One of these was Joe Pasternak, a much-traveled thirty-five-year-old producer who had come to America from Hungary as a boy and started his movie career working as a busboy in Paramount's commissary in the early 1920s. He worked his way up to assistant director, and just before sound came in he moved to Universal, which sent him to Berlin. There he met Henry Koster, a young journalist and cartoonist who soon became the most prolific screenwriter at the Berlin studio. By the early 1930s Koster was directing, and when Universal's German-based operation folded, he came with Pasternak to Universal City.

Pasternak had produced a few successful musicals in Germany, and Rogers suggested that he look for something along those lines for himself and Koster. Making the most of the opportunity, Pasternak developed a project for a young soprano named Deanna Durbin, who also was a recent arrival at Universal City. Rogers had signed her after Louis Mayer decided MGM wasn't big enough for both Durbin and Judy Garland, another musical ingenue. By midsummer Pasternak had a modest musical ready for Durbin; it was entitled *Three Smart Girls*, budgeted at $261,750, and scheduled for a twenty-seven-day shoot. The story was a blend of romantic comedy and family melodrama, with Durbin playing the youngest of three sisters who is determined to reunite her parents after her father (Charles Winninger) is enticed away from the family fold by a gold digger (Binnie Barnes). The story gave Durbin the chance to display not only her captivating innocence but also a remarkable vocal range that allowed her to sing popular ballads and opera. Pasternak and Koster started shooting in September 1936, with Joe Valentine on camera and Charles Previn as musical director.

This "Durbin unit" would be vital to Universal's survival over the next few years, but manager Martin Murphy treated the initial project like any other low-budget feature. In fact, Murphy doubted whether Koster was cut out for Universal, considering his work pace. Murphy expected four and a half script pages per day out of Koster, but he was getting only three. By the second week of shooting he informed Rogers that "Koster is far from a fast director [who] appears to lack planning in his work." By mid-October Koster had not picked up the pace, and Murphy was growing even more anxious. "This man should never be permitted to direct another [Universal picture]," suggested Murphy, "before you have a very definite understanding with him regarding maintaining a schedule as well as giving you quality in the production." Koster's deliberate working method was the primary problem, but the shoot also was slowed by California's child labor law, which restricted minors to eight-hour work days, three of which had to go for schooling. Rogers and Pasternak understood Murphy's concerns, but both were happy with what Koster was getting out of Durbin as an actress as well as vocalist. Besides that remarkable range, Durbin also displayed a vivacious spirit and an innocence that brought the rather flimsy story to life. Pasternak closed the picture in late October, eleven days behind but at a total cost of just $285,000. The figure would escalate to $300,000 by December, when *Three Smart Girls* was released, but it still was a bargain price for any musical—let alone a runaway hit that vaulted an unknown ingenue to stardom.

It would be a few months before the revenues from *Three Smart Girls* affected Universal's balance sheet, which was again showing losses at year's end even though the rest of the industry was coming out of the Depression. In 1936, for the second straight year, Universal was the only Big Eight company to report a net loss. It recorded $700,000 in losses for 1935, and $1.8 million for 1936. Those losses were written off to the Laemmles' regime, and things did look brighter for 1937. Fifty-one productions were planned, most of them budgeted under $200,000, and Universal had a hot property in Deanna Durbin. Rogers's top priority in 1937 was to establish a Durbin formula and regulate its output, and Rogers, acting as executive producer, took charge of the Durbin unit personally until this goal was accomplished. The move was Rogers's first mistake—and one that recalls Junior's administration. The second mistake was letting the Durbin formula inflate along with his own ambitions as a filmmaker. Rogers figured there was no way to keep her picture costs at the $300,000 level as her star ascended. Not only would Durbin's salary increase, but Rogers wanted to bring in stronger costars and generally upgrade the production values of her pictures to properly showcase her talent. Still Durbin's musicals would remain a bargain. She signed a new contract in April for $1,500 per week, committing to three pictures per annum. That broke down to roughly $20,000 per picture, compared with Pasternak's per-picture salary of $16,500 and Koster's $12,500. Thus the producer-director-star cost on a Durbin picture was under $50,000, only a fraction of similar charges for any other first-run production.

For Durbin's second picture, *One Hundred Men and a Girl*, Rogers allowed a budget of $606,000 and a shooting schedule of six weeks, confident that increased revenues would more than offset the expenditures. Top character actor and erstwhile leading man Adolphe Menjou was set to costar, and Rogers decided to bring Durbin's "classical" talents into the foreground. He had British conductor Leopold Sto-

Henry Koster (seated in center foreground) directs Leopold Stokowski and Deanna Durbin in One Hundred Men and a Girl.

kowski direct a hundred-piece orchestra playing Wagner, Tchaikovsky, and Mozart. The story of *One Hundred Men and a Girl* involved a girl who convinces a world-famous conductor (Stokowski, playing himself) to lead an orchestra made up of out-of-work musicians, including her widowed father (Menjou). Again Durbin would sing popular tunes as well as an aria or two, and the weightier social and familial themes were offset by her upbeat personality and a light comic touch. Pasternak, Koster, and Joe Valentine were back for this picture, along with staff writer Bruce Manning, who overhauled the rather flimsy original story for Durbin and then stayed on during production—as he would on the next five Durbin vehicles. Manning and the others concentrated their efforts on making a "Durbin picture." She was the focal character and governing sensibility of the picture, giving it a storybook quality that was perfectly skewed for a family-oriented market. So not only did the Durbin musicals provide an ideal complement to Universal's horror pictures, but they also broadened the audience base considerably—at a time when social conditions favored a more proper and uplifting type of product.

Production on the picture proceeded even more slowly than on its predecessor, though with Rogers overseeing the shoot, Murphy filed fewer complaints this time around. Pasternak closed production in late July after ten weeks' shooting, and by the time Rogers shipped the picture in August its cost was up to $750,000. Despite the inflated cost, Rogers was pleased with the results, and even before the September 1937 release of *One Hundred Men and a Girl*, he started Pasternak on Durbin's next vehicle, *Mad About Music*. Her first picture was still going strong commercially, and even the critics seemed to like it; apparently, Universal's new star-genre formula was money in the bank, if Rogers could reproduce it quickly enough. He did make one change in the Durbin unit in an effort to cut costs and speed up production: he replaced the methodical Henry Koster with Norman Taurog, a no-nonsense craftsman with a knack for working with kids (he had just done *The Adventures of Tom Sawyer* for Selznick). But otherwise the producer, writer, cameraman, musical director, and star remained the same for *Mad About Music*.

There were a few minor adjustments to the Durbin formula this time around—the story was set in Europe, for instance, and it featured religious songs rather than classical airs or opera to display Durbin's range—but the basics were all there. The plot involved a vain movie actress who banishes her teenage daughter (Durbin) to a boarding school in Europe, where the girl convinces a visitor, played by Herbert Marshall, to fill in as her surrogate father. As in her previous films, Durbin was cast as a virginal diva opposite an attractive older man, and her mission was not only to integrate different musical styles but also to integrate a father figure into a stable social and emotional context. In fact, in virtually all her films Durbin was depicted as a victim of a broken home and fragmented family who sought somehow to restore the traditional order.

Pasternak and Taurog took *Mad About Music* into production in November 1937, with a forty-four-day schedule and a budget of $700,000, both of which were virtually identical to initial estimates on her last picture. Whether replacing Koster would enhance the unit's efficiency remained to be seen—but Rogers and Cochrane wouldn't be around to find out. The Durbin pictures were widely applauded for having saved Universal from bankruptcy, but they were not being made as economically or as frequently as J. Cheever Cowdin wanted. And while Rogers concentrated on Durbin's pictures, the rest of Universal's program had suffered. By December rentals for *One Hundred Men and a Girl* were pouring in and the Academy nominated the picture for three Oscars, including a nomination for best picture. But all Cowdin could see at year's end was the balance sheet. As the industry continued to pull out of the Depression, Universal was again the only Big Eight company to lose money, finishing over $1 million in the red. So Cowdin sacked Cochrane and Rogers and brought in a new team. Nathan J. Blumberg was named Universal's new president, William Scully its sales manager, and Cliff Work the vice president in charge of production.

With the ouster of Laemmle's old crony Bob Cochrane, any vestige of the old regime was gone. But as anyone who ran Universal learned soon enough, the studio's production operation was inexorably wed to its market strategy, which Carl Laemmle had devised decades ago and set in concrete when he decided to maintain a huge production operation, but without a theater chain. Blumberg and Work, like their predecessors, had little choice but to churn out programmers, serials, and series pictures along with an occasional A-class feature. But the new team's background was in distribution and exhibition—that was why Cowdin hired them—and they were determined not to repeat the mistakes of the past. Rogers had started with the best of intentions, but like Junior Laemmle, he wound up pursuing the first-run market too aggressively, thus squandering his own time and talent as well as Universal's limited resources. Neither Laemmle nor Rogers was a filmmaker or even much of a production executive, and each proved as much. Cliff Work was not about to follow suit. His role, as he saw it, was to cut expenses and oversee plant operations, concentrating on low-grade features and subfeatures while he let Murphy and a handful of producers take care of the A-class pictures.

Thus Pasternak was crucial to Universal's fortunes, and Work assigned him as producer to other pictures as well as Durbin's. But the Pasternak-Durbin musicals were still the most important features on Universal's schedule, and Work wanted more efficiency and productivity from the Durbin unit. Replacing Koster with Taurog on *Mad About Music* had not improved things; the picture closed in February 1938, twenty-nine days behind and $150,000 over budget. Work decided to make an even more radical replacement for the next Durbin picture, *That Certain Age*, bringing in low-budget director Edward Ludwig. Otherwise the Durbin unit remained intact. Pasternak and writer Bruce Manning were still the principal architects of the series, and Cliff Work made it clear that Pasternak was to stay on top of *That Certain Age* and keep it within the $650,000 budget.

Pasternak and Ludwig held the line on the picture, which was every bit as big a hit as *Mad About Music*. By late 1938 Durbin's stardom was secure and her pictures were sure moneymakers, which Universal acknowledged with retroactive bonuses of $10,000 for her last three pictures. That brought Durbin's total compensation to $130,000 that year, and for the moment it quelled her escalating salary demands. Her demands were not unreasonable, though; she was Universal's only bankable personality and, along with MGM's Mickey Rooney, the fastest rising star in Hollywood. Durbin and Rooney had been all but unknown a few years earlier, and now the two sixteen-year-olds were national icons—idealized projections of American adolescence. They embodied the movies' capacity for wish fulfillment and naive optimism, a capacity that seemed to intensify throughout the 1930s. It was fueled by myriad forces, from the PCA and Legion of Decency (with their efforts to legislate an innocent and upbeat world view) to the Depression and the Dust Bowl, which uprooted families and changed the American landscape, and seemed to demand a palliative in our collective fictions that couldn't be found in our lives. A good many Hollywood movies of the era expressed a longing for simpler times and celebrated simpler folk. Will Rogers was Hollywood's biggest star in 1934, and after his untimely death, Shirley Temple held that special spot for four straight years. Hollywood's top filmmakers were Frank Capra and John Ford, who also evoked a way of life that was fading or had already vanished for most Americans—except on movie screens.

The Academy acknowledged Durbin and Rooney's role in evoking that lost era by awarding them both special Oscars in 1938 for "their significant contribution in bringing to the screen the spirit and personification of youth." Universal was also impressed with Durbin's economic "contribution," of course. Every one of her films had turned a sizable profit, invariably doing as well in foreign as in domestic markets. In fact, her films were so successful that Universal was able to charge exhibitors a 35 percent rental fee to run them rather than the usual 25 percent. Her two pictures in 1938 grossed $3.5 million at the box office—fully one-sixth of Universal's entire take on forty-seven releases. "It has long been a common Hollywood assumption," said *Fortune* magazine in a 1939 article, "that Durbin had been keeping that underprivileged studio [Universal] from bankruptcy single-handed."

A S important as Durbin was to Universal, Cliff Work did not involve himself with her pictures—or any other A-class productions for that matter. Work was a consummate company man with no qualms about concentrating his own efforts on the low end of studio operations. That was Universal's strong suit, and the one area that simply had to be regulated to ensure a steady supply of product and thus steady revenues. And it was obvious to Work when he arrived at Universal City that more discipline was needed in subfeature production. When he stepped in, Beebe and company were just completing *Flash Gordon's Trip to Mars*, a fifteen-part serial whose $168,700 budget had swollen to $192,600. Work gave Beebe the go-ahead on another sci-fi serial, *Buck Rogers*, but with explicit instructions to stay within its $177,000 budget. Western series production also was modified, with Work cutting the budgets for these B-grade sagas from $50,000 to $40,000. Even Johnny Mack Brown, the studio's reigning sagebrush star, was allowed only eight shooting days and budgets of $35,000 to $42,000 for his five-reelers. The heaviest cuts, though, came in program features, the sixty-to-seventy-minute melodramas and thrillers that ran as second features on the top half of double bills. Work held schedules to three weeks and cut budgets from the earlier average of $125,000 to under $100,000.

While Work had little direct involvement in A-class production, he and Blumberg did have definite plans for the studio's top creative talent. Both appreciated what Stahl, Whale, and Pasternak had done for Universal, but only Joe Pasternak was deemed essential to the present setup. Whale had done three films since swearing off the horror genre and doing *Show Boat* in 1936, but since then his value to Universal had fallen drastically, along with the quality of his films. Work intended to sustain the horror genre, but without Whale, who was headed for early retirement in the late 1930s as both his health and his spirits faded. Stahl presented a different problem altogether. He was a relic of the Laemmle regime, but one that still had to be accommodated, since Junior had signed him to a long-term deal in 1935 after his back-to-back hits, *Imitation of Life* and *Magnificent Obsession*. That contract gave Stahl $4,000 weekly and considerable authority over story and casting, but only by "mutual agreement" with the studio, something that Stahl and the studio had not reached since signing the contract. Stahl's only film since 1935 was a loan-out to MGM for *Parnell*, a ponderous biopic and one of Clark Gable's rare box-office failures.

Work was well aware of Stahl's bloated and excessive style, but he was determined to find something for his highest-paid director, and he finally did with *A Letter of Introduction*. Shades of *Frankenstein*, the project was a monstrous assemblage: part weepie, part screwball comedy, and part vaudeville show, sewn together to keep a half-dozen stars busy—including two wooden ones working with ventriloquist Edgar Bergen. The basic story was classic Stahl material, centering on an aspiring actress (Andrea Leeds) who shows up at the door of a fading, alcoholic film star (Adolphe Menjou) with a letter indicating she is his daughter by one of his previous marriages—a daughter he never knew existed. Complications arise when Menjou's vanity prevents him from admitting publicly that he is the girl's father, and she is mistaken for his "protégée"—i.e., his mistress—by everyone from the press and the public to her boyfriend and Menjou's fiancée. Despite the comic possibilities, Stahl played most of this to the melodramatic hilt, culminating in Menjou's suicidal leap in front of a taxi and a death-bed reconciliation with his daughter. Remarkably enough, the heavy-going drama was interspersed with comedy sketches featuring Edgar Bergen and his sidekick dummies, Charlie McCarthy and Mortimer Snerd. This was Bergen's first dramatic feature, but he was already well known from his work in vaudeville, radio, and comedy film shorts, for which he won a special Academy Award in 1937. He earned a flat fee of $100,000 for *Letter of Introduction*, which was $25,000 more than what top-billed Menjou drew. The vignettes with Bergen, McCarthy, and Snerd were oddly disconcerting, since Stahl seemed to have little idea how to integrate them into the melodramatic goings-on. He simply found an opportune time to interrupt the story and then shot Bergen as a virtual stage act, straight on from medium range to showcase his talents, cutting away occasionally to catch the reactions of the audience that invariably gathered—which was liable to happen anywhere given the illogic of the picture. Bergen and McCarthy did impromptu performances on the street, in their boardinghouse, even at Menjou's breakfast table.

The Bergen routines aside, *Letter of Introduction* had all the earmarks of an overblown Stahl melodrama. It was budgeted at $1.1 million and scheduled for fifty-four shooting days. On top of the $175,000 paid to Menjou and Bergen, Stahl's salary took another $240,000, since sixty weeks of accumulated time had to be charged against the production. The picture actually scored fairly well at the box office, but its success did not diminish Blumberg and Work's desire to get Stahl off the lot and thus off the payroll. Stahl did one last melodrama for Universal, in 1939. With *When Tomorrow Comes* he closed out a decade-long tenure with the company and headed into free-lance work.

Letter of Introduction was something of a watershed film for Universal, signaling not only Stahl's waning influence but also a shift to comedy vehicles for established radio and vaudeville stars, most of whom had already gone into movies. Blumberg signed a number of one- and two-picture deals in the late 1930s with such stars, including Bing Crosby, Edgar Bergen, W. C. Fields, and Mae West. Crosby had actually made his screen debut for Universal in 1930 before becoming a major star with Paramount. But by decade's end his career was declining and Paramount loaned him out freely, particularly to Universal for a series of second-rate musicals. Edgar Bergen and W. C. Fields were much more important to Universal's fortunes in the late 1930s. Once Bergen, McCarthy, and Snerd proved they were ready to graduate from comedy sketches to features, they were teamed with W. C. Fields for his Universal debut, *You Can't Cheat an Honest Man,* a star vehicle of considerable—and considerably offbeat—proportions.

The Fields-Bergen picture was budgeted at $700,000, with $100,000 paid to each of its stars. Fields was paid another $25,000 for the story, which he later claimed he'd scribbled on an envelope. As with most of the thirty-odd features he had done by 1938, the "story" was little more than a premise for Fields, who ad-libbed freely as the cameras turned. Director William Marshall started shooting in November 1938, with two staff writers trying to keep pace with Fields, quite literally writing the script while the picture was being shot. Production manager Murphy found this maddening, of course, though four weeks into the shoot he did receive "a form of a script" that Marshall and company "agreed would be adhered to after a fashion."

Actually, the lack of a shooting script and Fields's chronic ad-libbing were less of a problem than Fields's temperamental behavior, especially in dealing with his costar. The animosity that developed between Fields and Edgar Bergen became so intense that eventually, some six weeks into the shoot, Work decided to separate the two. He brought in veteran comedy director Edward Sedgwick and split the company into a "Fields unit" under Sedgwick's direction and a "Bergen unit" under Marshall. But Fields soon alienated Sedgwick as well, so Work turned to Eddie Cline, a seasoned comedy director whose career extended back to Mack Sennett's two-reelers in the teens. Remarkably, Marshall and Cline closed production on budget and only three days behind schedule. Due to the straightforward production style that required minimal editing, dubbing, and scoring, the picture involved very little postproduction. In a display of efficiency that would have been inconceivable at any of the major studios, *You Can't Cheat an Honest Man* was previewed six days after closing and shipped out a week later for a January 1939 release.

The box-office returns on *You Can't Cheat an Honest Man* were somewhat disappointing, but Blumberg and Work were encouraged by the project. Fields got along well with Cline, who could deal with Fields's erratic behavior and who, as a veteran of silent comedy, had little interest in complex stories or elaborate camera work and cutting. So Cline was able to counter Fields's anarchic approach to comedy with an efficient technical approach. Blumberg and Work signed Fields to a second picture, this time working with Mae West, another vaudevillian turned movie star who by 1939 was on the downside of her career. The project was *My Little Chickadee*, with Eddie Cline directing and Fields collaborating with West on the script. The Fields-West combination was a volatile one, and, wary of one another, both demanded approval of the script and the final cut of the picture. The script and Cline's directing style allowed them plenty of room for improvisation, which suited West as well as Fields. But by keeping one another in check, they brought an unexpected discipline to the production, which Cline had no trouble keeping on schedule and within its $625,000 budget.

Such discipline was altogether rare for a Universal feature during the Blumberg-Work regime. Work kept subfeature production under tight control, but developed an increasingly laissez-faire attitude toward top-feature production. What's more, he made little effort to beef up the supervisory ranks. Consequently, despite Murphy's efforts, feature filmmaking was a sustained exercise in crisis management. Most top features started shooting without finished screenplays—let alone continuity scripts and shooting schedules—and without detailed budgets as well. This tolerance for disorganization was becoming standard operating procedure, even for low-cost horror pictures. Consider *The Son of Frankenstein*, a 1939 release that was produced and directed by Rowland V. Lee, an experienced filmmaker and recent arrival at Universal. Lee took the picture into production in November 1938 with only a story outline and a budget range of $300,000 to $400,000. What story there was involved the son of Dr. Frankenstein, played by Basil Rathbone, who vies for control of his father's creature with a crazed and deformed shepherd. Karloff was back as the monster, but without the latent humanity and sensitivity of the earlier Whale-Balderston versions. Lugosi played the shepherd, Ygor, a condemned killer who has survived his own hanging (thus the deformity) and is using the creature to exact vengeance on the jurors.

The script was credited to Willis Cooper, who wrote the scenario as Lee shot. Even without a shooting script, Murphy fashioned a "very rough" budget and schedule in early December, once production was under way, which he set at $300,000 and twenty-seven days. There still was no script as Christmas approached, although Lee assured Work and Murphy that he would close before the holidays to avoid carrying any free-lance talent on salary during vacation. Work also was concerned about a January 10 shipping date. But Lee was still shooting on December 30, at which point Work devised a schedule with Murphy that kept the picture going day and night, with Ford Beebe and Lee alternating shifts. Production closed at 1:15 A.M. on January 5, and somehow the picture was cut and ready to preview by January 7 and was shipped three days later. The final cost on *The Son of Frankenstein* was $417,000, but the overages and production crises were forgotten when it emerged as Universal's first hit of 1939.

There would be other crises and other hit features for Universal that year. And like the Frankenstein sequel, each was a case study in chaotic filmmaking that somehow came together during and after production, despite Murphy's insistent efforts to establish more disciplined preproduction policies. As he lamented during production on *The Son of Frankenstein*, the problems "could have been materially remedied if we had had a completed script in the beginning from which an economical shooting schedule could have been prepared." He echoed that lament throughout the summer and fall of 1939 as one major project after another was started without script, budget, or schedule. In August Rowland Lee started shooting another horror film, *The Tower of London*, without the benefit of a script—though this time the situation was a bit less unnerving since the picture was a thinly veiled remake of *Richard III* and Lee could always turn to Shakespeare for inspiration. Again Lee came through, closing *The Tower of London* well under the $500,000 budget that Murphy finally devised. A rough cut revealed severe problems with the picture's finale, so Lee and Ford Beebe took it back into production for another week. That pushed its cost to $558,000, but the results were well worth it. *The Tower of London* was Lee's second horror hit for Universal that year, and he was being touted as another James Whale.

A more costly and crisis-ridden 1939 production was *First Love*, Durbin's fifth picture, with Pasternak and Manning devising the story and overseeing production, and Henry Koster back as director. By now Manning and Pasternak were much in demand all over the lot, and so little time was spent on script development before production opened in July. Murphy urged Work not to start the picture without a script, but Blumberg needed a Durbin picture by Christmas. Pasternak and

Together again: director Henry Koster (left) was reunited with Deanna Durbin and producer Joe Pasternak in 1939 for Durbin's fifth Universal musical, First Love.

Manning went ahead, confident they could turn out a routine Durbin hit if they stuck to the formula. This time around Durbin would play an orphan who plies her redemptive powers on a rich uncle and his snobbish family. In the process she falls for a local prep-school type, played by Robert Stack (in his screen debut, at age twenty), who was to bestow on Durbin her first screen kiss.

Pasternak's confidence and the formulaic nature of the story notwithstanding, *First Love* was the most chaotic shoot of the year at Universal City. Four weeks into production, Martin Murphy reported that the project was still without shooting schedule or detailed budget, "even though Bruce Manning is now back on the script which we were in hopes would prove our salvation." Two weeks later Koster and the writers were "evidently set on the story line," although the problems were far from over. "Unexpected sets are being called for," Murphy told Work, "even though we already have two of our largest stages completely filled with sets for this picture." All-day script sessions were held every Sunday, with Pasternak shuttling between the *First Love* meetings and those for *Destry Rides Again*, an offbeat comedy western with Jimmy Stewart and Marlene Dietrich that he was also producing—and that also went into production without script or budget. Even with the weekend script conferences, Murphy reported ten weeks into the shoot that Koster and company "continue writing from day to day and appear to be groping for material." Their problems were amplified by Durbin's lack of time on the set. As she matured physically and emotionally, Durbin became more concerned about her appearance and was spending over two hours daily on makeup, hairdressing, and wardrobe—besides the three hours mandated by state law for schooling. With the law limiting her to eight hours per day (and forty-eight hours per week), she was on the set less than three hours per day.

Pasternak finally closed *First Love* in mid-October, after ninety-one days in production; he had kept its cost just under $1 million. *Destry Rides Again* closed two weeks later, but only after Pasternak used Ford Beebe to shoot second-unit material both day and night. The Stewart-Dietrich western was previewed and shipped before Thanksgiving, at a final cost of $765,000. Both *First Love* and *Destry* benefited from the heavy holiday traffic, as did *The Tower of London*. All three were solid hits, contributing to Universal's year-end net profits of $1.2 million. Finishing well ahead of Columbia, UA, and RKO in 1939, Universal experienced its first profitable year since 1934 and best year since the silent era. Universal's success owed a great deal to Blumberg, who had the company's distribution network in excellent shape, as Cowdin expected he would when he hired him. But Cliff Work deserved most of the credit. Subfeature and B-movie production were cranking away, providing grist for the distribution mill. And as the new management team had hoped, Universal's A-class features were generating additional profits without draining resources.

Thus Universal's late-thirties surge involved a curious combination of discipline and disorganization, challenging the conventional wisdom about assembly-line filmmaking and the importance of continuity scripts as blueprints for feature productions. Work's "system" limited preparation to casting and crew assignments, setting a start date, and then proceeding with only a sort of vague conception of both the production and the finished product. Scripting and production design, more often than not, came together during shooting in a collaborative effort. The familiarity of the collaborators with one another and with certain star-genre formulas enabled them to somehow pull things together, and generally with minimal need for retakes or heavy postproduction.

This was no way to run a railroad, and it scarcely jibed with the widespread perception of Universal as the most factorylike of all the Hollywood studios. But there was really little else Blumberg and Work could do. They had low-budget and subfeature operations in ideal shape; indeed, this was the golden age of serial and B-western production for Universal. But the studio's financial margin for error was simply too slim to even attempt the same continuity and productivity at the high end of its operations. If the previous administrations had proven anything, it was that Universal could ill afford to expand and regulate first-run filmmaking—not without building up the technical staff and contract talent, and developing a solid production-management setup. Thus the lack of preparation and the reliance on outside talent, the undisciplined shoots and uneven feature output. Still it was working, thanks largely to Murphy and Pasternak, who maintained some semblance of order and quality control in top-feature production and turned out a few solid pictures per year. Perhaps *First Love, The Tower of London*, and *Destry Rides Again* weren't quite up to industry-wide standards in those glory years in Hollywood, but they were strong enough to win Universal a piece of the first-run market. And together with the rest of its output, they kept Universal in the thick of the action.

14

MGM:
Life After
Thalberg

While three successive adminis-
trations were struggling to keep Universal going in the late 1930s,
Louis Mayer kept MGM in its now-customary position far ahead of the
pack. Metro was the antithesis of Universal at the time—a profitable,
talent-laden studio geared to first-run productions and financed by revenues from an affiliated chain of prosperous first-class theaters. And
while the mood at Universal was one of sustained desperation, at Metro
there was a calm self-assurance, even a certain complacency. Thalberg's death in September 1936 had shaken that confidence, of course,
but Metro went on to finish the year stronger than ever, scoring profits
of over $10 million. There was continued success through 1937, when
MGM's net reached an all-time high of $14.3 million. Mayer credited
his new regime for the surge, though in fact it was the momentum
generated by the projects Thalberg had set in motion that was still
carrying Metro. In late 1937 that momentum waned, Mayer's management setup took hold, and the studio's profits and its lead over the
other majors did indeed begin to taper off.

And the longer Thalberg was gone, the more obvious it was that he
had been a vital counter to Louis Mayer. While Mayer was an administrator, Thalberg was a creative executive; while Mayer was cautious
and conservative, Thalberg was a risk-taker and innovator. Mayer was
straightforward and pragmatic, while Thalberg had a subtle, complex
mind. Both favored love stories, but Thalberg was a romantic and a

cynic, while Mayer was hopelessly sentimental. And both favored "quality" pictures, but Thalberg gauged quality in terms of style and inventive technique, while for Mayer it was a function of glamour, polish, and production costs. Thalberg also had supreme confidence in his own abilities and instincts as a filmmaker and he was willing to bet the studio's money on them. Back in 1933 he wrote a piece for the *Saturday Evening Post* suggesting that "the intelligent producer will go on experimenting—which in pictures means going on spending— until he believes in his own mind that he has made the best possible product." Such talk never sat well with Mayer, who did not mind heavy spending so long as he knew exactly what he was getting for it—a standard technicolor operetta with Jeanette MacDonald and Nelson Eddy, say, or a costume drama with Greta Garbo.

In spite of the long-standing dominance of Loew's theaters and Metro's resources, Mayer saw no reason to take the kinds of chances that Thalberg and Selznick seemed to thrive on. He favored more predictable and conventional products even at the prestige level, and thus he had always been more comfortable with Hunt Stromberg, who shared his preference for typecasting and star-genre formulations. But Mayer promoted these practices across the board—even in low-budget and series production, which became standard fare at Metro in the late 1930s.

Mayer's tastes and interests, no longer checked by Thalberg, steadily permeated Metro's operations in 1937–38. Mayer did not impose them directly, since he had virtually no involvement in day-to-day filmmaking. Rather, they filtered through the layers of management control that Mayer developed during his regime. Mayer was essentially a bureaucrat, presiding over an elaborate management-by-committee system. Production operations were run by an "Executive Committee" whose nine members still reflected the Schenck-Mayer-Thalberg triumvirate. There was committee chairman Mayer and his longtime associate and general manager, Eddie Mannix. There were two recent additions to the studio's executive staff, Sam Katz and Al Lichtman, who had been sent West by Nick Schenck in 1935 and 1936, respectively. The others were Thalberg men: Harry Rapf, Hunt Stromberg, Benny Thau, Bernie Hyman, and Larry Weingarten. Mayer renegotiated his own contract in 1937 and brought all of the committee members into the profit-sharing plan that once had been limited to Mayer, Thalberg, and Robert Rubin—the so-called Mayer group. The new arrangement gave Mayer $3,000 per week plus an annual bonus of 6.77 percent of Loew's profits, and it gave Rubin $2,000 per week plus 1.4 percent. The other executives' salaries and profit shares varied, with the largest shares (1.5 percent) going to Mannix, Stromberg, and Lichtman. The new pact boosted Mayer's 1937 income to $1.3 million, making him the highest-salaried individual in the United States that year, according to the U.S. Treasury Department.

The management glut, more than any other quality of the Mayer regime—more than the cautious and complacent market strategy, more than the predictability and cloying sentimentality of its pictures—was Metro's most distinctive and perhaps its most destructive characteristic. It was obviously a departure from Thalberg's central-producer setup. Back in 1927, MGM had produced seventy pictures with only seven supervisors, and Thalberg oversaw virtually all production. By 1937, the same number of pictures required twenty producers, eight of whom were also on Mayer's Executive Committee. With this shift to a more complex bureaucracy and a more heavily populated management system, filmmaking at MGM grew more rigidly efficient, the films themselves became more conventional, and innovation was implicitly discouraged. None of Metro's producers, not even the ones on the Executive Committee, had the kind of authority and creative control that Thalberg, Selznick, and Stromberg had during the mid-1930s.

The day-to-day efficiency and regimentation of Mayer's system was displayed daily in the studio's "Bulletin of Activities." The function of these fifteen- to twenty-page reports was stated on the cover:

> This Bulletin is issued Daily to familiarize you with:
> 1. Release schedule
> 2. Production shooting schedule
> 3. Production cutting and editing schedule
> 4. Advance production schedule
> 5. Producers assignments
> 6. Directors assignments
> 7. Writers assignments
> 8. Music assignments
> 9. Stock company assignments

These bulletins provide a blueprint of Metro's operations, and it's worth taking a close look at one from November 1937, just over a year after Mayer's committee system was installed. The bulletin of November 23, which ran sixteen pages, listed eighteen projects that were either in preparation, shooting, or editing. The schedule was designed for a one-picture-per-week output, with releases staggered by exactly seven days. The eighteen projects required thirteen different producers and fifteen directors. Those with more than one assignment were among MGM's less distinguished producers and directors, and their projects reflected as much. Producer Harry Rapf, for instance, had the heaviest load, with four assignments. All four were B-grade productions, and there were eight B pictures in all on the late-November bulletin—although the designation was made in the margin of Rapf's bulletin *in pencil,* since Mayer prohibited any formal reference to an MGM product as a B picture.

This skew toward second-rate productions marked a departure from Thalberg's system, as did the middle-management glut. But otherwise the above-the-line assignments worked much as they had under Thalberg. The star vehicle was still the prime organizing principle of Metro's production and marketing strategies. Producers were assigned on a per-annum basis, generally as caretakers of specific stars or star-genre formulas, while directors were assigned per picture. Thus producers knew well in advance what projects they would be handling and began working with writers long before directors were assigned. The November 23 bulletin specified sixty-six "advance productions"—that is, projects still in some stage of development. Of these, producers had been assigned to fifty-eight, writers to fifty-six, and directors to only four. The bulletin also makes it clear that both preproduction (especially story and script development) and postproduction (especially the cutting, dubbing, and scoring that occur after previews and retakes) were still very much in the producer's realm of authority. As with Thalberg's system, directors came on only during final preparation and stayed on a project only through its early editing stages.

The writers' assignments were a more complicated affair. There were a total of ninety-seven writers assigned to the fifty-five pictures still being scripted. Only twenty-nine projects had a single writer assigned to them; the others involved a combination of writers, working either in collaboration or separately. The amount of time spent on individual assignments varied widely—from 2 days to 167½ weeks. Of the ninety-seven different writers assigned, thirty-eight had been on the same project for at least ten weeks. Of those, twenty-two had been on for at least twenty weeks. Nine of those had been on the same assignment for at least thirty weeks, and two had been on for more than a year. As might be expected, the ones who had been on a single project thirty or more weeks were MGM's top writers—Charles MacArthur, Robert Hopkins, Robert Sherwood, Dashiell Hammett, and the like.

On November 23 there were five pictures actually shooting. Four were standard features with schedules of four to five weeks; the fifth was a MacDonald-Eddy operetta with a nine-week schedule. Only one picture was on schedule, but while the rest were behind, they were all moving at a reasonable pace. The cutting-editing schedule indicated that six Metro pictures were then in postproduction. The editing time required for all MGM pictures ranged from two to four weeks, with another six weeks in the lab for final processing and printing.

I F any project on the November 1937 docket exemplified MGM's changing direction under Mayer, it was "Family Vacation." Consider the project's pedigree. In 1935, Hunt Stromberg had produced an adaptation of Eugene O'Neill's play *Ah, Wilderness!*, a bittersweet portrait of male adolescence and coming of age in small-town America. It was a prestige production all the way, with Clarence Brown directing and with a cast that featured Lionel Barrymore, Spring Byington, Eric Linden, Cecilia Parker, and Mickey Rooney. Then some two years later, in a seemingly unrelated development, low-budget producer Lucien Hubbard was preparing a vehicle for Lionel Barrymore based on *Skidding*, a second-rate Broadway play. The play was a courtroom drama, centering on a Judge Hardy, to be played by Barrymore, whose home life was of only marginal importance to the story.

At about the same time, Mayer and the committee were looking for a project to showcase Mickey Rooney, who was then MGM's third-ranked male juvenile, behind Freddie Bartholomew and Jackie Cooper. A favorite of Mayer's, Rooney was a natural actor and gifted entertainer who had yet to find a proper outlet for all that manic energy and swaggering self-assurance. Mayer and company decided to expand the domestic subplot in *Skidding* by interjecting a nostalgic, romanticized family portrait such as that in *Ah, Wilderness!* In fact, the entire cast from Stromberg's production would be used again, except for Eric Linden. This time Mickey Rooney, who only had a bit part as the kid brother in *Ah, Wilderness!* would play the adolescent male. Mayer instructed Kay Van Riper, who was scripting *Skidding*, to add more humor and enlarge the role of Andy Hardy, the judge's son, who was mentioned only once in her initial treatment. The movie title was

MGM's impressive lineup of prepubescent stars, circa 1936, included (from left) Freddie Bartholomew, Mickey Rooney, Deanna Durbin, Judy Garland, and Jackie Cooper.

changed to A *Family Affair* and Hubbard produced it on a seventeen-day schedule, with the efficient George B. Seitz directing.

A Family Affair did a tidy business, and soon exhibitors were clamoring for another "Hardy picture." Mayer was delighted and the Executive Committee immediately set producers J. J. Cohn and Lou Ostrow to work on "A Family Vacation," with the prospect of developing a series of Hardy pictures. They were not to be like MGM's Tarzan or Thin Man pictures, though, which came out every one or two years. Metro would go all out with the Hardy pictures. The rationale was obvious enough. Not only the casting but the sets, props, music, even the story formula itself could be standardized, rendering what was already a low-budget enterprise that much more efficient and economical. There would have to be casting changes, since Barrymore was too important an actor to be tied up with a series; MGM also had bigger plans for Byington. So Judge and Ma Hardy were played by Lewis Stone and Fay Holden in "A Family Vacation," which further reduced costs and shifted the focus to Rooney's character. When the second Hardy Family installment started shooting in October 1937, Van Riper started "Family Affair #3." By late November "A Family Vacation"—whose title was changed to *You're Only Young Once* for release—was cut, dubbed, and scored. Mayer shipped it to New York before the holidays, just as shooting started on *Judge Hardy's Children*, the third series installment.

The Hardy series was under way. O'Neill's *Ah, Wilderness!* had "degenerated" into a low-cost movie formula that MGM turned out at a remarkable pace, and that indicated Mayer's commitment to cost-efficiency and his conviction that Metro could spoon-feed sentimental Americana to audiences in regular doses. Satisfying Mayer's—and the public's—longing for the naive innocence of small-town life, the stories celebrated home and family and, especially once Rooney's character took hold, the myriad rites of male adolescent passage. Lewis Stone, a longtime featured player who had never quite ascended to star status at MGM, provided an ideal father figure, but it was Rooney who carried the series. His Andy Hardy was a kind of centripetal narrative force that picked up speed with each picture, as character and actor steadily merged into a cultural icon of perpetual motion and perpetual adolescence. The women in the series were necessary but peripheral. Fay Holden's Ma Hardy was a low-key matriarch, much less visible and dramatically significant than the Judge, while Cecilia Parker was only a token sibling as Andy's sister. The most important females in the Hardy pictures, of course, were the objects of Andy's burgeoning sexual desire—the likes of Ann Rutherford, Lana Turner, Judy Garland, Ruth Hussey, and various other MGM ingenues.

With *Judge Hardy's Children* and the three subsequent installments in 1938, the basic cast and crew members of the Hardy unit were set. Its key members included:

STAFF AND CREW	CAST
Executive producer: J. J. Cohn	Judge Hardy: Lewis Stone
Associate producer: Lou Ostrow	Ma Hardy: Fay Holden
Director: George B. Seitz	Marian: Cecilia Parker
Writer: Kay Van Riper	Andy: Mickey Rooney
Script supervisor: Carey Wilson	Aunt Millie: Sara Haden
Cinematographer: Lew White	Polly Benedict: Ann Rutherford
Sound: Ralph Shugart	
Cutting: Ben Lewis	

The Seitz unit, as it came to be called at Metro, turned out Hardy pictures virtually nonstop for two years, averaging about one every three months. Even as the profits soared and the Hardys became the most familiar clan in the Western world, Metro stayed with the Seitz unit, and for good reason. Given MGM's superior resources, even these relatively low-grade products were on a par with the A-class output of any other studio. Still the Hardy pictures lacked the slick, superficial polish and sophistication of so many MGM releases; they had a certain innocent charm that was a function of both the subject matter and the modest production values. Equally important, these pictures involved an ideal melding of Metro personnel on both sides of the camera, and not even Rooney's meteoric rise to top stardom upset the unit's balance and productivity. Rooney's ascent did affect the series, though, as was apparent from the titles alone: the focus shifted from the entire family to the younger generation and finally to Andy himself with *Love Finds Andy Hardy,* the fourth installment. Of the dozen subsequent films in the series, only two would carry titles without Andy's name or some direct reference to his character, and both of these were scripted in 1938, when Rooney's impact was just becoming evident and before *Love Finds Andy Hardy* had even been conceived.

In fact, *Love Finds Andy Hardy* was put together virtually overnight, in an effort not only to exploit Rooney's popularity but also to team him with Judy Garland, another promising juvenile at MGM. The two had recently costarred in *Thoroughbreds Don't Cry,* a low-grade horse-racing picture, and in the spring of 1938 both were between assignments. Garland was penciled in to play the lead in an upcoming blockbuster musical, *The Wizard of Oz,* which was bogged down in preproduction. Rooney was free until *Boys Town,* which was set to shoot that summer. The Executive Committee wanted an interim project for the pair—a musical, possibly, or another Hardy picture. In late

March the story department turned up a tale of teenage courtship, "Oh, What a Tangled Web," published in the September 1936 issue of *Cosmopolitan*. Van Riper was on another assignment, so the project was given to William Ludwig, who by April 11 had transformed the story into a Hardy family scenario with a few musical numbers. Producer Lou Ostrow supplied the title "Love Finds Andy Hardy," and he met with Ludwig, Seitz, and Carey Wilson in mid-April for two days of rewrites. Ostrow also sought the counsel of Judge Hardy himself, sending the script to Lewis Stone and asking him to "please read this for me and come in with that armful of swell criticisms and suggestions you always have."

Ostrow scheduled the Hardy picture to start shooting May 1 for a midsummer release, but he ran into trouble with executive producer J. J. Cohn about the title and the overall emphasis on Andy Hardy. Cohn felt that "one more picture is needed to hammer home the Judge Hardy and Hardy family idea." Mayer agreed, and in late April his administrative assistant, Frank Whitbeck, sent a memo indicating Mayer's decision "to abandon the title 'Love Finds Andy Hardy' for the next Hardy picture." New titles were solicited, with the customary $50 prize offered to the person whose suggestion would actually be used. By May 5, 176 new titles had been proposed, each displaying Mayer's preferred emphasis, but in the meantime Mayer had Whitbeck confer with Loew's market research people. The result was that Whitbeck recommended "the title 'Love Finds Andy Hardy' be retained because this definitely points up Mickey Rooney and, of course, Rooney is hot at the box office right now." Title intact, *Love Finds Andy Hardy* went into production on May 16.

Ostrow and Seitz scheduled a nineteen-day shoot, plus another week for musical numbers. Rooney was slated to work all nineteen days. Judy Garland was slated for seventeen shooting days during principal photography, and she also dominated postproduction. Seitz closed the shoot on schedule, June 7, only five and a half weeks ahead of the July 15 release date. Ostrow, Seitz, and editor Ben Lewis spent three days on a rough cut, and then Ostrow and Seitz prepared a program of retakes requiring only eight setups—less than one day's shooting. These were done on Monday, June 20, with the rest of the week devoted to Garland's three musical numbers, which were arranged and recorded by Roger Edens, Garland's vocal coach and studio Svengali. Seitz shot the musical numbers at week's end, with Garland lip-synching the songs after each had been recorded. The last of these was done on Saturday, June 25. Exactly one week later a rough cut of the picture was previewed at the United Artists theater in Long Beach.

Despite the phenomenal speed of the postproduction process, Os-

Publicity photo for Love Finds Andy Hardy, *the series installment that put Rooney's title character squarely in the driver's seat. To Rooney's right is Judy Garland; in the background are series regulars Lewis Stone, Cecilia Parker, Fay Holden, and Sara Haden.*

trow and company were convinced that they had a quality product. Spirits were high by July 13, 1938, when *Love Finds Andy Hardy* opened at Loew's State in New York City and at Grauman's Chinese Theatre in Hollywood. They soared even higher a day later when Loew's sales department reported that in the past year only six pictures, all of them expensive prestige jobs, had opened to better business in the two first-run palaces. Lou Ostrow deserved much of the credit—though, following the Thalberg tradition, he refused screen credit. Ostrow was listed among MGM personnel as "attached to the J. J. Cohn unit," and when New York inquired about producer credit on *Love Finds Andy Hardy*, the studio explained that "Lou believes that neither his name nor that of the majority of producers sells tickets at the box office."

Stars sold tickets, of course, and in 1938 Rooney was among Metro's top pitchmen. Just as *Love Finds Andy Hardy* hit, he started *Boys Town,* an A-class production that teamed him with Spencer Tracy, who since coming over from Fox in 1935 had established himself as the studio's consummate dramatic actor. Tracy's understated portrayal of Father Flanagan, founder of Omaha's home for wayward boys, perfectly balanced Rooney's histrionics as a cynical street tough who is redeemed by patience, love, and understanding. Tracy's performance salvaged the otherwise maudlin melodrama, and it won him a second straight Academy Award (he won in 1937 for *Captains Courageous*, in which Rooney played a supporting role) and a slot, along with Rooney, on the exhibitors' coveted top-ten list of stars for 1938. The top spot went to Fox's Shirley Temple for the fourth straight year, but five of the next six on the 1938 list were Metro stars: Gable was No. 2, Rooney No. 4, Tracy No. 5, Robert Taylor No. 6, and Myrna Loy No. 7. Temple faltered the next few years, while Tracy and Rooney kept climbing. Soon Tracy and Gable were in a dead heat, but neither could keep pace with Mickey Rooney. Two of the 1939 series installments, *Out West with the Hardys* and *The Hardys Ride High*, were among the biggest hits of the year, and in late 1939 America's theater owners named Rooney the industry's top box-office star—the first of three con-secutive years for Rooney atop the poll.

Rooney's ascent in 1938–39 ran parallel with Deanna Durbin's, but it's worth noting that Durbin never made the exhibitors' poll. This may have had something to do with their different screen images. Rooney was the center of a rock-solid nuclear family in small-town America, while Durbin invariably was depicted as a victim of broken homes and fragmented families. More likely, though, the difference was more a function of the production and marketing operations of their respective studios. Universal lacked leverage in the first-run market and also lacked the resources to exploit Durbin's popularity—at least to the extent that MGM exploited Rooney's. Not only did her pictures make less money, but she made fewer films. From late 1936 through 1940, when her popularity peaked, Durbin made only nine pictures, a total that Rooney equaled with his Andy Hardy vehicles alone. All told, Rooney did twenty-seven pictures from 1937 through 1940, three times Durbin's output.

M E T R O ' S low-cost Hardy pictures proved invaluable when a late-Depression slump hit the industry in 1938–39. Profits for Loew's/MGM held at around $10 million both years, equaling the combined net profits of all the other major studios. Of the top fifteen moneymak-ers in 1938–39, five were MGM products, and Rooney starred in three. Rooney clearly was a bright spot in the studio's late-1930s fortunes, and one that indicated its newfound capacity for efficiency and star-genre formulation. But Mayer and his Executive Committee were growing concerned about the high end of MGM's production spectrum —about the high-cost, high-stakes pictures that had been Metro's spe-cialty, but no longer were paying off as they once had. Stromberg could still deliver MacDonald-Eddy operettas like *Maytime* and *Sweethearts* or lavish costume melodramas like *Marie Antoinette* and *Pride and Prejudice*, but these rarely displayed the wit, sophistication, or romance —or the box-office returns—that typified Thalberg's and Selznick's productions. Nor was there anyone at the studio who understood how to vary the roles of MGM stars and thus continually revitalize their careers. This was where Thalberg had best complemented Mayer over the years, and after Thalberg's death Mayer grew acutely aware of the need for a "creative executive," a producer who could handle a few prestige productions per annum and also oversee story selection and script development to maximize the studio's most important resource, its stars.

Significantly, Mayer had to look beyond Metro's core of bureaucrats and company men to find such a filmmaker. His choice was Mervyn LeRoy, who became the top producer at MGM in the late 1930s. LeRoy had impressed Mayer back in 1934 when he came over from Warners to direct *Tugboat Annie*, Metro's biggest moneymaker that year. His continued success at Warners convinced Mayer that he was the type of creative producer and administrator that MGM needed, and after a period of intense courtship following Thalberg's death, LeRoy bolted Warners in late 1937 to join Metro. From the moment he arrived at Culver City, it was obvious that LeRoy was not just another MGM producer. He was given an executive office on the third floor of the new Thalberg Building, alongside the offices of Benny Thau, Sam Katz, and Eddie Mannix, and a weekly salary of $6,000—which Mayer announced as $3,000, to avoid resentment from the other producers. LeRoy immediately began consulting with the Executive Committee on Metro's entire program. He was given four top assignments, including *The Wizard of Oz*, MGM's biggest production of 1938–39.

Scheduled for four months of principal photography and musical recording, *Oz* was far beyond the scope of anything LeRoy had done at Warners. It was excessive even by MGM's standards. A MacDonald-Eddy operetta might push a million dollars, a few projects like *Captains Courageous* reached $1.5 million, and only *Ben-Hur* and *Mutiny on the Bounty* had topped the $2 million mark. *Oz* was budgeted at well over $2.5 million—five times Metro's investment in its recent Hardy musical—and its final costs reached $2,777,000.

The inspiration for *Oz* in terms of scope came from David Selznick, who was putting together *Gone With the Wind* at the time and working out a deal with Metro for the services of Clark Gable. The inspiration for *Oz* in terms of story, subject, and tone came from Walt Disney's debut feature-length production, *Snow White and the Seven Dwarfs*, an animated musical fantasy that was released in December 1937.

When *Snow White* began breaking box-office records nationwide, Mayer took over negotiations for the rights to *Oz*, closing the deal for Frank Baum's classic children's fantasy for $75,000. By then LeRoy had initiated script development and casting, both fairly difficult tasks because of the fantasy angle and the fact that *Oz* was by no means a star vehicle. In fact, LeRoy was a bit nervous about using Judy Garland —a talented but untested $500-a-week ingenue—for the lead. But Garland would be getting able support from such top vaudeville troupers as Ray Bolger, Bert Lahr, Jack Haley, and Frank Morgan, each of whom earned five to six times her salary. LeRoy felt better after he saw Garland's work in *Love Finds Andy Hardy*—and so did Louis Mayer, who had begun to wonder whether he did the right thing back in 1936 by keeping Garland instead of Deanna Durbin.

The Wizard of Oz confirmed Mayer's judgment about Garland, and it also indicated that LeRoy had the makings of a top producer. But in the long run, *Oz* was most significant as a breakthrough project not for Garland or LeRoy but for another Metro producer, Arthur Freed. Mayer and LeRoy knew going into the project that its most important elements were the music and the below-the-line factors like art direction, set design, costuming, and the overall production values. In these areas Mayer relied on Arthur Freed, who had come to Metro a decade earlier as a lyricist. Over the years Freed had been heavily involved in musical production at MGM, and also had become Louis Mayer's chief confidant and troubleshooter. It was because of Freed's encouragement that Mayer first went after *Oz*, and Mayer in turn assigned Freed —working uncredited at $1,500 per week—to keep LeRoy and the project on track for its nine months of preproduction. Freed collaborated with art director Cedric Gibbons, set designer Edwin Willis, and Adrian, whose department created hundreds of costumes. He also worked closely with composer Harold Arlen and lyricist E. Y. (Yip) Harburg, whose music was essential to the film's success—not only as musical interludes but as a key factor in both story and character development.

Most of this work Freed completed before Mayer and LeRoy decided on a director in mid-September 1938. Second-rate staffer Richard Thorpe got the nod, indicating that Mayer was satisfied with the preparation of the picture and that he assumed LeRoy, who had been a top director at Warners, would be acting as a virtual producer-director. But after two weeks of shooting it was evident that LeRoy needed more than a mechanic to direct *Oz*, and Thorpe was taken off the picture. There followed a succession of top MGM directors—George Cukor, Victor Fleming, and King Vidor—who contributed to *The Wizard of*

Until his work on The Wizard of Oz *and* Babes in Arms, *Arthur Freed was known at MGM primarily as a lyricist. Here he rehearses a group of chorines for a number in* Broadway Melody of 1938.

Oz and also worked on David Selznick's *Gone With the Wind,* in production at the same time. MGM had a sizable stake in that picture—$1.25 million plus the services of Clark Gable in exchange for distribution rights and half the net profits—which explains Mayer's willingness to loan his directors to Selznick. The shuttling of directors disrupted both projects, but it had little effect on the quality or integrity of either picture. Fleming received director's credit on both, but each was ultimately a producer's picture.

A R T H U R F R E E D was all but oblivious to this game of musical directors' chairs in late 1938 and early 1939. Once he finished the preproduction work on *Oz,* he turned his attention to *Babes in Arms,* his debut project as a full-fledged MGM producer. His work on *Oz* had won him the task of adapting this 1937 Rodgers and Hart stage hit, and once he started preparing, his only real concern about *Oz* was when he would be getting Judy Garland, who was to costar in his picture with Mickey Rooney. LeRoy and his directors were running well behind on *Oz*—the picture was actually in production for a hundred days—but Freed didn't mind waiting. LeRoy's projected five-month postproduction schedule would put *Oz* out just before *Babes in Arms*, and Garland's performance was bound to give Freed's picture added momentum at the box office. *Oz* also was giving Garland invaluable experience and confidence as a musical performer.

Babes in Arms would be quite another enterprise, though, and infinitely better suited to Metro's resources and changing house style. In fact, Rooney was more important to Freed's conception of the project than Garland, since Freed saw it as a melding of the backstage musical and the Andy Hardy formula—brought together with an eye to the balance sheet since Mayer insisted on a budget ceiling of half a million dollars. Rodgers and Hart's play was one of those "Hey kids, let's put on a show" types, with the musical numbers passed off as "rehearsals" leading up to a climactic "amateur" show. The kids were supposedly offspring of vaudeville stars, a premise that provided a modicum of credibility for their musical talents and show-biz savvy. But no more than a modicum was required in this upbeat musical fantasy. Still, the obvious ties to Warners' backstage musicals in terms of both story and budget constraints sent Freed after Busby Berkeley, whose work at Warner Bros. was ideal training for *Babes in Arms*. Berkeley was still at Warners, although the musical was no longer a studio staple. With help from LeRoy, who first brought Berkeley to Warners back in 1932 for *42nd Street*, Freed convinced the director-choreographer to sign with MGM. Berkeley took a sizable pay cut for the job (from $2,250 per week at Warners to $1,500 at MGM), but the cut seemed well worth it since Metro had a greater investment in musical production and the best resources in the business. Berkeley also knew that MGM rewarded box-office success with salary hikes.

When Berkeley's contract with Warners lapsed in January 1939, Freed already had *Babes in Arms* well into preproduction. But with the delays on *Oz* preventing them from going into production, Freed and Berkeley took the opportunity to fine-tune the musical arrangements and the screenplay. While Berkeley worked on the choreography and production design, Freed and Roger Edens reworked the arrangements and orchestration on several of the Rodgers and Hart songs, including such classics as "The Lady Is a Tramp," and "Where or When." Freed also had time to put the script through another rewrite. He still felt there were serious story problems, and in late April he asked Kay Van Riper to do a complete overhaul while she was between Andy Hardy pictures. Van Riper knew the Rooney persona inside out, and her two-week rewrite added just the energy and innocent charm Freed wanted. Her contribution was significant enough, in fact, to warrant shared screen credit with Jack MacGowan, who had worked on the script six months earlier.

The script was squared away by early May, and Freed sent *Babes in Arms* into production. It was budgeted at $664,000, and the fifty-day schedule called for ten days rehearsing, thirty-four days shooting, and six days recording. The first week was spent recording with Edens and rehearsing with Berkeley, and the cameras started rolling on May 12. Berkeley and cinematographer Ray June started with the "book," averaging about ten setups and three and a half script scenes daily through the first four weeks of production. By the time they started the musical numbers on June 20, the budget had inflated to just over $700,000 but the picture was still on schedule. The shoot began to fall behind at that point, due mainly to the frequent skull sessions involving Freed, Berkeley, and Roger Edens, who continually reworked the musical numbers during production. These sessions were crucial, however, and not only to *Babes in Arms*. Freed, Berkeley, and Edens were laying the conceptual, artistic, and personal groundwork for years of collaboration—which included several hit variations on this same juvenile backstage formula with Garland and Rooney.

Even with the rehearsal days written into the schedule, shooting was interrupted fairly regularly from mid-June onward for conferences and unscheduled rehearsals. Consider, for example, an excerpt from The Daily Production Report describing how Berkeley, Freed, and company spent the day of June 19, when they had the entire cast and crew on call for rehearsals.

900–1005	Mr. Edens playing orchestration of Minstrel Number for Mr. Berkeley. . . .
1005–1055	Mr. Berkeley, Mr. Edens, and Mr. Stoll [the conductor] discussing presentation of number with Mr. Freed.
1055–1145	Mr. Berkeley outlining sequences in number and discussing wardrobe. . . .
1145–1220	Mr. Berkeley outlining requirements for number with Ray June. . . .
1220–110	Mr. Freed and Mr. Berkeley discuss lyrics of "Babes in Arms."
110–210	LUNCH
210–300	Wait for director—Mr. Freed had wanted him to see music number from *Rose Marie*—running same in Projection Room.
300–400	Rehearse.

The "Minstrel" and "Babes in Arms" numbers made up the finale and were the two most important sequences in the picture. The last four weeks of production were devoted exclusively to these two numbers, with the time split fairly evenly between rehearsing and shooting.

Mickey Rooney and Judy Garland in the finale from Babes in Arms, *Arthur Freed's first musical production at Metro.*

Roger Edens worked closely with Berkeley on both numbers, and Freed was consulted throughout, often by phone from the set. Garland was occasionally tardy, and one entire day was lost when she was called unexpectedly for retakes on *Oz*, costing Freed's production $8,563. But there was none of the difficult behavior that plagued Garland's later career. The production closed on July 18, eleven days behind schedule and $82,000 over budget. Its cost by early August, which included retakes, was just under $750,000—two million dollars less than *The Wizard of Oz*.

Oz premiered at the Loew's Capitol in New York on August 17, 1939, after a massive promotional campaign. It was accompanied during its Capitol run by a stage show with Garland and Rooney. This was the first time in almost five years that the Capitol had offered a live act along with a feature film, and the added entertainment undoubtedly contributed to the box-office records *Oz* set during its initial weeks in release. On opening day alone it played to a phenomenal 37,000 paid admissions. By week's end it had generated $93,000 in receipts at the Capitol, roughly twice the usual take on a prestige hit. But despite its quick start, *Oz* slowed in the hinterlands and actually ran out of steam in its initial release—a remarkable fact, considering its stamina as an annual television event throughout the decades. By the time MGM released *Babes in Arms* in mid-October, *Oz* had settled into a solid but unspectacular run. As these weekend figures from late October indicate, it was lagging behind *Babes in Arms* and several other top MGM releases, even in major markets:

DENVER	*Babes in Arms*	$6,527
	The Women	5,766
	Andy Hardy Gets Spring Fever	5,467
	The Wizard of Oz	5,400
BALTIMORE	*Babes in Arms*	8,948
	Boys Town	8,668
	The Women	6,787
	Andy Hardy Gets Spring Fever	5,811
	The Wizard of Oz	5,308

After *Babes in Arms* completed its domestic and overseas run, its gross totaled $3,335,000, resulting in a tidy profit for Loew's/MGM. *Oz* grossed $3,017,000, which, given its production cost of $2.77 million plus heavy promotional and distribution expenses, translated into a loss of nearly $1 million on its initial release. The picture itself was partly to blame. *Oz* is now considered a classic and a masterpiece, and rightly so, but critical and popular response at the time was mixed. Even more important was Loew's sales and marketing campaign, which was aggressive by prestige-picture standards but simply not up to the demands of a blockbuster musical. Selznick would demonstrate with the December release of *Gone With the Wind* what it took to exploit a picture of that magnitude—inflated prices, reserved seating, six-figure advertising budget, carefully orchestrated release strategy. Loew's/MGM assisted in Selznick's efforts and scored a sizable profit, but those efforts only reinforced the fact, for Schenck as well as Mayer, that the risks and headaches of gargantuan blockbusters were best left to independents like Selznick, Goldwyn, and Disney.

The Wizard of Oz was not Metro's only disappointment in 1938–39. Other ambitious pictures also failed to meet box-office projections— films like *Marie Antoinette, Broadway Serenade,* and *The Great Waltz.* These were designed to entertain the moviegoing masses as well as more sophisticated audiences, but they were not doing well in either first- or subsequent-run markets. In fact, Metro's most consistent success was coming via second-rate releases, particularly its low-cost series pictures, which were multiplying rapidly in the late 1930s. Besides the Hardy and occasional Tarzan and Thin Man pictures, which all had strong first-run potential, there were the Maisie pictures with Ann Sothern and the Dr. Kildare pictures with Lew Ayres and Lionel Barrymore. These were designed and marketed as virtual programmers, subpar features destined to open in second- or third-run theaters at the top half of a double bill.

This change in production and marketing strategy put MGM and Loew's on less compatible terms than in earlier years. Loew's theater chain was still solid and profitable, with its 128 houses in the United States and Canada, 76 of which were in the New York area. Of those outside New York, all but five were first-run houses in cities like Denver and Baltimore. But while these theaters were profitable for Loew's, they now accounted for only about 15 percent of MGM's revenues, since the studio was steadily skewing its productions away from the first-run market, and thus away from Loew's strengths. Loew's, in turn, had to rely more heavily on other studios for first-class product. What's more, the Loew's sales staff, forced to develop a different strategy for selling MGM's pictures, now concentrated more heavily on the nation's 16,000 subsequent-run houses. In the past, when Loew's had promised so many Garbos or Gables or all-stars to exhibitors, practically all MGM pictures were classed together. Now, with the growing disparity between MGM's features, Loew's had to sell them in different categories. Four or so top pictures were marketed as "super-specials," which returned 40 percent of their receipts to Loew's as a rental fee. Another ten high-quality features would command a return of 35 percent, and ten lesser features brought 30 percent. The rest were relegated to the program class, distributed on a flat-fee rental basis, and returned only a fraction of what a top feature earned.

This sales policy clearly was not as profitable as a straight first-run strategy, but it ensured profits to both MGM and Loew's—though it also contributed to the steady erosion of MGM's economic and artistic superiority. Metro was still very much on top at decade's end, though

Mayer was feeling less complacent than he had been a few years earlier. MGM had three nominees for the best-picture Oscar in 1939: *Gone With the Wind,* a Selznick production that Loew's/MGM simply distributed; *The Wizard of Oz,* a million-dollar loser at the box office; and *Ninotchka,* a Garbo picture that was doing subpar business because of the war-torn European market which had always been essential to the success of Garbo's pictures. Oddly enough, MGM's $9.5 million in profits in 1939 came primarily from Rooney's pictures and a few other mid-range features. The kind of prestige-level hits that had seemed to roll off the assembly line a few years before—pictures like *Grand Hotel* and *Mutiny on the Bounty,* *A Tale of Two Cities* and *The Great Ziegfeld*—were rare commodities by the late thirties. Given the studio's resources and Loew's market skew, MGM had to keep turning out big pictures. But all too often the results were overpriced, overproduced deadweights like *Broadway Serenade* and *The Great Waltz.*

MGM, it seems, had peaked early and now was curiously out of synch with Hollywood's golden age. There's no telling how Thalberg would have handled the changing tastes and improving market conditions as the Depression wound down, but the fact is that neither Schenck nor Mayer was willing to take the kinds of risks that Thalberg considered essential to the picture business when he was supervising production—risks that had put MGM at the top of the industry. Nor were they willing to give Metro's producers the kind of authority and creative control Thalberg and Selznick were given in the mid-1930s. Metro was only as good as its producers, and as long as filmmakers like Arthur Freed worked their way up through the system and could deal with Mayer's management-by-committee setup, there was hope that quality would be defined in something more than technical and budgetary terms. But few others were emerging from the bureaucratic ranks, and without them, Metro-Goldwyn-Mayer was looking more and more like just another major studio.

15

Selznick and Hitchcock:
Balance of Power

In early March 1939, Kay Brown finally closed the Hitchcock deal. Signing the portly British director had been one of her first assignments after being promoted to "eastern representative" of SIP in 1937. Knowing how badly both Selznick and Hitchcock wanted the deal, Brown assumed it would be a brief courtship. The only problem, she figured, would be dickering with Myron Selznick, who happened to be Hitchcock's U.S. agent. But the Selznick-Hitchcock courtship dragged on for nearly two years and proved to be as difficult as the eventual seven-year marriage, which was one of the most complex and fruitful alliances between a producer and a director in Hollywood's history. Only the Darryl Zanuck–John Ford coupling over at 20th Century-Fox even came close. The marital metaphor was apt in each case; the Selznick-Hitchcock and Zanuck-Ford unions were very much like difficult marriages, sustained by mutual dependence and a shared commitment to their offspring—only it was motion pictures, not the kids, that kept them together.

T H E Selznick-Hitchcock courtship began in May 1937, just as Hitchcock finished shooting *Young and Innocent* in Britain and as Selznick was writing *Nothing Sacred* in a hotel room with Ben Hecht in New York City. At the time Selznick was hitting his stride as an independent producer and Hitchcock was the top producer-director in Great Britain. Hitchcock's stock was also up in the States, due especially to the success of *The Man Who Knew Too Much* and *The 39 Steps*. As political and financial conditions in England deteriorated during the late 1930s, Hitchcock relished the idea of working in Hollywood. Selznick offered him a one-year, two-picture deal for $100,000, but Hitchcock declined, content for the time being to play Selznick off against other interested studios, particularly MGM. But Selznick was determined, and on June 11, the day before he opened production on *Nothing Sacred*, he sent a wire to Kay Brown and his other New York executives: "IMPORTANT! I think it would be a great mistake to pass up Hitchcock or let him go without a struggle." Selznick was even willing to share Hitchcock with Metro, if necessary, but he insisted that Brown do all that she could to sign him. "What makes the Hitchcock matter so important," said Selznick, "is that he is a producer as well as a director actually." Selznick desperately wanted to increase SIP's output and satisfy UA's product demand, and a producer-director like Hitchcock could shepherd projects from conception through release with Selznick simply monitoring production while he developed his own personal projects.

Hitchcock was not the only producer-director Selznick was after at the time. He was also courting Frank Capra, Mervyn LeRoy, Gregory La Cava, and Leo McCarey in mid-1937, hoping to sign one or more of them into the SIP-UA fold. In fact his most ardent courtship involved not Hitchcock but Capra, who Selznick felt was "unquestionably the ranking producing director in the business." Capra had outgrown Columbia, where he turned out such hit comedies as *It Happened One Night* and *Mr. Deeds Goes to Town* but felt stifled due to the company's meager resources and its belligerent studio boss, Harry Cohn. Selznick offered Capra a flat fee of $200,000 per picture or 25 percent of the net profits, whichever was greater; he also promised million-dollar budgets and top stars, and even gave vague assurances of creative freedom. It was an attractive deal, as were Selznick's offers to the other filmmakers. But not attractive enough—none of them ever worked for SIP. Nor did William Wellman or George Cukor, both of whom Selznick expected to stay on after *Nothing Sacred* and *Gone With the Wind*. Whatever the salaries and resources at SIP, Hollywood's top directors preferred to take their chances elsewhere, particularly now that prestige pictures were being turned out by every important company in Hollywood.

The reaction of Hollywood's "producing directors" to Selznick's overtures was scarcely surprising, considering the reputation he was quickly developing in that one-industry town. Though Selznick rarely interfered with directors on the set, his tight control over story selection and script development was already legend, and was bound to concern any director accustomed to acting as his own producer. And Selznick always was looking for ways to control camera work and editing as well. In the summer of 1937 William Cameron Menzies became SIP's production designer, and Selznick praised the "splendid and efficient manner" in which Menzies, under his supervision, "laid out the cutting and continuity" on several sequences in *Tom Sawyer*. Selznick felt this might provide something he had "long sought for, which is a pre-cut picture" with up to "80 percent on paper before we grind the cameras."

Selznick displayed his desire for preproduction control even more openly that same summer in an incident involving director John Ford and SIP executive Merian Cooper. The duo had worked together at RKO during the mid-1930s, and when Cooper left RKO to create Pioneer Pictures, he took Ford with him under personal contract, thus drawing Ford into the SIP-Pioneer merger in 1936. Cooper, as a vice president and executive producer for SIP, had his own unit, and in the spring of 1937 he gave Ford the go-ahead to develop a story he liked in *Collier's* called "Stage to Lordsburg." Ford put Dudley Nichols on a script and lined up Claire Trevor and a B-western star named John Wayne for the leads. But when Selznick caught wind of the deal, he pulled rank on Cooper and nixed the project. In late June 1937, Selznick informed Whitney and Wharton of his decision and his rationale. "I feel strongly that we must select the story and sell it to Ford," said Selznick, "instead of him picking some uncommercial pet of his." That decision cost SIP dearly. Cooper resigned from SIP on what he considered a "point of honor" and dissolved the SIP-Pioneer partnership. Cooper and Ford formed their own independent company called Argosy Pictures, set to distribute through UA, whose only assets were the two filmmakers. Ford's uncommercial pet was produced two years later by Walter Wanger and released by UA under the title *Stagecoach;* it was a huge hit.

CONSIDERING the pace with which Selznick was alienating the top filmmakers in Hollywood, it was fortunate that his courtship with Hitchcock was something of an extended blind date. The two finally met during Hitchcock's first trip to America in August 1937, when he came over to celebrate his thirty-eighth birthday. By then he had been corresponding regularly with Kay Brown, and the two got along so well that Hitchcock, his wife Alma, and his coscenarist Joan Harrison all stayed for several days in Brown's home on Long Island. Brown had the negotiations moving but Hitchcock still was not ready to commit, although by the time he returned to England he was leaning toward Selznick. Selznick figured the deal was close enough in November 1937 for him to dispatch Brown and SIP board chairman Jock Whitney to London to sign Hitchcock. Whitney found Hitchcock charming, but he was so disappointed with the newly released *Young and Innocent* that he wired Selznick that he had "held up all negotiations." Kay Brown felt differently, however. "Regret do not agree with Jock," she wired Selznick a few days later, and she encouraged her boss not to make any decisions until he saw Hitchcock's new film, which would be "available for you in about ten days."

Actually, Brown was less concerned with *Young and Innocent* than she was with another project altogether—something neither Whitney nor Selznick was even vaguely aware of, but that soon became a key issue in the negotiations. Hitchcock had just finished shooting *The Lady Vanishes,* and for his next picture he planned to adapt Daphne du Maurier's novel *Jamaica Inn.* As Hitchcock and Du Maurier worked out the deal, she showed him the manuscript of her next novel, *Rebecca.* Hitchcock read the manuscript and gave it to Kay Brown to read while she was in England. Brown was absolutely bowled over by the gothic romance and the quality of its telling—the mood, the atmosphere, the characterizations, the attention to detail. She saw *Rebecca* as an ideal SIP project—just as she had *Gone With the Wind.* Knowing that Selznick already had a massive disaster film in mind for Hitchcock, she didn't push the point, though. The project was *Titanic,* and although Hitchcock had no real interest in doing it, he assured Brown that he and her boss eventually would come to terms. In fact Hitchcock was quoted later that spring in *World Film News* as saying, "If I do go to Hollywood, I'd only work for Selznick." That was encouraging, although in the same interview Hitchcock asserted that the film director "will become obsolete unless his status and power expand to that of producer."

Selznick learned of the interview via Marcella Rabwin, his personal secretary, who had conducted a discreet investigation into Hitchcock's working methods for her boss. Rabwin turned up other comments of Hitchcock's that were equally unsettling to Selznick. A year earlier in *Footnotes to the Film,* for instance, Hitchcock described his ideal preparation for film:

> With the help of my wife, who does the technical continuity, I plan out a script very carefully, hoping to follow it exactly, all the way through, when shooting starts. In fact, this working on the script is the real making of the film, for me. When I've done it, the film is finished already in my mind. Usually, too, I don't find it necessary to do more than supervise the editing myself. . . . If the scenario is planned out in detail and followed closely during production, editing should be easy.

Interestingly enough, Hitchcock's role in the filmmaking process was much the same as Selznick's. Rabwin suggested that that was due to the disorganized production conditions at the Gaumont-British studio where Hitchcock worked, and she also figured that those conditions slowed Hitchcock down considerably. "Being the only one at G-B who knew anything about pictures," she told Selznick, "he was allowed to be his own boss and, consequently, took his time doing everything he wanted. Also, he is a fat man and a little lazy." But Rabwin thought Selznick would take care of that. "With prompting of such an energetic person as yourself," she suggested, "Hitchcock would do whatever you wanted in the way of schedule."

Selznick was less upbeat in his appraisal—and indeed, at moments like this, he had to confront his own contradictory impulses regarding authority and creative control. He wanted "producing directors," all right, but this man sounded too much like a producer. Hitchcock even had his own pet property, the Du Maurier novel that he wanted to do instead of *Titanic*. Kay Brown had sent Selznick the manuscript, which he forwarded to his story department. He received a reader's report on *Rebecca* a few days after getting Rabwin's report on Hitchcock, and it only deepened his concerns. Du Maurier's novel was categorized as a "murder mystery romance" and described thus: "A poor but delightful young companion marries a distinguished Englishman twice her age but is cowed by consciousness of his first wife's perfections. Gradually she learns that Rebecca was a fiend whom her husband killed. He is freed." There followed an eight-page plot summary with no indication of the novel's quality or appeal. The closing "Comment" dismissed the novel's "rather hysterical plot" as mundane melodrama, though it did allow that "melodrama has been responsible for some box-office classics." The novel lacked "a good major climax," though it contained "good roles for Ronald Colman and Carole Lombard," both of whom Selznick hoped to use and had instructed his readers to keep in mind as they evaluated projects.

The report dampened Selznick's interest in *Rebecca*, as did his anticipation of Joe Breen's reaction. He knew all too well Breen's obsessive concern for "compensating moral values," and that letting the hero get away with murder simply would not do at the PCA. By June 1938 a favorite pastime at SIP was inventing plot twists that would render the story morally acceptable. Kay Brown had suggested that Rebecca die by suicide. Val Lewton, who like Selznick had seen only the reader's report, thought he could persuade Breen to buy a "mental anguish as moral retribution" angle. If that didn't fly, said Lewton, he favored Kay Brown's suicide idea. Selznick tried to ignore all of this; as far as he was concerned, Hitchcock would be doing *Titanic*. Hitchcock planned a return trip to the States in July, and Selznick wanted both the project and contract offer ironed out before his arrival. On July 2 he met with Myron at the Beverly Wilshire for lunch, and they worked out a tentative one-picture deal, paying Hitchcock $50,000 for twenty weeks' work, with his assistant Joan Harrison coming in at $125 per week. If all went well, they would consider a long-term arrangement.

Hitchcock arrived carrying the galley proofs of *Rebecca* (due out in print August 5), which he was as eager as ever to adapt as a film. His enthusiasm was so high, in fact, that Selznick backed off on the *Titanic* pitch and agreed to look over the *Rebecca* galleys. Instead of reading them himself, though, he gave them to Val Lewton, who was already talking informally with the Breen office about the story. At that point Lewton had only read the reader's synopsis, and his attitude toward the project changed quite literally overnight once he read the novel. The following morning Lewton reported to Selznick that Du Maurier's novel was "superb"—far better than anything indicated in the readers' reports. Three days later, on July 14, 1938, Selznick and Hitchcock signed the one-picture agreement David and Myron had discussed, but without specifying the project. The next day Hitchcock left for England and Selznick received another memo from Val Lewton. "The more I think of it," wrote the SIP story editor, "the more I feel that we have got ourselves a tiger. It is as good as *Jane Eyre* and I think that women will be wild about it." He closed the memo urging Selznick to get moving on the screen rights.

After all this hype and intrigue, Selznick himself finally got around to reading the novel, and like everyone else he was much impressed. Without question it would make an excellent film, and one very much in line with his own tastes and interests. On August 4, the day before *Rebecca* went on sale, he wired Brown that it would be an "ideal" strategy to have Hitchcock represent SIP in dealing with Du Maurier for the rights. But the novel took off immediately and Selznick found himself in a bidding war with another UA producer, Sam Goldwyn. In late August he authorized Brown to close the deal for up to $40,000. "Because of the Goldwyn situation," wrote Selznick, "I think Hitch should be used as much as possible since I imagine he would have more weight in buying it than either Goldwyn's representative or our own."

On September 29 the deal finally was closed for $50,000, the same amount Selznick had paid for *Gone With the Wind*. Selznick was heavily into preproduction on *Wind*, and the idea of following it with another adaptation of an international best-seller seemed altogether logical. By now Whitney had read the novel and he too was won over

—and also a bit sheepish about his earlier concerns since *Young and Innocent* was cleaning up at the box office. When *The Lady Vanishes* opened in England to an even stronger response, Whitney began urging Selznick to go with a multiple-picture deal right away rather than risk losing Hitchcock or having the price hiked up if *Rebecca* hit. Selznick agreed, so again Whitney and Kay Brown journeyed to England to meet with Hitchcock. They lunched with the director and discussed the treatment of *Rebecca* he and Joan Harrison were doing and also the problems with the Production Code. They came away "enthusiastic," as Jock put it, especially when Hitchcock seemed interested in the idea of a four-picture deal. For the time being, Hitchcock agreed to a flat fee of $5,000 for the *Rebecca* treatment, and he said he would consider a multiple-picture deal at a minimum of $40,000 per picture.

That same month Selznick sold Orson Welles the radio rights to *Rebecca*, which he planned to use on his "Mercury Theatre of the Air" program. Welles had caused quite a sensation only a few weeks earlier with his radio dramatization of *War of the Worlds*, so this was an ideal opportunity to further publicize *Rebecca*. It also gave Selznick a chance to hear how the talented young radio dramatist would handle various story problems, particularly the heroine's first-person voice-over narration. Selznick sent Hitchcock a transcript of Welles's radio version in December, just before shooting started on *Gone With the Wind*. He expected to be totally immersed in that project, but when the American release of *The Lady Vanishes* emerged as the hit of the holiday season, the Hitchcock negotiations were back in session. After considerable maneuvering on both sides, a deal was signed on March 3, 1939, committing Hitchcock to seven years, starting at $40,000 per picture. It was an exclusive contract, so Hitchcock could do outside pictures only on Selznick's approval and on the terms of his SIP pact. On March 15, Selznick informed the press of the deal and that Hitchcock's first assignment would be *Rebecca*.

B Y the time Hitchcock went on the SIP payroll in April, he and Harrison already had finished a ninety-page treatment of Du Maurier's novel, complete with camera angles, dialogue, specifications for set and costume design, and various other details. Selznick hired Philip MacDonald to transform the treatment into continuity form, and it was then submitted on June 3 with the byline "story line by Philip MacDonald and Joan Harrison." Hitchcock hoped to start shooting in July —a reasonable enough expectation since *Wind* was nearing completion. Selznick took precious time away from the *Wind* shoot (which by early June was in production almost around the clock, with three separate production units) to read and analyze the *Rebecca* "story line."

He then offered Hitchcock and his collaborators a detailed critique of their effort, couched in a "memo" that ran several thousand words. Selznick's estimation was obvious from the opening sentences: "It is my unfortunate and distressing task to tell you that I am shocked and disappointed beyond words by the treatment of *Rebecca*. I regard it as a distorted and vulgarized version of a provenly successful work."

As Wellman had learned with his first draft of *A Star Is Born*, Selznick's initial reaction to any project indicated both his anxiety and his desire to remind his employees—particularly newly signed directors—of their subordinate position in the SIP power structure. But besides blowing off steam and asserting his control over a high-stakes production, Selznick also was working out his theory of literary adaptation—something that was very much on his mind as he took *Wind* into post-production. His governing precept was that when adapting so successful a novel, fidelity to the original was essential. "We bought *Rebecca* and we intend to make *Rebecca*," he asserted. "I don't hold at all with the theory that the different medium [of cinema] necessitates a difference in storytelling, or even a difference in scenes." Selznick re-

Alfred Hitchcock's fidelity—or lack of it—to Daphne du Maurier's original novel was a source of constant concern to Selznick during the scripting of Rebecca.

minded Hitchcock that he had already adapted "many classics successfully and faithfully," and he had learned that in doing a successful (i.e., popular) play or novel, the adaptation itself "will succeed in the same manner as the original succeeded if only the same elements are captured and if only as much as possible is retained of the original." Selznick even felt that the "alleged faults of dramatic construction" should be retained, since "no one, not even the author of the original work, can say with any degree of accuracy why a book had caught the fancy of the public."

Selznick was particularly distressed over Hitchcock's alteration of the principal characters. Maxim de Winter, the mysterious aristocrat and widower who marries the young heroine early in the story, was more foreboding and enigmatic in Hitchcock's version than he had been in the novel. And the unnamed narrator, referred to simply as "I" in the script, had become less passive and subdued. It should be noted that while Hitchcock, Harrison, and MacDonald were adapting the novel, a number of actresses were being considered for the lead. They ranged from newcomers Anne Baxter (then age seventeen) and Joan Fontaine, both of whom seemed quite close to Du Maurier's conception of the narrator, to more extroverted and vital types like Carole Lombard, Margaret Sullavan, and Katharine Hepburn. Ronald Colman had been considered ideal for the lead early on, although he confided to Val Lewton back in November that he feared the role of a murderer —or even a suspected murderer—might "prejudice his public" against him. With the release of Sam Goldwyn's *Wuthering Heights* in April 1939, however, Laurence Olivier had become the leading candidate for the role, and he signed for the part in June. Hitchcock clearly conceived of Maxim de Winter along the lines of Heathcliff, the menacing, sulking hero in Goldwyn's picture, while the heroine seemed to have been adapted with someone like Hepburn or Lombard in mind.

Selznick insisted that these characters be returned to their original conception, and that the story itself be brought in line with Du Maurier's. He told Hitchcock that he wanted *Rebecca* to "seem to be an exact photograph of the book"—much as he believed *Wind* was being done. If this were an original screenplay or an adaptation of a less successful novel, said Selznick, such creative license would not only be permissible but necessary. "But my ego is not so great that it cannot be held in check on the adaptation of a successful work. I don't think I can create in two months or two years anything as good with the characters and situations of *Rebecca* as Du Maurier created; and frankly, I don't think that you can either." After this lecture, Selznick proceeded with a scene-by-scene critique of the treatment. He closed the memo by saying: "It is my regretful conclusion that we should immediately start on a new treatment, probably with a new writing setup."

Hitchcock was sufficiently chastened, and he immediately started a rewrite. He submitted a revised treatment in late June with the assurance that "this follows the exact line of the novel and contains rough dialogue by Du Maurier. It will serve as a basis for discussions in order to decide what deviations may be permitted." Selznick, meanwhile, told Kay Brown to inform Du Maurier "that I have thrown out the complete treatment on *Rebecca* because of insufficient faithfulness to the book, and that it is my intention to do the book and not some botched-up semi-original as was done with *Jamaica Inn*." Without question, this would be a project where the "master of suspense" adjusted his own style to the story, rather than adjusting the tale to suit his own interests and skills as a director.

T H E same week that Selznick received Hitchcock's new treatment, he closed *Gone With the Wind*. Figuring he had earned a brief respite, he wired Jock Whitney in New York: "I am going on the boat Friday night and you can all go to the devil." Selznick soon returned to face the monumental task of postproduction on *Wind*, though he also devoted a few days to *Rebecca*'s final preparation and began looking for a writer to script Hitchcock's revised treatment. Eventually he signed Robert Sherwood, an American playwright who had done some screenwriting in England and was considered an excellent dialogue writer. Having seen a number of his own Broadway plays transformed into films, Sherwood also knew something about adaptation. By mid-August Sherwood, Harrison, and Hitchcock had completed a draft that was a fairly straight translation of Du Maurier. The only really important change involved the finale, wherein Maxim explains Rebecca's death (which occurred before the story began) to his second wife. In the novel, the black-hearted Rebecca flaunts her infidelities and goads Maxim into killing her. Selznick and the others, knowing that for the film they had to create a suspicion of murder but maintain Maxim's innocence, decided to have Maxim, despite Rebecca's taunts, stop short of killing her. Instead, Rebecca falls and strikes her head during a confrontation with Maxim, who then scuttles Rebecca's sailboat and sends her to the bottom of the sea. As in the novel, the court of inquiry would decide after discovering her body that Rebecca, who knew she was dying of cancer, had committed suicide. This long and fairly complicated finale was worked out by Selznick, Hitchcock, and Sherwood in a series of all-night story conferences, with Joan Harrison transcribing and later rewriting it in continuity form. Selznick thrived on such sessions—partly because of the regular injections of amphetamines and vitamin B_{12} he was getting to help him handle the demands of both *Wind* and *Rebecca*. Hitchcock had trouble staying awake, though it probably wouldn't have mattered all that much what state he was in. Immersed in preproduction on one project and postproduction on another, Selznick was in his element at a time like this. Only then was his control over a project secure, his conceptualization clear, and his input of real value.

With *Rebecca*'s story finally in focus, Selznick could complete the casting. He had long since decided on Olivier as Maxim, but he purposely held off casting the female lead until the heroine's characterization was worked out. In August, there were three leading candidates for the role: Margaret Sullavan, Anne Baxter, and Joan Fontaine. Hitchcock's earlier conception of the story, with its comic undertones and more spirited heroine, favored Sullavan. But the recent story sessions had reverted to Du Maurier's original conception of a timid, insecure type. As far as Selznick was concerned, that took Sullavan out of the running. She had tested well, and was favored by SIP executives on both coasts, but Selznick felt that Sullavan's established screen persona was at odds with the role as they'd decided to play it. He could not imagine the feisty Sullavan being intimidated by any woman—let alone a dead one. Equally important was Selznick's Pygmalion complex, which had been forming since he put Katharine Hepburn in *A Bill of Divorcement* back in 1931 and now was in full bloom. Besides giving Vivien Leigh a breakthrough role as Scarlett O'Hara, Selznick had recently brought in a young actress from Sweden named Ingrid Bergman, who was starring in an SIP production, *Intermezzo*. Baxter and Fontaine also were relative unknowns; either one could emerge as yet another of Selznick's female "discoveries"—Selznick's third Galatea in as many pictures. Not only would this mean terrific press for all three pictures, but lower production costs. Fontaine or Baxter undoubtedly would sign a long-term deal to get the part, just as Leigh and Bergman had done, and on terms vastly preferable to those he would have to accord a star like Sullavan.

After nixing Sullavan in mid-August, Selznick asked George Cukor and John Cromwell to help him decide between Baxter and Fontaine. Together with Hitchcock, they looked at the screen tests. Cukor, who was then directing *The Women* for Metro and was highly regarded as a judge of female screen talent, felt that Selznick was right about Fontaine. She was insecure and inexperienced, but those qualities would only heighten her performance. Cukor's views seemed to sway Hitchcock, so Selznick decided on August 18 to go with Fontaine.

Signing Fontaine enabled Selznick to set both the schedule and the budget on *Rebecca*, which actually was a relatively inexpensive picture. It was to be a thirty-six-day shoot, starting September 8, with a budget of $689,238. That was barely half of what Selznick was now spending on routine SIP projects, and only a fraction of the $4.25 million price tag on *Wind*. Much of the savings on *Rebecca* were due to its above-the-line total of only $270,000, with $77,000 going to Hitchcock, $51,000 to his two stars, and another $80,000 for story and continuity. The only other SIP production whose budget was anywhere near that was *Intermezzo*, which was estimated at $691,000 and came in at $770,000. The costs of *Rebecca* would edge over a million dollars, leaving *Intermezzo* the only SIP production since *Little Lord Fauntleroy* (the first SIP project) that was done for only six figures.

One reason for *Intermezzo*'s low cost is particularly instructive. When Selznick signed Bergman, he also bought the rights to her recent Swedish hit, *Intermezzo*. To cut costs, minimize preproduction efforts, and ensure Bergman's readiness for her American debut, Selznick decided to simply reproduce the Swedish picture, right down to the camera angles, lighting, framing, and character blocking. (He got the idea from Walter Wanger, who in 1938 made *Algiers* by "adapting" *Pepe Le Moko*, a successful French film.) That process severely constrained director Gregory Ratoff, who deviated somewhat from the Swedish original but did follow the same basic structure and design. The project indicated that Selznick was still looking for ways to go into production with a precut picture. And Ratoff's willingness to accommodate him indicated that there were filmmakers in Hollywood who had little concern for creative control. Selznick also had tried to exert his control over *Gone With the Wind*, demanding approval of every camera setup before Cukor called for a take. Cukor refused to comply, which was one of the key reasons for his removal—along with his legendary confrontations with Clark Gable, who felt he was engulfed in a woman's picture. Selznick considered his own handling of both *Wind* and *Intermezzo* to be perfectly reasonable. "I do not mean to put the director in a straightjacket," Selznick told his production manager in the summer of 1939, but "we must have a director who is willing to cooperate."

Hitchcock had been more than cooperative during story and script development on *Rebecca*, which he accepted as the producer's realm of authority. But he considered the set his own domain, and he had no plans to change to suit Selznick. So the climate was right for a confrontation, and there might have been one had Selznick not been so obsessed with *Wind*, which had its first preview September 9, the day after Hitchcock started shooting *Rebecca*. Selznick's continued preoccupation with *Wind* was a blessing for Hitchcock, enabling him to establish his own working methods and his authority on the set, free from the kind of interference that was becoming increasingly common on other recent SIP productions. Selznick was aware of his detachment from *Rebecca*. As he confided to Jock Whitney, "If we had *It Happened One Night* in the studio right now, it would seem like nothing compared to *Gone With the Wind*, so it is pretty tough for us to get enthusiastic about any picture, even a very good one, other than *Wind*."

Once production opened, Selznick did make an effort, though from an administrative distance, to assert his control over the picture. It was obvious from the outset, in fact, that Fontaine would need a tremendous amount of coaching and support during the shoot, and this would further hamper the slow, deliberate, and meticulous Hitchcock. After a week of shooting, Selznick began complaining to both his studio manager Henry Ginsberg and his production manager Ray Klune about rehearsal time, and particularly Hitchcock's refusal to rehearse a scene until all the lights were ready and he had absolute quiet on the set. Selznick also asked for "a summary of the amount of work achieved by each of our directors" in order to verify his "impression" that Hitchcock was getting "materially less footage daily" than any previous SIP director, and was doing fewer setups as well. A few days later Klune reported that Hitchcock averaged twelve setups daily for the first two weeks in production, which translated into a forty-eight-day shoot if he maintained the same pace. "If we can improve our day's work even by two legitimate setups," wrote Klune in a memo to Selznick, "this can be reduced to forty-two days. The thirty-six-day schedule was predicated on approximately sixteen setups per day." (Earlier in the summer, Hitchcock had suggested a sixty-day schedule, and apparently he knew his business and his own pace well enough—*Rebecca* took sixty days to complete, including retakes.)

One aspect of Hitchcock's working method that posed a real threat to Selznick's control of the picture was the director's ability to "cut with the camera." This had implications for Hitchcock's control of not just shooting but postproduction as well, and that genuinely disturbed Selznick. The standard procedure of most directors was to shoot a "master scene," usually a wide shot including all the principal action in a given sequence, and then to "cover" the sequence from various angles in medium shots, medium close-ups, and tight shots. During the editing process the shots would be assembled and reassembled to satisfy the demands of dramatic, temporal, and spatial continuity. Thus the amount of "coverage" shot during production—often called "protection," for obvious reasons—determined the range of options available during editing. Because Hitchcock so carefully conceived and preplanned his pictures, he shot very little coverage, getting only what he envisioned as essential to the final cut.

On September 19, ten days into production, Selznick drafted a memo to Hitchcock that addressed this issue. It began, "Dear Hitch: I am putting this in writing because there seems to be some difficulty on the part of Henry [Ginsberg] and the Production Department in making our complaints clear." He cited Hitchcock's frequent "failure" or "refusal" to acknowledge those complaints, so Selznick felt compelled to spell them out. "Cutting your film with the camera and reducing the number of angles required is highly desirable," allowed Selznick, "and no one appreciates the value more than I do; but certainly it is of no value if you are simply going to give us less cut film per day than a man who shoots twice as many angles. Eliminating additional angles without eliminating the time that is spent on these additional angles . . . is no feat." Selznick admitted that "it takes time to get the performance out of Joan Fontaine" that they both wanted, and he was even a bit apologetic about the lack of a finished shooting script—Sherwood still hadn't worked out the finale in which Maxim explains his role in Rebecca's death. But Selznick felt that neither of these factors should be slowing him down all that much. "There are things about your methods of shooting which I think you simply must correct," said Selznick, now becoming a spokesman for standard operating procedure throughout the industry. "Nobody in Hollywood would stand for them, so we might as well clamp down on you for this picture." He finished the memo by acknowledging that "this studio has never been famous for its speed of production," but he said that he "had hoped to correct this on *Rebecca*."

On the face of it, this was simply another studio executive's time-is-money harangue. But on a deeper level it revealed Selznick's growing realization that Hitchcock was a filmmaker whose work he could not prepare, control, and reshape to suit his own tastes. After finally signing a top producing director, Selznick was facing the necessary consequences—the same consequences he undoubtedly would have faced with Capra or Ford or La Cava. The present situation was more acute, perhaps, due to Hitchcock's meticulous preparation and penchant for cutting with the camera. Both practices extended Hitchcock's influence well beyond the actual shooting of the picture—even on a project where he was supposedly doing a straight adaptation of a best-seller. What would happen, wondered Selznick, with one of Hitchcock's own pet projects? Selznick let his temper cool, however, and decided not to send the memo. Instead he rewrote it and sent it to Henry Ginsberg, with instructions to relay his concerns to Hitchcock. "I have looked over with interest the report on Hitchcock's record to date," Selznick told Ginsberg, noting that it "shows [Hitchcock] to be the slowest director we have had." Selznick went on to lament Hitchcock's working methods and "the extra angles he is so proud of not shooting," and

he encouraged Ginsberg to keep the production on schedule and ignore excuses about Fontaine's inexperience or the incomplete script.
Ginsberg replied that Hitchcock was picking up speed somewhat, but
that *Rebecca* was already seven days behind schedule after eighteen
shooting days. In early October, Ray Klune compiled some figures for
Selznick on Hitchcock's first four weeks in production that indicated a
respectable but by no means fast pace:

—average number of setups per day: 10½
—average time to line up and light each setup: 21 minutes
—average time to rehearse (from the completion of lighting until the
first camera take): 16 minutes
—average time to shoot (from the start of the first take to the end of
the last take on each setup): 11 minutes

Selznick realized he could do little to speed things up without risk-
ing a confrontation with his director—something he certainly did not
want, given the quality of the dailies he had been screening each
morning in his projection room. Perhaps the clearest indication of Selznick's grudging acceptance of Hitchcock's command over *Rebecca*
came in an October memo that Selznick wrote after screening a complex scene involving a number of characters seated at a table for a
luncheon. The dramatic interplay in the scene was important, and a
good deal of information had to be communicated through glances
rather than dialogue. Selznick viewed Hitchcock's rushes, then wrote
him a memo saying that the luncheon "will make a good—if very cutty
—scene," and asking Hitchcock to "find the time to help the boys in
cutting this sequence as you see it."

Selznick was getting something he had wanted, a "pre-cut picture,"
but without his customary authority over the process. Still he tried to
exercise some influence through a steady stream of memos. He voiced
his concern, for example, about Olivier's slight frame, insisting that
both his height and his shoulders be artificially built up as they had
been for *Wuthering Heights*. He complained that Fontaine's legs appeared "singularly unattractive" in the rushes and encouraged Hitchcock to keep them off screen whenever possible. Selznick also complained about Fontaine's makeup: he argued that Bergman's "natural" look was more appropriate for Fontaine's character and her facial
qualities than the heavy makeup Fontaine was wearing. Selznick urged
Hitchcock and makeup artist Monty Westmore to study Bergman's
close-ups in *Intermezzo*. "Her eyebrows look natural," Selzick pointed
out; "she isn't smeared with Hollywood makeup. . . . what can I do to
get you makeup men to throw away your kits and your tweezers?"

There were occasions when Selznick's input went well beyond this kind of cosmetic or superficial concern, though. After looking over the rushes of a scene shot in early October in which Maxim and the girl initially profess their love for one another, Selznick instructed Hitchcock to retake Fontaine's close-ups. "I think Joan has been handled with great restraint," Selznick wrote his director on October 11, "but I think we have to be careful not to lose what little variety there is in the role by underplaying her in her emotional moments." Selznick suggested "a little more Yiddish Art Theatre in these moments, and a little less English Repertory Theatre."

By mid-October Sherwood's rewrites were completed and sent to Breen's office for approval. But still Selznick was not satisfied. He dictated a twenty-one-item list of subjects "for discussion," with his primary concerns centering on the nature of Rebecca's death and the "confession scene" wherein Maxim tells Fontaine the truth about Rebecca. "I think we must make it clear that Rebecca intended Maxim to kill her," wrote Selznick to Hitchcock, Sherwood, Lewton, et al. Although the Breen office refused to let them follow Du Maurier's story,

"A little more Yiddish theater." Hitchcock rehearsing Joan Fontaine for a crucial scene in Rebecca.

which portrays Maxim as a killer who goes unpunished, "that's no reason to lose the point that Rebecca *wanted* him to kill her." Val Lewton urged Selznick to avoid any direct confrontation with Breen's office, and assured him that Geoffrey Sherlock, one of Breen's associates (and his eventual successor), was sympathetic with their efforts not to rob the story of its complexity or Rebecca of her inherent evil. After meeting with Sherlock and Breen on Sherwood's rewrites, Lewton informed Selznick: "As we all expected, the confession scene in *Rebecca* passed all the censors without exception." Lewton also said that Sherlock had told him to expect a letter "written in what Jeff termed a 'cagey' fashion . . . [saying] that if what they see on the screen has the same flavor as what they have seen in the script, then it will be OK."

T H E S E were crucial issues for *Rebecca,* of course, but still Selznick's attention was riveted on *Gone With the Wind.* On October 13, director Vic Fleming—the last of four directors on Selznick's Civil War saga—restaged the opening scene wherein Scarlett and the Tarleton twins discuss the upcoming barbecue. It was the fifth time that particular scene had been shot, and it was also the final retake on the picture. With the Atlanta premiere scheduled for mid-December, Selznick immersed himself in *Wind's* postproduction, working closely with Hal Kern on the editing. But completing the retakes on *Wind* did free up effects expert Jack Cosgrove and production designer William Cameron Menzies for *Rebecca,* where the two were needed for the opening and closing sequences depicting the burning of Manderley, Maxim's estate. (The film opens with the aftermath of the fire; Fontaine, in voice-over, initiates an extended flashback relating the events leading up to the fire, which serves as the story's climax.) Selznick's decision to edit alongside Kern also freed up assistant editor Jim Newcom, who started a rough cut of *Rebecca.* Selznick would have preferred to supervise the editing himself, since he still felt there was an outside chance for a December release. But the premiere and release of *Wind* were already locked in, so work on *Rebecca* would have to proceed without him.

Hitchcock closed production on November 20, 1939, twenty-six days behind schedule and $400,000 over budget. Selznick, Kern, Hitchcock, and Newcom spent four days editing the picture, and when they finished it was apparent that more than the fire scene needed work. The picture was overlong, and only a complete overhaul of certain scenes would bring it down to a reasonable length. Cinematographer George Barnes had a commitment at Fox beginning December 11 and would not be available again until late January or early February. Selznick's own specialists—Menzies and Cosgrove—could handle the fire scenes, since they were mostly miniature and effects shots. But both Selznick and Hitchcock wanted Barnes on camera for the extensive retakes to ensure consistent lighting and compositional values. These complications, along with the December 15 premiere of *Wind* in Atlanta, dashed any hopes of releasing *Rebecca* before New Year's. On December 2 Selznick formally told the New York office that they would have to "toss in the sponge" on a 1939 release date for the Hitchcock picture, and he took most of the responsibility for the delay. "The combination of my exhaustion," he wrote, "plus my natural nervousness about every detail connected with *Wind*, hardly leaves me in a mood to do the big editorial job that is necessary on *Rebecca*."

One of those last-minute details on *Wind* was getting a finished score out of Max Steiner. Selznick had hoped that Steiner might have time to score *Rebecca* as well, but the composer still hadn't finished *Wind* in mid-November. Selznick began to fret that Steiner wouldn't even finish that job on time, so he hired Herbert Stothart from MGM to prepare an alternate score for *Wind*. Stothart was generally dismissed as a second-rate composer by his peers in Hollywood, and he turned out to be a fairly indiscreet one, too. He bragged of the assignment, and word quickly got back to Steiner, who demanded that either he or Stothart be taken off the picture. Pulling Stothart, Selznick noted that "musicians out here are even more jealous of each other . . . and more cliquish . . . than producers." Steiner's score was completed on time and it was certainly up to par. In fact the score was nominated for an Oscar, though Steiner was one of the few *Wind* nominees to lose out— to Herbert Stothart, who won for his work on *The Wizard of Oz*. When it became evident that Steiner would not have the time to score *Rebecca*, Selznick hired Franz Waxman, who proved even more difficult to work with. In a now familiar lament, Selznick complained to Ray Klune, "There is no reason on earth why a score shouldn't be written from a rough assembly," a point that he felt "ought to be hammered into Waxman." Selznick eventually did get a first-rate score for *Rebecca* —and another Oscar nomination—although Waxman worked so slowly that some of Steiner's music for *A Star Is Born* was incorporated into the *Rebecca* score.

In Waxman's defense, it should be said that there was not even a "rough assembly" of the Hitchcock picture to work with in early December, and the composer was not about to get one, considering Selznick's preoccupation with *Wind*. Selznick was working around the clock with Hal Kern on the final details, and on December 11 he sent Whitney in New York and Kay Brown in Atlanta identical wires: "Have just finished *Gone With the Wind*. God bless us one and all." After a successful press preview the following day, Selznick departed for Atlanta with an entourage that included virtually everyone who had worked on the picture except Vic Fleming. The publicized reasons for Fleming's decision not to attend the premieres in Atlanta and New York were exhaustion—he had in fact suffered a severe physical and nervous collapse during production—and also the death of his old friend, Douglas Fairbanks. But there were other reasons as well. Fleming was furious over a suggestion, which he mistakenly attributed to Selznick, that the other three directors who had worked on the picture be given some kind of screen credit and that Selznick's producer credit appear in the same-size type as Fleming's. (George Cukor, Sam Wood, and William Cameron Menzies all had directed portions that were included in the release version, as had Selznick.) After threatening to send the case to arbitration with the Directors Guild, Fleming received solo credit as director. And though there were few in Hollywood who thought of *Wind* as anything but a Selznick picture, the incident did underscore the growing power of the director—something Selznick was even more acutely aware of on *Rebecca*.

While Selznick was away for the Atlanta premiere, Hitchcock and Newcom finished a two-and-a-half-hour rough cut of *Rebecca*. Selznick screened it when he returned to Los Angeles, and he felt that the picture was finally coming together. On December 26, the night before the L.A. premiere of *Wind*, he decided on impulse to take *Rebecca* out for a sneak preview. He later told a UA executive that he "took it out with fear and trepidation because the picture was in the roughest kind of assembly form and was thousands of feet over length." Still he thought the film generated "a splendid audience reaction." By January 6, he and Hitchcock had agreed what portions of the film had to be retaken, and also what portions might be consolidated to eliminate footage. There was some disagreement over the issue of acceptable length, but Selznick was adamant about this particular matter. With *Wind* going out at over three and a half hours, he was painfully aware of lost revenue due to reserved seating and fewer screenings per day. He was determined to get *Rebecca* down under two hours to maximize its profit potential.

Hitchcock and Harrison did the necessary rewrites, and on January 18 the picture went back into production. Retakes were completed by February 3, at an additional cost of about $60,000. At that point Selznick and Kern began reediting while Hitchcock holed up with Charles Bennett, his British collaborator, to work on the screenplay for *Foreign Correspondent*, his next picture. Selznick had arranged for Hitchcock to write and direct this picture for independent producer Walter Wanger—and at $5,000 per week, twice what he was being paid by Selznick, who pocketed the "overage."

Selznick held another sneak preview of *Rebecca* on February 13 in Santa Barbara, and again the picture was well received. But Selznick still was dissatisfied with both the opening and closing sequences. He spent the following day studying both scenes and decided they had to be redone. This was no display of ego or petty interference; Selznick's ideas added immeasurably to the atmosphere of the opening and to the dramatic power of the fiery finale. During the prologue, when the burned-out remains of Manderley are glimpsed in the moonlight and Fontaine's character frames the story in voice-over, Selznick felt that the camera work and the timing of Fontaine's narration were slightly off. In a February 15 memo, he told Cosgrove and Menzies to reshoot the miniature of Manderley, and gave precise directions about the lighting, the camera movement, and the synchronization of the visuals with Fontaine's voice-over narration.

That same day Selznick, indicating what portions of the existing footage could be used, rewrote the entire fire scene. He wanted to foreground the role of Mrs. Danvers, the sinister housekeeper who had been preserving Rebecca's memory and had started the fire in an act inspired by that memory. Selznick quite literally choreographed both Mrs. Danvers's moves and the progress of the fire, being careful to match the action with Barnes's work. His primary interests were to establish Mrs. Danvers as more central to the action, and to trace the fire as it gradually engulfed Rebecca's bedclothes, which Danvers had kept intact all these years. Selznick called for a close-up in which we would see in Danvers's eyes the full extent of her vengeful madness. She would then look up, and in a glance-object cut we would see the burning ceiling fall directly upon us. After her demise, the camera was to follow the fire across the room until it reached the bed and engulfed the nightdress. Selznick also wanted to see the fire actually "devour the R" on Rebecca's bedding, thus providing "a natural curtain of flames as a background for our end title."

Cosgrove's unit immediately began reshooting the Manderley miniatures, while Selznick planned to restage the climactic fire. A few days later, RKO sent word to Selznick to confirm "the burning by you on February 19, 1940, of the 'Rebecca's Bedroom' set located between stages 10 and 11 at our studio in Culver City, California." So for the second time in little over a year, fires were started and filmed by Selznick on an RKO lot. Back in December 1938, Selznick had initiated the most intense year of his career with the burning of Atlanta (which was actually made up of redressed sets left over from the filming of various

RKO pictures, including *King Kong*); the burning of Manderley provided an apt, apocalyptic finale. Once the fire scene was shot, all that remained to do on *Rebecca* was the final editing and trimming, and the redubbing of dialogue. Still Selznick fretted through the last week of February; he was anxious about the Academy Awards—*Wind* had been nominated for a dozen Oscars—as well as the completion and release of *Rebecca*. On the twenty-seventh he ordered retakes of the "R" on Rebecca's address book and also a camera move-in on a magazine that he thought was too slow. He also fired off a nervous letter to Kay Brown, asking her to let Daphne du Maurier know that the picture was a faithful adaptation, although "there is one drastic change that was forced on us by the Hays office . . . which is that Maxim did not kill Rebecca." Selznick hoped that Du Maurier would not "hurt the picture" by saying anything "publicly or privately" about this.

Du Maurier's novel was now the second-biggest hit in modern publishing annals after *Gone With the Wind*, and Du Maurier reportedly was delighted with the adaptation. But Selznick needn't have worried about her reaction or her public comments. Nothing could have slowed the momentum created by her novel's success or by *Gone With the Wind*, which had been out a little over two months but had already grossed a phenomenal $5 million. The Academy Awards on February 29 further increased public interest. *Wind* captured an unprecedented ten Oscars, including best picture, and brought Selznick the Irving Thalberg Award for outstanding achievement in motion picture production. Selznick planted *Rebecca* firmly on *Wind*'s coattails, principally through a series of trailers designed to sell both pictures. This was a fairly complicated procedure, since *Wind* was already a known commodity but *Rebecca* actually was preceding it into general release. Selznick instructed his assistant Dan O'Shea to work on a general trailer "selling the three female stars we have discovered . . . the popularity of the novel, the fact of Hitchcock's first American picture, the current rave, Olivier, etc., etc." He also wanted two separate *Rebecca* trailers, both of which tied the film directly to *Wind*—one for the first-run theaters where *Wind* was presently playing and *Rebecca* would play later, the other for the theaters where both pictures had future play dates. The trailers were produced in early March, while final dubbing and recording on *Rebecca* were completed, and the film went into national release March 27.

T H E immediate success of *Rebecca* secured Selznick's position as Hollywood's top producer, independent or otherwise, and along with *Wind*, *Rebecca* provided an excellent example of prestige production at the height of the studio era. Both pictures were lush, romantic, well-crafted love stories that transposed best-selling fiction to the screen in consummate Hollywood style. They reinforced the most basic tenets of commercial filmmaking, but at the same time they extended the limits of spectacle and excess in Hollywood films. After *Gone With the Wind,* in particular, production values at the prestige level would never be conceived of in quite the same terms. Nor would sales and marketing. *Wind's* blockbuster status held through the entire year, so Loew's sustained its exclusive release strategy, booking the movie only in cities of 100,000 persons and up, and in theaters seating at least 850. Exhibitors continued to charge $.70 at the door—two to three times the going rate—and Loew's, in turn, charged the exhibitors 70 percent of the box-office revenues, twice the usual fee for a top feature, which Loew's then split with Selznick. The resulting profits for SIP and Loew's were staggering. By late summer, when it finally went into widespread release, *Wind* had grossed $20 million.

In 1940 SIP had only three pictures in release—*Wind, Rebecca,* and *Intermezzo*—while the five major studios along with Columbia and Universal were releasing roughly one feature per week. But none of those massive production companies took in anywhere near the $10 million in net profits that Selznick International earned that year. Only MGM, at $8.7 million, was even close, and half of its profits came from the deal with SIP to distribute *Wind.*

All of the majors benefited from the success of *Wind* and *Rebecca,* of course, since both pictures ran in their first-run theaters. And the industry was equally gracious in recognizing *Rebecca's* value. Just as *Wind* had the year before, *Rebecca* won the Academy Award for best picture in 1940, bringing SIP the industry's highest kudos in what was Hollywood's greatest era. To get only a general idea of Hollywood's output, consider the other best-picture nominees from those two years. In 1939 they were *Dark Victory, Goodbye, Mr. Chips, Mr. Smith Goes to Washington, Ninotchka, Stagecoach, The Wizard of Oz, Of Mice and Men, Love Affair,* and *Wuthering Heights.* In 1940 they were *Foreign Correspondent, The Letter, Our Town, The Grapes of Wrath, The Great Dictator, Kitty Foyle, All This and Heaven Too, The Long Voyage Home,* and *The Philadelphia Story.*

Selznick's commercial and critical success in 1939–40 put him on top of the industry, but the two pictures that carried him there took a heavy toll. The enormous effort he put into *Wind* and *Rebecca* left him physically, mentally, and emotionally spent, and the two pictures did in SIP as well. As the profits from *Wind* and *Rebecca* poured in, it became evident that the company was the victim of its own success. Without either a massive facility or a full program of productions, the profits could not be amortized, reinvested, or otherwise defrayed, so

Selznick at the 1940 Academy Awards ceremony, accepting his second straight Oscar for best picture.

the tax bite was enormous—especially for Selznick and Jock Whitney, whose incomes in 1940 threatened to reach about $4 million apiece. In August of that year the major stockholders in SIP decided to dissolve the company, sell each other portions of the assets, and let the profits be taxed as capital gains rather than personal or corporate income. Selznick and Whitney retained their interest in *Wind* (44 percent and 48 percent respectively) and made plans to rerelease it periodically. Selznick announced to the press not only that he was liquidating SIP but that he was taking an indefinite leave from active production—though he did create David O. Selznick Productions that summer, so he wouldn't be out of the picture altogether.

Besides doing in SIP and redefining the limits of prestige and profitability in Hollywood filmmaking, *Wind* and *Rebecca* also marked something of a watershed in terms of individual power and initiative. Selznick's success with SIP signaled the arrival of the independent producer as a dominant force in the industry. Filmmakers like Sam Goldwyn and Walt Disney had paved the way and would continue to push the limits—with pictures like *Fantasia*, for example, which Disney then had in production. The success of their pictures contributed to Hollywood's golden age, but they also indicated an important shift in its balance of power. The majors still dominated the marketplace and controlled the overall system, though individuals outside any studio's purview now were reshaping the products, the production process, and even the marketing strategies. And while *Wind* was the consummate producer's picture, *Rebecca* suggested that this power shift involved directors as well—or rather what Selznick had termed the "producing director." The movie director's authority had been subdued for some two decades, since the rise of the studio system and of the producer as its key functionary. But Selznick and Hitchcock were proving that the producer and director could break free, if not from the system at large, at least from direct studio control. That freedom enabled them to create some of the studio era's greatest pictures, while it also heralded the system's ultimate disintegration.

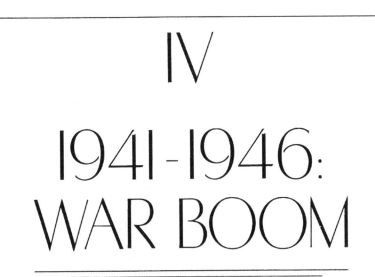

IV

1941-1946: WAR BOOM

16

Warner Bros.:
Warfare at Home
and Abroad

The war years were good ones for the American film industry. For the first time since the 1920s, dollars were plentiful, attendance was steadily climbing, and the mood in Hollywood was upbeat. There was concern over the international market, of course, as fighting in Europe and the Far East escalated. But the domestic market had never been more robust, with Hollywood playing a crucial role in nationalizing the U.S. war effort. This role began long before Pearl Harbor, and by 1940–41 movie screens were dominated by war-related fare. There were calls to arms like *Sergeant York, I Wanted Wings,* and the Abbott and Costello "service comedies" *Buck Privates, In the Navy,* and *Keep 'Em Flying.* There were dramatizations of the Battle of Britain, like *Dive Bomber, International Squadron,* and even a Warners-released British documentary, *Target for Tonight.* There were also a few espionage thrillers, most notably Hitchcock's *Foreign Correspondent.* With the official U.S. entry into the war in December 1941, Hollywood's support was effectively mandated by the Office of War Information (OWI), which wielded as much influence over movie content during the war as the PCA. Immediately after Pearl Harbor, the OWI requested that Hollywood concentrate on six subjects: the enemy, the Allies, the armed forces, the production front, the home front, and the issues. The studios readily complied, and within a year the war had infiltrated everything from the Sherlock Holmes and Tarzan quickies to top features, including *Mrs. Miniver* and *Casa-*

blanca, winners of the Oscar for best picture in 1942 and 1943, respectively.

Americans flocked to see these and other movies in increasing numbers, with weekly attendance climbing from 80 million in 1940 to nearly 100 million by 1946. Gearing up for the war effort meant a healthy economy and virtually full employment, especially in those industrial centers where Hollywood traditionally did its best business. By the early 1940s there were 17,000 movie theaters in some 8,500 American cities and towns, with a total seating capacity of over 10,500,000. There were only forty-nine U.S. cities with populations of more than 200,000; these urban centers held one-fifth of all the theaters and one-third of all the theater seats, but generated over two-thirds of the industry's box-office revenues—a disproportion that was due to the concentration of first-run theaters in these cities. So the first-run market was more lucrative than ever during the early- to mid-1940s as the war machine was being assembled. Airplane factories and munitions plants were running around the clock, rationing and rampant shortages limited outlets for spending money, and the movies provided an ideal form of recreation and diversion.

Thus the action at the box office was as heavy as that on-screen. The Big Eight saw their combined profits leap from $19.4 million in 1940 to $35 million in 1941, when war-related industrialization really began to pick up. Combined profits neared $50 million in 1942 and then surpassed even pre-Depression totals, reaching $60 million in each of the next three years. The momentum carried into 1946, Hollywood's best year ever, when combined profits soared to $122 million. The five integrated majors, netting $114 million, accounted for well over 90 percent of that total. Without question, the prime beneficiaries of the war boom were Hollywood's traditional powers.

Though the movie business had never been better, especially for the majors, the balance of power in the industry continued to shift away from the studios during the war years. After a decade of growth and consolidation in the 1930s, there was an equally significant diffusion of power and resources during the 1940s. And just as the federal government had facilitated that consolidation, primarily through the NRA, now it was helping to effect an overall destabilization of the movie industry. The first step in the process came in late 1938 when the Justice Department filed an antitrust suit against the Big Eight on behalf of independent exhibitors. The suit was later modified to focus on the five integrated majors, which, in November 1940, signed consent decrees agreeing to limit block booking, blind bidding, and other unfair trade practices. The decrees were to remain in effect for three years while the feds and the studio owners worked toward a more equitable system.

All the studios were affected by the antitrust action and consent decrees, since they could no longer compel theater owners to take weaker pictures in order to screen more desirable ones. But the majors felt the heaviest impact due to their concentration on the first-run market, which quickly became even more competitive than it had been in the late 1930s. The majors had little choice but to cut back B-movie production and to upgrade overall feature quality in 1940–41—which, ironically, put them in an ideal position once the war hit. With climbing attendance and the wartime economy putting dollars in America's pockets, particularly in the first-run cities, it soon became obvious that the court-induced adjustments in production and marketing were well suited to current conditions. With market demand at an all-time high and their affiliate theaters doing phenomenal business, the majors actually reduced all production during the war to further maximize profits. While Universal, Columbia, and UA maintained their prewar output, MGM, Paramount, Fox, Warners, and RKO slashed production. They had released 1,268 pictures from 1937 to 1941, an average of 50 per company each year; from 1942 to 1946 they released 788 films, for an average of about 30 annually.

The short-term profits were welcomed by the majors, though the antitrust suit hung like a sword of Damocles over their heads. That sword wouldn't fall for a few years, due to the consent decrees and the war, but another federal effort—albeit one not intentionally directed at the movie business—had a more immediate and destabilizing impact. The government needed billions of dollars to finance its defense buildup, which began in earnest early in 1940 at the time of increased Nazi aggression in Europe. Roosevelt made it clear that much of the funding would come from taxes, particularly from personal income taxes. The tax burden on high-salaried individuals steadily increased, peaking with the Revenue Act of 1941, which not only raised income taxes across the board but lowered the top tax bracket to only $200,000. That put someone earning a salary of $200,000 in the 90 percent tax bracket, resulting in take-home pay of only $20,000 after taxes. Hollywood's high-paid talent could avoid that tax bite only by decreasing their work load (and thus their income level) or finding some alternative to a salaried income. Thus top industry talents grew wary of long-term contracts and salaried income; instead they pursued profit-sharing and one-picture deals whereby their salaries could be invested into a picture and taxed as capital gains at a rate of only 25 percent.

These changing tax laws had a staggering effect on both the studio system and the star system. It's worth suggesting, in fact, that the Revenue Act posed as great a threat to the stability of the studio system as did the federal antitrust suits. Contract personnel were essential to the efficient running of the studios, especially the above-the-line talent— the stars, producers, directors, writers, and composers who turned out the studios' first-run movies. With these changing tax laws, either the studios would have to adjust how they did business with their top talent or risk losing that talent to "independent" status when their contracts expired. The growing power of guilds and unions was already giving studio employees unprecedented leverage, and now the tax laws encouraged producers and directors and even writers and stars to bolt for free-lance status or create their own companies. So there was a curious paradox in Hollywood. On the one hand, vastly improved market conditions meant huge earnings for the studios; on the other, individual personnel were gaining unprecedented power over their pictures, their careers, and the filmmaking process in general.

W A R N E R   B R O S . was more heavily affected by these industry changes than any other major studio. It was the most factory-oriented of the majors, with formulaic product, typecast stars, and a B-movie unit that cranked out roughly half its output. All that changed in the early 1940s. Bryan Foy's B-movie unit was phased out altogether in 1940, and there were severe production cuts among A-class features as well. While the majors' overall output dropped 38 percent during the war in comparison with the preceding five years, Warners' fell over 55 percent—from up to sixty releases per annum in the late 1930s to as few as twenty by the war's end. Warners also increased prestige production in 1940; some of it involved outside artists who were looking for one-picture profit-sharing deals to escape the heavy tax bite, and who could satisfy Warners' sudden demand for quality product. Early in 1940, for example, Warners cut deals with producer-director Frank Capra for *Meet John Doe,* and with independent producer Jesse Lasky for *Sergeant York.* Both films starred Gary Cooper, whose deliberate, soft-spoken, and heroic demeanor was at odds with the Warners type, but he was among the industry's most bankable stars in 1940—and besides, Warners had no real say over casting. The company simply provided financing and distribution, along with facilities and necessary personnel, while Capra and Lasky called the shots. Warners was hardly the only studio developing this strategy; RKO and Universal in particular were looking to "outside producers" for first-run product in the early 1940s.

Meet John Doe and *Sergeant York* were both huge hits, but both also were expensive films that took over a year to produce. During the

Los Angeles premiere of Warner Bros.' All This and Heaven Too, a top-flight Bette Davis melodrama released in 1940; the crowd indicates the robust movie market even before the war boom.

sixteen-month period that the two Cooper vehicles were in production, Warners released a succession of star vehicles with homegrown talent that were all A-class features but not as costly—in terms of time and resources as well as dollars—as *Doe* and *York.* Nor were they all standard star-genre formulations. Changing industry conditions demanded that the studio deliver more than just the usual batch of "Cagneys" and "Flynns," and Warners was displaying a growing penchant for off-casting and for genre variation before the war, especially with Cagney, Robinson, and Bette Davis. The widest range was displayed by Davis, who did a run of excellent melodramas and also starred with Cagney in a screwball comedy, *The Bride Came C.O.D.,* and with Flynn in a biopic, *The Private Lives of Elizabeth and Essex.*

Warners' stars welcomed these variations—all except for Errol Flynn. He was happy to let Warners shape his persona and had grown comfortable playing the role first established in *Captain Blood:* the heroic, single-minded Brit who resists tyranny and fights to restore some form of benevolent aristocratic rule. When Warners cast Flynn in *Dodge City,* a 1939 release, Myron Selznick's agency wrote Jack Warner that Flynn was "a little dubious about his ability to play a part that is so essentially American." But Flynn proved to be a natural as Westerner Wade Hatton, and the ever dependable Flynn unit—Olivia de Havilland, director Mike Curtiz, cameraman Sol Polito, et al.—transplanted the swashbuckler to the Old West with remarkable ease. *Dodge City* was released while the Flynn unit was doing *The Sea Hawk,* which turned out to be the last movie with one of Flynn's British heroes. After that Flynn generally played American heroes, though the characterization varied little from the likes of Captain Blood and Robin Hood.

Davis, Cagney, and Robinson had none of Flynn's qualms about off-casting; indeed, Cagney and Robinson virtually demanded it now that each had role-approval clauses in their contracts. Late in 1938 Robinson signed a three-year, six-picture deal at $85,000 per picture, with approval of both story and role. A few months later Cagney signed a three-year, eleven-film pact for $150,000 per picture, plus 10 percent of the gross receipts on all profits above $1.5 million, and he too gained story and role approval. Both Cagney and Robinson realized the importance of Warners' gangster films to their market value, and they continued to play urban toughs in pictures like *Brother Orchid* and *The Roaring Twenties,* so long as these were only occasional roles and only when the quality of the project warranted it.

With Cagney and Robinson edging away from the urban crime film, Warners turned to John Garfield and George Raft to carry its signature genre. When Garfield scored as a suicidal misfit in a 1938 melodrama,

Four Daughters, Warners signed him to a long-term deal starting at
$1,500 per week. Over the next few years he portrayed all manner of
criminals, convicts, and lowlife types in films like *They Made Me a
Criminal* and *Castle on the Hudson,* and on occasion he came close to
the kind of manic intensity and amoral charm of Cagney's early work.
Raft was put through much the same routine after he signed with Warners in 1939, but with less success. In fact, given Raft's rather lackluster
career with Paramount (after early stardom as Muni's coin-flipping
sidekick in *Scarface*), it's difficult to figure why Warners even signed
him, let alone why he merited $55,000 per picture—more than either
Davis or Flynn was earning at the time. It's even more difficult to figure
why Raft, who clearly was hired to portray criminal types and tough
guys, turned down roles that were so well suited to his emerging Warners persona. After mild success in two 1939 prison films, *Each Dawn
I Die* and *Invisible Stripes,* and in a 1940 crime thriller, *They Drive By
Night,* Raft refused to take two of the choicest roles in studio history:
"Mad Dog" Earl in *High Sierra* and Sam Spade in *The Maltese Falcon.*

Both parts were played by Humphrey Bogart, of course, who more
than any other star in the 1940s was the embodiment of the Warners
style. Neither Raft nor Garfield reached stardom at Warners, and both
Cagney and Robinson left the studio to go free-lance in 1942. But they
were scarcely missed as the Bogart persona steadily took hold, revitalizing the Warners crime thriller in ways that no one quite anticipated.
In fact, Bogart's rise in the early 1940s confirmed the continued viability of Warners' house style and its generic traditions, and the flexibility
of that style when it came into contact with new elements. *High Sierra*
and *The Maltese Falcon,* the key films in Bogart's ascent, were low-
cost, fast-paced, unpretentious studio jobs, in the tradition of the gangster sagas of a decade earlier. But they were somehow different, distinguished by the vulnerability and odd romantic appeal of Bogart's
persona, by a curious blend of cynicism and inner resolve that brought
an offbeat, almost existential quality to the Warners hero.

T H O U G H Bogart was the on-screen catalyst for the changes in Warner's male action pictures, there was also a new generation of filmmaking talent at the studio—notably Raoul Walsh, Mark Hellinger, John
Huston, and Jerry Wald—who were equally influential in the reshaping of the crime thriller and its hero. If any film should be singled out
in that process it would not be *High Sierra* or *The Maltese Falcon* but
The Roaring Twenties, a gangster saga released in late 1939 that starred
Jimmy Cagney and marked a turning point in the genre's development
and an influx of key studio talent. A throwback, the picture traced the
rise and fall of a mob boss (Cagney) and his conniving, heartless lieu-

tenant (Bogart). The story was by Mark Hellinger, a well-known New York journalist and syndicated columnist who signed on with Warners in September 1937. Hellinger's contract described his duties as being "of a diverse nature, which will include writing, story consultant, possibly producing," at a salary of $1,100 a week, plus $10,000 for each original story he sold to the studio. Among those originals was "The World Moves On," a fifty-one-page treatment Hellinger sent to Jack Warner in June 1938. Warner bought the story for Cagney, and Wallis assigned the script to a veteran staff writing team, Jerry Wald and Richard Macauley. To direct he brought in veteran Raoul Walsh, who signed on in May 1939 for ten weeks at $2,000 per week, with the picture set to start in July.

Walsh was then in his early fifties with a quarter-century of directing experience and with most of his movie career behind him—or so it seemed. But his masterful direction of *The Roaring Twenties* suggested that, like Howard Hawks, Walsh was an outsider whose temperament and narrative sensibilities were distinctly in tune with those of Warners. The opening reel, which plays like a nonstop montage, is even more intense and elliptical than LeRoy's work in *Little Caesar* or *I Am a Fugitive from a Chain Gang*. But once Cagney's initiation into crime and his hopeless love for the proper and middle-class Priscilla Lane are established, the story takes on an even, deliberate pace as it traces Cagney's inevitable fall. The finale is perfect: Cagney executes a cowering Bogart, who has taken over his mob and threatened Lane's family, and then Cagney himself is gunned down by rival gangsters. He stumbles along a snow-covered street and finally collapses not in the gutter but on the steps of a church, dying in the arms of an aging whore, who tells a cop, "He used to be a big shot."

Though it was an epitaph for Warners' classic gangster and his era, *The Roaring Twenties* also marked the birth of a production unit that would dominate the early-forties crime films and launch Bogart to stardom. The success of *The Roaring Twenties* won Hellinger full-fledged producer status and Walsh a long-term director's pact. And they immediately went to work with Wald and Macauley on another crime thriller, *They Drive by Night,* which costarred George Raft and Ida Lupino, with Bogart in a key supporting role. This was Hellinger's first crack at supervising a standard feature after he'd done two Foy-unit jobs, and he made the most of it. The story of two truck-driving brothers involved in hijacking and murder was based on a pulp novel entitled *Long Haul,* which Warners bought in March 1940 for $2,000. Hellinger hammered out the story with Wald and Macauley (who also had come up through the Foy unit), using the truck-driving saga for the first half and reworking *Bordertown* for the second.

A moderate hit, *They Drive by Night* enhanced Walsh's and Hellinger's status and moved Bogart a step closer to a starring role. Bogart's breakthrough came with their next project, *High Sierra*, a Walsh-directed, Hellinger-produced picture that again paired him with Ida Lupino, only this time Bogart was the sole male lead and principal character in the story. *High Sierra* had the earmarks of a classic urban crime film, but it pushed beyond the concrete confines of the gangster milieu and featured a sympathetic, self-conscious hero whose fall assumed near-tragic dimensions. There were premonitions of this in *The Roaring Twenties,* when the city-bred Cagney gradually realized that Priscilla Lane and all she represented—the bourgeois dream of home and family, secure behind a white picket fence in the suburbs—were out of reach. In *High Sierra*, the dream is more elusive and the hero's awareness more acute, which makes the story even more poignant.

The quality of the story and of the picture in general owed a good deal to John Huston's screenplay, which was several cuts above the Wald-Macauley scripts for *The Roaring Twenties* and *They Drive by Night.* Huston adapted the story from W. R. Burnett's novel, which Warners purchased for $12,500 immediately after its publication in March 1940. On March 21, Huston sent a memo to Hal Wallis with his ideas for the project. "It would be easy for this to be made into a conventional gangster picture," said Huston, "which is exactly what it should not be. With the exception of *Little Caesar*, all of Burnett has suffered badly in screen translation." Huston wanted to retain the "spirit" of Burnett's story, which he considered "the strange sense of inevitability that comes with our deepening understanding of the characters and the forces that motivate them." Huston spent four months on the script, assisted by Burnett himself, who was brought in for rewrites. The final draft was submitted on July 31, a week before Walsh and Hellinger took the picture into production. Huston stayed through the first four weeks of shooting, and he soon realized that Bogart was ideal for Burnett's story. "Bogie was a medium-sized man," Huston recalled later, "not particularly impressive offscreen, but something happened when he was playing the right part. Those lights and shadows composed themselves into another, nobler personality: heroic, as in *High Sierra*."

Bogart played a middle-aged ex-con, Roy Earl, who is sprung from prison at the outset by his former associates to mastermind a heist. The first thing Earl does is to head for a nearby park to commune with nature—and from that point on it's obvious that this is no routine gangster saga. In the course of the story, Earl befriends a displaced rural family and falls in love with the farmer's daughter; at the same time he creates his own "family" from the assorted losers preparing for the heist. All this comes to naught, of course, and neither the viewer nor Roy Earl himself expects otherwise. But he finds redemption and love en route to his violent end, and in the process redefines the nature and appeal of the hard-boiled Warners hero. Bogart's Roy Earl also provided the first real glimpse of the Bogart persona: stoic, self-reliant, vulnerable, romantic, a man with a past and little hope for the future. But Bogart's performance had no immediate impact on his status at the studio. After *High Sierra* was released early in 1941, he was assigned a secondary role in a low-budget western: the role of Cole Younger in *Bad Men of Missouri*. Bogart refused to report and Jack Warner put him on suspension.

While Bogart battled Jack Warner, several other members of his impromptu unit became caught up in battles of their own on the lot, all of which played into the ongoing drama of Bogart's rise and the changing crime genre at Warners. While Bogart was on suspension, Raoul Walsh continued to establish himself as Warners' top action director. After doing *Strawberry Blonde*, a romantic costume piece costarring Cagney and Olivia de Havilland, Walsh was back in his element with *Manpower*, another Hellinger action picture scripted by Wald and Macau-

Humphrey Bogart's doomed hoodlum, Roy Earl, befriends a migrant farmer (Henry Travers, left) in High Sierra, a watershed crime film for the studio and a breakthrough to stardom for Bogart.

ley. The three writers lifted the story from *Tiger Shark*, a 1932 Edward
G. Robinson vehicle directed by Howard Hawks that seemed to get
remade at Warners every few years. In this version Robinson battled
George Raft for the girl, played here by Marlene Dietrich, and the
protagonists were power linemen rather than tuna fishermen. *Manpower* was plagued by feuds both on and off the set. The most visible
rift involved Raft and Robinson, whose feuding during production
reached a point where Walsh had to avoid shooting with both men on
the set—thus pushing the production one week beyond its six-week
schedule, and its cost to $920,000. A more significant though less pub-
licized rift developed between Hellinger and Hal Wallis. Hellinger
was headstrong, gifted, and a genuine character—a "Broadway type"
who wore dark suits and white silk ties and was outspoken in his
estimation of his own talents. Wallis was more subdued but no less
self-assured, and what with the production cutbacks, he had fewer
administrative responsibilities and began to take a more active role in
individual productions, including *High Sierra* and *Manpower*.

With the success of *The Roaring Twenties*, Hellinger considered
himself a bona fide producer and he resented having to submit to
Wallis's authority. When Wallis somewhat arbitrarily stepped in as
coproducer on *High Sierra*, Hellinger accused him of using his other
producers "as messenger boys and involuntary ass-kissers," and he told
Wallis not to expect the same from him. Hellinger was equally put off
by Wallis's interference during preproduction on *Manpower*, and he
finally decided he had had enough. In February 1941 he asked Jack
Warner for his release and wrote an amicable letter to Wallis informing
him of the decision. "There is no great problem here," said Hellinger;
"it is simply a matter of two men who are unable to agree under a
business roof." He asked to stay on long enough to produce *Manpower*,
but even that proved impossible. On March 10, two weeks before
Walsh started shooting, Warners formally released Hellinger from his
contract.

After Hellinger's departure, Wallis asked Jerry Wald to take over as
associate producer on the picture. Ever the politic opportunist, Wald
parlayed that request into a step up the career ladder. On March 18,
Wald's agent wrote Warners that "Wald would rather not assume the
additional burdens and responsibilities of Associate Producer" without
added compensation. Two weeks later the $800-a-week writer was an
$1,100-a-week production executive. (Wald, as legend has it, was the
role model for Sammy Glick in *What Makes Sammy Run?*, Budd Shul-
berg's scathing portrait of a Hollywood producer.)

Shortly after *Manpower* closed there was another flare-up on the set,
one with much heavier repercussions for Walsh and the studio. *They*

Died With Their Boots On, a romanticized biopic of George Armstrong Custer, was to be the eighth Flynn epic directed by Michael Curtiz. By now Curtiz was Warners' top director, and his patience with Flynn was wearing thin. Flynn was becoming more difficult to control on the set, and his notorious antics—his "wenching" and heavy drinking— were seriously undermining his performances, not to mention the quality of his close-ups. For his part, Flynn cared little for the autocratic Curtiz, and the simmering resentment erupted in July 1941, when the two got into a fistfight on the set of the Custer picture. Curtiz refused to work with the obstreperous star, so Wallis brought in Raoul Walsh, who had recently proven his worth not only as an action director but as a peacemaker as well. *They Died With Their Boots On* took seventy-four days to complete, at a cost of $1.35 million, but production went smoothly after Walsh took over and the picture turned out well enough. So it appeared that Flynn had found himself another director and that Walsh had graduated to the first rank of Warners' filmmakers.

W H I L E the shift of Flynn's heroic epic into an American idiom proceeded under Walsh's direction, Bogart's revitalization of the classic Warners tough guy continued as well in considerably more modest productions—a series of low-cost energetic crime thrillers. The film that took Bogart to the top was *The Maltese Falcon.* It was Warners' third attempt to translate Dashiell Hammett's hard-boiled detective story to the screen, and it came as close to being a B-grade production as any at the studio after the Foy unit closed down. This time around the adaptation was done by John Huston, who by 1941 had become a prominent writer at Warners and was one of the few with ambitions to direct. He happened to be renegotiating his contract while he was adapting the Hammett thriller, and besides a pay raise to $1,500 per week, he asked for a rider in his contract whereby Warners agreed "to assign the 'Author' during the term hereof . . . the direction of one motion picture."

Huston already had his sights on *The Maltese Falcon.* He'd seen the studio's 1931 and 1936 versions of the Sam Spade yarn, and he felt that both had missed the flavor of the novel. Huston lifted much of Hammett's dialogue verbatim—in fact, he later claimed that the first draft was little more than a straight transposition of the book. He submitted that draft on May 15, 1941, while his new contract was being drawn up, and he was assigned to direct *The Maltese Falcon* that same week. On May 22, studio manager Tenny Wright met with Huston, associate producer Henry Blanke, and all department heads. They came up with a budget of $381,000 and a June 10 start date, which left Blanke little time for casting. He had already sent Huston's script to Mary Astor, who was then drawing raves for her performance opposite Bette Davis in *The Great Lie,* another Blanke production that Warners had released a few weeks earlier. Astor was eager to play the duplicitous *femme noire,* Brigid O'Shaughnessy, and on May 23 she signed a free-lance contract for four weeks at $2,500 per. Within the next few days Blanke also signed free-lance deals with Peter Lorre (five weeks at $2,000) and Sidney Greenstreet (four weeks at $2,500), uniting one of the most eccentric and delightful screen couples in 1940s Hollywood.

By June 5 the crew assignments for *The Maltese Falcon* were set, but the lead role had yet to be cast. Bogart shot wardrobe tests with Astor on June 4 at Blanke's request, though Blanke knew the role had been formally offered to George Raft. Blanke also knew that Raft planned to turn it down. Raft did not have story or role approval, but there was a clause in his contract ruling out any B-movie work. This wasn't at all uncommon at Warners—even Huston's contract specified that "the Author shall not be required to [write] . . . any so-called 'B' productions." Raft took that kind of thing seriously, however, as he indicated in a June 6 letter to Jack Warner. "I feel strongly," said Raft, "that *The Maltese Falcon,* which you want me to do, is not an important picture." Bogart had no such reservations about the project, and by June 10 he was off suspension and officially assigned to the picture.

Despite a relatively meager budget and his lack of directing experience, Huston mounted a disciplined, first-class production. In preparation for each day's shooting, he made sketches of every camera setup, which he then went over with Blanke and his old friend William Wyler. Huston considered Blanke his "champion and mentor," but Willie Wyler seems to have had the greatest influence on his working methods and directorial style. Following Wyler's approach to *Jezebel,* Huston carefully plotted each setup and conducted heavy rehearsals with both cast and crew, occasionally spending an entire day working out a scene without printing a single take. This set Huston apart from the more efficient Warners directors, although his output when he was shooting made up for the time spent rehearsing. During his first week on *Falcon,* Huston averaged nine setups and 4'00" of finished film per day. These figures indicate high productivity in terms of minutes but also, judging from the minutes-to-setups ratio, rather long takes—yet another similarity to Wyler's formal style.

By the third week of production Huston was two days ahead of his thirty-six-day schedule, although the unit manager reported that he was "carrying the picture on schedule" since he expected Huston to fall behind after the arrival of Sidney Greenstreet, who had no movie experience. The immense British actor reported to the studio in mid-June, weighing in at 357 pounds and causing more concern for the

A still used to check Bogart's makeup in The Maltese Falcon, *a film that solidified Bogart's stardom and marked John Huston's debut as a director. In future years, crew members would learn the correct spelling of Huston's name.*

wardrobe department than for Huston. Greenstreet did require added rehearsal, but Huston and cinematographer Arthur Edeson maintained their pace: seven setups and 4'00" of finished film per day during Greenstreet's first full week. The pace slowed somewhat for the extended climactic scene in Spade's apartment with Bogart, Astor, Greenstreet, Lorre, and Elisha Cook, Jr. The finale demanded extensive choreography and rehearsal, and took nine days to shoot. In the hands of a less gifted director it might have ground the story to a halt, but Huston handled it with apparent ease. In fact, it was the prototype for a recurring motif in Huston's pictures: the group of disparate, dog-eared individuals (usually males) who unite in an obsessive quest, continually testing one another's loyalty and ability, ultimately less interested in the object of their pursuit than in the quest itself.

On July 18, 1941, the unit manager on *Falcon* reported to Warner and Wallis: "34th shooting day . . . at Blanke and Huston's request we eliminated the ending, as written in the script, which takes place on stage 3 in SPADE'S OFFICE. These gentlemen feel they can cut the picture without this ending." So the picture closed two days ahead of schedule and $54,000 under budget, with a total cost at that point of $327,182. Wallis and Warner were delighted, particularly since they no longer regarded *Falcon* as a B-grade production. Composer Adolph Deutsch was assigned to score the film, and Jack Warner planned a series of previews to make sure viewers could understand the story's complex exposition—which, in fact, Warner himself never quite did, although the opening was reshot and a prologue was added to provide background on the "black bird." By September, preview audiences were uniformly enthusiastic and *Falcon* was set to open in October at the Strand in New York. And in a telling display of Bogart's changing status, Jack Warner decided on a billing change. A year earlier Wallis gave Ida Lupino top billing in *High Sierra;* he explained to Warner that "Lupino has had a great deal of publicity on the strength of *They Drive by Night,* whereas Bogart has been playing the leads in a lot of 'B' pictures." For *The Maltese Falcon,* the initial plan (as of June 1941) was to give Bogart second billing after Mary Astor, to run his name below the title and at 75 percent its size. In October, Warner formally acknowledged *The Maltese Falcon* as Warner Bros.' first "Bogart picture," and he gave his new star first billing, with his name above the title and in the same-size type.

Released on October 3, *Falcon* immediately established Huston and Bogart as the darlings of the New York critics. Kate Cameron of the *Daily News* considered Huston's direction to be "comparable to Alfred Hitchcock's at its best," Howard Barnes of the *Herald Tribune* stated that "Bogart is so good as Spade that it is hard to think of anyone else playing the part," and Bosley Crowther of the *Times,* calling the picture "the best mystery thriller of the year," praised Huston's "brisk and supremely hard-boiled" style. The picture scored several Oscar nominations, including best picture, best screenplay, and best actress, and it made a number of annual ten-best lists. *Falcon's* box office was mildly disappointing, but this Wallis felt was due to the fact that the advertising and sales departments "were not sufficiently sold on the picture in New York to get behind it importantly."

The boys in New York could scarcely have expected *The Maltese Falcon* to hit, but still Wallis's point was well taken. Unlike Warners' other top releases in 1941—*Sergeant York, Meet John Doe, The Great Lie, The Bride Came C.O.D., The Letter, They Died With Their Boots On*—the modest Bogart thriller had not been conceived, designed, and marketed as an "important" picture. Wallis would make certain that didn't happen on the next Bogart project, which he planned to handle personally. He believed now that Warners could do without Garfield and Raft, that Bogart could sustain the Warners crime thriller all by himself. What's more, Bogart provided an ideal complement to Errol Flynn. Where Flynn was vigorous and athletic, Bogart was contemplative and a bit sedentary. Flynn was hyperkinetic; Bogart was quintessentially "cool." Flynn flashed youthful good looks and exuded sexuality; Bogart was rumpled, world-weary, and pushing middle age. Flynn was a figure in motion and slightly out of breath, whether in tights or on horseback; Bogart was a figure in repose, with his collar unbuttoned, his tie loosened, and that perpetual cigarette dangling from his lips. But Bogart was also capable of violent action and romantic attachments, and in his own way he was as sexy and heroic as Flynn.

Wallis began looking for Bogart material, and in mid-December he received a promising report from a studio story analyst. The report, which provided a twelve-page synopsis of an unproduced play, "Everybody Comes to Rick's," closed with this comment: "Excellent melodrama. Colorful, timely background, tense mood, suspense, psychological and physical conflict, tight plotting, sophisticated hokum." The analyst saw the story as a "box-office natural" whose central character, an expatriate American saloon keeper in Casablanca named Rick Blaine, was especially suitable "for Bogart, or Cagney, or Raft in out-of-the-usual roles and perhaps Mary Astor." Wallis was certain he had found his Bogart vehicle—and a "timely" one indeed. The play was submitted to Warners on Monday, December 8, 1941, the day after the Japanese attacked Pearl Harbor; the story analyst's report reached Wallis's desk on December 11, the day the United States declared war on Nazi Germany.

W A R N E R S was already gearing up for the war, due largely to Harry Warner's intense anti-Nazi sentiments. He had begun pushing the studio's campaign against Hitler's Third Reich back in 1938, with *Confessions of a Nazi Spy*. But still Pearl Harbor brought sudden and significant changes to the studio. Besides the predictable increase in war-related pictures, there were massive cuts in feature production, prestige deals with outsiders like Capra and Lasky were eliminated, and the production management system was overhauled.

These changes were based on four related assumptions: first, that there would be limited materials and manpower during the war; second, that the heavy employment and heated-up economic activity of wartime would keep the theaters full, even with the supply of pictures limited; third, that the marketplace would become steadily less competitive, and thus the cost and complexity of prestige production, particularly with outside talent, was unnecessary; and fourth, that with feature production cut from forty-eight releases in 1941 to thirty-four in 1942, and then to only twenty-one in 1943, there was little need for the same elaborate system of studio management. Hal Wallis himself could handle most of Warners' more important pictures, with Jack Warner and a handful of producers and producer-directors handling the rest.

So Warners' associate producers graduated to producer status in 1942, and in the early months of the same year a number of important deals were cut to realign production management. The key transaction was with Hal Wallis. On February 2, he signed a new contract stating that "for several years past" Wallis had been "the executive having general charge and supervision of substantially all of the Class-A motion picture photoplays produced by the Company." Because Wallis no longer wished to be responsible for "as large a number" of productions, he and Warners now agreed to limit his output to four pictures per year. The contract was for four years at a salary of $4,000 weekly in years one and two, and $3,500 in years three and four. The drop in salary would be more than compensated for by an additional agreement: Wallis was to receive 10 percent of the gross receipts once his productions returned 125 percent of their production costs. Each of his films would be billed as "A Hal B. Wallis Production," at 50 percent the title size, and if a producer-director had a similar agreement, Wallis would receive straight producer credit on a separate title card following the screenwriter's. Wallis was to have first choice of story properties, directors, performers, and other contract talent, and Warners agreed to hire any outside talent whom Wallis deemed "essential to the proper production" of his projects. Wallis also was to cut his own pictures, but any disputes over final cut were to be resolved by Jack Warner.

Wallis's move from production executive to producer did not entail a reduction of authority. On the contrary, he had even more power and control over actual filmmaking than he did as an administrator. Eliminating his role as production chief did signal a shift in the studio's overall power structure and in production management, though, and Warners continued in that direction by signing new deals with Mark Hellinger and Howard Hawks. With Wallis leaving his supervisory role, Hellinger was now willing to return to Warners; he signed a five-year pact starting at $3,000 per month, with his duties to be those of a "producer and/or executive and/or director and/or writer." Hawks signed a five-year, five-picture deal with Warners on February 12, for a salary of $100,000 per picture plus bonuses and other incentives. The contract described Hawks as "Director and/or Supervisor," whose function was "to prepare or assist in the preparation of original stories, adaptations, continuities, and dialogue" and also "in the cutting, titling, and editing" of his Warners productions. No other director would do the retakes or added scenes on his pictures, and he would never be assigned to more than one project at a time. Warners agreed to bill each of his films as "A Howard Hawks Production," with his name above the title and at least 25 percent its size.

This clearly was a sweet deal for Hawks, giving him considerable authority and creative control. But Warners protected itself in several ways. The deal was an exclusive one, meaning Hawks could work for no one else for the duration of the contract. All projects were to be set through mutual agreement, with Warners reserving ultimate approval over both the shooting script and the final cut. Hawks also agreed, despite his contractual status as "supervisor," to submit to an executive producer. The contract stated that Hawks "shall work under the direct supervision of Jack L. Warner or a producer appointed by [Warner]." When the deal was signed, in fact, Warners and Hawks had already agreed that Hawks's first project would be a war picture starring John Garfield entitled *Air Force*, and that the executive producer would be Hal Wallis.

It was obvious from this and other projects that Wallis would still be overseeing most of Warners' prestige-level productions. When Wallis signed, he already had two top features set: *Now Voyager*, a Bette Davis melodrama, and *Desperate Journey*, Flynn's first war picture. By late February he added *Air Force* and decided to do "Everybody Comes to Rick's" with Bogart, under the title *Casablanca*. Later that spring he took on another Davis vehicle, *Watch on the Rhine*, and a wartime comedy, *Princess O'Rourke*, costarring Olivia de Havilland and Robert Cummings. These were among Warners' most ambitious productions in 1942, and Wallis's track record was remarkable. Each was a solid box-office hit, and all but the Flynn vehicle were critical successes as well. Wallis's initial half-dozen productions received eighteen Academy Award nominations and actually won seven, with *Casablanca* bringing Warners a best-picture Oscar—its first since *Zola* and only the second in the studio's history.

U N T I L Wallis signed his new pact, *Casablanca* did not appear to be destined for greatness. In December 1941 Wallis sent the reader's report to Jerry Wald and Robert Buckner, who supervised the studio's lesser fare, and several trade papers in January 1942 announced that Warner Bros. was planning to do the picture with Ronald Reagan and Ann Sheridan, two feature players who had just scored in *Kings Row*, a Christmas 1941 release. But as soon as Wallis became a producer he took on *Casablanca* as his own project and tapped Humphrey Bogart to star as Rick Blaine. Sheridan still was in the running for costar, and so was Mary Astor after her success with Bogart in *The Maltese Falcon*. But as the project was upgraded and the story reworked, Wallis decided to cast a European as Bogart's love interest. After considerable maneuvering, a straight swap was worked out with David Selznick in April, exchanging Olivia de Havilland for Ingrid Bergman.

The idea to cast a European in the female lead emerged during script development, which proved rather complex as "Everybody Comes to Rick's" was transformed into *Casablanca*. Much has been made over

the years about how the Epstein twins and Howard Koch wrote separate screenplays that were blended during production, but actually the
scripting of *Casablanca* involved more personnel and considerably
more convolution than that. The first two writers on the project were
Aeneas Mackenzie and Wally Kline, who did a treatment in January
after coscripting *They Died With Their Boots On*. They were instructed
by Wallis to flesh out the love story in the original play and remove any
censorable elements, particularly those involving the female lead. The
heroine in the play was Lois, a wanton American and classic *femme
noire*. Her earlier affair with Rick in Paris had broken up his marriage,
and as the story opens she arrives in Casablanca as the mistress, not
the wife, of celebrated Resistance leader Victor Laszlo.

Kline and Mackenzie tightened the story, but still Wallis was dissatisfied with the Lois character. In February he took them off the project
and asked Casey Robinson for some help. Robinson was Warners'
house specialist in romantic melodrama, having scripted such Davis
hits as *Dark Victory*, *The Old Maid*, and *All This and Heaven Too*, and
at the time he was scripting *Now Voyager* for Davis. He agreed to work
in his spare time on Lois's character and on the love story in general.
That same month Wallis officially assigned the project to Philip and
Julius Epstein, sibling staffers and the top script doctors at Warners.
Their forte was lightening up otherwise ponderous material, which
they had just done for *Yankee Doodle Dandy*, a musical biopic of
George M. Cohan starring Jimmy Cagney. The Epsteins overhauled
the dialogue on *Casablanca* and also reworked the character of Louis
Renault, the local prefect of police (played by Claude Rains in the film)
whose rapport with Rick Blaine is countered by a pragmatic cooperation with the Nazi occupational forces.

The Bogart-Rains relationship is in many ways the narrative and
thematic core of *Casablanca*, and credit for that goes to the Epsteins.
Casey Robinson, meanwhile, deserves credit for working out the more
conventional romance between Bogart and Bergman. Robinson got no
formal recognition for his work on *Casablanca*, since at this stage of his
career he refused to share screen credit with another writer. This was
a bit eccentric, to be sure—in this instance it cost him an Oscar—but
he was by now the studio's top writer and that was the way he chose to
operate. Robinson changed Lois, the libidinous American, into Ilsa,
the innocent European whose family had been ravaged by the Nazis
and whose fidelity to Laszlo and the "cause" both motivated her betrayal of Rick Blaine and ultimately absolved her from it.

By early April the love story had been reworked and both Bogart and
Bergman were cast—though there was a brief glitch when George Raft
suddenly began lobbying for the lead. Jack Warner sent a memo to

Wallis on April 2 suggesting Raft for the picture, but Wallis, refusing to even consider the prospect, flashed his confidence in Bogart and also his newfound contractual power at the studio. He sent Warner a reply the following day, assuring him that Bogart was ideal for the role, which was "being written for him." Actually, Wallis still had deep concerns about Bogart's character, Rick Blaine. Robinson had a handle on the romance and the Epsteins were fleshing out Rick's friendship with Renault, but Wallis felt that Rick's political sensibilities—and the geopolitical and war-related elements of the story in general—still needed work. On April 6 he assigned staff writer Howard Koch to rework Bogart's character, with instructions that he concentrate on Rick's political background and on the Nazi occupation angle. Or as Koch himself described the assignment in a later memo, he was to "develop a serious melodrama of present-day significance."

Koch got along well with both Bogart and director Mike Curtiz, and he stayed on to do rewrites during the shoot, which turned out to be extensive. Curtiz started shooting in late May, and it was not until the film was in production that the script really came together. Koch consulted frequently with both Curtiz and Bogart on the rewrites, and this

Tracking shot used in Casablanca *to film the arrival of the Nazi commandant, Strasser (Conrad Veidt), as he is met at the airport by the local prefect of police (Claude Rains).*

angered and confused Ingrid Bergman since she had no idea how her relationship with Rick and Laszlo would be resolved. As a matter of fact, Koch, Curtiz, and Wallis didn't know either. They went into the final scene—the confrontations at the airport between Rick and Ilsa, Rick and the Nazi commandant, and Rick and Renault—with several versions written. They planned to shoot them all, but everyone involved has claimed that they knew they had it when they shot Koch's preferred version—the one in the release version, wherein Rick sends Ilsa away with Laszlo, shoots the Nazi, and walks off into the fog with Renault. And as difficult as Bergman's uncertainty about the outcome must have been, it undoubtedly enhanced her performance, since Ilsa herself had no idea how things would come out until that moment at the airport when Rick told her to go with Laszlo.

Wallis and Curtiz closed the picture in early August, eleven days late and some $75,000 over the $878,000 budget. They very nearly shot yet another scene for the end of *Casablanca* after preview audiences expressed concern about the fate of Rick and Louis after they walked off in the fog. Wallis wanted to shoot an epilogue with the two men in uniform aboard a fog-shrouded freighter, discussing their plans to take on the Nazis. But before Wallis could arrange for the retakes, the Allies landed in Casablanca for the North African campaign. The Warners decided to exploit the marketing potential of that event and rushed the picture into a Thanksgiving premiere and a January release. Instead of the tag scene on the boat being added, Rick's closing line to Louis was rewritten—by Wallis himself, apparently—to indicate their shared sense of mission. Thus was born one of Hollywood's most memorable closing lines: "Louis, this could be the beginning of a beautiful friendship."

In another stroke of good fortune, the picture went into general release just as the Allies opened a summit conference in Casablanca; the conference was headline news for weeks and gave Warners additional free promotion. *Casablanca* was an immediate hit—one of the biggest in studio history—and it became an anthem of America's commitment to the war. Early in the story, Rick Blaine is reminiscent of the archetypal Warners tough guy—cynical and self-reliant, repeatedly muttering "I stick my neck out for nobody." But by film's end, when he has rediscovered his love of woman and of country, he crystallizes the American shift from neutrality to selfless sacrifice. The film won Bogart an Oscar nomination and sent him into a spate of war pictures. But though he was now a top Warners star, the seven-year deal for $2,750 per week that he signed on January 1, 1942, just before starting *Casablanca,* still stood.

B O G A R T was altogether satisfied with his position at Warners in the early 1940s—star status, a good salary, steady work in first-rate pictures —and that made him something of an exception at the time. Cagney and Robinson had already left for free-lance status, and Warners had to give Bette Davis her own independent corporation, "B.D. Incorporated," to keep her on the lot. In June 1943 Davis signed a five-picture contract, which gave her 35 percent of the net profits on her pictures. After dickering with Davis, Jack Warner had little patience with Olivia De Havilland's continual complaints. But her talents were indeed being squandered at Warners, since she was no longer costarring with Errol Flynn and it was Bette Davis who landed most of the choice melodramas. The only decent roles De Havilland was getting were on loan—with Warners picking up sizable profits, since her $2,500-per-week salary hardly reflected her market value after her Oscar nomination for *Gone With the Wind*. De Havilland's indignation over the loan-outs and her second-class studio status grew, and after another suspension in the summer of 1943, she decided to honor a long-standing Warners tradition. In August, she filed suit against Jack Warner and the studio over its suspension policies. And as Warners' own attorneys had been anticipating for years, the courts finally sided with the plaintiff. Warners appealed, and in November 1943 the Superior Court of California agreed to hear the case. In May 1944 the court found Warners in violation of the state's antipeonage laws.

This was a watershed event in Hollywood's history, a significant victory for top stars and a huge setback for the studios. No longer could Warners or any other studio tack on suspension time to the end of a contract, thereby preventing an artist from sitting out and becoming a free agent. So there was yet another chink in Warners' armor, and another of its longtime employees was looking elsewhere for work. And like Cagney, Robinson, and so many others, De Havilland had no trouble finding it. She signed with Paramount and underscored her argument that Warners had been wasting her talents by winning Oscars for best actress twice in the next four years.

L O S I N G the De Havilland case did little to mellow Jack Warner's combative demeanor or diminish his appetite for power. In fact, by 1943–44 he was battling his producers as well as his stars. The fiercest battles were with Hal Wallis, whose success with *Casablanca* brought Jack's simmering resentment to a boil. In June 1943, as *Casablanca* completed its run, several papers reported that Darryl Zanuck wanted Wallis as a unit producer at 20th Century-Fox. Jack Warner fired off an angry memo reminding Wallis of his contractual obligations and demanding that Wallis respond, "denying any such contemplation." But as Wallis's successes continued throughout the year, and especially after the attention Wallis received when the Academy Awards were announced, Warner began to wonder whether he'd be better off without his top producer. In late November, he had studio attorney Roy Obringer inform Wallis that the studio would consider releasing him from his contract if he felt the present deal was a "handicap" on any "capital gains basis." Wallis insisted he was pleased with his present deal, but within another few days Warner was back on his case. Wallis had done an interview for *The New York Times* and Jack Warner was not mentioned in the piece; Jack demanded an explanation from Wallis, who contended that the oversight was the *Times*'s and not his own. Warner, meanwhile, wired publicity chief Charlie Einfeld in New York that he would "definitely take legal action if this isn't stopped" adding that he was "sick and tired of everyone taking credit" while he was "doing most of [the] work."

At that point Warner took a more aggressive tack. He assigned Wallis a routine feature project in December, claiming it was within his rights to do so because Wallis had fallen behind in his contractual obligations. Technically this was true, since Wallis was obligated to deliver four pictures per year; after producing six pictures in the first year of his new contract, he had delivered only two—*Saratoga Trunk* and *Passage to Marseilles*—during the second year. Wallis refused the assignment, and much of January and February were spent haggling over legal technicalities. Then at the Academy banquet the feud reached a flash point. A number of Oscars went to Wallis's films, and Wallis himself received the Irving Thalberg Award for distinguished achievement in motion picture production. The evening marked a high point in his twenty years with Warners, and he hoped it would culminate in *Casablanca* winning the best-picture Oscar. When the award was announced, recalled Wallis, Jack Warner "leapt to his feet, ran to the stage, and received [the Oscar] ahead of me." Writing in his autobiography some thirty-five years later, Wallis admitted that he still hadn't "recovered from the shock."

The morning after the ceremony Wallis called Jack Warner's office and demanded the statuette. Warner had already told studio publicity director Alex Evelove to handle the situation, and Evelove reported back to Warner that he told Wallis that he would not be given the Oscar "under any circumstances" and that "we would photograph him with the Thalberg Award only, not with the Oscar." The story immediately hit the L.A. papers, and they were not squelched by Wallis's insistence in *The Los Angeles Times* that he was "glad to see Jack Warner accept the award" and that any suggestion of a feud between them "is totally unjustified." Wallis's efforts to work things out came to naught; within the next few weeks Warner began to pull writers off Wallis's projects and deny him access to stars and other personnel. By month's end Wallis had had enough. On April 1, 1944, his attorney wrote the studio that he was willing to cancel his contract on two conditions: first, that the studio continue to honor its profit-sharing commitment after he left; and second, that he be allowed to complete the five projects presently in production. Warner replied that since Wallis had not honored that contract, the studio had no obligations and that Wallis was "terminated" as a Warner Bros. employee. This initiated a lengthy legal battle that the studio was destined to lose, but Jack Warner persisted quite literally out of spite—in fact, a bone of contention was $7,040 worth of projection equipment that Warners had installed in Wallis's home, which Jack demanded that Wallis return.

As the Wallis case dragged on, Jack Warner fell out with Mark Hellinger as well. In February 1944, William Randolph Hearst personally asked that Hellinger be given a leave without pay to cover the war in the Pacific. Jack Warner agreed to a six-month leave, and Hellinger was away from the studio until the end of the summer. On his return, Hellinger found Warner hostile and distant, and his standing as both a writer and a producer had slipped. As Hellinger recounted in a letter to Warner written in November: "I had come back safely from a tough jaunt, and I had gathered what I thought were four hot yarns, and I had a new perspective and new hopes of a closer association than ever with you. Unfortunately, the picture did not remain bright very long." The letter accompanied his resignation.

Warner gave Hellinger his release, and a few weeks later the studio settled the Hal Wallis suit as well. In December 1944 Warners agreed to pay Wallis the profit shares on his pictures even after his contract was terminated, and all other contractual obligations were settled by a lump sum of $1 million, to be paid to Wallis over the next seven years (minus $3,872, the depreciated value of the studio-installed projection equipment).

H A L   W A L L I S ' S departure signaled the end of an era at Warner Bros. He had worked his way up through exhibition and publicity in New York, apprenticed under Zanuck before a decade-long stint as production chief, and then emerged as Warners' top filmmaker during the war. But Jack Warner was convinced that the studio could do without him—just as it could do without Hellinger—and in fact Warner was right. With output down to only twenty pictures per year, Blanke and Buckner and the other producers could easily cover things. And Jerry Wald, an expert at stroking Jack Warner's delicate ego, was also proving he could handle the studio's more ambitious projects. So with the market holding strong and power once again consolidated under Jack's control, the Warners were feeling upbeat as the war wound down.

17

David O. Selznick Productions: Packaging Prestige

Even though *Gone With the Wind*
and *Rebecca* left David Selznick thoroughly burned out and in temporary retirement from active production, the movie marketplace was
simply too hot to pass up in the early 1940s. At age forty, and after SIP's
three-year, nine-picture burst, Selznick wasn't sure how many more
blockbusters he had in him, and in fact it would be four years before
he produced another picture of his own. But he was not in hibernation
during that period—far from it. When he liquidated SIP in August 1940
to avoid heavy tax losses, he created David O. Selznick Productions.
Through that company he took a run at the wartime market from an
altogether different tack, loaning out his top personnel and "packaging" several pictures, which he then sold to other studios during preproduction. Thus Selznick had more in common with his brother
Myron and other top agents in the early forties than he did with other
filmmakers. Years of prestige production had schooled him well, and
since going independent he had learned the process of loaning out,
swapping, and otherwise negotiating for talent and story properties.
He had generally been on the receiving end at SIP, but in the early
1940s he found that dealing talent, stories, scripts—and even entire
projects—was financially rewarding and much less trying, both physically and emotionally. In the process, he redefined the role of both
agent and producer, creating something of a prototype for the packaging agents who would dominate the New Hollywood decades later—

individuals who assembled a picture's principal elements, particularly the star, script, and director, and then sold the package to a production company.

Due to the increasing mobility of top stars and the demand for first-run product in the early 1940s, this turn in Selznick's professional direction made perfect sense. A vital feature of the studio system by the 1930s was the cooperation among the various studios and production companies, particularly through loan-outs of above-the-line talent and top technical artists. An industry study funded by the Rockefeller Foundation at the time revealed that from 1933 through 1939, there were over 2,000 loans among the seven major studio-distributors involving actors, directors, and cinematographers under studio contract. This figure did not include writers, a particularly mobile group of Hollywood specialists. Nor did it include free-lancers, whose numbers grew enormously during the 1940s, since tax laws encouraged highly paid individuals to avoid salaried income in favor of profit-sharing deals and the like. Selznick's employees were somewhat rare cases in 1940s Hollywood, in that they were on salary and invariably had signed long-term deals. But the nature of prestige filmmaking, particularly its irregular production process and penchant for off-casting, put Selznick's top talent in the same high-mobility, high-demand market as free-lance stars, writers, and directors. And with the government's antitrust efforts bringing an increase in A-class production, there was a lucrative market for someone like Hitchcock, who was a writer as well as a producing director.

It was a Hitchcock deal, in fact, that first indicated to Selznick the real potential of dealing his talent. Like so many of Selznick's employees, Hitchcock was under long-term exclusive contract, which meant Selznick could loan him out and was obligated to pay only the designated salary, and he could "pocket the overage" paid for Hitchcock's services. During the fall of 1939, just before production opened on *Rebecca,* Selznick loaned Hitchcock to Walter Wanger for *Foreign Correspondent,* which Wanger was producing for UA. Wanger paid Selznick $5,000 per week for Hitchcock "to assist and collaborate in the writing, adaptation, script, dialogue, and continuity," and also to direct. That translated into an overage for Selznick of $40,000, and it cost him nothing in terms of lost time on *Rebecca.* Hitchcock worked on the script for Wanger while *Rebecca* was in postproduction, and then he directed *Foreign Correspondent* during the spring of 1940, after *Rebecca*'s release. Wanger's picture was out by the summer and was a solid hit in the States, although the events it so accurately predicted—the Nazi blitz and the bombing of England—cut off its international market. But Hitchcock's stock was up, particularly with *Rebecca* doing so

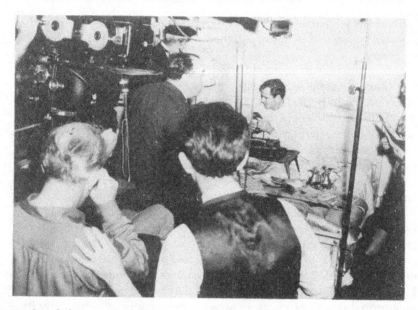

Hitchcock directing Joel McCrea in Walter Wanger's production Foreign Correspondent, *the first of many Hitchcock loan-outs by David Selznick during the 1940s.*

well, and there was suddenly quite a bit of interest in Hitchcock, and in Joan Fontaine as well.

During that summer of 1940 David O. Selznick Productions was born, and Selznick's career as a packager and talent agent began in earnest. While he dickered with RKO over a possible two-picture deal for Hitchcock, Selznick reached an agreement with Universal for Fontaine, who was to star in a remake of *Back Street*, the 1932 weepie. Universal also wanted director Robert Stevenson, whom Selznick had recently brought over from England, for the project. Selznick was delighted, since the female lead in *Back Street* was ideal for Fontaine, and the picture would quickly establish Stevenson's market value in Hollywood. Universal agreed to pay $45,000 for ten weeks of Fontaine's services, and the same fee for Stevenson over thirteen weeks. That translated into a clear profit of $56,000 for Selznick.

The deal fell through in late July, however, due to Fontaine's displeasure with the script and the part. Selznick exploded and told Fontaine that her contract gave her no option regarding roles or stories. Still she persisted, so he fired off a long and virulent letter, outlining her legal obligations and reminding her that *Rebecca* had cost SIP "many extra expensive days of shooting, many retakes, many wild lines —at a total cost of perhaps $75-100,000—to get a performance worthy of the picture, a performance which we could have had with such ease from a professional such as Maggie Sullavan, who was dying to do the role." Selznick also questioned Fontaine's capacity to judge screen roles. "I must say that I have known few film actors, even those with vast experience," counseled Selznick, "who have had sound judgment about what they should do." He mentioned stars like Gloria Swanson "who drove themselves into obscurity with startling speed and efficiency" once they gained control of their careers and were "in a position to substitute their own judgment for that of the people who have developed and exploited them."

Selznick sent Fontaine the letter on August 15, 1940, the same day that he closed the RKO-Hitchcock deal, committing his director to two pictures and a minimum of thirty-two weeks at $5,000 per week. Hitchcock was to direct *Mr. and Mrs. Smith,* a Carole Lombard vehicle, and then he would prepare and direct a project of his own, "Before the Fact"—later titled *Suspicion.* Fontaine still refused to do the Universal picture, however, but Selznick managed to turn the situation to his advantage. He suspended Fontaine in September for refusing to take *Back Street*—a role that went to Margaret Sullavan, coincidentally— and when Hitchcock had *Suspicion* ready in December, Selznick convinced RKO to take Fontaine for the lead at $7,500 per week. Thus Selznick made several thousand dollars per week more than he would have on the Universal deal, and Fontaine wound up with a part that brought her an Academy Award in 1941 for best actress, increasing her commodity value and solidifying her emergent screen persona.

The Hitchcock-Fontaine project for RKO was not without its complications, though. In *Suspicion,* as in *Rebecca,* Fontaine played a young spinster who is charmed by a somewhat mysterious gentleman (played by Cary Grant), whom she marries and eventually begins to suspect of being a murderer. This time her fears are justified—or at least they were in the original version. Hitchcock ended the film with Grant poisoning his wife after promising her to post a letter she had written to her mother. The letter tells all, and the story ends with the murderer mailing a letter that assures his downfall. That delightful Hitchcock twist met with disapproval at RKO, which feared it might damage the screen image of its biggest star, Cary Grant. So Hitchcock tacked on an utterly illogical ending wherein Fontaine suddenly realizes her husband is as innocent as the driven snow and they embrace joyously—even though only moments before it seemed certain he was about to kill her.

Neither Hitchcock nor Selznick liked the alternate ending, but it remained intact since Hitchcock was committed to start *Saboteur* for Universal. Frank Lloyd, one of Universal's producers, agreed to pay $70,000 for the script and $130,000 for fourteen weeks of Hitchcock's services as director, plus 10 percent of the gross revenues. Thus Hitchcock was now worth over $9,000 per week, some $6,000 more than Selznick was paying him. Hitchcock was growing increasingly resentful of the disparity between his salary and his market value, since the difference wound up in Selznick's pocket. Not that he was being grossly underpaid. At that point Hitchcock, after two years and ten weeks on Selznick's payroll, had earned $354,375, including various bonuses and commissions. That put him among the higher-paid directors in Hollywood, although the overages were putting Selznick in a class by himself as an agent—particularly since most Hollywood agents took only 10 percent of a client's pay, while Selznick was taking almost 70 percent. In 1942 Selznick cut two more excellent deals for Hitchcock's services. In April Universal producer Jack Skirball agreed to pay Selznick $150,000 for eighteen weeks of Hitchcock's services on *Shadow of a Doubt*, based on a script Hitchcock wrote with playwright Thornton Wilder. And in November, 20th Century-Fox signed Hitchcock to direct *Lifeboat* at $300,000 for eighteen weeks.

Selznick's success in these endeavors created an unexpected conflict with his brother Myron, whose agency represented Hitchcock and several other employees of David's. Myron and David had been intensely competitive since childhood, and when David was an active filmmaker Myron had treated him like any other producer or studio executive when it came to getting the most for his clients' services. Now it was David who was soaking the studios, and Myron resented having his authority usurped by his younger brother—though Myron had little to complain about considering the increasingly larger cuts his agency was making as David jacked up the asking price on his employees. David was feeling resentment as well, since he was paying Myron for the privilege of doing his job for him. As he told one of Myron's associates in January 1942, "If and when we should decide to sell Hitchcock for further pictures, we don't consider that we need to pay 10 percent to do so; we can sell him by telephone for as many pictures as we want to let him go for." That was one of countless letters and memos that went back and forth between the Selznicks in the early 1940s, most of them involving Hitchcock and Ingrid Bergman, who also was under contract to David and was a client of Myron's. In 1940, David worked out a deal for Bergman with MGM, paying $35,000 for seven weeks of her services opposite Spencer Tracy in *Dr. Jekyll and Mr. Hyde*. By 1942 her asking price had risen from $5,000 per week to $15,000, with David loaning her to Warners for *Saratoga Trunk* and *Casablanca*, and to

Paramount for *For Whom the Bell Tolls*. The latter two pictures secured Bergman's stardom, and a year later Selznick loaned her to Metro to star in *Gaslight*, this time for a flat fee of $250,00—and an overage of $180,000.

By then Myron was publicly taking credit for deals David was making—thus enhancing his agency's reputation—and he also was trying to finagle another 10 percent on certain deals by levying his agent's fee against both the individual artist and David O. Selznick Productions. David was predictably upset, and his complaints grew louder and more frequent with each successive deal. In a particularly emotional epistle, written in November 1943, he railed at length (eleven pages) about both Hitchcock and Bergman. But although Selznick believed—and with good reason—that he had done much more than Myron to establish the "market price" of both the director and the star, still he was not about to change his current methods. David undoubtedly would have been doing the agent's work regardless, given his obsessive concern for his contract talent—especially his female stars—and he was committed by various labor agreements and industry regulations to use agents when loaning out his contract talent. There was no question but that he preferred to work through Myron's outfit, and that their frequent quarrels kept them locked in an old familial intimacy. What's more, Myron's alcoholism and chronic depression were growing worse, and David knew that these business deals were one way of keeping tabs on his brother.

By 1942–43, Selznick was devoting as much energy to packaging projects as to dealing individual stars, writers, and directors. He prepared a few of these projects with the intention of producing them himself, and so the preparation was extensive, meticulous, and characteristically obsessive. The most ambitious and obsessive was *Jane Eyre*, which Selznick cultivated for some two years before selling it to 20th Century-Fox. A stage version of Charlotte Brontë's classic gothic romance toured successfully in the late 1930s, with Katharine Hepburn and later Janet Gaynor in the title role. Selznick's interest in the property began with *Rebecca*, which he considered a veiled adaptation of *Jane Eyre*. The success of Du Maurier's novel and Selznick's adaptation inspired a series of film melodramas, to the point where a "Jane Eyre formula" was emerging in Hollywood during the early 1940s although the novel itself had yet to be adapted. A succession of moody love stories, including *Suspicion*, were created in Hollywood that turned on the same basic premise: a naive young heroine falls in love with a wealthy, captivating, but mysterious older gentleman who seems to be hiding something—not only in his own past but in some secluded wing of the family mansion as well.

Before the formula gained currency—indeed, even before *Rebecca* was released—Selznick had begun thinking about doing the Brontë novel itself. Early in 1940 he instructed story editor Val Lewton to research *Jane Eyre* as a possible property. Lewton reported that "*Jane Eyre* appears in every listing of our book of statistics. It is listed as the sixth greatest novel in the English language among the twenty best English novels selected by librarians all over the world. It is listed as tenth among the sixty greatest novels of the world as chosen by a committee of American and English university professors. Among the list of classics most read in public libraries, it . . . is listed in the sixteenth position." After all his research, Lewton concluded that *Jane Eyre* should be situated "somewhere between *Wuthering Heights* and *David Copperfield*"—a high rank considering that Dickens was far and away the most popular and most frequently adapted of all English novelists.

Lewton also appraised a Mercury Theatre radio production of *Jane Eyre* that was broadcast in April 1940. As with the Mercury broadcast of *Rebecca* several months earlier, Selznick wanted to hear how Orson Welles would dramatize the popular novel. Welles adapted the novel and he also played Rochester opposite Madeleine Carroll in the title role. Lewton found the production subpar for Welles, "far below his very good rendering of *Rebecca*. . . . As you know, *Rebecca*'s genesis is *Jane Eyre*, and Rochester's character is exactly that of De Winter. Welles played it as if it were the Hunchback of Notre Dame." Lewton found Carroll less "mealymouthed" than usual, though, and felt that she brought "zip and sparkle" to Jane's character. Selznick had a detailed synopsis of the novel prepared, and he confided to Kay Brown in May that "despite some pretty corny situations, even for a book as old as this one, I am confirmed in my opinion of it as a perfectly swell picture story, and I definitely want to make it." He had production manager Ray Klune prepare a preliminary budget in June while he began looking for a writer to do the adaptation.

Late that year he began talking with John Houseman, a fast-rising producer and playwright, and cofounder with Welles of the Mercury Players (although the two had fallen out while making *Citizen Kane*, their initial motion picture effort). In January 1941, Selznick signed Houseman to adapt the story and supervise the project, which he hoped to have Hitchcock direct. *Saboteur* kept Hitchcock tied up, so Selznick put Robert Stevenson on *Jane Eyre* with Houseman, and he planned to bring Hitchcock in later, if possible. An entire year was spent developing the script and trying to coordinate Hitchcock's schedule, but in December 1941 Selznick told his assistant Dan O'Shea "to forget the idea of Hitchcock for *Jane Eyre*." Still Selznick wanted to do the picture, and later that spring he hired George Gallup's polling and market research outfit, Audience Research Incorporated (ARI), to test various stars and combinations. Gallup's assistant, David Ogilvy, sent Selznick a report "on the relative box-office contributions of Fontaine, De Havilland, Garson, and Hepburn in the role of *Jane Eyre,* and . . . of Pidgeon and Colman in the role of Rochester." ARI also tested different stars for the supporting role of Rivers, Jane's suitor, although "previous experience" indicated that "when you add a marquee name to a cast which already contains two, you add very little to the picture's box-office potential." In his summary of ARI's nationwide poll, Ogilvy reported that with moviegoers not familiar with Brontë's story, De Havilland "wins," primarily because of her "marquee value." Those familiar with the story preferred Fontaine, due to an "attempt at type-casting on the part of the public." Similar typecasting generated "a widespread belief that both Garson and Hepburn would be definitely miscast as Jane." Ogilvy also noted the "widespread recognition of the resemblance between the situations in *Jane Eyre, Rebecca,* and *Suspicion.* If you are anxious to minimize this recognition, it might be wise not to use Fontaine."

For the male lead, Walter Pidgeon was preferred over Ronald Colman, but there was something of a trade-off involved. "With Pidgeon you are on a rising market," reported Ogilvy, especially with "ticket buyers under eighteen years of age," whereas Colman "still carries implications of *action.*" Male viewers "look to Colman to retrieve a story which is basically feminine in appeal." The ARI study indicated that "when the ballots are sorted by teams, Fontaine and Pidgeon win with those who are most familiar with the story, and with those who react favorably to the synopsis," while "Colman and De Havilland win with those who do not react favorably to the story." Ogilvy closed his summation with a curious addendum: "In a supplementary poll, Orson Welles was included with Pidgeon and Colman. He received only 14 percent of the total vote [versus 48 percent for Pidgeon and 38 percent for Colman], being particularly weak with females."

While he fretted over casting, Selznick continued to monitor the script's development; eventually he brought in British novelist Aldous Huxley, who had done a solid adaptation of Jane Austen's *Pride and Prejudice* for MGM in 1940. Huxley worked at his own pace, which Selznick found agonizingly slow, so he put two other writers on the project, who would work independently of one another and of Huxley. During the summer of 1942, Selznick had his scenario assistant Bobby Keon sort through the various drafts and rewrites. She continually reassembled the script in accordance with Selznick's and her own estimation of the most effective scenes. Stevenson, meanwhile, began preparing the film for production. Then in the fall of 1942, Selznick announced that he would not be producing the picture. He had decided instead to include it in a massive deal that would send several scripts and numerous personnel to 20th Century-Fox. The deal was announced on November 16, 1942, and it involved the following transactions: the *Jane Eyre* package, for $250,000, which included the rights to Brontë's novel, a half-dozen script drafts, and the services (on loan) of Joan Fontaine as star, Robert Stevenson as director, and W. L. Pereira as production designer; the *Claudia* package, for $150,000, which included the rights to Rose Franken's play and the services of Dorothy McGuire (whose long-term contract would be split between Selznick and Fox); *The Keys of the Kingdom,* a $102,500 package that included the rights to A. J. Cronin's novel and the services of Gregory Peck; and miscellaneous Selznicks personnel on loan, including Gene Kelly, Alan Marshal, Alfred Hitchcock, and cameramen George Barnes and Stanley Cortez.

T H E R E were various reasons for Selznick to unload these projects. He still was reluctant to resume active production, and the timing and the price were right on the Fox deal. Bill Goetz, who was Selznick's brother-in-law though not a close friend or associate, was running Fox while Darryl Zanuck was away in the service. Goetz had designs on Zanuck's throne and was putting as many of his own projects in the works as he could while the studio boss was away. So he was a willing suitor, and Selznick felt that the half-million-dollar price was right. *Jane Eyre* was a tough project to give up, but Selznick still considered himself the shaping force on the picture and assumed that he would continue to influence it from a distance. He told Fox producer Kenneth Macgowan that he was responsible for "the vast bulk of the construction of both the script as a whole and of the individual scenes," and also for "the detailed camera and lighting treatment." He was mentioning this, Selznick told Macgowan, "only so that you will know that I am in a good position to be helpful should there be any trouble about the credits."

There was indeed "trouble about the credits" on *Jane Eyre,* due primarily to Orson Welles, who wound up costarring as Rochester and who also coscripted, codirected, and produced the picture. Ironically enough, Selznick had actually encouraged Welles to do the picture when the latter started having second thoughts about taking a costarring role. He recognized that Hollywood's most recent boy wonder was an enormous talent and figured that he would only enhance the project. But Welles's conception was distinctly more gothic and stylized than Selznick's, and he quite literally overhauled Selznick's entire "construction." Selznick's first inkling of this came in April, when he learned that Fox was planning to give Welles producer credit and top billing. Selznick told Bill Goetz that he was "frankly surprised" about Welles's producer credit and "incredulous" about the top billing. Selznick should have guessed that after *Citizen Kane*, "it would be too much of a comedown [for Welles] from the job of producer-star-director to that of costar receiving second billing."

Once Selznick saw the rough cut of *Jane Eyre* and talked with various Fox personnel about Welles's role in the production, however, he changed his tune. As his assistant Dan O'Shea explained in a letter to Fox president, Joe Schenck, Selznick had "been informed by people from your studio that Mr. Welles worked on the sets, changes in the script, in casting, among other things, and that he had charge of the editing." Selznick also recognized "the additional prestige value of Mr. Welles as producer." Welles obviously deserved producer credit—certainly more so than Stevenson or the "executive producer," Bill Goetz. Selznick's only requests were that Fontaine be given equal billing with Welles as costar and that Stevenson receive "directorial credit with a separate [title] card . . . in type not less than two-thirds the size used for Mr. Welles's credit as producer." Schenck complied with Selznick's request on the credits, but he simply ignored any suggestions about the final cut or release of the picture. Selznick had expressed his feeling that *Jane Eyre* needed "an extensive program of retakes, including a return to the original script," and that Fox should test-market it in a few key cities "to get a very thorough reaction before releasing it nationally."

There was little chance of Fox acting on Selznick's advice, what with Darryl Zanuck back from the war and very much in charge of the studio (despite Goetz's efforts to upgrade his own power and status by signing deals with outsiders like Selznick). Zanuck was a scrapper and a macho extrovert, a self-made man who respected Selznick's accomplishments but little else about him. He was well aware that *Jane Eyre* was one of several productions then in the works at Fox that involved stories, scripts, and/or personnel acquired from Selznick. But he wasn't about to let an outside producer tell him how to run his company. "As I told you the other night," Zanuck wrote to Selznick in August 1943, "the picture will do business, and because business is phenomenal, it will recoup its costs." He was right. When *Jane Eyre* was released it did a solid business, and without Selznick's suggested retakes.

A M O N G the Fox projects in which Selznick had a stake during that summer of 1943, *The Song of Bernadette* concerned him more deeply than *Jane Eyre*, or even Hitchcock's *Lifeboat*. His concerns centered on the picture's star, Jennifer Jones, who represented yet another dimension of Selznick's efforts as packager and agent in the early 1940s —namely, his role as star-maker, particularly of female "discoveries." Now that Ingrid Bergman, Vivien Leigh, and Joan Fontaine were established stars, Selznick's Pygmalion complex was approaching Shavian proportions. The celluloid image he now craved to enliven was that of one Phyllis Walker (née Isley, screen name "Jennifer Jones"), whom he had tested during the summer of 1941 and signed to an exclusive contract. She was wed at the time to Robert Walker, but the marriage was a troubled one. When Phyllis tested and signed with Selznick, Walker was living back East with their two children. Selznick was enthusiastic about the young actress and wondered in an August 1941 memo whether he should "sign the husband as an element of protection" and also to "preserve his pride," though he hoped Walker might turn out "to be a good bet himself." Selznick arranged a test for Walker at MGM, where the young actor did indeed catch on. Meanwhile Selznick planned to star Phyllis Walker in *Claudia*, a story he'd recently purchased. This plan was undone by Rose Franken, though, whose contract with Selznick for the screen rights to her novel and hit play gave her casting approval on the film version. In September 1941, she nixed Walker, insisting on Dorothy McGuire, who had starred in the stage version.

Selznick with three of his female contract stars: (from left) Ingrid Bergman, Shirley Temple, and Jennifer Jones.

Selznick began looking for another vehicle to launch Phyllis Walker, and he also began looking for a new name. He wrote his staff in January 1942 that he wanted as good a name as Veronica Lake, which he considered "the best synthetic name in pictures," and by the end of the month they came up with "Jennifer Jones." Selznick approved the name and continued to scout for a suitable role. There were lesser parts offered. Val Lewton, for example, who had left Selznick in April 1942 to become a unit producer at RKO, wanted to test her for the second female lead in *Cat People*. Jones had already done B-picture work, having signed with Republic Pictures briefly in 1938 and costarred with John Wayne in *New Frontier*. But Selznick was convinced she had genuine star potential and declined even to test her for Lewton's picture. It was some months later that he found the right role, that of the innocent peasant girl in Fox's *Song of Bernadette*, whose visions of the Virgin Mary evoke wonder and then consternation, but finally are recognized as miracles by the world and by the Catholic Church. The role could not have been more appropriate for both Jones and Selznick, introducing a dimension of Divine Intervention to Selznick's fascination with star-making.

Jennifer Jones was not among the "miscellaneous personnel" in the November 1942 deal with Fox, but both Selznick and Bill Goetz were well aware of her importance to the transaction. Selznick wrote his brother Myron that same month that he had been "selling her on a systematic campaign to Bill Goetz for month after month, and finally I showed him her test. I then personally suggested her for *Bernadette*, a role it looks as though we are going to get for her." *The Song of Bernadette* was then in preproduction and scheduled to start shooting March 15, 1943. Jones was given the lead in January, and Selznick put her through intense preparation for the role. As soon as Henry King started shooting in March, it was clear to all involved that Fox had a potential hit on its hands, due mainly to the innocent charm and pristine beauty of the twenty-four-year-old lead actress. Selznick was certain that Jones would emerge from *Bernadette* a star, and he was determined to follow it up with an equally strong picture. That determination was more acute than it had been with Fontaine or his other discoveries, though, and indeed Selznick was developing more than just a professional interest in Jennifer Jones. His interest was keen enough, in fact, to bring him back to active filmmaking.

Selznick had been thinking about doing a home-front melodrama to showcase several of his contract players—an American *Mrs. Miniver*, as he put it—and with Jones in the fold he decided to go ahead with the idea. In the spring of 1943, while *Bernadette* was in production, he began poring over synopses of home-front war stories prepared by his story department. He finally settled on *Since You Went Away*, a serial in the *Ladies' Home Journal* about the experiences of a mother and her two daughters on the home front, while the family patriarch is overseas. Selznick adapted the story himself, designing the screenplay as both a sentimental weepie and a rallying cry for the women whom America's fighting men had left behind. As he developed the screenplay, he felt the obsessive thrill returning, and by midsummer he was into serious preproduction and planning to start shooting in the fall. He saw the story as an ensemble piece featuring Jones and two other recent additions to his stable, Shirley Temple and Joseph Cotten. Jones and Temple would play the daughters, with Cotten as the suave military officer who befriends the family and provides a fleeting, innocent romantic interest for the mother during her husband's absence. The mother's role was crucial, and for that part Selznick signed Claudette Colbert, agreeing to a flat fee of $265,000. To direct he lined up the always amenable John Cromwell, though Selznick planned to oversee every detail of the production himself. Production opened in September 1943, was scheduled for seventeen weeks, and was budgeted at just over $2 million.

Selznick was back into a productive mode, a fact he underscored that fall by creating Vanguard Films, another independent company designed to turn out moderate-priced features. The way Selznick saw it, the market was simply too good not to take full advantage of it, and Vanguard also would ensure maximum use of his facilities and personnel. Selznick hired writer-producer Dore Schary away from MGM to be Vanguard's executive producer, paying him a salary of $2,500 per week plus 15 percent of the net profits on all Vanguard releases. For his debut production, Schary purchased a story titled "Double Furlough," a wartime romance that he retitled after a popular song, *I'll Be Seeing You*. The story centered on a shell-shock victim who, while home for Christmas, falls in love with a woman on a holiday furlough from prison. Selznick was excited about the project, which seemed an ideal complement to *Since You Went Away* and a perfect follow-up for Cotten. So he approved Schary's suggestion that Ginger Rogers be cast in the lead and insisted that Joseph Cotten play the soldier. As the ARI tests for *Jane Eyre* indicated, Cotten was among Hollywood's fastest rising male actors, but there was some question as to whether he would graduate from supporting player to full-fledged star. Selznick intended to find out with *I'll Be Seeing You*. There were questions, too, about Shirley Temple, who was apparently on the downside of her career at age fifteen. Selznick had recently signed her to a long-term deal and planned to use her as well as Cotten in both pictures.

Since You Went Away was the consummate Selznick picture, a heart-felt melodrama whose lavish production values and cloying sentimentality ran rampant. And as always, Selznick's perfectionism and his compulsion to adjust the material during production took its toll. Principal photography lasted nearly five months, with retakes spanning another three months, and the final cost reached $3.25 million. Selznick ran roughshod over Cromwell and everyone else involved, and his usual anxieties were even more intense this time out because of his personal and professional interest in Jennifer Jones. At one point he fired off a memo to production manager Ray Klune about "the miserable way in which we're presenting Jennifer Jones in this picture, mindful of my hopes that she would be another Bergman or Fontaine for us within the next six months." He also worried about the consequences "if we, the supposed great star-makers and star-builders, don't follow up on *Bernadette* with a proper delivery." He reminded Klune that Jones's role was one "which I deliberately created for her, having it in mind as a sensational contrast with *Bernadette*, and one calculated to cinch her claims to important stardom."

Selznick was especially sensitive about his reputation as star-maker,

Director John Cromwell and Selznick confer between takes of a scene in Since You Went Away.

since *Look* magazine was running a piece in its January 1944 issue on "The Selznick Girls"—Fontaine, Leigh, Bergman, Jones, Dorothy McGuire, and Shirley Temple. Selznick had provided extensive background material for the piece, and he pointed out that star-making had long been one of his strong points; during the 1930s he had either initiated or revived the careers of William Powell, Jean Arthur, Myrna Loy, Kay Francis, Katharine Hepburn, and others. But when a draft of the article was sent to Selznick to look over, he felt he had been misrepresented. "This article has little or nothing about me as a producer, and places me in the position of being a flesh peddler," wrote Selznick to Jean Herrick of *Look*. He then reminded Herrick of his accomplishments as a filmmaker: "I have won more honors than any producer in the business. I am the only producer to win the Academy Award two years in a row. I am the only producer to have been nominated every year since its inception (with the exception of last year, due to my inactivity) as one of the three or four men to be considered for the Irving Thalberg Award for the most consistently high quality of production. . . . "

The piece was rewritten to play up Selznick the filmmaker, but Herrick obviously had struck a nerve. There was no denying that even as he moved back into active production, Selznick's years as agent and packager had a subtle but important impact on his role as a producer. He became increasingly obsessed with the power and commercial value of stars, to a point where he seemed to evaluate any project only on its merits as a star vehicle. When Dore Schary was casting *I'll Be Seeing You*, for instance, he dismissed Schary's suggestion that Joel McCrea be used for the male lead, since McCrea was no more than "an alleged star" whose market value was less than Cotten's. Selznick was more positive but equally pragmatic about Rogers. "At least Ginger Rogers is an important star," Selznick wrote O'Shea after nixing McCrea, "and even though we're overpaying her greatly, we are at least buying a commodity that we know will sell an enormous number of tickets and to a certain extent insure the investment."

T H E piece in *Look* was excellent promotion for Selznick's upcoming picture, but it only increased his problems with Myron. Their relationship was already strained due to Hitchcock's recent decision to go with another agency, which Myron blamed on his brother. There were also David's repeated efforts in recent months to get Myron help for his acute alcoholism. By now Myron's condition was severe enough to require institutional treatment, which David set up, monitored, and even paid for. The treatments always looked promising for a time, but Myron always fell off the wagon, and he fell further and harder with each relapse. His mental health and his physical health were failing badly, and he began alienating his friends, clients, and associates alike. David's letters to his brother in 1943 and early 1944 are laden with references to his drinking and what it was doing to their relationship and to Myron's agency.

David's blasts at Myron were more than sibling rivalry or a means of relieving production-related stress. David genuinely wanted to save his drowning brother, and he even suggested that Myron consider starting his own production outfit to reinvest his life with some meaning and motivation. The same changing power structures that enabled David to compete with Myron as an agent might also enable Myron to compete with David as a producer. In October 1943, David suggested that Myron stop "fiddling around" with his agency and start a production company of his own—something a number of other top agents had been doing at the time. But Myron had been burning his bridges for years. He had an adversary relationship with virtually every studio boss and producer in the business, so there was little chance of his moving as effectively into David's bailiwick as David had moved into his.

M Y R O N ' S condition and postproduction on *Since You Went Away* were major distractions for David in February 1944, as were the upcoming Academy Awards. He had no pictures in contention this year, but several of his employees were in the spotlight. He was especially concerned about the Oscar for best actress, since the nominees included Jennifer Jones for *The Song of Bernadette,* Joan Fontaine for *The Constant Nymph,* and Ingrid Bergman for *For Whom the Bell Tolls.* The awards ceremony carried even more notoriety than usual this year, since for the first time the public would have direct access to the event. Figuring it lacked genuine mass appeal, NBC had declined to broadcast the event nationally, but local stations were picking it up and the public could buy tickets to attend the awards ceremony in person. Considering the attendant publicity for his three stars, Selznick was pleased to see Oscar night becoming a media event. His sentiments were with Jennifer Jones, not only because an Oscar would enhance the value of *Since You Went Away* but also because of their growing personal involvement. In fact, Jones was waiting until after the ceremony to announce that she was divorcing Robert Walker.

Knowing her husband's emotional state, Jones was terrified of the prospect. Walker had played her love interest in *Since You Went Away,* and working on the same set with his wife had not gone well. Clearly the marriage was all but over, a fact Walker found difficult to accept. Selznick knew an Oscar would take Jones's mind off the trauma of her impending divorce; it also would enable him to tighten his grip on her life and her career. By now Walker was at MGM, largely through Selznick's intervention, and still Selznick did what he could to advance Walker's film career. In mid-February 1944, only days after closing *Since You Went Away* and some two weeks before Oscar night, Selznick wrote Louis B. Mayer another in a series of letters pertaining to Walker's career. The purpose this time was to relay a feeling of "sincere regret" about the obvious typecasting of Walker as the "shy enlisted man" in a series of MGM productions. "I think a little encouragement through and from you," confided Selznick, "and a little understanding of him by you, would do much toward preserving and advancing one of the few young men who has come along in recent years who might become a great asset to Metro; a star worth countless millions if he isn't cast without imagination; if he isn't assigned to play the same role over and over again." Louis B. Mayer chose to ignore Selznick's advice despite his reputation as a leading authority in the industry on casting and star quality. Perhaps Mayer believed he could build Walker even on so limited a portrayal, or perhaps he felt that Walker was not up to the psychological demands of top stardom. Or perhaps Mayer sensed his son-in-law's deeper motives for advancing Walker's career, and he was thinking more about the future of his daughter, Irene Mayer Selznick, than he was about Walker or anyone else.

Jennifer Jones won the Academy Award for best actress, and she went ahead with her plan to announce the divorce. The trade wags and gossip columnists made note of the story, although it was overshadowed by another Oscar flap and divorce—the one at Warners between Hal Wallis and Jack Warner over *Casablanca*, which along with *For Whom the Bell Tolls* dominated the ceremony. Selznick had actually expected Bergman to win, but that would come a year later for her performance in *Gaslight*. Thus in the six-year span from 1939 through 1944, four of his female stars—Leigh, Fontaine, Jones, and Bergman—each won an Academy Award for best actress and accumulated a total of eight Oscar nominations. Significantly enough, only Vivien Leigh won in a Selznick production, and this reinforced the growing perception of Selznick as agent and "flesh peddler."

Selznick took *Since You Went Away* into heavy postproduction immediately after the Oscar ceremony, but some three weeks later his work came to a full stop. On March 23, 1944, Myron died suddenly—though not all that unexpectedly. The technical explanation was portal thrombosis, but in fact Myron Selznick, at age forty-five, drank himself to death. David had long since resigned himself to his brother's self-destructive nature and the inevitability of his early death, but still he was crushed when it finally came. He was virtually paralyzed with grief and unable to work for well over a month, even though he had several projects that demanded his attention. He personally responded to all the expressions of sympathy he received after Myron's death; this included writing to a number of the psychologists and doctors who had treated Myron over the years.

T H E sudden success of Jennifer Jones and the near-suicidal demise of Myron edged David Selznick's life closer to his art, to *What Price Hollywood?* and *A Star Is Born*, stories that David had used to exorcise his own personal demons. Now those stories hit closer to home than he ever could have imagined back in the 1930s, when he and Myron were young and their careers were ahead of them. He had watched his father and now his brother crash and burn after trying to take on Hollywood, and he began to wonder whether his own hubris might not take him down, too. With the help of Irene and Ben Hecht and his few close friends, he steadily overcame the depression that followed Myron's death. By late spring his energy was back and he was determined to make the loss work for him. He threw himself into his work as completely and obsessively as he had some five years before with *Gone With the Wind* and *Rebecca*. Between May and July 1944, he finished postproduction on *Since You Went Away*, he guided Dore Schary through production and a rough cut of *I'll Be Seeing You*, and he collaborated with Hitchcock and Hecht on the script and final preparation of *Spellbound*. After years on the sidelines, Selznick was back in the thick of it—he was making pictures again.

18

Universal: The Best of Both Worlds

The war years were not as volatile or as profitable for Hollywood's major minors, Universal and Columbia, as they were for the major studios. There were changes at Universal and Columbia, and the revenues were up, but for these studios, without theater chains of their own, the effects of the antitrust action and the war boom itself were considerably diminished. As far as the antitrust suit was concerned, the changes at the major minors were less a response to the suit itself than to the way the majors dealt with it. The five integrated studios had signed consent decrees in 1940 that outlawed blind selling and reduced block booking to groups of five pictures. Consequently, the majors cut back production overall to concentrate on top features, virtually eliminating B movies, since the sale of low-grade pictures could no longer be tied to their quality products. This strategy meant huge profits for the majors once the wartime economy took off, and it also opened things up for the major minors. On the one hand, limiting block booking and blind selling meant easier access to the first-run market, since independent exhibitors were no longer forced to take large blocks of films from the majors, sight unseen. On the other hand, the majors' reduction of B-movie production enabled Hollywood's lesser powers to dominate the low end of the market. The subsequent-run market was not significantly changed by the consent decrees, and the demand for low-budget pictures held strong throughout the war—so strong, in fact, that the major minors and the minors like Monogram and Republic actually stepped up B-movie production.

Thus the war was an ambivalent period for the major minors, which were now in a better position than ever to exploit both the first run and subsequent-run markets. The one drawback, of course, was that they were geared to the middle and low end of the movie business, and they lacked the personnel and the working capital to make an aggressive run at the high end. That drawback did discourage Columbia from top-feature production, but not Nate Blumberg and Cliff Work at Universal. They realized that their in-house resources were inadequate for consistently high-grade feature production, but the growing supply of free-lance talent and package deals could be tapped to complement their studio output. So Cliff Work scouted for outside talent and deals while production manager Martin Murphy kept operations at Universal City up to speed, with the usual emphasis on low-grade features and subfeatures.

The only in-house efforts that were targeted for the first-run market were Durbin's musicals and the vaudeville-inspired comedies with W. C. Fields. As the first-run market opened up in the early 1940s, though, it was becoming obvious that neither Durbin nor Fields would be of much value in Universal's upgraded operation. After eight straight hits for Universal from 1937 through 1940, Durbin's box-office appeal quite suddenly faded. Durbin turned eighteen in 1940, and unlike her MGM counterpart Mickey Rooney, who was suspended in a stage of perpetual adolescence, she couldn't withstand the vagaries of time and human biology. She simply outgrew her narrowly defined screen persona, and her mentor Joe Pasternak had no recourse but to adjust her roles—which was evident even in the titles of her 1941 films, *It Started With Eve* and *Nice Girl?* The pictures failed, and this marked not only Durbin's downturn but the breakup of the Pasternak-Durbin unit at Universal. Pasternak left Universal in late 1941 to work for MGM (where he began charting the career of another musical ingenue, Kathryn Grayson), and Universal director Henry Koster eventually followed suit. Meanwhile writer Bruce Manning was promoted to producer at Universal and was left with the task of salvaging Durbin's career.

Fields's decline was even more abrupt than Durbin's, though less economically significant. After a slow start for Universal in the late 1930s, Fields delivered successive hits with *The Bank Dick* in 1940 and *Never Give a Sucker an Even Break* in 1941. But he was in his early sixties and in failing health, and these proved to be his last features. (He died in 1946.) His retirement did not diminish Universal's interest in vaudeville-inspired comedy, though, particularly after Paramount's success in 1940 with *Road to Singapore,* which teamed Bing Crosby and another radio-vaudeville star, Bob Hope, in an inspired blend of comedy, music, romance (thanks to costar Dorothy Lamour), and vaudevillian shtick. Scouting for a team of its own, Universal began combing the comedy circuit in upstate New York and also the radio networks and the theater district in New York City. It pinned its hopes on the team of Ole Olsen and Chic Johnson, who brought their stage hit *Hellzapoppin'* to the screen in 1941. The picture did well, but the success of Olsen and Johnson was nothing compared to that of another Universal comedy team, whose surge to top stardom in 1941 took the studio and the industry by complete surprise.

"ABBOTT AND COSTELLO" were a genuine movie industry phenomenon and a tremendous windfall for Universal. Durbin's Depression-era impact may have been more dramatic, given the studio's desperate financial shape at the time, but she had nowhere near the economic and popular success, nor the longevity, of Abbott and Costello. The duo's breakthrough picture was *Buck Privates,* a February 1941 release that Universal parlayed into a quick succession of comedy hits that vaulted Abbott and Costello to the top of the industry. This rise indicated the importance of Universal's access to the first-run market in the early 1940s, which ensured maximum return on the studio's investment. It indicated, too, the studio's increased efficiency during the war years. Blumberg and Work could be ruthlessly pragmatic when the right opportunity came along—much more pragmatic than Cochrane and Rogers had been back in 1937 when Deanna Durbin first hit.

Bud Abbott and Lou Costello—a long, lean straight man and a short, fat dervish—first teamed up in 1931, playing burlesque and vaudeville circuits back East. They broke into radio and then Broadway in the late 1930s, and signed with Universal in 1940. Their debut came as feature players late that year in *One Night in the Tropics,* a second-rate Universal comedy. They then costarred in *Buck Privates* as two draftees who wreak havoc in an Army induction center and then bumble their way through basic training. In this picture the Andrews Sisters, another popular radio act, provided musical relief from the slapstick absurdity. *Buck Privates* was another low-budget project, directed by Arthur Lubin and produced by Alex Gottlieb, two B-grade staffers whose weekly salaries were $350 and $300 per week, respectively. Once the picture was in the can, Cliff Work started Lubin and producer Burt Kelly, another refugee from the B-movie ranks, on *Hold That Ghost.* Sensing that Abbott and Costello might have some appeal as a costarring team, Work gave them first billing and built the entire picture around them. The story involved a pair of inept waiters who lose their jobs and inherit a haunted roadhouse from a murdered mobster. Abbott and Costello utterly dominated the picture, which was a nonstop diet of slapstick and verbal lunacy in a clever melding of the gangster and horror genres.

Lubin and Kelly closed on *Hold That Ghost* in late February, some two weeks after *Buck Privates* was released. Within a week they had a rough cut, which Cliff Work found disappointing. The comedy was manic and unrelenting, laden with physical humor and elaborate in-jokes. There was no music, no romantic subplot—and worst of all, no real connection with *Buck Privates*, which was rolling up record grosses nationwide. Nate Blumberg was demanding a surefire follow-up as quickly as possible, preferably another "service comedy," and Work doubted that *Hold That Ghost* was the ticket. He met with Lubin, Gottlieb, and writer John Grant, and they decided to "shelve" *Hold That Ghost* and, working as quickly and economically as possible, to crank out something along the lines of *Buck Privates*. Meanwhile, they would devise musical routines with the Andrews Sisters and a bit of

Lou Costello (center) and Bud Abbott (right) with director Arthur Lubin, who directed most of the duo's low-cost comedies for Universal.

romantic diversion for *Hold That Ghost,* thus bringing it more in line with the service comedies. If all went well, the second service comedy would be in circulation by late May and the overhauled horror-gangster comedy by late summer. That decision set the trajectory of Universal's Abbott and Costello pictures over the coming years, establishing the basic ingredients of both the production unit and the screen formula. As with the Hardy unit at Metro, the Abbott and Costello unit was composed of B-picture personnel who were used to working at top speed. They turned out the duo's comedies at roughly the same rate as their counterparts in the Hardy unit at Metro, a picture every three or four months, with that second service comedy setting the pace.

Actually, a Navy version of *Buck Privates* was already under way when Work and the others conferred. Arthur Horman, who scripted *Buck Privates,* had just started work on a picture that was going to be called "We're in the Navy," and after the plan was devised he and John Grant completed the script in a matter of days. Copies were sent to the Department of the Navy and the Breen office in early March. Within another week, studio production manager Murphy and supervisor Alex Gottlieb had prepared a shooting schedule of twenty-three days, beginning April 8, with an estimated budget of $335,000. Their plans hit a slight snag on March 14, when Murphy received word from Commander Bolton that the "cooperation and approval" of the Navy Department "would not be forthcoming on material of this sort," since the picture would not "reflect credit on the service and do the Navy some tangible good." Bolton did close on a vaguely upbeat note, suggesting that if the picture "can be kept in the spirit of good, clean fun, you probably will avoid the wrath of the powers that be. Naturally it is a lampoon from start to finish and must be kept in that spirit." Bolton also suggested a few script changes—that the naval officers be portrayed in a more "dignified manner," for example, and that a shore-leave brawl be toned down or eliminated.

Universal desperately wanted Navy approval, which would give them access to the Navy's own documentary footage, and possibly even the use of their facilities and personnel. Bolton's reference to "the powers that be" was telling, however. There obviously would be outside pressures on war-related pictures, and the studios would have to learn to deal with them. For starters, Gottlieb ordered a rewrite of the script to accommodate Bolton's suggestions, then he and Murphy went to Joe Breen, who agreed to intervene on behalf of the MPPDA. Breen took the case directly to the Secretary of the Navy, and on March 31 Lubin reached a verbal agreement with a group of military brass in Washington, D.C., who granted official approval of the film. The following day Lubin received a wire giving him the OK to shoot at a naval training station near Los Angeles on the condition that Universal agree to submit the picture for "Navy approval" upon completion. At that point Murphy firmed up the production schedule, Work set a shipping date, and Blumberg initiated theater bookings. When Lubin started shooting "We're in the Navy" on April 7, 1941, play dates were being set for late May.

To hedge their bets on the project, the Universal powers brought in another star to share top billing with Abbott and Costello, who still hadn't proved they could carry a picture. Their costar was Dick Powell, who signed on for five weeks at $6,000 per week, and once he signed, the official release title of the picture became *Abbott and Costello and Dick Powell 'In the Navy.'* Powell played a radio star who enlists to escape his overly enthusiastic fans, and teams up with Bud and Lou during basic training. The Andrews Sisters, who enlivened *Buck Privates* with songs like "Boogie Woogie Bugle Boy from Company B," were back with "Gimme Some Skin" and other numbers to complement Powell's more conventional crooning. Again the musical interludes—which took up thirty-five minutes of the eighty-five-minute release version—were carefully interspersed with Abbott and Costello's routines. (The numbers in *Buck Privates* took up only 20'30" of eighty-two total minutes.)

Once shooting started, Lubin maintained a frantic production pace, getting vital assistance from choreographer Nick Castle and from cameraman Joe Valentine, who shot most of Durbin's musicals. Alex Gottlieb and M. F. Murphy monitored the shoot, which stayed right on schedule. A full day's shooting was devoted to each of the musical numbers, with another twenty days spent on the book. The picture was finished in twenty-eight days, with Lubin and Valentine averaging over fourteen setups and 3'30" of film per day—a remarkable pace for a top feature. (On only two days did they execute fewer than ten setups, and they did more than twenty setups on seven different shooting days.) Production involved up to two hundred extras, many of them Navy personnel, but still it proceeded like clockwork. The only problems involved John Fulton's special effects and miniature work, which were held up due to bad weather. Noted for his effects in horror and fantasy films, Fulton was called on here to create a complicated ship-maneuvers routine that goes haywire due to Abbott and Costello's botched signaling. The sequence would require elaborate lab effects, which meant extra time for film processing. Murphy grew more anxious as the weather held things up in early May, and he reminded Fulton at one point that "the sales force has already accepted definite bookings on over a hundred key situations for May thirtieth," and advised him to come up with an alternative plan if the weather refused to cooperate.

The weather broke before production closed on May 9, and the effects scenes were inserted into the rough cut Lubin prepared for a Navy screening on May 15. Still there were problems with the ship maneuvers—in fact, for a desperate seventy-two-hour period it looked as though the sequence might impede release of the picture. The Navy brass felt that Lubin's seagoing Keystone Kops routine cast the Navy in a bad light, and they refused to approve the film. So Gottlieb huddled with his writers and came up with a solution. They decided to have the manic Lou Costello unwittingly take a dose of a sleep-inducing drug, thus transforming the bungled ship maneuvers into a hallucinatory dream sequence. Rewrites were done May 17, added scenes shot the eighteenth, the picture was recut on the nineteenth, and on May 20 Maurice Pivar, head of Universal's editorial department, flew a print to Washington for another Navy screening. On the following day Lubin received the following wire from the Navy Department: "Your picture passed 100 percent. Have accomplished three weeks work in one day. Congratulations." A few days later Commander Bolton, now more appreciative of the picture's public relations value, wrote Work that he found the picture "delightful," and he added, "The ingenious twist of having Costello drink the sleeping potion eliminated the only possible objectionable material."

Congratulations were certainly in order. It had been only ten weeks since Cliff Work started Gottlieb and the others on a reformulation of *Buck Privates*, and they had managed not only a finished product but a remarkably cost-efficient one. The final cost of *In the Navy* was $379,207, with the heaviest expenses going to star salaries. Abbott and Costello earned a flat fee of $35,000, Dick Powell earned $30,000, and the Andrews Sisters $15,000. The remaining above-the-line costs were negligible, with producer Gottlieb earning $6,350, director Lubin $5,166 (including a bonus), and writers Horman and Grant each earning just over $3,000. Subsequent series installments would not be produced quite so quickly—and thus so inexpensively—but Universal did manage to keep costs in the half-million-dollar range. *Hold That Ghost* turned out to be relatively more costly since it had to be sent back into production to graft the musical numbers and a romantic subplot into the gangster-horror parody, but the picture was ready by early August and was another hit. By then Lubin and Grant had started *Keep 'Em Flying,* an Air Force variation on the established service-comedy formula which Universal had out by late November. It was Abbott and Costello's fourth hit in eight months, and it carried them to third place among the exhibitors' top ten—an elite group that not even Deanna Durbin had cracked.

At that point Work and Blumberg figured that the service formula was wearing thin and also that the U.S. military warranted a more positive treatment, so Abbott and Costello stayed strictly with genre parodies in 1942. In quick succession, the duo took on the then-popular "singing cowboy" westerns with *Ride 'Em Cowboy*, the equally popular radio mysteries with *Who Done It?*, and the Hope-Crosby "Road" pictures with *Pardon My Sarong*. All three were produced by Alex Gottlieb and coscripted by John Grant, who continued to let Abbott and Costello's dim-witted bumblers trash one social institution after another—only here the institutions were movie genres rather than branches of the armed servies. The genre parodies feature the same unique melding of physical comedy, slapstick, and absurdist wordplay, and again the comic onslaught was interspersed with musical interludes. Audiences took to the genre parodies as they had to the service comedies, and at year's end the nation's exhibitors put Abbott and Costello in a class by themselves among Hollywood's stars, naming them the number-one box-office draw in movies.

T H E success of Abbott and Costello was that rarest of industry phenomena, a low-cost formula with widespread appeal. The duo's distinctive comedies gave Universal another light entertainment genre just when Durbin's musicals were fading, and this time around the studio exploited the star-genre combination much more effectively. What's more, Abbott and Costello's success gave Blumberg and Work ready cash to go after the first-run market even more aggressively. They were determined to make the most of the opportunity by purchasing "prepackaged" A-class projects that could be produced and released through Universal. The prospects for these package deals were increasing in the early 1940s—David Selznick was only one of several independent filmmakers putting them together—and the advantages to such a plan were clear enough. It would save time and expense on preparation, it would keep the studio operating at full capacity, and it would enable Universal to recoup production costs and pocket the distribution fees (usually 30 to 35 percent of the gross receipts) before splitting the net profits with the outside producer. Cliff Work and company, meanwhile, could crank out Universal's routine fare.

The first independent deals were cut in November 1941. Universal was gearing up for "serious" treatment of the war, and the transactions that November involved two war-related projects. One was *Eagle Squadron*, a Walter Wanger project that traced the air war over England, and the other was *Saboteur*, a Hitchcock thriller involving munitions plant espionage which David Selznick had put together. Both projects were started for other companies—for UA and RKO, respectively—but problems with UA and RKO coincided neatly with Univer-

Abbott and Costello at a banquet where they were crowned as the movie industry's top box-office stars of 1942.

sal's decision to begin courting outside producers, so the Wanger and Selznick pictures wound up on Universal's 1942 schedule.

Saboteur was essentially a one-shot deal with Selznick, who sold the script to Universal for $70,000 and loaned Hitchcock's services for fourteen weeks at $130,000. The deal for *Eagle Squadron*, conversely, initiated a long-term affiliation between Wanger and Universal, one that would produce fourteen pictures over the next seven years. In fact, Wanger quickly assumed the mantle of "prestige producer" at Universal City, one that Joe Pasternak had worn before his recent departure for MGM. But Wanger was an even more singular figure at Universal than Pasternak, since he remained technically an outside producer even after he set up shop at Universal City. That obviously put Wanger in an ambivalent position, but he had always been a contradictory character in Hollywood. Born to a wealthy family and educated at Dartmouth, Heidelberg, and Oxford, he was often described as a champion of high culture in a crassly commercial industry. But in fact Wanger was as shrewd a businessman as any top Hollywood producer, and one with fewer "artistic" inclinations or pretensions than many of his colleagues. He was not a creative producer, nor did he consider himself a filmmaker per se. He was a production executive and an administrator with a keen awareness of the business who learned early on how to maintain considerable freedom and control while operating within the system. His apprenticeship paralleled David Selznick's. He worked his way up through the ranks as a studio executive at Paramount and Columbia before joining MGM as a unit producer in 1933, just after Thalberg's illness. After feuding with Mayer in 1934, he left Metro to set up Walter Wanger Productions, making an exclusive arrangement with Paramount Pictures that set the tone for his future career.

Wanger signed a series of multipicture contracts with Paramount, which set strict budgets and paid Wanger a weekly salary and a percentage of the net profits. His productions were described in his contracts as "strictly first-class in artistic, pictorial, and dramatic quality" and suitable for "the highest-class motion picture theaters in the U.S. and elsewhere." Wanger was to "plan and supervise" his pictures from scripting through release, though Paramount retained veto power at every stage of production. He produced fourteen pictures in two years for Paramount, then left to sign a long-term deal with UA. That agreement raised his budget ceiling from $300,000 to $750,000 per picture and also gave him certain executive responsibilities. After a slow start, he produced three consecutive hits for UA in 1938: *Algiers*, *Trade Winds*, and *Stagecoach*. But a half-dozen commercial disappointments in 1939–40, including Hitchcock's *Foreign Correspondent*, had him on shaky ground with UA when he started *Eagle Squadron* in 1940.

The package for *Eagle Squadron* that Wanger sold to Universal in November 1941 was really quite different from the project as it had been conceived and developed for UA. The difference is instructive, because it indicates Wanger's savvy and flexibility as a producer, and also his willingness to adjust the product to suit the market, the production context, and even the war itself. Wanger planned to do *Eagle Squadron* with Merian C. Cooper, who had been a flying ace during World War I before getting into motion pictures. What's more, Cooper had started as a documentarian and only later became a dramatic filmmaker and a production executive. *Eagle Squadron* was to be a semidocumentary about a group of American pilots who helped the Royal Air Force hold off the German Luftwaffe during the Battle of Britain— a nine-month Nazi blitz over England (especially London) in 1940–41. Wanger and Cooper wanted to incorporate actual combat footage and to have the American pilots portray themselves, though certain scenes —the conversion of the Yank mercenaries to the British cause, for instance—would have to be dramatized. But for the most part, this would be a factual account of Squadron 71 of the RAF, and thus quite innovative for a Hollywood feature. To shoot and direct, Wanger hired two top documentarians: Harry Watt, a Brit who had just finished an acclaimed documentary about the blitz, *Target for Tonight* (released in the United States by Warners in 1941), and Ernest Schoedsack, Cooper's longtime friend and associate.

UA announced *Eagle Squadron* in July 1941, and by then Watt and Schoedsack already had shot several thousand feet of film. Problems cropped up almost immediately, though. After nine months of intense bombing and aerial warfare over England, the Battle of Britain ended in May 1941 and London was enjoying a "blitzless summer." Thus the film would have to focus more on the fliers and less on the combat, and this led to further problems. The filmmakers told Wanger that they still felt "there is a fine film" to be made about the squadron, but they also believed "the problem of getting a picture of feature length on the screen, using the boys of 71 Squadron in their actual parts, presents to us almost insurmountable difficulties." By September Watt was convinced that "the only way this film can now be made is as a fictional one, using actors as the key members of the squadron, but always against a very factual and realistic background." The dramatic interplay of the fliers on the ground probably could not be "put across by amateurs," said Watt. "In any case, their feelings would not allow them to reenact the most poignant episodes"—especially those involving the deaths of their fellow fliers.

Wanger had already come to much the same conclusion and had assigned screenwriter Norman Reilly Raine to do a dramatization. He informed the UA board of directors of the decision, expecting them to be relieved. But the UA board was growing increasingly unhappy with Wanger due to his streak of box-office flops, and they pulled out of the project altogether rather than sink any more development funds into it. This led to a decisive battle between Wanger and UA, and finally to Wanger's release from his ten-year contract in October 1941. The split was a clean one; Wanger let UA keep his profit share on his latest production—the as yet unreleased *Sundown*, which did turn a profit— in exchange for the 14,000 feet already shot for *Eagle Squadron*. He began shopping the project around Hollywood—though without Cooper, who had taken a commission in the Army Air Corps. The best offer came from Universal, which agreed to buy the script for $60,000 and the aerial footage for another $50,000, and to hire Wanger at $2,500 per week as producer. Wanger's contract stipulated that he "shall have complete supervision and control of this production," although Universal had ultimate approval of director, cast, and final cut. Wanger had full use of Universal's personnel and facilities, and was allowed a budget "contemplated" in the $700,000 range. All net proceeds were to be split fifty-fifty between Universal and Wanger.

This was the beginning of a long and complex rapport between the producer and the studio, and it began on a rather intimate note since

Wanger had to use Universal personnel to stay within his budget range. He started principal photography on *Eagle Squadron* in January 1942, with Arthur Lubin directing and several of the studio's promising contract players as the fliers, including Robert Stack, Eddie Albert, and Jon Hall. The picture closed in April, but retakes and a revised ending held up release until summer. By then its cost was just over $900,000 and the market was glutted with combat movies, but the Watt-Schoedsack footage gave a distinctive edge to the otherwise routine wartime drama and the picture did well, grossing $2.4 million. After Universal recouped its production costs and a $635,000 distribution fee, there was nearly three-quarters of a million dollars for Wanger and Universal to divvy up.

W H I L E *Eagle Squadron* was still in production, Wanger decided to do another project with Universal as an in-house independent. He signed a deal to produce *Arabian Nights*, a costume romance with Jon Hall and Maria Montez that was to be the studio's first Technicolor picture using the three-color process. The project was ambitious by Universal's standards—its budget was just over $900,000—and the contract set a trend for future Wanger-Universal productions. As sole producer, Wanger took a weekly salary during production and then split any net profits. He supplied the story idea, and after its approval he was advanced $50,000 for script development. Once the script was ready, he and Work agreed on cast, crew, and budget, and Wanger then had complete control until the preview stage. Most of Wanger's films were scripted by Norman Reilly Raine and directed by Jack Rawlins; otherwise he depended on contract talent at the studio. Thus Wanger maintained considerable autonomy and creative control while providing Universal with a virtual in-house unit capable of turning out a consistent flow of first-class product. This arrangement was followed in a half-dozen pictures in 1943–44, all of which turned a proft for both Wanger and Universal.

Despite Wanger's relative autonomy and his profitability, though, his feature output was not all that distinctive. Once he signed that second deal, he quickly adapted to Universal's personnel, facilities, and market strategy, falling into step with the studio's in-house producers and seemingly content to leave the more ambitious—and riskier—projects to others. In fact in April 1942, the same month he signed to do *Arabian Nights,* Universal bought from David Selznick the *Shadow of a Doubt* package, which included the services of Joseph Cotten and producer-director Alfred Hitchcock, and the screenplay that Hitchcock had co-authored with playwright Thornton Wilder. Wanger went to work on *Arabian Nights,* which he himself disparaged as a second-rate "tits and sand" epic. But the picture did well for Universal (considerably better than Hitchcock's offbeat domestic psychodrama, which had a disappointing release). It had a lengthy international run and grossed just over $4 million; Wanger's share of the profits came to three-quarters of a million.

The success of *Arabian Nights* generated a quick succession of exotic Technicolor romances with Jon Hall and Maria Montez, and these in turn generated a cycle of second-rate costume romances costarring Yvonne De Carlo and Rod Cameron, mostly set in the Old West to vary the formula and exploit Cameron's popularity as a B-western star. Wanger himself initiated the De Carlo–Cameron cycle with *Salome, Where She Danced*, a project that indicated Wanger's willingness to do straight formula jobs for Universal. Wanger wasn't complaining. It was widely reported in the trade press that his income in 1944 was well over a million dollars, second only to Louis B. Mayer's among studio executives. And with his profit-sharing deal, Wanger was able to write off a good portion of his income as capital gains.

C L E A R L Y Wanger had come to understand that the name of the game at Universal was to parlay every success into formula. The war boom reinforced that tendency by bringing steady profits but also a mood of complacency to the studio and a formula-bound consistency to its products. This was evident in virtually all its in-house productions, and most notably in the dozen Abbott and Costello comedies turned out during the war years. The team was able to hold its top box-office rating for only a single year, 1942, but they lingered in the top ten and their pictures were still money in the bank. So Blumberg and Work saw little reason to change things. Abbott and Costello were wed to one another and to their screen formula, for better or worse—and for the time being, anyway, it was for the better. Their screen formula was so bankable, in fact, that even MGM wanted to cash in on it. Mayer borrowed the duo for *Rio Rita* in 1943 and for two 1944 projects, *Lost in a Harem* and *Abbott and Costello in Hollywood*.

Between the 1944 MGM loan-outs Universal produced *Abbott and Costello in Society*, which displayed how routine and predictable their projects had become after a dozen outings. This time out the object of comic mayhem was the leisure class, with the duo portraying a pair of bumbling plumbers who disrupt a weekend of upper-crust rituals on a posh estate. And significantly, they did it without name costars or well-known musical performers. Abbott and Costello now had the marquee value to sell a picture on their own, and apparently audiences were sufficiently accustomed to their lunacy to endure it without much letup for the picture's eighty minutes. The sole remaining member of the original production unit was John Grant, who had scripted most of Abbott and Costello's earlier pictures—and also *Lost in a Harem* for Metro—and was now earning $750 per week as writer and associate producer, with veteran low-budget director Jean Yarbrough calling the shots. *In Society* was budgeted at $640,000 and scheduled for thirty-one days, and Grant brought it in on target and without mishap.

An interesting complement to the Abbott and Costello comedies—and another offbeat "buddy" formula—was the Sherlock Holmes series, which thrived during the war years. Universal purchased the rights to Sir Arthur Conan Doyle's stories from 20th Century-Fox in the early 1940s, along with the contracts of Basil Rathbone and Nigel Bruce. Universal transplanted the nineteenth-century detective into a contemporary wartime milieu, thus cutting production costs (no costumes or period sets were required) and exploiting the popularity of military espionage films. In all, producer-director Roy William Neill guided Holmes and Watson through a dozen such wartime mysteries over three years, attending less to the geopolitical intrigue than to the rapport between the two principals. Rathbone and Bruce were an effective costarring team, and under Neill's direction they struck an ideal balance between melodrama and understated humor. The series' life span was directly related to the war, though its real strength was the Holmes-Watson rapport, which put the series in a class by itself among Universal's steady stream of low-grade espionage thrillers.

The espionage thrillers, Abbott and Costello comedies, and Technicolor costume epics all emerged as standard Universal screen formulas during the war, complementing the studio's most flexible and dependable of formulas, the horror film. The low end of the horror spectrum was dominated by newcomer Lon Chaney, Jr., who portrayed werewolves, vampires, mummies, and the like in a succession of sixty-minute programmers throughout the war. Occasionally Chaney was given a slightly more ambitious vehicle like *Son of Dracula*, produced by former serial maestro Ford Beebe and directed by Robert Siodmak in 1943. But for the most part Chaney was banished to the nether regions of Universal City—a fate that would have horrified even his father, whose specter was invoked in a 1943 remake of *The Phantom of the Opera*, starring Claude Rains in the title role. This picture, a genuine prestige effort, was less notable for Arthur Lubin's direction than for the color cinematography and art direction, which won Academy Awards—quite an achievement for Universal in those years, when even a nomination for in-house work was rare. And in an apt display of Universal's traditional regard for reformulation and cost-effectiveness, the same sets, costumes, personnel, and story idea were used a few months later for *Climax*, with Boris Karloff playing a physician for an opera company who is actually a deranged hypnotist with designs on a young diva. George Waggner, who had come up from the B ranks to produce *Phantom*, was producer-director on *Climax* and used the same Technicolor camera crew and art directors he had used for that earlier remake.

As Universal's high-grade horror pictures went to a more opulent visual style, with their color cinematography and their lavish, well-lit, and fully dressed sets, the studio's long-standing Germanic influence began turning up in other genres altogether. Indeed, one of the more intriguing aspects of Universal's house style during the war was the redirection of its Expressionist tradition from the horror film to the crime thriller and the psychological drama. Many of the latter films were done in the *film noir* style, so called because of both the visual and the thematic darkness. And just as the Expressionist style had given the horror films a certain vitality and creative energy a decade earlier, so it now had a similar effect on these thrillers and psychodramas. In fact, Universal's *films noirs* were really the only wartime product that did not lapse into utter predictability.

Surprisingly enough, the most distinctive of all Universal's wartime thrillers was produced in 1945 by Walter Wanger, by then the studio's prime purveyor of overblown formula pictures. Wanger had no intention of disrupting that formula output, whose profits were as predictable as their plots. Indeed, he signed another five-picture deal in April 1945 to deliver more of the same. But a month later, he signed another set of contracts that created a new, independent company, Diana Productions, and initiated its debut project, *Scarlet Street*, to be done as a Universal coproduction. The deal, which was as offbeat as the picture, indicated that both Universal and Wanger were willing to risk more radical ventures in their pursuit of the first-run market. It indicated, too, how complex and fragmented the control over these outside projects could become, since unconventional pictures often also involved unconventional and headstrong talent.

Diana Productions was essentially a partnership involving Wanger, director Fritz Lang, and actress Joan Bennett. The trio had a fairly complex history. Wanger and Lang went back to *You Only Live Once* in 1936, Wanger's debut project for United Artists and Lang's second picture in Hollywood after leaving Ufa. Wanger and Bennett went back even further. He signed her to a personal contract during his Paramount tenure in the early 1930s, when she was known primarily as the sister of screen star Constance Bennett. Joan's career took off in 1938 when Wanger put her in *Trade Winds* and convinced her to switch from blonde to brunette. Bennett stayed with the new look—and she stayed with Wanger as well. She starred in another Wanger/UA production in 1940 and married him that same year. Bennett's career flourished during the war, when she worked with Lang on two pictures; the most recent one had been *Woman in the Window*, a stylish thriller released by RKO in 1944.

Diana Productions was created as a private corporation with Fritz Lang as the majority stockholder and controlling entity. The only initial capitalization was for $75,000 to finance the development of a screenplay for the company's inaugural project, *Scarlet Street*, an adaptation of a French novel and play, *La Chienne* ("The Bitch"). Just over half the start-up money came from Lang and a third came from Bennett, who actually borrowed her share from Wanger, although he himself bought no stock. Lang was Diana's chief executive and, so far as film production was concerned, he was to be producer-director while Wanger was executive producer. Lang would prepare, direct, and edit Diana's productions, while Wanger negotiated contracts, arranged financing and distribution, and so on. Or as Wanger's contract put it, Lang would control "matters of purely artistic nature" while Wanger would attend to "all financial aspects of the production, including matters involving any substantial increase in costs." Lang had a reputation for being "difficult," and Universal demanded certain clauses to protect its investment of half the production costs plus any facilities and

Diana Productions' three founding partners—Walter Wanger (left), Joan Bennett (second from right), and Fritz Lang (right)—on the set of Scarlet Street.

personnel necessary for the project. If Lang departed from the approved script or went more than $50,000 over budget, Universal could take over production on forty-eight hours' notice. Once Lang finished shooting, he had sixty days to complete his cut for a first preview; thereafter Universal reserved the right to reedit the movie to meet "censorship requirements or export requirements or [to avoid] litigation or to enhance its commercial value."

This reediting clause ensured Universal's ultimate authority over the project, and left Wanger in a very difficult position. Lang assumed that his partner would run interference with the studio, while Universal clearly expected Wanger to keep Lang in line. So Wanger's allegiances were divided and his responsibilities somewhat contradictory. Besides tending to his production duties for Universal and his administrative duties for Diana, he would have to act as a buffer between Lang and the studio executives. This would be a delicate task, but Wanger was confident that any differences between Universal and Diana could be worked out, since the deal had such obvious benefits for all involved. Bennett was assured quality star vehicles, Lang was assured creative control of a handpicked prestige-level project from conception through first preview, and Wanger could devote at least some of his energies to more costly and ambitious productions. Universal, for its part, could further upgrade its A-class feature output, diminish its overhead costs (since Diana was putting up half the costs), and sustain productivity without increasing financial obligation or risk.

Wanger arranged financing through the Bank of America for Diana's share of the estimated $1.15 million in production costs, which included flat fees for Lang of $75,000, for Joan Bennett of $75,000, and for Wanger of $45,000. Another $50,000 went to Dudley Nichols for his screenplay. Lang took *Scarlet Street* into production early in the summer, with Bennett and Edward G. Robinson costarring and Dan Duryea in a key supporting role. The uncompromising, downbeat story, the stuff of nightmares, was ideal for Lang's dark visual style and his keen sense of cynicism and irony. Robinson played a self-loathing middle-aged cashier for a clothing store who finds solace from his failed marriage and failed ambitions as an artist in the arms of his mistress, played by Bennett. At the encouragement of her sadistic lover (Duryea), Bennett convinces Robinson to embezzle from his employer and she then takes not only the money but credit for his unsigned paintings as well. Robinson finally catches on and kills her in a rage, but the evidence implicates Duryea, who eventually is convicted and executed for the crime. But this scarcely extricates Robinson. Unable to paint, ravaged by guilt, and failing to convince authorities of the truth, he loses everything—his job, his marriage, his paintings, and finally his sanity.

Lang was firmly in control of the production and worked at his usual deliberate pace. He fell behind schedule, and though Universal could have exercised its option to take over the project, Cliff Work kept his distance—at least until postproduction. While the *Scarlet Street* shoot itself represented something of a "honeymoon" period between Diana and Universal, the romance ended when Lang's preview cut came in over two hours long. Honoring the contractual agreement, Universal previewed the picture, and then Work began talking about a recut to allay concerns about both "censorship requirements" and "commercial value." Lang, who was off doing a picture for Warners, insisted the picture be left intact. Wanger, caught between allegiances to both Lang and Universal, went along with Universal. Wanger was not pressured into the decision—in fact, he tried to persuade Lang of the reasoning, both aesthetic and economic, behind Universal's position. Wanger knew well enough from Lang's Ufa output of his proclivity for three-hour thrillers, and he also realized that Lang had little appreciation for the power structure and "commercial interests" in Hollywood that demanded a denser and more economical narrative style. Wanger believed that tightening *Scarlet Street* would improve its quality, and he supervised a recut that brought the picture to a hundred minutes.

The results seemed to bear out Wanger's position. *Scarlet Street* was a triumph for Diana, a money-maker for Universal, and one of Hollywood's consummate *noir* dramas. And despite Lang's protestations, it was scarcely a butchered masterpiece. In fact, the Universal-Diana setup seems to have been ideal for a filmmaker of Lang's talents and his self-indulgent excesses; the studio provided the necessary resources while Wanger provided both the protection and the discipline that Lang clearly needed. The success of *Scarlet Street* did little to assure Lang of all this, however, or to ease his abrasive temperament and flashes of paranoia. Lang's reaction troubled Wanger and Bennett, who were quite pleased with the picture and were still optimistic about the prospects for Diana. Cliff Work was pleased as well, and wired Nate Blumberg in November 1945 that *Scarlet Street* was "the best picture that has ever been made at Universal, and will measure up to the standard of any picture made in the industry in past years."

Scarlet Street was indeed a top Universal release in 1945, and it confirmed the company's commitment to outside productions as a complement to its own more predictable output. In fact, with the war ending and the Justice Department reactivating its antitrust efforts, it looked as if the first-run market and the outside deal would become even more prevalent at Universal. Blumberg signed Mark Hellinger in August 1945, giving him much the same inside/outside status enjoyed by Wanger, and there were other such deals in the works. *Scarlet Street* indicated that these deals could be troublesome, but that they were well worth the hassle in terms of revenues and credibility. They also enabled Cliff Work to focus his and the studio's energies on what it did best: low-cost formula pictures that the public and exhibitors consumed as fast as Universal could turn them out. Despite the phenomenal success at the high end of the market in the mid-1940s, the movie business still relied on a steady flow of standardized products, and Universal was there to provide it.

19

MGM:
The High Cost
of Quality

The war years brought a definitive end to Leo's decade-long reign as king of the Hollywood jungle. MGM did well during the war boom, but no better than several other studios —quite a comedown after the 1930s, when Metro's domination of the industry had been nothing short of phenomenal. From 1931 to 1940, the combined net profits of Hollywood's Big Eight companies totaled $128.2 million; MGM's net profits for the decade were $93.2 million, nearly three-quarters of the industry total. At the close of the decade, Metro still seemed invincible, but during the early 1940s its lead quickly evaporated. In 1942–43 it was struggling just to stay even with Paramount, Fox, and Warners, and by the end of the war Mayer and company had fallen well behind those three in terms of annual net profits. From 1941 through 1946, when the Big Eight's net profits soared to $398.8 million, Metro's cut was $81.5 million—barely 20 percent.

MGM's relatively mediocre economic performance during the war was directly related to Loew's limited theater chain, of course. The robust wartime economy and heavy theater attendance were a tremendous advantage to Paramount, Fox, and Warners. (By 1945, they had built up chains of 1,400, 635, and 500 theaters, respectively, while Loew's totaled only 135.) Equally important, though, was the effect of the Depression on filmmaking and marketing operations at MGM's three chief competitors. While Metro grew fat and complacent in the

1930s, Paramount and Fox fought back from economic collapse and, falling in line with Warners, developed leaner and more efficient systems. Those strategies persisted and paid off during the war years, resulting in ever wider profit margins. MGM led the industry in terms of annual gross income during the war years, but those revenues were not translating into industry-leading net profits. Metro's profits went from $11 million in 1941 to $18 million in 1946, an increase of some 60 percent. That was not bad, except in comparison to its major competitors, whose profits increased by 400 to 500 percent during the same period. Paramount's net revenues jumped from $9 million in 1941 to $39 million in 1946, Fox's from $5 million to $25 million, and Warners' from $5.5 million to $19.5 million.

The principal reasons for Metro's dwindling profit margin were its bloated production operation and chronic overhead costs, which in turn were related to its management setup and its corps of executives and producers. Back in December 1935, just as David Selznick was leaving MGM, he gave Nick Schenck some cogent advice about the studio's overhead costs and its management system. Because MGM was intent on maintaining top facilities and personnel, said Selznick, its budgets would "average $200,000 per picture higher than your competition," even without top producers. But he warned that if Mayer and Schenck weren't careful to cultivate a corps of top producers, "you will find the difference between cost with quality and cost without it." The warning proved prophetic, as Metro's management system itself became the consummate example of waste and excess. As soon as Mayer installed his management-by-committee system after Thalberg's death in 1936, there was a veritable population explosion in MGM's executive and producer ranks. In the early years Thalberg had required a half-dozen supervisors to produce roughly forty-five pictures; in 1937 Mayer was using twenty producers for the same number of pictures. The trend continued. By 1941 there were forty producers at the studio —five times the number required in 1927 to produce virtually the same number of pictures (forty-eight). The number of producers on staff actually expanded during the war, even though MGM cut its output to only about thirty pictures a year.

Metro's producers went by a variety of titles and had a range of duties and responsibilities, and all understood that to be a producer at MGM was to be a bureaucrat as well. All authority emanated from Mayer and proceeded downward through several levels of administrative authority. Mayer was Vice President in Charge of Production, and immediately under him was an executive staff of vice presidents—Harry Rapf, Al Lichtman, Sam Katz, and Eddie Mannix. Outside this elite group were another three dozen producers with varying degrees of authority.

The top rank consisted of eight executive producers; five were former Thalberg men, including Hunt Stromberg and Bernie Hyman, and the other three—Mervyn LeRoy, Robert Z. Leonard, and Joe Mankiewicz —were as close as anyone at MGM came to being "creative producers." Each of these executive producers had an assistant, several of whom also produced pictures, and there were an additional eighteen staff producers, including such capable filmmakers as Arthur Freed, Edwin Knopf, and Pan Berman.

The myriad decisions that Thalberg had made on his own or in consultation with Mayer or Mannix were now made by a hierarchy of committees, with the overall production operations still governed by Mayer's Executive Committee. By 1942 this committee included Mayer and his executive staff, along with B-movie chief J. J. Cohn and two writer-producers, Joe Mankiewicz and Dore Schary. The committee met weekly to keep tabs on current productions, to decide what properties were to be bought and who would develop them, and to make important cast and crew assignments. In a broader capacity, the committee set studio policy and decided on contract renewals and salaries for top personnel. As always, MGM's production agenda was geared to its stars, so the committee's weekly agenda invariably consisted of a list of the active top players or star vehicles that were currently in production. For the meeting of April 21, 1942, for example, the first twelve entries on a fifteen-item agenda were:

1. Myrna Loy
2. Spencer Tracy
3. Joan Crawford
4. Red Skelton
5. Lana Turner
6. Greer Garson
7. Hedy Lamarr
8. Mickey Rooney
9. Judy Garland
10. Van Heflin
11. Robert Taylor
12. Kathryn Grayson

This roster offers a pretty good idea of Metro's talent pool at the time, but it's also notable for the stars—and implicitly, the genres—that were not included. Metro was still very much a woman's studio, although in 1942 the sophisticated ladies of the 1930s were on the way out. Greta Garbo and Norma Shearer were easing into retirement, and Joan Crawford's popularity was fading fast. On the formula front, the studio was phasing out the MacDonald-Eddy operettas, the Marx Brothers comedies, and Johnny Weissmuller's Tarzan series. The war was already taking its toll as well. Jimmy Stewart had just joined the service; Clark Gable intended to enlist, though at the time he was mourning the death of his wife, Carole Lombard, who was killed in a January 1942 plane crash while on a war bond drive. Robert Taylor would also spend time in the service, though for the present he was doing extra duty at the studio. As of that April 21 meeting, Taylor was set for five pictures and possibly a sixth, "The Bugles Blow at Midnight," a project that awaited a decision from Gable. "If Gable refuses to do this picture," the committee ruled, "we can start with Taylor immediately."

That proposal indicated the wealth and penchant for extravagance at Metro in the early 1940s, and also that the growing power of individual stars could be offset by the sheer size of the studio's star stable. In fact, Metro was strategically developing second-rank players who could sub for its stars if the reluctance of a star or a scheduling conflict demanded it. Two rather obvious examples of this effort were Greer Garson and Hedy Lamarr, who had been developed as successors for Shearer and Garbo. By early 1942 the two were on very different career tracks, and this indicated both the positive and negative side of Metro's interchangeable-star strategy. Lamarr was mired in her second-rate Garbo persona, and there was no sign that she would pull out of it, even with Garbo's retirement. Garson, however, was emerging as a top star in her own right. Mayer had brought her over from England several years earlier when Shearer was becoming more selective and difficult to cast. Though still in her early thirties and eight years younger than Shearer, Garson had many of the same qualities—poise, maturity, breeding— and thus the makings of an MGM "leading lady." In her early films, Garson played the role of the resolute, dutiful wife, as exemplified by the title role she played in *Mrs. Miniver*—a part that Shearer turned down. *Mrs. Miniver* was in postproduction in April 1942, and Garson was on the committee agenda for her next assignment, *Random Harvest*. Those were MGM's two biggest hits in 1942, and they elevated Garson from an ersatz Shearer to being Louis Mayer's singular ideal of the wartime madonna: a dignified beauty of rare courage, repressed sexuality, and indomitable spirit who nurtured orphans, offspring, and husband (usually Walter Pidgeon) in one lavish melodrama after another.

Joan Crawford was an interesting contrast to Garson, not only in terms of screen type but also in terms of box-office appeal and control over her projects and her career. Crawford's popularity was declining in the early 1940s, and though she was four years older than Garson she refused to play maternal types and clung to her image as glamour queen and romantic costar. Past successes had solidified that glamorous persona and also had won Crawford all kinds of approval clauses, so developing projects for her was now a challenging and troublesome affair. The committee decided in the April meeting to send Crawford (via her agent) scripts for *Reunion in France* and *Three Hearts for Julia*, and Al Lichtman was to talk with her about the committee's plans for the two projects. Crawford agreed to do *Reunion in France*, even with little-known European actor Philip Dorn as her costar. The committee then decided to put low-budget director Jules Dassin on the picture, "if Mr. Mayer could get Miss Crawford's consent." Mayer managed to sell her on Dassin, but Lichtman had no luck on the other project. He reported that Crawford "refused to do *Three Hearts for Julia* unless a recognized star appeared in it as her leading man." Melvyn Douglas was the proposed costar, and in fact even the committee considered him a second-rate William Powell. So Lichtman suggested that they forget Crawford for the picture and go with Ann Sothern instead.

There were a few other headstrong female stars at Metro, some of whom were hooked up with male costars. If the union had been formalized on-screen, which happened more often at MGM than at any other studio, this could create rather interesting casting problems. The most durable of MGM's screen couples was Nick and Nora Charles, and Myrna Loy's name was on the April 1942 agenda for "The Thin Man's Rival," her fifth appearance opposite William Powell. She had already been sent the script, and the committee set a start date for mid-June. But Mayer and the others were due for a shock; Loy was tiring of the Nora Charles role and also was determined to do her part for the war effort. She refused the assignment and took an indefinite leave to work for the Red Cross. Loy was one star that Mayer and company had not anticipated having to replace, but they were not about to abandon the successful Thin Man series. In a meeting later that year, the minutes recorded "a lengthy discussion about 'The Thin Man' with regard to the replacement of Myrna Loy." The candidates included Marsha Hunt, Jean Arthur, and Loretta Young, but none proved satisfactory, so the series was suspended for the time being.

While Myrna Loy threatened to disrupt Nick and Nora's marriage, another actress was exercising her authority to create a screen couple whose union—both on screen and off—would prove more successful and durable than even Loy and Powell's. Katharine Hepburn's name was not on that April agenda, although by then it was implicitly linked to Spencer Tracy's. Tracy and Hepburn had just completed their first picture together, *Woman of the Year*, and Tracy was on the April 12 agenda for the committee's casting approval of another costarring venture with Hepburn, *Keeper of the Flame*. Approval was virtually automatic, since Hepburn set up the project and was the most powerful star on the lot at the time. Her power had not been won easily. In 1938 Hepburn was written off by several top exhibitors as "box-office poison," at which point she bolted RKO and went back East. She starred on Broadway in Philip Barry's *The Philadelphia Story*, and she had the foresight to waive her salary in exchange for the screen rights to the play. When it hit, Hepburn sold it to Louis Mayer for $250,000 as part of a package deal that included director George Cukor and a costarring team of Cary Grant, Jimmy Stewart, and Hepburn herself.

The Philadelphia Story was Metro's biggest hit of 1940, and a year later Hepburn was back in Mayer's office with another project and another list of demands. The project was *Woman of the Year*, and Hepburn wanted George Stevens to direct and Spencer Tracy—whom she had never met—as her costar. She also wanted a long-term MGM contract giving her story, script, and director approval. Mayer and his committee had little choice but to acquiesce to her demands, so Hepburn joined the MGM fold, and very much on her own terms. Joe Mankiewicz had been instrumental in selling *The Philadelphia Story* to the committee, and he was the nominal producer on *Woman of the Year* as well. But Hepburn was the chief architect on her initial MGM pictures, and she drew up the blueprints with Mayer's reluctant blessing. He did appreciate the commercial and critical success of her pictures, and he also welcomed Hepburn's influence on Tracy, whose chronic alcoholism and failed marriage (which was never legally dissolved) had in many ways gotten the better of him by 1942. Hepburn provided a stabilizing influence, and Tracy did some of his best work as her costar.

Mickey Rooney and Judy Garland were another top screen couple on the committee's agenda in April 1942, and Garland was yet another headstrong actress set on controlling her career and screen roles. But Garland was not yet out of her teens and had only recently reached top stardom, so she had considerably less control over her career or her assignments than other studio stars—even though she and Rooney both made the exhibitors' poll in 1941. Garland worked in a range of musical vehicles and with different costars, but her most successful pictures were with Rooney, especially in the Freed-produced, Berkeley-directed musicals. After *Babes in Arms* in 1939, Garland and Rooney did *Strike Up the Band* in 1940, *Babes on Broadway* in 1941, and the April 1942 agenda had them slated for *Girl Crazy*, which Freed planned to start after Rooney completed his latest Hardy assignment. The formula was wearing thin—this time the "kids" were putting on a musical rodeo at a dude ranch—and though Rooney was content enough with his situation at Metro, Garland's displeasure grew with

Spencer Tracy and Katharine Hepburn first worked together in Woman of the Year *at the insistence of Hepburn, who was then the most powerful star at Metro.*

each reformulation. She was nearly twenty years old and already had gotten married (disastrously, to band leader David Rose), but she had no luck dissuading Mayer from typecasting her as the virginal, naive adolescent.

Garland was signed to a long-term deal, and she knew there was little hope of breaking away from Freed, considering his rapport with Mayer and the success of his musicals. But she was so determined to redirect her career that she decided to form an alliance with another producer, namely Joe Mankiewicz. In 1942, Mankiewicz was (at age thirty-three) the youngest, the most aggressive, and possibly the most talented producer on the lot. He served on the Executive Committee and his stock was up at the time after he'd produced Hepburn's two recent hits. He shared with his older brother Herman a cynical attitude about the Hollywood power structure, only he was more ambitious and politic about it. He had a grudging regard for matters of protocol and such—there was little choice considering MGM's byzantine operations —but this scarcely stopped him from seizing the initiative when an opportunity presented itself.

Mankiewicz's involvement in Garland's career was a case in point. The two became lovers in 1942 as Garland's marriage to David Rose disintegrated, and Mankiewicz also played the role of Garland's mentor and confidant, encouraging her to hold out for more mature screen roles. Late that year he came across what he thought might be a breakthrough vehicle for Garland. In December 1942 Mayer and a few other executives were in New York for a new Broadway play, *The Pirate*, which Mayer thoroughly disliked even though it was doing solid business and seemed readily adaptable to the screen. After considerable discussion about the property in an Executive Committee meeting later that month, Sidney Franklin and Joe Mankiewicz were dispatched to New York to check it out. Mankiewicz was much impressed with the dreamlike fantasy about a girl on a Caribbean island who, while under a hypnotic spell, falls in love with a traveling troubadour she believes is Mack the Black, a legendary pirate. Upon returning to the studio, Mankiewicz suggested that *The Pirate* was an ideal movie project. Indications are that Mankiewicz had Garland in mind for the lead, but he did not push the idea with the committee. Mayer and the others were still not persuaded even to purchase the property, and they seemed to see it as a straight farce like the play, with someone like Myrna Loy in the lead. In a late January meeting Mankiewicz suggested that they make a sound track of the play and the audience reaction, a tactic he had used to win over the committee on *The Philadelphia Story* a few years earlier. Mayer agreed to the $6,000 expenditure for the recording, and several weeks later he purchased the property and assigned Joe Mankiewicz to write and produce the picture.

T H I S bit of palace intrigue with Garland and Mankiewicz was far from over, but already it indicated how complex the shifting studio alliances were in 1942–43. With most of Metro's big stars making only one or two pictures per year, and with the studio continuing to rely heavily on presold story properties, the infighting and studio politics were becoming troublesome. So much so, in fact, that the Executive Committee held a special session in January 1943 to discuss stories, stars, and the power relations at MGM. The discussion resulted in the following policy statement:

> *It is definitely understood that from this time forward* no scripts are to be sent to any of our stars without Mr. Mannix's approval. The vice presidents are to *emphatically* bring this to the attention of their producers. Mr. Mannix should also bring this to the attention of the directors . . .
>
> – – – – –
>
> Mr. Thau [Mannix's assistant] is to discuss with [publicity chief] Howard Strickling the elimination of the publicity department giving

out any advance stories about properties that we may acquire with regard to who will play in them. These publicity stories should only be confirmed by Mr. Mayer, Mr. Mannix, and Mr. Thau.

Although this eased the problems for the publicity department, it scarcely reduced the infighting over properties and producer-star alignments. Indeed, the potential for discord was there whenever MGM secured an established "commercial" play or novel and gave it to a producer to develop for a certain star. Once Mayer agreed to buy *The Pirate*, for instance, Mankiewicz knew that if he could convince the committee to mount it as a Garland vehicle, Metro was not only locked into the project but was already marketing a finished product. Mankiewicz also knew that once such a decision was made, he had a piece of Garland's future and Freed's command over her career diminished. He scarcely expected to take over her career, considering Freed's success with Berkeley, Rooney, and Garland—and considering, too, that he was no musical producer. In fact, because Freed and Garland were strictly musical personnel with an established track record, they did have a more intense rapport than any other top producer and star on the lot with the exception of Joe Pasternak and Kathryn Grayson, who formed a similar musical alliance. The degree of specialization involved in musical production demanded this kind of teamwork, even though MGM's market strategy did not. With production cutbacks and a more competitive and profitable first-run market, most top stars were looking for a wider variety of roles and story types, which they were more likely to find by working with different producers. There were a few quasi-formal units at Metro, as with Sidney Franklin and Greer Garson, who did four pictures together during the war, three of them directed by Mervyn LeRoy (who had given up producing altogether by 1942). But for the most part the high-grade production unit, at least as a coalition of above-the-line personnel working regularly together, was fast disappearing at MGM.

W H I L E the production cutbacks and increasingly competitive first-run market discouraged unit production at the high end of Metro's operations, Mayer saw no reason to eliminate disciplined, cost-efficient filmmaking altogether. So to stabilize the overall studio process during the war, he developed the so-called Schary unit. In 1941, Dore Schary was a thirty-six-year-old writer who was earning $1,000 a week at MGM and had solid screenwriting credentials and ambitions to produce. Late that year, Schary and Mayer became embroiled in a dispute over the making of *Joe Smith, American,* a modest home-front melodrama starring Robert Young as a worker in a munitions plant who faces problems at home and on the job. The picture was budgeted at $279,856 and was destined from its inception to play subsequent-run houses and double bills, and Schary felt that it was being undervalued and thus underproduced due to its low-budget status. Schary challenged Mayer directly not only about the picture but about the studio's low-budget operation generally, which he felt had begun running in virtual isolation from A-class feature production.

What Schary suggested was a closer association between A and B production at Metro. There were two main reasons for this strategy. One was scheduling: it enabled top personnel to keep busy between major productions. Equally important was the marketing angle, particularly where stars were concerned. The presence of Robert Taylor or Judy Garland in a low-budget release, like the presence of Rooney or Lionel Barrymore in the series jobs, elevated the picture above a B-grade standard. As significant were the production values that top writers, directors, cinematographers, and others could bring to Metro's lesser productions. The style and polish they provided, along with the presence of top stars, would offset even the appearance of B-grade production at MGM. In terms of production management, Schary proposed that low-budget operations, presently supervised by Harry Rapf and J. J. Cohn, be reorganized much like the Executive Committee— that is, a group of producers who would meet regularly to decide on stories, casting, scheduling, and so on. He also recommended that the B-level committee interact with Mayer's committee in order to utilize top personnel who were between assignments.

Mayer liked Schary's overall plan, and he also liked the way *Joe Smith, American* came in $40,000 under budget and promptly took off at the box office. And despite Schary's questionable political views (Schary was a left-leaning liberal and New Deal Democrat), Mayer saw the youngster as a creative complement to J. J. Cohn. As production supervisor, Cohn's strengths were financial and administrative—he was essentially the B-level equivalent of Eddie Mannix, a capable executive who oversaw day-to-day operations. But Cohn had no real sense of the technical and dramatic aspects of filmmaking, which were Schary's strengths.

On November 5, 1941, Schary signed a new one-year deal for $1,750 per week as the Executive Producer of Metro's B-movie operation, which was formally titled the Rapf-Schary unit—although it was referred to on the lot as simply the Schary unit. Schary also joined Rapf as a member of the Executive Committee, not only to tap into available personnel but to keep Mayer's group apprised of the new unit's activities. The Rapf-Schary unit comprised a dozen or so producers—the total varied as successful producers graduated to the A ranks and as less productive unit members were siphoned off. The group met weekly with Rapf and Schary to discuss ten to fifteen story synopses and to monitor the projects already in the works. Rapf's role was remarkably similar to Mayer's with the Executive Committee. If Schary or some other unit member liked a story, it was given to someone in editorial to "read and tell to Mr. Rapf," who then acted as a sounding board and voice of experience.

Schary's role, meanwhile, recalled Thalberg's under the old regime. He acted as story editor and facilitator during script development, handled casting and crew assignments, screened dailies, and monitored actual production. Schary also supervised editing, which demanded a special brand of creativity, since budgetary constraints usually made retakes impossible. In fact, limited budgets and resources were a constant concern to Schary and his producers, especially as they evaluated story properties. The Rapf-Schary unit decided in a February 1942 meeting, for instance, that a certain property that was "greatly liked" by producer Irving Asher could be produced "within the unit's budget" and that the story should "be told in the executive meeting today." At the same meeting another project was "deemed too expensive for the Rapf unit" and passed on to the Executive Committee for its consideration.

The Schary unit turned out roughly one film per month from late 1941 until early 1944. The budget ceiling for its first year was $300,000; only three of thirteen productions exceeded that figure, and the average cost on all thirteen pictures was $275,000. The unit concentrated on crime thrillers, westerns, home-front melodramas, and combat films. The westerns tended to be the most costly films, because of location work and other logistical problems, while the more topical war-related dramas were by far the most successful. During the unit's second year of operation Schary used more top personnel and the projects were more ambitious, pushing the average cost to nearly $400,000. The two most expensive projects were *Journey for Margaret*, a rehash of *Mrs. Miniver* that cost $463,000, and *Lassie Come Home* at $564,000. Both were sizable hits, less notable for the established talent they used than for the new talent they introduced: Margaret O'Brien, a precocious five-year-old who played a London waif orphaned by Nazi bombs in *Journey for Margaret*, and eleven-year-old Elizabeth Taylor, a real-life evacuee of London who costarred in *Lassie Come Home*. Schary actively developed the two child stars. He was motivated not only by their obvious talents but by the cost-effectiveness they stood for since even after their first hits, they still commanded only a fraction of what their established counterparts earned. In a meeting in January 1943, just after *Journey for Margaret* was released, the Executive Committee picked up O'Brien's option for another six months for a mere $150 per week. Two weeks later, on February 9, after a successful preview of *Lassie Come Home*, Liz Taylor's option was renewed for three months at $75 per week.

By late 1943 it appeared as if the Schary unit's association with A-class production was having just the reverse of the intended effect. One of Schary's pet projects in late 1943, for example, was *Bataan*, an all-star war film that featured Robert Taylor, Thomas Mitchell, and Robert Walker; it was directed by Tay Garnett just before he shot a Greer Garson picture. The final cost of the picture was $789,000. As promised, Schary upgraded the overall quality of Metro's low-budget output and provided greater continuity to its production operations. But what he was giving MGM, finally, was a "B-plus" unit. And despite pronouncements by Mayer, Schary, and various other personnel, the unit was not a profitable enterprise for Loew's/MGM. In fact, its prototype, *Joe Smith, American*, with profits of around $450,000, was by far its most successful production. After a full year in operation, the unit was operating at a net loss of $38,648, and it remained at this break-even level throughout Schary's tenure as Executive Producer.

Louis Mayer could live with that, considering what the Schary unit contributed to the overall efficiency and continuity of Metro operations. But Dore Schary was feeling less agreeable. In November 1942 when Mayer picked up Schary's option and raised his weekly salary to $2,000, there had been vague allusions to top assignments. None were forthcoming, however, and though projects like *Bataan* offered some satisfaction, Schary's ambitions extended beyond MGM's B-movie unit. Clashes with Mayer became more frequent as 1943 wore on, and in November when his option again came up, Schary decided to leave MGM and take over Vanguard Films for David Selznick—graduating, in effect, from B-plus to A-minus production. Selznick's offer was an attractive one. Vanguard's output would be limited enough to allow Schary to personally produce several pictures each year, and besides his weekly salary of $2,500, he would receive 15 percent of the net profits on all Vanguard releases.

T H E rising cost of the Schary-unit pictures was symptomatic of conditions at Metro during the war years, when record-setting revenues were offset by the studio's enormous production and overhead costs. MGM's heaviest costs during the war were in musical production. In the 1940s, the genre underwent an industry-wide renaissance, most notably at MGM. By 1944 one-sixth of all Hollywood's releases were musicals, roughly twice the prewar percentage, and MGM's ratio was even higher. In 1943–44, one-quarter of Metro's releases were musicals. Almost all of MGM's musicals during the war were handled by Freed, Joe Pasternak, and Jack Cummings, whose relative success was in some sense a function of each producer's capacity to develop a stable production unit. Cummings, the least successful of the three, never developed a consistent rapport with any musical stars or directors. Pasternak's unit orientation involved little more than his repeated outings with Kathryn Grayson, which did result in some mildly successful pictures. Henry Koster's arrival from Universal in 1944 promised a more coherent unit for Pasternak and Grayson—something like the unit they developed at Universal to produce Durbin's musicals in the late 1930s—but the promise was never fulfilled.

Arthur Freed was by far MGM's most successful musical producer during the 1940s. His best work early in the decade was in the series of Judy Garland musicals, most of them with Busby Berkeley directing and Mickey Rooney as costar. That was Freed's novitiate as a musical producer, a period that ended in 1943 when he produced four hit musicals including *Girl Crazy,* the last of his Berkeley-directed vehicles for Garland and Mickey Rooney, and *Cabin in the Sky,* a musical fable with an all-black cast directed by Vincente Minnelli. All four were adaptations of stage musicals, which Freed had come to see as something of a mixed blessing. They could be mounted and produced rather quickly since they already had been scripted and "visualized" onstage. But the screen rights were costly and their stage-bound nature tended to stifle innovation.

Freed broke free of those constraints in 1944 with *Meet Me in St. Louis,* a Garland musical directed by Minnelli. Rather than another transplanted Broadway show, *Meet Me in St. Louis* was an original "movie musical" that integrated the musical numbers into the story without recourse to a backstage plot, thus bringing fantasy and narrative reality into a delicate balance. It was not quite as imaginative technically as later Freed-Minnelli productions, nor did it rely as heavily on an innovative blending of story, song, and dance. But these qualities were certainly evident in *Meet Me in St. Louis,* and they signaled a change in MGM's musical style and the first glimmering of its musical golden age.

Meet Me in St. Louis also indicated what such an age would cost Metro. Freed's pictures had grown steadily more expensive and time-consuming over the past five years, but with *St. Louis* he was definitely kicking into a higher gear. In the year before he started serious preparation on it, he put five musicals through production. But once he started *St. Louis,* it would be a full year before he sent another musical into production. He devoted six months to script development and another seven months to preproduction; shooting and editing took another six months. While all this was exceptional compared to previous Freed productions, it established a pattern for most of the subsequent musicals with Minnelli. They would be characterized by budgets well over $1 million, preproduction schedules of a year or longer (including scripting), shooting schedules of three to six months, and another six months or more for postproduction.

A L T H O U G H *Meet Me in St. Louis* didn't originate on the Great White Way, its lineage did reach back to New York and Broadway. The movie was based on the "Kensington stories," a series of sentimental sketches written by Sally Benson for *The New Yorker* in 1942 which chronicled a family's experiences in St. Louis just after the turn of the century. Further inspiration for the film came from the massive Broadway hit *Life With Father,* another nostalgic family portrait that had been running since 1939. Freed convinced Louis Mayer to purchase the rights to Benson's stories for $25,000 soon after their publication in early 1942. Mayer also agreed to hire Benson for the adaptation, which was to trace the family through four seasons, culminating in the spring of 1904, the time of the St. Louis World's Fair. While Freed took the script through its early stages, Minnelli worked with the overall design of the film. His background was in set and costume design, and he worked closely with Lemuel Ayres to reproduce the American gothic look in the sets, and with art director Preston Ames to capture the evocative quality of Thomas Eakins's paintings. (Eakins was not only a leading artist, but also a popular magazine illustrator at the turn of the century, something of a predecessor to Norman Rockwell.) Influenced, no doubt, by Orson Welles's *The Magnificent Ambersons,* a 1942 RKO production, Minnelli himself came up with the idea of introducing each season with a greeting-card illustration of the family home which would dissolve into a live-action shot.

While the design of *Meet Me in St. Louis* came fairly easily, the script required a half-dozen different writers, all of whom struggled with the lack of motivation and conflict in the idyllic story. Benson worked with a staff writer to establish the characters, the setting, and the lyrical innocence of the era. But as with her stories, there was no pressing issue or situation to keep the plot moving. So Freed brought in the writing team of Sarah Mason and Victor Heerman, who spent several months in mid-1942 creating a bit of intrigue via a blackmail plot involving the central character, Esther Smith—a rather unlikely twist for so pristine and innocent a character in so idyllic a community. Freed found the plot device inappropriate and turned to staff writer William Ludwig, a specialist in adolescent romance, who promptly cut the blackmail plot and built up the courtship stories of Esther and her

Turn-of-the-century St. Louis, as recreated on the back lot at Culver City in 1944 for Meet Me in St. Louis.

sister Rose. Freed now felt that the script was satisfactory, and in February 1943 he ordered copies of the Ludwig script sent to all department heads and to the principal cast members.

Garland was not satisfied, however; her agent informed Mayer and Freed that she found the story lacking in plot and that her character was too "juvenile." Actually the critique originated not with the actress or her agent but with Joe Mankiewicz, who had just started work on *The Pirate* with Garland still in mind. Mayer agreed with the criticisms, so Freed brought in another pair of screenwriters to overhaul Ludwig's draft. They immediately wove a new plot line into the story: Mr. Smith, the family patriarch, is being transferred by his firm from St. Louis to New York. Freed liked the new line, but when he recirculated the script Garland again voiced her displeasure. There was no doubt of Joe Mankiewicz's influence by this time, since he had nearly completed a workable draft of *The Pirate* and was about to start preproduction on the picture. And despite Freed's persuasive pitch of the new story angle, Mayer began thinking that the Mankiewicz project might be ready to go before Freed could lick the problems with *St. Louis.*

But it would be another two years before Garland did *The Pirate*, and the producer would be Arthur Freed, not Joe Mankiewicz. The young writer-producer's ambition and his effort to win Garland over to his project were acceptable enough, but in the summer of 1943 he pushed a little too far. Mayer understood the power trips and sexual politics of Hollywood well enough—they were part of the business for producers and executives. But his paternalistic attitude toward ingenues like Garland and June Allyson was genuine, and so was his close friendship with Arthur Freed, whom he still considered Garland's mentor. Mankiewicz, for his part, was equally concerned about Garland's well-being, and he was convinced that Mayer's interference and paternalism were responsible for both her personal and professional problems. As he developed *The Pirate* and grew more intimate with Garland, Mankiewicz began to realize how terribly unhappy and confused she really was. Garland was heavily dependent on amphetamines, which she initially took to control her weight but now relied on to bolster her energy level and her confidence. Mankiewicz knew the dependency was severe, but he also began to suspect that Garland's emotional instability and her frequent flashes of hysteria were the result of something more than overwork and uppers. He was so convinced, in fact, that he arranged for Garland to meet with Karl Menninger, whose psychiatric clinic in the Midwest was a haven, at one time or another, for many Hollywood casualties. Menninger in turn referred Garland to a doctor in the Los Angeles area for treatment. At that point Mayer and Garland's mother, a classic show business shrew, learned of Mankiewicz's efforts. That brought an abrupt end to the affair, to Mankiewicz's musical, and to his tenure at MGM. On August 4, 1943, Joe Mankiewicz submitted a completed screenplay of *The Pirate*, his last official act before joining 20th Century-Fox.

A T that point *Meet Me in St. Louis* became a go project. By late August Freed and Minnelli had prepared a budget of $1,395,000 and set a start date for early October. Various problems at the studio and also with Technicolor's heavy schedule held up the project for another two months, though, and it finally went into production on December 7. By then its shooting schedule was projected at fifty-eight days and the estimated cost had swelled to over $1.5 million. Predictably enough, the heaviest line items were the sets and music, which comprised fully half the total budget at $497,000 and $234,000, respectively. Story and continuity costs were also pretty steep—the total was $132,250—due to the extensive rewrites. The cast was large, but Garland was the only star aboard and earning $2,500 per week then. The other key cast member was Margaret O'Brien, set to play Garland's precocious little sister; her salary was $250 per week. Even Vincente Minnelli came at a relatively low cost—$1,000 per week for forty-three weeks—since his career was just taking off.

Minnelli earned his salary on this particular production, since his skills not only as a director but also as a cheerleader and psychologist were necessary to get Garland through the picture. Her emotional and physical problems were acute in 1943. The Mankiewicz flap left her angry with Mayer, and she still was unhappy with the script for *St. Louis* and especially with her role, which she found rather vapid and juvenile. And despite her frequent demands to play more mature characters, she was also unsure of herself as a "leading lady" at a studio known for its glamorous female stars—particularly in a film like *Meet Me in St. Louis* in which she was the sole star. She got off on the wrong foot with Minnelli when she balked at the heavy rehearsals and prerecording sessions Minnelli had scheduled from November 10 until shooting started on December 7. He prevailed in this initial confrontation, and as the picture progressed he gradually won her confidence —and her affections. Minnelli and Garland were living together by the time *St. Louis* was in postproduction, and they were wed just after its release, with Mayer and Freed's blessings. In fact, Mayer gave away the bride at the ceremony. But despite her growing rapport with Minnelli and his patient efforts, Garland continued to be a difficult star to work with. She suffered from a host of maladies, both real and imagined, which led to fits of hysteria and frequent disruptions of the production. The daily production reports indicate that Garland was habitually late and occasionally failed to arrive at all, and that she often interrupted shooting for any number of reasons—the most frequent being her migraine headaches.

There were a host of other problems on the shoot, but Freed and Minnelli's chief worries throughout centered on Garland. Her problems were more persistent and less manageable than any others, and she was absolutely crucial to the success of the picture. Her character was the vital narrative agent in the film, providing what Minnelli termed the "continuity thread in the integration of the songs to the story." What made things especially tough for Minnelli was that Garland's key scenes tended to be the most trying and chaotic. On January 13, for instance, Minnelli and cameraman George Folsey were set to shoot the intricate sequence in which Garland and Tom Drake, who played her beau, walk through the house in the evening, lowering the gaslights. In the process, they exchange their first tentative avowals of love. Garland and Drake were the only actors on call that day, and were due on the lot at 9:00 A.M. and on the set (in wardrobe) at ten. Minnelli and his crew spent the early hours lining up and lighting the scene, a task they had started the previous evening. Garland should have been in hairdressing and wardrobe by nine, but assistant director Al Jennings reported otherwise. His description of her activities from nine onward was as follows:

> Judy Garland phoned A.D. [assistant director] that she was well enough to work, but unable to drive because eyes were bothering her, and would he please send a car for her. At 910 car left—returned with Miss Garland at 945. At 950 Mr. Freed's office phoned Unit Manager on stage that Miss Garland . . . had lost her toothbridge, her dentist Dr. Pincus had a spare set and to send car for them. [Unit Manager] Friedman called Transportation for O.K. to send car. At 1000 car was sent for bridge, returned at 1040 with them. Miss Garland arrived on stage at 1040—made up and hair dressed but in street clothes.

The cast and crew rehearsed for an hour, and then Garland got into her wardrobe. From 12:16 P.M. to 1:30 P.M., Minnelli made eleven takes of Garland and Drake turning out the lights. Another camera setup was necessary, which was selected before breaking for a one-hour lunch. The entire afternoon, from 2:37 P.M. to 6:15 P.M., was spent lining, lighting, and rehearsing the next setup. The only disruptions came when Garland left the set for a wardrobe adjustment (thirty-one minutes) and to be "treated for a headache" (ten minutes). Minnelli finally shot six takes of the new setup, plus one additional take after discussion with Garland, who, as the assistant director noted, demanded "a better one." This turned out to be one of Garland's stronger scenes in what was overall a thoroughly polished and convincing performance. In fact, the quality of her work—and indeed of the picture itself—is a testament to Garland's enormous talent, and to Minnelli's as well.

The problems due to Garland were overshadowed some six weeks into production when several other cast members fell ill. Mary Astor, who played the matriarch of the Smith clan, contracted pneumonia in mid-January and was out for several weeks. Margaret O'Brien, who played Tootie, the youngest of the four daughters, took sick two weeks later, and at that point Freed decided to suspend production for a few days rather than try to shoot around her. When key supporting player Joan Carroll underwent an emergency appendectomy in early February, Freed and Mayer closed down the shoot indefinitely. Minnelli made the most of it, though, using the time to work on the two most demanding scenes involving O'Brien. One was a Halloween scene,

Director Vincente Minnelli rehearses with Judy Garland for the pivotal love scene in Meet Me in St. Louis.

played out at nightfall as the costumed children build a bonfire in the street and prepare to haunt the neighborhood. Minnelli wanted to capture a child's exaggerated sense of wonder and terror through O'Brien's character, as she boasts "I'm the most horrible" and braves the wrath of the neighborhood crank. The delays enabled Minnelli to devote a full week's rehearsal to the Halloween sequence, and also to work on the climactic winter sequence, in which Tootie, inspired by Garland's rendition of "Have Yourself a Merry Little Christmas," explodes into tears and runs outside in her nightdress to demolish a "family" of snowmen in the yard. Each scene was a tour de force for O'Brien, who played each to perfection when shooting resumed in mid-February.

Other problems cropped up during the shoot. There were serious rains and flooding in the L.A. area in late February and early March, for instance, which held up exterior shooting. Freed and Minnelli finally closed the picture twelve shooting days behind schedule—plus an additional thirty-four "layoff" days accumulated before they finished shooting on April 7, 1944. By then they were $125,500 over budget, with the costs edging toward $1.8 million. There was also concern over the length of the rough cut, which ran over two hours. Freed called meetings with Minnelli and his writers, each of whom came up with suggestions for tightening the cut. During the previews in June and July they trimmed it down to 113 minutes, about average for an MGM musical.

Preview audiences indicated that the picture itself was anything but average, however, so Mayer and Schenck decided to hold up release until the holiday season. That would maximize the picture's profit potential in terms of theater bookings and attendance, and it would also give the New York office plenty of time to mount a strong sales campaign. The premiere was held in St. Louis on November 22, and the picture opened in New York a week later. It was easily MGM's biggest hit of the season, critically as well as commercially. Most of the kudos in the general press went to Garland and Minnelli, but the trade papers repeatedly singled out Freed. *Box Office Digest*, for example, stated that "Arthur Freed has seized on the well-known Sally Benson book to produce something of a minor miracle—a musical that is miles away from the formula." *Variety* said that *St. Louis* had "unusual warmth and appeal for a musical, which had to be credited to the professional understanding supplied by Arthur Freed's producership, as well as splendid direction and vivid performances." *Variety* also predicted that *St. Louis* "will be unquestionably a hefty grosser," and by March it was listed as second only to Selznick's *I'll Be Seeing You* among the month's "Box-Office Champions." The picture's success enhanced both Garland's and O'Brien's marquee value, putting them on the annual exhibitors' poll along with MGM stars Greer Garson, Spencer Tracy, and Van Johnson. O'Brien went on to win a special Oscar as the industry's premier child actor—no small feat in 1944, when movie screens were overrun by kids and awash with sentimentality.

T H E box-office success of *Meet Me in St. Louis* and several other Metro productions, notably *Gaslight* and *Mrs. Parkington*, pushed the gross revenues for Loew's/MGM in 1944 to $166 million, an industry record. MGM's net profits were $14.5 million, a record for the studio but actually a disappointing figure, given Loew's gross receipts and also the reported net profits of Paramount and 20th Century-Fox, which continued to pull away from MGM. The success of Freed's lavish musical did not bode well where Metro's profit margin was concerned, but at least with Freed the production costs translated into quality product. That was not the case with a number—perhaps the majority —of MGM's producers. The days of Selznick, Thalberg, and Stromberg were long gone, of course, and so were such promising producers as Joe Mankiewicz and Dore Schary. Most of the former Thalberg men still at Metro were now bureaucrats, weighing down the management structure and discouraging, though perhaps not consciously, the more talented and imaginative young producers. The two most active and successful producers at Metro were Freed and Pasternak. They were responsible for one-quarter of the twenty-eight productions on MGM's schedule for 1945; no other producer handled more than two projects. But Freed and Pasternak were producing Metro's most expensive and least efficient pictures, and as their projects became more ambitious they were contributing to the ever-increasing overhead.

The rising costs of musical production were symptomatic of virtually all of MGM's operations. Consider how quickly Schary's B-unit costs climbed from $275,000 per picture to over $400,000 in 1942–43. Clearly Mayer's late-1930s strategy of offsetting more lavish spectacles with low-cost formula pictures had gone awry. By 1945 virtually every MGM production carried a prestige budget, although few were performing at that level at the box office. MGM's penchant for high-cost productions was spelled out in a report published in *Box Office Digest* in January 1945 which related the costs of three hundred features produced by Hollywood's eleven biggest production companies in 1944. The data in that report can be broken down as shown in the table on the following page, grouping each company's output according to budget range.

These figures bear out various wartime trends besides MGM's inflated costs. They indicate the phasing out of B-movie production among the majors, the increasingly balanced output of RKO and the major minors (which in all three cases was accomplished by relying on outside talent for top features), and the steady supply of bargain-basement products by the three dominant minor studios. It's especially interesting, given the escalating budgets among the leading majors, that Monogram and PRC (Producers Releasing Corporation) were able to keep costs under $100,000 on the majority of their productions. As these B-picture factories were demonstrating, the general expense of feature filmmaking had not really changed since the late 1930s. In fact, a 1938 study of 251 features indicated that 30 percent cost at least $500,000 to produce, roughly the same percentage indicated in the above chart for 1944 releases. But while the industry at large spent over a half-million dollars on less than one-third of its output, MGM spent at least that much on 80 percent of its pictures.

MGM's high-cost/low-profit dilemma worsened in 1945. Loew's set another industry record with gross receipts of $175 million, while its net profits actually declined to $12.9 million. That year Paramount and Fox both netted over $15 million, and now even Warners, with profits of $9.9 million, was threatening to overtake MGM. Mayer and company were generating enormous revenues and profits for both Loew's and MGM, but the studio's top-heavy management structure and extravagant production operation were squandering millions per annum. As Nick Schenck surveyed the situation, he wondered how much longer he could put up with the inefficiency of Mayer's management-by-committee system. He began to wonder, in fact, whether it wasn't time to start looking for another Irving Thalberg.

	OVER $500,000	$200k–500k	$100k–200k	UNDER $100k
MGM	21	5	0	0
Paramount	17	2	4	4
20th Century-Fox	20	2	3	1
Warner Bros.	12	2	2	0
RKO	9	12	9	1
United Artists	3	10	0	0
Columbia	5	10	24	3
Universal	10	17	17	5
Republic	1	3	12	7
Monogram	0	2	3	21
PRC	0	0	2	19
TOTALS	98	65	76	61

20

Selznick and Hitchcock: Separate Ways

With the wartime market going strong, it was inevitable that David Selznick would return to active production. It was inevitable, too, that he would work again with his star director, Alfred Hitchcock. Since *Rebecca*, Selznick had loaned Hitchcock out in successive deals with UA, RKO, Universal, and 20th Century-Fox. Hitchcock, after a half-dozen projects on loan, usually writing as well as directing, found that his stock was up, and he was feeling comfortable and self-assured in Hollywood. He had yet to equal the success of *Rebecca*, but he was understandably wary of working again with Selznick. As he grew more confident in Hollywood and more accustomed to its mode of production, he was increasingly aware of how different his working methods and personality were from Selznick's. He was a disciplined, meticulous filmmaker whose approach to both preparation and actual production was deliberate and subdued. Selznick was an excessive extrovert who seemed to regard filmmaking as a sustained existential dilemma, an exercise in crisis management.

This apparent incompatibility did not bother Selznick, however. After returning to active filmmaking in 1944, he served as producer on Hitchcock's next three pictures: *Spellbound, Notorious,* and *The Paradine Case.* These films, along with *Rebecca* in 1940, constituted the best work either filmmaker did during the decade, and they indicated that Selznick and Hitchcock still had a great deal in common in terms of taste and story interests. In many ways, *Spellbound* and *Notorious,* like *Rebecca,* were consummate Selznick pictures. All of them reflected his long-standing fascination with ill-fated love affairs, and they favored the woman's point of view. Selznick's star-crossed lovers generally were victimized by external events beyond their control, events that often lent a sense of spectacle but little psychological complexity to his films.

While *Spellbound* and *Notorious* reflected Selznick's interests, however, each film also gave them a distinct inflection, thanks not only to Hitchcock but also to Ben Hecht, who coauthored both screenplays and ran interference with Selznick. Like Hitchcock, Hecht considered Selznick's story interests to be superficial and melodramatic, and indeed they were. The two men tried something different in both *Spellbound* and *Notorious,* creating sexual psychodramas wherein the narrative is driven by external events, but only as a pretext for getting inside the characters and questioning how well they really know their spouses or lovers or colleagues—or themselves. And while the external conflict is resolved, the "happy ending" is blatantly arbitrary and unsettling. Like all Hitchcock's best work, *Spellbound* and *Notorious* leave a lingering concern, if not a sense of downright dread, about a destabilized personality and relationships that can never again be fixed, whole, or in balance.

Though Hecht was Hitchcock's principal collaborator on both pictures, Selznick's participation also proved crucial at various stages of production. His interest was hardly surprising; the combined budgets for *Spellbound* and *Notorious* came to over $4 million, and they were designed for his most valuable star, Ingrid Bergman, just off an Oscar-winning performance in MGM's *Gaslight.* But as important as Bergman and her two pictures were to Selznick, he was considerably more concerned with Jennifer Jones, whom he was showcasing in two of his own productions, *Since You Went Away* and *Duel in the Sun.* Both displayed Selznick's growing fascination with blockbusters, motivated by the success of *Gone With the Wind,* but these were degenerating into overblown displays of ego and excess. They did preoccupy him, however, while *Spellbound* and *Notorious* were under way, just as *Wind* had while Hitchcock was doing *Rebecca.* Consequently, Selznick's involvement in all three Hitchcock projects was perhaps subpar relative to his usual level of interference, but wound up being what Hitchcock and the projects in general actually needed. On *The Paradine Case,* conversely, Selznick was between projects of his own and ran roughshod over scripting and shooting as well as editing. The result was by far the weakest of the Selznick-Hitchcock collaborations, and one that brought an abrupt end to their personal and professional relationship.

This distinction is crucial, given not only the general direction of each man's career at the time, but also of independent filmmaking and the studio system at large. Selznick quite literally overwhelmed his own "personal" productions, nullifying even the possibility for productive collaboration and creative interaction, for mere efficiency let alone artistry. From *Gone With the Wind* through *Since You Went Away* and *Duel*, Selznick's pictures were progressively less interesting and less memorable—except perhaps as monumental and cinematic curiosities—and they were indicative of independent filmmaking at its unbridled, self-indulgent worst. *Spellbound* and *Notorious*, on the other hand, were among the best Hollywood films of the 1940s, and their production struck an ideal balance of power and melding of talents, particularly those of Hecht, Hitchcock, Ingrid Bergman, and Selznick himself. Selznick's inability to strike or even to seek a similar balance on his own pictures underscored the potential dangers as filmmaking became more genuinely "independent" and excessive in the mid-1940s, while the Hitchcock collaborations evidenced an altogether more positive potential.

E A R L Y on, *Spellbound* involved neither Selznick nor Hecht, nor was it conceived as a vehicle for Ingrid Bergman. Acting on his own initiative in August 1943, Hitchcock spent 500 pounds for the screen rights to *The House of Dr. Edwardes*, a tale of insanity and murder written in 1928. He planned to do the picture for Fox after *Lifeboat*, as the second in a two-picture deal that Selznick had arranged in 1942 with Bill Goetz. When Darryl Zanuck returned from his stint in the Signal Corps, however, he and Goetz had a falling out that resulted in Goetz leaving the studio and Zanuck pulling out of the second Hitchcock picture. But Hitchcock owned the story rights so he simply pressed on, convinced that the story had possibilities and eventually would be produced. The novel's protagonist was a woman psychiatrist named Constance who is hired by a Dr. Edwardes to work in a mental asylum in the Alps. On arriving, she finds that Edwardes is away and the asylum is being run by a Dr. Murchison, who wields charismatic, almost mystical power over his patients and staff. One patient, a man named Gladstone, has been locked away after killing his driver en route to the asylum and then being subdued by Murchison. Constance eventually discovers that Murchison is actually Gladstone, and she helps the real Murchison escape the asylum. They are overtaken by the diabolical Gladstone as they flee, only to be rescued by Dr. Edwardes as the villain plunges to his death down a mountainside.

Anyone familiar with the film should realize that this narrative bears little resemblance to the actual film. Its transformation into *Spellbound* is illuminating not only in terms of Hecht's and Selznick's contributions, but also Hitchcock's strengths and weaknesses as a screenwriter. Just after the release of *Rebecca* a few years earlier, Val Lewton was looking for Hitchcock material and suggested in a memo to Selznick that "we need something better and more substantial than the old-fashioned chase pictures which he [Hitchcock] turns out when left to his own devices." The early treatments of *The House of Dr. Edwardes* displayed just that shortcoming, although the story showed greater potential when British screenwriter Angus MacPhail began working with Hitchcock. In January 1944, they submitted a revised treatment for what they now called "The Mind of Dr. Edwardes." In this version an amnesia victim impersonates the incoming asylum director, Dr. Edwardes, who apparently has been murdered en route to his new post. Constance falls in love with the amnesiac and subjects him to psychoanalysis after she discovers he is not really Dr. Edwardes. She discovers that his amnesia is the result of a guilt complex for having blinded a classmate decades earlier. Eventually she breaks through and he remembers seeing the murder of Edwardes, and this precipitates the final confrontation. Selznick took time away from *Since You Went Away* to confer with Hitchcock, and in February the writing team worked out another important story angle, setting both the death of Dr. Edwardes and the hero's eventual breakthrough—when he comes to terms with his guilt and remembers seeing the murder—on the ski slopes. Hitchcock also began working detailed production notes into the February treatment; clearly he was preparing to do the picture.

The death of Myron Selznick proved to be a catalyst of sorts in the project's eventual production. Ben Hecht, long a proponent (and subject) of psychoanalysis, encouraged Selznick to try it as a way of dealing with his own personal problems. Selznick's commitment to analysis increased with his brother's death, and by late spring he was more interested than ever in the Hitchcock project. After a series of conferences with Hitchcock and Hecht, Selznick decided to do the picture as a Vanguard production starring Ingrid Bergman. He saw it as the ideal follow-up for her to *Gaslight*, a Cukor-directed psychological thriller. He also considered the amnesiac's role perfect for Gregory Peck, a promising actor whom he had recently signed.

Selznick hired Hecht to overhaul the story and do a continuity draft, which Hecht cranked out with his usual dispatch. In less than two weeks, Hecht came up with the story as Hitchcock eventually filmed it. In Hecht's draft the heroine Constance is a cold, professional psychiatrist on the staff of a clinic whose director, Dr. Murchison, is resigning because of work-induced fatigue and stress. His replacement, Dr. Edwardes, arrives and the heroine immediately falls in love with him, only to realize that he is actually an amnesiac who may have killed Dr. Edwardes. She learns that his condition had been induced by guilt over his brother's death, which he inadvertently caused when they were children. Seeing the real Edwardes killed on the ski slopes has reactivated that guilt, and when Constance pulls him out of his amnesia he remembers seeing the outgoing Dr. Murchison, who could not face giving up his clinic, kill his replacement. In a reworked finale, Constance confronts Murchison in his office once she learns that he killed Edwardes. Murchison pulls a gun but fails to use it until she leaves the room; she then hears him commit suicide from the hallway outside his office. Besides these invaluable story changes, Hecht also added the visual motif of parallel lines that repeatedly trigger the hero's associations between ski tracks and the fence posts on which his brother was impaled—and thus the association between the two deaths. And to embellish the visual element even further, Hecht and Hitchcock convinced Selznick to commission surrealist painter Salvador Dali to do a series of paintings that could be incorporated into the hero's hallucinatory dreams and visions while he was undergoing psychoanalysis.

Selznick and Hitchcock agreed that Hecht's script, now titled "The Guilt Complex," was ready to take into production. Selznick also decided to supervise the project himself. He had finished cutting, dubbing, and scoring *Since You Went Away*, which was due for release later in the summer, and he was ready for another project. After meetings in early June with Selznick's psychoanalyst, May Romm, who served as technical adviser, Hitchcock started final preparation and Selznick set the budget and schedule. Production was to open in early July with a fifty-seven-day shoot at a cost of $1,670,000. It was a top-heavy budget, with above-the-line expenses of just under $600,000. Selznick paid himself a flat fee of $50,000 to produce. He paid Hitchcock $150,000 to direct and $40,000 for the rights to the original novel, and Hecht earned $70,000 for his rewrite. Bergman's salary of $17,500 per week would accumulate to over $220,000 during the shoot, while Peck's $3,125 per week would total $33,850. The other costs were fairly routine, except for the "dream sequence allowance" of $20,000.

On July 10 Hitchcock started production on the picture, not quite sure what to expect from Selznick or his production crew. There had been extensive changes on the lot and in the front office since *Rebecca*. Various key personnel like production manager Ray Klune, designer-turned-director William Cameron Menzies, and story editor Val Lewton had left; they had tired of the inactivity between productions and of Selznick's abrasive temperament when a project finally did get under way. Selznick had always been most abrasive when dealing with his directors, and this was again the case on *Since You Went Away*. He had been on the set almost daily, criticizing and often overruling director John Cromwell's decisions on camera angles, lighting, and even performance. So Hitchcock had reason for concern, but he found Selznick even more amenable on *Spellbound* than he had been on *Rebecca*. Hitchcock's success on *Rebecca* and his assurance as a "producing director" had a lot to do with Selznick's distance from *Spellbound*, of course, but equally important was Selznick's growing distraction due to the impending release of *Since You Went Away*, his first production in five years. Selznick threw himself into the marketing and sales campaign of that home-front melodrama with the same fervor he had displayed during shooting. He orchestrated the entire release campaign, from the film's New York premiere in late July until its nationwide release in October.

The trajectory of that campaign, as it turned out, coincided neatly with Hitchcock's shooting schedule of *Spellbound*. As soon as Hitchcock started the picture, it was clear that he could do quite well without heavy input from Selznick. After two weeks, production manager Richard Johnston reported that he had "seldom seen . . . as obviously efficient a company as the 'Dr. Edwardes' unit," which was averaging nine setups and over two and a half minutes of film per day, a pace that Hitchcock maintained throughout the shoot. Selznick later marveled that Hitchcock "secured such remarkable quality with such prompt efficiency," and that he did so "without the slightest set supervision on my part." Selznick even endorsed Hitchcock's authority in those rare instances when it was challenged. George Barnes, whose camera work on *Rebecca* had won an Oscar, disputed Hitchcock's composition and depth of focus on several shots early on in the production. Johnston related this to Selznick, who suggested that Barnes "be reasoned with," and that Johnston let him know that Hitchcock was in sole creative control of the picture. "I shall appreciate your giving Mr. Hitchcock every support on this," said Selznick. "It is untenable nonsense to have to put up with expensive retakes and with a limitation on Hitchcock's style."

The Barnes flap was one of the rare occasions during shooting that Selznick's services as producer were required on *Spellbound*. The rest of the shoot went smoothly, although there was a major interruption late in the production. Hitchcock had never been quite satisfied with Hecht's version of the finale, so he closed the picture nine days early without shooting that sequence. Hecht's scene specified that the camera stay with Constance after she confronts Dr. Murchison (Leo G. Carroll) and talks her way out of his office. From the hallway she hears the suicidal gunshot and faints, and the screen fades to black. Hitchcock and Hecht brainstormed during production and decided to shoot

Gregory Peck in a fitting pose—"on the couch"—with Ingrid Bergman and Alfred Hitchcock on the set of Spellbound.

the confrontation and the suicide itself from Murchison's point of view —thus creating one of the more memorable and visually stunning moments in any Hitchcock film. The rewrite was no problem, but Hitchcock's second unit required an entire week to prepare the shot. It was a difficult shot not only because it involved considerable camera movement (since Murchison was aiming a pistol at Constance as she gradually worked her way out of the room), but also because of a focus problem. Given the technological limitations of camera lenses at the time, the only way to keep both the pistol and Constance in focus, assuming that both were seen from the eyes of Murchison, was to create an oversize hand and gun that could be placed several feet in front of the camera. This hand and gun had to move with the camera, and also had to swivel toward the camera at the end of the scene for the suicide. On September 21, the second unit shot nineteen test takes of the "Gun Shot" scene, and on the following day Hitchcock brought Bergman in to shoot it. (Leo G. Carroll was not required on the set, of course, since the scene was shot entirely from his viewpoint.) Gregory

Peck and Michael Checkhov, who played Constance's mentor, Dr. Bru-lov, also came in to work with Bergman in a perfunctory tag scene in which the paternal doctor blesses the young lovers as they leave for their honeymoon.

Selznick and Hitchcock were both pleased with the revised finale, so all that remained were the ski scenes with Bergman and Peck, which required rear-projection effects, and also the Dali-designed dream se-quences. Hitchcock shot the ski slope sequences in four days during early October, and this brought the total cost of the picture to $1.79 million. So far as Hitchcock was concerned, that was it. He gave the picture to Selznick to cut and score, suggesting that they forgo the dream sequences altogether. He "shot around" them, making sure that any pertinent information was contained in Constance's analysis rather than in the dream itself. This left considerable leeway for surrealistic treatment if they did shoot the dreams, and it also made for some very talky demonstrations of Constance's ability as an analyst. Selznick ten-tatively agreed to do without the dreams and Hitchcock left for an extended holiday, fully expecting the picture to be cut, scored, and released before the year's end so that it would qualify for Oscar consid-eration.

Selznick initially intended to comply, but consciously or otherwise, he was bent on reestablishing control over the project. He previewed a rough cut of the picture—now officially titled *Spellbound*—to see how it would play without the dream sequences. The response was positive and the picture might have been rushed out, but Selznick decided it was nowhere near ready for scoring and release. He tinkered with the cutting for a few hours a day, week after week, even after preview audiences continued to indicate that the picture worked quite well. The more he tinkered and previewed it, the more convinced he was that Dali-inspired dream sequences would improve both the pic-ture and the promotional campaign. Psychoanalysis and surrealism were all the rage, and Selznick already had paid Dali for a series of paintings that could be used to design the scenes. In early November, Selznick made arrangements with Columbia to borrow William Cam-eron Menzies to design, supervise, and direct the dream sequences. That same month, composer Miklos Rozsa started work on the musical score, which Selznick encouraged him to make as "unusual" as pos-sible to accommodate the psychological theme.

Clearly Selznick was taking charge now that the picture was back in his domain and he was between projects of his own. Hitchcock had no complaints; postproduction was Selznick's forte, and Hitchcock re-membered what Selznick's contributions during postproduction on *Re-becca* had done for that film. He also was pleased with Menzies's work on the dream sequence, which was far enough along for Selznick and Hal Kern to cut some of that dream work into the picture for a December 1944 preview. Rozsa's "Love Theme" also was ready by then, so Selznick used it over the titles and had musical director Lou Forbes lay in stock music for the rest of the picture. Again the reaction was favorable, and Selznick started planning an early spring release date. Menzies finished the dream sequences in January, and Selznick and Kern began cutting in earnest so they could deliver the picture to Rozsa for scoring.

At this point, however, progress on *Spellbound* stalled. There was a serious snag in February when the PCA nixed the suicide scene, citing a Code provision that suicide was "to be discouraged as morally questionable and as bad theater—unless absolutely necessary for the development of the plot." With Val Lewton now off on his own, relations with the Breen office were generally more difficult and disorganized; in fact, Breen was never even notified of the changes in the finale. Selznick handled the negotiations personally, and he finally convinced Breen and Sherlock in a late February meeting that the scene, as photographed, was essential to the plot. Another hitch came a few days later when Bergman won an Oscar for her role in *Gaslight*. This should have delighted Selznick, but instead it had him worried that the similarities between *Gaslight* and *Spellbound*—Bergman's roles, the titles, the psychological angle, the *film noir* style—might bring the pictures too close to one another in the public's mind. So Selznick was inclined to delay release, and when Rosza, who refused to compose without a final cut, left for Paramount to score Billy Wilder's *The Lost Weekend*, Selznick had yet another excuse to put *Spellbound* aside and concentrate on the script development of *Duel in the Sun*.

Selznick procrastinated into the summer, and the distractions only increased. *Duel* was in production and Selznick was in the midst of an elaborate deal with RKO that included a half-dozen packages and the services of production executive Dore Schary. In mid-July he told his studio manager to schedule Rozsa for scoring within two weeks. "The delay has been entirely my fault," admitted Selznick. "I estimate that it will take me about a week, working a couple of hours a day, to finish the final editing of *Spellbound*. After that I want another preview . . . to determine whether the new ending works. I should think we could turn it over to Rozsa for final scoring not more than two days after the final preview." Rozsa was much in demand those days, especially after his "Spellbound Suite" was released as a recording—an idea of Selznick's to promote the picture. Selznick also had heard that Rozsa's score for *The Lost Weekend* was first-rate. What Selznick hadn't heard was that Rozsa had used the same exotic instrument—a device called

a theremin, which generated a high-pitched electronic warble—to sig-
nify Ray Milland's alcoholic cravings in *The Lost Weekend* that he had
used to indicate Peck's psychological lapses in *Spellbound*. Rozsa
thought nothing of it, since he assumed that Selznick's picture would
be released earlier. But *Spellbound* was still awaiting Selznick's final
cut in late September when *The Lost Weekend* was released, and Selznick was furious with Rozsa when he heard the score. Even after Rozsa's score for *Spellbound* won an Oscar, Selznick continued to berate
the composer and vowed he would never use him for another project.

Selznick had no one to blame but himself, of course, and by early
autumn it appeared that his preoccupation with *Duel* might cost him
dearly on the *Spellbound* project. In November *Spellbound* was finally
ready for release, but the timing was disastrous. *Gaslight* had completed its run months ago, so the promotional value of Bergman's
Oscar-winning performance in that picture was nil. Then in October
Jack Warner decided to release *Saratoga Trunk,* which he had shelved
two years earlier until the market for the Ingrid Bergman–Gary Cooper
costume picture improved. And RKO was about to release *The Bells of
St. Mary's,* with Bergman playing a nun opposite Bing Crosby. So three
Bergman pictures would be opening in New York within weeks of one
another. What's more ARI, George Gallup's research outfit, reported in
October that the interest in *Spellbound* had dissipated, that it was
likely to open in New York to the "lowest penetration of all Mr. Selznick's pictures," and at that point he saw the project as "a spectacular
publicity and advertising failure."

Finally moving, Selznick initiated a three-week advertising blitz to
precede the picture's November release. He spent $59,000 in New
York City alone, with a series of ads that played off ARI's assertion that
"selling Hitchcock and the mystery angle over the love elements in-
creases Want-to-See among men." Selznick also told his sales department in New York that Hitchcock's "marquee value ... is the
equivalent of that of a star," and he had Hitchcock's name put above
the title and in relatively large type size to increase the marketability
of the picture. He sent out this revised billing setup in October:

Selznick International	[35%]
presents	
INGRID BERGMAN	[75%]
GREGORY PECK	[75%]
in	
ALFRED HITCHCOCK'S	[50%]
"SPELLBOUND"	[100%]

There was no predicting the impact of the last-minute blitz or the competing Bergman releases and the Rozsa score on *Spellbound*'s box-office performance. Selznick's sales executives in New York and his ARI consultants in Princeton told him to expect the worst, but they were dead wrong. *Spellbound* was an immediate hit and one of the top releases of 1945–46. In its first three days at the Fox Westcoast it took in $45,336, a house record. In its first week at the Astor in New York, it grossed $57,238. It opened strong in the hinterlands as well, grossing $19,500 in its first week in Cincinnati—another record. In fact, its performance in the first-run markets across the country was phenomenal, especially on the coasts. By December 6, *Spellbound*'s total gross in New York and Los Angeles alone, where it was playing in four theaters, was just over $500,000. By the time the picture finished its Astor run in mid-April, its receipts from that one theater were $875,000.

In fact, *Spellbound* did so well in first-run houses that Selznick, speculating that "80 to 85 percent of our business" on *Spellbound* came "from the big cities," had Vanguard's Neil Agnew run a study of its release. Agnew's findings supported Selznick's diagnosis and had considerable impact on his release plans for *Duel*. They also reinforced Selznick's inclination to put more faith in his own intuition than in his sales department and the market research experts at ARI.

Still Selznick needed ARI, and he knew it. Without the market research or sales departments of the big studios, and without continual box-office feedback to gauge audience interests and changing trends, he had to have some means, however unreliable, of monitoring the public pulse. Still he didn't mind seeing ARI proved wrong, especially on a relatively offbeat and unpredictable project like *Spellbound*. It proved yet again the value of talent, intuition, and innovation. ARI could measure "want-to-see" and "penetration" during a promotional campaign, perhaps, but those number-crunchers struck Selznick as having no capacity whatever to sense a breakaway hit. And in this case the box-office tallies proved it. In its first forty-four weeks of release, *Spellbound*'s total gross was $4.67 million.

T H E success of *Spellbound* reaffirmed Selznick's market savvy, but his procrastination over the final cut and his investment of time, energy, and money into *Since You Went Away* and *Duel* raised serious questions about his judgment and sense of proportion. *Spellbound* actually outgrossed *Since You Went Away*, even though the latter had over twice the budget and a much more costly and aggressive marketing campaign. And now Selznick was hopelessly bogged down in *Duel in the Sun*, which pushed his filmmaking obsessions to new extremes.

A monstrous "psychological western" designed specifically for Jennifer Jones and costarring his two leading male stars, Gregory Peck and Joseph Cotten, the picture had a budget of over $5 million and a six-month production schedule, and it was destined for two years in post-production, with one year spent battling the PCA and Legion of Decency over cuts and another devoted to a million-dollar advertising and sales campaign.

The production of *Duel* also indicated that Selznick's penchant for interference was actually intensifying—in fact, it became company policy on that picture. "There were strict orders on the set," said Selznick just after *Duel* was completed, "that not a single scene was to be photographed, not even a single angle of a scene, until I was telephoned to come down on the set to check the lighting, the setup, and the rehearsal." He also claimed that "ninety-nine times out of a hundred," he changed the direction of the scene. Clearly Selznick was rethinking the status and the role of the director—at least on his personal projects. Eight individuals contributed to *Duel*, including King Vidor, William Dieterle, Josef von Sternberg, and William Cameron Menzies. Vidor was credited, though he directed less than half of the finished film, and he never thought of *Duel in the Sun* as anything but a David Selznick picture.

Throughout 1945, while Selznick was putting off the trim job on *Spellbound* and slowly sinking into the quagmire of *Duel*, Hitchcock and Hecht were working on their next Vanguard project, *Notorious*. Again they worked with only minimal input from Selznick, whose temperance was as paradoxical as ever, given his obsessive interference with *Duel*. While Selznick's regard for the division of filmmaking labor and for the separate spheres of creative control steadily diminished on his own blockbusters, he yielded more and more authority to Hitchcock. Significantly enough, Hitchcock did not abuse that authority or overstep his bounds, even though on *Notorious*, he would wind up actually producing the picture. As with *Spellbound*, Ben Hecht was a principal collaborator throughout production, and again the story was designed for Ingrid Bergman.

Hecht and Hitchcock's idea for this Bergman vehicle came to them while they were working on *Spellbound*. They wanted to cast Bergman as a "fallen" woman who adopts another identity and plunges into an espionage caper, forming romantic attachments with men from opposing political camps. Hecht worked out an outline for the story while Hitchcock shot *Spellbound*, and Selznick registered the title, "Notorious," in October 1944. Hitchcock was growing more fascinated with —and attracted to—Ingrid Bergman, as happened with most of the leading ladies he worked with more than once. He was intrigued by this story about a beautiful woman who assumes an identity and immerses herself in an artificial dramatic realm at a man's behest, since it clearly invoked the director-star rapport. And considering how effectively Hitchcock worked with Bergman, tapping the passion she kept suppressed beneath that cool exterior, she was perfect for the part.

Selznick, motivated by the story's dramatic possibilities but also by Bergman's contractual commitment, was anxious to get the project under way. He hoped to get at least two more pictures out of her seven-year contract. In December 1944, he gave it a go-ahead, okaying a budget of around $2 million and a start date of February 1, in which case, Selznick anticipated, "we would have time to make another Bergman." This wasn't unreasonable, given Hecht's speed and the fertility of his imagination when he worked with Hitchcock. Indeed, the Hecht-Hitchcock combination was both paradoxical and productive; Hecht's undisciplined, high-speed working methods were countered but not stifled by Hitchcock's more deliberate approach to script preparation. Moreover, Hecht's mastery of dialogue and plot machinery complemented Hitchcock's genius for coming up with dramatic and highly cinematic situations, though without any real idea of how to get his characters from one such situation to another.

Hecht went back on Selznick's payroll in December at $5,000 per week, and within four weeks he and Hitchcock had a detailed treatment. The basic story of *Notorious* was there, and somehow it survived the ten months of countless rewrites and revisions, which were mandated by everyone from Selznick and Joe Breen to J. Edgar Hoover. The story centered on Alicia Huberman, a German-American who is drawn into a geopolitical intrigue after her father is discovered to be a Nazi spy. The story opens with her father's conviction for espionage, which leads directly to his suicide. Alicia's own "notorious" reputation and wanton, self-destructive behavior are apparently the result of her guilt and confusion over her father's treachery. American FBI agents, exploiting that reputation and her father's connections, recruit Alicia to penetrate a Nazi spy ring in South America. In an effort to redeem both her father and herself, Alicia takes the job, which requires that she win the confidence of Alexander Sebastian, a former colleague of her father. But Alicia falls in love with the agent who recruits her, a man named Devlin, who himself is torn between love for Alicia and duty to his country—a duty that demands he encourage her to make love to and eventually marry another man.

This was the basic story premise that Hecht and Hitchcock came up with, and the numerous variations generated from January to November 1945 all turned on three basic issues: first, the characterization of Alicia, which ranged from an innocent and long-suffering victim to an outright whore and drunkard; second, the fate of Alicia and Devlin, both individually and as a couple, after she is found out by Sebastian and his clutching, diabolical mother; and third, the nature of what Hitchcock referred to as the "MacGuffin." Hitchcock used that term (and by now both Selznick and Hecht did as well) to describe the plot device—the government documents, the plans for the secret weapon, or whatever—that kept things moving but finally was only incidental to the interplay of personalities and emotions, which was the real focus of the story. In the initial version, the MacGuffin was uranium ore needed by the Nazis to fuel some newfangled weapons system. In this version, Alicia is introduced as a decidedly wanton woman; she wins redemption by film's end but loses Devlin, who is killed rescuing her from the Nazis. The tag scene has her back in the States, going to Devlin's parents to show them a commendation from the President that cites both her and Devlin for their heroic deeds.

The initial story changes came not from outside pressures, or even from Selznick, but from Hitchcock and Hecht's own initiative. By mid-February they had revised the final third of the story, and Hitchcock described the changes in a long letter to Selznick. This time Devlin's "drinking and carelessness" result in his being fired by his superiors, but Devlin proceeds with the mission on his own because of his love for country and for Alicia. Two major scenes were added, one involving a murder in an opera (harking back to Hitchcock's *The Man Who Knew Too Much*, made a decade earlier), and the other a lavish party in Sebastian's mansion. The party scene provided the climax. Devlin preoccupies the Nazis long enough for Alicia to escape, but he is way-laid and killed as she waits outside. "The mood of this ending," Hitchcock explained to Selznick, "is that Devlin who never said 'I love you' to Alicia, who never admitted that she was worth loving, finally said 'I love you' to her by dying in order to save her life." There was also a new tag: "Picture goes to Miami, where we find Alicia with her group of drinking friends again. She is a more notorious and low-cast wench than ever, but in her own heart is a memory of a man who loved her and died for her, and to her this is the same as if she had achieved a life of marriage and happiness."

At this point *Duel* was on location in Arizona, so Selznick had time to devote to *Notorious*. He assembled a second unit to shoot background and montage footage in Rio de Janeiro, and he also began consulting with Hitchcock and Hecht on casting. They agreed on Cary Grant for the male lead and Bergman's costar, and they also agreed that the roles of Alex Sebastian and his mother should be played either by lead actors or top character actors: their first choices were George Sanders and Ethel Barrymore. In early March, Vanguard's Neil Agnew wired Selznick from New York that he favored the Bergman-Grant pairing and liked the title, but that he was unsure of the need for name stars in the supporting roles. Selznick in turn instructed his assistant, Dan O'Shea, to do everything he could to close the deal for Grant, whom Selznick considered to be "worth literally at least a million dollars in gross." Sanders had already turned down the role of Alex, but still Selznick felt that they should pursue a top actor. "The part of Sebastian is practically as important as the other two," said Selznick, "and in some ways more important. Hitchcock talked me out of Clifton Webb, which I think is a pity . . . I am not interested in any but a really top star, preferably someone who has played straight leads and not heavies." This strategy saw another setback that month when Ethel Barrymore turned down the role of Mme. Sebastian; she was so sour on the role, in fact, that she refused even to talk to Hecht about rewriting the character to suit her.

While Selznick fretted over casting and the daily problems in Arizona with *Duel,* Hecht and Hitchcock continued to rework the story. By late March they had yet another sequence outline. This version did away with the opera and moved the party to an earlier point in the story, with Devlin discovering the uranium ore in a bottle down in the wine cellar while the party goes on upstairs. This event sets the final act in motion and leads to the finale, in which Devlin, who is still in the good graces of the FBI, confronts the Nazis in Sebastian's home and then flees with Alicia, whom Sebastian and his mother had been poisoning since discovering her treachery. The couple escapes but Alicia dies in the process. An epilogue finds Devlin alone in a Rio cafe where he overhears people discussing the death of Sebastian's wanton and traitorous wife. Devlin lets this pass and concentrates on a letter he has been reading—a commendation from Truman citing Alicia's bravery and her contribution to the national security. Devlin pockets the letter and finishes his drink.

This was essentially the story as Hitchcock would eventually film it, although actual production was months away and both story and script still had to withstand a steady onslaught of criticism and concerns. In late March Selznick first learned that the FBI, which had been sent a rough outline of the story, was not happy with the way the Bureau was depicted. Selznick relayed this to his writers, and he himself expressed concern about Alicia's character. They had not yet submitted anything to the PCA, but already Selznick was anticipating Breen's reaction. "I feel the girl's character is vastly overdrawn in its toughness, to a point where it is not amusing," wrote Selznick, "and is actually unpleasant without even being entertaining." Selznick also had trouble with her salty language, although he was "in sympathy with the notion of having the character talk in a Tallulah fashion." Alicia's character was so vulgar, said Selznick, that even the foulmouthed Tallulah Bankhead "would be shot before she would say anything like these lines." The writers, too, were concerned about the inevitable problems with the PCA, but Selznick's complaints were simply patronized and then dismissed. Hecht and Hitchcock figured he was too distracted to follow up on such suggestions, especially now that the *Duel* company had returned from Arizona. Within the next few weeks there were additional setbacks and distractions. President Roosevelt's death on April 12, 1945, sent the industry and entire nation into a period of mourning; all Hollywood shut down on the sixteenth for his funeral. Only days later a series of strikes in Hollywood closed down all active production indefinitely. Selznick hoped for a quick settlement but welcomed the opportunity to work on rewrites for *Duel* and the casting of *Notorious*, which hit a snag when Bergman refused to okay Grant as her costar. Selznick eventually brought her around, and in May Grant was signed for $50,000 in salary, to be deferred in lieu of 10 percent share of the gross receipts.

In early May Hecht and Hitchcock completed a continuity script, which provoked Selznick's usual diatribe. "I have devoted the last 3½ hours . . . [to] the Hitchcock script," Selznick wrote to Dan O'Shea on May 14, "and I am convinced it is in need of a drastic and serious rewrite. I am terribly depressed and distressed that the most expensive script in the history of my career should be in this condition." Selznick's concerns about the script costs were well taken. Although the story cost was nil, he was paying Hecht $5,000 per week and Hitchcock $7,500 per week; at that rate, he had already invested roughly $250,000 in their original screenplay. He suggested that O'Shea tell Hitchcock that "Ben [Hecht] is in no mental frame judging from my last talks with him and from the quality of this work" to continue on the project. Selznick wanted Bobby Keon, who had attended all the story and script conferences, to "coordinate" the rewrites. He also suggested bringing in another writer.

Keon, O'Shea, and Hitchcock were all too familiar with this type of reaction from Selznick, but this time the project really was in serious jeopardy. The continued strikes and other problems with *Duel* had Selznick financially and emotionally spent, and outside pressures on *Notorious* were growing heavier by the day. On top of FBI objections, the Office of War Information sent word in late May that it objected to the depiction of a highly organized Nazi underground operating in South America—the OWI wanted no implicit suggestion that the Allies had scored anything less than a total victory over Hitler's minions. One day after this news arrived, Selznick received a letter from Joe Breen advising him that the script was "definitely unacceptable" to the Code Administration. Breen described Alicia's character as a "grossly immoral woman . . . who, eventually, is portrayed as dying a glorious heroine." What's more, Breen was worried about the political and international elements in the story. He urged Selznick to "take some counsel about this story with representatives of the FBI, the Navy Department, and the Brazilian government."

The strikes continued into June, and so did problems over the Hecht-Hitchcock script. Selznick received a personal letter from J. Edgar Hoover, requesting "that all references to the Federal Bureau of Investigation be omitted." He received somewhat better news from the State Department, which approved the story so long as Devlin and his colleagues be portrayed as "U.S. Secret Agents" operating at the behest of the Brazilian government. Hecht also received a letter from Assistant Secretary of State Archibald MacLeish stating that, so far as he was concerned, nothing in the script "troubles foreign policy in any way." This obviously relieved Selznick, who passed it all on to Bobby Keon and the writers, who in turn transformed Devlin and his superiors —the Three Fates, as Hecht liked to call them—into generic government agents. Selznick also passed on his own concerns at this point about the weakness of what he termed the "thriller plot." Selznick wanted clearer motivation for the antagonism between Sebastian and the head Nazi, whom Alex must face at film's end after Alicia's identity as an American agent is revealed. He also felt that the script displayed a "lack of imagination on our parts to use wine for both the McGuffin [sic] and the poison." As an alternative MacGuffin Selznick proposed "a bomb that could be held in the palm of one's hand." At some point in the film, experiments with this device might culminate in the blowing up of a mountain, which "will give the picture size and spectacle." Selznick's suggestions, which were typical of his concern for surface plot at the price of subtlety and subtext, were again simply ignored by Hecht and Hitchcock.

H E C H T and Hitchcock were familiar with Selznick's brainstorms and his bursts of energy and inspiration. They also knew he was feeling somewhat desperate about the myriad problems on *Notorious*. They did not know, however, that Selznick had grown desperate enough to start looking for a buyer for the *Notorious* package. He wanted to clear the decks so he could concentrate on *Duel*, and he also needed an immediate infusion of cash. Selznick was paying a production unit that sat idle because of the strike, and it now was certain that *Duel*'s costs would surpass even the $4.25 million spent on *Wind*. In the past, Selznick had hedged his bets on a blockbuster with another, more reliable investment, and after *Spellbound* the Hecht-Hitchcock-Bergman project looked like a good bet, whatever the story and script problems. But Selznick's famed gambler's instinct—not to mention his sound business judgment—was not in evidence in that summer of 1945.

Selznick nearly had a deal in late June with Hal Wallis at Paramount, but it fell through and he turned to RKO. They reached an agreement in early July whereby RKO agreed to pay Vanguard $525,000 for the *Notorious* package—which included the various script versions, the footage shot in Rio, and some preliminary design work. The deal meant an immediate profit for Selznick and also a possibility of future bene-fits, since he and RKO would split the net profits fifty-fifty. RKO agreed to finance and distribute the production, and to use Bergman in the lead and Hitchcock as producer-director. Bergman was to go on salary at $17,500 per week no later than September 5, and Hitchcock's weekly rate of $6,000 per week began immediately. (His total compensation for the project, including its preparation, came to $339,000.) The deal was finalized on July 23, 1945, with production scheduled to start within another four to six weeks. Cary Grant, who had been on and off contract with RKO since 1937, actually was out of the deal altogether for a few days early in July, when it appeared Joseph Cotten would play Devlin. But the Grant deal eventually was worked out, with his salary set at $100,000 against 10 percent of the profits.

RKO soon realized it had bought into a slew of problems with the Hecht-Hitchcock script, and production was steadily pushed back for further rewrites and continual negotiations with the PCA. The heaviest revisions were done by playwright Clifford Odets, who was hired in early September to polish the dialogue, add a touch of class to Berg-man's character, and rework the end of the story. Although Hitchcock was outspoken in his displeasure with Odets's work, there was a brief period when it appeared that RKO would approve a shooting script credited to "Ben Hecht and A. B. Clifford" that featured one of Odets's more outrageous finales: Alex and his mother flee the Nazis with Dev-lin and Alicia, the four of them riding in Devlin's car with Alex at the wheel and his mother holding the lovers at gunpoint. There is a terrific crash when Madame Sebastian grows so enraged at her son that she shoots him. All ends well, however. The Sebastians are killed, the lovers survive, and the Nazis' plans are disrupted. In a tag scene, Alicia and Devlin sit in a café with his superior, and they smile knowingly after overhearing gossip from the next table about Alicia: "She's noto-rious—she's a spy!"

Hecht was back on *Notorious* in early October, largely because of Hitchcock's efforts as producer and Selznick's as a not-so-silent partner in the production. He turned out one more rewrite before the film went into production a few weeks later, this time concentrating on Alicia's character and the finale. The climactic finale has Devlin boldly taking the semiconscious Alicia out of the Sebastian house in full view of the Nazis—he knows that Alex and his mother dare not stop him since it would reveal that they have been duped by a foreign agent. They drive off, and Hecht then cuts to a brief epilogue in which three secretaries in a government office are updating Alicia's file. One of them crosses out "Sebastian" after her name, letting us wonder for a moment whether Alicia died en route to the hospital; but then the secretary writes "Devlin" in as her new married name.

The revised ending satisfied Hitchcock as well as the RKO executives, but the changes in Alicia's character had to satisfy the PCA, too. Joe Breen had informed RKO in late September that "before this picture can be approved it will be necessary to remove the present indications that your sympathetic lead is a woman of loose sexual habits." Breen also objected because "these officials know they are hiring a promiscuous woman." Instead, suggested Breen, they might stress "that Sebastian was once very much in love with her, omitting all innuendo as to her immoral character." The rewrites accommodated Breen—though they scarcely did away with the "immoral flavor" and "sexual innuendo" that so concerned him. By 1946, as evidenced not only by *Notorious* but also by pictures like Warners' *Mildred Pierce* and Metro's *The Postman Always Rings Twice*, sexual motivation and desire worked just as well—and perhaps even better, depending on the imagination and abilities of the filmmakers and actors involved— when treated as subcurrents of the story, as an unspoken but palpable dimension of the drama.

In this sense *Notorious* is one of the sexiest movies ever made in Hollywood, even though the lovers spend most of the film separated from one another. The script, the direction, and the performances create a sexual current that flows just beneath the surface story—the passion behind Bergman's stoic exterior, the insecurity and longing buried beneath Grant's studied nonchalance, the contradictory impulses of love and duty, guilt and redemption. Add to this the deep and genuine passion that Alex, played to perfection by Claude Rains, feels for Alicia, and also Devlin's apparent willingness to maneuver her into Alex's arms—and his bed—and *Notorious* seems not only sexy but somewhat perverse, a case study of repressed sexual desire and of confused audience identification, particularly where Devlin and Alex are concerned. Oddly enough, this sexual charge was precisely what Selznick was after in *Duel in the Sun* but failed to produce. He simply could not get beyond the spectacle and the surface of things, down to what made his characters tick. *Notorious* is indicative of Hitchcock's more subtle and psychological approach to the medium—not that he didn't appreciate and exploit the cinema's more spectacular capabilities. But Hitchcock's fascination with chase scenes, particularly in the most public of places, actually belies more discreet forms of pursuit—his characters' sexual pursuit of one another, for instance, or the hero's inevitable search for his or her own identity in a world of shifting values and endless duplicity.

An excellent example of Hitchcock's ability to integrate cinematic spectacle with the psychological, to push beneath the surface of events and behind the outward masks worn by his characters, occurs in a single shot midway through *Notorious*, at the outset of the cocktail party scene. The party takes place in the Sebastian mansion, and its purpose is for Alex to introduce his new bride, Alicia, to Rio society. The sequence opens with a distinctive establishing shot: from high overhead in the massive foyer, we view the host and hostess welcoming guests to the party. After establishing the scene and situating the characters, the camera begins to crane slowly and steadily down, not stopping to frame the couple or even the heroine, but continuing until it frames a tight close-up of Alicia's left hand, clasped at her side and out of Alex's sight, nervously gripping a key. In the previous scene, Alicia took this key from Alex's key ring, and now she intends to slip it to Devlin so that he can investigate the wine cellar, where she feels that Alex is hiding something.

So by the time Hitchcock takes us to the key in Alicia's hand, it is a highly charged object, and the dynamics of the shot itself—traversing in a single take from an omniscient establishing shot to a tight close-up that gives the viewer a privileged piece of narrative information—reveals Hitchcock's capacity to shift our attention from the obvious and observable to the highly personal. The key signifies Alicia's betrayal of Alex and her love of Devlin, and it also propels us into the coming scene. In the course of the party, Alicia must pass the key to Devlin and then maneuver him to the cellar, though she knows that Alex is jealous of Devlin and will be watching the two of them as he also attends to his guests; Alicia realizes, too, that the diminishing supply of champagne might lead Alex to the cellar at any moment. So the dramatic stakes represented by the key are heightened during the party scene, and culminate in the discovery of the uranium ore in the cellar and then Alex's discovery of the two of them together. The scene, as Hitchcock has choreographed and filmed it, is a cinematic tour de force, a complex interplay of viewpoints and personal desires, of both sexual and political pursuit—it is a chase scene par excellence. As a

Scaffolding was required for the elaborate crane shot that introduces the party scene in Notorious. *Inset, Hitchcock whispers instructions to his camera operator as he frames the critical culmination of the forty second shot, a tight close-up of Ingrid Bergman's left hand.*

backdrop, the party itself provides a sense of spectacle, but Hitchcock is interested in it primarily—if not exclusively—as a familiar, rule-bound social ritual that at once constrains and intensifies the action.

Weeks were spent choreographing and shooting the party scene, and weeks were spent during postproduction on its editing. This was a scene that Hitchcock would not have been content to let anyone else cut, and since he was producing, there was no question of yielding to anyone else's authority, not even Selznick's. Hitchcock had been willing to let Selznick take over during editing on *Rebecca* and *Spellbound*, and Selznick apparently hoped to have some input on the cutting of *Notorious* as well. By February 1946 he and Kern had finished a rough cut of *Duel* (which would remain in postproduction for another fifteen months), and Selznick sent a confidential memo offering to "contribute any ideas I might have" to the cutting of *Notorious*. But Hitchcock had already taken the picture through a rough cut, and by now he was secure in his role as producer and postproduction supervisor. Selznick's offer was politely declined, and Hitchcock cut the picture with RKO's editor, Theron Warth.

By far the most carefully edited scenes in *Notorious* were the party scene and the climactic walk down the stairway—down to the same foyer seen earlier in the fabulous crane shot—as Devlin, accompanied by Alex and his mother, helps the semiconscious Alicia out of her room and past the Nazi conspirators waiting below. Hitchcock edited most of *Notorious* from the projection room, where he dictated shot-by-shot instructions to Bobby Keon, who passed them on to Warth. The first set of cutting notes for the stairway scene, dictated in early February, 1946, broke the scene down into fifty-six shots, each one identified by camera distance, angle, and point of view. In late March, when he made the following adjustments, the scene finally was cut to Hitchcock's satisfaction:

> Lose second establishing shot.
> Lose pair of cuts before [Alex says] "I'm not afraid to die."
> 4-shot for [Madame Sebastian's line] "We can handle her."
> Lose next CU [close-up] Sebastian.
> 4-shot instead of next establishing shot.
> After [Madame says] "Talk to them quick" cut to Devlin and Alicia—
>   then to individual Sebastian.

Once this scene was cut, Hitchcock decided it worked so well that he would end the picture with it and forgo the tag scene and close on Alex instead. Rains's oddly sympathetic little man, in love with Alicia but tied to his mother and in league with the Nazis, pretends to help Devlin as he spirits Alicia outside and into the car. As the others look on, Devlin locks Alex out of the car and drives off, not only revealing that Alex has been duped but leaving him and his tyrannical mother to face the Nazis' deadly wrath. This simple and most effective closing left the viewer to ponder not only the lovers' fate but that of the Sebastians as well.

Even though *Notorious* was a straightforward melodrama confined almost exclusively to the controlled environment of the studio, it took seventy-six days to shoot, plus another seven days of retakes, and came in at $2,375,000. The disparity of above- and below-the-line costs is remarkable; over $1.15 million, roughly half the total budget, went to script, direction, and stars. *Notorious* was a star vehicle of the first magnitude; even its director and writer enhanced its marquee value. The importance of the stars and director as "names above the title" was reflected in the title and promotional billing.

Cary Grant	[100%]
Ingrid Bergman	[100%]
in	
Alfred Hitchcock's	[50%]
"NOTORIOUS"	[100%]
with	
Claude Rains	[75%]
Louis Calhern	[50%]
written by	
Ben Hecht	[25%]

RKO spent just over $500,000 on publicity for *Notorious,* and neither Selznick nor his name figured in any of these efforts. The picture was released in August to mixed reviews but a solid public response. It grossed nearly $5 million during its first domestic run and took in another $1.7 million abroad. After RKO recouped its production costs plus $1.6 million in distribution fees, the net profits came to about $2 million, which were split evenly with Selznick.

T H E packaging of *Notorious* and completion of *Duel in the Sun* marked another watershed in Selznick's career. By late 1946, he was back where he had been some six years earlier after releasing *Gone With the Wind* and *Rebecca,* only this time the situation was even more severe. He no longer had the conviction, the organization, or the resources to continue making movies, and he knew it. He had already lost his key staff members and technical personnel, and one after another of his stars reached the end of their option periods and refused to renew their contracts. Among the last of his long-term contract employees to leave was Alfred Hitchcock—though not until he did one final Selznick project, *The Paradine Case*, which only reinforced his determination to go.

The Paradine Case began as another Hitchcock-Hecht collaboration, but this time Selznick had no project of his own in the works to temper his involvement. The film was based on a pet project of Selznick's, a story he had purchased for MGM back in 1933 and then picked up for his own company in 1944. Perhaps Hitchcock and Hecht, left to their own devices, might have managed something interesting with the wordy and claustrophobic courtroom drama, but Selznick scarcely gave them the opportunity. He dominated preproduction and eventually scripted the picture himself, which only intensified the verbal and stage-bound nature of the story. It also earned Selznick solo writing credit, since Hecht bolted the project midway through the preparation. And Selznick's chronic rewriting and restructuring meant that the cameras rolled without a finished continuity script, although by this time Selznick had neither the personal reserves nor the corporate support system to pull things together during production. Hitchcock was only lukewarm on the project to begin with, and as Selznick asserted his power and authority during the shoot, Hitchcock became a mere functionary on the set. *The Paradine Case* finally has little of the dramatic complexity or cinematic vigor of the other Selznick-Hitchcock collaborations, precisely because it was a Selznick picture and no collaboration at all.

Actually, Selznick realized even before taking the picture into production that he was nearing the end of his tether—and not just with Hitchcock, but as an independent producer generally. In early December, 1946, he wired O'Shea in New York that he was "on the verge of collapse and not thinking clearly," and that he was "planning no new production by us whatsoever beyond *Paradine*, and until we can get organized." He also felt that they had no alternative but "to package almost everything we have on the calendar." Much of that packaging had already been done when Selznick cut the deal with RKO for *Notorious*, which intitiated the sale of a half-dozen packages. The deal also included the services of Dore Schary, who wound up taking over the RKO studio in 1946. Selznick's continued efforts to sell off his projects infuriated the executives at United Artists, who still considered Selznick a partner and had been advancing him development money for pictures. In fact, Chaplin instigated a lawsuit against Selznick for breach of contract and misapplication of UA funds. The suit was dropped, but Selznick's relationship with UA had soured to a point

Hitchcock and Selznick with the cast of The Paradine Case, *their final collaboration.*

where the distribution of *Duel* could not be worked out and another company, Selznick Releasing Organization (SRO), had to be created for the release of *Duel* and *The Paradine Case.* Selznick welcomed the break from UA, convinced as he was that Hollywood's long-standing distribution methods were "archaic, outmoded, and very wasteful." He was confident that SRO, an autonomous network of film exchanges that he set up in only a matter of weeks, would enhance his independent status and revitalize production operations. And for the moment, at least, that did appear to be the case. The new company enabled Selznick to cut his distribution costs by some 60 percent, and he actually turned a sizable profit on *Duel*—quite an accomplishment, considering the high cost and questionable quality of the picture.

The $10.75 million gross and $2 million profit on *Duel in the Sun* in 1947 put Selznick back in the fray, and he seemed well positioned indeed for the postwar era. It was clear enough that although the industry was enjoying its best year ever in 1946, its success was due to the momentum created during the war. There was little hope that either the record theater attendance or the national economy could hold up for long, and the Justice Department was reactivating its anti-trust campaign. So the winds of change were blowing, and they clearly favored Hollywood's independent filmmakers. The independent ranks were growing after the war as producer-directors like Frank Capra and John Ford looked to start their own companies. Well schooled after some eight years with Selznick, Hitchcock too would turn successfully to independent production. But while Hitchcock and others thrived in the changing movie industry, Selznick did not. Though Selznick was still a relatively young man—he was only forty-four years old in 1946, three years younger than Hitchcock—his career as an active and important filmmaker was virtually over.

There were personal reasons for this: emotional exhaustion, his separation from Irene and his family, and his commitment to Jennifer Jones. His domineering management style also had alienated nearly everyone who had worked with or for him, and after the war he found himself increasingly isolated in Hollywood. An equally important reason for Selznick's decline had to do with his odd, symbiotic attachment to the studio system. Selznick's tastes were remarkably consistent with those of the classical Hollywood; his conception of prestige filmmaking was shaped during the studio era, and his sense of dramatic qualities and production values, and of marketing and exhibition practices, had been very much in line with the industry's. Although he was nominally an independent after 1935 and was somewhat aloof from the factories around him, still he and the integrated system had been bound together. He needed the stable market, with its first-run theaters and its steady supply of routine features and its free-lance talent. Only in that environment could he produce and market his own differentiated products, which were not really all that different from the romantic melodramas churned out by the majors—they were only "more so." Hollywood had also needed Selznick. It needed the revenues that his blockbusters generated for the majors' affiliated theaters, and it needed the respectability and notoriety that his productions invariably brought the industry. Just as any studio needed its occasional prestige picture to reinforce its artistic credibility, so had the industry at large needed independent producers like Selznick and Sam Goldwyn to define the high-class motion picture—so long as they were not too independent and their pictures reinforced rather than challenged or changed the dominant notions of value and quality in feature filmmaking.

Still, Selznick had helped plant the seeds of the studio system's destruction with mammoth blockbusters like *Gone With the Wind* and *Duel in the Sun*, which were far beyond the production and marketing capabilities of any individual studio. And given his own unorthodox working methods and now the creation of SRO, it looked as if Selznick had become too independent for his own good. SRO gave him more liberty in marketing and sales than he bargained for—certainly more than he had with United Artists. In his decade-long stint with UA, Selznick had gotten excellent terms (the distribution fee on his pictures in the mid-1940s was a mere 10 percent), and UA assured him access to the nation's top theaters. That had resulted in a maximum profit potential for Selznick's pictures, while keeping him in close contact with the integrated majors, whose talent and resources he still required. UA also pressured Selznick for more product, and though his output had been meager since 1940, it was almost nil after the releases of *Duel* and *The Paradine Case.*

Equally important to Selznick's slide was his growing disdain for established filmmaking practices. In usurping more and more control over the entire production process, Selznick upset the delicate balance of power and division of labor that was so essential to effective filmmaking, particularly in the heady realm of prestige production where Hollywood's top artists were involved. The growing power of above-the-line talent still demanded cooperation and creative interaction, with or without a stable studio setting. On *Spellbound* and *Notorious* that kind of interaction had been very much in evidence, as producer, director, writer, and star developed an ideal working rapport. Hitchcock would continue to rely on a collaborative unit-production approach as he built a successful independent operation in the coming years. Selznick, conversely, found himself in an inevitable downward spiral, working in self-indulgent isolation on occasional overblown Jennifer Jones vehicles like *A Portrait of Jenny* and *A Farewell to Arms.* So Selznick had finally realized his lifelong ambition of genuine independence as a movie producer, but his rapid descent once he reached that status only underscored how fundamentally collaborative the Hollywood studio system really had been, even for so-called independents like David O. Selznick.

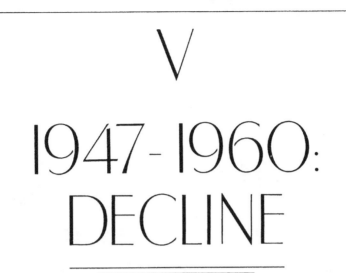

V
1947-1960: DECLINE

21

Warner Bros.: Top of the World, End of the Line

Dealing with change was nothing new to Hollywood, but the studios had never faced anything like the changes that came at the end of World War II. The war had proved to be a blessing in disguise for the industry, what with the artificially stimulated movie market, the vigorous economy, and the government's suspension of its antitrust efforts. Everyone in the industry expected those trends to reverse after the war, though the extent of the reversals was hardly anticipated. By 1945 the Justice Department was already gearing up to resume its crusade against the majors for restraint of trade and other monopoly practices. The studios had never fully eliminated block booking and blind bidding, and both picked up late in the war when the consent decrees expired. The Justice Department redoubled its antitrust actions, and now the feds actually were clamoring for "divorcement" of the major's theater chains—a devastating prospect, to say the least. What's more, the department was now going after the large theater chains and "circuits" of 150 to 300 houses, which were not affiliated with an integrated major but had worked out privileged deals with one or more studios and had come to control certain cities or market areas.

It was obvious that what the Justice Department and the federal courts had in mind was the elimination of these special arrangements as part of a wholesale effort to dis-integrate the movie industry. Their ultimate objective was an industry in which movies were produced and sold on a picture-by-picture and theater-by-theater basis. This would undermine the entire studio system, which relied on a stable and consistent market for its standardized products, which in turn generated the cash flow that enabled the studios to pay their operating (overhead) costs and maintain their contract personnel. The growing independence of top talent was already undermining the system from within; now the possibility of independence at the exhibition end threatened to destroy the system altogether.

The postwar "market adjustment" also looked ominous, since it was tied to larger social developments that did not bode well for the movie business. After the war, millions of servicemen returned from overseas and millions of women left the work force. In the short term there was a surge in courtship and thus in moviegoing, and this helped boost the industry's record performance in 1946. But soon enough the young couples were marrying, moving to the suburbs, and starting families— and investing less time and money in the movies. Suburban migration and the baby boom had their heaviest impact on the downtown deluxe theaters, where profit potential was highest. And now that the war-induced shortages and restrictions were over, there were new outlets for disposable income and new sources of diversion, from night baseball and bowling to night classes on the GI Bill. The most serious threat to the movie industry came from commercial television, of course. Since the 1920s, the radio networks and electronics giants like RCA had been heralding TV's imminent arrival, but it was stalled first by the Depression and then by the war. In the late 1940s it looked as if the social, economic, and technological conditions were ripe, however, and indeed the commercial television industry was finally taking shape.

I T would be several years before either the antitrust actions or the threat of television really hit Hollywood, and during the immediate postwar period the studios, and especially the majors, continued to ride the wave of war-induced prosperity and to ignore the storm clouds gathering on the horizon. Hollywood enjoyed its best years ever in 1945 and 1946 as Paramount surged back into industry leadership and both Fox and Warner Bros. pulled even with MGM. This was heady company for Warners, which had struggled for decades to gain real parity with the long-standing industry powers. Harry and Jack were confident that their company could keep pace, and their attitude even grew a bit complacent as revenues and profits continued to climb in the mid-1940s. The emphasis at Warners was on first-run star vehicles, with Davis, Flynn, and Bogart getting most of the choice projects. Jack Warner habitually griped about spending, but as both costs and profits escalated in 1945–46, there was less and less evidence of the efficient, factory-oriented system of old at Warner Bros.

The last vestige of that system left with Hal Wallis, whose lengthy court battles with Warners were finally resolved on December 31, 1944. Jack Warner considered this settlement an early armistice for the studio, and he had no doubts that with the reduced output he could personally control studio operations and monitor all production. Warners released only nineteen pictures in 1945 and twenty in each of the next two years, and Jack's self-assurance grew as profits soared from $10 million in 1945 to an all-time high for the company of $22 million in 1947. For administrative assistance Warner relied on Steve Trilling, who had been the studio casting director before becoming Jack's Executive Assistant in Charge of Production. Trilling was really nothing more than a glorified secretary, and Warner had no intention of letting him or anyone else have authority over production operations. Warner was the sole executive producer, and to supervise production he used a half-dozen producers, with Henry Blanke and Jerry Wald handling the more ambitious productions. Blanke had been with the company since the late 1920s and was very much a Wallis protégé, but he knew the studio and its resources well and had a tremendous track record over the last decade, particularly with the biopics of the late 1930s and the Bette Davis melodramas of the early 1940s. Warners demonstrated how highly Blanke was valued in April 1945, when he was given a new contract that put him in a class by himself among the studio's producers. It was a fifteen-year deal starting at $3,500 per week, and it committed Blanke to produce four pictures per year. None was to be budgeted for under $750,000, and at least one had to be a million-dollar production. He was granted "full charge and control of the editing of each motion picture . . . until after the first sneak preview." So once a project was initiated, it was Blanke's until after its first public screening. Warner, for his part, would decide on the story property, the casting and crew selection, the budget and scheduling, and the final cut.

Blanke took on most of Warners' top productions, and his first project under the new contract indicated where both Blanke's career and Warners' prestige efforts were headed after the war. The picture was *Deception*, a posh melodrama for Bette Davis involving high society and classical musicians. The picture's final cost was over $2 million and it grossed $3.2 million—a higher class of picture for Blanke, but one he would soon get used to. The average budget on his first nine postwar pictures was $1.65 million, and they consistently ran 25 percent over budget to a cost of $2 million. The average box-office take was only $2.15 million, which did not translate into profits for Warners. But Blanke did deliver big, respectable pictures and kept Davis relatively happy, which was no easy task after the war. Although Davis's dismal efforts with B.D. Inc., the in-house independent company Warners set up for her during the war, had proved that she was no producer nor much of a businesswoman, still she was a powerful force at the studio, earning $7,000 per week and wielding considerable control over her pictures. Blanke piloted her career after the war, and while there were no hits of the magnitude of those she routinely turned out in the early 1940s, he managed to keep her star aloft and her pictures at a break-even level.

Warners' other top producer, Jerry Wald, was both a complement and a contrast to Henry Blanke. In fact, if the Warners had decided to find another Zanuck, they would have had to look no further than the brash young writer-producer. Wald, who joined Warners in 1934 while still in his early twenties, was a screenwriter with a knack for the kind of fast-paced, captivating hokum that had been Zanuck's forte—and that Wald cranked out at nearly the same speed. In 1937 alone, Wald had fifteen screen credits, most of them for low-budget jobs that were cowritten with Richard Macauley. Scripts for hit pictures like *The Roaring Twenties* in 1939 won Wald more important assignments, and by 1941 they propelled him, at age twenty-nine, to producer status. He produced a dozen pictures during the war, and though he did little script writing he came up with the original story ideas on over half of them, including a few hit combat pictures like *Destination Tokyo* and *Objective Burma*. In April 1945, Wald's option was up and so was his value to the studio. He had another half-dozen projects in the works, each of which was based on one of his own story ideas, and he was currently producing *Mildred Pierce*. This promising project was adapted from a recent pulp novel, and though Wald hadn't come up with the story, he had figured out how to solve its difficult adaptation problems. Clearly Wald was a "creative producer" and thus was invaluable to the studio. Jack Warner decided to reward him with a new seven-year deal starting at $1,750 a week—only half of what he was paying Blanke but more than adequate for Wald, who signed the new pact in May 1945.

D U R I N G the run of his contract Jerry Wald emerged as Warners' leading producer, and he set the tone for these peak years with *Mildred Pierce*. The picture typified Warner's on-screen style in the mid-1940s, which more than any other studio's was keyed to the industry trend toward *film noir*. Warners had started going that route in the early 1940s with films like *The Maltese Falcon* and *Casablanca;* these were the two story types wherein Warners' distinctive *noir* stylistics were most evident, namely the hard-boiled detective film and the war-related espionage thriller. The studio's longtime commitment to black-and-white cinematography and to urban crime films predisposed it to *noir* intrigues, and now the style was even seeping into domestic melodramas like *Mildred Pierce*. Besides the narrative and visual style, the general production process on *Mildred Pierce* also typified Warners' postwar operations. Though Jack Warner had tight control over the studio, this was very much Jerry Wald's production. He initiated the project over objections from Warner, Joe Breen, and others; he orchestrated its lengthy and complex preproduction; and perhaps most important, he gave director Mike Curtiz considerable freedom once the picture was under way, while he himself ran interference with Warner.

Mildred Pierce was a star vehicle for Joan Crawford, a recent arrival at Warners whose contract gave her a sizable salary and implicit leverage over her pictures. Although bringing another sizable ego and creative force into the picture did further complicate things, Wald integrated all of these factors into a workable equation—which was more of a feat on *Mildred Pierce* than it had been on earlier prestige-level star vehicles at Warners. With Jack Warner now acting as both studio boss and production chief, there was no executive buffer between producer and top studio executive. And what's more, the growing power of above-the-line talent like Curtiz and Crawford made it all the more difficult to maximize their individual contributions while controlling the overall production.

Wald was up to the task, displaying the savvy and confidence of a top producer from the very initiation of *Mildred Pierce*. His interest in James M. Cain's steamy domestic melodrama dated back to 1941, the year of the novel's publication. Cain's title character was an ambitious, obsessive housewife whose blind devotion to her two daughters drives away her weak-willed husband, Bert, forcing her to fend for herself and her children. Mildred makes a determined climb from waitress to restaurateur, but her success has its downside. One daughter dies and the other, the perfectly wretched Veda, takes everything her mother can provide and continually wants more—including her mother's second husband, Monty, himself a manipulative hanger-on. The payoff in Cain's novel was Mildred's discovery that the heartless, conniving Veda has seduced Monty (or vice versa), which left Mildred with a broken heart, a fragmented family, a worthless fortune, and some heavy soul-searching. And it left Jerry Wald with a story that he could not possibly get past Joe Breen and the PCA.

Wald had a solution, however. His idea, basically, was to open the picture with the murder of one of the fornicators by the other, who would remain unseen; then Cain's story would be told in flashback as motivation and background for the murder. The flashback framework would enhance the drama and provide the "compensating moral values" and "moral retribution" that Breen valued so highly, since one of the lovers would wind up dead and the other in custody for murder. Wald approached Cain in the summer of 1943 with the idea, and Cain agreed to write a treatment. (Over at Paramount, coincidentally, writer-director Billy Wilder and novelist-turned-screenwriter Raymond Chandler were using a similar flashback frame to rework another of Cain's melodramas, *Double Indemnity*.) Cain struggled with the story for several weeks, and in late September he begged off the project. Jack Warner felt that Wald should do the same because of the obvious Code problems, but Wald persisted. A few months later Wald assigned Thames Williamson, a story analyst who had ambitions as a screenwriter, to work on the project. Williamson submitted a twenty-five-page treatment in late January 1944, which Wald felt was strong enough to show to Warner.

The studio boss reluctantly okayed the project, so Wald went after the screen rights and opened negotiations with the PCA. Cain agreed to $15,000 for the rights, but the story deal was held up by the PCA's predictable response. Judging from Williamson's treatment, Breen wrote Jack Warner on February 2, it was conceivable that "with certain important changes" the story might be brought into compliance with "the technical requirements of the Code." But still the picture would be highly questionable. After a lengthy rundown of the story's objectionable elements, Breen respectfully suggested that Warner "dismiss the story from any further consideration." The wording of the letter and spelling out of Breen's objections indicated that the Code office would yield on this one, so Wald and Williamson went ahead with another treatment. Three weeks later they met with Breen to go over the revised treatment, and on the following day Breen informed Warner that various "agreements with Mr. Wald" for further revisions would bring the story in line with Code policy.

At that point *Mildred Pierce* was officially a go project. Wald closed the deal with Cain and assigned the screenplay to Catherine Turney, Warners' top melodramatist. The story development to this point had already been complicated enough, but now Wald found that his flashback structure created two very different types of stories, a domestic melodrama and a murder mystery, which required different styles— and ultimately different writers. Turney's métier was the conventional woman's weepie with its linear plot trajectory, its domestic milieu, and its rather sordid sexual and marital concerns. But the opening killing, the police detective's grilling of Mildred to motivate the flashbacks, and the mystery angle were altogether foreign to her capacities as a writer. Turney worked off and on for a total of ten weeks through the spring and summer of 1944, fleshing out the melodrama but resisting the flashback structure and the thriller angle. So Wald turned to Albert Maltz, a specialist in male action pictures who had scripted *This Gun for Hire* and *Destination Tokyo* in recent years and currently was between rewrites on another Wald production, *Pride of the Marines*. Wald had Maltz write a brief (six-page) outline, strengthening the murder mystery and flashback structure, and recovering some of the "sex angle" of the novel, which Turney had downplayed. Wald liked the revisions and took Turney off the picture for three weeks while Maltz wrote a fifty-five-page prose version of the story with a distinctly masculine inflection. Wald then brought Turney back on the project, with strict instructions that she follow the Maltz version.

Wald now felt that the story was far enough along for him to start casting, which turned out to be as troublesome as getting the story and script straightened out. In retrospect, anyone but Joan Crawford as Mildred seems inconceivable, but the project was not developed with the former MGM diva in mind. In fact, there were several other major actresses, including Bette Davis, Rosalind Russell, Barbara Stanwyck, and Claudette Colbert, who were considered for the role ahead of Crawford. Even a few Warners' second-string stars like Ida Lupino and Ann Sheridan were in serious contention for the part. Davis backed away from the role early, and it looked as if it might go to Russell, who signed a three-year, three-picture deal with Warners in April 1944, and whose career was just peaking. Crawford also had signed a three-year, three-picture deal in April 1944, and though she was past her peak and came in at a lower salary—$100,000 per picture versus $150,000 for Russell—she was determined to get the lead in *Mildred Pierce*. Her tenacious pursuit of the role impressed Wald, Warner, and Trilling, who began to sense that she was better suited for the part than they initially realized. Crawford had resisted playing maternal roles at MGM or relinquishing her status as sex object and glamour queen. This image had faded in the early 1940s, and by now even Crawford was willing to admit it. But still her MGM tenure prepared her well for the part. Mildred's character, who pulls herself up by her bootstraps to join the ranks of the well-heeled, was very much in line with earlier variations on the Crawford persona—the Depression-era "shop girl" who makes good (and makes out), the seductive "man-eater" of the mid-30s, and the "clotheshorse" decked out in gowns by Adrian.

Crawford won the role, of course, and once she was assigned in early July Wald became even more anxious about getting a director set. In July he wrote Trilling that he wanted the director aboard at least six weeks before shooting started, and he asked whether Michael Curtiz was available after closing the Roz Russell picture, *Roughly Speaking* (Russell's first Warners picture). "At least once," Wald told Trilling, "I'd like to have Curtiz do a picture for me." Wald realized that Curtiz did not take just any assignment, but he was confident that he could "sell [Curtiz] on doing it." In September he approached him with the idea, and Curtiz was immediately interested. At the time Curtiz was not only Warners' top director but also its most flexible and wide-ranging filmmaker, as best demonstated, perhaps, in his recent back-to-back hits, *Casablanca* and *Yankee Doodle Dandy*. Curtiz was partial to the former, and to the visual and narrative dynamics of *film noir* in general, and he saw *Mildred Pierce* as an ideal subject for this kind of treatment. Wald pulled in writer Ranald MacDougall, and together with Curtiz they set about reworking the script and plotting the shoot, even before they were assigned to the picture in mid-October.

Wald and Curtiz worked well together and complemented one another's skills. Curtiz had an instinctive grasp of style and drama but real shortcomings as a writer and an administrator, which were Wald's strong suits. The two met with MacDougall on weekends to refine the story; then while MacDougall wrote the continuity and dialogue, they began preparing the actual shoot, scheduled to start December 7. The project was budgeted at $1,342,000 and scheduled for fifty-four days— par for Warners' more ambitious star vehicles at the time. Wald and Curtiz worked out the shooting schedule and locations (which included Curtiz's own beach house as the setting for the opening murder), and the two also consulted with Trilling on the casting and with studio manager Tenny Wright on the crew assignments. By early November all the principal parts were filled, primarily with Warners' feature players: Eve Arden as Mildred's coworker and confidante, Jack Carson as the slick real-estate hustler who forces Mildred's first husband out of business and later sets up her restaurant chain, and newcomer Zachary Scott as Monty, Mildred's decadent, cynical second husband. Wald wanted Ralph Bellamy to play Mildred's dull but dependable first husband, but in a cost-cutting move he settled for second-rate Warners player Bruce Bennett. Trilling was willing to go after a bigger name to play the heartless Veda, and they got Ann Blyth, a fast-rising ingenue at Universal.

Wald and Curtiz also worked together on the major crew assignments, and their search for a suitable cinematographer indicated a shared concern for the picture's visual style. Wald confided to Tenny Wright on November 6 "how worried Curtiz and I are becoming about the cameraman." Their worries were twofold. They wanted a picture steeped in the *film noir* style, but they also were concerned about having to light and photograph Joan Crawford, whose face was new to

Warners and not the easiest to shoot. Tests with Crawford were done by studio cameramen Ernie Haller, Bert Glennon, Sol Polito, and Carl Guthrie, and the results were deemed "not very satisfactory" by Wald and Curtiz, who were studying Crawford's MGM films. Curtiz wanted Arthur Edeson, who on *Casablanca* had done equal justice to the shadowy milieu and to the beauty of another non-Warners star, Ingrid Bergman. But Edeson was not available, and so Wald and Curtiz decided to have Ernie Haller do some more work with Crawford. After a series of tests over the next few weeks, they were convinced he could handle the assignment.

As the start date neared, Wald grew steadily more anxious about the script, which still had a patchwork feel to it because of the two very different types of stories and styles involved. But still he managed to

Joan Crawford, newly arrived at Warners after two decades at MGM, discusses her role in Mildred Pierce *with director Michael Curtiz.*

keep the project moving and to fend off Jack Warner, who wanted to hold up production until he approved a shooting script. Between November 6 and December 13, when production opened, Wald had the script rewritten three times by three different staff writers, including William Faulkner, who retitled it "House of Sand." MacDougall stayed on the project through all this, and he eventually shared screen credit (and an Oscar nomination) with Turney. But when production opened there was still no definitive shooting script. Wald was confident the problems could be solved without delaying the shoot, since they involved the "end" of the story, in which Mildred confesses to Monty's murder, is grilled by the police (and thus initiates the flashbacks), and finally is released when Veda is exposed as the killer. Wald and Curtiz decided to shoot the story chronologically, saving the murder of Monty —which actually opens the picture—and the police station material for later, once the rewrites were squared away. Warner and Trilling were continually on Wald's case about starting without a finished script, and Wald assured them that "Curtiz and I don't want to go through the headaches of having to shoot a film with the camera one paragraph ahead of the script." But that was pretty much the situation through the first eight weeks of shooting. Problems became so severe, in fact, that Jack Warner threatened to shut down production on December 29, when promised rewrites were not submitted.

Production was well under way by then, however, and Wald again devoted most of his time to coordinating the second-unit and montage shoots, getting the musical score started, and fielding Jack Warner's usual laments about rising costs and the alarming drop in efficiency at the studio. On January 11, 1945, for example, Warner sent Wald a copy of the previous day's production report and criticized Curtiz's working methods. "Curtiz is now one week behind schedule," Warner pointed out. "He should not really be behind as I feel he had competent actors and everything is organized." Warner wanted Wald to "have a talk with Mike and tell him we cannot use all these angles." This was a frequent Warner complaint, particularly where Curtiz was concerned. Once as fast and prolific a director as anyone on the lot, Curtiz had become a more calculated stylist in recent years. There had been inklings of this in the Flynn epics, since the romantic scenes and especially the "centrality" of the Flynn persona demanded more close-ups, reaction shots, glance-object cuts, and the like. But with his *noir* intrigues of the mid-1940s—*Casablanca, Passage to Marseilles,* and *Mildred Pierce*—Curtiz was spending even more time on lighting and camera work. This was also true of other Warners directors like Anatole Litvak and Jean Negulesco, who were equally adept as *noir* stylists and had a similar penchant for exotic sets and locales, complex patterns of light and shadow, and elaborate camera movement.

This meant increased cost to Jack Warner, who called a meeting of all studio cameramen and art directors in January 1945, while *Mildred Pierce* was in production, to warn them against extravagance and visual pyrotechnics. In a memo circulated before the meeting, Warner advised his employees that "technical perfection does not necessarily mean the success of a picture." He insisted that "with rising costs, [we] must use our ingenuity and devise new means of cutting corners without losing any of the quality." Set designers were going after "too much detail," claimed Warner, and cameramen were trying "more and more for the low camera angles and ceiling shots, which take time to light and slow us up." *Mildred Pierce* was just such a production, although set designer Anton Grot and cameraman Ernie Haller were less responsible for the overruns in time and money than was Curtiz, with his deliberate, meticulous direction. But as pressure from Warner increased toward the end of the shoot, Curtiz proved he could pick up the pace. After averaging only eight setups and under two minutes of footage daily up to that point, he breezed through the police station sequences during the last week of production, averaging thirteen setups and over 2′30″ of finished film per day.

Mildred Pierce closed in late February, thirteen days behind schedule, at which point Curtiz went to work with the montage unit. By then the anticipation over the picture had even gotten to James Cain, who wrote Wald that he was eager to see a rough cut since "the hearsay on 'M.P.' is so uniformly enthusiastic." Wald replied a few days later that it was indeed "a damn good picture!—one I hope you'll be proud to put your name on." But he wasn't about to let anyone outside the studio see the picture until it was ready—not even Cain. So he put Cain off through the spring and into the summer. The time was spent not only fine-tuning the editing and sound, but waiting for the right moment to release the picture. Wald and Warner were both convinced that it would play better in a postwar market, even though review audiences throughout the summer were enthusiastic. So they held on until September, a few weeks after V-J Day.

Their instincts and timing were perfect. *Mildred Pierce* tapped directly into the postwar mood of the country—generally upbeat, but with an undercurrent of anxiety about traditional notions of sexuality and marriage, which in a postwar milieu necessarily raised questions about women in the workplace, housing, and the economy in general. A huge hit, the picture brought in several million at the box office and a half-dozen Oscar nominations. The only nominee to win was Joan

Crawford for best actress—her first Academy Award after twenty years as a top star. The picture revitalized her career and led to a succession of choice Warners projects, including *Humoresque, Possessed,* and *Flamingo Road.* These were produced by Jerry Wald, who also found his career in high gear after *Mildred Pierce,* though the biggest career boost went to Mike Curtiz. Warners' consummate "house director," Curtiz had directed some seventy features for the studio since the 1920s, many of them hits. In 1946 Jack Warner repaid him with two exceptional contracts. Curtiz signed a seven-year pact starting at $4,200 weekly and requiring him to do only two pictures annually, well below his average output over the past two decades—though it was in line with Warners' reduced output and upgraded market profile. Warner Bros. and Curtiz also formed a profit-sharing partnership, Michael Curtiz Productions, Inc.

T H U S the payoff for Wald, Curtiz, and Crawford was a greater degree of freedom and authority on future Warners productions. Jack Warner had to assume, of course, that their filmmaking interests would continue to jibe with the studio's—a safe enough assumption even with a newcomer like Crawford, since Jerry Wald was producing her pictures. Though none of Crawford's subsequent pictures for Warners was quite up to the standards set by *Mildred Pierce,* Wald continued to restyle the Crawford persona, bringing a new "maturity" to the old MGM glamour. Henry Blanke did much the same with Bette Davis, who after the war also was easing out of her romantic costar phase and into early middle age. Both Crawford and Davis were somewhat difficult to work with and cast, but they were consummate professionals and neither Wald nor Blanke had any real trouble keeping them and their projects in line. This was certainly not the case with Raoul Walsh, who had been guiding Errol Flynn's career for several years and had had enough. Flynn was still in his thirties and should have been reaching his peak after the war, but professionalism was never his strong suit—nor was acting, really—and his star was flaring out rather quickly. *Objective Burma,* in 1945, marked the culmination of the Walsh-Flynn epics, and it also signaled the beginning of the end of the productive director-star rapport and of Flynn's popularity.

Objective Burma was the sixth picture that Flynn and Walsh had done together in three years, dating back to *They Died With Their Boots On.* Those two had been hits, as had the intervening films— *Desperate Journey, Gentleman Jim, Northern Pursuit,* and *Uncertain Glory*—with each one further refining Walsh's distinctive slant on the Warners style. Just as the heroic, flamboyant, unself-conscious Flynn was something of an "answer" to Bogart's subdued, vulnerable persona, so too were Walsh's expansive, fast-paced sagas an answer to the *film noir* style that Curtiz and others were refining at Warners, with its shadowy interiors, its psychologically complex characters, and its convoluted plot lines. During and after the war, Walsh established his own fix on Warners' tradition of male action dramas: energetic, linear stories, often framed in long shot and in wide-open settings, depicting heroic outsiders who invariably were hurtling to their own destruction, and apparently sensed as much, although they had neither the time nor the inclination to dwell on it.

Walsh's success with Flynn brought him a series of contract option renewals and raises, and Jack Warner even let him beg off *San Antonio*, Flynn's next picture after *Objective Burma*. But eventually Walsh had to come aboard (uncredited) to salvage the production when David Butler ran into trouble with Flynn. A short time later another Walsh-Flynn picture, *The Adventures of Don Juan*, was scrapped after extensive preproduction because Flynn was unhappy with the screenplay and with Walsh's apparent desire (along with that of the writers) to add an element of parody to Flynn's swashbuckling persona. With *Silver River*, a bloated and ponderous 1947 western that was far too much for Flynn to handle, Walsh's working relationship with Flynn broke down altogether. The picture was in production eighty-seven days, and its budget swelled to $3.2 million—unheard of for a Warners picture. When the picture was finished, Walsh flatly refused to work again with the dissolute star. Still convinced of Flynn's value, Warners signed him after *Silver River* to do three pictures over the next two years at $200,000 per picture. Walsh, meanwhile, was given his freedom and he never did work with Errol Flynn again.

W H I L E Warners faced a continual challenge in bringing the careers of Flynn, Davis, and Crawford in line with its own evolving style and interests, the career of Humphrey Bogart seemed to coincide quite naturally with the studio's development in the mid-1940s. Bogart was without question Warners' biggest star during both the wartime and the postwar era. He was named to the exhibitors' top-ten poll every year from 1943 to 1949, and was the only Warners star to make the poll at all after the war. His success generally came not in big, expensive pictures but in the same tight, relatively modest thrillers that carried him to stardom just before the war. John Huston had keyed this rise, providing the script for *High Sierra* and then writing and directing *The Maltese Falcon*. Vital to Bogart's late-forties surge as well, Huston wrote and directed *The Treasure of the Sierra Madre* in 1947 and *Key Largo* in 1948. But at mid-decade Bogart did his best work with Howard Hawks. They only did two pictures together in the 1940s—*To Have and Have Not* (1945) and *The Big Sleep* (1946)—but these were as important in defining the Bogart persona as any of the two dozen films Bogart starred in during the decade.

The two Hawks-Bogart pictures also were crucial to the development of Warners' burgeoning *noir* style in both of its usual manifestations— as an exotic geopolitical intrigue and a hard-boiled crime thriller. As was so often the case with his work at Warners over the years, Hawks managed both to articulate the studio's current stylistic bent and also to make distinctly "Hawksian" pictures: taut, economical thrillers whose action, pace, and penchant for violence were offset by elements of comedy and romance. Interestingly enough, Hawks accomplished this while acting as his own producer, for the most part, although the matter was subject to dispute on various projects—including the two Bogart pictures. Hawks had signed an exclusive five-year, five-picture deal in 1942 which specified that he was to work "under the direct supervision of Jack L. Warner or a producer appointed by [Warner]." Hawks chose to ignore this clause and had battled Hal Wallis through-out the production of *Air Force*, an immense hit in 1943. Thereafter he flatly refused to work under any direct supervision whatsoever.

Steve Trilling explained Hawks's feelings to Jack Warner in a February 1944 memo, just before Hawks was to begin his next project. "It does not seem to be a question of who is going to produce, but a question as to whether [Hawks] will have to work under a producer if he continues working at Warner Bros." Studio attorney Roy Obringer reminded Trilling of Hawks's contractual obligation regarding studio supervision; Trilling conveyed Hawks's response that "if he hasn't proven by this time that he can work without a producer, he doesn't want to continue" at the studio. Warner was not about to call Hawks's bluff, since his overall track record with the studio indicated an efficiency and professionalism that were rare in the industry, and also a capacity to get the most out of Warners' resources.

Hawks had more tangible leverage as well, having recently created an independent company that owned the rights to two very promising properties. The company was H-F Productions, created in 1943 by Hawks and agent Charles K. Feldman, and the properties were Hemingway's *To Have and Have Not* and Raymond Chandler's *The Big Sleep*, which Hawks planned to do as Bogart vehicles. H-F bought the screen rights to Hemingway's 1937 novel for $97,000 from Howard Hughes, who'd purchased them from Hemingway himself in 1939 for $10,000. In November 1943 H-F then sold the rights to Warners for $108,500 plus 20 percent of the film's gross receipts up to $3 million. Jack Warner had already given Hawks the go-ahead on script development, and Hawks in turn assigned the screenplay of two of his favorite writers: Jules Furthman, who had scripted *Only Angels Have Wings* for Hawks in 1938, and William Faulkner, who worked uncredited on *Air Force* and several other Hawks projects. Not too surprisingly, when the flap over production supervision came up after *To Have and Have Not* was in preproduction, Warner backed off and let Hawks produce the picture himself.

At first glance, *To Have and Have Not* had a great deal in common with *Casablanca*, which was certainly one reason for Warner's interest in the project. It, too, was a geopolitical intrigue-cum-romance set in an exotic locale, with Bogart's enigmatic hero shedding his cynical neutrality in the face of the ubiquitous Nazis. Again the action centered in a saloon, replete with ceiling fans, sunlight slanting in through the venetian blinds, and an array of colorful characters, including a piano-playing sidekick and an overweight heavy. But several qualities set the movie off markedly from *Casablanca*, most notably Bogart's relationship with the heroine, played by newcomer Lauren Bacall. As in virtually all of Hawks's films, whatever the genre, there was an offbeat romance at the heart of the story involving a self-reliant and resolutely unattached man and a wisecracking, aggressive woman who violates his space and his all-male group, eventually winning both his respect and his affections. Bacall played the role to perfection—to a point of displacing virtually all other dramatic concerns in the film.

Bacall herself was another H-F property, and one who would never have appeared in *To Have and Have Not* if Warners had had its way. "Betty Bacall" signed a one-year personal contract with H-F Productions in May 1943, at age nineteen, for $100 per week. She had a bit of stage work but no film experience; Hawks had signed her after his wife saw her picture on the cover of *Harper's Bazaar*. He felt that despite her lack of acting experience she would be ideal for the female lead in *To Have and Have Not*, but both Warner and Trilling were dismayed that he would use an untried teenager in so important a role. Trilling promised Warner during final preparation to "try, as much as possible, to talk [Hawks] out of Betty Bacall," but Hawks persisted. Within another year *To Have and Have Not* was a hit, Warners had purchased Bacall's contract from Hawks, and preproduction was under way for *The Big Sleep*.

Bacall's sudden stardom had quite an impact on *The Big Sleep*, as did her sudden romance with Bogart, though neither was at issue when the second Hawks-Bogart project went into production. Preparation on the picture followed much the same pattern as with *To Have and Have Not*. Hawks sold the rights to Raymond Chandler's detective novel to Warners for $20,000 in October 1944, several weeks after starting Faulkner and newcomer Leigh Brackett on the adaptation. By now there was no question of Hawks's authority as producer-director, and the process of script development on *The Big Sleep* indicated how loosely he operated during preproduction. Brackett and Faulkner each worked alone on different parts of the story and simply passed their work along to Hawks without even seeing one another's efforts, and without any input from Hawks while they were writing. "Most producers breathe constantly down a writer's neck," Brackett later recalled. "Howard Hawks sits down with you for a series of chats, giving you all his thoughts on what kind of story he wants, how it ought to go, etc., and then retires to Palm Springs and the golf course."

Actually, Hawks knew he would be rewriting the script during production—in this case with the aid of Jules Furthman, who came on after the shooting script was approved. It was Hawks's practice to shoot as close as possible to continuity and to revise the screenplay in the process, often with input from his leading actors. As it turned out, he and Furthman spent an inordinate amount of time rewriting during the first weeks on *The Big Sleep*—and without any input from Bogart, whose absence necessitated the rewrites. Bogart's already unstable marriage to Mayo Methot had begun to collapse once Bacall sauntered onto the scene, and the final crash came just as production opened on *The Big Sleep* in December. This apparently was the only time in Bogart's career that drinking or lateness affected his work, but Hawks managed to write and shoot around him. And once he was back on the set and his relationship with Bacall was in the open, the shoot proceeded smoothly and Bogart did some of the best work of his career as hard-boiled private eye Philip Marlowe.

Hawks closed production on *The Big Sleep* in the spring of 1945, just before *To Have and Have Not* was released. Not until that picture hit did anyone really realize the on-screen chemistry between Bogart and Bacall. Warners and Hawks also realized the opportunities they had missed on *The Big Sleep*, since Bacall had played only a supporting role that gave her little time on-screen with Bogart. What's more, *The Big Sleep* was previewed during the summer to lukewarm audience response. There was time to rethink the project, though, since Warners had decided to hold up release of *The Big Sleep* so it could rush out *Confidential Agent*, a war-related espionage picture co-starring Bacall and Charles Boyer. This gave Hawks and Feldman time to come up with a retake plan for the Bogart-Bacall picture, which Feldman relayed in a November 1945 letter to Jack Warner. Feldman reasoned that in *To Have and Have Not*, "Bacall was more insolent than Bogart, and this very insolence endeared her in both the public's and the critics' mind." He suggested that in retakes for *The Big Sleep* they "give the girl [Bacall] at least three or four additional scenes with

The Big Sleep *was sent back into production to build up the Bogart-Bacall relationship, exploiting the success of* To Have and Have Not *as well as the couple's off-screen romance.*

Bogart of the insolent and provocative nature that she had in *To Have and Have Not."*

Warner thought it over, and a few days later he sent the picture back into production for the Bogart-Bacall sequences, which added enormously to the appeal of the picture. When *The Big Sleep* finally opened early in 1946, critics roundly criticized its brutality and confused plotting—which was as much the result of Chandler's original story as the postproduction overhaul—but audiences were captivated by the romantic antagonism between Bogart and Bacall. Once again Hawks had fashioned a fast-paced thriller cloaked in darkness, cynicism, and despair, but one with light and heart at its center. There was a moment in *Casablanca* when Claude Rains told Bogart that despite his tough exterior, at heart Bogart was a sentimentalist. This was the key to Bogie's persona, and Lauren Bacall—whom he married while *The Big Sleep* was in production—brought home the point both on screen and off.

I N late 1946 Bogart's supremacy at Warners was underscored when Jack Warner tore up the seven-year contract Bogart had signed in 1942 and offered him a fifteen-year deal at $200,000 per picture. The new contract gave Bogart considerable authority over his projects, including approval of story, screenplay, and director; Bogart in turn gave blanket approval to five directors: Hawks, Huston, Curtiz, John Cromwell, and Delmer Daves. The contract designated the next two Bogart projects, *Dark Passage* and *The Treasure of the Sierra Madre,* and the disparity between the two indicated the kinds of risks involved in giving top talent that much creative control. The former was another *noir* thriller that paired Bogart and Bacall, and its success with critics and audiences was altogether predictable. *Sierra Madre,* conversely, was a much more ambitious and innovative picture, giving full rein to the darker side of the Bogart persona. He was off-cast as a paranoid prospector who descends into madness after he and two other down-and-out types, played by Tim Holt and Walter Huston, discover gold in the remote mountains of Mexico. Producer Henry Blanke persuaded Warners to let writer-director John Huston shoot the picture on location, which pushed its original budget of $1,879,000 to nearly $2.5 million. But the downbeat parable scored heavily, taking in $3.5 million at the box office and winning a Golden Globe for best picture, a spot on the National Board of Review's ten-best list, and Oscars for both John Huston (best director and best screenplay) and his father Walter (best supporting actor), along with an Academy nomination for best picture.

Despite its box-office performance, *Sierra Madre* failed to turn a profit because of its cost overruns, and this intensified Jack Warner's concerns about rising production and marketing costs. Industry conditions were deteriorating rapidly in 1947—so rapidly that Jack Warner was no longer inclined to approve high-cost, high-risk projects like *Sierra Madre.* In December 1947 he sent a memo to Steve Trilling on the subject. "I can't impress on you emphatically enough the importance of cutting budgets," he wrote. "There can be no prestige and all that stuff that goes with it. We are fighting a helluva battle and you must tell every director in no uncertain terms."

One project that was scaled down as a result of Warner's concerns about market conditions was *Key Largo,* a Bogart-Bacall drama set in the Florida Keys which was conceived as a location shoot early in 1947 but was finally done in the studio at Burbank, with John Huston directing and Jerry Wald producing. Wald had initiated *Key Largo* in late January 1947, when he sent Jack Warner a rough treatment of the Maxwell Anderson play. Wald was excited about the property, but he felt that they should add some humor, revise the ending (the hero dies in the play's finale), and "fatten up" the female lead for Bacall. Wald considered the story a "combination of *Petrified Forest* and *To Have and Have Not,*" two earlier Bogart vehicles. The story was a postwar drama about an ex-GI who travels to the Keys to pay his respects to the widow and father of a dead army buddy. He finds that their off-season resort has been taken over by a notorious mobster, who, though supposedly deported to Cuba, is using the resort as a base of operations for a counterfeit ring.

Wald got Warner's approval for *Key Largo*, and in late July paid $35,000 for the rights to Anderson's play. He sent a copy of the play to the Bogarts in early August, and their enthusiasm for the project effectively sent *Key Largo* into serious preproduction. Huston was tapped to write as well as direct, with newcomer Richard Brooks collaborating on the adaptation. During September and October, Huston fine-tuned *Sierra Madre* while Brooks researched *Key Largo* and Wald prepared the production. The three met regularly to hammer out the story line, which by late October was nearly set. At that point Huston and Brooks went down to the Florida Keys, where they holed up to write the continuity script—hardly a satisfactory alternative to taking the film itself down to the Keys, but the most they could hope for given the Warners' cost-cutting campaign. After a month in South Florida, Huston and Brooks had written roughly two-thirds of the script and soaked up some atmosphere. They returned to the studio in late November and finished the script by December 2 and planned to start production on December 15.

Joe Breen was not satisfied with the script, however, especially the gangster angle. Not only did the project recall Warners' classic gangster films, whose violence and tendency to valorize criminal types had been a subject of PCA concern when the agency was founded, but the heavy in the script also bore an obvious resemblance to Lucky Luciano, a mobster whom the U.S. government recently had deported to Cuba. Wald, Huston, and Brooks met with PCA officials in early December, and within a few days the script was revised and approved, with the reiteration that the characters "not in any way be identified with Luciano, a notorious gangster." A few days later Wald signed Edward G. Robinson (at $12,500 per week for ten weeks) to play Rocco—which meant that *Key Largo* was less likely to provoke associations with any real-world figures than with Warners' own history. That same week, Wald signed a free-lance deal with Claire Trevor (six weeks at $5,000 per week) to play Rocco's alcoholic mistress, and he borrowed Lionel Barrymore from MGM (ten weeks at $5,000 per week) to play the resort owner and father of Bogart's slain buddy.

Even with the constraints of Wald's supervision and the studio-bound shoot, *Key Largo* clearly was an ambitious and top-heavy production—particularly for Warners, which until the 1940s rarely put more than one star in a single picture. Star salaries alone totaled over

$400,000, and with the number of principal characters and plot lines, the direction would be demanding and difficult. The picture was scheduled for forty-eight days, but Wald had his doubts about Huston bringing it in on time. Unlike Curtiz, a staff director who was headstrong and self-indulgent at times but finally was a company man and a team player, John Huston was an inveterate maverick, an independent even when on studio contract. He had his own agenda, his own working methods, and little regard for Wald as a producer or a collaborator. In fact, once the various preproduction problems were worked out, Wald's influence over the picture diminished considerably and Huston took virtually complete control of the picture. This was a mixed blessing for the studio. Huston shared with Hawks a keen understanding of Warners' narrative and generic traditions, of its house style and resources. But he was an even more meticulous and deliberate director than Hawks, particularly in his use of camera movement and cutting to convey the story, and these qualities invariably meant expenditures of both time and money.

This equation was immediately borne out when production opened on December 15. Huston and cinematographer Karl Freund put the cast and crew through extensive rehearsals, all of which focused on a single scene—scene 47 in the script, the introduction of Rocco. Though Huston generally liked to shoot in continuity, he decided to start with this pivotal scene, which occurs some fifteen minutes into the picture. Rocco's entrance was set up by a brief sequence (scenes 42–46, four script pages), which Huston polished off during the first two days of the shoot. On December 21 he started shooting scene 47 (ten script pages), which consumed the next two weeks of production. The scene involved all five of the principals and most of Rocco's henchmen as well, and it served not only to introduce Robinson with a dramatic flourish but also to set up the various conflicts and relationships that would be played out in the course of the film. This demanded careful choreography, as is altogether evident from the following figures culled from the daily production reports:

DATE	SCENE	SETUPS	TAKES	PAGES	FINISHED FILM
12/22	47	12	37	½	0:31
12/23	47	10	33	1½	0:30
12/24 (½ day)	47	3	5	0	0:00
12/26	47	9	23	2¼	0:51
12/27 (Saturday)	47	6	20	2½	1:32
12/29	47	5	16	1	1:23
12/30	47	12	33	1¼	0:30
12/31 (retakes)	47	3	11	0	0:00

By January 2, 1948, some two weeks into production, Huston was already four days behind his forty-eight day schedule, having shot only 6 of the script's 150 scenes and generated about seven minutes of screen time. Sid Hickox, an efficient if undistinguished Warners cameraman, was assigned to the picture to speed things up, but it was apparent from his first day that he would have little or no impact. "The crew were in at 7 A.M. and Hickox was ready to shoot at 10:30 A.M.," reported unit manager Chuck Hansen on January 2. "Huston rehearsed with the camera and lined up, then he changed the setup. The result was that they did not get their first shot until 11:45 A.M." Hickox stayed on the project, but Huston actually worked more slowly as the film progressed. After completing scenes 42 to 47, he reverted to form and shot the script in continuity; as he went on, the visual treatment became more stylized, his rehearsals more extensive, and his coverage of the action more detailed. Predictably enough, this was maddening to Hansen, who felt that Huston was overly concerned with visual and narrative detail. As he stated in his report of January 30, Huston was continually "moving in with the camera and getting the necessary cuts of each player's reaction." And then came an especially telling comment: "In addition, HUSTON has stated he does not want the 'conventional' angles—he wants 'different' angles, and this also takes time."

Those unconventional angles and working methods proved costly; by February 14, 1948, the scheduled closing date, Huston was twenty-one days behind. Remarkably enough, there was very little pressure from Warner or Trilling, who had several reasons for keeping their distance, three in particular. First, Bogart and Bacall, who got along well with Huston and whose films were quite literally money in the bank for Warners, were happy with the shoot and doing good work. Second, since the picture was shot in the controlled studio environment, budget overruns were only about $6,000 to $7,000 daily. And third, Huston's "different" style of narration may have been maddening to Hansen—who was, after all, an one-the-set efficiency expert and thus committed to the conventional way of doing things—but Wald and Warner saw clearly enough in the dailies that Huston and company were creating something more than a routine romantic thriller.

The Bogart-Bacall romance was essential to the story and to the picture's eventual success, of course. But unlike the recent Hawks pictures, their relationship was not central to the narrative; indeed, the love story gradually recedes once Rocco surfaces. In *To Have and Have Not*, Bacall came out of nowhere to overwhelm Bogart and the geopolitical intrigue, transforming the film from a male adventure yarn into an offbeat romance. In *Key Largo*, Robinson's veritable return from the grave has much same effect on the love story. After Rocco's belated introduction, the film steadily assumes a darker and more threatening tone. The majority of the scenes are set at night, and Rocco's criminal activities seem somehow related to the fierce storm that is bearing down on the Keys. By film's end the romantic melodrama has moved beyond *noir* intrigue and crime thriller to become a virtual horror film, replete with "old dark house," violent storms, and a ghostly antagonist, Robinson, who only comes out after nightfall.

Whether this was a calculated transformation is difficult to say, even after studying the production records. Huston's penchant for shooting in continuity and the unique combination of resources and personnel —Robinson's gangster prototype, Freund's background at Ufa and then at Universal, where Huston himself got his start in the early 1930s when the horror genre was just taking off—certainly provided a context for this odd case of generic transformation and recombination. But the shift in narrative logic was lost on Jack Warner, who after a screening instructed the dubbing department to "play down the storm" on the sound track, and who agreed with Wald that they "should try to trim down Rocco's death at the end." The climactic scene takes place on a

Lauren Bacall huddles with director John Huston on the set of Key Largo, *as Humphrey Bogart listens in.*

A fitting culmination to Edward G. Robinson's twenty years of gangster roles came with his portrayal of Johnny Rocco in Key Largo.

fishing boat, and in an appropriate culmination of the gangster-as-vampire motif, Bogart waits above deck until sunrise to kill Rocco, having already killed off his henchmen. With Rocco trapped in the bowels of the boat and Bogart looming above in an open hatchway, the two exchange gunfire and Bogart prevails.

Robinson's death scene remained intact, which was a tribute not only to the staying power of his star persona but to Huston's own sense of defiance—and not simply of Warner and Wald, but of "conventional" narrative logic and film realism. Also defying the methods of studio production, Huston brought the picture in after seventy-two shooting days, exactly 50 percent over its projected schedule, though without going significanty over budget. Postproduction was handled much more quickly, with only three days in late March devoted to retakes. In April Max Steiner scored the film, enhancing the horrific dimension of the story, and in May the picture previewed. After additional editing and dialogue dubbing, *Key Largo* was ready for a June release. It was, along with *Johnny Belinda*, Warners' biggest picture of the year, taking in $3.5 million and finishing among the top twenty box-office hits in

1948. And in a tribute to Wald's growing stature as a producer, the Academy presented him with the Irving Thalberg Award.

Key Largo was the last Bogart-Bacall pairing, and it marked Huston's departure from Warners as well. Even before he had started production, Huston later recalled, "I had decided that my next film, *Key Largo*, was to be my last for Warner Brothers." He was fed up with Jack Warner, "dissatisfied with the studio in general," and feeling that "the complexion of the place was changing." He was not about to sign with another studio, though, since his displeasure with Warners extended in many ways to Hollywood at large. Instead, he teamed with producer Sam Spiegel to create an independent production company, Horizon Pictures, and he vowed to work outside Hollywood—and outside the country—whenever possible. He was particularly outraged over the rabid anti-Communist fervor that had emerged while he was doing *Key Largo;* it initiated what Huston termed "a wretched period in this country's history, truly a national shame." Congressional investigations of subversive activities and influences in the movie industry had begun during the spring of 1947, when the House Un-American Activities Committee (HUAC) targeted Hollywood's writing community. After a preliminary investigation, HUAC concluded that "scores of screenwriters who are Communists have infiltrated into the various studios, and it has been through this medium [of writing] that most of the Communist propaganda has been injected into the movies."

In the fall of 1947 as Wald and Huston were preparing *Key Largo*, HUAC opened a series of formal hearings on the matter. The committee sent subpoenas to nineteen "friendly" and nineteen "unfriendly" witnesses from the industry. Huston was no ideologue, but together with various other Hollywood luminaries—including his *Key Largo* costars Bogart and Bacall—he formed the Committee for the First Amendment. The group traveled to Washington to support the constitutional rights of the nineteen unfriendly witnesses and to voice their collective disapproval of the hearings, but their efforts came to naught. Eleven of the nineteen were called to testify, and ten of these refused to cooperate. The infamous "Hollywood Ten" were cited for contempt of Congress, they were abandoned by their studios and guilds, and by the time Huston closed *Key Largo*, their names were on a growing blacklist of suspected Communists who were denied employment in Hollywood. Huston was among the few who publicly criticized the studios and the blacklisting policy. He refused to take a loyalty oath required by the Directors' Guild, although he was vice president of the guild at the time, and on more than one occasion he upbraided Jack Warner for not supporting the Ten, six of whom had worked for Warners as screenwriters. The HUAC investigation and the threat of black-listing could not have come at a worse time, adding as they did to the internal and external pressures that threatened to tear the studio system apart. Blacklisting removed dozens—and eventually hundreds—of top artists from active production and created a climate of fear and repression throughout an already weakened industry.

It was obvious by early 1948, with revenues and theater attendance falling sharply, that the war boom was over. The Big Eight's combined profits fell from an all-time high of $122 million in 1946 to $89 million in 1947, and the decline accelerated in 1948. The majors were hard hit because of their theater holdings, but they took an even heavier blow in May 1948 when the Supreme Court handed down three decisions that effectively dis-integrated the Hollywood studio system. The anti-trust suit against the majors resulted in the *Paramount* decree (so called because Paramount was the first named in the original complaint), which abolished block booking, blind bidding, price-fixing, and all privileged arrangements between studios and theaters. In addition, the integrated majors were ordered to divest themselves of their theater holdings and function only as production-distribution companies. In separate but related cases against two large unaffiliated theater chains, the Griffith and Schine circuits, the Court abolished longstanding exhibition policies that gave these circuits first crack at top features, longer play dates, and other unfair advantages over smaller, weaker independents. What all this meant, finally, was that the filmmaking companies were mandated to handle production and marketing on a picture-by-picture basis, and this would bring an emphatic end to the studio-based production system, with its contract personnel, steady cash flow, and regulated output.

T H U S *Key Largo*, in terms of its stars and story and even its production values (the black-and-white cinematography, the sound-stage version of the Keys), was not just a throwback but an epitaph of sorts, signaling the end of an era at Warners. An even more dramatic epitaph came a year later in the low-budget crime thriller *White Heat*, which kissed off the past not with a whimper but an apocalyptic bang. The picture was conceived as a low-grade police drama about undercover work, but Jimmy Cagney's unexpected involvement had much the same impact on the project as Robinson's had on *Key Largo*, upgrading not only its budget and market value but also its potential as an exercise in institutional nostalgia. Warners had purchased Virginia Kellogg's original story early in 1948 for $2,000, and the writing team of Ivan Goff and Ben Roberts, who were well versed in low-budget thrillers, developed the project as a fairly routine cop story. In fact, the title originally referred to police pressure, and the criminal element was peripheral to the story.

Cagney had been away from the studio for five years, having set up his own independent production company. He was in need of ready cash at the time, and he asked Trilling about doing a picture for Warners. Cagney was apprised of projects in the works and when he expressed interest in *White Heat*, the project's status was substantially upgraded. Raoul Walsh was assigned to direct, while Goff and Roberts overhauled the story. They changed the focus from the cops to the bandits, changed the milieu from the Midwest to the Rockies, and changed the heavy from the sleazy Blackie Flynn to the doomed but dynamic Cody Jarrett. The script went through five rewrites between November 1948 and May 1949, with considerable input from Cagney and Walsh on the last few drafts. On May 6, 1949, the day that Walsh started shooting the picture, Cagney signed a nonexclusive contract with Warners that called for him to do three pictures over three years and gave him role and script approval and a quarter-million dollars per picture. *White Heat* was scheduled for a forty-two-day shoot and budgeted at just over $1 million, with roughly one-third of its cost going to Cagney and Walsh, who was now making roughly $100,000 per picture.

In its resurrection of a fading studio star and vanishing screen persona, *White Heat* recalled Walsh's first picture for Warners, a 1939 Cagney gangster epic, *The Roaring Twenties*, and also *High Sierra*, the seminal rural-bandit thriller Walsh did in 1941 with Bogart. *White Heat* displayed Walsh's usual expansive and freewheeling style, but its primary asset was the unique Cagney persona. From the opening train heist he pulls in the snow-covered mountains to his spectacular demise atop an exploding tank in the surreal landscape of an oil refinery, Cody Jarrett embodied a world of stark contrasts—between nature and technology, between freedom and entrapment, between our primitive and civilized instincts. Cagney pushed these conflicts to extremes that would have been unthinkable for any other actor, and indeed the film has a number of truly remarkable scenes: Cody's initial mental seizure and then his becalming on his mother's knee; the frenzied prison freak-out when he learns of his mother's death; his exuberant madness at the moment of his own destruction ("Made it, Ma—top o' the world!"). These scenes push the logic of genre and story and character into a realm that was Cagney's own, and one that neither the star nor the studio would ever reach again.

Warners released *White Heat* in the summer of 1949, and neither the critics nor the public knew quite what to make of it. Without a stabilizing narrative force—a love story, say, or a more appealing agent of law and order—the viewer is necessarily drawn to the doomed and anarchic Cody. At film's end the nominal hero, Edmond O'Brien, pumps one bullet after another into Cody with a high-powered rifle and mutters, "What's keeping him up?" The answer is obvious. It's what kept Robinson up at the end of *Key Largo*—that odd logic of stardom and genre and Hollywood mythmaking, accumulated through decades of films and roles. It's what gave stars like Cagney and Robinson, Davis and Muni, Bogart and Flynn the power to overcome conflict and loss and even death itself, and to be forever reborn and forever revitalized in another role, another life, another on-screen incarnation.

O R what seemed like forever, anyway. But the reproductive machinery that had generated and sustained Cagney and those other stars was grinding to a halt. Cagney played out his contract with two mediocre pictures in 1950 and then left the studio, returning only for an occasional one-shot deal over the next dozen years. This pattern was followed by virtually all of Warners' signature stars who were still working and affiliated with the studio in the late 1940s—Bogart, Davis, Robinson, Flynn, and second-rank players like Ann Sheridan and Sydney Greenstreet. And they weren't the only top studio talent to leave or to ease into retirement. In February 1950 Jack Warner began renegotiating Henry Blanke's fifteen-year contract, which had been signed back in 1945. In a letter to Blanke's agent-attorney, Warner argued that "the complete revamping of our entire industry calls for a great deal of caution and intelligent handling, otherwise I see nothing but chaos ahead." In May, Blanke's salary was cut from $5,500 to $3,500 per week —the first in a series of cuts he took as he shifted into an "advisory capacity" at the studio. A month later, in June 1950, Warner sold Jerry Wald's contract for $150,000 to Howard Hughes over at RKO. Wald could not get along with Hughes and he soon left RKO; and like so many other Warners stars and directors, he set up his own independent production company.

The demotion of Blanke and departure of Wald indicated that Jack was dead serious about "revamping" Warners' operations and reducing fixed studio costs. In what was perhaps the consummate irony in the company's history, Warners' net profits of $10.3 million in 1950 were higher than the profits of any other Hollywood studio. But these profits resulted, in large part, not from hit pictures but from the elimination of personnel to reduce overhead. So while the profit margin temporarily swelled, the potential for future profits was diminished considerably. In 1951 Warners again had the largest net take, at $9.4 million, and the cutbacks continued and began moving beyond the high-priced talent and into the studio's rank and file. In a single purge in April 1951, for instance, Warners fired 6 percent of its employees, reducing the publicity staff by two-fifths, the office staff by one-eighth, and eliminating the entire story department.

The studio's regulated and disciplined moviemaking system was leaving along with these employees, though other deals during the period indicated that Warners no longer valued this end of its operation as it once had. An important precedent was set when Warners agreed to serve as distributor for Transatlantic Pictures, the company created in 1947 by Alfred Hitchcock when he left Selznick. The first picture produced under the agreement was *Rope*, which Warners released in 1948, and as Hitchcock prepared *Stage Fright* in early 1949, he signed a six-year, four-picture deal with Warners for $250,000 per picture. Hitchcock was to produce as well as direct and thus was a virtual in-

By 1950 Warner Bros. was the most profitable studio in Hollywood, but industry changes left its future uncertain.

house independent; it also was a nonexclusive deal so he was free to work for other studios if he so desired. This was clearly an innovative agreement by Warners' standards, and another groundbreaking pact was signed in May 1951 when Warners agreed to do the financing and distributing for Fidelity Pictures. The Fidelity projects would be genuinely independent ones, with Warners having no direct control over their conception, development, or production.

Thus began the complete and relatively rapid transformation of Warner Bros. A good indication of the transformation was the kind of project that brought both Hawks and Huston back to the studio in the mid-1950s. Both had left Warners after their respective postwar hits, *The Big Sleep* and *Key Largo,* to become highly successful independent filmmakers. Hawks came back to Warners to produce and direct *Land of the Pharaohs,* a 1955 biblical epic with a cast of thousands in wide-screen and "Warnercolor." A year later Huston wrote, produced, and directed *Moby Dick,* another monstrous blockbuster that bore no resemblance to his earlier Warners pictures. Both *Land of the Pharaohs* and *Moby Dick* were prepackaged coproductions, with Warners providing facilities, limited financing, and distribution, but exercising very little control over their development and production. And both were so far afield from pictures like *The Big Sleep* and *Key Largo* that it's difficult to conceive how the same filmmakers, let alone the same company, could have done them. But Warners was indeed a different company by the mid-1950s, and Hollywood was a different industry. By 1955, Warners was shifting its regulated operation to series television and was a movie production company only in a marginal sense. Jack Warner still held on tenaciously to corporate control, but the actual filmmaking was governed by outsiders—whether independent movie producers or TV network executives. Jack was not about to admit it, but the glory days of Warner Bros. as a movie studio that shaped its own pictures, its own style, and thus its own destiny were gone.

22

MGM:
Last Gasp of
the Studio Era

Warners' response to the postwar transformation of the movie industry was typical of Hollywood's major studios, with one notable and somewhat predictable exception: Metro-Goldwyn-Mayer. As it had been during other periods of crisis and change in Hollywood, MGM was again distinctly out of step with the other majors. While its competitors steadily decentralized production, cut back contract personnel to reduce overhead, and made innovative deals with outside independents, Metro reverted to a centralized production setup, with its contract system, regulated output, and star-genre formulations. This scarcely jibed with the realities of the industry and the marketplace at the time, realities that Metro could not ignore indefinitely. By the late 1950s the studio system would be a thing of the past for MGM, just as it was for every other company in Hollywood. But Metro held out against the inevitable longer than any other company, turning out the last of Hollywood's studio-era productions, including some of the very best musicals in movie history.

MGM's postwar strategy meant heavy changes for the studio, in that it shifted from Mayer's management-by-committee system to the central-producer setup of the Thalberg era. The shift was motivated not by outside pressures from HUAC or the courts, but by MGM's failure to capitalize on the war-induced prosperity that was fattening the other studios' coffers. Metro had always spent more on its pictures and on studio operations generally than any other company—hence its ongoing reputation as the Tiffany's of the industry and its ever-diminishing profit margin. Gross revenues and net profits had climbed year after year during the war, and the trend continued through 1946. Loew's theaters were doing solid business, and its distribution outfit still moved MGM's pictures through the nation's—and the world's—theaters efficiently enough. But while income was up, MGM's year-end tallies fell further behind Paramount, Fox, and even Warners. Gross revenues for Loew's/MGM in 1946 were up to a record $180 million, and net profits reached an all-time high for the company of $17.9 million. But these profits were dwarfed by Paramount's $40 million, and they fell behind Fox's $25.3 million and even Warners $19.4 million.

Theater attendance fell in 1947 as operating costs climbed, and Nick Schenck grew increasingly concerned about the setup in Culver City. The closer he looked, the less optimistic he was about the ability of Mayer and his Executive Committee to turn things around. Metro's last solid commercial and critical hit had been *Meet Me in St. Louis* back in 1944, and the Freed and Pasternak units were still the only bright spots at the studio—but there, too, rising costs and lagging audience enthusiasm were a problem. The biggest success of 1946 had been *The Yearling*, a sentimental family story that grossed over $5 million and was MGM's lone nominee for a best-picture Oscar. But it also was a model of inefficiency. *The Yearling* had been in and out of production since 1941, with three different directors and a procession of writers, producers, and stars, so its gross receipts did not translate into heavy profits. Several other top Metro productions also ran into trouble in 1946–47, and none of them fared as well on release as *The Yearling*. The most notable was *Desire Me*, a Greer Garson melodrama that went so badly that director George Cukor refused to shoot retakes or to have his name associated with the picture. Mervyn LeRoy and Jack Cummings reshot much of the picture over a six-month period in late 1946 and early 1947. *Desire Me* was released without a director credit—hardly a sign of a steady and secure operation—and it fared poorly at the box office, contributing to both Metro's and Garson's postwar decline.

Mayer and his Executive Committee were not yet ready to give up on Garson's melodramas, but they had lost patience with several other longtime stars and series that no longer pulled their weight at the box office. The Hardy family, the Thin Man, Maisie, and Dr. Gillespie all were canceled in 1947 after a final series installment. The lone commercial hits that year were *Till the Clouds Roll By*, Freed's musical biopic of Jerome Kern, and *Green Dolphin Street*, an overblown costume drama. Both were long on production values—and thus on costs—but short on profit margin and critical acclaim. In fact, in 1947, for the first time in two decades, MGM did not earn a single Academy nomination for best picture. And after averaging three players per year during the war era on the exhibitors' poll of box-office stars, only Clark Gable made the top ten in 1947 (at number seven). MGM's profits were $10.5 million, the lowest total since before the war and far behind Paramount, Warners, and Fox.

Nick Schenck had seen enough. Mayer's high-cost, low-yield operation simply had to go. Schenck was not yet ready to unload Mayer himself, although it was well within his right as chief executive of Loew's/MGM to do so. Mayer and his chief associates—Eddie Mannix, Harry Rapf, Benny Thau—had been with the company since the original merger in 1924, and Loew's took pride in the longevity and continuity of the executive staff. (Schenck himself had been with MGM's parent company over forty years.) But production operations clearly needed something, which Schenck felt was a return to a central-producer system—one with a creative executive instead of a committee overseeing all production. So early in 1948 Schenck told Louis Mayer to "find another Thalberg."

T H A T was a tall order. No one presently at the MGM lot had the combination of creative and executive skills for the job—anyone who did had either quit or been fired. But it made sense to look for someone familiar with MGM's resources, so Mayer went after top production executives with experience at Metro. He started with David Selznick, who immediately declined the offer, as did Joe Mankiewicz and Walter Wanger. Mayer then conferred with Selznick, who suggested Dore Schary. Mayer blanched when he thought of Schary returning to MGM —and as production chief, yet—but he understood Selznick's reasoning. Schary obviously was a creative type who knew Metro, having spent six years there in the late 1930s and early 1940s as a writer and then as executive of the studio's low-budget unit. What's more, his function with the Schary unit had been similar to Thalberg's central-producer model: he supervised story and script development, monitored each production, and oversaw editing. After leaving MGM in late 1943 he took on more important projects, first as an executive producer for Selznick's Vanguard outfit and then as producer on the half-dozen packages that Selznick sold to RKO in 1946. Schary became production chief at RKO in January 1947, thus rounding out his education as a production executive. RKO's schedule that year included fifteen A-class features and twenty B's, with a total budget of some $20 million. Of this total, $15 million went to the high-grade features for an average of $1 million per picture, far below the MGM average, and Schary brought in RKO's twenty low-budget features for an average cost of only $215,000. These had included formula quickies featuring Dick Tracy and the Falcon which were of no real interest to Schenck and MGM except that they indicated Schary's experience with all phases of production.

One major concern about Schary that Mayer and Schenck shared was his ideological bent. Mayer and Schenck were archconservatives, and given the political climate in Hollywood and the nation at large, they could ill afford to have any executive at MGM who was perceived as being soft on Communism. In late 1947 Schary had been a principal figure in the HUAC hearings, and later he had personally crossed swords with Mayer, who had long regarded Schary's New Deal liberalism as a serious character flaw. Those confrontations were sparked by a provocative and popular RKO crime thriller, *Crossfire*, which had dared imply that there was a current of anti-Semitism in postwar America. The implication struck Congressman Parnell Thomas and his committee as distinctly un-American, and inquiries into the backgrounds of producer Adrian Scott and director Edward Dmytryk revealed prior left-wing affiliations. The two were among the nineteen unfriendly witnesses to receive subpoenas, and two of the only three nonwriters who eventually were called to testify. Dore Schary, as RKO's production chief, was also called—though not as an unfriendly witness—to discuss the infiltration of his studio by these and other subversives. In testimony given on October 29, 1947, he staked out a classic liberal position, arguing for individual rights guaranteed by the First Amendment. To make such an argument was actually courageous at the time, given the political climate. Schary testified that there was no set policy at RKO regarding the employment of Communists, and that he saw no need for one. "Up until the time it is proved that a Communist is a man dedicated to the overthrow of the government by force or violence, or by any illegal methods," said Schary, "I cannot make any determination of his employment on any basis except whether he is qualified best to do the job I want him to do." This assertion drew applause from the gallery, as did Schary's avowed desire to abide by, in his words, "a ruling of the Supreme Court which prohibits me as an American to arbitrarily refuse employment to a man purely because of his politcs."

Parnell Thomas drew even louder applause (according to the congressional records) when he castigated Schary for "the Rip Van Winkle opinion that has been permitting communism to grow throughout the world the way it has." But Schary denied that either Scott or Dmytryk were "subversive," let alone "foreign agents," as some had suggested. "I think there are Communists in Hollywood," admitted Schary, but he added that efforts by Communists, Socialists, and labor activists "to dominate guilds and unions have been defeated." He argued that the

"Communist line" had not worked its way into *Crossfire* or any other RKO pictures, and that he believed HUAC should focus its attention on "the actual things that get on the screen." In that regard, said Schary, "I don't know of any subversive films ever made, I just don't." Most of Hollywood's power elite agreed, even conservatives like Mayer and the Warners, though few were willing to say so publicly as the hearings picked up steam. Schary received moral support from several of his colleagues, including Walter Wanger and David Selznick. Wanger wired Schary the day he testified, praising his "great stand" and suggesting that Schary "stood out like a sore thumb amongst [his] colleagues." Selznick sent a telegram a few days later, telling Schary he was "proud" of the way he handled himself on the stand, and that "if there should be the slightest difficulty, you know that the light is still on in the window."

The resolve of Schary and other Hollywood liberals weakened in the coming weeks, however, as the committee made it clear that it intended to deal harshly with the Hollywood Ten—and with the industry at large—if it did not clean house. Thus came about the legendary Waldorf-Astoria meetings in late November, convened by Eric Johnston of the Motion Picture Association of America (MPAA)* to decide how to deal both publicly and privately with HUAC and the Hollywood Ten. Schary found precious little support at that meeting for his recent stand, and he also found an outspoken adversary in Louis Mayer. He recalled in later testimony that Mayer "spoke generally about the need for some kind of law against communism" in Hollywood, and that he had little regard for any arguments in defense of the individual's constitutional rights. Johnston proposed a guilty-until-proven-innocent policy for handling not only the Ten but also, as Schary recalled, "all persons charged by the committee with being Communists." The studio powers agreed, and they resolved to come out of the meeting with a "unanimous policy statement" condemning both Communist infiltration and the Ten. They also established a public relations committee to counter the negative press Hollywood was receiving from conservative journalists and special-interest groups.

The official MPAA statement, which held that the studios "will not knowingly employ a Communist," was drafted and released to the press on November 25, the same day Schary learned that RKO's board of directors had fired Scott and Dmytryk. Within a week it was clear that Johnston's policy of guilt-by-accusation was already being implemented. *Variety* reported on December 2 that "the Thomas committee

---

* In 1945, the Motion Picture Producers and Directors of America (MPPDA) changed its name to the Motion Picture Association of America (MPAA).

---

claims to have names of seventy-nine Communists working in the studios," and that Thomas was determined to keep all of them out of the movie industry. This was the first sign of Hollywood's blacklist, which swelled at a remarkable rate in the coming weeks and months. Schary tried in vain to distance himself from the witch-hunt as it gained momentum; in fact, as late as March 1948 he still refused to acknowledge the existence of any such blacklist. He was clearly in a tough spot, caught between his own liberal sentiments and his aspirations to join Hollywood's power elite, who were a conservative and cautious fraternity. Schary's own background as a writer and his penchant for "social problem" films put him squarely at odds with HUAC, but it grew increasingly obvious that one opposed the committee only at considerable personal and professional risk.

When Scott and Dmytryk were first subpoenaed as unfriendly witnesses, Schary received dozens of letters at RKO, and he personally responded to every one with a thoughtful, detailed defense of the filmmakers' rights. Once they refused to testify and incurred the wrath of HUAC, and MPAA, and RKO's board of directors, however, the number of negative letters increased and Schary sent neutral, perfunctory responses. He indicated that he could "condone" neither the committee nor the Ten; his only interest was in running the studio, though he hoped that "Scott and Dmytryk can clean up their reputation and come back to useful employment." There was little hope for this, of course, and it became obvious that the same fate was in store for hundreds of other employees in the movie industry. Although an ARI study of the public's attitudes toward Communist "infiltration" of Hollywood concluded that it was "easy to overestimate the extent of harm done to date" and that the hearings would have "little immediate effect on the box office," still the studio powers were caving in to pressures from HUAC, and Schary realized that if he wanted work in Hollywood, he would have to do the same.

So Schary certainly had reservations when Mayer approached him with the MGM offer, since it would mean supporting Mayer and Schenck's anti-Communist crusade. But these concerns seemed less prohibitive once Howard Hughes took over RKO in May 1948. Hughes was an industrialist, aviator, and occasional filmmaker whose anti-Communist fervor was of obsessive if not downright paranoid and hallucinatory proportions. He made it clear that any left-wing sensibilities on the screen or any fellow travelers on the RKO payroll would not be tolerated, and that he expected Schary's support in his efforts to ferret out any subversive activity at the studio. May 1948 also saw the Supreme Court hand down its Paramount Decree, and Hughes immediately stated that RKO would cooperate with the Court's demand for theater divorcement. Schary opposed ready compliance, siding with Mayer and the Warners, who felt that the majors should battle the ruling. But Schary had no luck convincing Hughes, which further deepened the division between the two top RKO executives. Word soon leaked out that Schary was unhappy and thinking of leaving RKO. On June 6 Schary addressed a memo to all personnel in an effort "to dispel all these rumors," especially those "concerning a change of management at RKO." He assured them that he and Hughes were "in complete accord on present policy and on the projected program for RKO."

Nothing could have been further from the truth. Schary saw no real hope of working with Hughes and he decided to take his chances with Mayer and Schenck. On July 1, 1948, Metro announced publicly that Schary was coming aboard as Vice President in Charge of Production at a salary of $6,000 per week. As an MGM press release put it, Schary was "assuming the production helm under the direction of Louis B. Mayer." Schary himself was quoted in the release as saying, "Under the leadership of L. B. Mayer, I offer my associates a program of work dedicated to the production of good films about a good world."

R H E T O R I C aside, Schary did not expect to work closely with Mayer. His main objectives at MGM were to streamline operations and reduce production costs, and since both the management glut and the high studio overhead were directly attributable to Mayer's regime, Schary foresaw little "direction" or "leadership" from Mayer as he cleaned house. In fact, his first objective was to dismantle Mayer's Executive Committee—the "college of cardinals," as Schary called them. "I never believed such a setup was practical," he said later. "I was going to be in charge of production and my contact would be with the individual producers." Schary kept the studio's executive staff intact, with Eddie Mannix as general manager of the plant, Joe Cohn doing budgets and schedules, and Benny Thau handling the actors' contracts and complaints. Mayer himself was kicked upstairs—his new title was Vice President in Charge of the Studio—though he still carried considerable weight with his former staff. But Schary was in charge of production operations, which he promptly demonstrated by calling a halt to all production and personally assessing the studio's personnel, story properties, and upcoming projects. On each scheduled production Schary read and evaluated the script, went over the production plans, and decided whether the project was worth pursuing. By mid-August he had settled on a dozen projects that would start production by September 1, with the possibility of expanding the schedule by another half-dozen projects before year's end.

Louis B. Mayer (right) signs Dore Schary as Metro's new production chief in July 1948.

The only area of studio operations that Schary really could not control was musical production. In fact, a governing irony of his regime was that it coincided with the golden age of the MGM musical, even though Schary's own commitment to the genre and his authority over musical production were limited at best. "We had a kind of musical stock company at MGM," he acknowledged in a 1973 interview, and he went on to state, "If we had ten good ideas for musicals [in any given year] . . . we made ten. If we had one, we made one. My feeling was, let's not count how many melodramas, or how many dramas or comedies, or musicals." This bit of selective recollection—all too typical of "oral histories" of the movie business—overstates Schary's individual authority while it understates the inevitable skew of Metro's production operation. The fact is that MGM produced eight to ten musicals per annum during Schary's tenure, year after year; given its resources, the studio could ill afford *not* to.

Despite Schary's efforts to build up more economical genres like the crime thriller and romantic comedy, Metro's commitment to musical production remained its most distinctive feature throughout the postwar decade. Only 4 percent of all Hollywood releases during this period were musicals, yet over 25 percent of MGM's total output—81 of 316 productions—were musicals. Indeed, MGM produced over half the musicals made in Hollywood from 1946 through 1955. Musical production at MGM was dominated by three men—Arthur Freed, Joe Pasternak, and Jack Cummings—who did sixty of those eighty-one musicals. Pasternak and Freed, the most prolific, turned out twenty-seven and twenty-one musicals respectively during the postwar decade, while Cummings produced a dozen. Most of Cummings's pictures were pretty routine, although he did produce a few important and memorable musicals like *Seven Brides for Seven Brothers* and *Kiss Me*

Kate. Pasternak's output, which was consistently superior, included such hits as *In the Good Old Summertime, Summer Stock, The Great Caruso,* and *The Merry Widow.* But it was Arthur Freed who orchestrated MGM's musical golden age, virtually defining its trajectory from 1944 with *Meet Me in St. Louis* to *Gigi* in 1958. Between the two he produced such musical masterworks as *The Pirate, Easter Parade, The Barkleys of Broadway, On the Town, Annie Get Your Gun, Royal Wedding, An American in Paris, Show Boat, Singin' in the Rain, The Band Wagon, Brigadoon, Kismet,* and *It's Always Fair Weather.*

Freed's star had been ascending back when Schary was first at MGM, and by the time Schary returned there was no question of Freed's status as the studio's top producer. His rapport with Louis Mayer was crucial to his rise, and the two remained close even after Schary's arrival—in fact, it was through Freed that Mayer exercised most of his authority after Schary took charge of production. It's worth noting, however, that Freed's productivity actually increased after Schary's arrival, because of the new production chief's demand for greater efficiency. But Freed's postwar surge had less to do with Mayer or Schary than with the production unit that Ford put together in the late 1940s. One member of that unit was composer Irving Berlin, who said of Freed: "His greatest talent was to know talent, to recognize talent and to surround himself with it." Freed had already proved the truth of this in the prewar years when he built a unit around Busby Berkeley, Judy Garland, and Mickey Rooney to produce backstage musicals. During the war his work with Vincente Minnelli started him in a different direction, and by 1948 Freed was developing a very different kind of musical with a different corps of above-the-line talent. This corps included directors, writers, composers, and stars, of course, but perhaps the most vital members of the Freed unit were the four choreographers—Gene Kelly, Stanley Donen, Charles Walters, Robert Alton—whom Freed developed into directors. The role of the director-choreographer was by no means common in Hollywood—except in the Freed unit, where it became prevalent by the early 1950s. The fact that MGM's director-choreographers worked almost exclusively with Freed underscores the importance of dance as an integral narrative element and also a defining characteristic of the Freed-unit musicals. Kelly starred in a few Pasternak films in the 1940s, and Donen directed *Seven Brides for Seven Brothers* for Cummings, but both worked most often and most effectively with Freed.

Other top artists at Metro had close associations with the Freed unit as well. Director Vincente Minnelli's alliance was the most intense; he directed all but one of his MGM musicals for Arthur Freed. All told, Kelly, Donen, and Minnelli worked in various combinations on half of

Freed's two dozen musicals from 1943 to 1958. Freed developed strong alliances with his performers, writers, and composers as well. Gene Kelly starred and danced in nine Freed musicals, and Fred Astaire in six. Alan Jay Lerner and the team of Betty Comden and Adolph Green wrote virtually all of the top Freed-unit hits—often the lyrics as well as the book. Lerner, Comden, and Green primarily did stage musicals, because they preferred Broadway's creative freedom (and greater financial rewards, since writers owned a piece of their productions) to the constraints of movie writing. But in Arthur Freed they found a collaborator whose taste and judgment they trusted and whose production unit could transform even their most stage-bound efforts into uniquely cinematic experiences. In fact, *An American in Paris* and *Singin' in the Rain*, arguably the Freed unit's greatest achievements, both were original screenplays—the former by Lerner and the latter by Comden and Green—and are inconceivable in any other medium.

Significantly enough, Pasternak and Cummings did not develop similar creative alliances at MGM, nor did they emphasize dance in their musicals the way Freed did. No Metro director worked regularly with Cummings; the only one who did with Pasternak was Richard Thorpe, a second-rate staffer who was as likely to crank out a mediocre thriller as a Pasternak musical. The only exclusive relationship that either producer formed with an above-the-line artist was Pasternak's with Mario Lanza. The massive tenor, who burst into stardom in four quasi-operas, peaked in 1951 with a huge hit, *The Great Caruso*, and then declined just as rapidly because of his alcoholism, drug dependency, and chronic weight problems. Other than that alliance, Pasternak and Cummings shared a number of MGM's second-class musical stars—including rather conventional talents like Kathryn Grayson and June Allyson, but also water-ballet specialist Esther Williams and flamenco dancer Ricardo Montalban.

T H E Freed unit came of age with a 1949 production, *On the Town*, its first all-out dance musical and its most effective effort yet in blending story and music, song and dance into a seamless, integrated whole. Back in 1944 when Gene Kelly was just emerging as an actor, dancer, and choreographer at MGM, he convinced Freed to buy the screen rights to Comden and Green's stage version of *On the Town*. A high-energy romantic fantasy in which three sailors dance their way through a twenty-four-hour shore leave in New York City, it was then a huge Broadway success. Freed in turn convinced Mayer to shell out $250,000 for the play, but when the war ended and the market for "service pictures" declined, Mayer decided simply to shelve the project. Dore Schary was certain that war-related pictures would return to favor in the late 1940s—in fact, he was then personally producing a combat picture, *Battleground*. He also could see no point in squandering a quarter-million-dollar property, so he urged Freed to go ahead with *On the Town*.

Freed was on a roll at the time—three of his last four pictures had grossed over $3 million—and he was ready to try something a bit less conventional. So he decided to have Gene Kelly choreograph and direct *On the Town*, which may have been Freed's single most important decision as an MGM producer. The picture initiated a remarkable surge for the thirty-seven-year-old Kelly. He had already reached stardom despite obvious limitations as an actor, but he was just coming into his own as a dancer, choreographer, and director. Concurrent with Kelly's rise was that of Stanley Donen, a former dancer who had been collaborating with Kelly as a choreographer, and whom Kelly brought on as his codirector for *On the Town*. Donen was then twenty-four years old and earning only $400 per week, and Kelly later recalled that Donen "was still considered by the studio to be my whipping boy" and that even Freed "had his doubts" about Donen's abilities. These doubts would disappear soon enough, although there was no question that the governing creative force behind *On the Town* was Gene Kelly.

By the time Kelly and Donen did *On the Town*, they had already choreographed two pictures and had demonstrated a knack for directing as well. Their most recent collaboration was on *Take Me Out to the Ball Game*, which had just finished shooting in October 1948. They had come up with the story for the film and had worked closely with Comden and Green, who did the dialogue and song lyrics. The nominal director was Busby Berkeley, but as shooting progressed the two choreographers took increasing control over the picture. Not only was Berkeley's energy waning—it was his last effort as a director—but he also had no real feel for this type of musical, with its tight integration of the musical sequences into the narrative. His forte was the backstage variation, with its clear separation of story and show. *Take Me Out to the Ball Game* was a solid hit, although its gay-nineties setting gave Donen and Kelly little opportunity to pursue their growing interest in modern dance and ballet. *On the Town* was more suitable to those interests, and when Schary and Freed indicated their support of the project, Kelly and Donen set to work with Carol Haney and Jeannie Coyne to create a series of routines specifically for the picture. Once Freed saw the routines, he was convinced that Donen and Kelly were ready for a project of their own and that *On the Town* would set a new direction in MGM's musical production.

Comden and Green were signed to do the screenplay for *On the Town*, and it was completed by late January 1949. By then preproduction was in full swing. Kelly concentrated on rehearsing with the other principals—Frank Sinatra, Jules Munshin, Ann Miller, Vera-Ellen, and Betty Garrett—while Donen prepared the location and studio shoots. By mid-February the budget estimate was set at $1.9 million; above-the-line costs were a hefty $690,000, largely because of the quarter-million-dollar property cost and the flat salary of $130,000 to Frank Sinatra. Production was scheduled for twenty weeks, and the increased cost and complexity of the dance-oriented musicals was further indicated by the heavy rehearsal time on the picture. Ten weeks would be devoted to rehearsing, and ten to shooting.

Considering the logistical demands of the location work and also Donen and Kelly's multiple responsibilities, the shoot went remarkably well. Most of the book portion was shot at the studio before the picture was taken on location in May to shoot the opening dance montage (with professional dancers filling in for Sinatra and Munshin whenever possible) and the close of the picture. The opening montage, which through intercutting integrates all of Gotham's landmarks into a

A breakthrough film for Gene Kelly and Stanley Donen as director-choreographers was Take Me Out to the Ball Game. *Here Donen (in white shirt) rehearses a number with that film's costars, Frank Sinatra, Jules Munshin, and Kelly.*

single dynamic dance routine, took two full weeks to shoot. By then costs had pushed just over $2 million, but both Freed and Schary were pleased with the results. Donen, Kelly, and company were back on the lot by late May, and after another two weeks all of the musical numbers except the final pas de deux with Kelly and Vera-Ellen had been shot. This ballet was rehearsed for two solid weeks and shot in four days, with production closing in early July. Because the musical numbers featured more dancing than singing, the postproduction for *On the Town* was relatively light by musical standards, and the picture was ready to preview by early September.

While *On the Town* took the MGM musical to a new level of accomplishment, it took it to a new level of cost and logistical complexity as well. The drain on studio resources was tremendous, and only a box-office performance of $3 million could justify that kind of investment. Freed was confident that the picture would hit that figure, and the recent Freed-unit productions certainly reinforced his conviction. *Take Me Out to the Ball Game* was doing excellent business, as were two other Freed-unit productions: *Words and Music,* a musical biopic of Rodgers and Hart starring Mickey Rooney, and *The Barkleys of Broadway,* which reunited Fred Astaire and Ginger Rogers, who hadn't worked together since their last musical pairing for RKO a decade earlier. Pasternak's *In the Good Old Summertime* and Cummings's *Neptune's Daughter* were also huge hits at the time, grossing about $3.5 million apiece. The fall previews for *On the Town* indicated that it, too, would be a hit, so MGM decided to hold it for a holiday release and maximize its box-office potential.

T H E success of these musicals during Schary's first full year at Metro underscored the studio's commitment to the genre. Schary was resigned to that commitment by now, and also to the parallel management system that the three musical producers maintained, conveniently removed from Schary's own central-producer system. But still he was determined to prove that MGM could succeed with more timely and less costly films as well. He hoped to close out his first year at Metro with a flourish of his own—outside the musical genre—and he succeeded. He had a virtual sure thing with *Adam's Rib,* the sixth Tracy-Hepburn pairing that closed in August and was released in October. The delightful marital comedy was directed by George Cukor and scripted by another marital team, Garson Kanin and Ruth Gordon. All were in top form, as were supporting players Tom Ewell, Judy Holliday, and Jean Hagen. *Adam's Rib* had executives on both coasts expecting box-office records, and they got them. There was less certainty, however, about *Battleground,* a pet project of Dore Schary's that was due out in December. Schary had been high on the project since his RKO days; in fact, one of the many contributing factors to Schary's leaving RKO was Hughes's lack of enthusiasm for the grim World War II saga about an infantry unit's efforts to survive the Battle of the Bulge. When Schary left RKO, he bought the screen rights to the property for $100,000 and resolved to do it at MGM. He personally produced the picture over the strenuous objections of Louis Mayer, whose feelings about realistic war dramas hadn't changed since Thalberg produced *The Big Parade* a quarter-century earlier. But Schary and director William Wellman went ahead, putting a number of Metro's male stars, principally Van Johnson and Ricardo Montalban, through their paces in a back-lot version of the war-torn, snow-covered European landscape.

Battleground was an immediate critical and commercial hit. Schary had pushed for a December release not only to exploit the holiday moviegoing traffic but also to qualify for the 1949 Academy Awards. *Battleground* did score several Oscar nominations, including one for best picture—MGM's first nominee for best picture since 1946. Schary's picture shared top commercial honors with *Adam's Rib*. In an era when $5 million in gross receipts was the gauge for blockbuster status, the Tracy-Hepburn picture pushed $6 million and Schary's war story took in just under $5 million. Along with its half-dozen musical hits then in release, all of which did at least $3 million at the box office, the studio boasted eight of the sixteen biggest box-office hits of 1949–50. And while all the other majors suffered declining profits in 1949, with RKO actually suspending production altogether for a time, Metro's profits climbed from a twenty-year low of $4.2 million in 1948 to $6 million in 1949.

Dore Schary was vital to the reversal of MGM's fortunes, building studio morale as well as a more efficient and profitable operation. As it became more obvious that the movie industry was in serious trouble, many saw Schary as the company's salvation—a present-day Thalberg capable of guiding MGM through an even more difficult period than the Depression. This attitude was best expressed, perhaps, in a letter to Schary received from Metro's longtime story editor and producer, Sam Marx. "It is just a few days over a year since you came back here," said Marx, "and in that time a lonely, frightened studio has changed back to a thriving, exciting place." After acknowledging that it was "a little old-fashioned to stay sentimental about Irving," Marx went on to compare Schary to Thalberg:

> Irving's integrity and quality were mighty contributions in themselves for what is often a tawdry industry. When one adds to these his

instinctive feelings for what is right in a script, we certainly have the best elements required to make a great motion picture producer . . . Irving helped elevate the business, but he did it in a period when films needed elevating and it was that lush intermission between the two world wars. . . . I often wonder if he would have kept up with these times. I like to think so, I hope so, but I don't know. However, we know about you. I saw *Battleground*, and I've seen what you have done in a year, and I can't think of a greater compliment to pay you than just that.

Not everyone at MGM shared this viewpoint, and particularly not Louis B. Mayer. By early 1950 it was obvious that beyond his rapport with Arthur Freed, Mayer had little or no impact on the production operations at MGM. He was now in his sixties and nearing retirement age, but he was not yet ready to let Schary take control of the studio he had been running for over a quarter-century. There was no denying the studio's turnaround, nor Schary's contribution. And Schary's tastes did seem to coincide with those of the public—and those of the Academy, which awarded Oscars to *Battleground* for its screenplay and cinematography. But Mayer had always resisted crime and violence as subject matter for Metro pictures, and a grim combat film hardly seemed an example of the "good pictures about a good world" that Schary had promised. Despite MGM's recent success, Mayer grew increasingly critical of Schary's rule and his filmmaking tastes. He focused his wrath not only on *Battleground* but also on two John Huston projects, *The Asphalt Jungle* and *The Red Badge of Courage*, that Schary had approved and that were both highly visible early in 1950. These two Huston pictures, in fact, set Mayer and Schary on a collison course that could only result in one of them leaving MGM.

Mayer was no fan of John Huston, the maverick writer-director who had refused to take a loyalty oath and continued to berate HUAC and anyone in the industry who supported the committee. Huston had set up his own production company after leaving Warners in 1948, but to hedge his bets and to keep busy between his Horizon productions, he also had signed on with MGM at $4,000 a week to direct one picture per annum. The first MGM project was to be *Quo Vadis?*, a biblical epic begun with Mayer's support and approval. But there were problems with the production, including a lack of enthusiasm on Huston's part, and eventually the project was suspended. By then the studio was firmly in Schary's control, and his artistic and political sensibilities jibed with Huston's. The two huddled to consider an alternative project and decided on *The Asphalt Jungle*, a taut thriller that Huston adapted from W. R. Burnett's novel. It was an ideal Huston vehicle in the tradition of *The Maltese Falcon* and *Key Largo*—a provocative, brutal crime film about an offbeat male group caught up in an ill-fated quest. Huston took *The Asphalt Jungle* into production in late 1949, with Sterling Hayden and Sam Jaffe costarring, and newcomer Marilyn Monroe in a key supporting role. When it was released in March 1950, Mayer was openly critical of the picture; he was widely quoted as saying, "I wouldn't walk across the room to see a thing like that." The public felt otherwise, though, and Huston's picture was an immediate sensation.

This scarcely deterred Mayer. He was even more critical of the prose treatment that Huston submitted that same month for his next project, an adaptation of Stephen Crane's dour Civil War story, *The Red Badge of Courage*, which traced the efforts of a raw recruit to overcome his abject terror in the face of battle. Like *The Asphalt Jungle* and *Battleground*, this picture disdained romance and sentimentality, and in fact it displayed precious little of what Mayer and many of his longtime cohorts, particularly those in the New York office, associated with commercial entertainment. But grim realism and downbeat ensemble pieces were in, it seems, and so was Dore Schary, who saw *Red Badge* as an ideal follow-up to *Battleground*. Even though Mayer's concerns were seconded by the sales executives in New York, Schenck gave Schary the go-ahead on *Red Badge*. Schary in turn gave Huston and his producer, Gottfried Reinhardt, a budget ceiling of $1.5 million and a shooting schedule of thirty days. As was altogether evident from Schenck's conversations with Lilian Ross, who did a series of feature articles for *The New Yorker* on the making of *Red Badge*, Schary, Mayer, and Schenck were well aware of the stakes involved in the production—which were a great deal higher than the $1.5 million budget. Schenck made it clear that he intended to back his new production chief, whose instincts had been proven right thus far. And Schary himself was willing to admit that he had little else to go on. "Call it instinct," he told Ross, explaining why he went ahead despite the "great resistance" from Mayer and others to his making *Red Badge*. "This picture has no women . . . no love story . . . no single incident," said Schary. "The story—well, there's no story in this picture." Still he was determined to proceed; he was certain that the film would score critically and had the makings of a surprise hit.

Huston and Harold Rosson, his cameraman on *The Asphalt Jungle*, shot *Red Badge* in thirty-eight days, with most of the work being done outdoors on the back lot at MGM and on location in the Los Angeles area. The picture starred Audie Murphy, the baby-faced and heavily decorated World War II hero who thus far had specialized in low-budget westerns. The other principals were relative unknowns, and they were supported by hundreds of anonymous extras for the battle scenes (at a cost of $145,000). Huston and Rosson created a strong sense of atmosphere, with a vivid contrast between the gruesome, chaotic battles and the quiet, almost lyrical interludes between skirmishes. Shooting was completed during the summer, and by early fall Huston and editor Margaret Booth had completed a preview cut. They had pared the film down to seventy-eight minutes, some twenty-minutes shorter than the average A-class feature. After a number of studio previews and then two public sneaks in Los Angeles, it was obvious that audiences were not drawn to the bleak study of cowardice, redemption, and the horror of war.

The previews were devastating to Schary, and though Huston was also concerned about the picture, he had no intention of hanging around Culver City to salvage it. While Schary and producer Gottfried Reinhardt were left holding the rough cut and the preview cards to *Red Badge*, Huston left to do *The African Queen*, one of his own Horizon Pictures projects that would take him to Africa for an arduous location shoot. Schary saw no choice but to recut the picture, and by late October he and Reinhardt had done a complete overhaul of *Red Badge*. Reinhardt came up with the idea of a literary framework (the movie opened on an image of Crane's novel) and a voice-over narration (spoken by James Whitmore, a costar and Oscar nominee from *Battleground*), which Schary scripted. Schary also insisted that some of the more gruesome images of death and carnage be cut, which made the viewing experience more palatable but further diminished what little motivation there was for the hero's initial cowardice.

Another disastrous preview sent Schary and Reinhardt back to the editing bench. This time they imposed a more rigid structure on the story, amalgamating the various battles into one climactic engagement. By then the picture's cost had reached $1.65 million, its length was down to a mere sixty-nine minutes, and Schary figured they had reached the point of diminishing returns with recuts. He had lost his enthusiasm for the project and simply wanted to get the picture off the lot and into circulation. But still Mayer was lobbying against *The Red Badge of Courage;* he now insisted that Loew's shelve it rather than waste even more money on its marketing and release. Hoping to erode Schary's credibility and authority at the studio, Mayer took his case to Schenck. The exchange grew heated, Mayer delivered an ultimatum, and his power play failed. Schenck had heard enough of Mayer's carping about Schary, and he welcomed the chance to be rid of it and to let Schary take full charge of the studio. On June 23, 1951, the press announced that Louis B. Mayer, after twenty-seven years at the helm of Metro-Goldwyn-Mayer, was leaving the company.

To anyone familiar with the palace intrigues at Loew's/MGM, Mayer's departure was no surprise. It had been coming for over a year, really; Huston's film simply provided the catalyst. There was no longer any question of Schenck's allegiance, nor of his willingness to edge Mayer away from the center of power at the studio. A clear sign had come a few months earlier in 1951, when Schenck announced that Schary and several other studio executives would receive sizable stock bonuses as Metro continued to improve its market position. Not only was Mayer left out of the deal, but he wasn't even consulted or asked to make the announcement. This made it altogether obvious that the company's highest paid executive (Mayer's 1951 salary was $300,000, Schenck's was $278,000) had become little more than a figurehead. It hardly mattered that Mayer had been right about *The Red Badge of Courage*. "I figured I would write that off to experience," Schenck told Lilian Ross, rationalizing both his and Schary's mistake in backing Huston's project. "You can buy almost everything, but you can't buy experience." Loew's unceremoniously dumped *The Red Badge of Courage* when it finally was released later that summer. The picture opened at a six-hundred-seat theater in midtown Manhattan and dropped from sight in a matter of weeks, leaving a sizable debit in Loew's year-end balance sheet. But otherwise business was good, with Loew's profits in 1951 holding steady for the second straight year at over $7.5 million while the other majors saw their second straight decline in net revenues.

L O U I S M A Y E R was livid about his ouster as chief executive at MGM, the studio that he had built and nurtured, and that still carried his name. He was determined to show the movie community and the public that his filmmaking career was not yet over, and that he could adapt to a changing industry and marketplace if he had to—and clearly he did have to. The current rage in Hollywood was the biblical epic done in "spectactular" proportions. Paramount's *Samson and Delilah* and Fox's *David and Bathsheba* had topped the box-office charts in 1950 and 1951, respectively, and even Metro got into the act in 1951, with Mervyn LeRoy finally completing *Quo Vadis?* The MGM epic grossed over $10 million and was the consummate example of the Hollywood blockbuster, circa 1950. It was a European coproduction that exploited the "ancillary" foreign markets, was shot on location outside the United States to ease the tax bite and bypass the union salary scales, was based on an international best-seller, and offered viewers a spectacle they couldn't see on their TV sets.

After leaving Metro, Mayer put together his own company to produce "Joseph and His Brethren." He spent two years trying to get the biblical epic off the ground, and throughout its development he consulted with David Selznick. Mayer considered his former son-in-law the master among Hollywood's big-scale producers, and he also wanted to use Jennifer Jones, who now was wed to Selznick. Selznick's initial enthusiasm about "Joseph and His Brethren" steadily diminished. He did not doubt its commercial viability, but he became increasingly concerned about Mayer's temperament and his limitations as a movie producer. In a lengthy epistle written in October 1953, he outlined his concerns and advised Mayer to abandon the project. He also provided some insights into Mayer's career and the changing industry. Praising Mayer for his "enormous contribution" to the movie industry "in the building of a great machine," Selznick suggested that the old machinery was breaking down and being replaced, and he wasn't sure that Louis Mayer was able to retool.

"There are two, and only two, important types of manpower in motion pictures," said Selznick, "and they are equally rare: the great top executive and the great individual picture-maker." With the end of the old studio system, there was no longer a need for executives like Mayer, and there was no way a studio boss from the old system could compete with "individual picture-makers" like Goldwyn and Wyler and Huston. Selznick closed his missive with advice of a more personal nature: he urged Mayer to consider something outside the movie business. "Hoover, Warren, Eisenhower—these men are your intimate friends," Selznick reminded Mayer, and he suggested that Mayer consider public service, perhaps as a diplomat or statesman. Selznick also wondered whether the deposed mogul was lingering in Hollywood out of bad faith more than anything else. "I am not alone in thinking that you are letting your bitterness about your mistreatment at M-G-M color your thinking to a dangerous extent," confided Selznick. But as Selznick feared, Mayer persisted with his independent production efforts, which came to naught. Mayer never did make peace with himself or with Metro, and he carried his bitterness toward Schenck and Schary to his grave four years later.

S C H E N C K and Schary, for their parts, were as unwilling as Louis Mayer to accept the idea that MGM's "great machine" was winding down and that the old order was rapidly changing. And for the time being, at least, they seemed to be holding off the inevitable through sheer inertia. Schary himself, as central producer, symbolized the studio's commitment to the old order, and so did its contract system, its continued output of some forty in-house productions per annum, and its refusal to cooperate with the Supreme Court ruling and divorce its theater chain. By the time of Mayer's ouster, Schary had stabilized operations and the studio was turning solid, steady profits. But for all Schary's efforts, there was little continuity, quality, or sense of direction in MGM's output, other than the Freed-unit productions. When Mayer left the studio, Freed had three projects in the works—*An American in Paris, Show Boat,* and *Singin' in the Rain*—which would mark the height of MGM's musical golden age. All three were enormous critical and commercial hits, taking a collective $13 million and a slew of Academy Awards. The Freed unit's critical acclaim crested at the awards ceremony in early 1952, when *An American in Paris* was named best picture of 1951, the Irving Thalberg Award was given to Arthur Freed, and a special Oscar went to Hollywood's consummate hyphenate, Gene Kelly, "in appreciation of his versatility as an actor, singer, director, and dancer, and especially for his brilliant achievements in the art of choreography on film."

Louis Mayer received none of the accolades on Oscar night, though he deserved a few. He had nurtured Freed as a producer, had schooled him in the art of judicious but heavy spending, and had run interference in New York as Freed's musicals taxed the studio's resources. After Mayer's departure, both the quantity and the quality of Freed's productions dropped sharply. Following the three-picture burst in late 1951, it was a full year before Freed even initiated another production, and he averaged only one picture per year from 1953 until 1958. Four of them were Minnelli-directed musicals, none of which displayed the dynamic, imaginative qualities of the earlier Freed-Minnelli efforts. The last of these was *Gigi,* which was also the team's most successful collaboration, grossing over $10 million in its international release and winning a phenomenal ten Oscars in 1958, including Awards for best picture, best director, and best screenplay (Lerner). But *Gigi* was an oddly static and ponderous musical, devoid of the dance routines and high energy that characterized the best Freed-unit productions.

By this time, the MGM dance musical had run its course, having taken a last, frenetic gasp in 1955 with *It's Always Fair Weather,* Freed's last collaboration with Kelly and Donen. It was based on an original Comden and Green script about three service buddies who meet in New York ten years after the war, and thus was something of a rehash of *On the Town.* It was also an extended lampoon of the television and advertising industries, which were the dominant media institutions in New York in the mid-1950s. The price tag for *It's Always Fair Weather* was $2.45 million, it was in rehearsal for fifty-three days and in production for fifty-six, and it was in postproduction for a full eight months, mainly because of the elaborate split-screen effects used in several musical numbers. The results were marvelous, but the complex production's excessive cost and drain on resources was no longer justified by market demand. In 1955 it seemed that only reworked stage hits like *Guys and Dolls* and *The King and I* were scoring big at the box office. *It's Always Fair Weather* was very much a movie musical with no presold appeal, and it failed to turn a profit.

Not that MGM didn't try to sell the picture—and this raises what may have been the most significant aspect of this last-gasp effort. Even though *It's Always Fair Weather* satirized commercial television and advertising, it wound up playing a key role in MGM's foray into commercial TV production. A year earlier, during the 1954–55 television season, Disney had made the leap to television with *Disneyland*, an hour-long, weekly TV series on ABC. *Disneyland* was essentially an extended advertisement for the new amusement park, though it incorporated plugs for Disney's pictures as well. The series was a solid success, and it started Schenck and Schary thinking about TV as a means of promoting both their own studio and its products. Loew's/MGM cut a deal with ABC for *MGM Parade,* in which host George Murphy took viewers behind the scenes at Culver City and also pitched upcoming MGM releases. The series premiered in September 1955, and the movie it promoted in its premier show was *It's Always Fair Weather.*

The TV series fared no better than Freed's movie—both were commercial failures—but it did signal MGM's grudging acceptance of the burgeoning TV age and its willingness to adapt to America's changing media marketplace. For the following season *MGM Parade* was overhauled: It had Walter Pidgeon introducing serialized versions of classic MGM productions, from dramas like *Captains Courageous* to Freed-unit musicals like *The Pirate.* In an even more telling move, Loew's cut a deal with CBS in August 1956 to provide the first feature film to prime-time network TV in a complete telecast. The film was *The Wizard of Oz,* which was leased to the network for four telecasts at $225,000 per showing. There was an option clause in the *Oz* deal granting CBS another seven showings at $150,000 each, but neither Loew's nor CBS expected the film to sustain much appeal beyond its initial telecasts. *The Wizard of Oz* was first broadcast on November 3, 1956, and its ratings performance sent shock waves throughout the industry. Over one-third of America's 40 million television sets were tuned to CBS on that autumn evening—an indication that both the movie and TV industries had quite a bit to learn about their relationship, and quite a bit to offer one another.

Clearly movies could help satisfy TV's voracious appetite for programming, and with product that was superior to what was being offered. TV, on the other hand, could provide the studios with sizable amounts of cash for their stockpiles of old movies, whose shelf life and "resale value" had hardly been of any real concern before the new medium emerged. Actually RKO, which had been mismanaged into the ground by Howard Hughes and was now out of active movie production, had already stopped thinking of television in adversarial terms —in early 1956 it had sold off its film library to a TV syndication outfit for $15 million. Following suit over the next few months, the other majors unloaded their pre-1948 titles for upwards of $20 million. Loew's had held off, and after the *Oz* telecast it decided to hang on to most of its classic hits. But a few months later, MGM did release seven hundred of its lesser pre-1948 features to television for $25 million.

The *Oz* telecast and the subsequent sale of the old features to television confirmed the passing of the old order at Loew's/MGM, as did a number of personnel changes on both coasts. Nick Schenck had resigned in late 1955 after a half-century with Loew's, and he was succeeded by Arthur Loew, Marcus's son, another longtime executive with the company. Arthur Loew quickly became embroiled in a power

Clear signals of the changes at MGM and in the film industry at large in the late 1950s.

struggle with Joseph Vogel, who advocated an even more conciliatory rapport with the TV industry. Loew was forced out and replaced by Vogel only weeks after the *Oz* telecast, and before the year was out Vogel summoned Dore Schary to New York. With a "golden handshake" and a settlement of $1 million, Schary's reign as MGM production chief ended. His departure was inevitable, really, since his efforts to sustain a centralized production system no longer jibed with the studio's overall strategy. By then Loew's/MGM had resolved its differences not only with the TV industry but with the Justice Department as well, having finally divorced its theaters—the last of the majors to do so. MGM was also the last of the majors to phase out its studio contract personnel, a move that began in earnest after Schary's exit. So the studio era came to an abrupt end for MGM in the mid-1950s, and while Schary may have looked like another Thalberg during Metro's brief surge in the late 1940s and early 1950s, clearly the studio—and the industry at large—no longer had any use for the likes of Dore Schary, or for the kind of filmmaking that he advocated.

23

Universal:
Blueprint for the
Television Age

If any Hollywood studio was pre-
pared for the coming media age, it was Universal. With its long-standing dual agenda of low-cost formula pictures and A-class productions
via outside independents, Universal had been gearing up all along for
TV and the New Hollywood. No one at Universal quite realized this at
the time, of course, and certainly not when the new age was first upon
them. Universal was simply another company struggling to survive in
a rapidly changing industry, with no better sense than any other studio
of what the postwar conditions and the emergence of commercial television might bring. But during the decade-long transformation of the
film industry in the 1950s, the various studio powers gradually, inexorably, came round to Universal's mode of operation. Universal itself
was the most stable and consistent production company during this
period of flux and confusion, and by the time the media industries
began to restabilize in the early 1960s, Universal found itself in an
unprecedented position of strength. After a half-century as a second-
rate Hollywood power, Universal quite suddenly emerged as the indis-
putable leader in both television and movie production.

Universal's steadiness during the 1950s and its success in the early
1960s were the result not of any accurate forecasting of the industry's
direction but of economic necessity. Universal sustained its strategy of
low-budget in-house production and high-grade outside deals because
that was all the chronically weak studio could afford to do. From all

indications, Universal would have pursued much the same course as its chief competitors after the war, had it had the adequate resources, personnel, and financial leverage. The clearest indication of Universal's general uncertainty about postwar conditions and its impulse to adjust its production and market strategy came in 1946, with yet another of its ill-advised forays into first-run feature production. In August 1946, as the war boom was peaking, J. Cheever Cowdin and Nate Blumberg merged Universal with International Pictures, a modest independent company that specialized in prestige productions. The merger gave the studio a new management team in Leo Spitz and William Goetz, International's founder and chief executive, who upgraded in-house production at Universal City and increased the studio's reliance on outside producers for top features.

Universal already had contracts with independent filmmakers like Walter Wanger, Fritz Lang, and Mark Hellinger, who leased studio space and distributed through Universal on what were essentially co-productions. Now similar deals were cut with Ben Hecht, Garson Kanin, Sam Wood, Douglas Fairbanks, Jr., and others. Straight distribution arrangements also were made with a few British producers, notably Arthur Rank and Alexander Korda. In terms of Universal's own production operations, Spitz and Goetz eliminated subfeatures and set all features at a minimum of seventy minutes in length. Universal still turned out double-bill fare, but the quantity of low-grade features was scaled back along with the overall output. Universal and Columbia had averaged fifty releases per year during the war—roughly twice the output of the five majors. Columbia maintained this pace into the 1950s, but Universal cut its annual output to thirty-five pictures.

The results of the Universal-International merger were critically favorable but commercially disastrous. For the first time in a decade, Universal pictures were on ten-best lists and were contenders for major Oscars. Not since Deanna Durbin's initial rise in 1937–38 had any Universal release been nominated for best picture, best director, best actor, or best actress. Then from 1946 through 1948, Universal scored ten nominations in these categories. All ten came via outside producers or imports, and seven went to nominees who never set foot on the Universal City lot—including Laurence Olivier, who directed and starred in *Hamlet*, which won Oscars for best actor and best picture of 1948. By then it was evident that Universal could ill afford the high cost of critical prestige. The company had gone into a tailspin immediately after the merger, falling from record profits of $4.6 million in 1946 to a net loss of $3.2 million in 1948.

So it was back to basics at Universal in the late 1940s, back to low-cost formula jobs designed for the subsequent-run market. And it was back to the old management regime as well. The deals with outside producers were phased out, along with the management team of Spitz and Goetz—though the two did remain at Universal City. Production was now under the authority of longtime plant manager Edward Muhl, who in his two decades with the studio had seen Junior Laemmle, Charles Rogers, and Cliff Work come and go. Indeed, Muhl must have had a sense of déjà vu when *Hamlet* won the Academy Award for best picture of 1948. The last time Universal had won the best-picture Oscar was in 1931, for Junior Laemmle's production of *All Quiet on the Western Front*, and it, too, had represented a market strategy that the studio had just abandoned in favor of low-cost formula pictures. Muhl had supported the move back in the early 1930s, since it meant relying on the studio's own resources and accepting its limitations, and he felt the same way in the late 1940s. No more would Universal bank on imports or outside producers to milk the first-run market, which grew more competitive and uncertain by the month after the *Paramount* decree in May 1948. That Supreme Court ruling not only dis-integrated the majors, but also removed all constraints and studio controls over the movie marketplace, thus opening the first-run market to all comers. Soon there was a backlash effect as escalating rental prices for top features began forcing the smaller exhibitors to settle for second-rate product— which Universal now planned to supply. Revenues would be steady but modest, and neither Blumberg nor Muhl expected to be celebrating on Oscar night. They were right on both scores. Profits held through the 1950s, and Universal was the only active company among the Big Eight to go through the entire decade without even a nomination for best picture.

T H E initial impetus for Universal's retrenchment plan came with the unexpected emergence of Abbott and Costello. The comeback started in February 1948 with a project tentatively entitled "The Brain of Frankenstein." It was another Abbott and Costello genre parody, one that in its own unassuming way was rather innovative—a bit of generic recombination designed not only to give the duo a much-needed boost, but also to revive the horror formula and reverse the decline of its two key stars, Bela Lugosi and Lon Chaney, Jr. There were no serious hopes for the horror genre, of course, which seemed rather antiquated after Hiroshima and the birth of the Atomic Age. But Muhl was convinced that Abbott and Costello had plenty of mileage left in them, even though the comedy team had fallen from the exhibitors' poll in 1945 and been sliding ever since. After the war, Universal tried them in a costume picture, then in a sequel to *Buck Privates*, and even in a fantasy in which they were introduced separately and teamed up halfway through the story. None of these worked, so producer Robert Arthur got together with writer John Grant, who had collaborated on Abbott and Costello's initial hits, and the two worked out the idea for the horror-comedy.

In "The Brain of Frankenstein," the duo played railroad porters whose freight includes the encased forms of Dracula, the Wolf Man, and Frankenstein's monster. Abbott and Costello were their usual bumbling selves, while Lugosi and Chaney did straightforward horrific versions of their signature roles. The result was an oddly appealing mix of genre conventions and viewer reactions, melding the studio's two most familiar and stimulating formulas to create something truly unique—and something distinctly cost-effective as well. Arthur and company cranked out the picture in six weeks on a budget of $760,000, with Abbott and Costello's salaries the only heavy line item on the budget. The picture closed in March, and before its summer release it was retitled *Abbott and Costello Meet Frankenstein* to play up the comedy angle. Despite poor reviews the picture was a huge hit, and Abbott and Costello surged to number three in the 1948 exhibitors' poll. Not surprisingly, the hit was reformulated the following year in *Abbott and Costello Meet the Killer (Boris Karloff)*—another melding of stars and genres that gave the studio another low-cost, high-yield hit. It also enabled Abbott and Costello to retain third place, behind Hope and Crosby, on the exhibitors' poll. The "Abbott and Costello Meet . . ." formula held up into the 1950s, and so did the duo's marquee value. By then Dean Martin and Jerry Lewis had burst to stardom, pushing the public's fascination with buddy-buddy comedy teams to a new extreme. In 1951 six of the nation's eight most popular stars were Abbott and Costello, Hope and Crosby, and Martin and Lewis.

The comeback of Abbott and Costello intitiated an upswing for Universal which continued through 1949 and into the fifties. In fact, while the rest of the Big Eight saw their net revenues decline during the early-to-mid-1950s, Universal's income climbed steadily. The $3.2 million loss in 1948 was reduced to just over a million in 1949, and then the studio was back in the profit column for the next eight years. The surge marked a return to the Carl Laemmle era, with Universal exploiting its own resources, disdaining A-class production, and supplying subsequent-run houses with a steady diet of formula pictures and lowbrow family fare. Besides Abbott and Costello, Universal's biggest stars in 1949–50 were a hick family and a talking mule, whose pictures were reformulated with ruthless economy and redundancy—and which, more than anything else being produced in Hollywood at the time, set the tone for the dominant "programming" strategy on commercial television.

Lobby card for Abbott and Costello Meet Frankenstein *makes graphically clear the studio's effort to meld two established Universal formulas whose popularity was waning in the late 1940s.*

Universal's top hit of 1949 was *Ma and Pa Kettle,* a cut-rate farce that recast the postwar baby/family/housing boom in comic-surrealist terms. The unlikely hit starred the cantankerous Marjorie Main as Ma Kettle and Percy Kilbride as her put-upon husband. The Kettles were first introduced in *The Egg and I,* a 1947 screwball romance starring Claudette Colbert and Fred MacMurray as city slickers who move to the farm (a comic situation that was reworked for TV in the 1960s as *Green Acres*). When *The Egg and I* grossed $5.75 million, Universal tried a low-grade spin-off by bringing only the Kettles back for a sequel. Ma and Pa Kettle reversed the urban-rural dynamic of the earlier picture, as Pa's slogan for a tobacco company wins the Kettles and their fifteen unkempt offspring a modern home. The result was another hit. *Ma and Pa Kettle* took in $2.5 million at the box office, nearly ten times its production cost, initiating a series that ran through nine installments during the 1950s. It also inspired a crop of rural sitcoms on TV a decade later, notably *The Real McCoys* and *The Beverly Hillbillies.*

An even more unlikely series was sired in 1949 by Francis the Talking Mule, who wisecracked his way through seven pictures in seven years and earned millions for Universal. This series was also reworked into a barnyard sitcom for TV called *Mr. Ed*, which was produced and directed for CBS by longtime Universal staffer Arthur Lubin. Unlike the Kettle series, which was grafted from a successful first-run release, *Francis the Talking Mule* was a low-grade operation from the start. It was based on a popular novel about an inept Army lieutenant, played by Donald O'Connor, who is lost behind enemy lines during the Burma campaign. He is saved by an Army mule and winds up playing straight man to the mule's running commentary on Army life, modern warfare, military intelligence, and life in general. *Francis* was budgeted at $580,000 on a thirty-day schedule, and the producer-director team of Robert Arthur and Arthur Lubin was a logical choice, considering their track record with low-cost comedy pictures in general and the Abbott and Costello pictures of 1941–42 in particular.

Francis was essentially another buddy-buddy service comedy in the tradition of Abbott and Costello's early hits, only this time a jackass instead of Lou Costello was delivering the punch lines. Francis was "played" by Chill Wills, an experienced character actor and bit player who actually had a minor role in the original as an army sergeant. When Lubin and Arthur ran into trouble finding the right voice for Francis, they decided to test Wills, who had a distinctive gravel-voiced drawl. The effect was perfect—Chill Wills transformed Francis into a four-legged Will Rogers. Arthur convinced Muhl to pull Wills from the picture, reshoot his scenes with another actor, and pay him an additional $2,500 to record the Francis dialogue during postproduction. The dubbing was done in July 1949 and by September *Francis* was ready to preview. The previews went so well that before the picture was even released, Blumberg and Muhl had a sequel in the works.

The Francis, Ma and Pa Kettle, and Abbott and Costello pictures were produced by Robert Arthur, one of the five unit producers who dominated studio operations at Universal City during the 1950s. The others were Aaron Rosenberg, Ross Hunter, William Alland, and Albert Zugsmith, who along with Arthur accounted for over half (53 percent) of Universal's total output from 1952 to 1959. All five were genre specialists, and each had an appreciation for the efficiency and economy of formula production that came with the job at Universal. Robert Arthur handled most of the comedies along with the series jobs. Rosenberg did the more ambitious projects, most of which were outdoor adventures shot on location in color. Ross Hunter did the bigger in-house projects and served as a mentor to Rock Hudson as his star rose throughout the decade. Hunter also produced many of director Douglas Sirk's stylized romantic melodramas, several of which—notably *Magnificent Obsession* and *Imitation of Life*—were remakes of John Stahl's 1930s weepies. William Alland, who generally worked with director Jack Arnold, concentrated on low-budget westerns and science fiction films. Their westerns were eminently forgettable, but the sci-fi films included some of the studio's more interesting and timely efforts: *It Came from Outer Space, The Creature from the Black Lagoon,* and *This Island Earth.* These sci-fi films tapped into two long-standing Universal traditions, the horror genre and the old Flash Gordon and Buck Rogers serials—though Alland and Arnold infused them with a contemporary fascination with nuclear destruction and atomic radiation. Albert Zugsmith was the most flexible and least genre-bound of Universal's unit producers; he was a troubleshooter who took on a range of projects and produced a number of memorable films—from a modest sci-fi masterpiece like *The Incredible Shrinking Man* to Douglas Sirk's manic melodrama *Written on the Wind,* to Orson Welles's *noir* thriller, *Touch of Evil.*

U N I V E R S A L ' S heavy reliance on contract producers for its top productions during the 1950s was somewhat ironic, considering its earlier arrangements with free-lancers like Wanger, Hellinger, and Lang. Indeed, Universal had paved the way for the kind of outside deals that were becoming commonplace in Hollywood, as the other studios steadily shifted away from active production in favor of financing-and-distribution deals with independent producers, which generally involved the leasing of studio facilities as well. These deals were diminishing the studios' authority and fragmenting the overall power structure in the industry—they were the clearest sign of a burgeoning New Hollywood, free from absolute studio control. At first glance, Universal's disdain for outside producer deals seemed to indicate an effort to maintain the Old Hollywood, with its base of studio power and authority. But in fact Universal cut an unprecedented outside deal in the early 1950s that signaled an even more severe fragmentation of the industry's power structure. The deal was with James Stewart, who did a succession of pictures for Universal which made millions for the studio and made Stewart the biggest star in Hollywood.

The chief architect and key figure in the Stewart deal was not the star but his agent, Lew Wasserman of MCA. Not surprisingly, both stars and agents were becoming more powerful in 1950s Hollywood, as studios shifted to a picture-by-picture operation and as free-lance status became routine for top industry talent. Not only did films have to be sold to exhibitors and audiences on their own merits, but often enough the initial project was financed and produced on its perceived merits and market potential. The most reliable gauge of any project's market value, especially in the competitive and volatile first-run market, was the marquee value of its star. In fact, as studios increasingly went to outside deals, coproductions and the like, the "bankable" status of a star became more than just a figurative term. Banks, too, were adopting a picture-by-picture mentality, financing individual projects rather than a studio's annual output or a production company at large. Invariably, such picture deals were built around individual stars and were packaged by talent agents. In fact, if any institution now had a long-term stake in a star's career, it was more likely to be a talent agency like MCA than a movie studio.

Music Corporation of America (MCA) had been created by Jules Stein back in the mid-1920s to handle bookings and promotion for Chicago-area bands. Stein steadily expanded his business and by the early 1940s MCA was becoming a force in Hollywood, thanks largely to Stein's protégé, Lew Wasserman, who joined MCA in 1936 at age twenty-two. By 1950 MCA was the dominant agency in Hollywood and Wasserman its most important agent—he was, as Stein put it, "the student who surpassed the teacher." Like Myron Selznick, Wasserman reveled in his ability to dicker with studio bosses and jack up his clients' salaries. It was Wasserman, for instance, who convinced Jack Warner to increase the salaries of Errol Flynn and Bette Davis after the war, when their careers were fading. And as these and scores of other contract stars went free-lance in the 1940s and 1950s, it was Wasserman who shaped their careers and packaged their talents. Thus he surpassed Myron Selznick and moved into David's bailiwick, playing agent and packager and even producer. By the early 1950s MCA had more talent under contract than any studio, and Wasserman was putting together more projects and star vehicles than any filmmaker or studio executive in Hollywood.

Of the countless free-lance deals that Wasserman engineered during the early 1950s, the Stewart-Universal deal was perhaps the most important. Like so many stars at the time, Stewart was looking for a degree of independence and control over his career, and also a way to avoid huge tax payments and thus to maximize his annual income. And as the profit potential of Hollywood's big pictures went up, Wasserman was looking for ways to tie his clients' income to the market performance of their pictures. Stewart's asking price by 1950 was $200,000 per picture, which was a considerable sum but hardly reflected his real value to a movie that grossed four or five million. Wasserman came up with the idea of having Stewart forgo an up-front salary on his pictures in lieu of a percentage of the net profits—in Stewart's case, a full 50 percent. These deferred payments would be tied to the economic life span of a film. Thus Stewart's income could be spread over two or three years, or even more if the film was sold to television. This strategy made good sense given the changing industry and marketplace, and it made especially good sense to Universal. The deal enabled the studio to produce top-star vehicles without paying a star-level salary up front, and payments could be avoided altogether if the picture failed to turn a profit.

The Stewart-Universal deal resulted in a string of hits during the 1950s, including *Winchester '73, Harvey, Bend of the River, The Far Country, The Glenn Miller Story,* and *Thunder Bay,* which were as close to first-run releases as anything in Universal's schedule. Many were done in Technicolor and wide-screen and were shot on location, and thus they could compete with the lavish spectacles that the other studios were releasing. Stewart's Universal pictures gave a sizable boost to his own marquee value as well as his annual income. In fact, for several years running he was both the highest paid and the most bankable star in Hollywood. Stewart first cracked the exhibitors' poll in 1950, and in 1955 he was named the industry's top box-office star. But significantly enough, Stewart was by no means a Universal "house" star at the time. He had a nonexclusive agreement with the

James Stewart, Universal's top star in the early 1950s, looks over the menu in the studio commissary with Shelley Winters, his costar in Winchester '73.

studio, and some of his best work in the mid-1950s was done with Alfred Hitchcock at Paramount—through an elaborate deal also arranged by Lew Wasserman. What's more, Wasserman persuaded Universal to let Stewart take Anthony Mann with him to do a few of their distinctive westerns for other studios: *The Naked Spur* for MGM in 1952 and *The Man from Laramie* for Columbia in 1955.

T H E Stewart deal was the most obvious manifestation at Universal of the fragmentation and shifting power relations in Hollywood during the early 1950s. An equally important behind-the-scenes development was a change in the ownership and management at Universal. In 1950 J. Cheever Cowdin retired as board chairman, and after he left there was considerable maneuvering for control of Universal both inside and outside the company. In 1951 Milton Rackmil, president of Decca Records, began buying Universal stock, including the holdings of Spitz and Goetz, who no longer fit into the studio's plans. Rackmil gained majority control in 1952, making Universal a subsidiary in Decca's entertainment conglomerate. He replaced Blumberg in New York, while Spitz and Goetz were replaced at Universal City by Ed Muhl.

While the James Stewart deal had signaled the newfound clout of stars and talent agencies in the early 1950s, the Decca takeover indicated the importance of diversification. Significantly enough, before the 1950s it had been the integrated majors that were most concerned about diversifying their media interests—and that had the finances and the power to even consider it. All of the majors had certain arrangements with electronics and broadcasting companies dating back to the rise of network radio and talking pictures in the late 1920s. Indeed, RKO's birth in 1928 represented an effort by RCA to expand its media interests beyond its radio subsidiary, NBC. The rise of television brought new opportunities for diversification, and again the majors led the way. Paramount and Warner Bros. were particularly aggressive in their efforts to exploit the emergent medium, with plans to buy TV stations in major markets and to develop video projection systems for their theaters so as to reduce the costs and complexity of film distribution. These plans were dashed by the Supreme Court's 1948 *Paramount* decree. Theater projection was clearly off the agenda after the Supreme Court ordered the majors to divest themselves of their theater holdings, and the government also undercut the studios' efforts to buy television stations. Regulation of commercial TV was in the hands of the Federal Communications Commission (FCC), which had the authority to deny station licenses to anyone charged with monopoly or antitrust practices. The FCC informed the Hollywood majors that it would block any of their efforts to reintegrate via TV station ownership, nor would it approve cross-ownership between studios and networks. The majors could supply television programs, of course, but they had no desire to play a game they could not control. So they abandoned their plans to diversify into commercial television altogether, and soon they were regarding the medium in competitive rather than cooperative terms.

With the majors out of the television scene, Hollywood's general courtship of the burgeoning industry actually intensified. Lesser studios and producers were eager to supply TV programming, and their more modest and cost-efficient operations were actually better suited to the demands and constraints of the new medium. TV had an enormous appetite for product, and the concerns about production values were minimal. So low-budget studios like Republic and Hal Roach Studios quickly retooled for "telefilm" production in the late 1940s, and they also began selling or leasing their old features and shorts for TV showings. Roach's was among the first converted movie companies to actually get a TV series on the air. A subsidiary, Hal Roach Television Corporation, was set up to produce *Fireside Theater*, which debuted on NBC in April 1949. This was an "anthology drama" modeled after successful TV series like *Kraft Television Theatre* and *Studio One* —live shows done in New York which presented a different hour-long drama each week. The obvious and important difference was that the Hal Roach series was shot on film in Hollywood rather than live from New York, and thus it could be shown at any time after production. (Video*tape*, which would allow for delayed broadcast of video productions, was still in the research-and-development stage and was not introduced until 1956–57.) Given the state of video production techniques circa 1950, Roach's telefilm dramas also had superior production values. But the dramas themselves were modest efforts. Each half-hour installment usually included two fifteen-minute vignettes that were produced in two or three days with the same speed and economy that had characterized Roach's two-reel comedy shorts starring Our Gang and Laurel and Hardy.

Hollywood's two major minors were equally interested in telefilm production, although they took a somewhat more cautious approach. Both Universal and Columbia set up subsidiaries in New York City in the late 1940s to produce TV advertisements. Universal moved its subsidiary to Los Angeles in 1949, but continued producing only TV ads. That same year Columbia created Screen Gems, a Hollywood-based telefilm company designed to produce entertainment programming. Screen Gems started actual TV series production in 1951, and by then the telefilm competition in Hollywood was rather intense. In September 1951 *Broadcasting* magazine, a television trade journal, reported that there were seventy-five independent telefilm companies in the L.A. area. Twenty-five of these had sold a total of forty series to the TV networks for the 1951–52 season, at an average cost of $15,000 per episode—and this in an era when movie budgets routinely surpassed a million dollars and B-movie costs were generally in the $250,000 range. In January 1952 *Variety* reported "the gradual but definite stabilization" of Hollywood-based telefilm production. According to *Variety*, "the 80-odd vidfilm companies existing in these parts in early 1951 have boiled down to around 20 financially stable outfits."

Those stable outfits included companies that would ascend to positions of considerable power in the next few years, although they barely qualified as B-movie units at the time. Perhaps the best example of such a company was Desilu Productions, which came virtually out of nowhere in the early 1950s and by 1957 had bought RKO and was producing far more hours of filmed entertainment than any of the established studio powers. The motivating force behind Desilu was Desi Arnaz, who represented a new breed of studio executive in 1950s Hollywood, although Desilu itself was something of a throwback to the B-movie factories of old. *I Love Lucy* and Desilu got started when, in 1949, CBS asked Lucille Ball to bring her popular CBS radio series, *My Favorite Wife,* to television. Ball was interested, but she refused to work in New York or to costar with anyone but her husband, Desi Arnaz. The deal stalled, so Arnaz decided to create Desilu and produce the series himself. Working out of a Hollywood rental facility, General Services Studio, Arnaz did a pilot for *I Love Lucy* that convinced CBS and a sponsor, Philip Morris, to back the series. They signed Desilu to deliver thirty-nine episodes of *Lucy* in 1951–52 on a budget of $24,500 per episode.

Premiering in September 1951, *I Love Lucy* was TV's first runaway hit series and the technical and narrative prototype for TV's foundation genre, the situation comedy. For director of cinematography, Arnaz had hired Karl Freund, who was sufficiently intrigued by the challenge of doing a respectable half-hour of film on such a demanding schedule and limited budget that he came out of semiretirement to do the series. CBS wanted a live audience and agreed to put up $50,000 to renovate a General Services sound stage so that it would seat some three hundred spectators. Arnaz and Freund worked out a system whereby each episode could be performed almost as a stage play—in a single evening, in continuity, and in front of an audience—while it was filmed by three cameras running at once. Later the processed film was run through three interlocked editing machines. This obviously cut the time, effort, and expense of both production and editing, and indeed it proved efficient enough to bring the series in on time and only about

Desi Arnaz, the moving force behind Desilu, represented a new breed of studio mogul in 1950s Hollywood.

$250 per episode over budget. All thirty-nine episodes were produced for $965,000, well below the going rate for a single first-run feature at the time. And though the results may have been subpar by feature filmmaking standards, they were vastly superior to the live video productions of the era. Besides the superior quality of the filmed series relative to video, this process also resulted in a tangible product that could be rebroadcast with no loss of quality. (Video, conversely, could only be rebroadcast via kinescope, a crude method of simply filming a video image.) At a point when the TV industry was just discovering the tremendous value of reruns, this made the telefilm series that much more attractive.

I Love Lucy was phenomenally popular, consistently drawing some two-thirds of the viewing audience and setting one milestone after another in TV's early years. In April 1952, for example, *Lucy* became the first show to reach ten million U.S. households and to be seen by at least thirty million viewers. When *I Love Lucy* hit, Arnaz immediately went to work on another telefilm series, *Our Miss Brooks*, which was adapted from a popular radio sitcom starring Eve Arden. The show debuted in October 1952 and gave Desilu another solid hit. By the following season Desilu had signed production contracts with several star-producers, including Danny Thomas, Loretta Young, Ray Bolger, and Jack Benny. Because of the growing production commitments, Arnaz moved Desilu out of the General Services facility and leased six sound stages in L.A.'s Motion Picture Center, each of which was renovated to accommodate a studio audience. Desilu continued to turn out its own series as well, which by 1955 included another sitcom, *December Bride;* a crime drama, *The Lineup;* and a western, *The Life and Legend of Wyatt Earp.* By then the company's annual output was approaching 350 half-hour episodes—far beyond what any Hollywood movie studio was turning out, and at only a fraction of the cost.

N I N E T E E N fifty-five, a watershed year in filmmaking history, marked the end of the majors' resistance to active television production and thus the beginning of a full-scale transformation and recolonization of Hollywood. The process had already begun, of course, but not until the big movie studios threw in did Hollywood really embrace the TV industry. The turnaround actually happened fairly quickly—in fact, early in 1955 it looked as if the networks and the major Hollywood powers were still very much at odds. *Fortune* magazine ran a piece in February, "The Comeback of the Movies," which expressed the conventional wisdom at the time regarding the big studios' market fix and their attitude to TV. *Fortune* noted the tremendous success of recent blockbuster movies and also of such recent technological developments as CinemaScope, Cinerama, and 3-D. The six-year decline in theater attendance finally seemed to have bottomed out at roughly forty-five million per week—barely half the mid-1940s total, but sufficient to keep the industry moving. Net revenues were up as well, with the combined profits of Hollywood's seven leading movie companies jumping from $23 million in 1953 to $34.6 million in 1954. From *Fortune's* perspective, the studios' success intensified their resolve to combat television. It was also suggested that among Hollywood's power brokers, only Universal's Milton Rackmil had an interest in TV series production. The closing paragraph of the article asserted: "Rackmil is perfectly honest when he says that he never thought of television as a threat to the movies, but his brother executives in the pictures felt differently. Their present scorn of television is the best evidence of their fear of it."

The *Fortune* piece was misleading for two important reasons. For one thing, Rackmil and Universal had no real plans to get into TV series production, even though the studio's formula and series fare provided a virtual blueprint for telefilm production. And for another, Rackmil's "brother executives" were by now well past feelings of fear or scorn regarding the TV industry. There was no longer any denying that televison was an idea whose time had come. The medium's penetration of American domestic life had already reached 67 percent—fully two-thirds of all the homes in the United States had TV sets—and this figure would continue rising as the cost of television sets declined and as both transmission and reception of broadcast signals improved. The quality of the programming also was improving. In fact, when the *Fortune* piece appeared in February 1955, the big studios were still gauging the impact of three crucial events that had occurred back in October 1954. On October 3, Screen Gems premiered its most promising series yet, *Father Knows Best*, a domestic comedy-drama built around former MGM star Robert Young. Three weeks later on Sunday the twenty-fourth, David Selznick made TV history with his production, "Light's Diamond Jubilee," a two-hour spectacular celebrating the seventy-fifth birthday of Edison's invention of the light bulb. Selznick's production, which aired simultaneously on all the networks, drew the largest audience in TV's brief history. Then three nights later, Walt Disney Studio premiered its flagship series, *Disneyland.*

All three events helped shake the Hollywood powers out of their complacency, but *Disneyland*'s impact was unquestionably the most pronounced. The show was an instant hit, and in early 1955 its popularity was peaking with the second and third installments of Disney's Davy Crockett saga. Like all of the weekly *Disneyland* segments, these were designed to promote one area of the recently completed theme park—in this case, Frontierland. The movie bosses were impressed by the general quality of *Disneyland*, and also with the framework it provided for recycling old product. But more than anything else, what impressed them was the promotional angle. They saw *Disneyland* as a sustained advertisement for the studio, the new amusement park, and the upcoming Disney films.

The Disney series proved to be something of a catalyst. Three of the majors—Warners, Fox, and MGM—started planning series of their own for the following season. *Warner Brothers Presents, The 20th Century-Fox Hour,* and *MGM Parade* all premiered in the fall of 1955, and they had two significant factors in common: They rehashed previous studio hits, and they actively promoted both the studio and its upcoming releases. *MGM Parade* provided a weekly behind-the-scenes glimpse of the studio and the moviemaking process. There were occasional excerpts from classic Metro pictures, but the emphasis was on the current output. *The 20th Century-Fox Hour* was basically an anthology drama that presented condensed, scaled-down remakes of earlier Fox hits. *Warner Brothers Presents* also relied on classic studio releases for its subject matter, but with a very different approach—and that difference proved crucial. Warners adapted three of its old films,

Casablanca, Kings Row, and *Cheyenne*, into ongoing series with continuing characters, rotating each week from exotic romance and intrigue *(Casablanca)* to small-town melodrama *(Kings Row)* to the Old West *(Cheyenne)*.

The Fox, Metro, and Warners series were major disappointments for all involved—for the studios, the networks, the sponsors, and the public. Somehow the self-promotion that was working so well for Disney simply didn't play for the other studios. The success of *Disneyland* was due largely to the appeal of the park itself, of course, which was quickly becoming a national institution. But the other studios' rehashed classics, studio tours, and endless promotion only turned off viewers—who promptly turned off their sets. Sponsors, too, were unhappy with the studios' self-promotion, since it diluted the strength of their own "commercial interruptions." So after that first season, at the behest of both the networks and sponsors, all three shows were revamped. But only Warners was willing to abandon the self-promotional format altogether and go with straightforward series production.

This was a tough decision for Jack Warner, because as he'd said in October 1955, the studio went into telefilm production "chiefly and only to secure advertisements through television" for its big-budget features. But that attitude quickly changed, as TV proved unfavorable as a means of pitching feature films, and also as the high-stakes movie market and the telefilm market came into clearer focus. Warner and his fellow studio bosses were increasingly concerned about their loss of control over the changing movie industry, with its wide-open markets and rising budgets, its free-lance talent and packaging agents, its outside deals and location shoots. These and other factors signaled the end not only of the studio system at large—that is, the integrated system of production, distribution, and exhibition—but also the end of the efficient, regulated, studio-based mode of production.

Telefilm series production was clearly one way to keep the studio system alive, at least where the production facilities themselves were concerned. Outfits like Desilu and Screen Gems were proving that TV series could be cranked out efficiently and profitably—that for studios like Warners or Fox or MGM they could serve much the same purpose as the 1930s-era B-movie unit. The constraints and product demands were severe; indeed, ABC had paid Warners only $86,000 for each hour-long episode in 1955–56. But if Warners and the other studios increased and further standardized telefilm production, they could stabilize studio operations and offset the rising costs of feature film-making. Television was also providing the Hollywood studios with a short-term boost in operating revenue after 1955, as they unloaded their pre-1948 features for programming fodder. All of the studios had opened their vaults by early 1958, with Paramount scoring the last and the richest deal when it leased 750 features to MCA for $50 million. *Variety* reported in October 1958 that some 9,200 features had been sold or leased to TV syndication companies. The feature film libraries of the TV stations in New York City alone contained 4,800 titles in 1958, and it was estimated that 25 percent of all sponsored television programming that year was made up of Hollywood movies.

B Y late 1958 all the studios had unloaded sizable portions of their vaults, and all but one had gone into TV series production. That one notable and most ironic exception was Universal, without question the movie studio best disposed to TV series production in terms of both production process and type of product. Universal had been leasing its facilities to telefilm producers for years, most notably Revue Productions, a subsidiary of MCA. Both Rackmil and Muhl were as eager as ever to make the leap into telefilm production themselves, but the company simply lacked the capital to produce TV series of its own. This was a major frustration for an old-timer like Ed Muhl, who stood by while the other studios adopted the series strategy for their telefilm productions that Universal had been refining for decades—and that Universal now had running to near perfection with its genre units and its Kettle and Francis series.

Universal finally did move into telefilm production in 1959, though scarcely by its own volition or on its own terms. In February 1959 MCA bought the studio itself, Universal City, from Decca Records. At the same time Jules Stein initiated a takeover of Decca and Universal Pictures, which he expected to take at least a year or two. For the time being, he was content simply to secure Universal City, since MCA sorely needed a studio facility for Revue Productions. The telefilm company had grown rapidly, and by 1958 Revue was producing one-third of NBC's prime-time schedule—eight-and-one-half hours of programming per week. Universal City gave MCA-Revue a centralized production facility, and it gave Lew Wasserman a suitable base for his ever expanding West Coast operations. Wasserman was now generally considered the most powerful man in Hollywood, and MCA was considered a model of diversification. The two judgments were not unrelated. Largely through Wasserman's machinations and his stable of clients, MCA had its fingers in as many pies as the Hollywood entertainment industry could bake—from movies and TV to publishing and pop music.

The MCA takeover of Universal City left Universal Pictures flush with capital and looking to a much brighter future—albeit one that the company could scarcely determine or control. Universal Pictures was still independent and separate from MCA, at least in a technical sense, with Rackmil and Muhl running the company and leasing studio production space from MCA. Some of Universal's top talent stayed on and a few of its established units and star-genre formulations remained intact, but feature output was cut by 50 percent—from thirty-five features in 1958 to only eighteen in 1959 and in the ensuing years. While output was reduced, budgets were jacked up to a point where even an Audie Murphy western or a sci-fi thriller was starting to look respectable. And unit producer Ross Hunter's pictures were now in another league altogether, judging from such 1959 releases as *Imitation of Life* and *Pillow Talk*. The former was a lavish remake of John Stahl's 1934 weepie that was among the biggest hits of the year, grossing over $6 million. *Pillow Talk* was an equally slick romantic comedy that teamed Rock Hudson and Doris Day, the top two box-office stars in the industry.

The unit-produced genre pictures, like the telefilm series, had their roots in the old Universal City factory system, but another production just after the MCA deal indicated how genuinely independent top-feature production was becoming even at Universal. The picture was *Spartacus*, a $12 million spectacular that went into production in early 1959 and finally was released in late 1960. This was an unprecedented production by Universal's standards, and its packaging was equally unconventional—though it was very much in line with current blockbusters like *Ben-Hur* and *Cleopatra*. *Spartacus* was a European coproduction put together by an outside producer, Edward Lewis, and directed by maverick free-lancer Stanley Kubrick. Much of the film was shot in Spain, and several in its international all-star cast owned a piece of the production. The picture was a sizable gamble—though not as sizable as *Cleopatra*, the Fox production that was driving that company to the verge of bankruptcy. In Universal's case the gamble paid off. *Spartacus* was a worldwide success, amassing net profits of over $14 million on its international release. As happened with so many projects after the takeover, though, Universal served as no more than the nominal producer, providing production facilities, personnel, and distribution. Thus *Spartacus* was by no means a "Universal picture" in any traditional sense.

There were precious few of those as the decade wore on and Universal fell in step with the other studios, turning out costly and distinctive pictures, most of them outside productions for an increasingly competitive and unstable movie market. Before long the clearest vestige of the old Universal operation was in telefilm production, with series like *The Virginian, Leave It to Beaver,* and *The Jack Benny Show* rolling off the Revue assembly line. Indeed, the facilities and personnel at

Universal City were so well suited to telefilm-series production that within two to three years of the initial MCA takeover, Universal was the most productive and profitable studio in Hollywood. Profits had started climbing as soon as MCA bought the studio facility in 1959, and in 1962, the year MCA completed the Decca-Universal buyout, studio profits jumped from a 1961 record high of $7.5 million to $12.7 million. That total, which included both feature and telefilm production, made Universal the unquestioned leader in the film industry. After a half-century as a second-rate power, Universal was quite literally in a class by itself among the Hollywood studios.

But Universal wasn't really a movie studio anymore—none of them were in this age of diversification and conglomeration. Universal's alliance with MCA-Revue ensured its continued dominance in Hollywood, but it also signaled a fragmentation of the film industry and the loss of studio control over the system at large. The TV networks had a lock on programming control, and independent filmmakers and packaging agents were calling the shots on most movie production. The studios were still key players, to be sure. They had the best production facilities in the business and, even more important, they still controlled film distribution and thus had considerable power over the movie marketplace. But the "studio system" that Universal and the others had built and maintained for decades was all but gone. The studios would survive—as production plants, as distribution companies, as familiar trademarks—but the studio era had ended, and with it Hollywood's classical age.

24

Epilogue:
Into the New Hollywood

Television was obviously a mixed blessing for Hollywood, revitalizing studio-based production but bringing a decisive end to the studio system as Hollywood had known it. For top industry talent, particularly the leading producers, directors, and stars, declining studio control meant unprecedented freedom and opportunity. This same contingent had mounted the first real challenge to the studios' collective authority back in the early 1940s, when they began going free-lance as a matter of routine. That brought greater leverage over their careers and their pictures, and a taste of autonomy and creative freedom as well. But not until the courts and the TV industry disintegrated the studio system altogether did these filmmakers gain any real independence.

Among Hollywood's top talent, no one made the transition into the New Hollywood more successfully than Alfred Hitchcock. Certainly none was better prepared. Hitchcock was the only major producer-director from the studio era who had never worked as a house director under long-term studio contract. Thus he had developed his administrative and business skills, and he was accustomed to dealing with studios as rental facilities and distribution companies. Equally important, Hitchcock had already developed his own trademark style. By the 1950s a "Hitchcock picture" was a known commodity in the movie marketplace, a story type and narrative technique that had become familiar to millions of viewers. That put Hitchcock at a tremendous advantage as the very notion of film style shifted from a studio-based to an individual context. Hitchcock continued to exploit that advantage in the 1950s, steadily adjusting his style to suit the changing marketplace. In fact Hitchcock's career throughout the decade, and especially the five-year trajectory from the 1955 debut of his TV series, *Alfred Hitchcock Presents,* to the release of *Psycho* in 1960, well indicated the options and opportunities available to Hollywood's leading filmmakers as the studio era wound down.

H I T C H C O C K began the 1950s as an in-house independent at Warners, supplying them with first-run features like *Strangers on a Train* and *Dial M for Murder.* Although he was very much an independent, he did have the benefit of stable management via his agent, Lew Wasserman. Hitchcock also assembled a production unit during the 1950s which was crucial to the development of his "personal" style. During Hitchcock's tenure at Warners, two key members of that unit came aboard: cinematographer Robert Burks and editor George Tomasini. In 1953 Hitchcock moved to Paramount on an innovative and very lucrative nine-picture deal set up by Wasserman which gave Hitchcock ownership of five of those pictures after their initial release. Hitchcock began at Paramount with two romantic thrillers: *Rear Window* (1954), costarring Grace Kelly and James Stewart, and *To Catch a Thief* (1955) with Kelly and Cary Grant. Both were hits, and it looked as if more would be coming. Hitchcock was gaining the confidence of the industry's biggest stars, whom Wasserman invariably could deliver, and he had added several more key members to his production unit: assistant director (and later associate producer) Herbert Coleman, costume designer Edith Head, and screenwriter John Michael Hayes.

With the move to Paramount, there was also a certain refinement of Hitchcock's style and story formula. He was now working with larger budgets and thus with higher production values. His films generally were done in Technicolor with elaborate sets and costumes, and they included exotic location work. Hayes's scripts were a masterful blend of romantic comedy and suspense; unlike the heavy dramas done by Hecht and others, these were lighter stories with considerably more emphasis on the romance. But still the essential Hitchcock elements were there, particularly the innocent bystander who is drawn, unawares and in broad daylight, into some inexplicable intrigue. Somehow that intrigue forces the protagonist to come to terms with himself as well as with the governing enigma, and thus the mystery involves not only an outward search—a chase after the elusive "MacGuffin"—but also an inward search. Equally evident was the characteristic Hitchcock technique, a delicate interplay of subjective camera work, whereby the audience is tied to the consciousness and viewpoint of the protagonist, and an occasional, curious omniscience—a bemused detachment from the protagonist which puts the viewer in league with Hitchcock the narrator.

Hitchcock was so pleased with the setup at Paramount that when Wasserman came to him in 1955 with the idea of doing a TV series, Hitchcock resisted. His moviemaking was going exceptionally well, he had little interest in television, and his Paramount unit was hardly suited to telefilm production. But Wasserman suggested that the TV series be done with another unit altogether, housed at Universal in MCA's telefilm company, Revue Productions. What's more, the series could be produced along the lines of the publishing ventures Wasserman had been setting up, whereby Hitchcock licensed his name and his "likeness" to publishers of mystery magazines and short-story anthologies. Although some of these included prefaces and such written under Hitchcock's name, he had virtually nothing to do with them. Wasserman conceived of the TV series in much the same terms: an anthology of thrillers and mysteries which would trade on the filmmaker's name, his style, and his familar visage.

Hitchcock finally acquiesced when CBS and Bristol-Myers agreed to put up $129,000 per half-hour episode, and to grant him full ownership of each series installment after its initial telecast. Hitchcock's only obligations were to serve as nominal executive producer and script supervisor, and to personally introduce each episode. Hitchcock brought his former coscenarist Joan Harrison out of retirement to handle actual production, though he did provide some of the series' key elements. Hitchcock designed the silhouette caricature of himself which became the show's logo, and he also came up with the idea of using Gounod's "Funeral March of a Marionette" as the musical theme. Most important were Hitchcock's deadpan comedy routines. Scripted by free-lancer James B. Allardice, these opened and closed each episode, framing the drama and often providing crucial narrative information in a delightfully offhand way. They also reinforced Hitchcock's public image as a witty, sardonic curmudgeon who refused to take the show, the sponsors, the network, or even himself very seriously.

Alfred Hitchcock Presents was an immediate success, and by the 1956–57 season it was the sixth-rated show on television. Hitchcock's involvement remained minimal, and he had no illusions about its production values. With each half-hour episode being shot in three days, Hitchcock acknowledged that "there can be no comparable quality" relative to movie production. There were no top stars nor dazzling techniques in the TV series, no location shooting nor Technicolor. But there were certain key elements of the familiar Hitchcock style. Each

"Good evening . . ." Hitchcock introduces another installment of Alfred Hitchcock Presents, *which was shot at the MCA-Revue Studio on the Universal lot.*

episode was a modest thriller, usually a psychological study of an offbeat character caught up in some weird or threatening situation. The
series writers exploited Hitchcock's penchant for wry humor and plot
reversals, with Hitchcock himself often supplying a final twist in his
closing monologue. And despite the production constraints and the
somewhat mechanical reformulation of Hitchcock's style, the series did
provide a kind of exposure that his movies, whatever their success,
simply could not. The series delivered Hitchcock to millions of viewers, week after week, transforming him into a veritable culture industry
unto himself and his name into a trademark that was more meaningful
in the media marketplace than that of any studio.

While the Revue telefilm crew reproduced the Hitchcock style in watered-down half-hour installments over at Universal City, Hitchcock concentrated his own energies on the Paramount features, most of which were ambitious productions with the size and scope of the New Hollywood blockbusters. The highlights of this period were two James Stewart vehicles, *The Man Who Knew Too Much* (1956) and *Vertigo* (1958), and also a huge hit with Cary Grant, *North by Northwest* (1959). The latter was produced not at Paramount but at MGM—another indication of how arbitrary and tenuous Hitchcock's relationship was with any one studio. Indeed, by then Hitchcock's primary affiliation clearly was not with a studio but with Wasserman and MCA. Like the Paramount releases, *North by Northwest* was a Wasserman package involving several of MCA's top clients, notably Hitchcock, Grant, and screenwriter Ernest Lehman. Wasserman also arranged to bring Hitchcock's key collaborators—Robert Burks, George Tomasini, Herbert Coleman, and composer Bernard Herrmann—from Paramount to MGM for the picture.

The *North by Northwest* deal was a striking indication of the changing power structure and production values in Hollywood, particularly where top stars and filmmakers were concerned. Grant and Hitchcock each received a flat fee for the picture—Hitchcock's was $250,000, Grant's $450,000—with the payments spread out over three years to ease the tax bite. Each also would earn 10 percent of all gross receipts above $8 million, to be paid in annual installments starting January 1962. MGM would provide the facilities and finance the picture, which was easily Hitchcock's most ambitious production to date. The initial budget for *North by Northwest* was set at $3.1 million for a sixty-day shoot, with twenty days on location in New York, Chicago, South Dakota, and elsewhere in California. Not surprisingly, the costs gradually mounted once the picture went into production. It ran twenty days behind schedule, and by the time it was ready for release in April 1959, costs had reached $4.3 million. There were no complaints from the studio, however, since MGM would recoup its investment "off the top" —that is, out of the initial box-office returns—and as far as the Metro powers were concerned, a Hitchcock-Grant project was money in the till.

Screenwriter Ernest Lehman, though new to the Hitchcock unit, well understood Hitchcock's unique commodity value—as a personality, a signature style, and a particular kind of movie experience. Lehman said that in writing *North by Northwest*, he was after "the Hitchcock picture to end all Hitchcock pictures . . . with glamour, wit, excitement, movement, big scenes, a large canvas, innocent bystander caught up in great derring-do, in the *Hitchcock* manner." The story

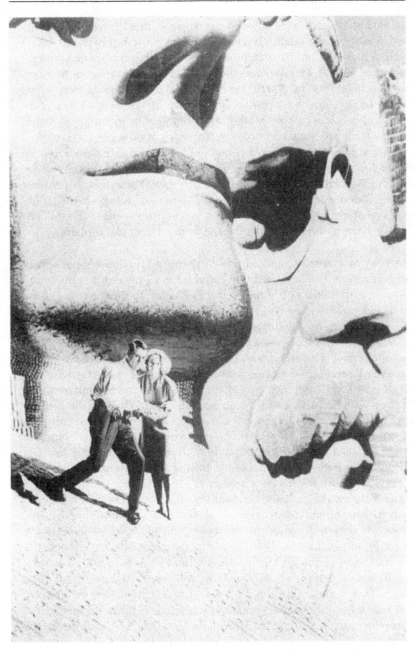

North by Northwest, *like most of Hitchcock's feature films in the late 1950s, was a star vehicle of blockbuster proportions.*

was an ideal melding of romance and geopolitical intrigue, with its Cold War spy story gradually yielding to the courtship between Grant and Eva Marie Saint. The outcome of that courtship is obvious throughout—one needn't look beyond the opening credits to figure that out. The predictability of *North by Northwest*'s outcome is part of its charm, finally, and so is the predictability of Hitchcock's signature style. Lehman's script resonated with memorable moments and plot devices from previous Hitchcock pictures, right down to the last cliffhanging moment as the hero reached out to save a figure dangling from Mount Rushmore—invoking the finale of *Saboteur*, only there the national monument had been the Statue of Liberty. *North by Northwest* also included a few very original set pieces, including one of Hitchcock's most memorable: the legendary crop-duster scene, as Grant flees across a barren midwestern landscape from a homicidal biplane.

NORTH BY NORTHWEST marked a high point in Hitchcock's popularity and commercial success, and few could have suspected that he would follow it with the likes of *Psycho*. But Lehman's reference to it as "the Hitchcock picture to end all Hitchcock pictures" turned out to be oddly prescient. *North by Northwest* did mark the end of an era, with *Psycho* taking Hitchcock's career—and the industry at large—in another direction altogether. The story, adapted from a recent Robert Bloch novel, concerned one Marion Crane, a woman of dubious character who embezzles $40,000 from her employer and leaves town, apparently to meet up with her divorced lover in a nearby city. While on the run she stops at a deserted motel, and after a soul-searching conversation with the motel proprietor, a singularly odd young man named Norman Bates, she decides to return the money. But that night she is brutally murdered by Bates, who turns out to be a serial murderer who also has killed—and stuffed—his own mother.

These themes of guilt and redemption, of confused sexual desire and Oedipal attachment, were typical of Hitchcock's films, but he had never taken them to quite this extreme. Nor had he done anything so brutal or so sexually explicit. Aware of the risks involved, Hitchcock did the picture quickly, economically, and under a veil of secrecy. *Psycho* was shot for only $800,000 in the Revue studios at Universal City, which Paramount rented for the project. Only a few members of Hitchcock's motion-picture unit were aboard, notably editor George Tomasini, composer Bernard Herrmann, and designer Saul Bass. Otherwise he used the crew from his TV series for the relatively low-grade black-and-white production. Contrary to usual preselling practices, Paramount let out no advance publicity and held no advance screenings. Instead it mounted an aggressive ad campaign aimed at younger audiences, who presumably would appreciate the dark humor and the excessive sex and violence. The highlight of the ad campaign was an elaborate movie trailer in which Hitchcock, playing off his TV monologues, conducted a tour of the Bates Motel and the ominous mansion nearby, describing just enough of the story to tantalize the viewer. Paramount further hyped *Psycho* by insisting that exhibitors refuse admission once the picture had started.

Psycho was a genuine industry phenomenon and one of the biggest box-office hits of 1960, second only to MGM's extravagant remake of *Ben-Hur*. *Ben-Hur* reinforced Hollywood's blockbuster mentality, taking in nearly $20 million in gross revenues and scoring a half-dozen Oscars, including that for best picture. But *Psycho,* which enraged critics, terrorized audiences, and grossed $8.5 million, was a vastly more significant film in the overall scheme of things. It was one of those rare movie experiences that forced viewers to rethink the very nature of narrative cinema and of screen entertainment. Here was a first-run feature that perverted the themes of heterosexual romance and mother love, that implicated the viewer as a sensation-seeking voyeur, that killed off its lead character barely halfway into the story, and that freely mixed low-grade telefilm values with dazzling cinematic techniques. *Psycho* also marked the coming of age of the "exploitation film," the low-budget formula thriller targeted for younger audiences which redefined the limits of sex and violence in movies and further fragmented the movie market. Within another decade, the screen would be overrun by second-rate "stalk and slash" films tailored for the growing youth market—though none would display the artistry or genuine perversity of *Psycho.*

A F T E R back-to-back movie hits in 1959 and 1960 and the continued success of his TV series, Hitchcock's stock was at an all-time high. Perhaps the clearest indication of Hitchcock's market value was a deal he made with MCA for the rights to *Psycho* and *Alfred Hitchcock Presents,* just after MCA's 1962 takeover of Universal. Hitchcock swapped those two very hot commercial properties for a sizable block of MCA stock, thus becoming MCA's third-largest stockholder after board chairman Jules Stein and president Lew Wasserman. For a Hollywood filmmaker to attain that kind of status was unprecedented, to say the least, and so were the properties involved in the deal: one an innovative and genuinely subversive motion picture that redefined the marketplace and Hitchcock's trademark style, the other a mass-produced series of 268 telefilm episodes that reformulated that same Hitchcock style, week after week, domesticated for home use and suitable for family consumption.

Hitchcock on the set of Psycho *with Janet Leigh, whose death in the "shower scene" midway through the film was among the more obvious on-screen indications that Hollywood's classical era had ended.*

Psycho and *Alfred Hitchcock Presents* indicated a split in Hitchcock's "personality," and they were harbingers of a split in the film industry as well. They reflected the contradictory impulses that would come to dominate the New Hollywood, as innovation and subversion gave way to a cinema of shock tactics and mindless excess, and as TV programming was standardized to the point of inertia. Hitchcock's own career continued on this dual trajectory. In 1962 the TV series was expanded and retitled *The Alfred Hitchcock Hour*; despite the boost in production values, the series grew more predictable and formulaic with each installment. That same year he produced and directed *The Birds*, a technically dazzling but oddly perverse movie punctuated by increasingly violent bird attacks that are never explained to the audience or fended off by the hapless protagonists. After that effort, Hitchcock returned to more routine big-budget star vehicles—though he himself was now the main attraction in his pictures, the epitome of Hollywood's burgeoning director-as-superstar mentality. And remarkably enough, now that Hitchcock could write his own ticket in an industry that seemed to be patterning itself after his career, both the quality and quantity of Hitchcock's work fell sharply. After *The Birds*, he closed out his career with a succession of what, for him, were decidely second-rate pictures—*Marnie, Torn Curtain, Topaz, Frenzy*, and *Family Plot*.

Advancing age and a curious complacency were partly to blame for Hitchcock's decline, but two other factors were equally important— and again they indicated crucial developments in the industry at large. One had to do with Lew Wasserman, who until 1962 was not only Hitchcock's agent but his virtual production manager, arranging deals and packaging projects while Hitchcock and his respective movie and telefilm units attended to the actual filmmaking. But during the MCA-Universal merger, the Justice Department threatened Stein and Wasserman with antitrust and conflict-of-interest charges if they did not divest either their talent agency or their production-distribution company. Consequently MCA sold its agency in 1962, leaving Hitchcock without the management executive who had guided his career since his early Hollywood years with David and Myron Selznick. Another reason for Hitchcock's decline was the dispersion of his movie production unit, which Wasserman had been instrumental in keeping together. Although Hitchcock consolidated all his filmmaking efforts at Universal City after making *Psycho*, he soon found himself without the services of Burks, Tomasini, Herrmann, Head, Coleman, Bass, and other key collaborators of the past decade. Nor did Hitchcock again hook up with individual writers or stars for a succession of pictures, as he had with the likes of John Michael Hayes and James Stewart.

By the mid-1960s, each Hitchcock film was an utterly independent venture, with Hitchcock himself providing the only real continuity from one project to another. But as Hitchcock was being canonized by critics and historians as the exemplary American auteur, his output suggested something quite different: that in order to turn out quality pictures with any consistency, even a distinctive stylist and inveterate independent like Hitchcock required a base of filmmaking operations, a pool of resources and personnel, a consistent production unit, and a stable management setup. As Hitchcock and others were learning, creative freedom and control were of little value without the resources and the constraints that had been basic to the old system but were sorely lacking in the New Hollywood.

Invariably, the most successful filmmakers in the New Hollywood were those who, like Hitchcock during his peak years, were basically unit producers able to maintain continuity and stability in an increasingly unstable and uncertain industry. A few successful producer-directors even tried to create their own studios, hoping to recapture the discipline, efficiency, and quality control of the studio system. Robert

Altman with Lion's Gate, Francis Coppola with American Zoetrope, George Lucas with Lucasfilm Limited—these were not simply independent production companies but studios in microcosm, where talent could be nurtured, production units developed, and multiple projects undertaken in a cooperative, productive, and creative environment. As Coppola said when he created Zoetrope, it was "time to return to the old studio system as it was in the '30s—a family of people working together from inception to final production without packages of bought talent."

There was no going back, of course, either to the social and economic conditions of the studio era or to the delicate equilibrium of the studio system itself. There had been a marvelous symmetry to that system, a balance of power and industrial forces which was evident throughout: in the creative give-and-take at every stage of the production process, in the symbiotic accord between the studio's creative community and its front office, and in turn between the studio's front office and the home office in New York. There had been waste and self-indulgence in some prestige-level production, to be sure, just as there had been deadening standardization at the low end of Hollywood's output. But each had its place in the overall scheme of things, and ultimately both blockbuster and B movie were ancillary to first-run feature production, which had always been the studios' strong suit—and which the New Hollywood has proved utterly incapable of turning out with any quality or consistency.

At the heart of the classical Hollywood and of each studio's house style were those star-genre formulations, the Davis melodramas and Karloff horror pictures and Gene Kelly musicals that seemed to flow so effortlessly from the filmmaking machinery. Those were the economic lifeblood of the studio system and the basis for the industry's popular appeal, and they still stand among the greatest cultural accomplishments in an age when art and industry, commerce and technology are so inexorably wed. As Hollywood classics like *Jezebel* and *Frankenstein* and *On the Town* are recirculated and rediscovered by successive generations, it is little wonder that filmmakers would want to revive the system that produced them. But those celluloid traces, at once so real and so remote, are all that remain of the studio system and of the vigorous, dynamic breed that created and sustained it.

Notes on
Sources

PRIMARY RESEARCH

In writing this book, I relied primarily on archival sources: studio files, production reports, interoffice correspondence, financial records, and other documents related to studio filmmaking. In fact, the decision to focus on MGM, Warners, Universal, and Selznick was based not only on their exceptional "fit"as four representative production entities from the classical era, but also on the availability of their corporate records in archives around the country.

The following is a listing of the collections and archives in which I conducted research for this book, including brief descriptions of their holdings:

Arthur Freed Collection, Department of Special Collections, Doheny Library, University of Southern California; hereafter Freed Collection (USC).

An exhaustive collection of the production records, studio correspondence, etc. of MGM's top producer in the late 1940s and 1950s, who produced most of the golden-age musicals.

Mark Hellinger Collection, Department of Special Collections, Doheny Library, University of Southern California; hereafter Hellinger Collection (USC).

This is a rather limited collection in itself, featuring legal, financial, and production-related materials from Hellinger's years as an in-house independent at Universal. It is well complemented, though, by the Hellinger material in the Warners Collection, also housed at USC.

Alfred Hitchcock Collection, Margaret Herrick Library, Academy of Motion Picture Arts and Sciences, Beverly Hills, California; hereafter Hitchcock Collection (Academy).

A massive collection of production-related records and materials, with emphasis on Hitchcock's later American pictures. An excellent complement to the Hitchcock holdings in the Selznick Collection at UT-Austin.

MGM Script Collection, Doheny Library, University of Southern California; hereafter MGM Script Collection (USC).

This collection includes a general inventory of MGM scripts and other script-related preproduction materials (treatments, screenplay drafts, etc.), including those for unproduced projects. It also contains story-conference notes and memos for some of MGM's pictures.

Dore Schary Papers, Wisconsin Center for Film and Theatre Research, State Historical Society, Madison, Wisconsin; hereafter Schary Papers (Madison).

Another limited and uneven but valuable resource, containing materials— mostly executive-level correspondence—from Schary's respective executive stints at MGM, Vanguard, RKO, and then back at MGM. Particularly illuminating are the minutes of MGM executive meetings from both the early and the late 1940s.

George B. Seitz Collection, Louis B. Mayer Library, the American Film Institute, Los Angeles; hereafter Seitz Collection (AFI).

A somewhat uneven but valuable resource, particularly strong in story and script development and preproduction for the Andy Hardy pictures, most of which Seitz directed.

David O. Selznick Collection, Hoblitzelle Theatre Arts Library, Humanities Research Center, University of Texas at Austin; hereafter Selznick Collection (UT-Austin).

This massive collection contains some materials from Selznick's early years as studio executive at MGM, Paramount, and RKO. Though these are rather limited, they suited the needs of this study since they focus on Selznick's own role and function at the studio. The bulk of the Selznick Collection involves his years as an independent (1935 and following), and here the materials are exhaustive, covering virtually every aspect of Selznick's filmmaking activities.

United Artists Collection, Wisconsin Center for Film and Theatre Research, State Historical Society, Madison; hereafter UA Collection (Madison).

This is an extensive and well-catalogued collection of UA's corporate and financial records prior to 1951. There are no production-related materials per se in the collection, but it provides a valuable complement to the collections of individual UA producers like Selznick and Wanger.

Universal Collection, Department of Special Collections, Doheny Library, University of Southern California; hereafter Universal Collection (USC).

This is a limited and remarkably uneven collection, but there are some valuable materials from the 1930s, 1940s, and 1950s: detailed budgets and production records on various titles, "shooting records" and weekly status reports on all productions through the 1930s, and various "recapitulations" and summary reports.

Walter Wanger Collection, Wisconsin Center for Film and Theatre Research, State Historical Society, Madison; hereafter Wanger Collection (Madison).

This is an excellent, well-catalogued, comprehensive collection that spans Wanger's career in the 1930s, 1940s, and 1950s. It includes his contracts, correspondence, financial reports, and the production records on many of his pictures.

Warner Bros. Collection, Department of Special Collections, Doheny Library, University of Southern California, Los Angeles; hereafter Warners Collection (USC).

This massive, well-catalogued, and well-administered archive contains extensive production records, organized by title, as well as personnel records (legal records, contracts, studio correspondence, publicity materials, etc.), organized by individual employee.

Warner Bros. Legal Files, United Artists Collection, Wisconsin Center for Film and Theatre Research, State Historical Society, Madison, Wisconsin; hereafter Warners Legal Files (Madison).

This collection contains contracts, agreements, and other legal materials on virtually all Warners features. The materials are organized alphabetically by feature title and tend to favor the above-the-line aspects of production—i.e., contracts for director, writer(s), and star(s), contracts for motion-picture rights to story properties, and so on.

Warner Bros. Script Files, United Artists Collection, Wisconsin Center for Film and Theatre Research, State Historical Society, Madison; hereafter Warners Script Files (Madison).

This collection, like the MGM Collection at USC, includes a general inventory of scripts and related preproduction material, including scant story-conference notes.

SECONDARY RESEARCH

Besides the archival research for this book, I did extensive secondary research in trade papers and journals, biographies and memoirs, oral histories and interviews, anecdotal surveys of individual studios and histories of the movie industry in general. While these provided a general understanding of Hollywood and its history, I was struck time and time again by the superficial and frequently self-serving nature of these sources, by the inconsistent and often contradictory information they contained, and by the failure to consider larger economic and industrial factors in developing a systematic analysis of the film-making process. Indeed, my heavy reliance on primary archival sources was not initially intended, but became a virtual necessity as the value of those primary sources and the limitations of the secondary sources became more evident.

A book-length study of studio filmmaking and studio style could be based on secondary sources, and indeed two have been: *The Hollywood Studios* by Roy Pickard (London: Frederick Muller, 1978) and *The Hollywood Studios* by Ethan Mordden (New York: Knopf, 1987). Both provide a valuable survey of the studios, though they are limited somewhat by the same problems that plague their sources. What's more, the studio-by-studio approach (each book devotes single chapters to some eight different companies) precludes any coherent, comprehensive view of the studio system at large, of the ongoing interaction between studios, and of the overall impact of such external shocks as the Depression and World War II.

Other studies of the movie industry are more systematic, more rigorous, and more closely attuned to actual filmmaking practice, and thus I found them very useful in my research. Of particular value was the recent study by David Bordwell, Janet Staiger, and Kristin Thompson, *The Classical Hollywood Cinema: Film Style and Mode of Production to 1960* (New York: Columbia University Press, 1985). Another important recent work is Douglas Gomery, *The Hollywood Studio System* (New York: St. Martin, 1986), which provides a solid economic history of the studios during the classical era. Taken together, these two books are an ideal complement to this study. Bordwell, Staiger, and Thompson address the production process and film style in the industry at large, but provide only a cursory treatment of how these were put into practice at individual studios. Gomery examines Hollywood's important studios in some detail, but he emphasizes the financial and corporate structure of each company; his book is more concerned with each studio's New York office than with its filmmaking operations in Los Angeles.

Previous studies of American film history also were of value in researching and writing this book, particularly Robert Sklar, *Movie-Made America: A Cultural History of the Movies* (New York: Vintage, 1976), and Garth Jowett, *Film: The Democratic Art: A Social History of the American Film* (Boston: Little, Brown, 1976). Two anthologies that also proved valuable were Tino Balio, ed., *The American Film Industry*, rev. ed. (Madison: University of Wisconsin Press, 1985), and Gorham Kindem, ed., *The American Movie Industry: The Business of Motion Pictures* (Carbondale: University of Illinois Press, 1982). Balio's anthology is especially useful thanks to the detailed introduction he provides for each of the four historical sections of the book.

Inevitably, a study of this nature also relies heavily on general reference books. The ones I found most useful were Leslie Halliwell, *Halliwell's Film Guide*, 3rd ed. (New York: Scribner, 1982); Ephraim Katz, *The Film Encyclopedia* (New York: Perigee Books, 1979); Cobbett S. Steinberg, *Film Facts* (New York: Facts on File, 1980); and David Thomson, *A Biographical Dictionary of Film* (New York: William Morrow, 1976). An excellent compendium of statistical data on the movie industry, most of it culled from reliable trade papers and journals, is Christopher H. Sterling and Timothy R. Haight, *The Mass Media: Aspen Institute Guide to Communications Industry Trends* (New York: Praeger, 1978).

P R E C I S E and detailed notes on sources, particularly the archival sources, would be unwieldy and utterly impractical, requiring another hundred pages of text, at the very least. I hope the following notes on sources, broken down by chapter, will provide an adequate bibliographic guide.

INTRODUCTION: "THE WHOLE EQUATION OF PICTURES"

The opening quotation is from Ben Hecht's autobiography, *A Child of the Century* (New York: Simon & Schuster, 1954); Selznick's comments were found in his correspondence files in the Selznick Collection (UT-Austin). Andrew Sarris's auteurist pronouncements appeared in "Toward a Theory of Film History," the introduction to *The American Cinema: Directors and Directions, 1929–1968* (New York: E. P. Dutton, 1968). Leo Rosten's description of movie producers is from his massive study, *Hollywood: The Movie Colony, The Movie Makers* (New York: Harcourt, Brace, 1941). Frank Capra's open letter to the *Times* is quoted in his autobiography, *The Name Above the Title* (New York: Macmillan, 1971). F. Scott Fitzgerald's oft-quoted passage on Hollywood appears in *The Last Tycoon: An Unfinished Novel* (New York: Scribner, 1941). André Bazin voiced his misgivings about auteurism in his essay "La politique des auteurs," reprinted in Peter Graham, ed., *The New Wave* (Garden City, N.Y.: Doubleday, 1968).

1. UNIVERSAL: THE SYSTEM TAKES SHAPE

I found virtually no archival material on Universal's silent period, so I relied on secondary sources in this chapter more heavily than in any other in the book. Two key sources in this and the subsequent chapters on Universal were Douglas Gomery, "Universal," in his book *The Hollywood Studio System,* which provides a concise corporate and economic history of the studio, and Clive Hirschhorn, *The Universal Story* (New York: Crown, 1983), which surveys the general history of the studio and supplies plot synopses and principal credits on every Universal release. Another valuable summary of Universal's early history is I. G. Edmonds, *Big U: Universal in the Silent Days* (New York: A. S. Barnes, 1977).

Useful background information was found in an early biography of Carl Laemmle by John Drinkwater, *The Life and Adventures of Carl Laemmle* (New York: Putnam, 1931). The Laemmle-Thalberg period is also treated in two studies of Thalberg's life and career: Bob Thomas, *Thalberg: Life and*

Legend (Garden City, N.Y.: Doubleday, 1969), and Samuel Marx, *Mayer and Thalberg: The Make-Believe Saints* (New York: Random House, 1975). Another excellent resource was Kevin Brownlow's landmark study of silent filmmaking, *The Parade's Gone By . . .* (New York: Knopf, 1969).

In some ways, the year 1920 is a somewhat arbitrarily assigned starting point for the "studio system." The reason, of course, is that the factory-based mode of production, the bicoastal management structure, and vertical integration were coming together in a unified industrial process at about that time. The "studio system" as a specific mode of production, however, began to emerge during the early teens, as had been well documented by various historians. Of special note is the work by Janet Staiger and Kristin Thompson in *The Classical Hollywood Cinema*; see also Staiger, "Dividing Labor for Production Control: Thomas Ince and the Rise of the Studio System," in Gorham Kindem's anthology, *The American Movie Industry*, and "Blueprints for Feature Films: Hollywood's Continuity Scripts," in Tino Balio's anthology, *The American Film Industry*.

2. MGM: DAWN OF THE THALBERG ERA

Primary research for this chapter was done at the MGM Script Collection (USC) and the Selznick Collection (UT-Austin).

A relatively large amount of work of varied quality has been done on MGM. Two invaluable secondary sources for this and subsequent chapters on MGM are Douglas Gomery's concise economic and corporate history, "Loew's and Metro-Goldwyn-Mayer," in *The Hollywood Studio System*, and also John Douglas Eames, *The MGM Story* (New York: Crown, 1975), which surveys the studio's annual output, providing plot synopses and principal credits on every Metro release. Of the various histories of the studio, the most comprehensive and readable is Bosley Crowther, *The Lion's Share: The Story of an Entertainment Empire* (New York: E. P. Dutton, 1957).

Biographies and memoirs of Metro's top executives, filmmakers, and stars are plentiful. Three estimable treatments of Metro's top studio executives are Bosley Crowther, *Hollywood Rajah: The Life and Times of Louis B. Mayer* (New York: Holt, Rinehart & Winston, 1960), Bob Thomas, *Thalberg* (Garden City, N.Y.: Doubleday, 1969), and Samuel Marx, *Mayer and Thalberg: The Make-Believe Saints*. Also of note are reminiscences of their MGM screenwriting days by Frances Marion in *Off With Their Heads* (New York: Macmillan, 1972) and by Anita Loos in *Kiss Hollywood Good-by* (New York: Viking, 1974). One worthwhile treatment of silent filmmaking at MGM by a staff director is King Vidor's *A Tree Is a Tree* (New York: Harcourt, Brace, 1952).

3. SELZNICK AT MGM: CLIMBING THE EXECUTIVE RANKS

Primary research for this chapter was done in the Selznick Collection (UT-Austin) and the MGM Script Collection (USC).

Most of the sources cited in the previous chapter are pertinent here as well, along with two other books that are crucial to any study of Selznick: Rudy Behlmer, ed., *MEMO from David O. Selznick* (New York: Viking, 1972), and Ronald Haver, *David O. Selznick's Hollywood* (New York: Knopf, 1980). For a fairly routine and anecdotal biography see Bob Thomas, *Selznick* (Garden City, N.Y.: Doubleday, 1970).

4. WARNER BROS.: TALKING THEIR WAY TO THE TOP

Primary research for this chapter was done in the Warners Legal Files and the Warners Script Files (Madison), and in the Warners Collection (USC).

In this and subsequent chapters on Warners, important background information was culled from Douglas Gomery's chapter "Warner Bros." in *The Hollywood Studio System* and from Clive Hirschhorn, *The Warner Bros. Story* (New York: Crown, 1979), which surveys the company's annual output, providing plot synopses and principal credits on every Warners release. Charles Higham has written a passable anecdotal history of the studio, *Warner Brothers* (New York: Scribner, 1975), and a sibling's biography of the studio's founders can be found in Michael Freedland, *The Warner Brothers* (London: Harrap, 1983). Of the numerous biographies and memoirs of studio executives, of special interest are Jack L. Warner, *My First Hundred Years in Hollywood* (New York: Random House, 1964); Hal Wallis and Charles Higham, *Starmaker: An Autobiography of Hal Wallis* (New York: Macmillan, 1980); and two biographies of Darryl F. Zanuck: Mel Gussow, *Don't Say Yes Until I Finish Talking* (Garden City, N.Y.: Doubleday, 1971), and Leonard Mosley, *Zanuck: The Rise and Fall of Hollywood's Last Tycoon* (Boston: Little, Brown, 1984).

Extensive work of a somewhat revisionist nature has been done in recent years on Hollywood's conversion to sound. Of particular note are David Bordwell, "The Introduction of Sound," in *The Classical Hollywood Cinema*; Douglas Gomery, "The Coming of Sound: Technological Change in the American Film Industry," in Tino Balio's anthology, *The American Film Industry*; and Gomery, "The 'Warner-Vitaphone Peril': The American Film Industry Reacts to the Innovation of Sound," in Gorhan Kindem's anthology, *The American Movie Industry*.

5. SELZNICK AT PARAMOUNT: FROM BOOM TO BUST

Primary research for this chapter was done in the Selznick Collection (UT-Austin).

Useful background information was supplied by Douglas Gomery's chapter "Paramount" in *The Hollywood Studio System*. Again, I found Rudy Behlmer's compilation, *MEMO from David O. Selznick*, useful, and also Ronald Haver's *David O. Selznick's Hollywood*. For a solid summary-overview of Paramount's output during the classical era, see Leslie Halliwell, *Mountain of*

Dreams: The Golden Years at Paramount Pictures (New York: Stonehill, 1976). Douglas Gomery examines theater operations in the 1920s and the Paramount-Publix merger in his essay "The Movies Become Big Business: Publix Theaters and the Chain Store Strategy," in Gorham Kindem's anthology, *The American Movie Industry*.

6. UNIVERSAL: RENAISSANCE AND RETRENCHMENT

Primary research for this chapter was done in the Universal Collection (USC).

Secondary source material for my discussion of the making of *All Quiet on the Western Front* was found in Kingsley Canham, "Milestone: The Unpredictable Fundamentalist," in *The Hollywood Professionals*, vol. 2 (New York: A. S. Barnes, 1972). A valuable secondary source for my treatment of the horror genre was Rudy Behlmer's chapter on the making of *Frankenstein* in *America's Favorite Movies: Behind the Scenes* (New York: Frederick Ungar, 1982).

7. MGM AND THALBERG: ALONE AT THE TOP

Primary research for this chapter was done in the MGM Script Collection (USC) and the Selznick Collection (UT-Austin).

Many of the same secondary sources cited in chapters 2 and 3 were referred to for background information. For a particularly telling account of William Fox's downfall, see Upton Sinclair, *Upton Sinclair Presents William Fox* (Los Angeles: published by the author, 1933). See also "Metro-Goldwyn-Mayer," *Fortune* 6 (December 1932). The case study of the story conferences for *Grand Hotel* was reconstructed entirely from the story and script files in the MGM collection at USC.

8. SELZNICK AT RKO: AT THE HELM OF A FOUNDERING STUDIO

Primary research for this chapter was done in the Selznick Collection (UT-Austin).

Background information on the financial conditions and corporate machinations at the studio was found in Douglas Gomery's chapter "Radio-Keith-Orpheum" in *The Hollywood Studio System*. For a survey of the studio's annual output with plot synopses and principal credits, see Richard Jewell and Vernon Harbin, *The RKO Story* (New York: Arlington House, 1982). An excellent studio history is Betty Lasky's *RKO: The Biggest Little Major of Them All* (Englewood Cliffs, N.J.: Prentice-Hall, 1984).

9. WARNER BROS.: THE ZANUCK ERA

Primary research for this chapter was done in the Warners Legal Files and the Warners Script Files (Madison), and in the Warners Collection (USC).

The biographies and memoirs cited in chapter 4 were useful for preparing this chapter as well, as was Mervyn LeRoy's autobiography, *Take One* (New York: Hawthorne, 1974). For a comprehensive survey of the studio's leading house directors, see William R. Meyer, *Warner Brothers Directors* (New York: Arlington House, 1978). Two important recent books on Warners in the classical era are Nick Roddick, *A New Deal in Entertainment: Warner Brothers in the 1930s* (London: British Film Institute, 1983), and Rudy Behlmer, ed., *Inside Warner Bros. (1935–1951)* (New York: Viking, 1985). Although both books concentrate on the "Hal Wallis era" (1933 and following), they do provide excellent surveys of the Zanuck era.

10. MGM IN THE MID-THIRTIES: CHARMED INTERVAL

Primary research for this chapter was done in the MGM Script Collection (USC), the Wanger Collection (Madison), and the Selznick Collection (UT-Austin).

For excellent though in some ways conflicting acounts of the impact of the Roosevelt administration and the NIRA on Hollywood, see Robert Sklar, *Movie-Made America,* and Douglas Gomery, "Hollywood, the National Recovery Administration, and the Question of Monopoly Power," in Gorham Kindem's anthology, *The American Movie Industry.* Of the various biographies and memoirs already mentioned, particularly useful in writing this chapter were Bosley Crowther's biography of Louis B. Mayer, *Hollywood Rajah,* Sam Marx's *Mayer and Thalberg,* Bob Thomas's *Thalberg,* and Anita Loos's *Kiss Hollywood Good-by.*

11. SELZNICK INTERNATIONAL PICTURES: GOING INDEPENDENT

Primary research for this chapter was done in the Selznick Collection (UT-Austin) and the MGM Script Collection (USC).

For an exhaustive and first-rate study of United Artists, see Tino Balio, *United Artists: The Company Built by the Stars* (Madison: University of Wisconsin Press, 1976).

12. WARNER BROS.: POWER PLAYS AND PRESTIGE

Primary research for this chapter was done in the Warners Legal Files and the Warners Script Files (Madison), and the Warners Collection (USC).

For more information on the Hays Office and the PCA, see Ruth A. Ingliss, "Self-Censorship in Operation," in Tino Balio's anthology, *The American Film Industry*. An excellent essay on Hollywood's self-censorship during the early 1930s is Richard Maltby, " 'Baby Face,' or How Joe Breen Made Barbara Stanwyck Atone for Causing the Wall Street Crash," *Screen*, March–April 1986. Two useful studies on the Legion of Decency are J. C. Turner, "Public Reaction to the National Legion of Decency as Reflected in the Popular Press, 1934–1952" (M.A. thesis, University of Texas at Austin, 1984), and Paul W. Facey, *The Legion of Decency* (New York: Arno Press, 1974).

Rudy Behlmer's annotated compendium of studio correspondence, *Inside Warner Bros.*, was especially useful in preparing this chapter, as was Nick Roddick's *A New Deal in Entertainment*. (Roddick's single in-depth case study, by the way, traces the making of *Anthony Adverse*, a rather curious selection since it was hardly representative of the studio's output at the time.) Rudy Behlmer also conducts a case study of the making of *The Adventures of Robin Hood* in his book *America's Favorite Movies*. There are numerous star biographies and memoirs of Warners' leading players, but none is all that illuminating about the production process at the studio. Two scholarly articles on individual Warners stars that did prove useful were Cathy Klaprat, "The Star as Market Strategy: Bette Davis in Another Light," in Tino Balio's anthology, *The American Film Industry*, and Kevin Hagopian, "Declarations of Independence: A History of Cagney Productions," *The Velvet Light Trap* 22 (1986).

13. UNIVERSAL: PLAYING BOTH ENDS AGAINST THE MIDDLE

Primary research for this chapter was done in the Universal Collection (USC).

Douglas Gomery's chapter on Universal in *The Hollywood Studio System* was especially useful in sorting out the shifting power structure and financial fortunes at the studio in the late 1930s, as was "Deanna Durbin," *Fortune* 22 (October 1939).

14. MGM: LIFE AFTER THALBERG

Primary research for this chapter was done in the MGM Script Collection (USC), the Seitz Collection (AFI), the Selznick Collection (UT-Austin), the Freed Collection (USC), and the Schary Papers (Madison).

For a detailed case study on the production of *Oz* and the general conditions at the studio in 1938–39, see Aljean Harmetz, *The Making of The Wizard of Oz* (New York: Limelight Editions, 1984). Mervyn LeRoy's autobiography, *Take One,* also provides some insight into that production and that period, as do Bosley Crowther's *Hollywood Rajah* and *The Lion's Share*. For an excellent survey of MGM's parent company and the general distribution and exhibition status in the late 1930s, see "Loew's, Inc.," *Fortune* 20 (August 1939).

15. SELZNICK AND HITCHCOCK: BALANCE OF POWER

Primary research for this chapter was done in the Selznick Collection (UT-Austin) and the Hitchcock Collection (Academy).

An excellent biography of Hitchcock—and a useful source of background material for this chapter along with Ronald Haver's *David O. Selznick's Hollywood*—was Donald Spoto, *The Dark Side of Genius: The Life of Alfred Hitchcock* (Boston: Little, Brown, 1983). Hitchcock's 1937 essay, "Direction," first printed in *Footnotes to the Film*, is reprinted in Albert J. LaValley, ed., *Focus on Hitchcock* (Englewood Cliffs, N.J.: Prentice-Hall, 1972).

For a more detailed treatment of the working relationship between Selznick and Hitchcock, see Leonard J. Leff, *Hitchcock and Selznick* (New York: Weidenfeld, 1987), which was published after I completed this manuscript.

16. WARNER BROS.: WARFARE AT HOME AND ABROAD

Primary research for this chapter was done in the Warners Legal Files and the Warners Script File (Madison), the Warners Collection (USC), and the Hellinger Collection (USC).

For an excellent study of the general economic conditions in the movie industry in the early 1940s, see Mae D. Huettig, *Economic Control of the Motion Picture Industry* (Philadelphia: University of Pennsylvania Press, 1944). For a detailed legal account of the ongoing antitrust battles in Hollywood, see Michael Conant, *Antitrust in the Motion Picture Industry: Economic and Legal Analysis* (Berkeley: University of California Press, 1960). An interesting complement to these two studies is the massive ethnography of Hollywood conducted in 1940 by sociologist (and later screenwriter and novelist) Leo Rosten, *Hollywood: The Movie Colony, The Movie Makers.*

Again Rudy Behlmer's *Inside Warner Bros.* proved useful, as did his chapters on the making of *The Maltese Falcon* and *Casablanca* in *America's Favorite Movies*. For remarkably different and self-serving accounts of the studio power structure and filmmaking process during the war, see Hal Wallis's autobiography (with Charles Higham), *Starmaker,* and Jack Warner's memoir, *My First Hundred Years in Hollywood*. One autobiography that offers considerable insight into this period is John Huston, *An Open Book* (New York: Knopf, 1980).

17. DAVID O. SELZNICK PRODUCTIONS: PACKAGING PRESTIGE

Primary research for this chapter was done in the Selznick Collection (UT-Austin), the Hitchcock Collection (Academy), the Schary Papers (Madison), and the Warners Legal Files (Madison).

This period and dimension of Selznick's career has been sorely neglected.

(Haver, for instance, devoted fewer than three pages to it in the otherwise excellent *David O. Selznick's Hollywood*.) As with the previous chapters on Selznick as an independent, Tino Balio's *United Artists* provided valuable background information. See also "United Artists: Final Shooting Script," *Fortune* 22 (December 1940).

18. UNIVERSAL: THE BEST OF BOTH WORLDS

Primary research for this chapter was done in the Universal Collection (USC), the Hellinger Collection (USC), the Wanger Collection (Madison), and the Selznick Collection (UT-Austin).

For an insightful essay on the upsurge in independent production by the studios in 1940 and after, see Janet Staiger, "Individualism Versus Collectivism," *Screen*, July–October 1983. For a detailed treatment of Diana Productions, see Matthew Bernstein, "Fritz Lang, Incorporated," *The Velvet Light Trap* 22 (1986).

19. MGM: THE HIGH COST OF QUALITY

Primary research for this chapter was done in the MGM Script Collection (USC), the Freed Collection (USC), the Schary Papers (Madison), and the Selznick Collection (UT-Austin).

An exceptional study of the Freed unit and MGM's golden-age musicals is Hugh Fordin, *The World of Entertainment* (Garden City, N.Y.: Doubleday, 1975). See also Vincente Minnelli's autobiography, *I Remember It Well* (Garden City, N.Y.: Doubleday, 1974).

20. SELZNICK AND HITCHCOCK: SEPARATE WAYS

Primary research for this chapter was done in the Selznick Collection (UT-Austin), the Hitchcock Collection (Academy), and the Schary Papers (Madison).

As in the previous chapter on Selznick and Hitchcock, useful material was culled from Ronald Haver's *David O. Selznick's Hollywood* and from Donald Spoto's *The Dark Side of Genius*. When their respective analyses of *Spellbound* and *Notorious* are compared, however, especially in terms of individual film authorship and their emphasis on the autobiographical and psychotherapeutic aspects of filmmaking, the rather severe shortcomings of each author's "one man, one film" mentality are altogether apparent.

21. WARNER BROS.: TOP OF THE WORLD, END OF THE LINE

Primary research for this chapter was done in the Warners Legal Files and the Warners Script Files (Madison), the Warners Collection (USC), and the Hitchcock Collection (Academy).

Douglas Gomery's chapter on Warners in *The Hollywood Studio System* and Rudy Behlmer's annotated compilation, *Inside Warner Bros.*, both proved useful, and it's worth noting that both books mark the "end" of Warners' classical era as circa 1950.

Several studies of the HUAC investigation of Hollywood and of the industry's ongoing political struggles in general have been written: see in particular Larry Ceplair and Steven Englund, *The Inquisition in Hollywood: Politics in the Film Community, 1930–1960* (New York: Arbor House, 1980); Victor Navasky, *Naming Names* (New York: Viking, 1980); and David Talbot and Barbara Zheutlin, *Creative Differences: Profiles of Hollywood Dissidents* (Boston: South End Press, 1978).

22. MGM: LAST GASP OF THE STUDIO ERA

Primary research for this chapter was done in the MGM Script Collection (USC), the Freed Collection (USC), the Schary Papers (Madison), and the Selznick Collection (UT-Austin).

The downfall of RKO during and after Schary's tenure there is chronicled briefly by Douglas Gomery in his chapter on RKO in *The Hollywood Studio System*, and also in "RKO: It's Only Money," *Fortune* 47 (May 1953). Background material on the Freed-unit musicals was culled from Hugh Fordin's *The World of Entertainment* and from Vincente Minnelli's autobiography, *I Remember It Well*. See also Rudy Behlmer's chapter on the making of *Singin' in the Rain* in *America's Favorite Movies*, and Donald Knox, *The Magic Factory: How MGM Made an American in Paris* (New York: Praeger, 1973). For a star bio with more than the usual attention to the business of making movies, see Clive Hirschhorn, *Gene Kelly* (New York: St. Martin's, 1974).

John Huston, in his autobiography, *An Open Book,* provides considerable insight into the HUAC investigations, the Schary-Mayer flap at MGM, and the making of *The Red Badge of Courage.* The making of that Huston film as well as Mayer's ouster are also chronicled in Lillian Ross, *Picture* (New York: Rinehart, 1952).

23. UNIVERSAL: BLUEPRINT FOR THE TELEVISION AGE

Primary research for this chapter was done in the Universal Collection (USC). Like the opening chapter in this book, this closing chapter relied more heavily than the others on secondary research owing to the lack of primary archival resources—particularly on the role of talent agencies and the impact of television on Hollywood during the 1950s. For a general survey of the role that MCA and Lew Wasserman played in Universal's fortunes during the 1950s, see Michael Pye, *Moguls: Inside the Business of Show Business* (New York: Holt, Rinehart & Winston, 1980). Two timely *Fortune* essays on the Hollywood-TV interplay in the mid-1950s are "TV: The Coming Showdown" (September 1954) and "The Comeback of the Movies" (February 1955). The two trade-press articles cited in this chapter are Dave Glickman, "Film in the Future—As Television's Horizons Expand," *Broadcasting*, September 10, 1951, and Dave Kaufman, "Vidpix Weed Out Shoestrings," *Variety*, January 9, 1952.

Two solid general histories of American network television are Erik Barnow, *Tube of Plenty: The Evolution of American Television* (New York: Oxford University Press, 1975), and Lawrence Bergreen, *Look Now, Pay Later: The Rise of Network Broadcasting* (Garden City, N.Y.: Doubleday, 1980). Neither of these, however, deals with the integration of the movie and TV industries in any real detail. That issue has been a topic of considerable research more recently: see the special issue of *Quarterly Review of Film Studies*, Summer 1984, particularly Robert Vianello, "The Rise of the Telefilm and the Networks' Hegemony Over the Motion Picture Industry," and Douglas Gomery, "Failed Opportunities: The Integration of the U.S. Motion Picture and Television Industries."

Three recent and as yet unpublished doctoral theses address the Hollywood-TV relationship in much greater detail: Dennis Dombrowski, "Film and Television: An Analytical History of Economic and Creative Integration" (Ph.D. dissertation, University of Illinois, 1982); William Boddy, "From the 'Golden Age' to the 'Vast Wasteland': The Struggle over Market Power and Dramatic Formats in 1950s Television" (Ph.D. dissertation, New York University, 1984); and Christopher Anderson, "Hollywood TV: The Role of Television in the Transformation of the Studio System" (Ph.D. dissertation, University of Texas at Austin, 1988). Anderson's study is especially pertinent vis-à-vis the present book because of its emphasis on the studio system, and also because of its case studies of Selznick's failed effort to move into TV production in 1954–55 and Warners' successful effort a year later.

24. EPILOGUE: INTO THE NEW HOLLYWOOD

Primary research for this chapter was done in the Hitchcock Collection (Academy) and in the Warners Legal Files (Madison).

Michael Pye's *Moguls* was a valuable resource on the Universal-MCA-Hitchcock connection. Donald Spoto, in *The Dark Side of Genius*, does a good job suveying the complex business arrangements Hitchcock was involved in during the 1950s, in publishing and TV as well as movie production. For a particularly provocative analysis of the impact of Hitchcock's later work, especially *Psycho*, on the New Hollywood, see David Thompson, "Alfred Hitchcock and the Prison of Mastery" and "*Psycho* and the Roller Coaster," in *Overexposures: The Crisis in American Filmmaking* (New York: William Morrow, 1981).

For more on the New Hollywood, see Robert H. Stanley, *The Celluloid Empire* (New York: Hastings House, 1978); Michael Pye and Linda Myles, *The Movie Brats* (New York: Holt, Rinehart & Winston, 1979); James Monaco, *American Film Now* (New York: Oxford University Press, 1979); Les Keyser, *Hollywood in the Seventies* (New York: A. S. Barnes, 1981); Saul David, *The Industry: Life in the Hollywood Fast Lane* (New York: Times Books, 1981); David McClintock, *Indecent Exposure: A True Story of Hollywood and Wall Street* (New York: William Morrow, 1982); Todd Gitlin, *Inside Prime Time* (New York: Pantheon, 1983); and Steven Bach, *Final Cut: Dreams and Disaster in the Making of Heaven's Gate* (New York: New American Library, 1985).

PHOTOGRAPH CREDITS

The author and publisher wish to thank the following for permission to reproduce the photographs on the pages listed:

CINEMA COLLECTORS: pp. 23, 101 (bottom), 104, 114, 137, 206, 210, 219, 260, 278, 310, 316, 324, 343, 401 (inset), 405, 419, 427, 467, 485, 490

KOBAL COLLECTION: pp. 26, 35, 38, 59, 117, 149, 153, 224, 238, 240, 249, 256, 286, 306, 373, 377, 387, 401, 432, 433, 438, 447

MUSEUM OF MODERN ART/FILM STILLS ARCHIVE: pp. 27, 52, 56, 73 (bottom), 93, 170

PHOTOFEST: pp. 20, 65 (top and bottom), 73 (top), 77, 91, 96, 101 (top), 129, 131, 146, 154, 165, 171, 178, 181, 185, 193, 215, 230, 267, 293, 301, 332, 335, 348, 355, 365, 461, 487

MARC WANAMAKER/BISON ARCHIVES: pp. 17, 19, 33 (top and bottom), 43, 49, 83, 109, 126, 264, 451, 471, 475

INDEX

CPSIA information can be obtained
at www.ICGtesting.com
Printed in the USA
LVHW092009160721
692882LV00007BA/438

9 780805 046663